. . People

D1450143

Identifying information is given on the inside of the back cover.

AMERICAN GOVERNMENT

INSTITUTIONS, POLICIES, AND POLITICS

Paul A. Dawson
Oberlin College

SCOTT, FORESMAN AND COMPANY
Glenview, Illinois   London, England

To Linda, especially, and Amy, Carrie, and Mike, of course.

Credit lines for the photos, illustrations, and copyrighted materials appearing in this work appear in the Acknowledgments section beginning on page 618. This section is to be considered an extension of the copyright page.

Library of Congress Cataloging-in-Publication Data

Dawson, Paul A.
  American government.

  Includes bibliographies and index.
  1. United States—Politics and government. 2. United
States. Constitution. 3. Political participation—
United States. 4. Civics. I. Title.
JK274.D37   1987   320.973   86-22096
ISBN 0-673-16557-4

PREFACE

This preface to *American Government: Institutions, Policies, and Politics* tells what is distinctive about this textbook and why you might find those distinctive features useful and, very likely, exciting.

Distinctive Features

- *American Government: Institutions, Policies, and Politics* has more to teach than other introductory American government texts. It has all the information it should have about governmental institutions plus lots of material on what governmental institutions do—make public policy—plus lots of material on why they do it—because of politics.
- It integrates its coverage of governmental institutions, public policy, and politics. The text does not just include several chapters on institutions, followed by some policy chapters, with a few on politics sprinkled in. Instead, the text shows the whole cloth of American government, with institutional characteristics, policy outcomes, and political dynamics woven together.
- *American Government* provides more real-life cases of the political system at work. It is rich with both historical and current examples of policy making and politics. Each chapter, for example, starts with a briefly presented Case. Also, every chapter is packed with examples to illustrate major points.
- This text has a well-conceived and well-executed pedagogy. The format of each chapter is as follows:

  A short opening paragraph answers the question that all students ask as they start to read something: "Why should I care?"

  A brief Case immerses the student in a policy-making episode.

  The Case leads to several clearly stated Insights.

  Each Insight is then elaborated as a major chapter topic.

  Each topic ends with a short paragraph or two summarizing key points.

  "Vantage Point" inserts, one or two per chapter, provide additional material that is related to major topics.

  A concluding chapter Summary pulls together all the major topics.

  Review and Reflection questions at the end of the chapter encourage synthesis.

  Key Terms are listed at chapter's end in the order in which they appear in the narrative.

  A brief bibliographic essay precedes the list of Supplemental Readings in each chapter, explaining why the readings might be interesting to students.

- The text's language also makes it distinctive. I think a text can teach a lot, but only if it involves students in their own learning. To do that, I've kept the tone personal, the voice active, and the language accessible. (There's no law that we can't enjoy serious work.)
- *American Government* offers a unique opportunity for instructors and students to listen in on a fascinating dialogue between two famous scholars of American government, Aaron Wildavsky and Nelson Polsby. This dialogue starts on pages 26 and 27 and other portions of it appear throughout the text.
- There are two full-color photoessays—one using postage stamps to show some of the issues and policies that have made it onto the national government's agenda; the other illustrating political participation as part of the fabric of peoples' daily lives.
- To accompany the text, there also are some special ancillary materials:

    The Instructor's Manual, co-authored with James C. Foster of Oregon State University and Richard Balkema of Valparaiso University, in addition to all the traditional materials, also includes some suggested Classroom Activities. Each of these activities puts students in a situation where they have to do something. By doing something, students experience some political dynamic or policy dilemma, start thinking about what they are experiencing, and become more enthusiastic about what they are learning.

    Videotapes of me and my students demonstrating some of these Classroom Activities are available, so that you can see how they work or use them as the basis for class discussion. (In my own classes, I'll run the Activity, conduct the class discussion of it, draw out of the experience certain insights, and then use the insights to introduce major lecture topics.)

    The Study Guide, prepared by James C. Foster of Oregon State University, includes chapter summaries, learning objectives, key terms and definitions, self-test questions with answers keyed to the text, and chapter case study topics.

    The Test Item File, prepared by Ted Carageorge, John Rees, and Conrad Cotter of Pensacola Junior College, and Stefan D. Haag of Austin Community College, contains 100 questions per chapter—multiple-choice, true-false, and short answer. The multiple choice items are based on two levels of an educational testing taxonomy; each question is labeled factual or conceptual.

    Sixty *transparencies* reproduce charts and graphs from the text.

As you might expect, I couldn't have done all this without a great deal of help.

I owe a tremendous debt to Arnold Meltsner. Arnold, a professor at the Graduate School of Public Policy of the University of California at Berkeley, was with the project from beginning to end, insisting that the world did not need another ordinary American government textbook, helping me focus my mind on chapters I had yet to write, critically reacting to many drafts, and spurring me on as only a very astute policy analyst can.

James C. Foster, author of the Study Guide and coauthor of the Instructor's Manual, and Richard Balkema, coauthor of the Instructor's Manual, gave more of themselves, their energies, imaginations, and insights than anyone had a right to expect.

Others have provided expert guidance and critical review of different parts of the textbook. These include:

Doug Amy
Mount Holyoke College

Chris Belavita
University of Southern California

William M. Bulger
President of the Senate
The Commonwealth of Massachusetts

Charles Elder
Wayne State University

Mark Ferber
Resident Manager, New England
The First Boston Corporation

Daniel J. Givelbar
Dean
Northeastern University School of Law

Isebill Gruhn
University of California at Santa Cruz

Stefan D. Haag
Austin Community College

Marilyn Hoskin
University of Buffalo

William H. Hudnut, III
Mayor
The City of Indianapolis

Loch Johnson
University of Georgia

Michael Johnston
Colgate University

Vera Katz
Speaker
House of Representatives
State of Oregon

Kenneth Kennedy
College of San Mateo

Henry Kenski
University of Arizona

Burdett Loomis
University of Kansas

Robert Nakamura
Dartmouth College

Charles Pearson
New York University

Nelson Polsby
University of California at Berkeley

Ron Rapoport
College of William and Mary

Robert Scigliano
Boston College

Steve Sinding
Chief of the Population Division
Agency for International Development

Robert E. Whelan
Comptroller
The City of Buffalo

Aaron Wildavsky
University of California at Berkeley

Barbara Wolanin
Curator of the Capitol
Washington, D.C.

Tom Wolanin
Staff Director
Subcommittee on Post-Secondary Education
U.S. House of Representatives

Alan J. Wyner
University of California, Santa Barbara

My students over the years, here at Oberlin College and, for one summer, at the University of Wisconsin at Madison, helped me learn how best to teach, by engaging their capacity to learn.

I also owe a special thanks to my colleagues at Oberlin who read and commented on the manuscript: Louis Fernandez, Joe Gurtis, Ron Kahn, Hirschel Kasper, Richard Levin, Bob Piron, Ben Schiff, Bob Tufts, Harlan Wilson, and Jim Zinser. Oberlin College's librarians, with professionalism and good cheer, graciously accommodated basically outrageous requests.

I'd like to thank, for their professional guidance and goodwill, the extraordinary people associated with Scott, Foresman and Company, especially Jim Levy, Dick Welna, and Bruce Borland, College Division management; Scott Hardy, Paula Fitzpatrick, and Ginny Guerrant in editorial; Carolyn Deacy in design; Leslie Cohn in picture research; Tana Vega-Romero in marketing; Jim Boyd who first brought me on board; Kathryn Jandeska who prepared the index; and Iris Ganz who provided secretarial help.

Finally, my deepest appreciation goes to those whose selfless love and support turned aspirations into reality—my parents, Marion and Charles Burke; my wife Linda; my children, Amy, Carrie, and Michael; and my sometimes student, sometimes mentor, Mark.

Paul A. Dawson

OVERVIEW

CONTENTS

VANTAGE POINTS

PROLOGUE

WHAT CAN GOVERNMENT DO?
THE CASE FOR LESS, AND MORE

W*hat can government do for, or to, you? Can it loan you money to go to college? Can it make your working parents financially support my retired ones? Can it make sure there is a job waiting for you after school? But, what if government does not do these things? If it does not make these decisions, who, or what, will? And if these decisions are made without government, will you, or society, be better off?*

This introductory chapter begins with a short Case, based on the story of Robinson Crusoe, after he was washed ashore on the Island of Despair. Through this Case, we see what Crusoe had to do and we begin to understand what any society must do.

Crusoe's experiences suggest three insights. First, every society must make certain decisions about how it will use its resources. These decisions are unavoidable; they will be made—one way or another. Second, very few of these decisions must be made by anyone in authority, whether a Crusoe or a government. Third, at the other extreme, all of these decisions can be made by a central authority.

The extremes define the range of possible roles that government can perform. What remains, for us and for society, is to sort out the role that government should perform. This will not be easy; as you will soon see, there are good arguments both for less and for more government. Nevertheless, you might want to try to understand these arguments and begin to make up your own mind. Since the people who advance these arguments are debating America's, and your, future, you might want to have something to say about it.

1

WHAT CAN GOVERNMENT DO?

> Whether the matter under consideration is
> auto emissions or auto imports, the health of
> individuals or the health of the economy, the
> central policy question . . . is likely to be:
> What role for government?
> —*Richard Zeckhauser and Derek
> Leebaert,* What Role for
> Government?

The Case   Robinson Crusoe's Choices

September 30, 1659. I, poor, miserable Robinson Crusoe, being ship-
wrecked, during a dreadful storm in the offing, came on shore on this
dismal unfortunate island, which I called "the Island of Despair," all the
rest of the ship's company being drowned, and myself almost dead.

All the rest of the day I spent in afflicting myself at the dismal circumstances I was brought to. . . . (namely) I had neither food, house, clothes,
weapon, or place to fly to, and in despair of any relief, saw nothing but
death before me, either that I should be devoured by wild beasts, murdered by savages, or starved to death for want of food.[1]

Things looked better the next morning. From his ship floundering on the rocks,
Crusoe salvaged some of the necessities of life. No longer in immediate peril, he
took stock of his situation.

Even on the Island of Despair, Robinson Crusoe had resources, both those
from the ship and the natural ones of the island. Some he came by accidentally.
After a month or so, Crusoe noticed, for example, some green stalks sprouting in
a place where he had shaken out a feed bag, thinking it empty of grain.

This touched my heart a little and brought tears out of my eyes, and I
began to bless myself, that such a prodigy of Nature should happen upon
my account. . . . [2]

After the corn matured, Robinson appreciated its value and was determined to
act prudently:

I carefully saved the ears of this corn, you may be sure, in their season,
which was about the end of June; and laying up every corn, I resolved to
sow them all again, hoping in time to have some quantity sufficient to
supply me with bread; but it was not till the fourth year that I could allow
myself the least grain of this corn to eat, and even then but spar-

---

[1]Daniel Defoe, *Robinson Crusoe* (New York: New American Library, Signet Classic, 1961), p. 72.
[2]*Ibid.*, p. 80.

Robinson Crusoe and Friday, from Luis Bunuel's 1954 film based on Daniel Defoe's well-known novel.

ingly . . . for I lost all that I sowed the first season by not observing the proper time. . . . [3]

In spite of his adversities, Crusoe survived and, after four years on the island, was totally content.

> I had nothing to covet; for I had all that I was now capable of enjoying. I was lord of the whole manor; or if I pleased, I might call myself king, or emperor over the whole country which I had possession of. There were no rivals. I had no competitor, none to dispute sovereignty or command with me.[4]

And so he remained, until Friday.

Friday's arrival might have upset Robinson's contentment, since Friday had different tastes and preferences, including a hankering for human flesh. But Crusoe quickly expressed his abhorrence of the practice and provided, as a substitute, roasted goat meat.

> . . . he took so many ways to tell me how well he liked it that I could not but understand him; and at last he told me he would never eat man's flesh any more, which I was very glad to hear.[5]

Because of his success in socializing Friday, Crusoe was able to maintain his state of tranquility.

There was one other thing that helped: Crusoe's gun and the knowledge of how to fire it, both of which he kept from Friday. For some background information on Daniel Defoe, see the **Vantage Point**: Daniel Defoe, the Author of *Robinson Crusoe*.

---

[3]*Ibid.*, p. 81.

[4]*Ibid.*, pp. 128–129.

[5]*Ibid.*, p. 209.

DANIEL DEFOE, THE AUTHOR OF ROBINSON CRUSOE[1]

Daniel Defoe.

Defoe (1660–1731) was a prolific English novelist and political journalist. Credited by some as the father of the English novel, Defoe engaged the reader in realistic narratives, such as those in *Robinson Crusoe* and in his other outstanding novel, *Moll Flanders*.

As a political journalist, Defoe often wrote anonymous tracts for both sides in the political debates of his day. Writing under his own name, his political pamphleteering also landed him in jail briefly.

Robinson Crusoe, one of the most popular novels in the English language, is both highly entertaining and, some think, profound. The book's narrative style entertains, by moving quickly from one scene to another, showing every aspect of Crusoe's struggle to survive. But the story also reflects a particular system of values, one that stresses individualism, hard work, thrift, and personal redemption borne of suffering.

[1]See, for example, Frank H. Ellis, ed., *Twentieth Century Interpretations of Robinson Crusoe: A Collection of Critical Essays* (Englewood Cliffs, NJ: Prentice-Hall, 1969).

Insights

Let us draw some insights from this Case and make their relevance clear to the study of American government.

Insight 1.   *There are certain decisions that every society must make.* In Crusoe's, and society's, case, resources are scarce. Therefore, decisions must be made about how they will be used. In Crusoe's case, for example, decisions had to be made about whether corn would be eaten or planted, about who would fish and who would farm, about who would shoot the gun. In society's case, comparable decisions must be made: What will be produced? In what manner? To whom will goods and services be distributed? All of these decisions must be made and will be made—by someone, somehow.

Insight 2.   *Government's role in making societal decisions can be minimal.* Before Friday arrived, Crusoe made his own decisions about the use of the island's resources. And, as shown by the contentment he achieved, this decision-making mechanism worked; in his own private world, Crusoe was content. Likewise, a society might let all of its resource allocation decisions be made by a private mechanism, the voluntary transactions among buyers and sellers, for example. If it did, there would be little need for a government, except as an

Like the meat these Muscovites are standing in line for, society's resources are scarce, and therefore, decisions must be made about how they will be used.

impartial referee to make sure people strike only bargains, not each other, and that they actually keep the bargains they strike.

Insight 3. *Government's role in making societal decisions can be extensive.* After Friday arrived, the situation changed in a potentially drastic way. Since Friday and Crusoe had such different preferences, some mechanism was needed to make what were now collective choices about the use of resources. Crusoe, and his gun, filled that need; he was the "Master" who made all the decisions. Similarly, a government may exercise total control over all of a society's resources, producing what the government wants, distributing goods and services as it sees fit, and promoting whatever values it deems proper.

Each of these insights introduces a major theme which is elaborated next.

DECISIONS THAT SOCIETY MUST MAKE

Let them eat cake.

There are three **mandatory social decisions** that every society must make about the allocation of its resources: (1) What will be produced? (2) In what manner will things be produced? (3) To whom will goods and services be distributed?

These decisions are mandatory because resources are scarce. The idea of **scarcity** is easy to grasp; it simply means there is not enough of what people

As this scene of the Boston Commons illustrates, societies sometimes decide to produce public goods. These goods provide benefits for all to enjoy.

desire. What is it that you value, for example? Is it time? Space in your dorm room? Money? Whatever it is, it's scarce. And that is why you have to make choices about how you will use your resources. It is also true of society.

What Will Be Produced?

One way or another, with less or more governmental involvement, every society will decide what to produce. The possibilities are as diverse as human desires.

Will society use its resources to produce wine coolers—or Twinkies? Will we kill alligators for shoes or sew symbols of them on clothes? Will land be used for houses or parking lots? Will we build hospitals or health spas?

All of these products have something in common; they are **private goods**, because, once consumed by someone, they can not be consumed by anyone else. Private goods, therefore, have specific benefits; no one, for example, shares directly in whatever benefit you get out of the Twinkie you eat or the clothes you wear. In addition to these kinds of goods and services, a society may produce goods that provide more general benefits. Again, the possibilities are almost endless.

Will society use its resources to produce open green spaces? Theater in the park? Clean air? Freedom from the fear of crime? Research on the causes of cancer? Protection against foreign invaders?

All these products are **public goods**, because the benefit that one person gets from them does not lessen the benefit that anyone else can derive. Public goods, therefore, have general benefits; they provide a wide stream of benefits from which many may drink simultaneously.

A society also must choose to produce either private or public goods, or some combination of the two. Will we have more private automobiles or adequate mass transit systems? Will we launch space shuttles for spying or advertising campaigns for selling soup? Will we build meat markets or medical

Every society must decide who will do what. In this society, for example, some glean, while others write, as, for example, the author (on the right) does here.

WHAT CAN GOVERNMENT DO? THE CASE FOR LESS, AND MORE

schools? Will we produce fancy clothes for the rich or adequate shelter for the poor? All these choices involve trade-offs between private and public goods.

For all these and other possibilities, this society, or any society, will decide what to produce. But, how will things be produced and who will get them?

In What Manner Will Things Be Produced?

One way or another, with less or more governmental involvement, every society will decide on its methods of production.

For a society to design a production process, there are a number of subsidiary decisions that must be made: Who will produce the things society wants? Where will they be produced? At what level will they be produced?

A society may decide among alternative uses of its resources. Should it, for example, produce fancy clothes, or a shelter for street people?

Who Will Produce What Society Wants? For Crusoe, the answer was obvious—at least until Friday arrived. Then a decision had to be made: "Who will fish and who will hunt?" Similarly, any society must make a variety of decisions about who will do what: Will national defense be supplied by women in fighting units of the armed services? Will crops be harvested by illegal aliens? Will blacks be business executives? Will those who choose not to join a union be allowed to work next to those who do?

Where Will Things Be Produced? Crusoe had to decide where to plant his crops and where to keep his goats, for example. Similarly, any society must decide on the sites of production. Again, many particular decisions may present themselves: Will there be a glue factory in a residential neighborhood? How about a plutonium factory? Can a factory move and throw a whole town into the rust bucket? Will orchestras perform throughout the land, or only in big cities? Will megacomputers be made in America?

At What Level Will Things Be Produced? Seeing that what he could not use was wasted, Crusoe cut back the corn he planted and the trees he felled. Similarly, any society must find a way to decide among alternative levels of production: Will we increase the production of guns and lower the supply of food stamps? Will we look for additional sources of energy or try harder to conserve current supplies? How much grain will be milled for bread and how much will be diverted into the production of beef?

For all these and many other things, every society will decide, one way or another, upon the manner in which things are produced.

To Whom Will Goods and Services Be Distributed?

In addition to its decisions about what to produce and the methods of production, a society must decide who will receive goods and services.

Imagine some of the things that might be available and who could get them: Will food go to those with empty stomachs or full bank accounts? Will the chance to attend a prestigious college go to the most qualified or the best heeled? Will mass transit systems stretch into the suburbs? Will health care delivery systems reach into the inner city?

To make these and many other decisions about who will receive what is produced, every society needs some mechanism to distribute its goods and services. And every society will find, or invent, a mechanism for doing this— with or without government.

■ From Robinson Crusoe, we learned that there are certain decisions that every society must make. By elaborating this insight, we now know much more.

In any society, things are scarce. Therefore, choices between different ways of using things must be made. These are decisions about the allocation of society's resources. These decisions will be made—one way or another—in every society. Taken together, they form society's agenda of things it somehow must do.

What can be government's role in the making of society's resource allocation decisions? Conceivably, government could get involved in the making of every decision about how a society should use its resources. You, for example, are a social resource. You could be used to dig coal or pull teeth. Could government then get involved in deciding your vocation? Absolutely. In this, and every other resource allocation decision, government can get involved—if it wants to and tries hard enough.

Government, therefore, can get less or more deeply involved in the making of all a society's resource allocation decisions. There are good cases to be made for both less and more governmental involvement.

THE CASE FOR LESS GOVERNMENTAL INVOLVEMENT

> Still one thing more, fellow citizens—a wise and frugal government, which shall restrain men from injuring one another, which shall leave them otherwise free to regulate their own pursuits of industry and improvement, and shall not take from the mouth of labor the bread it has earned.
> —President Thomas Jefferson, in his first inaugural address, March 4, 1801

The case for less governmental involvement in the making of resource allocation decisions rests on a desire to let the private economic market make these decisions, a belief that the market allocates resources in an efficient manner, and a hope that the market will promote other important social values.

The extent to which resource allocation decisions are made:

Publicly,
by
Government

Privately,
by the
Market

FIGURE 1
The Range of Possible Social Choice Mechanisms

This is a continuum representing the extent to which resource allocation decisions are made publicly, by government, or privately, by the economic system. The public end is on the extreme left and the private end is on the extreme right.

Let the Private Market Make Social Choices

We know that every society needs some kind of mechanism for making decisions about the uses of its resources. What are the possible mechanisms?

Imagine a continuum, running from right to left, like the one in **Figure 1**. Along this continuum, visualize a number of different mechanisms for making resource allocation decisions. On the extreme left end of the continuum, picture a compulsory mechanism for making these decisions, a total dictatorship, for example. Toward the extreme right end of the continuum rests another possible mechanism for allocating society's resources: the private market. The **private economic market** is all the transactions that buyers and sellers engage in voluntarily. These transactions, of course, are not made in a face-to-face manner and do not involve barter; they are impersonal transactions, made on the basis of price. Nevertheless, because of these transactions, decisions are made about what to produce, how it will be produced, and who will receive the resulting goods and services. Because of these transactions, trees, for example, are turned into textbooks, not toothpicks; workers, for example, are increasingly not unionized; and legal advice, for example, goes mostly to those who can afford it. In such ways as these, society's resource allocation decisions can be made by the private market.

In this country, the private market is the preferred mechanism for making resource allocation decisions. This cultural preference for the private market mechanism is largely a matter of tradition, but it also is based on a belief that the private market works efficiently.

The Private Market Works Efficiently

Americans believe that the private market is capable of **economic efficiency**; it can allocate resources in a way that reduces waste and thereby increases human welfare. On the Island of Despair, for example, Crusoe planted more corn than he needed and, rotting and rat-infested, it went to waste. But Crusoe could correct this situation; by reallocating his time to other activities, he reduced waste and increased his satisfaction. In a similar way, the private market can eliminate inefficient uses of resources.

The private market, many believe, automatically senses waste and then reallocates resources in a more efficient manner. This can happen in many ways. When there is too little beef in the stores, prices go up and encourage producers to raise more cattle, thereby increasing the supply of beef. When jobs are scarce, the unemployed will be willing to work for less and businesses will be encouraged to take advantage of cheaper labor by expanding production. When your school raises its tuition too high, you can transfer to another one which you think is just as good, only cheaper. In all these cases, the private market can work efficiently.

When it works efficiently, the private market produces the best possible outcome: resources are allocated in such a way so that as many people as possible are as satisfied as possible. Moreover, most Americans assume, as did Jefferson, that the private market works best when there is little governmental involvement. Ideally, government need act only as a referee, so that coercion does not distort voluntary agreements and people actually live up to the agreements they make.

The Private Market Promotes Important Values

Most Americans also prefer the private market because they hope it will promote other important values. The hope is well founded. Because of the way resources are allocated, certain values are rewarded and thereby reinforced. On the Island of Despair, for example, Crusoe could survive only through hard work and thrift, values he acquired and clung to. In a similar way, reliance on the private market helps Americans realize other things they value, especially liberty, the right to pursue their own self-interest without regulation, and privacy, the right to do what they want without supervision. In both cases, the private market is a sanctuary; within it, these values thrive.

■ As Crusoe knew before Friday arrived, there may be little need for any central authority to decide on the uses of society's resources. In general, the case for a minimal governmental role rests on beliefs about the way the private market enhances economic well-being and other important values. But what happens when the market does not work this way?

THE CASE FOR MORE GOVERNMENTAL INVOLVEMENT

> The test of our progress is not whether we add more to the abundance of those who have much; it is whether we provide enough for those who have too little.
> —President Franklin D. Roosevelt,
> in his second inaugural address,
> January 20, 1937

The case for more governmental involvement in the making of resource allocation decisions rests on a conclusion that the private market has failed. In general, **market failure** occurs when the private economic market fails to work efficiently, when it fails to work fairly, or when it fails to promote other things of value to society.

The Private Market May Fail to Work Efficiently

The case for more governmental involvement rests on a belief that the private market has failed to produce what society wants and to produce it in an acceptable manner. The market, for example, may produce too little of what people want or too much of what they do not want: too few affordable houses; too little health care; not enough clean water; too much crime; and too few jobs. The market also may produce things in a manner that society finds unacceptable: too many children in textile mills; too short life spans for chemists; too many foreign-made goods; too few female professors; too many robots on automobile assembly lines. When it does such things, the private market fails, because it is not allocating resources in a way that people find desirable.

Moreover, the private market can easily fail, especially when buyers have bad information about goods and services, when there is little competition among sellers, and when people want public goods.

The private market fails when buyers have bad information. If people do not know what smoking can do to them, too many cigarettes will be consumed; if they do not know what good medicine is, there will be too many quacks in practice; if they do not know what a college education can do for them, there will be too few in school. In all these examples, the market will fail, because people have bad information about the consequences of their actions and, therefore, can not accurately measure the satisfaction, or the harm, they derive from their action.

The market also fails when there is not enough competition among sellers. If there is only one grocery store in town, food prices will be higher than they would be otherwise; if only General Motors made automobiles, there will be fewer cheap cars; if only one train runs from New Haven to New York, the cost of commuting will be higher than it needs to be. In all these examples, the market will fail, because, without competition, people will pay artificially high prices for goods and services and, therefore, have money available for other things they desire.

Finally, the private market will fail to produce public goods. There are many public goods and services that a society may desire: national defense, public seashores, and clean air. Since public goods provide freely accessible benefits, it is difficult to withhold benefits from anyone or to collect from those who derive them. For example, suppose you went into the clean air business; many might benefit, but few would voluntarily pay you anything for the good you provide. Since there is no profit in producing them, the private market will not produce public goods.

For all these reasons, the private market may fail to work efficiently. And, when it does, the resulting public dissatisfaction can fuel a demand for greater governmental involvement.

The private market may fail to work—or work fairly.

The Private Market May Fail to Work Fairly

The private market can be efficient but not fair. Markets are efficient when they produce what people want and when they do so with a process that people view as desirable. But **fairness** requires that goods and services be distributed in a manner that society approves of. An agricultural market, for example, may be very efficient; it may produce the greatest amount of food with the fewest resources. But this market still could be unfair. The food that is produced could be distributed in a manner that the society sees as unfair. Whether or not something is fair is, clearly, a highly subjective matter. Moreover, a society may change its view; at different times, it may be more or less offended by certain levels of unemployment, infant mortality, or farm foreclosures, for example. Whenever it happens, however, the belief that the market is unfair also can heighten the demand for governmental involvement in decisions about the uses of society's resources.

The Private Market May Fail to Promote Other Social Values

Other than the values of liberty and privacy, the private market may fail to promote important social values. The private market, for example, does not necessarily produce economic stability. Instead, the market may produce wild swings in the economy, booms of great prosperity and busts of great depression. This may be unacceptable; a society, instead, may value economic stability and demand that government provide it. In addition, other things like civil rights, can not be bought in the private market; people who value free speech or the right to cast a secret ballot must go outside the market to realize these values. In general, whenever society wants things that can not be provided by the private market, the case for governmental involvement is strengthened.

■As Crusoe knew, after Friday and his different tastes arrived, there may be a great need for some central authority to decide on the uses of society's resources. In general, government's role in making societal decisions can be extensive. It is unlikely to be, we know, because of America's cultural preference for the private market. But the market can fail and we know it will under certain conditions. When these occur, faith in the market is replaced by societal dissatisfaction and sometimes by political demands for greater governmental involvement in making decisions about the uses of society's resources. The case for more governmental involvement is built, therefore, on the failures of the private market—just as new cities are erected on the ruins of old.

SUMMARY

Every society, whether it consists of two or two hundred million, must make certain decisions about the uses of its scarce resources. There are three major mandatory resource allocation decisions: (1) What will be produced? (2) In what manner will it be produced? (3) To whom will goods and services be distributed?

A society, however, may use different devices for making these decisions. At one extreme, it could let these decisions be made as the result of the workings of the private economic market, a voluntary system of transactions made on the basis of price. At another extreme, a society could let all these decisions be made by government, a compulsory system of transactions made on the basis of law.

Most Americans act as though they prefer letting the private market make decisions about the allocation of societal resources, because they believe it works efficiently and promotes important social values, especially the values of personal liberty and privacy. This preference and these beliefs are the basis of the case for less governmental involvement in the making of resource allocation decisions.

Americans, however, can become dissatisfied with the private market, because it fails to work efficiently, or because it does not distribute goods and services fairly, or because it fails to nurture other important values, such as economic stability or civil rights. This dissatisfaction and these beliefs are the basis of the case for greater governmental involvement in the making of resource allocation decisions.

Key Terms

mandatory social decisions	private economic market
scarcity	economic efficiency
private goods	market failure
public goods	fairness

Review and Reflection

1. In what ways did Robinson Crusoe act like a government?

2. What *can* government do? Define its potential role in the broadest possible terms.

3. Describe, with examples, the resource allocation decisions that every society must make.

4. Define "private economic market."

5. Can both the private market and government make mandatory resource allocation decisions?

6. Imagine a continuum representing the extent to which resource allocation decisions are made publicly, by government, or privately, by the economic system. Let the public end be on the extreme left and the private end be on the extreme right, as below:

The Degree to Which Decisions Are Made

Publicly,   Privately,
by   ——————————————   by the
Government   Market

Where would you place the American case on this continuum? Why is it there? Where would you place other systems? How is it, do you suppose, that other political systems end up where they do on this continuum?

7. Some people believe that government's role in society should be as small as possible. What, if anything, justifies this view?

8. Other people believe that government should play a much bigger role than it does today. What, if anything, justifies this view?

9. What do you believe? Where do you think the American national government *should* be on the public-private continuum in Question 6? Why?

Supplemental Readings

Since the late 1970s and especially in the 1980s, those who argue in favor of more governmental involvement have been on the defensive; few, today, argue in favor of a bigger federal government or new, expensive federal responses to domestic social problems.

The attack against big government has been pressed by conservatives who, like *Friedman*, argue that social welfare is enhanced through the operations of the private market. Government, therefore, according to *Silvas*, should get smaller, as public responsibilities are returned to the private sector.

Liberals, today, take another tack. Instead of arguing that government, or the federal government in particular, should get bigger, contemporary liberals criticize the conservative approach while groping for one of their own. A common criticism made, for example, by *Edsall*, is that conservative policies are unfair, because they redistribute wealth upwards, into the pockets of the already wealthy. Others, such as *Tsongas*, also argue that there remain social and economic problems that must be solved and we must find new ways to solve them. There are some, still vague, emerging alternatives. The "neo-liberals" for example, as *Rothenberg* shows, would try to stimulate economic growth and public investment through new forms of cooperation between government and the private sector.

But you can jump into the middle of this debate yourself. Start by reading these books:

Edsall, Thomas. *The New Politics of Inequality*. New York: W. W. Norton & Company, 1984.

Friedman, Milton, and Rose Friedman. *Free to Choose: A Personal Statement*. New York: Harcourt Brace Jovanovich, 1979.

Rothenberg, Randall. *The Neoliberals: Creating the New American Politics*. New York: Simon and Schuster, 1984.

Silvas, E. S. *Privatizing the Public Sector: How to Shrink Government*. Chatham, NJ: Chatham House Publishers, Inc., 1982.

Tsongas, Paul. *The Road from Here*. New York: Knopf, 1981.

PART ONE

FOUNDATIONS OF AMERICAN GOVERNMENT

"Each generation . . . has a right to choose for itself the form of government it believes most promotive of its own happiness."
—*Thomas Jefferson*

CHAPTER ONE

WHAT SHOULD GOVERNMENT DO?
THE CENTRAL QUESTION

What should government do? Should it try to help American farmers, or let them go bankrupt? Should it hire college graduates who refuse to pay off their federally guaranteed student loans? Is it wrong for the federal government to ignore the needs of the hungry at home or abroad? Is the federal government's support for Israel justified?

"Should" questions are questions about what is correct, or justified, or proper. These kinds of questions can not be avoided; they dominate our history and the way we think about governmental institutions, public policies, and politics.

This chapter begins with a brief Case, drawn from one of the most crucial periods of the Civil War. In this period, President Lincoln wrestled with his deepest dilemma: should he accept defeat and disunion or try to preserve the Union by committing the North to the destruction of slavery?

The Case suggests four insights. First, in Lincoln's presidency and in the political life of this nation, the central question is: "What is the proper role of government?" Second, **governmental institutions** are places where binding decisions are made about the use of society's resources. Third, **public policies** are governmental attempts to remedy societal problems. Fourth, **politics** is the way we fight over what government should, and should not, do.

These definitions provide useful insights. For complementary ones, see the **Vantage Point**: Complementary images of governmental institutions, public policies, and politics.

GOVERNMENT'S PROPER ROLE

> The legitimate object of government is to do
> for a community of people whatever they
> need to have done, but cannot do at all in
> their separate and individual capacities.
> —*Abraham Lincoln*

The Case President Lincoln's Decision to Issue the Emancipation
Proclamation

Summer, 1862. President Lincoln had counted heavily on General McClellan and
now McClellan's failure at Richmond weighed even more heavily on the President. The failure extended the Civil War two and one-half more years and forced
Lincoln to adopt a new policy for fighting the war.

It was to have been a short war, fought quickly for limited aims. And it would
have been—if only Richmond, the capital of the Confederacy, would fall. In the
West, the war had been mostly won after General Grant forced the Confederate
retreat and reopened the Mississippi and Tennessee Rivers. Through this action,
the border states of Kentucky and Tennessee were no longer threatened and the
Confederacy was increasingly isolated. If only Richmond would fall.

General McClellan was supposed to take Richmond, but he showed "a
singular genius for making war in low gear."[1] Moving guns weighing up to nine
tons into carefully constructed fortifications, "Tardy" McClellan slowly prepared
to lay siege. But before he could even start his bombardment, General Lee
attacked McClellan's right flank and broke through. As McClellan retreated from
his trenches, the siege of Richmond was over before it began. Lee's Confederate
forces then swung north to Manassas, Virginia, when they again defeated the
Union Army in the Second Battle of Bull Run.[2] Despair dominated Washington,
D.C., and privately Lincoln could not escape the conclusion: "We must change
our tactics or lose the war."[3]

It was no longer possible to fight a limited war to restore the Union. Before
Richmond, Union soldiers had sufficient resolve and enthusiasm; expecting quick
victory, they swelled the Union ranks. Finding instead defeat in a protracted war,
Union resolve and often the soldiers themselves fled. Voluntary enlistments
plummeted and with them Lincoln's hope for a limited war. He could no longer
resist the demands of the abolitionists to fight a larger war for a broader purpose;
now their resolve and enthusiasm was needed to feed the war machine.

---

[1] Bruce Catton, *Terrible Swift Sword* (New York: Doubleday and Company, 1963), p. 371.

[2] For a fictionalized account of the Second Battle of Bull Run, or Second Manassas, as it was known
in the Confederacy, see Tom Wicker, *Unto This Hour* (New York: Viking Press, 1984).

[3] Catton, *Terrible Swift Sword*, p. 365.

President Lincoln at General McClellan's camp.

Abolitionists flooded Congress with petitions calling for an immediate end to slavery. By July, 1862, military necessity had pushed the North to the edge of a momentous decision; accept defeat and disunion or try to destroy slavery. Without embracing the cause of abolition, Congress passed the Confiscation Act which permitted the army to confiscate the property and free the slaves of those fighting against the Union. But the law was only half a step, a military tactic to encourage slaves to escape and join in the fight against their former masters. The tactic lacked moral conviction; the law was poorly implemented, and in one scandalous case, a Union General refused refuge to escaping slaves and turned them back, away from Union lines. Appalled abolitionists called on the President to countermand his general and enforce the policy of confiscation; Lincoln refused.

Outrage mounted. Horace Greeley, the flamboyant editor of the *New York Tribune,* published an open letter to the President. This letter, the "Prayer of Twenty Million," argued that the North was losing the war because of its soft stand on slavery. Greeley urged the President to enforce the Confiscation Act and take the additional decisive step of emancipation. Lincoln's reply to Greeley was printed five days later: ". . . My paramount object in this struggle is to save the Union, and it is not either to save or destroy Slavery. If I could save the Union without freeing any slave, I would do it; if I could save it by freeing all the slaves, I would do it; if I could do it by freeing some and leaving others alone, I would do that. . . ."[4] Lincoln, however, had already plotted his course.

---

[4] Quoted in Howard Zinn, *A People's History of the United States* (New York: Harper and Row, 1980), p. 186.

Lincoln and his cabinet were committed to the Emancipation Proclamation a full month before the exchange of letters in the *Tribune*. But Lee's march had taken him north of the Potomac River; moving across Maryland with an unbeaten army, Lee threatened the defense of Washington. Under those conditions, issuing the Emancipation Proclamation would have seemed a desperate act which signalled weakness rather than new purpose. The document, therefore, awaited a Union victory—the battle of Antietam Creek, outside of Sharpsburg, Maryland.

Antietam was pivotal; after Lee retreated, the Emancipation Proclamation was issued. And a limited war, fought to conserve the status quo, became an unlimited war, fought for the revolutionary purpose of giving freedom to slaves.[5]

Insights

Insight 1. *The central question in American political life is: "What should government do?"* Throughout his presidency, Lincoln struggled with the question: What was the proper course of action? Was it, for example, proper to confiscate or emancipate slaves? Or was it proper to refuse to do so? Lincoln's struggle epitomizes America's. Throughout our history, Americans have struggled to define government's proper role. Was it, for example, proper to rebel against Great Britain? Should the national government have let the Great Depression run its course? Is it right for the state to require integrated schools, free of prayer? In one guise or another, the underlying concern with government's proper role is the central theme in Lincoln's presidency and in the continuing political life of this country.

Insight 2. *Governmental institutions are places where binding decisions are made about the use of society's resources.* During the Civil War, the President and the Congress decided what resources the North would enlist in its cause. President Lincoln, for example, decided whether General McClellan would press the attack or wait for more supplies; whether blacks would be enlisted in battle or relegated to the rear; whether the energies of the abolitionists would be mobilized behind the war or behind opposition to his presidency. Moreover, once he made up his mind, Lincoln's decisions were binding; if necessary, force could be used to carry out his orders. Today, national governmental institutions can make binding decisions about alternative uses of different kinds of resorces: Should environmental resources be consumed by this generation or saved for subsequent ones? Should all citizens serve in the Armed Services? Should wealth be concentrated in the pockets of the few?

Insight 3. *Public policies are governmental attempts to remedy societal problems.* President Lincoln clearly knew the problem to be remedied but he still needed a cure. This he hoped the Emancipation Proclamation would provide. Today, America suffers from different problems, although, like Lincoln, we ago-

---

[5] Stephen W. Sears, *Landscape Turned Red: The Battle of Antietam* (New York: Ticknor & Fields, 1983).

WHAT SHOULD *GOVERNMENT DO? THE CENTRAL QUESTION*

nize over alternative remedies. Should we counter threats to national security by developing the capability of knocking down incoming missiles? Should the federal government cure poverty among the elderly by increasing taxes on young workers? Should state and local government try to make up for federal cuts in social services, by taking money out of the pockets of consumers?

Insight 4. *Politics is the way we fight over what government should, and should not, do.* As long as they have different values and are free to pursue them, people will disagree over what government should do. During the Civil War, for example, underlying values implied different war policies: Lincoln was primarily concerned with restoring the Union, while Greeley placed a higher premium on ending slavery; Lincoln was more interested in winning battlefield victories, while McClellan seemed more interested in avoiding defeats. Today, many different values imply many different policies: some value free trade and would reduce governmental involvement in the economy, while others are more concerned with protecting American jobs and would have the federal government reduce imports; some value civil rights and would have the federal government do more to protect racial minorities, while others are more concerned with their personal liberty and believe that government has done enough. In these and many other examples, different values dictate different, and often competing, courses for government. How are such conflicts to be settled? Through perpetual civil war or through politics? In general, our society relies on politics, as it tries to chart government's proper course.

Each of these insights reveals something about the nature of government, policy, and politics in America; their elaboration, next, reveals much more.

THE CENTRAL QUESTION IN AMERICAN POLITICAL LIFE

> Government (in a democracy) can not be stronger or more tough-minded than its people. It can not be more inflexibly committed to the task than they. It can not be wiser than the people.
>
> —Adlai Stevenson, Democratic nominee for President, 1952

The central question is: What is the proper role of government? The question has been, and we believe, always will be, central in the political life of this nation. It also is vital; how it is answered determines what we as a nation strive for and scorn, what we as a people value and despise, and whether or not our

This cartoon expressed its own view of whether Great Britain was behaving properly, or at least, more improperly than the young man in the middle.

government has a right to exist. The question also lacks an unambiguous and final answer, since people invariably disagree about what government should, and should not, do. All answers, therefore, will be viewed by some as incomplete, if not incorrect. All courses of governmental action will be viewed by some as incorrect, if not improper.

The question provokes struggle. No one struggled harder than President Lincoln. But his was only the hardest of many; American history is littered with past attempts to decide on government's proper role:

- Was it proper to incite rebellion against Great Britain?
- Was it right for the federal government and its courts to insist on bussing as a way of combating racial segregation in public schools?
- What should have President Carter done to free the American hostages in Iran?

The struggle, moreover, is more than a curious historical artifact; it is an ongoing, and, probably, never-ending process, reflected in many contemporary controversies:

- Does the government have an obligation to feed the hungry and house the homeless?
- Should the federal government prohibit any form of prayer in public schools?
- Should the Interior Department sell public lands—or pieces of the Statue of Liberty?

There are many different perspectives one could take on America's continuing effort to answer this central question. Many of them are woven into subsequent chapters, as we describe governmental institutions, public policies, and politics.

To complement this text's perspective, we have asked Professors Nelson Polsby and Aaron Wildavsky to grapple with the question of government's proper role. Other portions of this Dialogue appear throughout the book in chapters 4, 5, 6, 7, 10, 11, 13, 15, and 16.

■ For President Lincoln in the gloomiest days of the Civil War, for Professors Polsby and Wildavsky in their Dialogue, and for the rest of us in this course—and later—the central question is: What is the proper role of government?

The question also dominates the life of democratic governmental institutions, since they are especially concerned about their legitimacy and about their need to cultivate public support.

Should state and local governments provide bilingual education? The debate over these and many other questions about government's proper role continues.

GOVERNMENTAL INSTITUTIONS

> If democracy loses its touch, then no great war will be needed to overwhelm it.
> —*Vannevar Bush, science advisor to Presidents Roosevelt and Truman*

We have defined governmental institutions as places where binding decisions are made about the use of society's resources. The decisions are binding because government has the right to use force, if necessary, to make sure that people accept them. The right to use force is conditional, not absolute, however. To maintain the right, a government, especially a democratic one, needs legitimacy and will react to signals that this is lacking.

Democratic Governments Need Legitimacy

Governmental institutions, especially ones in democratic political systems, need legitimacy; their right and their ability to rule depends on it.

The Nature of Legitimacy. **Legitimacy** is a collective sense that governmental actions are consistent with popular preferences. Thus, governments have legitimacy when there is a good fit between the rulers and the ruled, especially between the government's policies and the people's preferences. The fit between policies and preferences, of course, is a subjective one that depends on personal perceptions, on people's beliefs that their government is acting in their interests. The apparent fit is hard to achieve and easily lost, however. When it is, it also is easy to doubt the political system's legitimacy. Throughout

Aaron B. Wildavsky, a past President of the American Political Science Association and Professor of Political Science at the University of California at Berkeley, is the author of many books and articles on all aspects of policy making, including *The Politics of the Budgetary Process* (Boston: Little, Brown, 1964) and (with Nelson Polsby) *Presidential Elections: Strategies of American Electoral Politics*, 6th ed. (New York: Scribner, 1984).

Nelson W. Polsby, a past Managing Editor of the *American Political Science Review* and Professor of Political Science at the University of California at Berkeley has published many books and articles on American politics in general and the United States Congress in particular, including (with Aaron Wildavsky) *Presidential Elections: Strategies of American Electoral Politics*, 6th ed. (New York:

Scribner, 1984) and *Political Innovation in America: The Politics of Policy Initiation* (New Haven, Conn.: Yale University Press, 1984).

The dialogue between Professors Polsby and Wildavsky ranges widely, beginning here with the proper role of government and progressing into specific areas of American political life that are bound up in this overarching question of government's proper role: possible threats to liberty, the nature of American political culture, interest groups, political parties, the news media, the Reagan presidency, the performance of the major institutions of national government, and the effects of public policy on social welfare and national security. These other portions of the Wildavsky—Polsby Dialogue can be found in Chapters 4, 5, 6, 7, 10, 11, 13, 15, and 16.

A DIALOGUE BETWEEN PROFESSORS AARON B. WILDAVSKY AND NELSON W. POLSBY ON THE PROPER ROLE OF GOVERNMENT

AUTHOR: What's the proper role of government? For example, would you have the federal government do more or less? And why?

WILDAVSKY: I'm in favor of reducing agricultural subsidies, tobacco subsidies, dairy subsidies to zero. We're the only country in the world that manages to subsidize milk production in a way that results in higher costs for consumers. I would reduce every single subsidy to business. Why am I subsidizing the President of U. S. Steel? What, is he one of the downtrodden of America? Let him go out and earn a living.

[handwritten margin note: A GRANT BY GOV. TO A PERSON OR COMPANY TO ASSIST AN ENTERPRISE DEEMED BENIFICAL TO THE PUBLIC]

POLSBY: Workers are obviously the ones you have to worry about.

WILDAVSKY: If we're going to go to workers, why is it a matter of social justice that workers in the auto and steel industry should get two and a half to three times the average wage in industry? In my opinion, until the federal government stops subsidizing Chrysler and other American cars by putting pressure on Japan and others to limit their imports here, Lee Iacocca should not get more of a salary than anybody else on government welfare. I'm going to think he's wonderful and great when he actually competes in a free enterprise system and not in a government subsidized system. And then

. . .until the federal government stops sub-sidizing Chrysler and other American cars by putting pressure on Japan and others to limit their imports here, Lee Iacocca should not get more of a salary than anybody else on government welfare. —Wildavsky

I'm going to say he's entitled to whatever his board and his stockholders will pay him.

POLSBY: I was going to raise the issue of government subsidized product liability insurance for the makers of drugs. Drug manufacturers will simply get out of the immunization business if they think that they're going to lose their shirts. Or even worse, consider the case of "orphan drugs," drugs for diseases that occur so infrequently that it's simply not economic for a drug company to work on them.

WILDAVSKY: In the end, all these costs come back to citizens. I'm worried about government being the insurer of last resort because I think that this will lead to unconscionable verdicts. Since Uncle Sam has virtually no budget limits, the result will be to intensify what is happening now, namely, to increase greatly the cost of manufacturing these drugs and to undermine our competitive position in the world market for them. I would rather revise the law of tort, the law of personal injuries, so that those who have been harmed through someone else's error can collect substantially and those who have poor cases won't collect at all.

I recently read a Rand Corporation study of thousands of cases in Chicago which goes something like this: If you are unfortunate enough to be in an accident and get hurt badly, you collect x dollars from the other person's insurance company. But, if the other person is a city, you get four times x dollars. And, if the other party is a corporation, you get six to eight times x dollars. The idea is that fat cats can pay.

So long as we view insurance as a form of income redistribution, as a part of the struggle over equality in America, the results will be totally haphazard and a lot of money will go to lawyers who should be engaged in more socially productive labor.

POLSBY: Redistribution is socially productive labor, according to some. In fact, lawyers are in the business of redistribution, in a fundamental sense. Without the capacity to sue and assert one's rights, your status determines your just desserts. With this capacity exercised the way it is in the United States, which is to say frequently, maybe it isn't your status but rather the quality of your case that determines your benefit.

Above: A scene depicting the Whiskey Rebellion of 1794. Here, rebels jeer at a federal official whom they have tarred and feathered. Below: George Washington reviewing the Western army which was called in to supress the rebellion.

GENERAL GEORGE WASHINGTON.
Reviewing the Western army at Fort Cumberland the 18.th of October 1794

our history, there have been times when the policies of government and the actions of governmental officials seemed out of touch with popular preferences. These times raised to crisis levels doubts about the system's legitimacy, especially the legitimacy of the increasingly strong national government:

- In the Whiskey Rebellion of 1794, farmers in western Pennsylvania objected to the federal tax on liquor and the national government had to resort to force to suppress the rebellion.
- During the Civil War, when President Lincoln moved toward emancipation too slowly for some and too quickly for others.

WHAT SHOULD *GOVERNMENT DO? THE CENTRAL QUESTION*

- In the Great Depression, the apparent inability of either the economy or government to meet human needs stimulated social unrest and political radicalism.
- With the escalation of the American war effort in the mid- and late-1960s, President Johnson's Vietnam War policies provoked violent protest and heavy-handed repression.
- During the height of the Watergate crisis, revelations of impropriety in the Nixon White House and reelection campaign forced the first resignation of a sitting President.
- Failing to deliver the promised government "as good as its people," Jimmy Carter dejectedly returned to Georgia after the presidential election of 1980. In all these cases, the apparent lack of legitimacy was especially disturbing in a democratic political system.

The Nature of Democracy. A **democracy** is a political system in which the government's right to rule depends on maintaining the consent of the governed. This has been true since the founding. In the words of Seymour Martin Lipset, a prolific political sociologist, the United States of America was the "first new nation."[6] The new government in 1776 was founded on the radical doctrine of **popular sovereignty**: the idea that, unlike the divine rule of absolute monarchs, a democracy's right to rule was derived from the governed. This new government, therefore, would be a **republic**, a form of government in which sovereign power remained with the people, although it was exercised by governmental officials. In theory, power flowed from the people to the government. In rhetoric, it was "We the people . . ." who declared independence from the Crown, *not* "We the states . . ." In practice, the new democratic government would have to keep its "touch" to maintain a close relationship with the people. Here then was the implied promise: the democratic government would ensure a fit between what it did, the policies it adopted, and what the people wanted, the things that were consistent with their preferences and underlying values.

In a democracy, a good fit between public policies and popular preferences can come about through elitist, participatory, and representative forms of government.

Elitist Democracy. An **elitist democracy** relies on the few to act in the interests of the many. This form of democracy rests on the premise that the people know what they want, but they do not necessarily know what is good for them. The people, for example, defer maintenance on society's infrastructure, its roads, bridges, and water systems—even though neglected repairs cost more in the long run. Elitists conclude that the people do not always know what is good for them and someone will have to figure it out for them. The argument is especially appealing to governmental officials; everyone likes their

---

6 Seymour Martin Lipset, *The First New Nation* (New York: Basic Books, 1963).

COMPLEMENTARY IMAGES OF GOVERNMENTAL INSTITUTIONS, PUBLIC POLICIES, AND POLITICS

We have defined governmental institutions, public policies, and politics in straightforward, traditional terms:

- *Governmental institutions* are places where binding, or authoritative, decisions are made about the use of resources.

- *Public policies*, the decisions, embody societal goals and government's plans for realizing them.

- *Politics* is the way people with different values fight over what government should, and should not, do.

To deepen your understanding of the American political system, you might find it useful to keep the following images in mind as you read subsequent chapters:

The Car. A governmental institution is an automobile, the collection of parts and the way they fit together. Policy is direction and movement. Politics is fuel. (Note that there are many different cars, going in different directions, at different speeds, some running better than others.)

The Theater. Government is the stage and the written parts to be spoken. Politics is the life actors breathe into their roles. Policy is what makes it over the footlights.

The Football Game. Government is the rules, the field, the stadium. Politics is the skill and the competitive urges of the players and the coaches. Policy making is the play: the drive, the fumble, the pass, the interception, the end run, the score, the victory, the defeat—and the next meeting.

The Where, the What, and the Why. Government is where it happens, policy is what happens, and politics is why it happens.

own discretion and room to exercise it. The argument has been severely criticized, however, as too undemocratic.[7]

Participatory Democracy.   A **participatory democracy** counts on the people to represent themselves directly and thereby affect the fit between their interests and the government's policies. The participatory impulse is endemic in the American democracy, as was noted earlier by the nineteenth century political observer, Alexis de Tocqueville: "In no country in the world has the principle of association been more successfully used, or more unsparingly applied to a multitude of different objects, than in America. . . . If a stoppage occurs in a thoroughfare . . . the neighbors immediately constitute a deliberative body; and this extemporaneous assembly gives rise to an executive power, which remedies the inconvenience, before anybody has thought of recurring to an authority superior to that of the persons immediately concerned."[8]

[7] The rebuttal comes in Jack Walker, "A Critique of the Elitist Theory of Democracy," *American Political Science Review*, 60 (1966): 285–95 and is elaborated in Peter Bachrach, *Theory of Democratic Elitism: A Critique* (Boston: Little, Brown, 1967).

In a representative democracy, people communicate their preferences to policy-making elites, as these farmers are before the Capitol.

which remedies the inconvenience, before anybody has thought of recurring to an authority superior to that of the persons immediately concerned."[8]

This participatory impulse is not an historical oddity; efforts to make public policy more public by democratizing the way it is formed pervade American history.[9] From the procedural reforms of the progressives to the demands of modern day public interest groups, the impulse makes strident the cry to open, to public scrutiny and participation, the decision-making procedures of all kinds of political and governmental institutions—political parties, congressional committees, and bureaucratic agencies, including, some suggest, the Central Intelligence Agency.

Representative Democracy. A **representative democracy** strikes a balance between democracy's elitist and participatory extremes. Elected representatives act like elites, trying to decide what is in the best interest of the people. But the people have access to various avenues of political participation and, through them, attempt to keep their representatives on a short leash. Democratic representatives therefore have a difficult task; they must maintain enough discretionary judgment so that they can act responsibly to do what they believe right and they must be sufficiently well-constrained by the people so that they act in a manner that is responsive to the will of the people.[10] Edmund

---

[8] Alexis de Tocqueville, *Democracy in America*, vol. 1, trans. Henry Reeve (New York: Random House, 1981), p. 101.

[9] For historical examples, see Richard Hofstadter, *The Age of Reform* (New York: Vintage Books, 1955).

[10] See Hanna Pitkin, *The Concept of Representation* (Berkeley, Calif.: University of California Press, 1967).

Burke, a Member of the British Parliament in the 1770s, found out how hard it is to maintain this balance when campaigning for re-election before his Bristol electorate: "Your representative owes you, not his industry only, but his judgment; and he betrays instead of serving you if he sacrifices it to your opinion." But Burke went too far; he lost the balance between elitist and participatory views—and he lost the election.

Representative democracy relies on political competition to bring about a fit between people's interests and public policy. Electoral competition reins in discretion, making representatives responsive by making them fearful of their jobs and therefore, hopefully, attentive to the felt needs of their constituents—especially to those who are well-organized and politically assertive. This is the kind of democracy Joseph Schumpeter had in mind: "The democratic method is that institutional arrangement in which individuals acquire the power to decide by means of a competitive struggle for the peoples' vote."[11] Through the competitive electoral struggle, unworthy representatives are replaced with ones whose actions might better match the wishes of the people. In general, the American democracy tends to rely most heavily on representative forms of policy making, although it includes both elitist and participatory forms as well.

No matter how it is acquired, legitimacy sustains—and energizes—democratic governmental institutions. With legitimacy, democratic governmental officials are empowered to achieve great public purposes. Without legitimacy, democratic governmental officials have no good choices; if they do nothing, they are resented and if they try to do something by force, they are soon replaced.

Democratic governmental institutions and those who occupy them, therefore, react strongly to expressions of popular dissatisfaction that raise doubts about their legitimacy, especially when those cries are amplified through representative political processes and institutions.

Democratic Governments React to Dissatisfaction

Democratic governments react to popular dissatisfaction about their policies. Popular dissatisfaction is a fault line through society that signals a poor fit between governmental actions and popular desires. Democracies, therefore, usually react to popular dissatisfaction before it can shake their foundations. When they do, democratic governmental institutions react either by adopting new policies or by rallying public support for old ones.

Government in America is mostly reactive—pushed into action by the press of events, as Lincoln was pushed by military necessity. Remember that government is subject to the same laws of inertia that affect us all; government usually does not initiate action spontaneously. Like us and most other objects at rest, government tends to move only when some outside force or political pressure is applied.

---

[11] Joseph A. Schumpeter, *Capitalism, Socialism, and Democracy* 2nd ed. (New York: Harper and Brothers, 1947), p. 269.

'Henry—it's the thermostat police!'

To illustrate the reactive nature of American government, let us quickly scan some major events in American political history:

- *The Declaration of Independence.* On July 4, 1776, representatives from the thirteen states unanimously declared their independence from the British Crown. They were reacting to a "long train of abuses and usurpations" which revealed a despotic plan to suppress the people. They made explicit this justification by using more than half the Declaration to list the specific grievances that drove them to declare their independence.
- *The Revolutionary War.* The war too was reactive, fought by the colonists in response to the loss of their rights as English subjects. In the words of Samuel Eliot Morison, a famous historian of this period, "Make no mistake; the American Revolution was not fought to *obtain* freedom, but to *preserve* the liberties that Americans already had as colonials. Independence was no conscious goal, secretly nurtured in cellar or jungle by bearded conspirators, but a reluctant last resort, to preserve 'life, liberty, and the pursuit of happiness.'"[12]
- *The New Deal.* The New Deal was born out of necessity, in reaction to calamity. In the four years before Roosevelt took office, the American economy shrunk almost in half. Banks failed, farms and homes were lost through foreclosure, and unemployment rose above twenty percent for the nation as a whole. Inaugurated on March 4, 1933, President Roosevelt called the Congress into a special session. During the next "Hundred Days," the Congress reacted and government's role grew as never before, extending into banking, stock market practices, farming, employment practices, and the generation of electrical power.

---

[12]Samuel Eliot Morison, *The Oxford History of the American People* (New York: Oxford University Press, 1965), p. 182.

The conditions of the New Deal's birth are conveyed in the photograph by Margaret Bourke-White, even though these were flood victims, lined up for free food.

- *School Integration.* President Dwight Eisenhower was no fan of big government; yet on September 24, 1957, he took control of the Arkansas National Guard and ordered it to integrate peacefully the Central High School in Little Rock, Arkansas. Eisenhower acted only after he was pushed by Orville Faubus, the then-Governor of Arkansas, who had used the Guard to block a federal court order that the schools be integrated. The stakes were high in this direct challenge to the supremacy of federal over state law and to Eisenhower's credibility as President. Neither could be sacrificed; Eisenhower had to react.
- *President Reagan's Counter Revolution.* Reacting to almost fifty years of growth in government, President Reagan promised relief when he took office in 1980. A generation of resentment found a champion in Reagan's promises: "The taxing power of government must be used to provide revenues for legitimate government purposes. It must not be used to regulate the economy or bring about social change."[13]

From these historical examples, a main theme of American political history emerges: American government tends to react to political events, to past problems and pressing concerns. Pushed more by current pressure than pulled by future considerations, democratic governmental institutions often appear to

---

[13] Quoted in the *New York Times*, 2 November 1981.

LOOKING AHEAD . . .

The rest of this text covers all the traditional material on the American political system and does so in a way that should deepen your understanding of governmental institutions, public policies, and politics.

Thus, as you encounter material on the Constitution, on civil liberties, political parties, the presidency, or whatever, ask: "What relevance does this have for governmental institutions? For public policy and the way it is made? For politics?"

Let us preview the relevance of subsequent chapters for your study of American government. (Their relevance for understanding public policy is previewed on p. 279 and for politics on p. 187.)

What are you about to discover about the nature of American governmental institutions? Many things, once you realize that much of American government can be understood as a struggle for legitimacy.

Part I. *Foundations of American Government.* The Constitution (chapter 2) was a statement of what the Founders hoped would be a legitimate, and therefore, powerful form of government. Federalism (chapter 3) reveals the ongoing struggle over the proper roles of different levels of government. Civil Liberties and Civil Rights (chapter 4) describes some of the boundaries on government, boundaries that attempt to define what government should and should not do.

Part II. *The Political Environment.* Chapters 5, 6, and 7 show that the struggle to maintain legitimacy forces governmental institutions to cope with the demands of their political environments.

Part III. *Public Policy: Organizations, Processes, Goals.* Chapters 8, 9, and 10 reveal the ways in which governments try to relieve popular dissatisfaction by transforming environmental resources into public policy.

Part IV. *Governmental Institutions.* In chapters 11, 12, 13, and 14, the major institutions of American national government struggle to maintain legitimacy, while working toward organizational and societal goals.

Part V. *Policy Evaluation.* The concluding chapters 15 and 16 evaluate the federal government's pursuit of policies to alleviate human misery and to provide for national security. These chapters ask of the American political system: Has it met the needs of the American people?

stumble toward answers to the question: "What is the proper role of government?"

■ President Lincoln correctly sensed the constraints on his decision to issue the Emancipation Proclamation: he needed to act in a manner that at least maintained and hopefully increased his, and the nation's, legitimacy. In a democracy, it always is so. Democratic governmental institutions and those who lead them need legitimacy. Since they do, they will tend to react to dissatisfaction that signals the lack of fit between their policies and the people's preferences.

POLICIES

> . . . as new conditions and problems arise beyond the power of men and women to meet as individuals, it becomes the duty of the Government itself to find new remedies with which to meet them.
>
> —*President Franklin Roosevelt*

We have defined public policies as governmental attempts to remedy societal problems. Societal problems are like health problems, however; the symptoms often are more obvious than the cure. Government, therefore, has two difficult tasks: (1) diagnose the problem and (2) administer the cure.

Diagnosing the Problem

It is hard to argue with the advice: "If it's broken, fix it." But it is easier to tell if your leg, or your heart, is broken than it is to tell what, if anything, is wrong with our society or with the way its resources are being used. Therefore, much of what goes on in and around governmental institutions is concerned with the diagnosis of societal problems.

During the Civil War, President Lincoln did not find it hard to diagnose the problems facing the nation. Others, however, in both the North and the South, often saw things differently. Because people see social conditions differently, they may either disagree that a problem exists at all or on what the problem is. Following are some examples of events and situations in our nation's history that reflect this societal disagreement:

- Before the adoption of the Constitution, it was hard to get people to see that the Articles of Confederation left the new nation too weak to protect itself from either foreign or domestic threats.
- Before the Civil War, it was hard to convince most Americans that slavery was a problem; after the Civil War, it was hard to convince most Americans that all people were equal.
- Before the 1930s, most people thought that periods of economic decline were inevitable, beyond human reach.
- Before Pearl Harbor, it was hard, apparently impossible, to convince Americans that the World War was their problem.
- During the 1960s and 1970s, people were not sure whether the federal government was the solution to social and economic problems or their cause.
- In the presidential election campaign of 1984, Walter Mondale found it hard to convince people that President Reagan's age (then seventy-three) was a problem.

- From 1982 to 1986, when economic growth was going up, unemployment down, and inflation holding steady, Democrats found it hard to convince most people that President Reagan's economic policies were undesirable.

In all these cases, since people saw things differently, it was hard to forge an agreement.

The diagnosis of the problem is a crucial step in the making of public policy. When people disagree about the existence or nature of a problem, the ensuing public controversy will make it very hard to administer any remedy.

Administering the Remedy

It also is hard for government to design and implement public policy. Even when there is agreement on the existence and nature of a societal problem, there are many other obstacles to the making of public policy:

- Since it is open to interpretation, people easily disagree on the Constitution's meaning and implications. Resulting doubts about the constitutionality of public policies weakens their impact and erodes government's legitimacy.
- Since they place such a high premium on their civil liberties, most Americans are quick to oppose any form of governmental intervention that appears heavy-handed or restrictive.

These mothers, kneeling in prayer against the bill to lend military equipment to Great Britain, were not convinced that the war against Nazi Germany was their problem.

LOOKING AHEAD . . .

What are you about to discover about the nature of public policy? First, start with the idea that much of American government can be understood as either an obstacle to the making of public policy or as a way around an obstacle.[14] Then, each of the major sections and chapters in the rest of this textbook also can be seen this way:

Part I. *Foundations of American Government.* (chapters 2, 3 and 4) Disagreements about the foundations of the American political system frustrate policy making. These include, for example, disagreements about the Constitution, federalism, civil liberties, and civil rights.

Part II. *The Political Environment.* (chapters 5, 6, and 7) Disagreements in the political culture about the proper spheres of public and private action threaten the legitimacy of all forms of governmental intervention. These disagreements also are often magnified by the political process, through the activities of interest groups, political parties, and the media.

Part III. *Public Policy: Organizations, Processes, Goals.* (chapters 8, 9, and 10) To find ways around obstacles to policy making, political organizations build agreement about the existence and nature of societal problems, orchestrate political support for governmental intervention, and match up policy goals and procedures. As these chapters reveal, the routes have been used successfully in the making of education policy, civil rights policy, and economic policy.

Part IV. *Governmental Institutions.* (chapters 11, 12, 13, and 14) Disagreements among the major institutions of national government frustrate coordinated action. In addition, the internal structure of these governmental institutions weakens their capacity to act decisively and with common purpose.

Part V. *Policy Evaluation.* (chapters 15 and 16) America's pursuit of the goals of social welfare and national security has been wracked by disagreements over fundamentals. Are Americans better, or worse, off when the national government expands its social welfare responsibilities? Is the nation more, or less, secure when defense spending goes up and America's allies chart their own foreign policy courses?

- Since there are only blurred lines of authority, it is easy to dispute any shift in the allocation of national, state, and local governmental responsibilities.
- Since America's political culture glorifies individual values, it is hard to mobilize sentiment for public purposes.
- Since they are free to form political interest groups, people with intense concerns often block effective policy making.
- Since the media is preoccupied with short-term, political controversies, it is hard to educate people about long-term societal problems.

---

[14] The growing literature on policy making includes, for example, Larry N. Gerston, *Making Public Policy: From Conflict to Resolution* (Glenview, Ill.: Scott, Foresman, 1983); John W. Kingdon, *Agendas, Alternatives, and Public Policies* (Boston: Little, Brown and Company, 1984); and Robert T. Nakamura and Frank Smallwood, *The Politics of Policy Implementation* (New York: St. Martin's Press, 1980).

- Since they disagree about its costs and benefits, Americans freely dispute governmental attempts to regulate, or deregulate, the economy.
- Since Americans disagree over what is fair, it is hard to sustain political support for policies that redistribute wealth from the rich to the poor.
- Since so many disagree over whether increased military expenditures make us more, or less, secure, and since there are so many involved groups and governmental agencies, it will continue to be hard to make foreign and defense policies that protect the nation's security.

In all these cases, political disagreements and institutional obstacles make it very hard to make public policy. Many of these disagreements are firmly established in deeply held personal values. Most of the institutional obstacles are an expected and not unintentional part of the American political system.

■ As he moved toward issuing the Emancipation Proclamation, President Lincoln encountered many obstacles. So will any policy maker interested in nontrivial accomplishments.

There are both subjective and structural obstacles to the making of public policy. Subjective obstacles are those that make it extremely hard to diagnose the problem. For the most part, these subjective obstacles grow out of human disagreements over the existence and nature of societal problems. Structural obstacles are those that frustrate attempts to administer a remedy. For the most part, structural obstacles are a natural by-product of the American political system.

The obstacles, of course, can be overcome. Doing so, however, is a very political process.

POLITICS

> Observing politics is like watching pigs wrestle under a blanket; we usually see only the surface repercussions of an underlying struggle.

We have defined politics as the way we fight over government's proper role. The fights come about because of underlying conflicts among personal values.

Conflicts Among Values

When we observe politics, we often see only the boiling surface, not the fire underneath. We see Presidents pushing policies, convention delegates in funny hats, budgets made and broken, speeches made and more speeches made. The pot boils, but why?

Values are the fire, the source of the conflict that brings about political activity. This is a society with diverse desires. Some want more wilderness, others more paper pulp; some want a government more protective of civil rights, others want less government; some want political power so they can try to do good for society, others want political power so they can do well by themselves or simply because they are driven to seek power for its own sake. People hold these diverse desires or preferences because of their underlying values and values often conflict. When they do, politics is the mechanism we use to try to settle underlying value conflicts. Since the beginnings of America, it has always been so.

- Federal troops protecting pioneers valued national expansion over the rights of native Americans.
- Tariffs that protected new industries valued economic development more than free trade.
- The Eighteenth Amendment imposed dry on wet values.
- The New Deal valued economic recovery more than freedom from governmental interference.
- The nation found domestic peace more valuable than continued agony in Vietnam and withdrew.

In all these and many other instances, underlying values are what Americans fight over. Politics is the way we fight.

The Way We Fight Over Government's Proper Role

Value conflicts sometimes spill over (or are made to spill over) into the public domain. The process by which this happens is called agenda building and is dealt with in chapter 9. When value conflicts become public, people attempt to drag the government in on their side, hoping that it will settle the controversy in their favor. In this way, governmental involvement usually comes about in reaction to political pressure.

There are many historical examples of outside political pressures that precipitated change in governmental policies.

- McClellan's failure at Richmond made Lincoln change his war policy.
- Popular dissatisfaction with the stalemated war in Korea doomed the Democratic party in the 1952 presidential election.
- When Americans seemed fed up with their own complacency, John F. Kennedy won the presidency in 1960 with a pledge to "get the country moving again."
- Public outrage over Watergate and the presidential pardon of Richard Nixon helped Jimmy Carter win the presidency in 1976 by promising to restore honesty and trust to government.
- Public disgust toward the Carter administration's inability to end the occupation of the American Embassy in Iran and more diffuse resentment toward a government that seemed too big, too bossy, and too inefficient assisted Ronald Reagan's successful drive for the presidency in 1980.

In all these examples, political action came in response to other events—as a people, we fear the devil we know more than the one we have yet to meet.

Political action produces political reaction and, as a result of this dynamic, change is continuous. Why is this so? Part of the answer lies in the nature of public policy; most public policies create winners and losers since policies distribute benefits to some but impose costs on others.[15] All of the following policies, for example, unevenly distribute benefits and costs: defense policies help aerospace workers more than welfare mothers; agricultural subsidies help farmers but impose costs on consumers; expanded social security benefits lower the standard of living of young workers; an MX missile system might increase national security but it lowers property values when placed next door. Other policy changes produce huge crops of losers, as, for example, the American Revolution did when it generated a huge number of political refugees (the equivalent of about 12 million if it happened today, given the current population of the United States).

The second part of the answer lies in human nature; those who lose refuse to stay losers. Instead, they react politically and seek redress for their losses. For example, the Democratic Party seemed dead after the presidential election of 1972, buried under the Nixon landslide, but came back to life and recaptured the presidency in 1976; isolated from the Carter presidency and the policies of the Reagan administration, organized labor helped its candidate,

---

[15] For various ways of classifying politics in an attempt to understand the kinds of politics they generate, see James Q. Wilson, *Political Organizations* (New York: Basic Books, 1973), especially chapter 16 and Theodore J. Lowi, "American Business, Public Policy, Case Studies and Political Theory," *World Politics*, 16 (July 1964): 677—715.

Public policy, even when trying to promote national defense, creates winners and losers.

Walter Mondale, win the Democratic presidential nomination in 1984. In all these cases, political action produced reaction.

Now we know why politics is reactive: public policy creates winners and losers. Losers are terribly important because theirs is the voice of dissatisfaction that demands new and more favorable policies. Wanting change, losers create political pressure on government which, over time, causes it to alter its policy course, seeking to increase popular satisfaction and its own legitimacy.

The course of American history reveals a cyclical pattern of action and reaction, of oscillation between periods of expansion in government's role, followed by contraction and a deference to the private sector, followed by social dissatisfaction and a new wave of public action. As Arthur Schlesinger, Jr., has written: "In general, we go through periods of action, passion, idealism, and reform that continue until the country is worn out by the process and disenchanted with the results. Then we enter a period where public action recedes and private interest dominates. . . . The recoil against Reagan . . . will likely produce, somewhere shortly before or shortly after 1990, a shift in the nation's direction as vivid in its effects as when Theodore Roosevelt took over in 1901, or FDR in 1933, or JFK in 1961."[16] The process, and questioning behind it, continues.

---

[16] Quoted in *The New York Review*, 16 August 1984, p. 36. See also Arthur M. Schlesinger, *Political and Social Growth of the American People, 1865–1940* 3rd ed. (New York: Macmillan, 1941). The view that history exhibits cyclical patterns has intellectual precursors, of course, including Henry Adams, *The Tendency of History* (New York: Macmillan, 1919). For an economist's powerful explanation of these patterns, see Albert O. Hirschman, *Shifting Involvements* (Princeton, NJ: Princeton University Press, 1982).

LOOKING AHEAD . . .

What are you about to discover about politics? This time, think about the forces that drive the making of public policy. Once you do, then each of the major sections and chapters in the rest of this textbook can be seen this way:

Part I. *Foundations of American Government.* (chapters 2, 3, and 4) The Founders were political problem solvers when they drafted the Constitution, as was Supreme Court Chief Justice John Marshall when his decisions advanced national over state values, and as are those who fight to protect their civil liberties and civil rights.

Part II. *The Political Environment.* (chapters 5, 6, and 7) The political culture is packed with competing values, each seeking advantage through political agents and processes.

Part III. *Public Policy: Organizations, Processes, Goals.* (chapters 8, 9, 10) Conflict that produces shifts in values comes before, and after, the making of public policy.

Part IV. *Governmental Institutions.* (chapters 11, 12, 13, and 14) Government's binding decisions are made only after intense political struggles.

Part V. *Policy Evaluation.* (chapters 15 and 16) Social welfare and national security policies invariably fail to please everyone. And popular dissatisfaction often produces a political action, as people seek to improve the fit between their preferences and the actions of their government.

■ Politics comes about because of underlying societal conflict over the relative importance of different values. Since it also comes about in response to political events and pressure, politics, like government, tends to be reactive. Once initiated, moreover, political action tends to produce political reaction, as public policies create winners and losers and as losers seek political change and redress.

Therefore, the proper role of government evolves through an ongoing and never ending political struggle.

SUMMARY

Where are you and where are you going?

You have some preliminary understanding of the nature of democratic governmental institutions, public policies, and politics.

You know:

• Governmental institutions are places where binding decisions are made about the use of societal resources; democratic governmental institutions, especially, need legitimacy and need to be sensitive to expressions of popular dissatisfaction.

- Public policies are governmental attempts to remedy societal problems, and, in this society, it is often extremely hard to diagnose the problem and very hard to administer the cure.
- Politics is the way we fight about what, if anything, government should do about societal problems.

And where are you going?

Hopefully, toward an increased ability to deal with the central question in American political life: What is the proper role of government?

The question of government's proper role is at the heart of our political life because Americans have values which they want to see supported and because both governmental action and inaction favor some, but not all, values. This unavoidable question therefore is a recurring theme in American political history and in this textbook.

There is no final, unambiguous answer to the question of government's proper role. People have different, conflicting, and changing values; it is not surprising therefore that the sense of what is proper will also change and evolve over time. All answers to the question are tentative; all political battles between competing values are incomplete and all the resulting policy victories are temporary—unless defended. The only certainty is the promise of disharmony, as Samuel Huntington has shown.[17] Everything changes—except the continuing need to struggle politically with the question of government's proper role.

Key Terms

governmental institutions	popular sovereignty
public policies	republic
politics	elitist democracy
legitimacy	participatory democracy
democracy	representative democracy

Review and Reflection

1. What question did President Lincoln have difficulty answering?
2. What are Professors Nelson Polsby and Aaron Wildavsky talking about?
3. Define *governmental institution*.
4. What do democratic governmental institutions need? Why?
5. Does dissatisfaction drive democracy? To do what?
6. Define *public policy*.

---

[17] Samuel P. Huntington, *American Politics: The Promise of Disharmony* (Cambridge, Mass.: The Belknap Press of Harvard University Press, 1981).

WHAT SHOULD GOVERNMENT DO? THE CENTRAL QUESTION

7. Why is it hard to make public policy? *ITS HARD TO DIAGNOSE THE PROBLEM & ADMINSTER A CURE*
8. Define *politics*. — *THE WAY WE FIGHT ABOUT WHAT GOVERNMENT SHOULD DO ABOUT SOCIETIES PROBLEMS.*
9. Why is there politics? *EVERYONE HAS DIFF. VIEWS OF THE ROLE OF THE GOV. IN OUR LIVES*

Supplemental Readings

At this stage, there are two kinds of additional works that might interest you: ones that further describe the structure of democratic political systems and those that dissect its dynamics.

Works that expose structure include *Easton's* metaphor shattering accomplishment—the introduction of the concept of "system" to political science; *Schumpeter's* classic treatment of relationships between economic and political systems; *Dahl's* formal analysis of the nature of democracy; and *Bachrach's* critique of elitist forms of democracy.

Works that expose underlying dynamics include *Lindsay's* account of the historical development of modern democratic government; *Kristol's* speculations on the typically American drive to democratize policy making; *Lipset's* attempt to understand the development of governmental institutions as the result of the interplay between the values of equality and achievement; *Hirschman's* analytically rigorous explanation of recurring cycles of public enthusiasms and private retrenchment; and *Huntington's* explanation of political upheavel in America.

Bachrach, Peter. *Theory of Democratic Elitism: A Critique*. 2nd ed. London: University of London Press, 1970.

Dahl, Robert A. *A Preface to Democratic Theory*. 4th ed. Berkeley, Calif.: University of California Press, 1985.

Easton, David. *The Political System: An Inquiry into the State of Political Science*. 2nd ed. Chicago: University of Chicago Press, 1981.

Hirschman, Albert O. *Shifting Involvements: Private Interest and Public Action*. Princeton, NJ: Princeton University Press, 1982.

Huntington, Samuel P. *American Politics: The Promise of Disharmony*. Cambridge, Mass.: The Belknap Press of Harvard University Press, 1981.

Kristol, Irving. *On the Democratic Idea in America*. New York: Harper and Row, 1973.

Lindsay, A. D. *The Modern Democratic State*. New York: Oxford University Press, 1970.

Lipset, Seymour Martin. *The First New Nation*. New York: Norton, 1979.

Schumpeter, Joseph A. *Capitalism, Socialism, and Democracy*. 3rd ed. New York: Harper Brothers, 1962.

CHAPTER TWO

THE CONSTITUTION
BALANCING LIBERTY AND ORDER

Can you be totally free to do whatever you want? If you think so, try smoking in a crowded elevator, running naked through your library, or driving down the sidewalk. If you do not think you are totally free to do whatever you want, you probably have some sense of the many ways in which personal desires for liberty are balanced by society's need for order.

No person can be totally free. If everyone were free to do whatever they wanted, then the rights of some would suppress the rights of others. If all people were able to shout down unpopular opinions, on your campus or in the nation, for example, then no one would be free to speak. Personal liberty, therefore, is limited by a need for social order.

But too much order can extinguish liberty. If there is too much emphasis on the need to maintain social order, then people are not free to act in ways that may be personally and socially desirable. If all colleges taught the same things, for example, then professors and students would not be free to teach and learn what they found relevant or valuable. The need for order, therefore, is limited by a desire for the fruits of liberty.

Without balance between the two, personal liberty is not secure and social order is not desirable. Therefore, some way must be found to balance the desire for liberty with the need for order. One way is through a **constitution**, law that describes the structure of government, its authority to maintain order, and its proper relationship to a people.

This chapter begins with a brief Case, based on the Constitutional Convention. When the delegates to the Convention gathered in Philadelphia, they were united by their desire for liberty and their recognition of its perilous state. But they disagreed over what kind of order was needed and how it might best be achieved.

The Case reveals four insights. First, in their attempt to balance liberty and order, the Founders were politically skilled analysts and problem solvers. Second, the Founders' sense of the proper balance between liberty and order was shaped by prior political experiences and by intellectual traditions. Third, the Founders made some fundamental decisions about the national government's right to impose order. Fourth, unable to forge complete agreement and mindful of the future need to modify the agreements they had struck, the Founders provided a legal framework within which Americans could continue to seek a more perfect balance between liberty and order.

THE BIRTH OF NATIONAL GOVERNMENT

> Order without liberty and liberty without
> order are equally destructive.
> —*Theodore Roosevelt*

George Washington.

The Case **When Passion Wrestled with Reason During the Drafting of the Constitution**

Philadelphia, 1787. Later—much later—they would be known as "The Founding Fathers" and subsequently, in a less sexist way, simply as "The Founders." Then, however, it was much different; they surely did not know what they would be founding. The delegates to the Constitutional Convention came knowing only the problems they faced, not the solutions they would find. But they had to try. So they came, dubious of success, fearful of failure.[1]

The Convention began inauspiciously. The delegates slowly straggled in, except for the ever energetic James Madison, the first out-of-state delegate to arrive. Madison had been at work for ten days before George Washington reached Philadelphia on Sunday, May 13. Washington's arrival was greeted with enormous enthusiasm—with "the thunder of artillery, the pealing of bells, and the flash of the sabers of the City Light Horse."[2] It was a heady time, buoyant with high hopes for a new beginning. But euphoria trickled away.

Since they had to wait for latecomers, the delegates postponed their deliberations. By Monday, only the other delegates from Virginia had joined those from Pennsylvania who lived within sight of the State House where the convention would meet. The mood turned sour; boredom, irritation, and concern replaced the initial rush of enthusiasm that had accompanied Washington's arrival. Nevertheless, the delegates waited—because the nation's problems could not be avoided.

The main problem, consistently, was liberty. Before the Revolution, the problem was winning liberty. After the Revolution, the problem was protecting the liberty that seemed threatened, both from abroad and at home. The Founders knew the foreign threat. Under the Articles of Confederation, the new nation had suffered the continuing humiliation of foreign domination. The Founders also sensed the domestic threats to liberty. Under the Articles of Confederation, the rights of people in many states had been trampled by the unchecked powers of state legislatures. In Philadelphia, the delegates struggled with the problem: Was it possible to create a central government strong enough to protect liberty—but not so strong as to extinguish liberty?

The Founders met amid a growing suspicion that central government had to be strengthened. This idea had to be coaxed along, while assuaging fears that a

---

[1] This account is drawn largely from Clinton Rossiter, *1787: The Grand Convention* (New York: The New American Library, 1968) and Max Farrand, *The Framing of the Constitution of the United States* (First published in 1913.) (New Haven, Conn.: Yale University Press, 1974).

[2] Rossiter, *1787*, p. 159.

strong central government might stifle liberty. After two weeks of preliminaries, Madison struck boldly; his proposed **Virginia Plan** would have established a true national government, armed with the power to overturn state laws and force compliance with the laws passed by the central government. Madison's vision would eventually triumph at the convention—but it would be an incomplete and tentative victory over competing visions and political values.

James Madison.

The Virginia Plan, as the first specific proposal put before the convention, captured the delegates' attention and became the focus of debate. Thus it served as a touchstone for the emerging commitment to create a strong national government. The commitment took concrete form the next day when the key motion passed: Resolved . . . "that, a *national* government ought to be established consisting of a *supreme* legislative, executive, and judiciary." From that moment on, the convention was committed to the idea of a strong national government. Sensing the momentum, Virginia and Pennsylvania pressed ahead, attempting to link representation in the national legislature solely to the size of a state's population. But they drove "almost too blithely," too insensitive to the political needs of the representatives from smaller states. They too had come pledged to represent their states and they feared, correctly, that their voices would be lost in the new legislature, drowned out by a chorus of large states. Their fear was real and it helped precipitate what was about to become an ill-tempered and passionate struggle for power.

Threatened by proportional representation, the small states pushed back, trying to protect their liberty from the feared domination of large states. Politically astute enough to know that you cannot beat something with nothing, they drafted an alternative to the Virginia Plan. But, while insisting on equality of representation in the new legislature, the small states chose a lame horse. Their proposal, the **New Jersey Plan**, promised only mild reform of the Articles of Confederation and therefore ran counter to the convention's growing nationalistic sentiment. With the defeat of the New Jersey Plan, contradictory currents whirled through the convention. Most were committed to a strong central government and the large states had the votes to adopt their preferred form of representation. But the small states still had trump; their votes would be needed later to ratify the Constitution. If they now bolted the convention, the new government, threatened from both home and abroad, would be stillborn. This was the crucial moment, "the most perilous" time in the life of the convention.

It was a time when passion wrestled with reason. Ironically, as the delegates moved closer to agreement, their disagreements became more heated and potentially more disabling. Frustration led some to warn that their states, not finding justice in Philadelphia, might seek comfort in foreign alliances. Angers rose and pushed tempers toward their flash point. Positions stiffened; "never was the word 'never' spoken so often and rashly in the Convention, as in these hotblooded days around July 4."[3] Eventually, perhaps moved most by the fear of failure, the delegates dragged themselves to middle ground.

The **Great Compromise**, proposed by the delegates from Connecticut, broke the deadlock. It let the delegates coalesce around a package: proportional representation for one house of the national legislature and equal representation

---

[3] Rossiter, *1787*, p. 190.

Alexander Hamilton.

of states for the other. It pleased everyone—and no one. It was an amalgam of conflicting values, a tenuous balance of the felt need for, and the ingrained fear of, a central government. As such, it only ambiguously defined the actual scope of the national government's powers and left a bit blurred the relationship between the states and the national government.

What they could not untangle in Philadelphia, the delegates left to the passage of time, to the course of events, and to the ongoing evolution of government's role.

Insights

Not knowing ahead of time what they would create in Philadelphia, the Founders relied on their own political skills, their predispositions, their principles, and their recognition of their own fallibility.

Insight 1. *The Founders were politically skilled analysts and problem solvers.* The Founders were neither gods nor divinely inspired, intent upon some holy quest for the perfect form of government. They were mortals, trying to cope with a situation that must have seemed almost beyond their control. To understand the problems they faced, they had to rely on their skills as political analysts. To deal with those problems, they had to rely on their skills as problem solvers.

Insight 2. *Many of the Founders were predisposed toward a strong central government.* The Founders did not react objectively to the problems they saw. They were biased by their political experiences and by their intellectual heritage, biased away from a central government as weak as the one they knew under the Articles and toward one sufficiently strong to protect liberty.

Insight 3. *The Founders agreed on the basis of the new central government's right to rule.* Under the Articles of Confederation, the states yielded little power to the central government. In Philadelphia, the Founders sought and found an alternative basis of power: the new central government's right to rule would be based on the people and would be maintained by procedures that derived their consent.

Insight 4. *The Founders established a legal framework within which government's role could continue to evolve.* The Constitution was an incomplete triumph; the Founders did not settle all their disagreements and could not anticipate fully all new disagreements. The Founders, however, did establish a legal context for future struggles over competing visions of government's proper role.

Each of these insights will be elaborated throughout the chapter.

THE FOUNDERS

Some men look at constitutions with sanctimonious reverence and deem them like the ark of the covenant, too sacred to be touched. They ascribe to the men of the preceding age a wisdom more than human. . . .

—Thomas Jefferson, "Letter to Samuel Kercheval"

Robert Morris.

The Founders were mortal problem solvers, struggling politically with pressing problems that threatened the life of the new nation.

The Mortal Problem Solvers: Contentious and Passionate

We do the Founders no special honor when we forget that they were men, not gods: worthy of respect, not reverence. We can better appreciate the Founders and what they accomplished when we think of them as mortal, when we raise them "from immortality to mortality," in John Roche's famous phrase.[4]

As a group, the Founders were remarkable people. George Washington, for example, enjoyed enormous prestige, more than we can easily imagine today. To comprehend Washington's public stature, you have to create a mental composite—a combination President, Pope, and rock star. In comparison, James Madison was less conspicuous—slight of build, simply dressed, not assertive in public debate. But Madison was the scholar in politics who gained enormous respect and influence because of the force of his intellect. Both were representative of the group of delegates, largely prestigious men of public affairs. Most had important roles during the Revolutionary War—leading troops, diplomatic missions, and efforts to raise money. After the war, most rose to political prominence in their states and in the Congress of the Confederated States. Yet there were human differences. Alexander Hamilton, inexplicably, was frequently absent and lacked influence. Robert Morris of Pennsylvania, on the other hand, was as brilliant as Madison but richer, more audacious, and more skilled in debate. Morris, in fact, lacked only trustworthiness, principles, morals, and the leg he lost ". . . jumping out of the window when one of our founding-husbands came home unexpectedly. . . ."[5] Some, like Washington, had distinguished themselves in battle, but not all. Alexander Martin, for example, had been dismissed from the army for cowardice in the battle of Germantown, although he later overcame his disgrace and

---

[4] The classic treatment of the Founders as problem solvers is John P. Roche, "The Founding Fathers: A Reform Caucus in Action," *American Political Science Review* 55 (1961): 799–816.

[5] Harry Golden, *Only in America* (New York: The World Publishing Company, 1958), p. 31.

rose to become governor of North Carolina. Some who one might have expected to find in Philadelphia, like Thomas Jefferson and John Adams, were abroad on diplomatic missions. In general, the Founders were highly talented, but also contentious and passionate. For an in-depth look at who the Founders were, see the **Vantage Point**: The Founders.

The Founders were fallible problem solvers. After the convention, James Madison would write that people will disagree among themselves as long as human reason is fallible and humans are free to exercise it.[6] A part of this insight, at least, must have come to Madison during the convention when the Founders split into two distinct groups. One group, later referred to as the **Federalists**, wanted to create a new constitution and a central government strong enough to turn back foreign threats and nurture the nation's economic development. The other group, unfortunately for them labeled nothing more politically inspirational than the **Antifederalists**, favored more modest reform in the Articles of Confederation that would prevent a central government from suppressing the rights of local governments and the life-style of agrarian interests. After heated debate, the Federalists prevailed, but not completely. Madison, for example, feared that a dire mistake had been made in Philadelphia because the Constitution did not make the national government strong enough to "prevent the local mischiefs" of state governments.

Since they disagreed over something as fundamental as the proper balance between personal liberty and the right of the national government to establish order, the Founders could not help but be passionate. The convention's debate, therefore, was not a bland battle over abstract structural designs; it was a fight over important political values and personal interests.

If there was to be a strong central government, it could better defend liberty against foreign threats but might threaten it and the sovereignty of states at home. A central government, emboldened by the growing nationalism of the times, also might seek greater national strength through economic development that favored the interests of merchants. On the other hand, too strong a central government might extinguish the local agrarian interests and virtues so treasured by the Antifederalists.[7] In addition, many of the Founders had their own economic interests which would have been well served by governmental backing of economic growth. (While no one should expect the Founders to have shot themselves in the pocketbook, too much has been made of the possible influence of economic motives on their deliberations.[8]) All these, and many other values and interests, made the blood boil in Philadelphia.

Amidst differences of opinion, deeply held values, and debilitating apprehension, the Founders forged a somewhat ambiguous and tentative consen-

(doubtful)

---

[6] Madison's analysis of the reasons for differences of opinion is found in Number 10 of the *The Federalist Papers*, his assessment of the causes of and remedies for human factiousness.

[7] See Jackson Turner Main, *The Antifederalists: Critics of the Constitution, 1781–1788* (Chapel Hill, NC: The University of North Carolina Press, 1961) and Cecelia M. Kenyon, ed., *The Antifederalists* (New York: Bobbs-Merrill, 1966).

[8] The original treatment of the economic motives of the Founders is Charles A. Beard, *An Economic Interpretation of the Constitution of the United States* (First published in 1913.) (New York: Macmillan, 1935).

THE CONSTITUTION: BALANCING LIBERTY AND ORDER

THE FOUNDERS

Who were "The Founders"? Sometimes the term is used inclusively, to refer to all who were elected to be delegates to the Constitutional Convention. But not all the delegates actually showed up in Philadelphia; some who did went home early, and others had little influence. The term "Founders" also is used a little more exclusively, to refer to those delegates who actually attended and participated on a fairly regular basis. Once in a while, however, the terms "Founders" or "Framers" are used quite exclusively, to refer to those who had some significant impact on the drafting of the Constitution.

Although they often acted autonomously, the Founders were members of state delegations. Each delegation cast one vote, determined by a majority of its delegation. In the final vote, on September 17, 1787, the state delegations that were present approved the Constitution unanimously. (There was no delegation from Rhode Island, since its legislature had not agreed to send one.) In an attempt to make it look as though the individual delegates were unanimous as well, the Convention passed a motion that invited all delegates to sign the Constitution, as witnesses to the agreement of the states. Of the fifty-five originally present, forty-one remained and, of them, only three refused to sign.

Here is a listing of the fifty-five delegates who came to Philadelphia, along with a capsule description of the role they played during the Convention.[1]

Name	State	Role
Abraham Baldwin (s)	Georgia	Useful, the best of the delegation
Richard Bassett (s)	Delaware	Inactive
Gunning Bedford, Jr. (s)	Delaware	Useful
John Blair (s)	Virginia	Visible; by siding with Madison and Washington against Mason and Randolph, Blair was the pivotal vote within the delegation.
William Blount (s)	N.C.	No activity, until the last day
David Brearly (s)	N.C.	Useful
Jacob Broom (s)	Delaware	Visible
Pierce Butler (s)	S.C.	Very useful
Daniel Carroll (s)	Maryland	Useful, before he left to avoid summer in Philadelphia
George Clymer (s)	Penn.	Visible
William R. Davie	N.C.	Useful, especially in selling the Great Compromise
Jonathan Dayton (s)	N.J.	Visible
John Dickinson (s)	Delaware	Made a useful contribution; old and tired, went home early, although had George Read sign for him
Oliver Ellsworth	Conn.	Influential, before leaving early
William Few (s)	Georgia	Visible
Thomas Fitzsimons (s)	Penn.	Invisible

[1]The characterization of the role played during the Convention is derived from Rossiter, *1787: The Grand Convention* (New York: The New American Library, 1968), p. 164–66 and 247–53.

Name	State	Role
Benjamin Franklin (s)	Penn.	Very influential, especially because of his prestige, affable manner, and negotiation skills
Elbridge Gerry	Mass.	Influential but refused invitation to sign
Nicholas Gilman (s)	N.H.	Invisible
Nathaniel Gorham (s)	Mass.	Influential
Alexander Hamilton (s)	New York	A disappointment, but influential during ratification
William Churchill Houston	N.J.	Left after a week to die a "slow and painful death"
William Houstoun	Georgia	Visible
Jared Ingersol (s)	Penn.	Invisible, until the last day
Daniel of St. Thomas Jenifer (s)	Md.	Visible
William Samuel Johnson (s)	Conn.	Very useful
Rufus King (s)	Mass.	Influential
John Langdon (s)	N.H.	Useful
John Lansing, Jr.	New York	Walked out in a huff
William Livingston (s)	N.J.	Useful
James McClurg	Virginia	Visible, since he opened his mouth three times, "put his foot in it twice, and went home to his patients"
James McHenry (s)	Maryland	Visible
James Madison (s)	Virginia	One of the most influential
Alexander Martin	N.C.	Invisible
Luther Martin	Maryland	Influential, "pigheaded," left in "disgust"
George Mason	Virginia	An influential contributor who refused to sign

sus about the proper roles of national and state governments. They had to; the problems pressing on the new nation were too great to be avoided.

The Problems: Foreign and Domestic Threats to Liberty

There were both immediate and long term threats to the new nation's liberty. The immediate threats came both from foreign governments and from the states of the nation.

The foreign threat to liberty remained after the Revolutionary War. Great Britain and Spain continued their efforts at domination; Great Britain kept its military forts within the nation's borders and closed the St. Lawrence River to American ships, as Spain did in a similar attempt to stifle the nation's fledgling economy by closing the Mississippi River. The nation's hopes for economic development also were frustrated by British policies that restricted America's overseas trade, particularly trade with the West Indies. Meanwhile, the war-torn economy choked on unregulated imports from abroad. Something had to

Name	State	Role
John Francis Mercer	Maryland	Present for only eleven days
Thomas Mifflin (s)	Penn.	Inactive
Gouverneur Morris (s)	Penn.	A key player, later praised by Madison
Robert Morris (s)	Penn.	Like Hamilton, a disappointing member
William Paterson (s)	N.J.	Very useful, until he left early
William Pierce	Georgia	After making a few sketches of the Convention, left in need of funds
Charles Pinckney (s)	S.C.	Influential, especially good at detail
Charles Cotesworth Pinckney (s)	S.C.	Influential
Edmund Randolph	Virginia	Like Mason, one who contributed a lot, but not his signature
George Read (s)	Delaware	Very useful
John Rutledge (s)	S.C.	Active and influential
Roger Sherman (s)	Conn.	The most influential member of his delegation
Richard Dobbs Spaight (s)	N.C.	A useful "plugger of holes"
Caleb Strong	Mass.	Visible
George Washington (s)	Virginia	The presiding officer who never missed a day, Washington's presence and manner smoothed the road to success.
Hugh Williamson (s)	N.C.	The most able North Carolina delegate
James Wilson (s)	Penn.	Second only to Madison in influence
George Wythe	Virginia	Left to attend his dying wife
Robert Yates	New York	Followed Lansing

(s) Signed the Constitution.

be done; the nation's integrity as an autonomous nation-state was flouted and, simultaneously, the economy could not grow and thereby sustain a national government strong enough to counter the foreign threat.

The new nation was weakened further by internal strife. The domestic threat to liberty came from the state legislatures and the popular reaction to them. During the war, the colonies had declared themselves states, each with their own constitution. Fighting one form of executive authority, the states overreacted and placed power mostly in legislatures, out of the hands of state executives. But the new legislatures ran amok; in retrospect, the internal strife resembled class warfare. In some states, Rhode Island, for example, those who favored debtors over creditors won control of the legislature and quickly issued paper money that could be used to cheaply pay off earlier debts. In other states, creditors controlled the legislature; in Massachusetts, for example, a legislature dominated by the rich proved insensitive to the needs of debtors. Farmers were hard hit, besieged by tax and debt collectors, hauled into court,

For the Founders, the central problem was protecting liberty. Even today, many people believe that this remains the major problem—and fear that recent growth in the role of the national government threatens liberty.

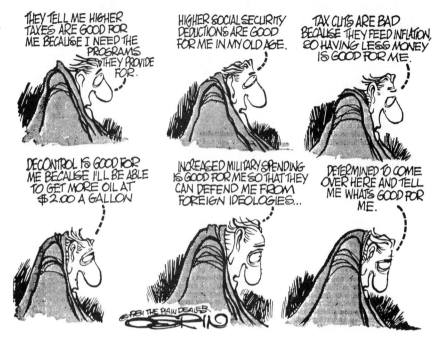

and removed from their lands which were sold for debt payments. Rebellion flared in western Massachusetts as unpaid Revolutionary War veterans organized farmers in armed resistance. Everywhere, it seemed, state legislatures threatened the liberties of some; capricious state laws provoked popular disgust and outright opposition. The situation deteriorated as state legislatures lacked the power and the stomach to enforce their laws. It was the worst of two worlds; state legislatures threatened the liberties of some and were unable to protect the liberties of others. The new nation, only loosely tied under the Articles of Confederation, must have appeared as a feuding collection of ill-governed principalities—with liberty the loser. Both foreign threats and domestic strife imperiled revolutionary ideals; these thorns had to be removed. In the long run, however, the nation's hide had to get tougher and that meant increasing national strength.

The long term threat to liberty came from the nation's weakness. In 1776, the nation declared its political independence but remained dependent, because it was weak. And the nation was weak politically because its economy was weak. Also in 1776, Adam Smith's *Wealth of Nations* had made explicit the connection; with economic development came national strength. The implications were clear; without economic development, the weak nation would remain dependent, vulnerable to foreign domination. But the obstacles to economic development were imposing. To grow, the largely agricultural nation had to export its crops; but foreign powers blocked the trade routes. To grow, infant industries had to be sheltered from foreign competition; but there was no central control over imports. To grow, business confidence was needed; but state legislatures overturned contracts, blocked the collection of debts, issued

THE CONSTITUTION: BALANCING LIBERTY AND ORDER

Shay's Rebellion of 1786. This armed resistance was but one of several against various state legislatures that threatened the liberties of some and were unable to protect the liberties of others.

worthless money, and confiscated property. These pressing problems had to be solved.

The Founders, therefore, could not avoid trying to solve the problems facing the nation. Much of their success was due to their political skills.

The Politics of Problem Solving

The Founders were successful problem solvers because of their remarkable political skills. The skills were essential because the problems themselves were intrinsically political, involving competing visions of the proper role of the central government and of the proper balance between personal liberty and social order. Alternative solutions to these problems inevitably favored some interests over others, the interests of large over small states or of manufacturers over farmers, for example. Even if they had tried, the Founders could not have taken the politics out of problem solving; they also were too smart to try.

Many of the Founders had impressive political skills that were revealed in at least the following three ways: first, the Founders were politically skilled in turning events to their advantage. Even after the Revolution, the new Americans had no sense of a common national identity. But, as Jack Rakove shows in his recent study of the beginnings of American politics, a national political consciousness would emerge in response to external events.[9] Some early American leaders saw the scenario unfold as misguided British policies con-

9 Jack N. Rakove, *The Beginnings of National Politics* (New York: Alfred A. Knopf, 1979).

Having convinced themselves, the Founders needed to convince the rest of the country of the need for a strong national government. Benjamin Franklin helped, with this, one of the first editorial cartoons.

JOIN, or DIE.

tinued to press on the new nation. For example, one American leader, John Langdon, wrote to Thomas Jefferson in 1785: "Great Britain seems determined to pursue the same ruinous line of conduct, that guided her thro' the late war . . . every step Britain takes to prevent our increase of commerce . . . will be eventually to our advantage, by driving us into manufactures," and by convincing us of "the absolute necessity of vesting Congress with full power to regulate our commerce, both external and internal."[10] The strategic situation was clear; you have to wait to strike when the iron is hot. And the Founders were very good at that because of their political foresight and sense of timing. The Founders foresaw the course of events and their likely result; anticipating the American political reaction, the Founders honed their arguments and prepared to strike.

Second, the Founders also were politically skilled in molding perceptions. Perceptions are important because they lead people to an understanding of the problem and of what should be done about it. During the convention, Madison showed his ability to mold perceptions by sequencing events. By striking first and boldly with his Virginia Plan, Madison shaped perceptions and set the convention's agenda. The delegates had convened amid uncertainty over the new nation's maladies and cure. They knew they were supposed to "revise" the Articles of Confederation. But, unsure about how far they could go, the Founders met without a detailed and confident plan of action. Madison exploited this uncertainty by taking the initiative and advancing his Virginia Plan. From that moment on, the delegates focused their attention on the need for a new constitution and argued over the proper form of a new national government. In this way, by molding perceptions of the problem and of the preferred solution, Madison, both the playwright and stage manager of the Constitutional Convention, structured its agenda and funneled its deliberations.

---

[10] *Ibid.*, p. 362.

THE CONSTITUTION: BALANCING LIBERTY AND ORDER

Third, the Founders were politically skilled in negotiation. Negotiation works when both sides are willing to modify important values. The Founders made negotiation work because they knew that change in underlying values was essential and because they were patient and persistent enough to bring it about. For example, they were skilled negotiators when the small states threatened to bolt, but did not, and when the large states demonstrated, but did not press, their numerical advantage. Almost torn apart by competing values, the Founders negotiated a principled settlement that they and the people could rally around.

■ As politically skilled analysts and problem solvers, the Founders were able to perceive the threats to liberty, articulate their visions of proper forms of government, translate their visions into structural designs, and partially reconcile competing interests. In the end, a balance was struck, one reflecting the predispositions of those who favored a strong central government.

THE BACKGROUND OF THE CONSTITUTIONAL CONVENTION

> The Constitution was "extorted from the grinding necessity of a reluctant nation."
> —John Quincy Adams, quoted in Max Farrand, The Framing of the Constitution

In reacting to the nation's problems, the Founders were influenced by their political and intellectual heritage. The Founders had deep and rich traditions, dating back to the first colony in the Americas, established in 1607. After 180 years of collective experience, the Founders would write the Constitution in 109 days. (The scale is hard to grasp; it would be like taking a four hour final examination in a course that met continuously for fourteen weeks!) During their brief stay in Philadelphia, the Founders distilled their heritage into an enduring document.

The Political Heritage

From their political heritage, many of the Founders drew tentative and sometimes competing conclusions about the proper and improper roles of government. In Philadelphia, these conclusions shaped the way problems were seen and biased the search for solutions in the direction of a stronger central government.

The Founders' political heritage was derived from the three major stages of

FIGURE 2.1 Constitution Writing in Perspective

Compare your years in school (about eleven) to the same amount of time that passed between the start of the Revolutionary War and the writing of the Constitution.

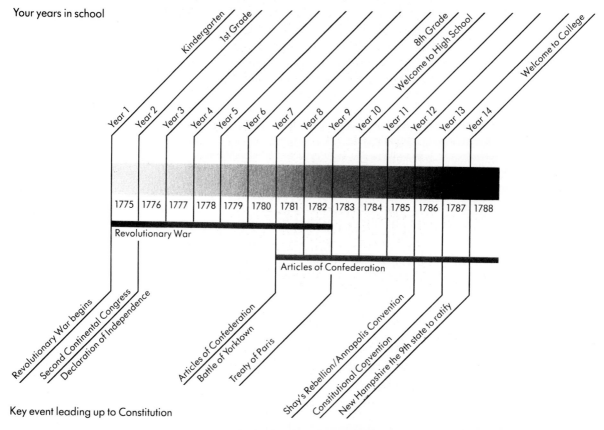

the American experience: the colonial period; the revolutionary period; and the period of the Articles of Confederation. (See **Figure 2.1.**)

The Colonial Period. Americans emerged from the colonial period with fears, customs, traditions, and well-learned political lessons. As colonists, the Americans knew the oppression of a monarch and a Parliament, both of which often ignored the traditions of colonial autonomy. Except for laws passed by the charter colonies of Rhode Island and Connecticut, the government of Great Britain could simply cancel colonial laws. The King was sovereign in more than name, since his sovereignty was dependent only on maintaining God's favor, not the popular approval of his subjects. From this period, the Americans emerged with a fear of absolute, unchecked power and a deep suspicion of "the ever-present, latent danger of an active conspiracy of power against liberty."[11]

---

[11] Bernard Bailyn, *The Ideological Origins of the American Revolution* (Cambridge, Mass.: The Belknap Press of Harvard University Press, 1967), p. 95.

The Bloody Massacre, when British troops fired into a mob protesting their presence, was a part of the Founders' political heritage.

The American colonists had continued the custom of recording in writing their understanding of government's proper role. They had known as English subjects that written documents could restrain arbitrary power; they knew the precedents of the Magna Carta (1215), the Habeas Corpus Act (1679), and the English Bill of Rights (1689). As colonists, they continued the custom, adopting written charters that described what colonial governments could and could not do. Over time, these practices formed a rich legacy of political traditions that were available for adoption at the Constitutional Convention. All of the colonial charters, for example, provided for **separation of powers**—the division of governmental authority among an executive (the governor), a legislature, and a judiciary. All charters, except Pennsylvania's, also embraced **bicameralism**, the division of legislative authority between two chambers. In addition, most charters favored mixed government in which the interests of people were represented in a popularly elected house of the legislature and the interests of private property were represented through appointments to the other house. Finally, all charters had bills of rights that listed what government should not do. All of these were prominent traditions; the Founders did not abandon them on their way to Philadelphia.

The American colonists had learned an important political lesson well; written laws could not always protect liberty. They had thought that written law, by defining the proper and improper roles of government, would be a sufficient protector of liberty. In the colonial period however, they learned that Kings and Parliaments could be fickle and capricious, willing to brush aside, at their own convenience, even written protections against governmental interference. In Philadelphia, the lesson was remembered; liberty must be protected by some law that is higher than the laws of humans.

The Revolutionary Period. During this period, political traditions grew up around new political units—the American states. Going into the Revolutionary War, the colonial assemblies were political staging areas for opposition to British policies; Great Britain retaliated by dissolving the colonial legislatures. In reaction, the colonies called for a congress—simply, a meeting of all colonies—to consider their common plight. The First Continental Congress convened in Philadelphia in 1774, nursing hopes for compromise. One of the important aspects of this assembly was that the colonies met together but retained a sense of their own identity; this was a congress of separate and distinct colonies—more of a block party than a family reunion. This sense of separateness developed into a new political tradition as war broke out and the colonies declared themselves autonomous states.

The states took themselves seriously. Everybody knows what the Declara-

The heart of old Philadelphia, scene of The First Continental Congress in 1774.

THE CONSTITUTION: BALANCING LIBERTY AND ORDER

tion of Independence declared. But whose independence was declared by the Declaration? You may think that is obvious before you begin to consider some of the alternatives: the people's, the colonies', the nation's, maybe. The fact is that the Declaration of Independence declared the colonies "to be free and independent states." And by the term "states," the Declaration did not mean what you and I mean by "Ohio," "California," or "New York." When the Declaration and the residents themselves used the term, "state" meant an autonomous nation-state—like the Soviet Union or France. In theory at least, the American states were empowered to do all the things that nations do—declare and fight a war with some other nation-state (maybe New Jersey against Spain) and enter into foreign alliances (maybe New Jersey and France against New York and Spain). In this full-blown sense, the colonies emerged from the revolutionary period as free and independent states and with them emerged a new political tradition.

The new political tradition was revolutionary; states took from the King what God had given him—his sovereignty. Out of this rape of the King's right to rule, a new political tradition was born. Even the most rabid revolutionary must have quaked a bit at the audaciousness; states now claimed and exercised the right of kings to rule without challenge within their own borders. The claim was serious and it quickly took root as a major tradition and force in American political life. Over time, the tradition of state sovereignty would serve as a major argument in the debate over the proper relationship between state and national governments and would persist as a major barrier to federal intervention in social problems. Even today, people who want to cut back the role of the national government point in horror at "federal meddling" in state affairs and cry, "tradition!"

During the revolutionary period, hope replaced fear. It was a time of youthful enthusiasm; the signers of the Declaration of Independence surely hoped that a better form of government would be found, one that would secure, not squash, the rights of the people. But high hopes were poorly founded; little thought had gone into the search for a new form of government. Structural faults in the relationship between the states and the central government would soon shatter the euphoria.

The Articles of Confederation. This period lasted about six years, long enough to gain a better appreciation of the problems of protecting liberty. The Articles, after taking a while to be ratified, finally took effect in March of 1781. Later that same year, after the Battle of Yorktown in October, the war was mostly over and Americans were free to try out their new form of government—and it was a trying experience. Liberty seemed threatened from both above and below. From above, the defects of the Articles left the country almost headless, without a central government strong enough to cope with foreign nations. From below, the defects of state constitutions left the states powerless, without sufficient popular support to ensure voluntary compliance with their laws. During this six-year period, and especially with the development of a sense of national identity and the thirst for national economic development, the defects became more glaring and the need to search for new solutions became more pressing.

The Articles of Confederation were only a treaty among sovereign states, not a constitution binding together the parts of a whole; Article III specifically spoke of a "league of friendship," not a national government. There also were no branches of national government as we know them today; instead, the "Congress" was only a body representing the separate states. The Congress also had little authority and almost no power: it could coin money, but there was little to coin; it could conduct foreign policy, but it could not interfere in the foreign affairs of the states; it could appoint army officers to key positions, but it had to rely on state militias to supply troops; it could ask the states for money to pay for congressional operations, but it could not raise its own revenue or demand it from the states. Moreover, the Congress had no authority over commerce or commercial activity among the states. New York, for example, could tax the "importation" of goods from New Jersey, hurting their farmers and commerce between the two states. Similarly, commercial opportunities loomed but lay fallow in the West as the states quarreled over conflicting land claims which the Congress lacked authority to referee. Under the Articles, commercial chaos reigned; with no national mechanism for resolving disputes among states, conflicts boiled over state borders, disrupting commercial activity and frustrating economic development. There was no easy antidote to the chaos; the Articles had their own Catch-22 rule—the squabbling states could be brought into line only with their unanimous agreement to amend the Articles. As these and other defects became more glaring and as earlier hopes dimmed, Americans softened their fear of central political power. A new understanding became more broadly shared; liberty could not be protected without a strong central government.

Braced with a new understanding about the need for a stronger union, the Founders came to Philadelphia. Because of their political heritage, most of the Founders had a particular view of the problem and its likely solution: create a government strong enough to protect liberty but not so strong as to threaten it. This is a familiar problem; your campus security force needs some arms to keep the peace—night sticks, maybe even guns, but not tanks and ground-to-air missiles. Likewise, to protect their newly won liberties, most of the Founders believed they needed a strong, but well-controlled national government—a tiger on a short leash.

The Intellectual Heritage

The Founders also brought an intellectual heritage to Philadelphia and they drew heavily on this rich intellectual tradition of political theory and philosophy. The Founders themselves were aware of this heritage and self-conscious in its application. This was revealed, for example, in a letter to George Washington as early as 1783:

The foundation of our empire was not laid in the gloomy age of ignorance and superstition; but at an epoch when the rights of mankind

THE CONSTITUTION: BALANCING LIBERTY AND ORDER

were better understood and more clearly defined, than at any other period. The researches of the human mind after social happiness have been carried to a great extent; the treasures of knowledge acquired by the labors of philosophers, sages, and legislators . . . are laid open for our use, and their collected wisdom may be happily applied in the establishment of our forms of government. . . . [12]

This intellectual heritage contained three main ideas—natural law, natural rights, and a social contract—and each had a significant impact on the constitutional deliberations.

Some of the Founders' ideas about natural law had deep historical roots in the writings of philosophers and political theorists, most notably in John Locke's *Treatise of Civil Government*, which recent scholarship dates to either 1682 or 1683. The concept of **natural law** is very abstract; it is the set of immutable truths that should govern human relations. These truths are the law of God and Nature; their existence and their validity does not depend on whether or not people agree with them. The Founders believed, however, that the meaning of natural law could be discerned through human reason, that it could provide the basis for a new form of government, and that these fundamental truths were superior to the laws that would be made after the government was established. Moreover, since natural law described the proper relationships among people and between them and their government, these ideas implied both natural rights and a social contract.

According to Locke, natural law guaranteed certain rights. These **natural rights** existed in nature, before the formation of either society or government, and included the right to life, liberty, and property. Under natural law, no one was to infringe on natural rights. But nature can be a pretty tough place; for example, the strong may enslave the weak and slaves may rebel and slay their masters. The struggle to protect rights, therefore, is constant, worrisome, and exhausting. To secure rights, to prevent interference with natural rights, and to settle disputes once they erupt, people come together in a **social contract**— an agreement to form a civil society that will guarantee natural rights. In this way, the social contract comes first, before government. After a compact is formed, society needs a government to enforce the contract. Therefore, government exists to protect natural rights and should be strong enough to perform this role.

■ Most of the Founders were predisposed in favor of a strong central government because of prior political experiences and established intellectual traditions. Their political heritage convinced them of the need for a strong central government. Their intellectual heritage convinced them that one should exist. But, before it could be formed, the new central government needed a foundation, something that justified its right to rule.

---

12 Edward S. Corwin, "The Progress of Constitutional Theory Between the Declaration of Independence and the Meeting of the Philadelphia Convention," *American Historical Review* 30 (1925): 511–36, in Gordon S. Wood, ed., *The Confederation and the Constitution: The Critical Issues* (Boston: Little, Brown and Company, 1973), p. 16.

CONSTITUTIONAL FOUNDATIONS

> I know no safe depository of the ultimate
> powers of the society but the people them-
> selves; and if we think them not enlightened
> enough to exercise their control with a
> wholesome discretion, the remedy is not to
> take it from them, but to inform their discre-
> tion.
>
> —*Thomas Jefferson*

The Founders based the new government's right to rule on three enduring principles: republicanism, constitutionalism, and judicial review.

Republicanism

In the beginning the word was "the People." It was no fluke that the Constitution began: "We the People . . ." As opposed to: "We the States . . ." It made a big difference because the words said who had the right to form the government. Saying "We the People" meant it was the people who were coming together and the right to form the government was theirs; the people, therefore, not the states, were the basis for the new government and the source of its power. It made a significant difference. The difference also meant a radical shift of sovereignty, away from the states and toward the people. From those words on, the people had **popular sovereignty**—the right to create, alter, or abolish the national government and therefore any of its policies. Those words, however, made ratification difficult; many were reluctant to give up the sovereign rights of states while others feared the consolidation of power within the central government. But ratification came to pass and "the People" won. With ratification, a new form of government was created—and a new principle was established.

The principle of **republicanism** holds that the power to rule resides in the people and is only exercised by elected representatives who are responsible to the people. Remember the dilemma the Founders faced; find a form of government that was strong enough to protect liberty without threatening it. Republicanism was the solution: (1) the people would participate indirectly in governing through their elected representatives and (2) the representatives would exercise power but be held accountable for their actions by the people who retained ultimate sovereignty.

The principle of republicanism explains a lot about American government, policies, and politics. It explains, for example, why it was necessary to call a convention to revise the Articles of Confederation, rather than simply delegating the chore to the existing Congress; the people, not the states were the only source of just authority. The principle also helps account for the free-floating

In a republic, the people participate in policy making indirectly, and, sometimes indiscreetly, as in this portrayal of "The County Election."

antipathy of Americans toward their government; republicanism makes us suspicious of legislators and bureaucrats who act like they own the power we have only lent them.

Constitutionalism

The principle of **constitutionalism** holds that the proper role of government is constrained by a written contract or constitution. This principle is extremely important because it makes the Constitution supreme to governmental institutions, public policies, and politics. The principle starts with an assumption; through careful reasoning, people can discover the meaning of natural law. Once they figure out the difference between right and wrong, human understandings of natural law can be written down. This the Founders believed and they built their understanding of natural law into the Constitution. Doing so was a profound and powerful act, because it made the Constitution, as the codification of natural law, supreme.

The Constitution is supreme in three major ways: it is supreme over the national government; it is supreme over whatever laws the national government might make; and it is supreme over the constitutions of the states and whatever laws they may make. The Constitution, therefore, is supremely able to constrain national government so that it does not threaten liberty.

The Constitution constrained the national government by defining the proper structures of government, by assigning proper functions to these structures, and by prohibiting some activities. The proper structures consisted of a totally new federal government, three branches of government, a bicameral Congress, a single executive, and a federal court system. The assignment of functions provided the Congress with a long list, most of them empowering it to regulate commerce and defend the nation; provided the President with a shorter list, mostly commanding the army, appointing ambassadors and federal judges, recommending policies to Congress, and vetoing congressional actions; and provided the federal judiciary with only vague hints of its eventual role. The Constitution further constrained both levels of government. At the national level, Congress was prohibited from interfering with the rights in the Bill of Rights and (until 1808) from stopping the slave trade. At the state level, the Constitution prohibited state governments from doing what only nations do: making war, treaties, money, or charging tariffs on imported or exported goods. All of these were serious prohibitions that were intended to keep all forms of government distant, out of the private affairs of a newly freed people.

Judicial Review

Bill Cosby, the comedian and television star, once said: "If I had a kid, I wouldn't name it. I'd just let it run loose and see what the neighbors called it." Judicial review is like that. Nowhere is it mentioned in the Constitution; it is just a useful idea that developed.

The Constitution was supposed to restrain government. No government, whether national or state, was supposed to do anything that went against the supreme law of the land; doing so would be unconstitutional. But there was a problem; who would say whether or not something was unconstitutional? If the Constitution could be used to rein in government, who held the reins? The Founders anticipated this problem and, to deal with it, they included in the Constitution one half of a solution; they gave to the courts, only implicitly however, the power of **judicial review**—the right and the duty to declare unconstitutional, and therefore invalid, acts of the executive and legislative branches. Soon after the founding and in response to the pressure of political events, the Supreme Court would make explicit its implied constitutional duty and thereby fashion the remaining half of the solution.

Under Chief Justice John Marshall, at the opening of the nineteenth century, the Supreme Court of the United States forged for itself the power of judicial review. "It is emphatically the province and duty of the judicial department to say what the law is," Marshall would write in his decision in the famous *Marbury* v. *Madison* case (which is described in detail in chapter 3). From this decision on, the Court's role was set; as a coequal branch of government, the Supreme Court could set constitutional boundaries and thereby constrain all branches and levels of government.

After it was signed, the new Constitution still had to go through what turned out to be a highly political ratification process.

■ From the Founders' point of view, the principles of republicanism, constitutionalism and judicial review established the new government's right to rule. On this foundation would rise a new superstructure—a legal framework within which government's role would continue to evolve.

THE CONSTITUTIONAL FRAMEWORK FOR GOVERNMENT'S EVOLVING ROLE

> The Constitution of the United States was made not merely for the generation that then existed, but for posterity—unlimited, undefined, endless, perpetual posterity.
> —*Henry Clay*

The Founders were problem solvers who drafted a partial solution to the problems of protecting liberty. Theirs, however, was not the final solution: it was a legal context for ongoing problem solving. The Constitution serves as a framework for problem solving in three major ways: it incorporates and ratifies society's consensus of government's legitimate role; it relieves social strain by accommodating change; and it molds both public policy and the political processes by which it is made.

THE POLITICS OF RATIFICATION

*T*he Constitution specified that it had to be ratified by nine of the thirteen states. Article VII stated: "The ratification of the conventions of nine States shall be sufficient for the establishment of this Constitution between the States so ratifying the same." By requiring the approval of the delegates of state conventions, specifically elected for the purpose of voting on ratification, the Founders took their case directly to the people and bypassed state legislators, many of whom opposed the Constitution.

Ratification, however, was not a foregone conclusion. In some cases, it came about because those who favored ratification, the Federalists, were more skilled and influential than those, the Anti-federalists, who opposed it. In the end, the Federalists won their games of "propaganda and politics," because the Constitution embodied the people's emerging sense of nationhood.

Here is the chronology of the ratification process, along with some comments on the politics of each step.[1]

State	Date of Ratification	Vote (yeas/nays)	Comment
Delaware	12/7/1787	30/0	After only five days of discussion, Delaware, one of the smallest and weakest of the states, rushed to ratify.
Pennsylvania▲	12/12/1787	46/23	Aware of strong public opposition, the Federalists campaigned heavily and dominated the ratification convention. The ratification vote, however, was greeted by rioting in some parts of the state.
New Jersey	12/18/1787	38/0	Like Delaware, Georgia, and Connecticut, New Jersey was a small and weak state whose support was ensured by the provision of equal state representation in the Senate.
Georgia	1/2/1788	26/0	Defenseless against the Creek Indians, Georgia welcomed strength through union.
Connecticut	1/9/1788	128/40	With Connecticut's vote, the Federalists gained momentum.
Massachusetts▲★	2/6/1788	187/168	Most of the delegates initially opposed ratification; a majority formed after those favoring ratification promised to recommend to the new Congress a package of amendments that would guarantee personal liberties (what became the Bill of Rights, passed by the Congress in 1791).

[1]The comments are drawn, in part, from Rossiter, *1787*, p. 274–98.

Social Consensus

In drafting a document that had a chance to be ratified, the Founders were seriously constrained by the existing social consensus, one that was fearful, limited, and incomplete. For a chronology of the ratification process, see the **Vantage Point**: The Politics of Ratification.

The Constitution reflected a fearful consensus: a fear of central authority and a fear of the excesses of democracy. These fears would father both the

State	Date of Ratification	Vote (yeas/nays)	Comment
Maryland	4/26/1788	63/11	An easy victory, in spite of Luther Martin's complaints that the Founders had forged chains for their countrymen.
South Carolina	5/12/1788	149/73	Approved unconditionally, but with recommended amendments.
New Hampshire★	6/21/1788	57/47	Meeting at the same time as Virginia, New Hampshire moved first, becoming the ninth state to ratify, technically enough to approve the Constitution.
Virginia▲	6/25/1788	89/79	With Virginia's approval, three out of the big four (Pennsylvania, Massachusetts, Virginia, and New York) had ratified; political logic now pushed New York.
New York▲★	6/26/1788	30/27	In an attempt to win a majority of the delegates to the ratification convention, James Madison, Alexander Hamilton, and John Jay, under the pseudonym, "Publius," wrote a series of newspaper articles, arguing the case for ratification. This series, *The Federalist Papers*, has enduring value as an authoritative interpretation of the work of the Founders. Hamilton also outmaneuvered the Antifederalists, by arguing that New York City and the southern counties could secede to join the union and by postponing the vote, until news of Virginia's vote arrived. After the ratification vote, armed factions clashed in Albany and an Antifederalist paper was destroyed in Greenleaf.
North Carolina◆	7/2/1788	84/184	
North Carolina	10/21/1789	194/77	Over a year after voting it down and several months after the new government had been in business, North Carolina ratified the Constitution.
Rhode Island★	5/28/1790	34/32	After Federalists won control of the state legislature, a hastily called ratification convention narrowly voted in favor.

★Note the relative closeness of the vote.

▲One of the four largest, most populous, and wealthiest states; most historians believe these were "must wins" in the battle for ratification.

◆North Carolina's first vote, defeating ratification.

structure and the workings of government. The potential oppressiveness of government was diluted by the separation of powers and regulated through a system of **checks and balances**—an arrangement in which authority was shared so that the actions of any governmental official would be constrained by other officials. These two ideals, in practice, decentralized power; no one official or group would make, *and* implement, *and* interpret public policy. Still, the fear of the national govenment lingered, making ratification difficult.

But the people too were feared as a potential threat to liberty; by the weight of their number and with the force of their passion, mobs can crush liberty. The Founders had known this fear before the Convention and brought it to Philadelphia. One of them, Elbridge Gerry, spoke for many: "The evils we experience flow from the excess of democracy."[13] The fear of democracy also shaped government; popular passions were diluted through indirect forms of political participation and the dispersion of power removed it from the grasp of majoritarian factions.

The Constitution also reflected a limited consensus for a narrow governmental role. In its properly narrow role, the national government was supposed to protect the rights of persons, not provide substantive benefits to them. This limited consensus thus emphasized the rights of individuals and not the obligations of government to care for its citizens and shaped, through most of our history, popular expectations of government's proper role. Only in relatively recent times, and only after national traumas of economic depression and world war, did this view of government's narrow role weaken. Only then, say from the mid-1930s, did government's role as a direct provider of benefits swell, or bloat as some would argue. Nevertheless, the narrow or minimalistic conception of government's role persists and, from time to time, reasserts itself in demands to reduce the size and scope of government.

Finally, the Constitution reflected an incomplete consensus. All Americans did not agree on everything that government should, or should not, do; neither did the Founders. Moreover, forced to react to pressing problems, the Founders lacked the time to seek a more complete consensus and any assurance that they could find or impose one. The nation was new and time was short. On some issues, common beliefs easily led to agreement; on other issues, conflicting beliefs led to bargaining and compromise, as in the Great Compromise. On still other issues, the emerging consensus was imperiled by wildly conflicting beliefs, for example, about slavery and the question of the exact relationship between the powers of the national and state governments. On highly conflictual issues, the Constitution was vague or silent; to avoid disruptive issues, the consensus was left incomplete. Unavoidably, the Constitution incorporated in black and white the grays of the incomplete social consensus. But even the incomplete consensus shaped the evolution of government as questions left unanswered in Philadelphia continued to haunt Americans, begging for and sometimes demanding, answers.

Constitutional Change

The Constitution relieves social strain, by serving as a unifying symbol and through its ability to adjust to changing circumstances. The Constitution accommodates change in four ways: (1) by serving as a guiding principle, (2) by being flexible enough to settle new political conflicts, (3) by allowing govern-

---

[13] Quoted in George W. Carey, "The Separation of Powers," in George J. Graham, Jr., and Scarlett G. Graham, eds., *Founding Principles of American Government: Two Hundred Years of Democracy on Trial* Rev. ed. (Chatham, NJ: Chatham House, 1984), p. 115.

THE CONSTITUTION: BALANCING LIBERTY AND ORDER

President Nixon entering a helicopter on the White House lawn, after the Supreme Court forced him to turn over the Watergate tapes, thereby precipitating his resignation.

ment to adapt to new social problems, and (4) by being open to formal modification.

First, the Constitution works as a guiding principle, a rule that governs the making of other rules. Stable solutions to societal problems are found when people agree on the rules that will be followed in settling conflicts. The alternative is the use of force, which leaves no one's rights secure in the long run. A society, therefore, needs prior agreement on the rules of the game. The Constitution includes such agreements. For example, Article IV, Section 3 describes the process by which new states join the Union and Article I, Section 7 gives the procedure by which the national government shall attempt to decide upon its role—and pay for it.

Second, the Constitution is flexible enough to allow for the settling of new, usually unanticipated, political conflicts. And judges, armed with their power of judicial review, are strong enough to flex it. The Constitution, for example, was flexible enough in 1974 to reconcile the conflicting demands of a President who claimed executive privilege in refusing to turn over tape recordings and the demands of the Watergate Special Prosecutor who insisted that they were necessary evidence in a criminal proceeding. In this case, *United States* v. *Nixon*, the United States won as the Constitution proved flexible enough to settle a wholly unanticipated conflict.

Third, the Constitution makes government adaptive enough to respond to new social problems. After listing all the powers of Congress, for example, the Constitution adds what almost looks like an afterthought; the last point of

Article I, Section 8, gives Congress the power "to make all laws which shall be necessary and proper" for carrying out the previously enumerated powers. This power was used early on when Congress decided to create a national bank so it could more conveniently coin and borrow money, even though it had no explicit right to create banks. Nevertheless, Congress had the implied right to exercise this power, the Supreme Court would rule in *McCulloch* v. *Maryland*. (This case is described more fully in chapter 3.) Over time, the Court's broad interpretation of the "necessary and proper" clause would be used to justify government's intrusion into previously private areas of life as it sought to cope with new social problems.

Fourth, the Constitution is open to formal modification. Though the Founders believed that the Constitution incorporated natural law, they did not believe that they were infallible or that the Constitution was perfect. They expected that the human capacity to understand natural law would grow over time and that, therefore, the Constitution should absorb new and better understandings of natural law. In the words of Thomas Jefferson: "Laws and institutions must go hand in hand with the progress of the human mind."[14] To accomplish this, the Constitution, in Article V, provided these four avenues.

1. The normal procedure for amending the Constitution is that, after both houses of Congress propose an amendment (each by a two-thirds vote), amendments are ratified by the legislatures of three-fourths of the states. This route has led to all but one of the existing amendments.
2. Another procedure uses the normal route for proposing an amendment but then makes a detour around the state legislatures by allowing for an amendment to be ratified by specially called conventions in three-fourths of the states. This route was used in the one exception, the repeal of prohibition, to bypass the predominantly dry state legislatures.
3. and 4. The third and fourth procedures are extraordinary routes, never used. An amendment can be proposed by a national constitutional convention that is specifically created for this purpose by the legislatures of two-thirds of the states. The resulting amendment would then be ratified either by additional state conventions *or* by state legislatures. These are extraordinary routes because of the possibility that a national convention might propose a completely new constitution.

All of these are rocky routes because it is very hard to change the Constitution. That was intentional, since the Constitution incorporated natural law and since it was supposed to protect individual rights from majority rule. The Founders, therefore, made the Constitution hard to amend, in the hope that only certain kinds of changes would filter through the process—only those motivated by a deep commitment to the common good, not to narrow self-interests.

Finally, constitutional change does more than relieve social strain; it creates new public policy. During the drive to ratify the Constitution, for example,

---

[14] Thomas Jefferson, "Letter to Samuel Kercheval," in Saul K. Padover, ed., *The Complete Jefferson* (New York: Duell, Sloan, and Pearce, 1943), p. 291.

opposition coalesced around the fear that the central government was too strong, too threatening of liberty, and opponents demanded constitutional guarantees of individual rights. The proponents promised that these would be added—right after ratification. They kept their promise, as the Bill of Rights specifically protected a number of personal freedoms. Since the adoption of the Bill of Rights, additional policy outcomes have come through constitutional change—a federal income tax, for example. Most of these additional amendments have expanded the role of government and broadened opportunities for democratic participation in policy making, although others, such as a proposed balanced budget amendment, would put a lid on both.

The Constitution's Impact on Government, Policies, and Politics

The Constitution is not a neutral document; it is biased. This simply means that the Constitution has a number of significant effects on governmental institutions, public policies and the ways they are made, and politics.

First, the Constitution endows the President, Congress, and the Supreme Court with considerable, but limited, authority. Moreover, these governmental institutions also have elastic powers; under the pressure of events or compelling rhetoric, they stretch to accommodate new demands for action. Extensions of governmental authority are conditional, however; they are supposed to protect, not suppress, personal liberty. But people may, and probably will, disagree over which is occurring. For example, when the President tries to protect the nation's security by ordering widespread lie detector tests of federal bureaucrats, is this an expansion of presidential authority that protects liberty? Or would this practice protect the liberty of some at the expense of the liberty of others? Because of its conditional grants of authority and because of likely controversy around government's exercise of authority, the Constitution sets the stage for an ongoing drama over what government should and should not do.

Second, the Constitution has two especially significant effects on public policy: it makes some kinds of policy more likely than others and it makes it hard to coordinate the policy-making activities of governmental officials.

The Constitution makes some kinds of public policy more popular and therefore, more likely to occur, than other kinds. Because of its emphasis on the rights of individuals, the Constitution encourages the adoption of public policies that promote private activities—like making a profit in private enterprise. Because of this premium on the rights of private persons, the Constitution discourages the adoption of policies that would take away from some and give to others—like taxation schemes that blatantly redistribute wealth from the rich to the poor. The first type is called **distributive public policy**; the latter is **redistributive policy**.[15] And, in general, the Constitution has a bias toward the adoption of distributive, rather than redistributive, public policy.

---

[15] For an early but clear discussion of the differences between distributive and redistributive policy, see Theodore J. Lowi, "American Business, Public Policy, Case-Studies, and Political Theory," *World Politics* 16 (1964): 677–715.

The Constitution also makes it hard to coordinate the making of public policy. By dividing it among national governmental institutions, the Constitution fragments the power of the state to intervene in society. Since different branches have their own considerable, but limited, power base, it is hard to get all branches to act in concert. In general, the absence of coordination is the norm, as for example, when the President and the Congress cannot agree on budget cuts or when the Supreme Court stops the Internal Revenue Service from granting tax exemptions to certain private schools. The lack of coordination also extends to relations between national governmental institutions and state and local governments, as we show in the discussion of federalism in chapter 4. In addition, the lack of coordination will be found inside all governmental institutions, as we show in our treatment of the presidency, Congress, the federal bureaucracy, and the Courts (chapters 11, 12, 13 and 14, respectively).

Third, the Constitution's impact on governmental institutions and public policy means there will be politics. Since the powers of governmental institutions are somewhat elastic, people will fight politically over whether these powers should expand or shrink. Since they will disagree over whether an expansion of governmental authority protects, or suppresses liberty, people will mobilize in support, or opposition to almost everything government does. Since distributive policies are the norm, intense political pressure will be needed to bring about policies that redistribute wealth. Since so many policy-making activities are uncoordinated, both political leadership and organization will be needed to bring about significant changes in the direction of public policy.

■ The Founders' success can be measured by the Constitution's durability and flexibility. Americans argue over whether or not governmental institutions are behaving constitutionally, for example; but we do not argue over whether or not they should. We argue over whether or not a proposed policy would protect or stifle liberty; but we do not argue over the central importance of the value of liberty. We expect to differ in our beliefs about government's proper role; but we try to settle differences peacefully, through political, not military, activity.

SUMMARY

The problems of the day pushed the Founders to Philadelphia, where they tried to balance personal liberties with the need to establish social order.

Liberty was endangered by both domestic and foreign threats. At home, state legislatures rode roughshod over the rights of their citizens. From abroad, foreign nations ignored the rights of the new nation and stifled its economic development. These threats to liberty and the difficulties of meeting them under the Articles of Confederation inclined many of the Founders toward a new central government.

The Founders were politically skilled analysts and problem solvers. Many of them also were skilled in molding perceptions, especially the Federalists who eventually would convince a reluctant nation that the rights of states had to give way to the need for a strong national government. Many of the Founders had sufficient skill to negotiate a compromise among competing visions of government's proper role.

The Founders established foundations for the new government: a commitment to a republican form of government based on the doctrine of popular sovereignty; a belief that the Constitution, as a written account of natural law, could constrain government; and the expectation that the Supreme Court would uphold the Constitution.

Over time, the Constitution has provided a legal context for ongoing problem solving, as the nation continues its attempt to balance liberty and order.

Key Terms

constitution
Virginia Plan
New Jersey Plan
The Great, or Connecticut,
    Compromise
Federalists
Antifederalists
separation of powers
bicameralism
natural law

natural rights
social contract
popular sovereignty
republicanism
constitutionalism
judicial review
checks and balances
distributive public policy
redistributive public policy

Review and Reflection

1. Must liberty be balanced with order? Why? *YES O W/O LIB & LIB W/O O ARE EQUALLY DESTRUCTIVE*

2. When did passion wrestle with reason? Who won? *DURING DRAFT OF CONSTITUTION*

3. What were some of the issues that the Founders fought about?

4. Describe the foreign and domestic threats to liberty present at the time of the Constitutional Convention.

5. In what ways did their political heritage push the Founders toward a particular solution to the problems of liberty?

6. Define natural law, natural rights, and social contract. What's the relationship among these ideas?

7. The Constitution rests on what three foundations? Why are these important?

8. The Constitution serves as a legal context for ongoing problem solving in what three ways?

9. What do you think should be the balance between liberty and order? For example, should people be free to criticize the President even if doing so interferes with his responsibility to carry out the nation's foreign policy? Does it matter whether this happens during a war?

Supplemental Readings

The Constitution was a product of the experiences and values of its authors. Experience was a powerful teacher, as *Rakove* shows in his history of a time before the Constitution, when Americans unsuccessfully struggled with the problems of peace and as *Wood* shows in his account of the growth of ideas that would find their way into the Constitution. The values of the Founders both motivated their search and predisposed them toward particular solutions. Some, *Beard*, for example, argue that self-serving economic motivations dominated. Others, however, take a more inclusive view as *Rossiter*, for example, does in his comprehensive history of the Convention.

In Philadelphia, a certain viewpoint prevailed, one convinced that only a strong national government could protect liberty. This view can be described through the eyes of the Federalists, as *Morris* tries to, or through their own words, as recorded in the *Federalist Papers*. But there was another side to the struggle in Philadelphia, a view that feared the ability of a strong national government to stifle liberty. This view also was highly principled, as *Main* and *Storing* show in their studies of those who are known mostly for what they were against, the Antifederalists.

The Constitution is more than its times and its authors, however. The Constitution means something and it makes a difference. You will find it reprinted in the back of this textbook. After you read it, you might want to know more about its meaning and about the way it has been modified and interpreted over time. For a little help, see *Pritchett*; for a little more, see *Peltason*; for as much as you will need for now, see *Corwin*.

Beard, Charles A. *An Economic Interpretation of the Constitution*, New York: Free Press, 1979. (First published in 1913.)

Corwin, Edward S. (revised by Harold W. Chase and Craig R. Ducat), *The Constitution: And What It Means Today*, 14th ed. Princeton, NJ: Princeton University Press, 1978.

The Federalist Papers, available in many editions, including one with an introduction by Clinton Rossiter, published by The New American Library.

Main, Jackson Turner. *The Antifederalists: Critics of the Constitution, 1781–1788*, Chapel Hill, NC: The University of North Carolina Press, 1961.

Morris, Richard B. *Witness at the Creation: Hamilton, Madison, Jay and the Constitution*, New York: Holt, Rinehart & Winston, 1985.

Peltason, J. W. *Corwin's and Peltason's Understanding the Constitution*, 9th ed. New York: Holt, Rinehart, & Winston, 1982.

Pritchett, C. Herman. *The American Constitutional System*, 5th ed. New York: McGraw-Hill, 1981.

Rakove, Jack N. *The Beginnings of National Politics: An Interpretive History of the Continental Congress*, Baltimore, Md.: Johns Hopkins University Press, 1982.

Rossiter, Clinton. *1787: The Grand Convention*, New York: The New American Library, 1968.

Storing, Herbert J. (with the editorial assistance of Murray Dry), *What the Antifederalists Were For*, Chicago: The University of Chicago Press, 1981.

Wood, Gordon S. *The Creation of the American Republic, 1776–1787*, New York: Norton, 1972.

CHAPTER THREE

FEDERALISM
SHIFTING NATIONAL, STATE, AND LOCAL RESPONSIBILITIES

W*hen things that should be are not, and things that should not be are, disappointment grows and a question forms. When you cannot register for classes because the computer says you have not paid the term bill you did pay, when the election cannot be held because no one delivered the voting machines, when elderly Americans do not eat because their Social Security check was not delivered on time, disappointment grows and we ask, "Who is responsible?"*

Democratic governments, just like other kinds of institutions, can fail. When they do, we look around for someone to blame, demanding, "Who's in charge here?" Often, however, it seems as though there's never anyone around to blame. The reason is called federalism.

Federalism is the way authority is distributed among national, state, and local governments so that all have some degree of independence from one another. In our federal form of government, therefore, many governments have some separate and some shared responsibilities. As a result, it is difficult to fix ultimate responsibility in this political system. This is no accident.

As we saw in chapter 2, the Founders left blurred the lines of authority that divided the responsibilities and powers of the national government from those of the states. Gradually, some of these divisions were sorted out, largely through administrative, legislative, and judicial responses to political controversies. But some disagreements remain, and old controversies resurface, in an ongoing struggle to sort out the proper responsibilities of national, state, and local levels of government.

This chapter opens with a brief Case, a capsule description of the career of John Marshall, the Chief Justice of the Supreme Court from 1801 to 1835. The Case reveals some important insights. First, the landmark decisions of the Marshall Court allocated responsibility and, implicitly, power within the new federal system of government. Second, federalism evolves in response to political pressures and underlying value conflicts. Third, federalism has significant effects on government, policies, and politics.

THE FORMATION OF A FEDERAL SYSTEM

Proclaim Liberty throughout all the land unto
the inhabitants thereof.
—Inscription on the Liberty Bell

John Marshall, Chief Justice of
the United States Supreme
Court from 1801–1835.

The Case   The Career of Chief Justice John Marshall

January 19, 1801. The office of President John Adams, Washington, D.C.

This time he had failed in the mission given him by President Adams. Now he was back in Adams' office to report his failure; John Jay would not accept the President's invitation to return to the Supreme Court as its chief justice. Adams responded immediately: "I believe I must nominate you."[1] President Adams did and the Senate quickly ratified the nomination of John Marshall as Chief Justice of the United States Supreme Court.

Marshall's failed mission was fortunate—for him and for the nation. As Jay's substitute, Marshall would serve for the next thirty-four years. During his tenure, the Supreme Court would decide over 1100 cases with Marshall writing about one-half the decisions; he, more than any other person, translated constitutional theory into practice and thereby molded the federal system.

John Marshall's career spans the early development of the federal system and reveals much about its basic nature. Throughout it all, Marshall was an astute analyst of both law and politics—elevating the power of the national government over the states, establishing the Supreme Court as the final judge of both, and protecting the private sector from government. As his career unfolded, so too did the federal system.[2]

Marshall grew up on the edge of the colonial frontier, in a hollow of the Blue Ridge Mountains of western Virginia. There he acquired the easy natural charm and physical strength that would endure for the next eighty years, until his death on July 6, 1835. Life was difficult on the frontier; one survived by learning how to survive. Later, in the Revolutionary War, Marshall was more than a survivor. He was a brave and natural leader who could win and keep the respect of his men. After the war, Marshall's legal practice thrived as he previewed his intellectual skills: his ability to analyze complex issues, identifying key problems and isolating promising solutions; his ability to reason his way to a conclusion, overwhelming opposition like a tidal wave—but without rancor or lingering bitterness; his ability to articulate the conclusion, stating the case most clearly and resting it firmly on a foundation likely to endure. From his legal practice, Marshall moved on to public

---

[1] The quote is in *An Autobiographical Sketch of John Marshall*. As it appears here, the quote comes from Charles Fairman, "John Marshall and the American Judicial Tradition," in W. Melville Jones, ed., *Chief Justice John Marshall: A Reappraisal* (Ithaca, New York: Cornell University Press, 1956), p. 82.

[2] This brief description of Marshall's life and career is drawn from Albert J. Beveridge, *The Life of John Marshall* (New York: Houghton Mifflin Company, 1916); Edwin S. Corwin, *John Marshall and the Constitution: A Chronicle of the Supreme Court* (New Haven: Yale University Press, 1919); Leon Friedman and Fred L. Israel, eds., *The Justices of the United States Supreme Court 1789–1969* Vol. I. (New York: Chelsea House Publishers, 1969), pp. 285–351; and Jones, *A Reappraisal*.

service: in Virginia's legislature and its ratification convention, arguing in favor of the new Constitution; in Congress, defending President Adams' foreign policy against its Jeffersonian critics; in diplomacy, fighting foreign restrictions on American commerce. His background had prepared him well for that winter day in President Adams' office. Marshall was ready. Growing up on the frontier, fighting the war, practicing his craft, honing his intellectual and political skills, Marshall had acquired a certain kind of courage—what Albert Beveridge, his biographer, calls "that courage for action."[3]

John Marshall, left, shown speaking to a group of lawyers during his circuit-riding days.

The Supreme Court also was impoverished in its early years, as Marshall had been; when he took his seat, the Court had neither prestige nor a well-accepted role in national government. Jay knew the Court's tenuous position, having served as the Court's first chief justice before leaving for diplomatic service; he had refused Adams' invitation to rejoin the Court because he did not think the Court would "acquire the public confidence and respect which . . . it should possess."[4] Jay's view was well founded. The early Court was a subordinate body; it even met in the basement of what is now the Capitol's North (Senate) Wing. It did not meet much, only for about six weeks a year. The Court's short session probably was fortunate, however, because of Washington's swamp-like summer climate and malaria-laden swarms of mosquitoes. The justices were mostly out of town, since they also served as members of lower (circuit) courts. "Riding the circuit" meant just that, in horse-pulled carts carrying everything needed for the burdensome trip. Riding the Southern Circuit, for example, meant two trips a year, each taking two months to travel two thousand miles—all to hold a two-week session. The early Court also had not accomplished much, not enough to acquire much prominence. In its first four years, the Supreme Court decided only five cases—and only fifty-five up to the time Marshall took his seat. Moreover, the Court lacked leadership, a sense of purpose, and political allies—but not enemies.

As Marshall assumed his seat, the federal judiciary's already tenuous legitimacy was under new attack. Adams already had lost the election of 1800 to his, and Marshall's, bitter antagonist, Thomas Jefferson. Jefferson's sympathies for popular control of government would soon fuel the attack against the judiciary. Under Adams, the Federalists had passed the Alien and Sedition Acts, making it a crime to criticize the government or its officials—namely them. Some federal judges had enforced the hated acts too vigorously; now came the popular backlash. With Jefferson's blessing and often indirect support, some judges were impeached, tried, and removed from office. In other cases, judgeships were abolished and courts had their jurisdictions cut. The state governments, jealous of their powers, also were hostile toward the federal judiciary. It seemed a bad time to get into the business. Nevertheless, Marshall's courage in the face of political adversity both sustained him and nurtured the Supreme Court.

In coping with controversies that were pressed on the Court, Marshall drew and defended new lines of authority. Through a series of landmark decisions, the Supreme Court became strong enough to carry out its constitutional responsibilities, and the responsibilities and powers of the national government grew, often at the expense of those of the states. When he was finished, Marshall had led the Supreme Court to prominence as a coequal branch of the national

---

3 Beveridge, *John Marshall*, Vol. 1, p. 41.
4 Ibid., p. 24.

government. And he struck a new balance in the relationship between national and state government, one consistent with the needs of a growing economy and one necessary for a strong nation.

Drawing on his own vigorous nature, Marshall enlivened the national government, expanding its sense of purpose and direction. Drawing on his vision of the needs of a growing economy, Marshall cleared fertile soil, pushing back stunting state intrusions. Drawing on his political intuition, Marshall resisted the pre-Civil War pressures for states' rights. Increasingly, however, the Court found it difficult to cope with the strident insistence on states' rights. As the nation lurched toward fratricide, Marshall's career came to a close.

John Marshall died on July 6, 1835, in Philadelphia. As his body was carried through the streets in a hero's farewell, on its way to the docks to be returned to his beloved Virginia, the city's bells rang. Foremost among them was the voice of what we now call the Liberty Bell. "Then a strange thing happened. A great cleft appeared in the side of the bell and, like Marshall's voice, it too became still forever."[5] The bell was taken down and later displayed in front of Independence Hall, where all could read its inscription: "Proclaim Liberty throughout all the land unto the inhabitants thereof."

Insights

This glimpse into the career of Chief Justice John Marshall highlights his accomplishments, the way federalism evolves, and its consequences.

Insight 1. *The landmark decisions of the Marshall Court allocated responsibility and implicitly, power within the new federal system of government.* Because of Marshall's decisions and the skill with which he argued them, vague constitutional lines of authority became more specific. As a result, a strong national government emerged, one reflecting more of Hamilton's than Jefferson's vision of the proper balance between it and the states.

Insight 2. *Federalism evolves in response to political pressures and underlying value conflicts.* Marshall's decisions were tentative stands, taken in response to political pressures. The resulting divisions of governmental responsibilities were flexible, fluid divisions. Over time, new battles would be fought over constantly changing federal, state, local, and private responsibilities.

Insight 3. *Federalism has significant effects on government, policies, and politics.* Marshall's landmark decisions ensured that no one level or branch of government would totally dominate any other. Since then, other decisions, laws, and practices have built on this principle, further fragmenting governmental responsibility and power. The fragmentation has consequences: it makes responsibility elusive, it creates opportunities for both cooperation and conflict, it produces distinctive policies and often peculiar politics.

Each of these insights is elaborated in a separate section.

---

[5] Jones, *A Reappraisal*, p. xvi.

THE NATURE OF FEDERALISM

> In essence, federalism has been a device for forging the national power needed to build an effective economy and to defend the nation against external threats, while preserving the advantages afforded by smaller units of government.
>
> —Lewis B. Kuden, "Federalism in the Courts: Agenda for the 1980s," at a Conference on the Future of Federalism

Federal Forms of Government

We have defined *federalism* as the way authority is distributed among national, state, and local governments, so that each of them enjoys some degree of independence from one another. This definition lets us distinguish unitary from federal forms of government: **unitary governments**, such as those in Great Britain and Japan, concentrate responsibility, whereas **federal governments**, such as those in the United States, Canada, West Germany, and Australia, distribute responsibility among various levels.

Within federal political systems, responsibility may be distributed broadly and in complex ways. Within the United States, for example, there are many different types of governments, including all the following: the national government of the United States; the fifty state governments; the local governments of the United States, including over 3000 counties, over 16,000 townships, and over 19,000 cities and towns; the over 28,000 special-district governments that do a certain thing within a particular geographical area (run hospitals, libraries, airports); and the over 15,000 public school districts in the United States. Adding all these together, there are over 81,000 governments in the United States—more than the number of people that will fit in your college football stadium, unless you attend Michigan, Ohio State, Stanford, or UCLA. Moreover, these many different governments can be combined in many different ways. All of the following are examples of relationships among governments: national laws are supreme over state laws; states may create and abolish cities; federal funds may flow to states and cities which, in turn, may be required to follow federal regulations; federal commodities, like green beans, may be dished out in local school cafeterias. These examples, however, only scratch the surface of all the possible relationships among more than 80,000 governments, combined two or more at a time. For a different perspective, see the **Vantage Point**: Federalism Is Like a Milkshake (Unless You're in New England).

When focusing on the responsibilities of governments, we often overlook the role of private persons and organizations. This is convenient, but artificial.

FEDERALISM IS LIKE A MILKSHAKE (UNLESS YOU ARE IN NEW ENGLAND)[1]

To help understand the complex and changing nature of federalism, political scientists have employed many different terms and metaphors. (One recent study found 267 distinctions.)[2]

Most often, political scientists and even some governmental officials use cake metaphors to describe federalism. Morton Grodzins, for example, has written of federalism as a marble cake.[3] The marble cake metaphor is useful because it pushes our understanding away from a simple layer cake idea of federalism, with the federal layer on top of the state layer on top of the local layer.

As you might imagine, people, including members of Congress, have had a lot of fun with the metaphors of political scientists. Representative Raymond J. McGrath (R., N.Y.), for example, wrote in a letter to his constituents:

> Our government was founded as a layer cake, with strict lines of authority between the Federal Government and the states. Practicality changed the layer cake Federalism into marble cake Federalism, as the national Government merged efforts with the states in areas such as our armed forces.
> From a marble cake, we have progressed over the past 20 years into a system which many say resembles a fruit cake, with no particular pattern guiding the relationships between the different layers of government. Finally, we have ended up with a birthday cake Federalism, where dozens of special interests make their wishes known and receive presents in the form of Federal assistance.[4]

We prefer to think of federalism as though it were a milkshake, since this more fluid metaphor calls attention to the many different ways of mixing responsibility and power.

You, however, may have different tastes. But choose your metaphors carefully; they can obscure as much as they reveal.

---

[1]What the New Englanders among you probably call a "frappe."

[2]William H. Stewart, "The Function of Models and Metaphors in the Development of Federal Theory," paper presented at the 1979 annual meeting of the American Political Science Association, Washington, D.C., August 31–September 3, 1979.

[3]Morton Grodzins, "Centralization and Decentralization in the American Federal System," in Robert A. Goldwin, ed., *A Nation of States* (Chicago: Rand McNally, 1963), p. 3.

[4]Quoted in *The New York Times*, 18 November 1981.

After all, the whole point is to understand the way society allocates its resources and in America most of our resources are allocated by private persons and organizations working through the private economic market. To affect these resource allocation decisions, any government must count on at least the passive compliance of other levels of government and private entities and typically needs their active cooperation. If the national government wanted to conserve clean water, for example, it must affect not only municipalities that release inadequately treated sewage, but also industrial plants that dump untreated wastes, employees who look the other way, consumers who do not want to pay higher prices or taxes, boaters and gas station owners with leaky gas tanks, many of the states and a few regional authorities—plus Canada. This example illustrates one of the more imposing realities of American politics. In addition to interdependencies among levels of government, all levels of government routinely rely on a large number of actors in what is called the private sector.

The *private sector* consists of all those nongovernmental persons and entities that make decisions about the uses of society's resources. To get a fix on the relative sizes of the private sector and government or the public sector, compare their shares of the *Gross National Product*—the dollar value of all goods and services produced in a given year. In 1984, for example, the Gross National Product amounted to about $3,661,300,000,000.[6] About 34 percent of this was purchased by all levels of government in the form of health care for the aged, guns and tanks for soldiers, concrete and labor for roads, salaries for teachers and bureaucrats, and so on. From another angle, we see that the private sector is about two times bigger than the entire public sector, with all its thousands of governments.

U.S. SMELTING
"SQUANDERING OUR PRECIOUS RESOURCES SINCE 1932"

While you keep in mind the straightforward definition of federalism, do not overlook the complexity that Daniel Elazar and other students of federalism have exposed.[7] Because federalism is so complex and variable, it is hard to build a unified understanding of it, as Paul Peterson has complained.[8] But one thing is clear, accomplishing anything in this society requires a large number of relationships among governments and between governments and private persons and organizations. These are just a few of the possible relationships, with some of the consequences:

- Private persons act like federal bureaucrats when they fill out their income tax forms.
- Businesses bail out cities, like New York and San Francisco, when they loan them executives to find ways to save money and provide better services.[9]
- Labor unions get a boost at the table when the government forces businesses to sit down and bargain.
- Private colleges get more students when governments give grants and loans to students.
- Everybody pays more for electricity when a state taxes the coal dug within its borders.
- Private persons act like zookeepers when they adopt burros that are about to be shot by the National Park Service or like forest rangers when they act as though they really believe that only private individuals can prevent forest fires.

---

[6] *Economic Report of the President* (Washington, D.C.: United States Government Printing Office, 1985). Tables B–1 and B–74.

[7] Daniel J. Elazar, ed., *The Federal Polity* (New Brunswick, NJ: Transaction Books, 1979).

[8] Paul Peterson, *City Limits* (Chicago: The University of Chicago Press, 1981). See especially chapters 1 and 4.

[9] See, for example, the seven case studies in R. Scott Fosler and Renee A. Berger, eds., *Public-Private Partnership in American Cities* (Lexington, Mass.: Lexington Books, 1982).

All of these relationships, and many more, make federalism—and the way our society makes decisions—complex, fascinating, and often frustrating.

The Foundations of National Authority

To win agreement in Philadelphia and ratification throughout the nation, the Constitution left many things vague. It did not, for example, specify the exact relationships among the branches of the national government or between the central and state governments.

But the nation had to find a solution to the problem that faces any large emerging nation: the need to unify different and widely scattered interests behind a central government, without provoking a civil war. William H. Riker, in his classic treatment of federalism, argues that emerging large nations must choose between two alternatives. They can replace one colonial master for another, their own imperial central government. Or, they can join "in some kind of federation, which preserves at least the semblance of political self-control." For this reason, Riker sees federalism as "the main alternative to empire . . . a technique of aggregating large areas under one government."[10] The alternative had been embraced in Philadelphia; now, it needed refinement.

Through a series of Supreme Court decisions, Chief Justice John Marshall crafted a solution to the problems facing the new nation. In the process, Marshall laid the foundation for a strong judiciary within a strong national government. The foundation was erected on new constitutional advances: the principle of judicial review elevated the position of the Supreme Court within the national government; the doctrine of implied powers and the principle of national supremacy augmented the authority of the national government over the states and economic activity, while opening the way for the development of a strong federal judiciary and a vigorous national economy; the contractual rights of private persons were upheld and expanded in ways that fostered economic growth.

The Right of Judicial Review.   Under Marshall, the Supreme Court advanced its position in the national government by claiming the right of judicial review. Thus armed, the Court had the power to declare actions of the legislative and executive branches unconstitutional and therefore void. The Court asserted this right in the famous **Marbury v. Madison** case.[11] It was a complicated game, with many players but a low final score: Marbury 0; Madison 0; Marshall 1.

William Marbury was to have been a judge, one of those appointed by President Adams just before he left office. Adams hoped that his kind of judges would blunt Jefferson's radicalism and antipathy to the emerging powers of the

---

[10] William H. Riker, *Federalism: Origin, Operation, Significance* (Boston: Little, Brown, 1964), pp. 4–5.

[11] *Marbury* v. *Madison*, 1 U.S. 368 (1803).

As he was making his last minute appointments, President John Adams surely did not know that he was setting the stage for *Marbury* v. *Madison*.

national government. Besides, Adams had campaign debts to pay off and political allies to reward—more than 200 and Marbury was one of them. His appointment had been approved, but somebody in the Secretary of State's office erred; Marbury's official letter of appointment was not delivered before Jefferson took office. Jefferson and his Secretary of State, James Madison, simply took no action and Marbury's letter went undelivered. Marbury took his case directly to the Supreme Court, claiming that the Judiciary Act of 1789 gave it **original jurisdiction**—the authority to hear and decide cases as a trial court, rather than just as an appeals court that reviewed the decisions of lower courts. To force Madison to deliver the letter of appointment, Marbury sought from the Supreme Court a specific remedy: a **writ of mandamus**, a court order compelling the performance of a legal duty.

Chief Justice Marshall knew a political thicket when he saw one. It looked like the Supreme Court would lose, no matter what. If the Court ordered Madison to deliver Marbury's appointment letter, the Court would create for itself many thorny problems: they would be siding openly with the Federalists against the new administration; they would make Jefferson more hostile toward the Court; and they would lose credibility if Madison simply refused to obey. The other branch in the road looked just as prickly. If the Court did *not* order Madison to deliver the letter, then the Court would have a different set of problems: they would risk alienating their Federalist supporters; they would lose credibility by caving in to a hostile administration; by appearing weak, they might invite intrusions into the judicial domain. Personal embarrassment topped all this, since it was Marshall who, simultaneously with his chief judgeship, had been serving as Adams' Secretary of State—and since the clerk who misplaced the letter of appointment was Marshall's brother.

Marshall, astute in both law and politics, knew what to do and had the courage to do it. In one swift stroke, he asserted the right of judicial review and elevated the Supreme Court, while cutting the ground from under the Court's adversaries. Marshall took for himself the task of writing the Court's opinion, thereby presuming to speak for the Court as a whole, a practice he would continue throughout his judicial career, pulling together or "massing" the Court to emphasize the idea that the Supreme Court was an institution, not just a group of judges. In this opinion, Marshall did another thing he would do time and time again: he said more than he had to, thereby imposing his own view of federalism.

Marshall's decision led the Court safely through this political thicket—and it emerged stronger. He argued that Marbury had a point, he was entitled to receive his letter of appointment. In addition, Marbury was correct, Marshall agreed; the Judiciary Act of 1789 did give the Supreme Court the authority to issue a writ of mandamus in this case. But Marshall asked the prior question: "Should the court follow the Judiciary Act?" Only if the act is constitutional, Marshall argued. Here, Marshall went out of his way, saying more than he had to say to decide the case. He argued that the Court had a higher responsibility; before applying a law, the Court should first decide if the law is consistent with higher law; that is, with the Constitution. In this instance, Marshall argued, the relevant section of the Judiciary Act was *not* constitutional. Since the act was unconstitutional and therefore void, the Supreme Court had no constitutional right and no legal authority to order the delivery of Marbury's letter of appointment. And, therefore, it refused to do so. The final score: Marbury 0— he did not get his appointment; Madison 0—he and the Jefferson administration lost a chance to challenge the authority of the Supreme Court; Marshall 1—he claimed for the Supreme Court a potentially strong constitutional role.

In *Marbury* v. *Madison*, Marshall's assertion of the right of judicial review coaxed out of this "ticklish little suit" a strategic triumph for the Supreme Court.[12] The triumph was a prerequisite for a stronger role. Armed with the right of judicial review, the Supreme Court was able to referee competing claims and redraw lines of responsibility. From this moment on, sometimes broadly, sometimes narrowly, the Supreme Court would determine the constitutionality of law.[13]

The Doctrine of Implied Powers and the Principle of National Supremacy. Both of these new foundations of national authority emerged from the same case, **McCulloch v. Maryland**. The **doctrine of implied powers** was the view that the national government could do whatever was necessary and proper (or even just convenient) to carry out its constitutionally explicit

---

[12] Jones, *A Reappraisal*, pp. 87–88.

[13] John R. Schmidhauser, *The Supreme Court as Final Arbiter in Federal-State Relations, 1789–1957* (Chapel Hill: University of North Carolina Press, 1958).

powers. The **principle of national supremacy** advanced the view that the laws that result from the national government's exercise of its implied powers are supreme over the laws of the states.

In *McCulloch* v. *Maryland*, Marshall settled the immediate controversy before the Court.[14] But to do so, he broadly interpreted the language of the Constitution, advancing both the doctrine of implied powers and the principle of national supremacy. At first glance, the particulars of the case made it look like a poor place to fight over the respective rights of the national and state governments. The Constitution, after all, did not give the central government an explicit right to create a national bank. The Bank of the United States was widely despised, but its size and backing gave it a competitive advantage over state banks. To retaliate, Maryland and other states tried to tax the branches, increasing their costs of doing business and hopefully driving them out. In this case, the state of Maryland passed a law, requiring the Baltimore branch of the Bank of the United States to pay a tax of $15,000 a year. It was the cashier of the branch, James McCulloch, who refused to pay. The state took him to their courts, where they won, not surprisingly. McCulloch appealed to the Supreme Court.

The money issued by the Bank of the United States, as well as that of even more dubious value—that issued by local banks.

Marshall's decision went to the heart of the matter: "Did the central government have a right to create a national bank in the first place and, if so, could this be done without the interference of a state government?" Marshall's opinion drew inferences out of constitutional language. After enumerating explicit powers, Article I, Section 8, the **necessary and proper clause** of the U.S. Constitution, gave the national government the power "To make all Laws which shall be necessary and proper for carrying into Execution the foregoing Powers, and all other Powers vested by this Constitution in the Government of the United States, or in any Department or Officer thereof." Since the national government had the explicit right to raise money by taxation or borrowing, and since the establishment of a national bank was an appropriate means for doing so, Marshall argued, it then followed that the national government had the implied power to create the bank. Moreover, a state could not interfere since Article VI made the laws of the United States the "supreme Law of the Land."

Through this decision, Marshall simultaneously elevated the responsibilities and powers of the national government and circumscribed those of the states. Armed with this doctrine and this principle, the nation was poised to begin a process of nation building. But nation building required the law to be uniform throughout the land, as it could be only if the Supreme Court had the right to review all the decisions of state courts—even those in which the state was a party. That right, too, Marshall soon claimed.

In *Cohens* v. *Virginia*[15], the Supreme Court extended its appellate jurisdiction to cover cases in which a state was a party. In this case, Cohens was convicted of violating a Virginia anti-lottery statute. After exhausting his state appeals, Cohens appealed his conviction to the Supreme Court, claiming that

---

[14] *McCulloch* v. *Maryland*, 4 U.S. 415 (1819).
[15] *Cohens* v. *Virginia*, 5 U.S. 82 (1821).

there was a federal question involved, namely, an alleged conflict between the state law and a federal one that permitted lotteries. The state of Virginia tried to block Cohens' appeal to the Supreme Court and claimed that the Court had no authority to review the judgment of state courts, even when they rule on matters involving federal law. Not so, ruled Marshall, finding that the Judiciary Act of 1789 gave the Supreme Court the final authority to review cases involving federal questions. By framing the issue as a contest between the federal and state courts and by upholding Cohens' right to appeal, Marshall established the supremacy of federal courts and opened the way for the development of a strong federal judiciary. By allowing Cohens' conviction to stand, however, because of his faulty argument in the appeal, Marshall avoided a direct and potentially debilitating confrontation with the state court. Continuing to choose his cases well, Marshall next found an opening that would give the national government the right to oversee and direct economic development.

In *Gibbons* v. *Ogden*[16], Marshall's decision provided the basis for an expansion of the Congress' **commerce powers**—its responsibility to regulate various forms of economic activity. Thus empowered, the national government went on to perform an increasingly expansive role in helping shape the growth of a strong national economy and a strong nation.

The case grew out of the New York State Legislature's attempt to restrict navigation on the Hudson River, limiting it to Ogden's (New York) steamboats. But Gibbons also was in the steamboat business, operating from the New Jersey side under a federal permit that had been granted by Congress. Ogden, seeking to protect a good thing, got the New York courts to issue an injunction that blocked Gibbons from New York waters. New Jersey retaliated by barring Ogden's boats from its waters. When the case came before the Supreme Court, Marshall had to answer the narrow question: "Who had the right to regulate navigation?" But in providing the answer, Marshall characteristically found a way to advance the broad powers of the national government. The case involved the **commerce clause** of the Constitution: "The Congress shall have power . . . to regulate commerce with foreign nations, and among the several states, and with the Indian Tribes." (Article I, Section 8). In this case, Marshall expansively defined interstate commerce to include all kinds and forms of commercial intercourse—including transportation and navigation. Since then, the Congress has used its commerce powers to regulate many forms of economic activity, including such diverse matters as child labor, agricultural production, labor unions, wages and hours.

The Sanctity of Private Property Rights.   The Marshall Court upheld the sanctity of private property rights and thereby encouraged growth in the private sector. Nation building required a vigorous economy, one in which business could confidently invest and expand, protected from both foreign and

---

[16] *Gibbons* v. *Ogden*, 6 U.S. 1 (1824).

Relying on its commerce powers, Congress passed the Fair Labor Standards Act of 1938, outlawing child labor.

domestic interference. To lower risk and stimulate investment, the private sector needed the stability and predictability that only a central government could give as it extended uniform conditions over the entire territory of the United States. This investors received, as the Marshall Court drew out the implications of constitutional language in a series of decisions. To secure the rights of those who held private property, the Marshall Court relied on Article I, Section 10 of the U.S. Constitution. This section, the so-called **contract clause**, kept states from passing laws that relieved private persons (such as debtors) of their contractual obligations. Under Marshall, the Supreme Court made explicit the full dimensions of this prohibition and therefore, the extent to which private property rights were protected from state interference.[17] The cumulative effect of these decisions helped legitimize a proper sphere within which private business was free to act without fear of state regulation.

Because of these constitutional advances, conditions favored the growth of a strong national government, sustained by a vigorous national economy. In time both triumphed, invigorated by an emerging sense of nationalism. But competing visions remained to buffet the political system, producing ongoing change in the nature of federalism.

---

17 *Fletcher* v. *Peck*, 2 U.S. 328 (1810); *Dartmouth College* v. *Woodward*, 4 U.S. 463 (1819); *Cohens* v. *Virginia*, 5 U.S. 82 (1821); and *Gibbons* v. *Ogden*, 6 U.S. 1 (1824).

Federalism and Change

Federalism evolved in a manner at odds with the ideals of Thomas Jefferson.

Federalism constantly changes as it evolves.[18] But the evolution of federalism has not been predictable or orderly. Rather, federalism has evolved in complex ways: sometimes the responsibilities and powers of the national government expanded at the expense of those of the states; at other times, an expanded federal role has fed the expansion of state and local roles; and sometimes federal government expanded its role only after states had paved the way. The evolution of federalism also continues, in pace with current controversies.

Federalism evolves in response to underlying value conflicts. This evolutionary pattern is revealed throughout American history. Marshall, for example, took his seat on the bench amidst competing visions and fears.[19] The nationalist view, epitomized by Alexander Hamilton, for example, envisioned a strong central government and a strong national economy, sustaining and nurturing one another. Moreover, the nationalist view served a central value, and a belief about how it could be best realized. The nationalists valued personal liberty as highly as any and believed that it could best be served by a central government strong enough to protect it from domination by foreign and state powers. The nationalist view was challenged, however, by Thomas Jefferson and others. They disparaged the motives of mere merchants, embracing instead agrarian virtues and beliefs that freedom prospered when it was distant from central government and commercial activity.[20] The Hamiltonian view linked the development of a strong national economy with the development of a strong national government. In contrast, the Jeffersonian view denied this link, fearing that the concentration of economic and political power would stifle personal liberties. Whereas Hamiltonian values embraced national politics, government, and economic policy making, Jeffersonian values spurned all three. The dispute ran deep and Marshall could not avoid taking sides. Throughout his career, Marshall championed the cause of the national government, seeking to expand its responsibilities and powers. As he did so, and in part because he did so, federalism evolved in ways that augmented the authority of the national government and in ways that furthered the development of national economic strength and national military might.

Federalism continued to evolve in response to the often competing demands of different interests and concerns. In some cases the values were irreconcilable and the new federal solutions tentative or unstable. Roger Taney, Marshall's successor as chief justice, was, for example, unable to reconcile the competing interests of an industrial North, increasingly opposed

---

[18] For the historical evolution of federalism, see Daniel J. Elazar, *The American Partnership: Intergovernmental Cooperation in the Nineteenth-Century United States* (Chicago: University of Chicago Press, 1962); Samuel Beer, "Modernization of American Federalism," *Publius* 3 (1973): 49–74; and Harry Scheiber, "Federalism and the American Economic Order, 1789–1910," *Law and Society Review* 10 (1975): 57–89.

[19] Martin Diamond, "What the Framers Meant By Federalism," in Robert A. Goldwin, ed., *A Nation of States* (Chicago: Rand McNally, 1963), pp. 24–41.

[20] Herbert J. Storing, (with the editorial assistance of Murray Day), *What the Antifederalists Were For* (Chicago: University of Chicago Press, 1981).

Before collective bargaining, labor unions could do little more than disrupt production, as, for example, through sit-down strikes.

to slavery, and an agricultural South, increasingly dependent on slave labor. The uneasy truce that had postponed civil war was shattered by Taney's use of judicial review in the Dred Scott case to rule unconstitutional the Missouri Compromise of 1820, Congress' attempt to limit the spread of slavery.[21] The Civil War carved its own alterations on the landscape of federalism as the powers of the central government grew in response to the demands of re-unification—sometimes at the expense of the rights of others. During the war, for example, the civil liberties of private persons were consistently violated as those suspected of treason were imprisoned without being formally charged.

Later, social currents were strong enough to sweep along with them a Supreme Court that made accommodating adjustments in federal and state relations. For nearly a century after Marshall's death, the Supreme Court slowed expansion of the federal government's role, deferring to the powers the states claimed under the Tenth Amendment and deterred by the spirit of laissez-faire capitalism which stressed the virtues of unregulated private activity. For example, the Supreme Court upheld the states in the exercise of their sovereign powers regulating the sale of liquor within their own borders and in their practices allowing child labor.[22] [23] Even as late as 1935, the Supreme Court argued that the rights of states were infringed by federal law to

---

[21] *Dred Scott* v. *Sanford*, 60 U.S. 393 (1857).
[22] The License Cases, 16 U.S. 513 (1847).
[23] *Hammer* v. *Dagenhart*, 247 U.S. 251 (1918).

end cutthroat competition and improve working conditions.[24] In general, up to 1936, the era's hero was private business, with the states often ready to do its bidding.

The scales tipped by 1937, new values gained ascendancy, and political pressures welled up for a national government strong enough to curb the excesses of business corporations. Running on a reform platform for his second term in 1936, President Franklin Roosevelt carried all but two states. The Supreme Court apparently sensed the shift and upheld, as constitutional, new national legislation that guaranteed labor's right to unionize and required good-faith bargaining by business.[25] In this 1937 shift, the Supreme Court returned to Marshall's view of the relative dominance of the national government in federal and state relations. For the next forty years, the states got along with Washington the best they could, resisting where possible, cooperating where necessary, but always begrudgingly and often with a bitter taste of resentment.

Roosevelt's New Deal and the subsequent social welfare obligations of President Johnson's Great Society bred local resentment and produced a political reaction, first witnessed in the presidential election of Richard Nixon in 1968 and later in the election of Ronald Reagan in 1980. The political reaction found judicial expression in the renewed use of the Tenth Amendment as a basis for striking down federal law. On this basis, for example, the Supreme Court ruled in 1976 that the federal government had gone too far, infringing on "the separate and independent existence" of states, when it tried to require state and local governments to pay their workers according to federal standards for minimum wages and maximum hours.[26]

Today, the issue of federal and state relations remains in flux. Many wish for more of a shift of federal power back to the states. Justice Sandra Day O'Connor, for example, whose background in state politics and government seems to have predisposed her to local concerns, often rallies to the state side. Other Supreme Court justices, especially former Chief Justice Burger and now Chief Justice Rehnquist, sometimes join O'Connor in her view that the federal government conscripts state legislative powers and thereby undermines "the most valuable aspects of our federalism."[27] But Justice O'Connor need not despair; other cases and challenges to the expanded powers of the national government will continue to surface and federalism will continue to evolve.

■ Marshall's landmark decisions established the basic nature of the American federal system: a strong national government, but one that often shared responsibilities and powers with subnational governments. Since then, the roles of the national government and the many subnational governments have become bigger, more complex, and more interwoven.

---

[24] *Schechter* v. *United States*, 295 U.S. 495 (1935).

[25] *National Labor Relations Board* v. *Jones and Laughlin Steel Corporation*, 301 U.S. 1 (1937).

[26] *The National League of Cities* v. *Usery*, 426 U.S. 833 (1976).

[27] *Federal Energy Regulatory Commission* v. *Mississippi*, 456 U.S. 742, 791 (1982). See also Louise Byer Miller, "The Burger Court's View of Federalism," *Policy Studies Journal* 13 (1985): 576–83.

THE POLITICS OF FEDERALISM

> Federalism . . . is an improvisation promoted
> into a political theory.
> —*John P. Roche,* The Founding Fathers:
> A Reform Caucus in Action

The quotation from John Roche suggests a certain irreverence toward the concept of federalism and an encouragement to look behind it for the underlying reality. His encouragement is helpful because it suggests that federalism is a surface reaction; an important one to be sure, but still a surface reaction to the operation of underlying social and political forces. This section gets beneath the surface to identify the nature of those forces and to describe the ways they have affected the evolution of federalism.

Let us preview the argument of this section: federalism evolves through reactions to political pressures and competing values. It does *not* evolve spontaneously; rather, federalism evolves in response to pressing events and competing values that prompt a reshuffling of responsibilities and powers. In addition, different social values make competing claims on government and out of attempts to resolve political pressures and value conflicts, responsibilities and power are redistributed in new ways. All of the resulting rearrangements, as long as they do not destroy the independence of some governmental units, we recognize as forms of federalism. Let us build the argument, piece by piece.

Reactions to Pressure

As federalism evolves, public and private responsibilities are sorted out through a political, not a logical, process. Many note that the structure of federalism is not logical and therefore should be changed. We think this view is mistaken, although expressing it may be politically useful. The then-Governor of Utah, Scott M. Matheson, was taking a political posture, for example, when he supported President Reagan's proposed "New Federalism" and called on the President "to sort out, philosophically and in a logical way, just which programs ought to go back to the states . . ."[28] Granted, current federal arrangements often are not logical. The reason, however, is simply that they did not evolve in a logical manner; rather, federalism evolved as a result of a political process.

Political pressure to change the nature of federalism comes when people believe that existing arrangements for allocating societal resources have failed.[29] Political pressures, therefore, are rooted in dissatisfaction with the current performance of some level of government, some part of the private

---

[28] Quoted in *The New York Times*, 18 February 1982.
[29] Charles Wolf, Jr., "A Theory of Non-Market Failure," *Public Interest* 55 (1979): 114–33.

TABLE 3.1 Public Opinion Data on Use of Tax Dollars

Since 1972, Americans have changed their minds about the level of government that gives them the most for their money.

In a public opinion survey conducted in the years 1972 through 1984, Americans were asked: "From which level of government do you feel you get the most for your money—federal, state, or local?"

Each of these levels of government appear as rows in the table. Each percentage figure is the percentage of the sample that, in a particular year, thought they got the best deal from that level of government. In 1984, for example, only 24 percent of the people surveyed thought that the federal government gave them the most for their money, while 35 percent of the sample believed they got the best deal from local government.

Level Preferred	Year						
	1973	1975	1977	1979	1981	1983	1984
Federal	39%	31	36	29	30	31	24
State	18	20	20	22	25	20	27
Local	25	25	26	33	33	31	35

NOTES: The columns add up to less than 100 percent since some people (between 14 and 22 percent) said they did not know.

SOURCE: Advisory Commission on Intergovernmental Relations. *Significant Features of Fiscal Federalism* (Washington, D.C.: U.S. Government Printing Office, 1985), Table 87.

sector, or both. Historically, it has been mostly the perceived failures of state governments that have given rise to dissatisfaction and to political demands for an expanded national role. In the last decade or so, however, public opinion has turned around. As you can see from the data in **Table 3.1**, people have become increasingly dissatisfied with the way the national government spends their tax dollars and increasingly pleased with the performance of state and local governments.

The historical failure of state governments to accommodate the development of a national economy was one instance that led to pressures that expanded federal regulation of interstate commerce. State governments could not deal with the problems of destructive variation. For example, they permitted too much variation within the railroad industry and with different railroad companies running on different sized tracks, and shipments frequently unloaded and reloaded, individual companies profited but the national economy suffered. To avoid the problems of destructive variation, the federal government increasingly regulated interstate commerce, usually by adopting uniform standards—in airline flight plans, the voltage at which electricity is transmitted, the weight and length of trucks on interstate highways, and so on. In many instances, the expanded federal role reduced destructive variation, thereby increasing the efficiency, productivity, and growth of a national economy.

In other historical instances, the failure of state governments to protect the rights of all their citizens brought major change in the constitutional powers of the national government: through the Thirteenth Amendment which abolished slavery and gave Congress the power to enforce the amendment; through the Fourteenth Amendment which extended the Fourth Amendment's "due process" rights to the citizens of the states; through the Fifteenth and Nineteenth Amendments which gave Congress the power to protect the voting rights of blacks and women, respectively; through the Twenty-fourth Amendment which gave Congress the power to prohibit state taxes that discouraged voting; through the Twenty-sixth Amendment which gave Congress the power to extend voting rights to those eighteen years of age or older. In addition, the failure of state governments to cope with economic, natural, and civil disasters often led to new federal responsibilities as, for example, in the Great Depression of the 1930s, when most states and private pension plans were unable to meet their fiscal responsibilities; in the aftermath of floods, hurricanes, volcanic eruptions; in the disorder and destruction of civil riots; in the case of states that are overwhelmed by a flood of immigrants, as Florida was by Haitian refugees in the early 1980s. Finally, the historical drift toward more federal authority gained impetus from the failure of state governments to respond to the financial needs of cities, after both the white and the black middle classes fled to suburbia. The state governments have no exclusive claim on failure, however. More and more, people believe that many federal "solutions" to social and economic problems have failed; this perception, in turn, erodes political support for the current pattern of federal dominance. This shift of public opinion has been revealed by survey research; the percentage of people favoring the concentration of power in the national government, rather than in state governments, fell from a high of 56 percent in 1936 to only 36 percent in 1981[30] and probably continued to fall under the presidency of Ronald Reagan.

Public perceptions of governmental failure sometimes stimulate a search for ways to increase the involvement of the private sector in the solution of social problems, as in a number of examples:

- when the City of New York failed to maintain Central Park, private citizens and charities provided financial assistance;
- when governments failed to discourage smoking effectively, private insurance companies, private organizations like the American Lung Institute, and private citizens like Brooke Shields joined the effort;
- when the National Park Service failed to find a humane solution to the problems caused by too many wild burros in the Grand Canyon, private persons and wildlife groups helped to round up the burros and find homes for them;

The Fifteenth Amendment meant that blacks had a right to cast a ballot, although, as in this case, not necessarily a secret one.

---

30 *Public Opinion*, (Dec./Jan., 1982), p. 36.

Want to adopt a burro? After the federal government failed to deal humanely with the problem of burro pollution, private groups rounded up the burros and helped find homes for them.

- when the city government of Lincoln, Nebraska, could not meet its payroll, the city's Kawasaki motorcycle factory loaned its workers to the city;
- when San Francisco, California, found itself in a financial mess, private business executives donated their advice on personnel and financial management.

These cases illustrate the political dynamic. Federalism evolves as a response to political pressures that are rooted in perceptions that existing arrangements have failed to solve social and economic problems.

Struggles Among Competing Values

It is important that we not underestimate the force of ideas on human affairs; they are powerful social forces, not the playthings of intellectuals. As is shown in the writings of Max Weber, Seymour Martin Lipset, Henry Steele Commager, Louis Hartz, and elsewhere, ideas about what is valued have compelling force in structuring our economic and political order.[31]

Values are a society's moral imperatives; they are deeply held beliefs about things that should exist, things that should be realized. Most societies are relatively pluralistic—because they accommodate many different beliefs about what the society should do, about which qualities of life should be preserved or sought out, about what is worth fighting and dying for. American society is no exception to this general rule; it, too, is pluralistic in that it accommodates many different values. Nevertheless, we can isolate four key values that have competed for public approbation and governmental sanction throughout American history: liberty, national strength, economic efficiency, and equality.

These values are sources of pressure for change in the existing distribution of responsibilities and power. As a result of attempts to resolve the competing claims of these societal values, federalism evolves. In the name of liberty, federalism evolves as a system of government with built-in obstacles to majoritarian domination of minorities. To achieve national strength, the central government acquires sufficient power to subsidize the development of a vigorous national economy. To realize economic efficiency, the powers of all governments expand to correct for perceived failures in the private market and contract when people believe the private sector can do a better job. To redistribute societal resources in a more equal manner, the national government assumes additional responsibilities and the power to carry them out. Throughout American history, the allocation of governmental responsibilities and powers has been altered in ways that affect these values. Let us see how this has happened.

---

[31] Max Weber, trans. by Talcott Parsons, *The Protestant Ethic and the Spirit of Capitalism* (New York: Scribner's, 1930); Seymour Martin Lipset, *The First New Nation* rev. ed. (New York: Norton, 1979); Henry Steele Commager, *The American Mind: An Interpretation of American Thought and Character Since the 1880s* (New Haven, Conn.: Yale University Press, 1950); Louis Hartz, *The Liberal Tradition in America: An Interpretation of American Political Thought Since the Revolution* (New York: Harcourt Brace Jovanovich, 1955).

During the debate over ratification of the new national constitution, for example, federalism was defended as a form of government that would preserve the value of liberty. *The Federalist Papers*, the campaign literature of the day, presented arguments in favor of ratification. First, liberty was threatened by the factiousness of people. Factiousness means that people divide into warring groups, trying to advance their own self-interest—often at the expense of other groups in society. Farmers, for example, wishing to sell their crops at higher prices than consumers will pay, might want to restrict supplies and drive up prices. Second, some groups may try to win control of government so that they can use its authority to favor their own interests. Farmers, for example, might try to use government's authority to block the importation of cheap foreign grain. Protected from foreign competition, domestic farmers could raise prices and reap higher profits. By influencing governmental policy in this manner, a group could dominate other groups—thereby threatening their liberty. Third, by dispersing power throughout various levels and branches of government, federalism would frustrate factions by making it harder for any one of them to capture all of government's power. Fourth, federalism, therefore, is a friend of liberty. Factions will still be factions but their struggle for dominance will be inconclusive, as long as responsibility and power is widely scattered throughout the federal system. In time, however, it may be necessary to modify this conclusion. As Aaron Wildavsky has noted, these Madisonian premises have been undermined by modern communication and computer technologies that make it easier and cheaper to mobilize interest group pressure.[32]

The value of national strength has had an equally strong grasp on the evolution of federalism. In the early years of the Republic, for example, Alexander Hamilton and other ardent nationalists believed that economic wealth would be the backbone of national strength and sought public policies to stimulate economic development. Hamilton's "Report on Manufacturers" was nothing less than a blueprint for national economic planning to push America boldly into the industrial age. The concept seduced a nation hungry for its place in world affairs. Over time, an increasingly strong national government found various ways to stimulate economic development. During most of the nineteenth century, for example, the national government often used land grants to encourage states to develop agricultural colleges and to encourage railroads to expand their lines.[33] Today as well, the felt drive to augment national strength animates politicians and voters alike, as some call for new tariffs to protect American jobs and as others look for ways to improve cooperation among government, business, and labor.

Throughout our history, Americans have also valued highly economic efficiency, and its hoped for consequences—personal wealth and social progress.

---

[32] Aaron Wildavsky, "Bare Bones: Putting Flesh on the Skeleton of American Federalism," in Advisory Commission on Intergovernmental Relations (ACIR), *The Future Of Federalism in the 1980s* (Washington, D.C.: U.S. Government Printing Office, 1981), pp. 67–88.

[33] George F. Break, "Fiscal Federalism in the United States: The First 200 Years, Evolution and Outlook," in ACIR, *The Future Of Federalism*, pp. 39–65.

Thus, perceived failures in the operation of the private economic system are deeply disappointing and Americans are quick to seek corrective remedies. Economists call the causes of economic inefficiencies **market imperfections**—defects that keep the private market from operating efficiently. One enduring market imperfection is consumer ignorance—people's failure to know what they are buying, drinking, eating, or breathing. Once, for example, people did not know if they were eating decayed meat and today they do not know what the "flavor enhancers" are in their American-made cigarettes. Because of their ignorance, consumers waste money buying things they might not buy if they only knew better. Some economists reason that consumer ignorance is an imperfection in the private market that promotes economic inefficiency—one that governmental intervention can correct. Others argue either that consumers should look out for themselves or that governmental intervention only will prevent the private market from working, while creating opportunities for political corruption. Beginning with the presidency of Jimmy Carter, excessive governmental regulation began to be seen as a major cause of a weak economy and accordingly, the political prescription was to deregulate various forms of economic activity, such as air travel.

The value of economic efficiency has ambiguous implications for the evolution of federalism; it is used both to justify and condemn shifts of responsibility and power from the private sector to government as well as reallocations between the national and the state governments. There are examples on all sides. Some state governments, for example, convinced that they do the job inefficiently, have contracted with private businesses to run their prisons. At the federal level, President Reagan, for example, relied on the efficiency argument to justify his short-lived proposal to give state governments more responsibility over the administration of welfare programs: "I believe that there is much more chance of waste and fraud in trying to run it from the national level than there is in running it at the local level. These are your neighbors there that you are trying to help, and you are better able to know what to do for them than Washington is, 3,000 miles away."[34] Others suspect that inefficiency and even fraud flourishes best in local soil. And there are, of course, some things that the federal government does better than any other level of government; for example, after ratification of the Sixteenth Amendment in 1913 legalized the federal income tax, the national government became almost as efficient as organized crime in raising revenue. In the absence of clear and compelling answers over how to allocate responsibility and power efficiently, Americans do what they do best; they fight politically over subjectively held beliefs.

Finally, the value of equality has justified and sustained an historical expansion in the responsibilities and powers of the national government. Indeed, as has been pointed out by Samuel Beer, a noted Harvard political

---

[34] Quoted in *The New York Times*, 22 November 1981.

scientist, this is "one of the standard, classic functions of the central government in any federal system—to do a little evening up among regions."[35] Throughout American history, there has been a tendency for the national government to adopt mildly redistributive policies. In the area of welfare policies, for example, the federal government assumed, by 1971, the entire cost of the food stamp program so that all people, no matter where they lived, might have an equally nutritious diet. But disparities remained in other kinds of welfare programs. As a result of state discretionary practices, welfare payments for a family of three varied from $96 in Mississippi to $477 in New York. Such discrepancies are very expensive and therefore difficult to maintain. As one urban expert, Paul E. Peterson notes, "If a city expands its services to needy citizens, it only increases its attractiveness as a residence for the poor . . . consistent, concentrated pursuit of such a policy leads to bankruptcy."[36] Therefore, if income is to be shifted from the rich to the poor, the national government has to do it. To a limited extent, it has. By 1982, for example, the federal government had picked up 54 percent of the total cost of the country's main welfare program, Aid to Families with Dependent Children (AFDC). In general, however, the historical move of the national government to equalize the distribution of society's resources has not proceeded rapidly—and not without considerable political opposition.

Pressure to bring about a greater degree of equality through social welfare programs meets resistance. "Evening up" means redistributing wealth, generally from the well-off to the less-well-off, and the well-off may resist politically. In recent times, the redistributive policies of the national governmet have produced something of a conservative backlash, clearly evidenced in the election and policies of the Reagan Administration. President Reagan helped to legitimize this backlash by arguing that the national government should not try to redistribute the wealth of the society; the people themselves, not the national government, should try to push redistributive policies at the state level. In his own words: ". . . this is one of the built-in guarantees of freedom in our federalism . . . the right of the citizens to vote with their feet. If the state is badly managed the people will either do one of two things: they will either use their power at the polls to redress that or they'll go someplace else."[37] To preserve the value of liberty, therefore, Reagan was prepared to sacrifice some degree of equality and to tip the federal and state balance of responsibility and power accordingly.

Each of these major political values—liberty, national strength, economic efficiency, and equality—may lead to pressure to alter the distribution of responsibility and power in the federal system. In addition, these values often compete with one another and make contradictory demands on government.

---

35 Quoted in *The New York Times*, 5 May 1982.
36 Paul E. Peterson, *City Limits* (Chicago, Ill.: University of Chicago Press, 1981), p. 210.
37 Quoted in *The New York Times*, 22 November 1981.

The conflict between liberty and national strength, for example, often has pitted the civil liberties of the people against the war powers of the government. The conflict between economic efficiency and equality, for example, is one which Arthur Okun and other economists have said requires tradeoffs and compromise.[38]

Now we better understand the forces behind federalism and the way they cause it to evolve. Existing divisions of responsibility and power may produce public dissatisfaction and political pressure for change. In addition, as one political scientist, Frederick M. Wirt, has observed: there is a "long-standing tension between the values of central and peripheral authorities . . ."[39] As a result, underlying conflict among values is an inconclusive and therefore ongoing struggle that continuously shapes political perceptions, demands, and thereby, the nature of federalism.

■ In making his landmark decisions, Chief Justice John Marshall was both pushed by political pressures and pulled by his vision of the proper roles of the national and state governments. Marshall's decisions, favoring Hamiltonian over Jeffersonian values, often concentrated responsibility and power in the national government, at the expense of the prerogatives of the states. The struggle over competing values is an ongoing one, forcing continuing realignment in federal, state, and local governmental relations.

THE FEDERAL FRAMEWORK FOR GOVERNMENT'S EVOLVING ROLE

> . . . if American leaders, from the Constitutional Convention forward, have been ambivalent about the locus of power and responsibility within our federal system, that same ambivalence is still reflected within the broad mass of the American people.
> —*Robert E. Merriam,* American Federalism: A Paradox of Promise and Performance

Federalism is a many faceted thing with many consequences. It creates a network of interdependent relationships within government and between levels of government and the private sector. Within this network, responsibility

---

[38] Arthur M. Okun, *Equality and Efficiency: The Big Tradeoff* (Washington, D.C.: Brookings, 1975).
[39] Frederick M. Wirt, "The Dependent City? External Influences Upon Local Control," *Journal of Politics* 47 (1985): 83–112.

While they mostly prefer local control, many Americans think that political corruption and public indifference towards it is widespread in local government.

and power is dispersed through a variety of fiscal arrangements. This dispersion, in turn, has significant effects on government, policies and the way they are made, and politics.

Intergovernmental Relations

Federalism disperses responsibility and power throughout the society to create a network of intergovernmental relations. In the name of federalism, many hold and exercise governmental authority, creating opportunities for both cooperation and conflict. Illustrations abound: different agencies of the U.S. government arrive at different economic forecasts, while trying to agree on policies that are based on conflicting budget assumptions; the federal government creates and funds the food stamp program, but relies on state governmental officials to administer it; different state governments share responsibility for common resources like the Colorado River which winds through five states. In the final analysis, all exercises of governmental authority are constrained by those private persons whose behavior government is trying to modify, from the automobile driver who refuses to wear a seat belt to the chemical manufacturer who dumps toxic wastes late at night. In these and many other ways, governmental authority is dispersed throughout society in ways that make responsibility elusive and hard to pinpoint.

Federalism is an especially fluid way of shuffling responsibility for the uses of society's resources. At different times, in response to shifting political pressures and competing values, different mixtures of public and private arrangements have been tried, modified, and retried. As Americans found new ways of rationing responsibility, federalism evolved. Historically, American society has come to see its problems as increasingly national in scope, requiring national solutions. This crystallization of a national focus occurred on the eves of the Civil and World Wars, during the depths of the Great Depression, and at the beginning of more recent attempts to expand the socioeconomic welfare policies of the federal government. Since the 1960s, such social and economic problems as poverty, civil rights, economic productivity, and environmental degradation have been defined as synonymous with the nation's problems and therefore, as proper areas of federal governmental involvement. Accordingly, the federal government attempted to meet these expanded responsibilities in

"Sorry, but all my power's been turned back to the states."

President Reagan tried to return responsibility to state and local governments—whether or not they wanted it.

various ways, especially through the use of federal grants to state and local governments. The accumulation of federal responsibility and power is not irreversible, however. Under President Reagan, for example, the scope of federal responsibility shrunk, as did federal grants, making state and local governments, not to mention their clients, apprehensive about their fiscal future.

Fiscal Federalism

The term **fiscal federalism** refers to the network of interdependent relationships among levels of government that has been stitched together through different ways of using public revenues, usually the revenues of the national government.[40] In general, fiscal federalism has expanded the responsibilities and powers of the national government while at least maintaining, and sometimes enhancing, the responsibilities and powers of state and local governments.

The Growth of Fiscal Federalism. The national government, especially since the early 1960s, has tried to carry out its expanded responsibilities through various kinds of grants-in-aid to state and local governments. **Grants-in-aid** are financial grants made by the national government to aid state and local governments in carrying out certain responsibilities. These grants have grown enormously in recent times, taking an increasingly larger share of the federal budget and becoming an even more important percentage in the budgets of the states. As the first column of **Table 3.2** shows, the federal government's total dollar outlay for these grants added up to an estimated $92.9 billion in 1984, up more than fourteen times the 1960 level of $6.5 billion. In addition,

[40] Samuel H. Beer, "A Political Scientist's View of Fiscal Federalism," in Wallace B. Oats, ed., *The Political Economy of Fiscal Federalism* (Lexington, Mass.: D. C. Heath, 1977), pp. 21–46.

FEDERALISM: SHIFTING NATIONAL, STATE, AND LOCAL RESPONSIBILITIES

TABLE 3.2 The Historical Growth of Federal Grants-in-Aid

Year	Grants-in-Aid to State and Local Governments (in billions of current dollars)	Grants as a Percentage of	
		Total Federal Expenditures	Total State and Local Expenditures
1960	6.5	7.0%	13.0%
1962	8.0	7.2	13.8
1964	10.4	8.8	15.2
1966	14.4	10.0	17.1
1968	18.6	10.3	17.4
1970	24.4	11.9	18.3
1972	37.5	15.3	22.8
1974	43.9	14.7	21.4
1976	61.1	15.9	24.3
1978	77.3	16.8	26.0
1980	88.7	14.7	25.0
1982	83.9	11.0	20.6
1984 est.	92.9	10.6	19.7

SOURCE: *Economic Report of the President, 1985* (Washington, D.C.: U.S. Government Printing Office, 1985, Tables B–76 and B–77.

the middle column of the table shows that the federal government has set aside an even larger share of its total budget to grants-in-aid: 10.6 percent in 1984, up from 7 percent in 1960, but down from the high of 16.8 percent in 1978. The view from the states, as revealed in the third column of **Table 3.2**, is equally striking; the states have become more dependent on federal funds. Whereas states used to rely on federal grants for only about 13 percent of their total revenues in 1960, federal grants, as a percentage of state total expenditures, grew to a high of 26 percent in 1978 and were still at about 20 percent in 1984. Finally, although all these figures show some decline under the Reagan Administration, overall levels of federal aid to states and cities are unlikely to shrink much more, although they may be aimed at different targets or channeled through different mechanisms.[41]

---

[41] See Richard P. Nathan, "Reagan and the Cities: How to Meet the Challenge," *Challenge* 28 (1985): 4–8.

Federal grants may be targeted on different objectives. In his study of *The New Federalism*, Michael Reagan isolated some of the different objectives:

- establishing national minimum standards, as in highway construction;
- improving the efficiency of state and local governments;
- attacking national problems, such as infant mortality, or regional problems, such as economic development in Appalachia;
- equalizing the tax resources among the states;
- stimulating innovative approaches to problems.[42]

These objectives may be realized through different forms of federal aid.

Forms of Federal Aid. Federal grants-in-aid may also be channeled through different mechanisms, depending on the purposes to be served and the political pressures to be accommodated. Thus far, American ingenuity has come up with *four major grant-in-aid mechanisms* for funneling federal money to states and local agencies:

1. **Project grants**, given on application and for some specific purpose—like new highways.
2. **Categorical grants**, awarded on the basis of some objective formula and used for clearly defined purposes—like educating the children of federal employees whose parents work in facilities that are exempt from local taxation.
3. **Block grants**, also awarded on the basis of some formula but for broader purposes which are defined with large amounts of discretion by state and local governments—like health.
4. General **revenue sharing**, which allows states and local jurisdictions great discretion over the use of federal money, as long as they do not violate basic national policies, such as nondiscrimination policies.

The choice, or relative prominence, of one or another of these grant mechanisms is significant because of what it reveals about the underlying struggle within the federal system for responsibility and power.[43]

The responsibility and power of the national government varies directly with the narrowness of the guidelines for grants-in-aid. The national government enhances its own power and responsibility when it defines the objectives and lays down the procedures for administering the grant. Under Lyndon Johnson's War on Poverty, for example, the federal government took upon itself the task of trying to rebuild the central cities of America. Cities previously had been the stepchildren of state governments, ignored and abandoned to the poor and the increasingly nonwhite. To deal effectively with the hard-core

---

[42] Michael D. Reagan, *The New Federalism* (New York: Oxford University Press, 1972), pp. 66–72.

[43] See also Lawrence D. Brown, James W. Fossett, and Kenneth T. Palmer, *The Changing Politics of Federal Grants* (Washington, D.C.: The Brookings Institution, 1984).

minorities that otherwise might be shut out completely by local majorities. Blacks, for example, have been able to mobilize effectively at the national level, seeking civil rights protections, as have environmentalists who have overcome their minority status in many communities by banding together to seek national guarantees of environmental protection. In all these cases, those who may be frustrated at one level have recourse to other levels of government. The consequence, for any particular group, is opportunity to influence the making of public policy. The overall consequence is increased political stability, since those with political grievances who are frustrated at some level may be able to carry their political demands to other, hopefully more sympathetic, governmental officials.

Second, multiple centers of power also provide many opportunities for policy innovation and for the diffusion of innovation. By maintaining some degree of autonomy and discretion, the states serve as natural laboratories for trying out new policy proposals. The supporters of tax credits for private schools, for example, often pointed to the states of Louisiana and Minnesota, arguing that their tax credit policies had not bankrupted the state treasury or destroyed public education. In some cases, states broke new policy ground, as Montana did, for example, in outlawing life insurance rates that discriminated between men and women. In other cases, states have experimented with new ways of solving special problems they were experiencing, as Iowa did in reallocating gasoline taxes away from highways and toward economic development, in an attempt to cope with its depressed agricultural economy.

State experimentation with new policies can begin the process of building the sort of broad-based political pressure that is felt in Washington, D.C. This policy-making route has been employed by various groups which were first rebuffed at the national level. For example, those who favored an amendment to the U.S. Constitution that would require the federal government to balance its budget were frustrated at the national level for years before they refocused their lobbying efforts at the state level. They then tried a route never used successfully: getting enough states to call for a new constitutional convention, one that would write a balanced budget amendment into the federal Constitution. While this objective has not been reached, Congress was forced to make some conciliatory gestures toward the sentiment for a balanced budget amendment.

The spread of policy innovations has had a more clear-cut impact on national policy making in other instances. Congress, for example, was hurried by pressure from the states into adopting the Seventeenth Amendment, requiring the direct election of U.S. senators. In general, the federal system is a useful national laboratory, where policy innovations can be tested out before they are turned loose on the country as a whole.

Third, federalism also creates opportunities for political obstruction and delay. This is especially true when the country is trying to realize some new broad national purpose, such as expanding voting rights or an end to racial segregation in housing. To accomplish such major objectives, many different governmental jurisdictions, private associations, and private citizens must be persuaded to join in a coordinated effort. In general, it often seems as though policy making in a federal system is an interminable process, especially when intense opposition surfaces and exploits opportunities for delay, as, for example, in the legislative histories of civil rights policies in this country.

Fourth, federalism creates inefficient policy-making processes, as much time and effort is spent lining up political support and in winning policy agreements throughout the society. For example, the process of trying to make a national policy regulating the disposal of nuclear wastes was much more inefficient than it would have been if someone simply had the authority to decide the matter. Inefficiency in policy making, however, is tolerable to most Americans—especially when they consider the alternatives. Many, like the Founders, distrust efficiency because they fear that efficient policy-making processes require the concentration of too much power in too few hands.

Fifth, federalism, in addition to its impact on the policy-making process, also tends to produce somewhat incoherent policy outcomes—fragmented, inconsistent, and sometimes contradictory policies, rather than nicely integrated, mutually reinforcing ones. The national government, for example, requires states to withhold food stamps from those with significant personal assets, but states fail to allocate sufficient resources to accomplish the task. Ohio exports sulfur dioxide and acid rain eastward, while New York spends its tax dollars throwing crushed limestone into its lakes, trying to make the water fit for fish. The federal government adopts a law that requires young men to register for military service, but thousands fail to line up. In these instances and in general, the different policies and interests of multiple participants in the federal system may not coincide, and the result is jumbled bits of policy that fail to fit together in a coherent pattern.

The Political Consequences of Federalism. Federalism creates distinctive politics that include opportunities for both claiming credit and placing blame, for both cooperation and conflict. All these things are possible because none of the many governmental and private actors in this political system is strong enough to accomplish their objectives without at least the partial agreement of other persons and governments. As a result, political bargaining is unavoidable and political leadership is hard to find.

The history of federal grants-in-aid programs reveals these political dynamics. Project and categorical grant programs provided wonderful opportunities for credit claiming, as national politicians pointed to specific programs, with highly visible and narrowly focused benefits delivered to appreciative constituents.[50] Moreover, since it lacks the power to force the compliance of other parts of the political system, the federal government finds it necessary to bargain with other governments and private persons. The need for bargaining, in turn, opens up opportunities for both cooperation and conflict, since the various governmental and private actors in the federal system may have their own objectives and these may be at odds with the national government.

---

[50] George F. Break, "Intergovernmental Relations," in Joseph A. Pechman, ed., *Setting National Priorities: Agenda for the 1980s* (Washington, D.C.: The Brookings Institution, 1980), pp. 247–81.

■ Throughout our history, federalism has had many significant effects on government, policies, and politics. Our continuing struggle to find the proper allocation of responsibility and power has produced a tangle of interdependent relationships, in which no one governmental unit is clearly and consistently dominant. While it may deter infringements on personal liberty, that tangle also makes it hard for any one governmental official to display compelling leadership.

SUMMARY

The Constitution envisioned a strong central government. But, as a compromise that also had to win ratification, the Constitution only vaguely divided authority within the central government and between it and the governments of the states. Soon, and largely through judicial responses to political controversies, the vision took more specific form.

Through landmark decisions, John Marshall, as the Chief Justice of the Supreme Court, allocated responsibility and, implicitly, power: the Supreme Court was responsible for upholding the Constitution; the national government could do whatever was necessary and proper to carry out its constitutional responsibilities; Congress was responsible for the regulation of interstate commerce; private persons, not state governments, were responsible for decisions about the uses of private property.

Marshall's early decisions established the foundation for a federal form of government, one in which a national government shares some responsibilities with various subnational governments. This form of government provided the central leadership necessary for nation building, while accommodating the diverse and sometimes conflicting interests of a culturally diverse people

Federalism, however, is an ambiguous answer to a basic question: "Who should be responsible for deciding among the different uses of society's resources?" The answer is ambiguous because responsibility, and the power to carry it out, is widely dispersed in the federal system—within the national government, among the many levels and different types of government in the United States, and between various kinds of public authorities and all the persons, groups, and businesses in the private sector. It also is ambiguous because responsibilities and powers are loosely assigned and change over time in response to the shifting pressures of political events and competing political values. As a result, federalism has evolved and continues to evolve.

Federalism has significant effects on government, policies, and politics in America. Since governments often compete with one another, policies can become more extensive and more responsive, although complex patterns of intergovernmental relations also limit accountability. Since responsibility is dispersed throughout multiple centers of power, politicians compete in claiming their share of the credit for policy proposals, and in avoiding their share of the blame for policy failures. Since the national government shares responsibilities with state and local governments, federal fiscal controls tend to be applied gently and indirectly, usually after winning policy agreements through bargaining and compromise. The resulting federal framework accommodates seemingly inconsistent consequences. It creates opportunities for political influence and innovation, as well as opportunities for obstruction and delay; it extracts efficiency from the policy-making process and fails to produce well-integrated and coherent policy outcomes.

Key Terms

federalism
unitary governments
federal governments
Marbury v. *Madison*
original jurisdiction
writ of mandamus
McCulloch v. *Maryland*
doctrine of implied powers
principle of national supremacy
necessary and proper clause

commerce powers
commerce clause
contract clause
market imperfections
fiscal federalism
grants-in-aid
project grants
categorical grants
block grants
revenue sharing

Review and Reflection

1. What is the difference between a unitary and a federal form of government?

2. What was *Marbury* v. *Madison* about? Explain the significance of the Supreme Court's decision in this case.

3. What was *McCulloch* v. *Maryland* about? What was the significance of the Court's decision?

4. How would you distribute governmental responsibility and power if you were only concerned with protecting personal liberties? With increasing national strength? With improving the efficiency of the economic market? With equalizing the distribution of wealth?

5. What is fiscal federalism?

6. In what ways have federal grants altered relationships among national, state, and local governments?

7. How does federalism affect government, public policies and the ways they are made, and politics?

8. What do you think should be the proper allocation of governmental responsibility and power between the national, state, and local levels?

Supplemental Readings

Many people have a curious reaction to the term "federalism;" their eyelids begin to droop. And, if they then hear the term "intergovernmental relations," they're totally gone. The terms, unfortunately, obscure much that is fascinating in American government. To appreciate it, take a quick look at some of the state-by-state write-ups in *Peirce and Hagstrom's The Book of America*. (Neal R. Peirce also writes a consistently interesting newspaper column which is widely syndicated.) To see states as political actors, pressing their demands on the national government and experimenting with new policy approaches, check out the book by *Haider* and the article by *Walker*. The shifting relationships between the national and the various subnational governments is best revealed in the work by *Brown et al.* on federal grants. Federal aid does not always have the intended effect, however, as *Derthick* and *Pressman and Wildavsky* show. If you want to place things in a more general and theoretical context, spend some time with the classics: *Elazar, Riker,* and *Wright,* or with the only major political science journal that focuses on federalism, *Publius.* Finally, the *Advisory Commission on Intergovernmental Relations (ACIR)* is a governmental agency that distributes data and issues interesting reports; both can be found by looking for the Commission, as author, in your library's card catalogue.

Advisory Commission on Intergovernmental Relations. (Various reports)

Brown, Lawrence D., James W. Fossett, and Kenneth T. Palmer. *The Changing Politics of Federal Grants.* Washington, D.C.: The Brookings Institution, 1984.

Derthick, Martha. *The Influence of Federal Grants.* Cambridge, Mass.: Harvard University Press, 1970.

Elazar, Daniel J. *American Federalism: A View from the States.* 3rd ed. New York: Harper and Row, 1984.

Haider, Donald H. *When Governments Come to Washington.* New York: Free Press, 1974.

Pressman, Jeffery L., and Aaron B. Wildavsky. *Implementation.* 3rd ed. Berkeley, Calif.: University of California Press, 1984.

Peirce, Neal R., and Jerry Hagstrom. *The Book of America: Inside Fifty States Today.* New York: Warner Books, 1984.

Publius: The Journal of Federalism. Published by the Center for the Study of Federalism, Temple University.

Riker, William H. *Federalism: Origin, Operation, Significance.* Boston: Little, Brown, 1964.

Walker, Jack L. "The Diffusion of Innovations among the American States," *American Political Science Review* 63 (1969): 880–99.

Wright, Deil. *Understanding Intergovernmental Relations.* 2nd ed. Monterey, Calif.: Brooks/Cole, 1982.

CHAPTER FOUR

CIVIL LIBERTIES AND CIVIL RIGHTS
THE ENDURING STRUGGLE

You probably think freedom is free. The conclusion is easily drawn. Usually everyone talks about freedom as though it is available for the asking. It is natural to take freedoms for granted, as though nothing has to be done to make sure you can enjoy them. It is also wrong to do so.

Freedom has a price: the willingness to fight for it. Americans, through most but not all of their history, have been willing to pay the price. In the process, they have expanded two major classes of freedoms: civil liberties and civil rights. *Civil liberties* are guarantees that government will not interfere arbitrarily with people, their opinions, and their property. *Civil rights*, in contrast, are guarantees that government will protect people against discrimination, either by other persons or by some other part of the government. The expansions in civil liberties and civil rights have not come cheaply, however; they often have come only after great personal pain and political conflict.

This chapter opens with a Case about what happened after a reporter for the New York Times published the results of his investigation of a series of alleged murders. This true story, and its surprising conclusion, reveals four main insights. First, civil liberties and civil rights protect persons. Second, civil liberties and civil rights protect persons from government and from each other. Third, civil liberties and civil rights evolve. Fourth, civil liberties and civil rights help define government's improper and proper roles.

The rabbi, after listening to the old lady complain about her neighbor, said, "You're right." After she had left, the neighbor came to complain about her. When the neighbor had finished, the rabbi replied, "You're right." And the neighbor left happily, as had the old lady.

The rabbi's wife fumed. "You told the old lady she was right. And you told her neighbor that she was right. They both can't be right," she shouted.

"You're right," the rabbi agreed.

The Case   **For Digging Up a Crime, a Reporter Goes to Jail**

The thirteen people were not supposed to die; the reporter who uncovered the story was not supposed to go to jail; and the accused murderer was not supposed to be set free.[1]

The thirteen people came to the Riverdell Hospital in New Jersey with little in common. For example, Eileen Shaw, age 36, came to have her fifth baby. Everything went well until she went into shock and died the next day. Nancy Savino, age 4, woke up with a sore stomach on Saturday and the doctors operated the same day. Suspecting a burst appendix, they found and removed cysts in the small intestine. Nancy seemed to be recovering well, was alert and sitting up. By six o'clock the next morning, Nancy was looking forward to going home; by seven o'clock, she was dead. Margaret Henderson, age 26, was in serious pain, unable to stand erect when admitted to the hospital. An exploratory operation discovered nothing and Margaret seemed better until the next day when, tense and apprehensive, she told a nurse she was "going to meet her Maker." Half an hour later, Margaret Henderson died. The lives of Eileen Shaw, Nancy Savino, Margaret Henderson, and ten others were bound together in sickness and in death. They were not supposed to die; but they did—all in one hospital, all within one and one-half years, and all under mysterious circumstances.

Initially, there were two investigations into the deaths, both botched in ways that permanently deepened the mystery. The first investigation was unofficial, conducted by the hospital's doctors. We will never know what caused one of Riverdell's doctors to suspect another. But he did, and Dr. Harris, acting covertly, got the combination to Dr. Jascalevich's locker in the hospital. Because he was alone, we only know what Dr. Harris says he saw; eighteen mostly empty vials of curare, a deadly poison that paralyzes muscles, causing death by suffocation.

---

[1] This account is drawn from Myron Farber, *"Somebody Is Lying": The Story of Dr. X* (Garden City, New York: Doubleday, 1982).

Calling his superior, Dr. Harris reported what he saw and passed on the combination to the locker. Other doctors came, reopened the locker, and photographed the contents. This, the unofficial investigation, then spilled over onto the desk of the Bergen County prosecutor.

Guy Calissi, the county prosecutor, conducted the official investigation. Calissi knew somebody was lying; but he got confused, overwhelmed by contradictory answers and bewildered by scientific terminology. He developed new suspicions, wondering if Jascalevich was being framed by other doctors, jealous of his success and anxious to advance their own careers. But he could not pursue his suspicions; the trail was long, costly to follow, and increasingly cold. With news of Jascalevich's plans to resign from Riverdell, Calissi dropped the investigation.

There the matter lay for the next nine years, until Mike Levitas received a letter in late June of 1975. As a deputy editor of the *New York Times*, Levitas passed it to one of his reporters, Myron Farber. The letter alleged murder, committed on a mass scale, in a major hospital, by a chief surgeon; like Captain Ahab's arm, the letter beckoned men to their destiny. Farber's investigation led to a series of articles in the *Times* and it reopened another official investigation by the new prosecutor of Bergen County. This investigation got further, resulting in the indictment and trial of Mario Jascalevich for five counts of murder. Dr. Jascalevich was on trial, but so, too, were Myron Farber and the *New York Times* at the instigation of Jascalevich's attorney, Ray Brown.

Myron Farber leaving jail.

Attorney Brown was not interested in mysteries; he was interested in getting his client acquitted. In Brown's eyes, Farber's information led to the reinvestigation. For all Brown knew (and insinuated), Farber might have made up the whole story, weaving together the jealousies of greedy doctors and publicity-hungry prosecutors, hoping to enrich his own career with front-page stories and a bestselling book.

Goaded by these broadly hinted conspiracies, the judge became adamant; Jascalevich's right to a fair trial was more important than Farber's claim of freedom of the press. If Brown said he needed Farber's notes to prepare his defense, then the attorney could have the notes. The subpoena was issued; Farber was ordered to deliver to the court all notes and information in his possession. But Farber refused, claiming an obligation to protect his sources of information. Farber had promised them confidentiality and violating that promise meant more than breaking his word; it meant future news sources would not trust him to protect their identities. And, if cut off from sources of information, Farber, and the press in general, could not function. The refusal was necessary and highly principled, Farber and the attorneys for the *Times* argued; freedom of expression and of the press were at stake.

Judge Arnold listened impatiently. Close to retirement and frustrated with a case that had grown too long and too acrimonious, Judge Arnold heard Farber's refusal to produce the subpoenaed materials. He listened and ruled that he would decide this issue later. In the meanwhile, the *New York Times* was held in contempt and fined $5000 a day, and Myron Farber went to jail until he agreed to produce the subpoenaed information, or until the trial was over—whichever came first.

The trial dragged on, while the fine against the *Times* eventually reached over $100,000 and Myron Farber stayed in jail. From his cell window, Farber could watch the traffic in the street, two stories below. He was there when he saw Jascalevich, looking fresh and cool and free, waiting for a ride home after a day's session in court.

The longest criminal trial in American history finally ended. After more than seven months and the testimony of seventy-six witnesses, the jury took two hours to find the defendant "not guilty." Myron Farber emerged from jail and recovered from the experience; a bit battered and a little stronger, much like the freedom of press rights he said he was defending.

Insights

We can profit from the pain in this Case by appreciating these insights.

Insight 1. *Civil liberties and civil rights protect persons.* In this case, individual persons were protected, not organizations or society as a whole. It was Dr. Jascalevich who was protected, not the *New York Times* and not society. In general, the American system of justice is constructed as though it were an upside down pyramid, more based on a concern with the freedom of individual persons than on concerns with the interests of any organization or with the general social welfare.

Insight 2. *Civil liberties and civil rights protect persons from government and from each other.* In this case, Dr. Jascalevich needed protection from government, since only it could take away his liberty. His right to a fair trial guaranteed that he would not be imprisoned arbitrarily. In other cases, people need government to protect them, since others may discriminate against them.

Insight 3. *Civil liberties and civil rights evolve.* As was clear from the response, Judge Arnold was not impressed by the strength of the argument that the press had the right to protect the identity of its sources. As a result of this confrontation, however, the right became more secure; shortly after this case, New Jersey passed a "shield" law that guaranteed the right. In this case and in general, civil liberties and civil rights evolve, usually after someone has claimed a new protection and has been willing to fight for it.

Insight 4. *Civil liberties and civil rights help define government's improper and proper roles.* In both Jascalevich's and Farber's cases, civil liberties imposed limits on government; government could not jail Jascalevich without a fair trial and it could not keep Farber in jail after the trial was over; both actions were outside the bounds of proper governmental action. In general, civil liberties define what government cannot do to people and civil rights define some of the things that government should do for them.

Each of these insights is elaborated next.

PERSONAL PROTECTIONS

> Those who expect to reap the blessings of
> freedom must . . . undergo the fatigue of
> supporting it.   —Thomas Paine

The brief Case opening this chapter revealed some things that are true about
the American system of justice. But we postponed until now the question of
why they are true.

Consider the following two propositions and examples. First, people should
be free of arbitrary governmental interference; Dr. Jascalevich, for example,
should not lose his freedom without a fair trial. Second, people should not be
discriminated against, either by other people or by government; the children of
Vietnamese refugees, for example, should not be barred from public school.
You, like most of us, probably accept these propositions and examples automatically without pausing to ask "Why?" But do ask why does this society usually
insist that people be protected against discrimination and arbitary governmental interference?

Freedom and Progress

Personal freedoms are protected to ensure human, and therefore societal,
progress. American society is organized as though it believes that personal
freedoms must be valued before all other things. This is a bit peculiar,
considering all the other things that could be valued more highly—intelligence, artistic creativity, physical beauty, personal honesty. All these things
are valued, of course, but none as highly as freedom. The premium we place on
freedom stems from our concern for the well-being of individual persons and
from the underlying justification of this concern.

Classical liberalism is the doctrine that justifies our preoccupation with
personal freedom. The doctrine embraces three central ideas: the well-being of
individual persons is more important than anything else; it is necessary to rely
on individuals to know what is good for them; and individuals, if free to decide
upon and pursue their own interests, will do that which is good for them and
thereby for society. This, the classical variety of liberalism, is a central ingredient in our cultural heritage. As Supreme Court Justice Louis Brandeis
observed: "Those who won our independence believed that the final end of the
State was to make men free to develop their faculties."[2] This belief endures.

Our cultural heritage of classical liberalism shapes expectations of government and public policy; we ask of both, "Do they leave individuals free to
pursue their self-interest, as they themselves define it?" The preferred answer
is yes, since the heritage assumes that personal development and, therefore,
social progress flourish in the absence of interference.

---

[2] *Whitney v. California*, 274 U.S. 357, 375 (1927).

Patrick Henry. He recognized that freedom is not an absolute, but may be limited by many things.

The Limits of Freedom

When he said, "Give me liberty or give me death," Patrick Henry made it sound as though liberty was an absolute and as though he would accept nothing less, preferring death as the alternative. Well, Henry was a great political agitator who knew how to make the mob bubble, but he was no fool. When faced with the very real possibility of capture and execution, he spent most of the Revolutionary War hiding out in the hills of western Virginia. Patrick Henry, in other words, traded off a little bit of his liberty for a big bit of his life; he recognized, as we do, that freedom is not an absolute, but may be limited by many things. In general, freedom is limited by necessity, expediency, and— worst of all—by default.

Necessity. Necessity limits personal freedoms when one person's rights conflict with those of another. Consider the following examples: Myron Farber's right to keep confidential his news sources conflicted with Mario Jascalevich's right to a fair trial; your right to free speech cannot endanger me, as it might if you shouted "Fire" in a crowded sauna. In general, whenever the exercise of some freedoms interferes with the exercise of other freedoms, necessity requires that the intruding freedoms be limited. But it is not just necessity that limits freedom.

Expediency. Sometimes personal freedoms are limited when other considerations seem more important, at least in the passions of the moment. In the early days of the Republic, for example, the national government found it useful to enlist organized religion in its effort to subdue Native Americans. Through grants of both money and land, the national government supported the missionary work of religious groups among the American Indians—because it helped the government and in spite of the fact that it did not help all religions, especially not the Indians. More recently, state governments expediently scaled the wall between church and state when they used public school buses to transport students to parochial school and when they loaned publicly purchased books and computers to church schools. In both examples, intensely held policy objectives—the pacification of Indians and the education of youth—are used to justify constraints on human freedoms.

Default. Personal freedoms are most severely constrained when those who have them refuse, or are unable to exercise them; freedoms, like muscles, can atrophy. Myron Farber, for example, would have limited the rights of a free press if he had identified his sources, rather than go to jail. Similarly, Rosa Parks would have acknowledged limits on the rights of blacks to sit wherever they wanted on public buses if she had not been willing to go to jail for refusing to give up her seat to a white man. (The incident, described in more detail in chapter 8, sparked the bus boycott in Montgomery, Alabama, in 1955-1956.) But it is easier to write about defending freedom than to do it; in practice, the cost of defending freedom is high, often higher than individual persons can bear. In such cases, some argue, it is government's responsibility to bear the burden and thereby, protect civil rights.

CIVIL LIBERTIES AND CIVIL RIGHTS: THE ENDURING STRUGGLE

■ In the story of the investigation and trial of Dr. Jascalevich, some freedoms were clearly protected, while other interests seemed more vulnerable. Dr. Jascalevich's right to a fair trial was well protected, as, eventually, were Myron Farber's press rights. But many other interests went unprotected; the hospital's concern in protecting itself against law suits and patients' interests in protecting themselves against possible harm.

Civil liberties are like that; they protect individual persons against immediate threats, not formal organizations or society as a whole against more remote ones.

CIVIL LIBERTIES: PROTECTIONS FROM GOVERNMENT

> The history of liberty has largely been the history of the observance of procedural safeguards.
>
> —Felix Frankfurter, Associate
> Justice of the United States
> Supreme Court, 1939–1962

Civil liberties protect persons from government, from its ability to interfere arbitrarily with their personal freedoms and their personal property. The protection is necessary because government has something that no one else has—the right to use force to realize social objectives. Consider the following examples: to raise revenue, the government will penalize those who do not voluntarily comply with the tax laws; to defend the nation, the government will imprison those who try to evade military service; to ensure economic competition, the government will fine those who conspire to fix prices. In all these ways, fighting with the government is different than arguing with the neighbors over their wandering dog or dandelion seeds. When they fight legally, neighbors can only deprive one other of their peace of mind. Fighting with the government is more difficult and potentially more dangerous because government alone is authorized to use force in settling conflict—as Myron Farber found out when the state made him go to jail.

In general, civil liberties are both numerous and limited. Because it is so prized by Americans, liberty is protected in many ways. But they also are limited because the liberties of some may intrude on the liberties of others.

The Major Civil Liberties

Most of our constitutionally guaranteed civil liberties are found in the Bill of Rights, the first ten amendments to the Constitution. They can be easily identified by enumeration as shown in **Table 4.1**.

TABLE 4.1   The Bill of Rights

Freedom of Religion, Speech, Press, Assembly, Petition	**Amendment I.** Congress shall make no law respecting an establishment of religion, or prohibiting the free exercise thereof; or abridging the freedom of speech, or of the press, or the right of the people peaceably to assemble, and to petition the Government for a redress of grievances.
Right to Bear Arms	**Amendment II.** A well regulated militia, being necessary to the security of a free State, the right of the people to keep and bear arms, shall not be infringed.
Freedom from Quartering Troops	**Amendment III.** No Soldier shall, in time of peace be quartered in any house, without the consent of the owner, nor in time of war, but in a manner to be prescribed by law.
Protections Against Search	**Amendment IV.** The right of the people to be secure in their persons, houses, papers, and effects against unreasonable searches and seizures, shall not be violated, and no warrants shall issue, but upon probable cause, supported by oath or affirmation, and particularly describing the place to be searched, and the persons or things to be seized.
Rights of Suspects	**Amendment V.** No person shall be held to answer for a capital, or otherwise infamous crime, unless on a presentment or indictment of a Grand Jury, except in cases arising in the land or naval forces, or in the militia, when in actual service in time of war or public danger; nor shall any person be subject for the same offence to be twice put in jeopardy of life or limb; nor shall be compelled in any criminal cause to be a witness against himself, nor be deprived of life, liberty, or property, without due process of law; nor shall private property be taken for public use, without just compensation.
Rights of Defendants	**Amendment VI.** In all criminal prosecutions, the accused shall enjoy the right to a speedy and public trial, by an impartial jury of the State and district wherein the crime shall have been committed, which district shall have been previously ascertained by law, and to be informed of the nature and cause of the accusation; to be confronted with the witnesses against him; to have compulsory process for obtaining witnesses in his favor, and to have the assistance of counsel for his defense.
Right to a Jury	**Amendment VII.** In Suits at common law, where the value in controversy shall exceed twenty dollars, the right of trial by jury shall be preserved, and no fact tried by jury, shall be otherwise reexamined in any Court of the United States, than according to the rules of the common law.
Freedom from "Cruel and Unusual" Punishment	**Amendment VIII.** Excessive bail shall not be required, nor excessive fines imposed, nor cruel and unusual punishments inflicted.
The Protection of Unenumerated Rights	**Amendment IX.** The enumeration in the Constitution, of certain rights, shall not be construed to deny or disparage others retained by the people.
Reserved Rights	**Amendment X.** The powers not delegated to the United States by the Constitution, nor prohibited by it to the States, are reserved to the States respectively, or to the people.

There are three classes of civil liberties, those that protect against governmental actions that would interfere arbitrarily with privacy, political participation, and freedom from punishment.

Privacy Rights. Civil liberties include **privacy rights**, protections against arbitrary governmental interference in one's personal affairs. The concept of privacy rights, therefore, implies a sphere of private activity within which people can act without fear of governmental intrusion. Many privacy rights are securely lodged inside this private sphere. There is little doubt, for example, that all the following are well-protected privacy rights: the right to practice one's religion, to learn what is going on by reading the newspapers or by discussing current events with one's classmates, the right to sell, buy, and hold on to personal property. Most of these are especially secure privacy rights because they enjoy constitutional protection. The First Amendment, for example, prohibits Congress from making laws that interfere with the practice of religion, the freedom of speech, of the press, and of the people to assemble and petition government. In general, privacy rights have emerged as the most basic of civil liberties. In the words of Justice Brandeis, "The right to be left alone (is) the right most valued by civilized men."[3]

Government, through its police forces, can restrict personal liberty, as it does to those who sit in the street in front of the White House to protest U.S. foreign policy.

Privacy rights have significant consequences for American government and policy making; they map out the domain from which government should be excluded. This mapping function is well-recognized: ". . . the concept of a right to privacy attempts to draw a line between the individual and the collective, between self and society. It seeks to assure the individual a zone in which to be an individual, not a member of the community."[4] This privacy zone has expanded over time to the point where, by 1986, it encapsulates all the following rights:

- the right to abort a three-month-old fetus[5];
- the right to exclude officially approved prayer from public schools[6];
- the right to keep books that some think obscene on library shelves[7];
- rights that keep Ku Klux Klan members and black militants out of jail even when they advocate the forceful overthrow of the government[8];
- rights that stop the government from canceling the contractual relationship between you and your college.[9]

All these are only a few examples of that sphere of private personal action from which government is excluded.

Participation Rights.   In addition to privacy rights, civil liberties include **participation rights**, prohibitions against artificial restrictions on one's right to participate in government and in the making of public policy. These participation rights flow from the people's sovereignty; they are not favors graciously

---

[3] *Olmstead* v. *United States,* 277 U.S. 438 (1928).

[4] Thomas I. Emerson, *The System of Freedom of Expression* (New York: Random House, 1970), p. 545.

[5] *Doe* v. *Bolton,* 410 U.S. 179 (1973) and *Roe* v. *Wade,* 410 U.S. 113 (1973).

[6] *Engel* v. *Vitale,* 370 U.S. 421 (1962), *Abington School District* v. *Schempp,* 374 U.S. 203 (1963), and *Murray* v. *Curlett,* 374 U.S. 203 (1963).

[7] In *Roth* v. *United States,* 354 U.S. 476 (1957), the Supreme Court first tried to define obscenity and thereby chart a course between those forms of expression that could be regulated and those that are immune from governmental intervention.

[8] *Brandenburg* v. *Ohio,* 395 U.S. 444 (1969), first used to protect members of the Ku Klux Klan, was subsequently relied on to protect black militants who called for the violent overthrow of the government.

[9] *Dartmouth College* v. *Woodward,* 4 U.S. 463 (1819).

dispensed by a benevolent government. Participation rights are what (hopefully) keeps government reined in, by providing the people with opportunities to influence the direction of public policy and with a chance to hold accountable elected public officials. Over time, these opportunities to participate have become increasingly extensive. As a result, the policy-making process has been democratized by:

- the addition of younger (eighteen-year-old) voters to the electorate[10];
- the elimination of literacy and poll taxes as requirements to vote[11];
- a guarantee that poor people can run for elective office, even if they cannot afford the filing fee[12];
- the equalization of the size of electoral districts[13];
- a reduction in the fear of public exposure and possible harassment from political participation.[14]

In all these and many other ways, the civil liberties of Americans provide opportunities to participate in the making of public policy.

Punishment Rights.   Civil liberties also include **punishment rights**, protections against the arbitrary loss of life, liberty, or property. These rights protect alleged, or even convicted, criminals from governmental actions that could lead to a financial penalty, imprisonment, or even execution. Government can take away these freedoms, of course, but punishment rights specify the procedures that must be followed before it can do so. These procedures, what we describe later as the **due process of law**, are what protect against arbitrary loss. Many

---

[10] The Twenty-sixth Amendment.

[11] Literacy tests were outlawed by the Voting Rights Act of 1965; the Twenty-fourth Amendment barred poll taxes.

[12] *Lubin* v. *Panish*, 415 U.S. 709 (1974).

[13] *Baker* v. *Carr*, 369 U.S. 186 (1962) and *Reynolds* v. *Sims*, 377 U.S. 533 (1964).

[14] *NAACP* v. *Alabama*, 357 U.S. 449 (1958).

A poll tax receipt. The elimination of this tax further ensures a citizen's right to participate in government without any restraints.

CIVIL LIBERTIES AND CIVIL RIGHTS: THE ENDURING STRUGGLE

punishment rights also enjoy constitutional protection. The Fifth, Sixth, Seventh, and Eighth Amendments, for example, provide a number of specific protections against what might otherwise be arbitrary governmental persecution or deprivation. For example, people on trial must be informed of the charge against them; they must be brought to trial in a timely manner and be assisted by counsel; they have the right to confront their accusers (and their sources of information, the right Dr. Jascalevich's attorney insisted on); they cannot be tried twice for the same offense; they cannot be forced to testify against themselves; they sometimes have a right to a trial by jury; and, if found guilty, they still have a right not to be made to suffer any cruel or unusual punishment. In general and primarily through a series of landmark Supreme Court cases, the rights of those suspected or accused of crime have become increasingly better protected. A fuller discussion of due process and of these landmark cases appears in the **Vantage Point**: What Is Due Process?

A physically impaired child who is being "mainstreamed" in a public school classroom, in order to receive some benefit from a public school education.

Americans hold most of their various civil liberties very dearly, although they sometimes suspect that punishment rights make it too hard for police to fight crime and thereby hurt society as a whole. In general, though, we easily perceive what we take to be threats to our civil liberties.

Limits on Civil Liberties

The limits on civil liberties are quite inclusive; but they better protect some people than others and they fall short of guaranteeing tangible benefits.

The Inclusiveness of Civil Liberties. In the course of American history, the limits on civil liberties were stretched to cover more and more categories of persons. It was not always so. In 1776, for example, many people did not enjoy a full measure of civil liberty—blacks, Native Americans, women, the poor, and the unpropertied. With the passage of time, civil liberties became more inclusive, sheltering previously excluded classes. Today, almost everyone has civil liberties and "everyone" includes more people, and more different types of people, than you might guess. All of the following now have more civil liberties than they used to:

- mentally retarded persons in state institutions who have a right to some degree of training in caring for themselves[15];
- the children of illegal aliens who are entitled to a free, public education[16];
- physically impaired children who must receive some benefit from their public education, even though it is not enough to achieve their full academic potential[17];
- young public school children who do not wish to pray or stand out for their refusal to do so.

In addition, some people have more, and others fewer, civil liberties.

[15] *Youngberg* v. *Romeo*, No. 80–1429 (1982).

[16] *Plyler* v. *Doe*, 457 U.S. 203 (1982).

[17] *Bd. of Ed. of the Hendrick Hudson Central School District* v. *Rowley*, 458 U.S. 176 (1982).

WHAT IS DUE PROCESS?

*P*unishment rights are guarantees that people will be protected against governmental actions that arbitrarily restrict their freedoms. The definition implies that there are ways government can restrict freedom as long as it does so properly.

Government may restrict personal freedom as long as it follows the *due process of law,* the correct procedures for protecting the rights of those who are accused, tried, or convicted of a crime. But what are the correct procedures?

As you might expect, the concept of due process is somewhat elastic, sometimes expanding in an attempt to better protect alleged criminals and sometimes contracting in an attempt to protect the rest of us. In the struggle over its meaning, "due process" protections have become more explicit and generally, more inclusive. The

Clarence Gideon.

dynamic is well illustrated in the recent history of some Supreme Court decisions:

- *Gideon* v. *Wainwright.* In 1963, the Court agreed with Clarence Gideon and in the process, expanded the rights of those on trial for a crime.[1] Gideon had been convicted in

Florida of robbing a pool hall and sentenced to a five-year term in the state prison. While there, Gideon wrote the Supreme Court, arguing that he had been tried and convicted unfairly, because he had been too poor to afford a lawyer. After the Court decided in his favor, Gideon was released from prison, retried (with a public defender representing him) and acquitted.

- *Miranda* v. *Arizona.* In 1966, the Court agreed with Ernesto Miranda and in the process, expanded the rights of those suspected of a crime.[2] Miranda had been convicted in Arizona of the kidnapping and rape of an eighteen-year-old girl. When his case was appealed to the Supreme Court, Miranda's attorneys argued that he had been interrogated unfairly, without being told of his constitutional right against self-incrimination and without having an attorney present. The Court agreed: police are

---

[1] *Gideon* v. *Wainright,* 372 U.S. 335 (1963). Clarence Gideon's story is told by Anthony Lewis, *Gideon's Trumpet* (New York: Random House, 1964).

[2] *Miranda* v. *Arizona,* 384 U.S. 436 (1966). Ernesto Miranda's story is told by Liva Baker, *Miranda: The Crime, The Law, The Politics* (New York: Atheneum, 1983).

The Selectivity of Civil Liberties. Some people have extra civil liberties, while others have fewer. Minor political parties, for example, do not have to disclose the names of those who contribute money to their election campaigns when doing so might expose them to harassment. In addition, members of the press, like Myron Farber, think that they have the right to refuse to disclose confidential material and sources in court proceedings, although the courts seldom agree. Finally, some people have fewer civil liberties than others. These typically are public figures who, for example, find it more difficult than the rest

obligated to inform suspects of their rights to remain silent and to have an attorney during questioning. As a result of this decision, Miranda was retried and again found guilty—this time on the basis of an admission he made to his common-law wife when she visited him while he was in prison on his initial conviction.

- *Brewer* v. *Williams*. In 1977, the Supreme Court, in a 5–4 vote, agreed with Robert Williams and, in the process, further expanded the Miranda rights of those accused of a crime. Williams had been convicted in Iowa of the kidnapping, sexual molestation, and murder of a ten-year-old girl. Williams had surrendered to police in Davenport, Iowa, and they had informed him of his *Miranda* rights. The Davenport police also promised Williams' attorneys that they would not

interrogate Williams during the 160-mile trip to the site of the kidnapping and trial, Des Moines. During the trip, however, the police, knowing of Williams' professed religious convictions, encouraged him to think about the little girl's right to a "Christian burial." At that point, Williams led police to the girl's body. In their appeals, Williams' attorneys argued that police had violated some of his *Miranda* rights. When the case finally came before the Supreme Court, a majority of the justices agreed and ruled that Williams was entitled to a new trial. Chief Justice Warren Burger dissented, calling the decision "intolerable," because it continues "punishing the public for the misdeeds of law enforcement officers."[3]

- *Nix* v. *Williams*. In 1984, the Supreme Court disagreed with the same Robert Williams and,

in the process, limited the rights of those on trial by adopting an "inevitable discovery exception to the exclusionary rule." The exception permitted the courtroom use of illegally obtained evidence, if that evidence inevitably would have been discovered by legal means. The exception was made in the case of the appeal of the retrial and reconviction of Williams, because the Court agreed with the position that, even without his help, the police search then underway would have led to the child's body. This time in the majority, Chief Justice Burger wrote: "Exclusion of physical evidence that would inevitably have been discovered adds nothing to either the integrity or fairness of a criminal trial."[4]

Since 1984, the Supreme Court has continued to balance the rights of the accused with the rights of the rest of society. In the process, the meaning of *due process* has become more explicit.

---

[3] *Brewer* v. *Williams*, 430 U.S. 387 (1977).

[4] *Nix* v. *Williams*, 467 Official Reports of the Supreme Court 431 (1984) [Preliminary print].

of us to defend themselves against libel, although they are fighting back and sometimes winning.

The Failure to Provide Tangible Benefits.   Civil liberties do not include rights to enjoy tangible benefits, only the opportunity to pursue them without interference. In this sense, civil liberties are sometimes thought of as **negative rights**, which emphasize the absence of interference, and not **positive rights**, which are more concerned with the provision of tangible benefits. Civil liberties guarantee, for example, that people have privacy, but do not guarantee that they will do anything constructive with it; that people have access to the political process, but not that they will be able to elect whomever they want; that criminal suspects have an attorney, but not that their attorney will get them off; that newspapers have protected sources, but not that they will publish worthwhile stories. In these ways, civil liberties only concern the quality of the process by which people search for what they value and are not concerned with the outcomes of this process.

■ Civil liberties protect persons against arbitrary governmental interference. Governments do, of course, interfere with personal liberty, as both Dr. Jascalevich and Myron Farber learned. But, in these cases and in general, government cannot interfere arbitrarily. What is the difference between proper and improper forms of governmental interference? Civil liberties, demands that they be respected, and those who make the demands draw the boundary.

Whereas civil liberties are primarily concerned with what government should not do, civil rights emphasize what government should do.

CIVIL RIGHTS: PROTECTIONS BY GOVERNMENT

> Even though we face the difficulties of today and tomorrow, I still have a dream. It is a dream chiefly rooted in the American dream. I have a dream that one day this nation will rise up and live out the true meaning of its creed: 'We hold these truths to be self-evident: that all men are created equal.'
> —Reverend Martin Luther King, Jr., march on Washington speech, August 28, 1963.

Civil rights are guarantees that government will protect people against discrimination, whether by other persons or by some other part of the government. The rationale for civil rights is straightforward: discrimination is a burden that artificially constrains human development and, therefore, social progress. In spite of this logic, the elimination of discrimination has been anything but straightforward. In large part, the effort has been hampered by disagreements over four main issues: (1) Who are the targets of discrimination? (2) What should they be protected against? (3) What protections should government provide? (4) What compensation, if any, should be provided to victims of past

*Look guys. . .why don't we just say that all men are created
equal. . .and let the little ladies look out for themselves?*

discriminatory policies? Nevertheless, through past efforts to answer these
questions, Americans have reached some agreement about their major civil
rights, their scope and their limits.

The Major Civil Rights

Over the course of American history, but especially in the 1960s and 1970s,
civil rights were extended to many different kinds of people. Usually, these
were the members of racial or ethnic minority groups: black Americans,
Hispanic Americans, and Native Americans, for example. Sometimes the protected persons were members of other kinds of minority groups, such as the
physically handicapped, the elderly, and Vietnam veterans. In addition, special
governmental protections were extended to members of other groups, such as
women, who are not numerically in the minority. In such cases, protections
were extended against more and more forms of discrimination, in access to
public schools, jobs, promotions, housing, and credit, for example. Typically it
was the federal government that moved to guarantee equal opportunity in
these areas, usually by prohibiting continuing discrimination and sometimes by
trying to compensate those adversely affected by historical forms of discrimination.

Some of the major events in the history of civil rights are provided in **Table
4.2**. To indicate the rate of progress, we also have linked each event to a
timeline. One perspective on the uneven rate of progress was provided by a
federal judge, Damon Keith, when he wrote ". . . as with most revolutions or

TABLE 4.2   The Major Civil Rights

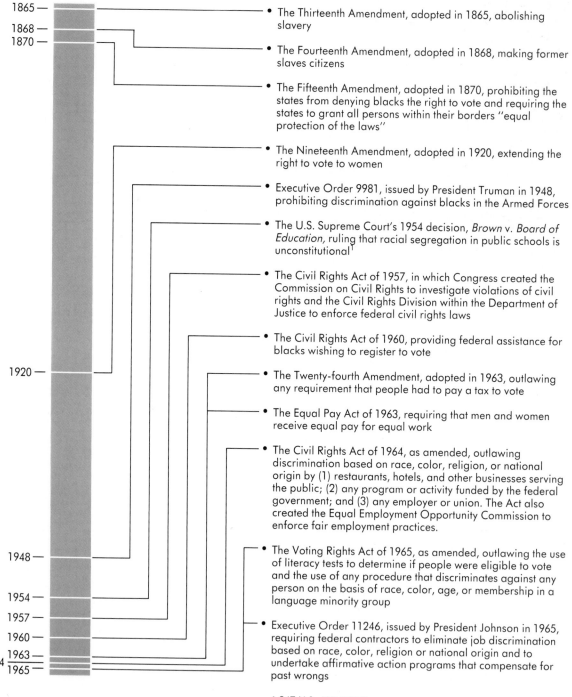

1865 —	• The Thirteenth Amendment, adopted in 1865, abolishing slavery
1868 —	
1870 —	• The Fourteenth Amendment, adopted in 1868, making former slaves citizens
	• The Fifteenth Amendment, adopted in 1870, prohibiting the states from denying blacks the right to vote and requiring the states to grant all persons within their borders "equal protection of the laws"
	• The Nineteenth Amendment, adopted in 1920, extending the right to vote to women
	• Executive Order 9981, issued by President Truman in 1948, prohibiting discrimination against blacks in the Armed Forces
	• The U.S. Supreme Court's 1954 decision, *Brown* v. *Board of Education,* ruling that racial segregation in public schools is unconstitutional[1]
	• The Civil Rights Act of 1957, in which Congress created the Commission on Civil Rights to investigate violations of civil rights and the Civil Rights Division within the Department of Justice to enforce federal civil rights laws
	• The Civil Rights Act of 1960, providing federal assistance for blacks wishing to register to vote
1920 —	• The Twenty-fourth Amendment, adopted in 1963, outlawing any requirement that people had to pay a tax to vote
	• The Equal Pay Act of 1963, requiring that men and women receive equal pay for equal work
	• The Civil Rights Act of 1964, as amended, outlawing discrimination based on race, color, religion, or national origin by (1) restaurants, hotels, and other businesses serving the public; (2) any program or activity funded by the federal government; and (3) any employer or union. The Act also created the Equal Employment Opportunity Commission to enforce fair employment practices.
1948 —	• The Voting Rights Act of 1965, as amended, outlawing the use of literacy tests to determine if people were eligible to vote and the use of any procedure that discriminates against any person on the basis of race, color, age, or membership in a language minority group
1954 —	
1957 —	
1960 —	• Executive Order 11246, issued by President Johnson in 1965, requiring federal contractors to eliminate job discrimination based on race, color, religion or national origin and to undertake affirmative action programs that compensate for past wrongs
1964 1963 —	
1965 —	

[1] 347 U.S. 483 (1954).

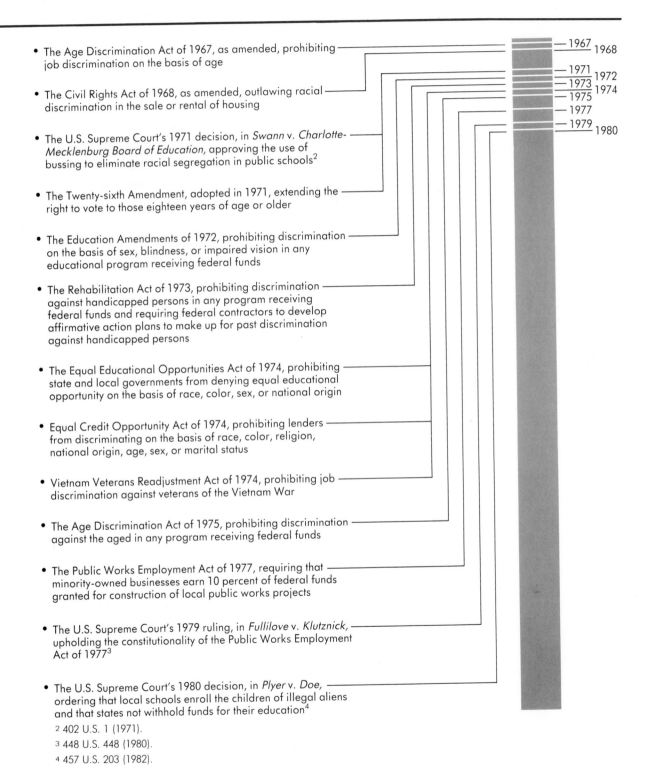

- The Age Discrimination Act of 1967, as amended, prohibiting job discrimination on the basis of age

- The Civil Rights Act of 1968, as amended, outlawing racial discrimination in the sale or rental of housing

- The U.S. Supreme Court's 1971 decision, in *Swann* v. *Charlotte-Mecklenburg Board of Education,* approving the use of bussing to eliminate racial segregation in public schools[2]

- The Twenty-sixth Amendment, adopted in 1971, extending the right to vote to those eighteen years of age or older

- The Education Amendments of 1972, prohibiting discrimination on the basis of sex, blindness, or impaired vision in any educational program receiving federal funds

- The Rehabilitation Act of 1973, prohibiting discrimination against handicapped persons in any program receiving federal funds and requiring federal contractors to develop affirmative action plans to make up for past discrimination against handicapped persons

- The Equal Educational Opportunities Act of 1974, prohibiting state and local governments from denying equal educational opportunity on the basis of race, color, sex, or national origin

- Equal Credit Opportunity Act of 1974, prohibiting lenders from discriminating on the basis of race, color, religion, national origin, age, sex, or marital status

- Vietnam Veterans Readjustment Act of 1974, prohibiting job discrimination against veterans of the Vietnam War

- The Age Discrimination Act of 1975, prohibiting discrimination against the aged in any program receiving federal funds

- The Public Works Employment Act of 1977, requiring that minority-owned businesses earn 10 percent of federal funds granted for construction of local public works projects

- The U.S. Supreme Court's 1979 ruling, in *Fullilove* v. *Klutznick,* upholding the constitutionality of the Public Works Employment Act of 1977[3]

- The U.S. Supreme Court's 1980 decision, in *Plyer* v. *Doe,* ordering that local schools enroll the children of illegal aliens and that states not withhold funds for their education[4]

1967 1968
1971 1972
1973 1974
1975
1977
1979 1980

2 402 U.S. 1 (1971).

3 448 U.S. 448 (1980).

4 457 U.S. 203 (1982).

struggles for fundamental change, further change is painfully slow after the initial fervor subsides. Progress is frequently accompanied by setbacks and obstacles."[18] For another perspective, see the **Vantage Point**: Linda Brown's View of School Integration. The rate of progress is not an accident of history, however, it is the result of a political process.

Limits on Civil Rights

At any one time, there are limits on civil rights, points beyond which government does not go to protect people or to ensure their progress. These limits may be written in law and recorded in court decisions, but they are not etched in granite. Rather, civil liberties are limited only by the ability of people to insist that government do more or by the ability of other people to insist that government has done enough.

In recent times, the political process for probing the limits on civil rights has included the following stages:

- Through the sorts of agenda-building activities that are described in chapter 9, civil rights leaders directly challenged segregation. By sitting at segregated lunch counters, by riding on segregated busses, by marching to register to vote when no one would register them, and by marching while under court order not to, civil rights activists refused to acknowledge the legitimacy of segregationist policies.
- In the face of massive noncompliance, the defenders of segregation had no politically defensible tactics. They only could acquiesce—or attempt to use force to bring about compliance.
- The use of force, however, was counterproductive. The use of force and its inevitable excesses, amplified nationally by newspapers and television, only made segregation appear less legitimate.
- Meanwhile, the balance of public support tipped and the rush of enthusiasm swelled the ranks of civil rights activists with people of all colors and religious persuasions. Blacks and whites, Catholics and Jews joined together in a formidable coalition that spanned the customary cleavages in American society.
- The broad-based coalition signalled the emergence of a new public support for civil rights. By the late 1960s, more than half the whites polled believed in integrated public schools; by 1976, the plurality had topped 75 percent.[19]
- Throughout the 1960s and 1970s, the pace of visible accomplishments accelerated as black citizens became voters and as black leaders became elected officials. In 1960, for example, only 29.1 percent of southern blacks were registered to vote. By 1982, seventeen years after passage of the

---

[18] Judge Damon J. Keith, "What Happens to a Dream Deferred: An Assessment of Civil Rights Law Twenty Years After the 1963 March on Washington," *Harvard Civil Rights-Civil Liberties Law Review* 19 (1984): 492.

[19] See D. Garth Taylor, Paul B. Sheatsley, and Andrew M. Greely, "Attitudes Toward Racial Integration," *Scientific American* 238 (1978): 430.

CIVIL LIBERTIES AND CIVIL RIGHTS: THE ENDURING STRUGGLE

LINDA BROWN'S VIEW OF SCHOOL INTEGRATION

Linda Brown as a child.

*I*n 1951, Linda Brown and her parents thought that pupils in the public schools in Topeka, Kansas, were segregated by race; in 1984, Linda Brown and her daughter thought that pupils in the public schools in Topeka, Kansas, were segregated by race.

Linda Brown naturally assumed that she would be going to school with her friends: "I only wanted to go to school with Mona and Guinevere because that's who I played with every day," Linda recalled later.[1] But the neighborhood school was all white. Unlike her friends, Linda was black; they definitely were not going to the same school—not in Topeka in the early 1950s.

Linda's father was one of a group of black parents who filed a class action suit against the Board of Education of the Topeka public school system, protesting their policy of segregating pupils by race. They were, of course, but they did not think it was illegal. The Topeka school board was only doing what the United States Supreme Court had said it could do in its 1896 ruling, *Plessy* v. *Ferguson*,[2] which held that states could provide sep-

arate facilities for whites and blacks, as long as those facilities were "equal." Linda's parents and the others felt differently and pressed the suit, first in Federal district court, where they lost. This began a process that eventually would bring the question of the constitutionality of the practice of racial segregation back before the United States Supreme Court.

This time the Court ruled differently, agreeing with the argument, advanced by Kenneth Clark and other psychologists, that racial segregation was harmful to black children. "To separate them from others of similar age and qualifications solely because of their race, generates a feeling of inferiority as to their status in the community that may affect their hearts and minds in a way unlikely ever to be undone," the Court concluded in its 1954 decision, *Brown* v. *Board of Education of Topeka, Kansas.*[3]

Almost thirty years later, Linda Brown, as Linda Brown Smith, the mother of two children in the Topeka schools, joined in another suit against the school board. In this suit, Mrs. Smith and others

objected to a continuing pattern of racial imbalance in the public schools. They noted that, whereas about 25 percent of Topeka's students were minorities, the proportion rose as high as 54.1 percent in some elementary schools and as low as 1.4 percent in others. Mrs. Brown argued that this was not integration and sought a court order that would have brought about more representative enrollments.

The Topeka School Board, however, defended the policy it had adopted after the 1954 Supreme Court decision, which assigned pupils to the school nearest their home, while permitting transfers if they would improve the racial balance. The board's lawyer, Charles Henson, noted that the original case was about Linda Brown's "right to attend her neighborhood school" and argued against those who were "now urging that people be assigned to a school on the basis of color to reach a predetermined mix."[4]

---

[1] Quoted in the *New York Times*, 17 May 1984.

[2] *Plessy* v. *Ferguson*, 163 U.S. 537 (1896).

[3] *Brown* v. *Board of Education of Topeka*, 347 U.S. 483 (1954) and its companion case, 349 U.S. 294 (1955) in which the Court ordered desegregation to proceed "with all deliberate speed."

[4] Quoted in the *New York Times*, 17 May 1984.

The doctrine of "separate but equal" began to crumble after the Supreme Court ruled (in *McLaurin* v. *Oklahoma State Regents*) that George McLaurin could not be forced to sit apart from other university students.

The Lieutenant Governor of Virginia, L. Douglas Wilder (left), the first black elected to statewide office in the South since Reconstruction, and the Governor, Gerald Baliles.

Voting Rights Act, that figure had jumped to 56.5 percent.[20] Similarly, before the passage of the Act there were fewer than 300 elected black officials nationwide. By 1985 there were over 6000, including the Lieutenant Governor of Virginia, L. Douglas Wilder, the first black elected to statewide office in the South since Reconstruction, and the mayors of four of the nation's six largest cities: Thomas Bradley of Los Angeles, Wilson Goode of Philadelphia, Harold Washington of Chicago, and Coleman Young of Detroit.

- Political gains did not always translate into economic gains, however. There were, of course, isolated examples of outstanding personal accomplishments and a suddenly growing black middle class. But millions of blacks living in poverty became more millions and the economic gap between white and black families widened, as the data in **Table 4.3** reveal. Whereas there were over 7 million blacks living in poverty in 1971, there were over 9 million in 1983 (Column 1). Whereas the median income of white families fell, in real terms, from what would have been $26,263 in 1971 to $25,757 in 1983, the median income of black families started lower and fell faster, from what would have been $15,843 in 1971 to $14,506 in 1983. (Compare Columns 2 and 3.) The conclusion is as inescapable as poverty seems to be: civil rights, by themselves, do not ensure economic progress.

- Believing that past forms of discrimination had held back the economic progress of blacks and women, civil rights advocates sought new approaches that would compensate people for past wrongs and help them catch up with those who had moved ahead. The new policy approaches called for **affirmative action**, employers' agreements to compensate people for past

---

[20] U.S. Bureau of the Census, *Statistical Abstract of the United States: 1984* 104th edition (Washington, D.C., 1983), p. 261.

TABLE 4.3   For millions of black Americans, civil rights did not bring economic well-being.[1]

Year	Number of Blacks Below the Poverty Level (in millions)[2]	Median Income of Black Families (in constant dollars)[3]	Median Income of White Families (in constant dollars)[3]
1971	7.4	$15,843	$26,253
1973	7.4	16,297	28,237
1975	7.5	16,251	26,412
1977	7.7	15,722	27,522
1979	8.1	15,886	28,054
1981	9.2	14,532	25,762
1983	9.9	14,506	25,757

[1] *Economic Report of the President* (Washington, D.C.: U.S. Government Printing Office, 1985), p. 264.

[2] To keep the "poverty level" comparable from year to year it is adjusted to correct for changes in the cost of living.

[3] Since these are "median" income levels, one-half the families had income greater than this amount and one-half had income less than this amount. The median income figures for blacks and whites are comparable, since the "constant" dollars are corrected for the effects of inflation. In this case, the "constant" dollars are calculated with 1983 as a base. Thus, the figure of $14,506 really was the median income of black families in 1983, since they received 1983 dollars. The figure of $15,843, for example, would have been the median income of black families in 1971 if they had gotten that income in the cheaper, more inflated, and more numerous dollars of 1983.

wrongs against all members of their race or sex by giving them preferential treatment in hiring and promotions. As broadly envisioned, it was not required that the persons who benefited from affirmative action programs also be the ones who were discriminated against—only that they be members of the class of persons who were discriminated against.

- During the 1970s, especially during times of growing unemployment, and especially among white ethnics whose own sense of identity and pride had been revitalized by the civil rights movement, federal affirmative action policies began to encounter intense opposition.[21]
- Meanwhile, the past successes of the civil rights movement also had created a more diverse group of civil rights activists who now found it increasingly difficult to coordinate fund raising and litigation strategies.[22]

[21] See John W. Blassingame, "The Revolution That Never Was: The Civil Rights Movement, 1950–1980," *Perspectives: The Civil Rights Quarterly* 14 (1982): 3–15.

[22] See, for example, the difficulties of the National Association for the Advancement of Colored People (NAACP) and the National Legal Committee, recounted in Stephen L. Wasby, "Civil Rights Litigation by Organizations: Constraints and Choices," *Judicature* 68 (1985): 337–52.

- The courts, too, posed an obstacle to further progress, especially when it appeared that civil rights gains could be purchased only at the expense of the rights of others. In 1978, for example, the U.S. Supreme Court ruled, in *Regents of University of California* v. *Bakke*, that the University of California at Davis had violated the rights of a white applicant, Allan Bakke, when it reserved some places for black medical school applicants.[23]
- Moving into the 1980s, the opposition to affirmative action became more broadly based. The opposition included, for example, Glenn C. Loury, a black economics professor at Harvard, who feared that it hurt the self-esteem of those who benefited from it, while perpetuating negative views among whites about the abilities of blacks to compete; President Ronald Reagan's attorney general, Edwin Meese III, who sought to weaken a previous president's executive order that required federal contractors to hire minorities and women, because the policy amounted to "reverse discrimination" and ran counter to the nation's attempt to create a color-blind society; and Thomas Sowell, a black economist at the University of California in Los Angeles, who argued that civil rights guarantee only equality of opportunity, not equality of condition.[24]
- Today, the opposition to affirmative action policies lingers—and so does the demand for compensatory treatment. The prospects for reconciling the two are dim. As Linda Chavez, a staff director of the U.S. Commission on Civil Rights has observed, "The greatest bitterness in the current civil rights debate is over how best to remedy the effects of past discrimination."[25]

When you look back over these stages, it should be clear that it has been easier to remedy past wrongs than to achieve full equality, especially when the efforts to do so appear to threaten personal liberties. This brief historical overview seems to substantiate the claim of one political theorist, Michael Walzer, when he said, "Liberty and equality are the two chief virtues of social institutions, and they stand best when they stand together."[26] Unfortunately, the reverse is true as well. In recent years, Americans, rightly or wrongly, seem swayed by the belief that social equality threatens personal liberty.

In the final analysis, the rights of minorities will not be secure until all people come to believe that discrimination against some makes both the target of discrimination *and* society as a whole less well-off. This will require that more accept the message of the Reverend Martin Luther King, Jr.: "Injustice anywhere is a threat to justice everywhere." And, perhaps, it will require that more accept the idea that no one should have to bow their head if they're not praying.

■ Sometimes, the absence of governmental interference is not enough to ensure human freedom because discrimination against some persons may block their attempts to express it. When this happens, most Americans believe

[23] 438 U.S. 265 (1978).

[24] See, for example, Thomas Sowell, *Civil Rights: Rhetoric or Reality* (New York: Morrow, 1984).

[25] "Civil Rights Since *Brown*: 1954–1984," *The Center Magazine* 17 (1984): 12.

[26] Michael Walzer, "In Defense of Equality," *Dissent* 20 (1973): 408.

that government should protect people's civil rights, although most Americans do not always agree on (1) the targets of discrimination; (2) the forms of possible discrimination against which people should be protected; (3) the protections that government should provide; and (4) the extent to which people should be compensated for the historical residue of discrimination.

LIBERTIES AND RIGHTS EVOLVE

> Without courage to assert rights, they weaken.
> —Roger N. Baldwin, founder of
> American Civil Liberties
> Union in an annual report

There are movable boundaries between government's proper and improper roles. This can be seen in a postscript to the Case which began this chapter. After the trial and after Farber was freed, New Jersey amended the law that protected or "shielded" a reporter and his or her confidential sources. The new law made explicit what Farber had claimed: the right to protect confidential news sources. With this change, new explicit language was added to the definition of government's improper role—and civil liberties evolved.

How do civil liberties and civil rights evolve? Mostly through testing and challenge—in society and through the political and judicial processes. But answering this question fully would be like trying to answer the question: "How has humankind evolved?" Imagine how difficult that would be. We would have to identify every branch and twig on the evolutionary tree, and then show all the details of the evolutionary processes. It cannot be done. What we can do is identify some of the major branches and some of the major processes in the evolution of liberties and rights.

Major Evolutionary Branches

There are two types of branches in the evolution of civil liberties and civil rights. Upward sloping branches are expansions of liberties and rights; downward sloping ones represent contractions. Both kinds span American history, although human freedoms have mostly expanded over time.

Expansions of Human Freedoms.   Most of the expansions of civil liberties and civil rights have a definite form. Many have come through formal amendments to the Constitution; others have been brought about by court decisions, especially decisions of the Supreme Court; and other statutory advances have come on the heels of electoral victories.

THE POLSBY—WILDAVSKY DIALOGUE CONTINUED . . .

AUTHOR: It seems to me that the concern with personal liberty has been an enduring theme throughout American history. Do you agree and, if you do, why do you suppose this is true?

POLSBY: I think it's true primarily because the basic economic problems in this country have been relatively easy to solve. I don't think it would have been true if this had been a poor country, but, because it isn't, personal liberty has been very important.

AUTHOR: What do you see as the main threats to personal liberty today, or in the foreseeable future?

> *Now, today, there is more, or as much, personal liberty in this country as there has ever been. It would be hard to find a society in which people can express themselves in more numerous ways . . .*
>
> *—Wildavsky*

POLSBY: As always, zealotry. On the whole, personal liberty in the United States, that is to say, the opportunity for persons to behave in ways that suit themselves, has vastly increased in the last fifty years. The reason, primarily, is because of personal geographic mobility in which the social controls of extended families have diminished markedly. The next set of problems has to do with how the backlash to this is handled in the legal system. What happens to laws with respect to abortion, pornography, the closing of bath houses, and all sorts of public conduct? What happens in these various spheres will determine, it seems to me, the state of personal liberty over the next arc of time. It's not necessarily a matter of a threat to civil liberties but a matter of handling balances among genuine public needs for order and personal needs for expression. These are very complex issues, as is, for example, the whole issue of finding an appropriate arena for making decisions about abortion. We haven't sorted that out yet and how we sort it out, it seems to me, will have a tremendous impact on who enjoys what liberties.

WILDAVSKY: It's a question, in part, of whether you look at what is evident now or what might come later. Now, today, there is more, or as much, personal liberty in this country as there has ever been. It would be hard to find a society in which people can express themselves in more numerous ways than we have now. However, there are possible threats. I do not see them entirely, yet, as actual threats. Of course they come from political extremes.

It's not necessarily a matter of a threat to civil liberties but a matter of handling balances among genuine public needs for order and personal needs for expression.

—Polsby

Let's start from the right. One sign is the effort to have polygraph tests used throughout federal government. One understands the motivation. You have something you try to keep secret. People are leaking information all the time. And, while it's not quite the same sieve as it was in the Carter Administration, it can be uncomfortable. My judgment would be, go with Secretary of State Schultz, that the losses from the use of polygraph tests are greater, by far, than the gains.

On the left, this is somewhat less obvious, but it will become more obvious. Things that, in the 1930s, 40s, and 50s, were thought to be settled among "right-thinking" people have now been opened up again. Should a communist teach in schools? People on the left used to say, yes, as long as they didn't try to indoctrinate their students directly or whatever. If the question were asked today about a racist, you would have more trouble now.

Or, for another example, take child abuse. Is child abuse worse now than it ever has been? I doubt it, because conditions of life are generally better. But there's a lot of abuse. This permits government at various levels to intrude into family life. Obviously, there's a great good to be obtained. But there also are possible evils. We see this in the effort to treat children in a super protective way, thus reducing the protections for defendants.

What I see, both on the far right and on the far left, are greater efforts to intervene in personal behavior. On the far left, the intervention is justified in terms of equality and, on the far right, intervention is justified on the grounds of morality or the need to re-establish hierarchy.

On the constitutional level, major expansions of civil liberties include the first nine amendments in the Bill of Rights; those constitutional amendments that freed the slaves, promised equal protection of the laws, and extended voting rights to blacks; other amendments that extended participation rights—to women in 1920, to residents of the District of Columbia in 1961, to voters who had not paid poll "or any other tax" in 1964, and to youth age eighteen and older in 1971. Judicial expansions in civil liberties have come about after the Civil War, because of the passage of the Fourteenth Amendment, and through subsequent Supreme Court decisions which required the states to respect the protections afforded by the Bill of Rights. More recently, major expansions came about because of many of the decisions of the Supreme Court under Chief Justice Earl Warren (1953–1969). Firmly in place by 1961, the majority led by Warren significantly expanded the scope of human freedoms—making electoral districts and representation more equal; protecting newspapers against libel suits; ruling prayer in public schools unconstitutional; enforcing laws against racial segregation; and protecting, in a variety of ways, those accused of crime. Finally, electoral battles too can advance the cause of human freedom, as they did after the Republican nomination of Barry Goldwater for the office of President in 1964. Goldwater's defeat was bad enough for him; he was buried under Lyndon Johnson's landslide of 486 electoral votes, losing forty-four of the fifty states, plus the District of Columbia. Goldwater's defeat was worse for the Republican party because he dragged down with him many Republican candidates for Congress. The deluge produced a bumper crop of Democrats—senators who slipped in unexpectedly during the 1958 elections and normally would have been wrung out six years later and representatives firmly attached to Johnson's coattails, thereby swelling his congressional majority. President Johnson was able to capitalize on this, calling on the 89th Congress to pass what became the Voting Rights Act of 1965 and the Civil Rights Act of 1968.

These, of course, are only some of the major spurts in the evolution of civil liberties and civil rights, but they suffice to show the expansionary trend. The story, however, is not totally uplifting because human freedoms can wither.

Contractions of Human Freedoms. War kills. It kills people, and often civil liberties, sometimes during the war and sometimes shortly after. Sometimes the threat of war is enough. During these times, civil liberties are pushed aside as less important than national survival or what some took to be national loyalty. This pattern repeats throughout American history.

With the passage of the Alien and Sedition Acts in 1789, the Federalists, having narrowly skirted a war with France, moved to suppress internal dissent by making it a crime to criticize the President or Congress. Although only ten Americans were jailed for violation of these acts, their convictions were upheld as constitutional.

During the Civil War, civil liberties were seriously suppressed in the North. Many opposed to the war were imprisoned without a trial, although the press was generally left free to criticize Lincoln and his generals and did so, often brutally.

These Japanese-Americans, awaiting inspection on arrival at an assembly center set up in the Santa Anita racetrack, appear to maintain their dignity in spite of the imminent loss of liberty.

World War I, and Imperial Russia, ended in 1918. In reaction to the rising red tide of communism, civil liberties were suppressed in America. During the first red scare of 1917–1920, the nation overdosed on fear. In an hysterical binge, thousands of persons were rounded up, tried for sedition, or deported. Under federal law, about a thousand people were convicted and under state sedition laws, many more were imprisoned. The fury subsided eventually, spent on battered traditions and ruined lives.

After Pearl Harbor, President Roosevelt caused nearly 120,000 Americans of Japanese ancestry to be forcibly removed from their homes on the West Coast. Justified in the interests of national security, the internment of Japanese Americans resulted in lost dignity, property, wages, and civil liberties. The image lingers, and haunts.

After the Second World War, a second red scare threatened civil liberties. Passed in 1940, the Smith Act made it a crime to advocate the forceful overthrow of the government. The Internal Security Act of 1950 also made membership in the Communist Party a crime. Both were used to try Communist party leaders, and their convictions for advocacy, not action, were upheld by the Supreme Court.[27] The formal prosecutions were the lesser threat to civil liberties; more threatening was **McCarthyism**, a new style of political discourse named after its creator, Senator Joseph R. McCarthy (R.,Wis.). He was chasing communism, a real threat to national security, but that was not the problem. It was how he did it, through the use of undocumented, defamatory charges that could not be refuted, or even effectively challenged by persons who lacked power and purse. Under both legalistic and rhetorical assaults, civil liberties shrank.

These examples are hills and valleys on our journey, landmarks in the evolution of human freedom in America. Now we need to get below the surface to try to understand what caused these eruptions; we need to examine the underlying forces that set the evolutionary processes in motion.

---

[27] *Dennis v. United States*, 341 U.S. 494 (1951).

Major Evolutionary Processes

Liberties and rights evolve through testing and challenge in reaction to fear, conflict, and political pressure. Each of these sets off evolution in human freedoms; sometimes expanding them, sometimes contracting them.

Reaction to Fear. Supreme Court Justice Louis D. Brandeis once wrote, "It is the function of speech to free men from the bondage of irrational fears."[28] Fear is the enemy of freedom; it frustrates human progress and robs people of their capacity to develop. And that, in a society founded on a desire for human progress, is the greatest loss of all.

Civil liberties and civil rights evolve in reaction to five specific fears: fear of government, fear of majorities, fear of technology, fear of crime, and, sometimes, fear of minorities.

Civil liberties evolve in reaction to a fear of government. In the Case, both Mario Jascalevich and Myron Farber feared government since it could deprive them of their liberty by imprisoning them. In the beginning, many thought the Bill of Rights sufficient to protect the people from the national government. After all, it did not look as though the national government would do much to, or for, people. Over time, however, the role of government expanded as it intervened more into what had been private concerns. As government became more intrusive, fear grew that any government strong enough to give things to people is strong enough to take things away. In reaction to bigger government, bigger and better protections were sought.

Civil liberties evolve in reaction to a fear of majorities. Majorities are dangerous because they are powerful and often intolerant. The fear of majorities has deep roots and recent offshoots. Its roots run to the founding of the Republic. In justifying the new form of government, Madison wrote that it would protect against the mischief of factions. Ever since, factions, especially majority factions, have been feared and with good cause, since it was not American Indians who drove white Americans eastward or newly arrived Irish Americans who refused to hire backbay Yankees. Today, large concentrations of ethnic minorities which are new to our shores, Haitians, for example, and other minority groups which are now more insistent about their rights, homosexuals, for example, evoke new fears. To protect themselves from discrimination and possible abuse, they too seek guarantees from government. In this way also, civil liberties evolve.

Civil liberties evolve in reaction to a fear of crime. One estimate clocks serious crime at one incident every two seconds of every day. No one is immune; President Ronald Reagan was an assault victim in 1981, as were over 600,000 other Americans the same year. There are two questions concerning crime. The first is easy: "Should society fight crime?" Society has no choice; crime robs people of their money and, more importantly, crime and the fear of crime rob people of the security they need for self-development. Crime, therefore, cannot be tolerated in a society that values human progress. The

[28] *Whitney v. California,* 274 U.S. 376 (1927).

second question is harder: "What should society do to fight crime?" Society finds it harder to answer this question, since ways of fighting crime often threaten civil liberties. Crime can be fought, for example, by rounding up suspects or by digging up evidence. Both approaches can erode civil liberties, if, for example, police rounded up people just because they looked suspicious or randomly tapped telephone lines.

In spite of possible adverse side-effects on civil liberties, society is under real pressure to protect itself, and people sometimes are willing to trade a little liberty for what they hope will be a lot of protection from crime. Some suspect that the fear of crime has eroded civil liberties, especially the punishment rights of suspects; others disagree. The controversy spills over into the judicial process and often ends up before the Supreme Court. Some of the Court's attempts to deal with it are reflected in the **Vantage Point**: What Is Due Process? on pages 128–29.

Endangered American Species

Civil liberties evolve in reaction to a fear of technology. Each of the following modern crime-fighting technologies pose unclear but often scary implications for civil liberties. The use of electronic devices that analyze stress in the human voice to show if someone is lying, for example, may short-circuit Fifth Amendment rights against self-incrimination. In addition, the FBI and most of the states now use a centralized computer file to keep track of crime. Problems arise, however, because errors creep into the files, giving criminal records to non-criminals and thereby threatening their liberty—not to mention their credit ratings and employment. Modern computing technology also suggests various ways of tracking such diverse crimes as tax fraud and the employment of illegal aliens, while simultaneously scaring those who fear that this would also increase the potential for abuse and intimidation. The fears are not far-fetched; for example, America's major spy organization, the National Security Agency (NSA), has a huge computer system at its heavily guarded Fort George Meade headquarters near Washington, D.C. The computer-based system works like a giant electronic vacuum cleaner, sweeping the airways of all electronic messages entering or leaving the United States. By using key "watch" words, NSA zeros in on suspicious conversations, makes a transcript, and passes it on to the FBI.

All these examples have something in common; in all, new technologies magnify the power of government—its power to improve society and its power to threaten liberty. The threat stimulates attempts to defend civil liberties, shoring up precious ground. In the process, civil liberties evolve.

Civil rights sometimes evolve in reaction to a fear of minorities. The fears may be real or imagined, the associated threat immediate or remote. During the economic hard times of the 1970s, for example, some workers had reason to fear the demands of blacks and women for affirmative action programs. In this instance, some white male workers acted as though they did feel a relatively immediate threat, a feeling that helps to explain the intensity of their opposition to this civil rights policy. In other instances, fears that eroded civil liberties were more imaginary than real, as when Americans of Japanese ancestry were interned during World War II. During the mid-1960s, President

Johnson, rightly or wrongly, felt justified in stifling American protest against the war in Vietnam, because he feared it sapped American resolve while increasing the determination of the North Vietnamese. During the 1980s, fear of the spread of Acquired Immune Deficiency Syndrome (AIDS) sometimes prompted new forms of discrimination against homosexuals. Invariably, fear of minorities erodes civil liberties.

Reaction to Conflict.   Liberties and rights may conflict with each other and with other rights. When they do, human freedoms often change, getting weaker, or stronger, but always evolving. In the opening Case, for example, two civil liberties conflicted: Jascalevich's right to a fair trial and Farber's right to report the news freely.

Even family conflicts can turn into issues of civil liberties. In 1980, for example, twelve-year-old Walter Polovchak, visiting in the United States, ran away from his parents rather than return home with them to the Soviet Union. Walter wanted political asylum; his parents wanted Walter. The Illinois chapter of the American Civil Liberties Union got involved on the side of the parents, arguing that government should not interfere with parents' rights. Walter, for one, was not convinced; in a letter to a supportive news columnist, Walter wrote: "Maybe ACLU should go to the Soviet Union and fight for the rights of people."[29]

In addition, political battles can inflict wounds on human freedoms. In the early 1950s, for example, the political ambitions of the late Senator Joseph McCarthy conflicted with the civil liberties of civilian federal employees. As we have seen in times of war, the nation's interest in survival conflicted, or was believed to conflict, with the civil rights of racial and ideological minorities.

In these examples, parents, federal employees, and racial and ideological minorities enjoyed only the rights they were willing to fight for. In all such cases, rights that either are not defended, or not defended effectively, provide scant protection.

Reaction to Political Pressure.   Political pressure explains much of the evolution of human freedom in America. In the beginning, for example, to calm political opposition, those who favored the new Constitution promised written guarantees, the Bill of Rights, to protect civil liberties. The promise worked; it won "popular backing for the new government."[30] In this, the first great logroll, civil liberties expanded because of a concession to political pressure.

More recently, in the early 1980s, there was almost overwhelming support for prayer in the public schools. A Gallup poll in 1980, for example, reported that 76 percent of a national sample supported a proposed constitutional amendment, permitting prayer in the public schools. The popular pressure was felt in Washington as the previously buried amendment resurfaced and as members of Congress sought some way of appeasing some without antagonizing others. Also in the early 1980s, the public became increasingly agitated over

---

[29] *The Plain Dealer,* 4 July 1982.

[30] Howard Zinn, *A People's History of the United States* (New York: Harper and Row, 1980), p. 99.

the role of the federal courts. Judges, especially federal court judges, had become more "activistic," more inclined to push federal policy into areas that had been state, if not private, concerns. The agitation was broad based, resting on opposition to federal policies about desegregation, school prayer, and abortion. The opposition crystallized around a new proposal; take away from the federal courts their jurisdiction over these cases. "If you do not like the decisions federal judges are making, take away their right to make those decisions," many reasoned. Within the first two years of the Reagan Administration, over forty bills were introduced; all would have stripped the federal courts of their jurisdiction over controversial cases and in the process, reduced the scope of civil liberties and civil rights.

Political pressures to expand civil rights sometimes produce frustrating counterpressures. In the drive to obtain constitutional protections for women's rights, for example, supporters of the Equal Rights Amendment (ERA) won the approval of Congress by 1972 and the ratification votes of thirty-five of the necessary thirty-eight states by 1980. Their drive for ratification was neither quick nor intense enough, however; opponents had time to organize and counterattack. Even with the deadline extended to 1982, the ratification effort was doomed by "Stop ERA" forces organized by Phyllis Schlafly of Alton, Illinois, and by the country's increasingly conservative political mood. Even worse for ERA supporters, Mrs. Schlafly understood the need to keep her forces mobilized; the Equal Rights Amendment, she said, was a cadaver that they had to "keep pushing back into the coffin."

In all these examples, political pressure pushed liberties and rights, sometimes up, sometimes down, but always in an evolutionary direction.

■ Going into his trial, Mario Jascalevich could not be sure he would be acquitted, and Judge Arnold could not be sure Myron Farber would stay in jail rather than relinquish his notes. In this case, people's civil liberties only gradually evolved, as the trial unfolded. It is generally true that civil liberties and civil rights evolve through testing and challenge. As a result, new boundaries are built around government, separating its proper from its improper roles.

BOUNDARIES ON GOVERNMENT'S ROLE

What's a Constitution among friends?
—*attributed to Grover Cleveland*

Whether or not President Cleveland really said this, the remark suggests that somebody had better look after the boundaries that separate government's improper and proper roles. Those boundaries do not maintain themselves; they need to be constantly patrolled—and repaired when necessary.

The Boundaries

Civil liberties and civil rights define government's proper role by saying what government cannot do and what it should do to. As civil liberties evolve, case by case, boundaries rise around government. They block what is improper and by default, suggest what government might properly do. In this way, government's proper role is an implied residue, the legacy of judicial and political battles. In a different way, civil rights define government's proper role directly, by saying what it should do to protect freedom. Thus, the struggle for civil rights expands government's reach into previously excluded areas, committing it to the cause.

Patrolling the Boundaries

As you can imagine, patrolling these boundaries is a big job, bigger than what individuals, acting alone, can accomplish. Moreover, individuals like you and me are usually busy looking out for our more immediate self-interests. This is why the job falls to others who are equipped to do it, and who will do it because it is in their self-interest. In this society, the task falls especially heavily on interest groups, political parties, the press, Congress, and the courts.

As we will see in subsequent chapters, each of these organizations and institutions perform many functions, including defending against arbitrary expressions of governmental authority that limit personal liberty and attacking discriminatory practices that violate civil rights.

■ Civil liberties and civil rights evolve in ways that help sort out government's improper and proper roles. But the process of enlarging human freedom is neither spontaneous nor automatic. It happens only when individuals, voluntary groups, profit-making organizations, and those in governmental agencies are willing to struggle and to persevere.

SUMMARY

To ensure human freedom, civil liberties guarantee that government will not interfere arbitrarily with people, their opinions, and their property. In addition, civil rights guarantee that government will protect people against discrimination, whether it comes from other persons or from some other part of the government.

Civil liberties and civil rights are meant to protect persons, so that they may fully develop their potential and thereby, make their greatest contribution to society. In spite of the value, however, human freedoms are limited by necessity, expedience, and default.

The protections afforded by civil liberties and civil rights cannot be taken for granted, however. These protections constantly evolve, usually in reaction to fear, conflict with competing values, and political pressure. Out of such struggles, protections that people are willing to fight for sometimes get stronger; undefended freedoms, however, always get weaker.

Civil liberties and civil rights bound government's improper and proper roles, separating what should not be done from what should be. The boundaries do not maintain themselves, however; they must be patrolled and repaired by those intermediary groups, organizations, and institutions that stand between individual persons and threats to their freedom.

Key Terms

civil liberties
civil rights
classical liberalism
privacy rights
participation rights
punishment rights

due process of law
negative rights
positive rights
affirmative action
McCarthyism

Review and Reflection

1. What is the difference between civil liberties and civil rights?

2. Why would a society want to protect personal freedoms? How would society benefit?

3. If freedom is such a good thing, why is it limited? And by what?

4. What are the major civil liberties?

5. What, if anything, limits civil liberties?

6. Do you think government is a threat to your civil liberties?

7. Do you think the federal government does enough to protect the rights of minorities? Too much? Why?

8. Would you be willing to support affirmative action programs if you were convinced that the lingering effects of past discrimination could not be removed without them?

9. Do you agree that there is an effective boundary between what government should, and should not do? Or do you believe that some governmental agencies do what they should not and fail to do what they should? If that is so, what might be done about it?

Supplemental Readings

The literature on civil liberties and civil rights includes great dramatic accounts as well as more traditional accounts.

The true stories, full of high drama, injustice, suspense, heroes and villains, human tragedy, and often, inspiration, include: *Bayley's* account of the general failure of the press to warn against the dangers of McCarthyism; *Friendly's* book, in contrast, shows Colonel Robert R. McCormick, publisher of the *Chicago Tribune* riding to the rescue by defending the rights of Jay Near and in the process advancing First Amendment rights; *Garrow* relates well the harrowing story of the FBI's harassment of Martin Luther King, Jr.; *Jones* exposes the U.S. Public Health Service's failure to treat more than 400 black Alabama sharecroppers and laborers so it could study the effects of syphilis; *Kutler* does a good job of putting flesh and blood on the broken bones of those who suffered during the second red scare; *Lewis* describes the expansion in punishments rights that came about after Clarence Earl Gideon, a prisoner in the Florida State Prison at Raiford, set out to convince the Supreme Court that he should go free because he had been convicted without a lawyer; and *Vassilikos* provides a somewhat fictionalized account of the suppression of democracy in Greece.

The more traditional works include *Abraham's* textbook on the interpretation of the Bill of Rights; *Levy's* explanation of what the Founders meant by freedom of speech and press; *Mill's* classic statement of liberalism; and *Sorauf's* account of the process of erecting the wall between church and state.

The dramatic accounts:

Bayley, Edwin R. *Joe McCarthy and the Press.* New York: Pantheon Books, 1982.

Friendly, Fred W. *Minnesota Rag: The Dramatic Story of the Landmark Supreme Court Case That Gave Meaning to Freedom of the Press.* New York: Vintage Books, 1982.

Garrow, David J. *The FBI and Martin Luther King, Jr.: From "Solo" to Memphis.* New York: W.W. Norton, 1981.

Jones, James H. *Bad Blood: The Tuskegee Syphilis Experiment.* New York: The Free Press, 1981.

Kutler, Stanley I. *The American Inquisition: Justice and Injustice in the Cold War.* New York: Hill and Wang, 1982.

Lewis, Anthony. *Gideon's Trumpet.* New York: Random House, 1964.

Vassilikos, Vassilis. *Z.* New York: Ballantine Books, 1969.

The more traditional accounts:

Abraham, Henry J. *Freedom and the Court: Civil Rights and Liberties in the United States.* 4th ed. New York: Oxford University Press, 1982.

Levy, Leonard W. *Legacy of Suppression: Freedom of Speech and Press in Early American History.* 2nd ed. Cambridge, Mass.: Harvard University Press, 1964.

Mill, John Stuart. *On Liberty.* (First published in 1859.) New York: Penguin, 1982.

Sorauf, Frank J. *Wall of Separation.* Princeton: Princeton University Press, 1976.

PART TWO

THE POLITICAL ENVIRONMENT

"We have met the enemy and he is us."
—*Pogo*

CHAPTER FIVE

POLITICAL CULTURE
WHAT DO AMERICANS CARE ABOUT?

What do Americans care about—what do they want from their political system? Governmental officials, policy makers, and politicians need to know if they are to maintain their legitimacy and advance their causes and careers.

The American people care about their values, their underlying beliefs about desirable ends and means, about what is worth realizing and about the ways in which it should be sought. Some of these are **political values**, beliefs about the proper role of government. Taken together, the political values add up to our **political culture**, our collective sense of what government should do and how it should do it.

The political culture endures and is freely expressed. It is passed on from generation to generation by a process of **political socialization**, the way we learn about our political environment and how we develop psychological reactions to it. The culture is also often manifested in **public opinions**, the verbal expressions of underlying attitudes and values.

It took a stranger to these shores to show us clearly the nature of America's political culture as we see in the following Case. While here to study America's prisons, Alexis de Tocqueville also discovered its soul. His insights endure. First, there is an American political culture which helps maintain democracy. Second, the political culture esteems the values of individualism, liberty, and equality. Third, the political culture is perpetuated by the people, not their government. Fourth, the political culture is expressed many ways, in the opinions of the public and in the actions of their leaders.

CULTURE AND DEMOCRACY

This photograph of Alexis de Tocqueville makes it hard to imagine him trekking around a primitive American countryside.

> No novelty in the United States struck me more vividly during my stay there than the equality of conditions. It was easy to see the immense influence of this basic fact on the whole course of society. It gives a peculiar turn to public opinion and a peculiar twist to the laws, new maxims to those who govern and peculiar habits to the governed.
>
> —*Alexis de Tocqueville,*
> Democracy in America

The Case   Alexis de Tocqueville's Search for America[1]

Alexis de Tocqueville's ship, the *Havre*, blown off course from its intended destination of New York, landed at Newport, Rhode Island, on May 9, 1831. From that point, Tocqueville and his traveling companion, Gustave de Beaumont, began a nine-month journey through most of the twenty-four states of the day. Persisting through physical hardship, seeking out and interviewing notables and common folk along the way, Tocqueville filled notebooks with observations and impressions—seeking nothing less than the soul of a nation and capturing it in his major work, *Democracy in America.*[2]

Although sent by France to study the administration of America's prisons, Tocqueville hoped to find the answer to what he saw as the question of his age: Could liberty and equality be reconciled? In his mind and in much of the recent experience of France, these two values, equality and liberty, seemed incompatible. To us, today, this might seem curious, but it did not to Tocqueville.

Liberty for Tocqueville and his class was indispensable. Theirs, however, was a special kind of liberty: the absence of interference. This is what is usually defined "as the 'negative' concept of liberty, seeing individual freedom as the absence of restraint and coercion by other men or conversely the possession of uncoerced choices in action."[3] Their liberty, however, was not an idle, private pleasure; liberty, as an aristocratic value, carried with it ethical and civic duties.

[1]This account of the life and work of Tocqueville is drawn from: Hugh Brogan, *Tocqueville* (Great Britain: The Chaucer Press, 1973); Doris S. Goldstein, *Trial of Faith: Religion and Politics in Tocqueville's Thought* (New York: Elsevier, 1975); Richard D. Heffner, ed., *Alexis de Tocqueville: Democracy in America* (abridged) (New York: New American Library, 1965); Jack Lively, *The Social and Political Thought of Alexis de Tocqueville* (Great Britain: Clarendon Press, 1962); J. P. Mayer, *Alexis de Tocqueville: A Biographical Study in Political Science* (New York: Harper and Brother, 1960); and George Wilson Pierson, *Tocqueville and Beaumont in America* (New York: Oxford University Press, 1938).

[2]Alexis de Tocqueville, *Democracy in America* J. P. Mayer, ed., trans. by George Lawrence (Garden City, New York: Doubleday and Co., 1969).

[3]Lively, p. 10. See also H. J. Laski, *Liberty in the Modern State* (London: Faber and Faber Ltd., 1930) and Isaiah Berlin, *Two Concepts of Liberty* (Oxford: Clarendon Press, 1958).

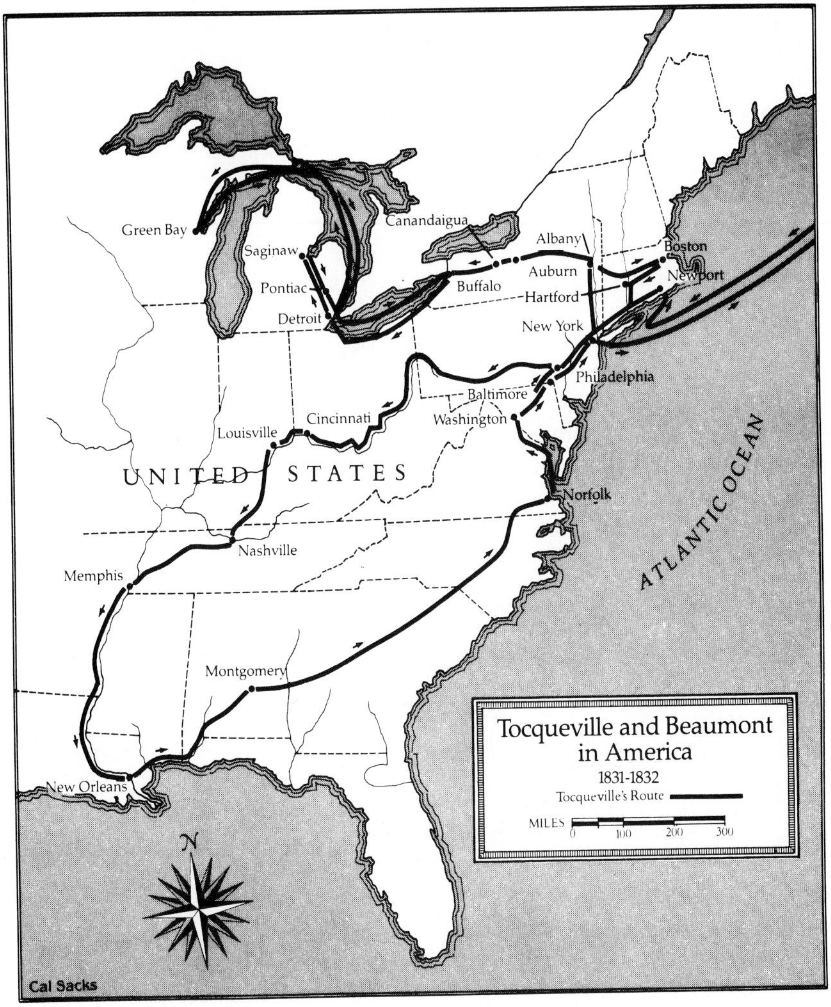

Tocqueville and Beaumont
in America
1831-1832
Tocqueville's Route

With liberty, people were unfettered and independent, willing and able to exercise their free choice, to decide for themselves what was moral and what was not, what their responsibilities were towards others, and most importantly, how one should interact with others to carry out voluntarily public responsibilities. In this way, liberty was a precondition for the good society.

But Tocqueville and his class feared that liberty was threatened by equality. The liberty Tocqueville loved he knew as "the finest, rarest product of the old aristocracy . . ."[4] which, he had believed, depended on social inequalities and personal uniqueness. The challenge came from the democratic impulse to make people more equal, leveling social disparities and enforcing, Tocqueville feared, a numbing sameness among people, thereby stifling human imagination and the capacity for moral action. The end result, most greatly feared, would be the total

[4]Pierson, p. 751.

domination of the individual by the masses and by popular demagogues; the tyranny of the majority that would extinguish personal liberty.

Tocqueville believed he could show that equality and liberty could coexist. The evidence to support this proposition lay in America, he thought. There the drive toward equality was further advanced, yet the democratic order had not suppressed personal liberties. Thus, Tocqueville saw America as a political laboratory, in the grip of a democratic experiment. In it one might glimpse the future and thereby better prepare for the arrival of democracy in France. With inspired but human guidance, liberty might be protected from the tyranny of the majority.

What better place to search? Arriving midway through the second term of President Andrew Jackson,[5] Tocqueville found an increasingly democratic nation committed to political equality—yet the commitment had not extinguished the personal liberties that allowed people to be different. Tocqueville began to unravel the apparent anomaly by examining the political culture of the American people.

The American people, Tocqueville saw, were enlightened by what he called their private morality. In particular, the American culture included a commitment to a protected sphere of action in which relatively autonomous individuals could decide for themselves their self-interest and then, without interference from others or government, try to realize it. In this way, the devotion to personal liberty could be a bulwark against anarchy and despotism.

Tocqueville realized that the sense of private morality, by itself, was an insufficient defense against tyranny. There were, he saw, other intellectual habits and social and political devices that helped protect liberty from the potentially oppressive masses. These included religious convictions that were rooted in a faith free of governmental control; well-practiced traditions of free speech and a free press; a decentralized system of political authority that relied on local government and voluntary associations to give people a sense of self-importance and public responsibility; a strong and independent judiciary that could protect against the potential excesses of popularly elected legislatures; a jury system that reflected peer judgments; a constitution that peacefully accommodated demands for change; the election of representatives indirectly, so as to dilute popular control of policy. In America, these habits and devices, reinforcing the cultural commitment to personal freedoms, also helped preserve liberty.

Upon his return to France, Tocqueville's analysis met with instant acclaim. But his analysis won him neither the political success he sought for himself nor the liberty he desired so desperately for his country. Although he did win political office, his too-aloof manner and the tenor of the times frustrated his desire for political influence. Liberty, too, continued to be battered in the turmoil of French politics and by 1851, when Louis Napoleon forcefully dissolved the National Assembly, Tocqueville's worst fears seemed realized. Withdrawing from public life, Tocqueville first sought intellectual refuge in an attempt to discover the underlying causes of anarchy and despotism. But Tocqueville began to run out of new ideas, research materials, and time. In a futile attempt to escape the ravages of tuberculosis, he fled south to Cannes and after seeking final refuge in his Catholic faith, Alexis de Tocqueville died on April 16, 1859.

---

[5] For an excellent history of the time, see Glyndon G. Van Duesen, *The Jacksonian Era: 1828–1848* (New York: Harper and Brothers, 1959).

Nothing better symbolized the new extremes of political egalitarianism, both its feverish exuberance and its feared excesses, than the raucous hordes that descended upon President Jackson's inaugural party in the White House.

Insights

Despite deficiencies in both methodology and factual assertion, *Democracy in America* has endured as a remarkably perceptive analysis of the nature and consequences of the American political culture. Tocqueville was the first to trace systematically the connections between a society and its government. Like a polarizing filter over a camera lens, he transformed what we see and the way we study a nation's political life. He also discovered some basic truths about American society and its implications for the American style of democracy. From his discoveries, we can still draw some important insights about our political culture.

Insight 1. *There is an American political culture that helps maintain democracy.* After Tocqueville, it was no longer possible to see governmental systems in a vacuum, ripped from their social context. Rather, we now understand that whether or not democracy endures, and the way it functions, is in part determined by its cultural environment.

Insight 2. *The American political culture esteems the values of individualism, liberty, and equality.* Arriving before the various waves of immigration, Tocqueville found the Americans a less diverse people than he would today. Still, there were many differences—along class, racial, sexual, and ethnic lines. It is a testimonial to his analytical powers that Tocqueville cut through this bewildering diversity to its central core. He saw clearly that Americans love equality but insist on keeping private and therefore safe their personal liberties.

Insight 3. *The American political culture is perpetuated by the people, not their government.* Tocqueville firmly believed that the character and in his words, the "private morality" of a people would shape the evolutionary course of their government. We have abandoned these terms today in our desire to be more secular and scientific, and speak instead of political culture. But Americans have not abandoned the practices Tocqueville observed: they are the ones, not their government, who instruct one another in the rights and duties of a democratic people.

Insight 4. *The American culture is expressed in many ways in the opinions of the public and in the actions of their leaders.* For Tocqueville, America's political culture permeated almost every aspect of American life: the American commitment to the perfectability of the individual, the relations between parents and children, the "quarrelsome" American national pride, and why Americans are so hard to offend in their own country but so easily offended in others. Today, other effects have become more visible, especially those that shape popular expectations about government's proper role and those that contribute to the stability of the political system.

Each of these are important insights, important enough to convince Tocqueville and his class that democracy could be made safe for their world. Each is elaborated next.

POLITICAL CULTURE

> Americans of all national origins, classes, regions, creeds, and colors, have something in common: a social *ethos*, a political creed.
> —*Gunnar Myrdal,* An American Dilemma

A culture includes all of the ways a people think about all the aspects of their society, its art, literature, and human relationships, for example. A political culture is more narrowly focused on a society's government, what it does, and how it does it. As we have defined it, America's political culture is our collective sense of what government should do and of how it should do it.

A Psychological View of Political Culture

To make sense of America's political culture, you have to allow for both its surface manifestations and its underlying core.

On its surface, America's political culture is an exhilarating array of varied symbols, feelings, opinions, and actions:

- the "irritable patriotism" of Americans which Tocqueville complained about and which still distinguishes Americans from the citizens of other Western democracies, as **Table 5.1** shows;
- the enduring patriotism that most Americans share, although the data in **Table 5.2** reveals some differences between whites and blacks, and between men and women;
- those pictures of George Washington on our school walls, looking down from his cloudy perch;
- the reactions of our loved ones, when we tell them we are thinking of running for political office;
- the hoopla of an election campaign, before we invented more electronic forms of fun.

But all these, like geysers, volcanoes and earthquakes, are surface manifestations of deeper, underlying forces.

Our definitions suggest the nature of a political culture's underlying forces. In their path-breaking cross-national study, Gabriel Almond and Sidney Verba, for example, defined political culture as "the particular distribution of patterns of orientation toward political objects among the members of the nation."[6] In a somewhat more comprehensive fashion, Lucian Pye, in his study of Burma's search for national identity, wrote that a political culture is "built out of the cumulative orientations of a people toward their political process, its dimensions include the limitations imposed by the realities of power and authority structures of the society, modes of calculation and of estimating causality,

TABLE 5.1 Americans, at least American youth, are more patriotic than their counterparts in other Western democracies.

Nationality	Question: Are you proud to be (an American/respondent's country named)?
American	97%
British	90
French	73
German	71
Swedish	70
Swiss	67

NOTE: Sample was young men and women between the ages of eighteen and twenty-four. Approximately 2000 respondents in each country.

SOURCE: *Public Opinion*, June/July 1981, p. 25. Survey by Nippon Research Center, Ltd. and Gallup International, November 25, 1977–January 6, 1978.

TABLE 5.2 Patriotism In America

Although most Americans say they are "very patriotic," this is less true of women and blacks.

Question	Percentage Responding "Very Patriotic."				
	Total	Whites	Blacks	Men	Women
"Do you consider yourself very patriotic, somewhat patriotic or not very patriotic?"	53	56	35	59	49

SOURCE: *The New York Times Magazine*, December 11, 1983, p. 89.

---

[6]Gabriel Almond and Sidney Verba, *The Civic Culture* (Princeton, NJ: Princeton University Press, 1963), pp. 14–15.

constellations of values, and patterns of emotional responses."[7] Significantly, both studies focus on psychological phenomena, people's subjective orientations toward things in their political environment. To understand a political culture, therefore, we need to understand the character of these psychological orientations.

Think of a political culture as though it consists of three kinds of psychological orientations: personal values, attitudes toward political objects, and expressed opinions about those objects.[8] Some of these psychological ingredients are more important than others. As in **Figure 5.1**, the most visible parts of the political culture are the opinions that people express about governmental institutions, public policies, and politics. These opinions, however, are expressions of underlying **political attitudes**: emotionally charged reactions toward these parts of one's political environment. These attitudes also have a source; they come about because of still deeper, underlying **personal values**, intense beliefs about goals worth realizing and preferred ways of trying to reach them. A person's goals, for example, could include such things as social equality or world peace. One's preferred methods of working toward goals could include, for example, sincerity and honesty.

Such personal values influence the ways people see their environment, their attitudes toward political things in their environment, and their expressed opinions about those political objects. (This relationship among personal values, political attitudes, and political opinions is portrayed schematically in **Figure 5.1**.) A political culture, therefore, consists of surface opinions and underlying attitudes, all organized around enduring personal values.

This psychological view of political culture is useful. It helps us see why, for example, Americans can share common values yet have diverse political attitudes and opinions.

---

[7]Lucian W. Pye, *Politics, Personality, and Nation Building: Burma's Search for Identity* (New Haven, Conn.: Yale University Press, 1962), p. 122.

[8]See in particular, Milton Rokeach, *The Nature of Human Values* (New York: Free Press, 1973) and Martin Fishbein, ed., *Readings in Attitude Theory and Measurement* (New York: Wiley, 1967).

POLITICAL CULTURE: WHAT DO AMERICANS CARE ABOUT?

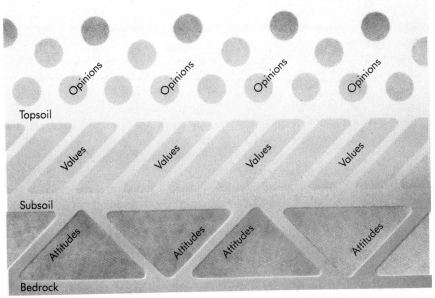

FIGURE 5.1
The Relationship Among Personal Values, Political Attitudes, and Political Opinions

Political Opinions: These are the oral or written reflection of underlying attitudes.

Political Attitudes: By relying on their personal values, people evaluate objects in their political environment: the governmental institutions, public policies, governmental officials and politicians and what they do. Objects that are consistent with personal values are evaluated positively; those that are not are evaluated negatively. These more or less positive and negative emotional reactions are political attitudes.

Personal Values: People have a few central values, core beliefs about ideal means and ends. Foremost among these in America are the values of individualism, liberty, and equality.

These relationships can be seen schematically. Think of values as though they were bedrock, supporting less deep attitudes (the subsoil), and think of attitudes as underlying more visible opinions (the topsoil).

The American Triumvirate: Individualism, Liberty, and Equality

Americans take their personal values very seriously. These deeply rooted beliefs about ideals drive our democracy, forcing it to live up to its promises if it is to maintain its legitimacy. Foremost among these, are three values in particular that animate American politics. Because of their importance—and to help you remember them—let's refer to them as the American triumvirate of values: individualism, liberty, and equality.

Individualism. **Individualism** is a value that glorifies the process by which unfettered individuals pursue what they judge to be their self-interest. It also sanctifies the results of this pursuit as a desirable end state. The value asserts that only individuals can best determine what is good for them and by implication, for society as a whole. In this sense, the value establishes a normative standard; if something is to be judged as "good," then it must be good for individuals and they themselves must concur. The standard of individualism, therefore, is a litmus test for evaluating political objects. People will view and react to governmental institutions, public policies, and politics on the basis of their effects on individualism.

Liberty. **Liberty** also is a valued means and end; it is something to be striven for and once attained, enjoyed for its own intrinsic value. Americans value liberty as a condition under which they are able to pursue other things of interest to them. In addition, as an ideal end state, liberty is valued for its own sake, without regard to what, if anything, people do with it once they reach it. This ideal is also central to the American political culture and has been since the founding, as we saw in chapter 2. It has been and remains a very important personal basis for evaluating political objects. If governmental institutions, policies, and politics are believed to promote liberty, people will tend to form positive attitudes toward them and express favorable opinions about them.

Equality. In America, the value of **equality** usually refers to means, not ends. There is, in fact, some hostility towards the notion that people are supposed to share equally in the benefits of society. As David Stockman, President Reagan's former budget director, put it while expressing his first year determination to cut into "sacred cow" social welfare programs, "Nobody is entitled to anything." The view is well-entrenched and well-reflected in popular opposition to affirmative action programs that would weigh sex and race more heavily than ability, as the data in **Table 5.3** reveals. In general, equality usually has meant equality of opportunity, not equality of result—the chance to succeed, not a guarantee of success. As a basis for evaluation, the standard of equality, especially of equality of opportunity, leads people to react favorably to things that remove barriers to personal progress and unfavorably to whatever imposes additional obstacles.[9]

These three key values, and what they imply, have persisted throughout American history as moral imperatives—as statements about conditions that society should enjoy. At different times in American history, the relative importance of these values has shifted, as the drive for equality softened the insistence on civil liberties during the Civil War, for example. At other times,

---

TABLE 5.3 Public Opinions Toward Affirmative Action

Affirmative action policies, as we saw in chapter 4, call for employers to give women and blacks preferential treatment in hiring and promotion. Most people disapprove of such practices and believe that ability should be the most important consideration.

This finding emerged from a Gallup poll in which people were asked the question: "Some people say that to make up for past discrimination, women and members of minority groups should be given preferential treatment in getting jobs and places in college. Others say that ability should be the main consideration. Which point comes closest to how you feel on this matter?"

	Percent Supporting		
	Give Preferential	Rely on Ability	No Opinion
Total	10%	84%	6%
Whites	6	87	5
Nonwhites	27	64	9
Men	9	85	6
Women	11	84	5

SOURCE: Gallup Report No. 224, May 1984, p. 29.

---

[9]See Jennifer L. Hochschild, *What's Fair: American Beliefs about Distributive Justice* (Cambridge, Mass.: Harvard University Press, 1981).

Sex was no barrier to elective office when Kay Orr (left) ran against Helen Boosalis for the governorship of Nebraska in 1986.

the implications of these values have pressed more or less intrusively on our collective conscience, as for example, the commitment to individualism recently helped lower barriers of race and sex as obstacles to personal advancement.

These value-laden roots of American political culture have deeply impressed different commentators and political analysts, although—like the blind philosophers describing the elephant—they have differed a little from one another in their hold on the beast.[10] Alexis de Tocqueville was one, for example, who was struck by the Americans' essential commitment to equality and to those conditions that allowed liberty to prevail. Writing fifty years afterwards, another foreign observer, James Bryce, focused on similar manifestations of underlying values: beliefs that individuals have sacred rights and that the people are the legitimate source of governmental power; the idea that written and natural law restrain government and limit its power; distrust of

---

[10]For empirical studies that measure Americans' commitment to underlying political values and their behavioral implications, see James W. Protho and Charles M. Grigg, "Fundamental Principles of Democracy: Bases of Agreement and Disagreement," *Journal of Politics* 22 (1960): 282–86; Herbert McClosky, "Consensus and Ideology in American Politics," *American Political Science Review* 58 (1964): 365–68; Frank R. Westie, "The American Dilemma: An Empirical Test," *American Sociological Review* 30 (1965): 531–32; Donald J. Devine, *The Political Culture of the United States* (Boston: Little, Brown, 1972); and Gabriel A. Almond and Sidney Verba, eds., *The Civic Culture Revisited* (Boston: Little, Brown, 1980).

central political authority; a tendency to trust majorities over minorities; a presupposition—held as a matter of faith, not evidence—that less government was better than more.[11] Samuel P. Huntington, following Gunnar Myrdal in reaching for a comprehensive grasp of the essential ethos (or spirit) of the society as a whole, also spoke of "the American Creed"—characterized by the core political values of liberty, equality, individualism, democracy, and the rule of law under a constitution.[12] In these illustrative ways, different social commentators, writing at different points in time, have mostly ended up with the same conclusions.

There is an amazing degree of agreement about central values in the American political culture. Even more amazing are the many ways our central political values shape public opinion in America. It is as though the values of individualism, liberty, and equality are major arteries through the body politic, each branching off and sustaining vital organs and functions.

■ In his travels through America, Alexis de Tocqueville found a distinctive political culture, one in which Americans insisted on acting as individuals and on reconciling liberty with equality. Since then, the political culture has endured from generation to generation.

POLITICAL SOCIALIZATION

> In my view, one of the primary responsibilities of parenthood is instilling in one's children a sense of moral values. This is not the responsibility of Government, an institution which is clearly unsuited for such a function.
>
> —*Nancy Landon Kassebaum, U.S. Senator (Rep., Kan.)*

The definition of political socialization is the process by which we learn about our political environment and develop psychological reactions to it. The reality is less systematic. In America, this process is surprisingly private, indirect, casual, and incomplete. As a result, the political culture is transmitted imperfectly and political attitudes are freely formed, but poorly rooted.

---

[11]This distillation of James Bryce's *The American Commonwealth* parallels Samuel P. Huntington's treatment in *American Politics: The Promise of Disharmony* (Cambridge, Mass.: Belknap Press, 1981), p. 22.

[12]Huntington, p. 14.

The Nongovernmental Nature of Political Socialization

Political socialization in America is mostly a nongovernmental affair. As a result, it is more likely to occur at the dinner table and in front of the TV than in school or at political rallies. Political socialization, of course, does not have to occur this way and some governments, especially non-democratic ones, are very careful and deliberate in their efforts to instill "correct" points of view. Nevertheless, this society's preference for mostly private agents of political socialization is well-established. Private socializing agents are so dominant because of the relative weakness of alternative role models. Indeed, when America does produce a public role model, it usually turns out to be a philanthropically inclined businessman who launched his public service career on his parents' highly profitable success in the private sector. As a rule, we simply do not esteem public service or hold up for emulation the careers of distinguished public servants.

Our distrust of government has helped produce a political culture that disapproves and thereby constrains direct governmental involvement in political socialization. Government's role, in practice, is indirect—palely reflected in the few public rituals and symbols that parade through our streets, wave from our buildings, and clutter up our money.

The Agents of Socialization

There are many different kinds of agents active in the process of political socialization: the family, the media, religious leaders and organizations, elementary and secondary schools, political interest groups and political parties, candidates for elective office and officeholders, political experiences, and, to a limited extent, governmental institutions.

The Role of the Family. Of all the possible agents of political socialization, the family is far and away the most influential.[13] Moreover, the family's central role in political socialization continues to be strong—in spite of mostly overstated concerns about a possible "generation gap" between the political attitudes of youth and their parents.[14] The family's premier role may be weakening, however. Some, especially Daniel Moynihan, a former Harvard professor and later Democratic senator from New York, fear that the breakup of the traditional two-parent family will result in youth poorly socialized in many ways.[15] So far, however, it is still true that many political attitudes are "inherited," thereby perpetuating the political culture in ways that enhance the stability of the political system.

---

[13]See Richard Dawson, Kenneth Prewitt, and Karen S. Dawson, *Political Socialization* 2nd ed. (Boston: Little, Brown, 1977) and Richard M. Merelman, "The Family and Political Socialization: Toward a Theory of Exchange," *Journal of Politics* 42 (1980): 461–86.

[14]M. Kent Jennings and Richard Niemi, "Continuity and Change in Political Orientations: A Longitudinal Study of Two Generations," *American Political Science Review* 69 (1975): 1316–35.

[15]Daniel Patrick Moynihan, *Family and Nation* (San Diego: Harcourt Brace Jovanovich, 1986).

Berry's World

American political culture produces few public heros. When it does, as in the case of Sally Ride and others, these people serve as public role models, worthy of esteem and emulation.

"My grandson, needless to say, is also pro-Reagan."

Drawing by Mulligan; © 1982 The New Yorker Magazine, Inc.

The family's influence on children's political orientations is indirect, casual, and incomplete. It is indirect, since parents are more likely to instruct their children about mostly private matters, not ones that are obviously political. The data in **Figure 5.2** reveals, for example, that most parents are much quicker to talk to their children about religion and even sex than they are about politics. The parents' role in political socialization is also mostly casual, more likely to occur as the unintended side-effect of a casual reference than as a result of deliberate indoctrination. (You, for example, might have heard your parents say unflattering things about Democrats, for example, but we will bet you spent little time with them discussing President Reagan's 1986 State of the Union Address.) Parental political socialization also is incomplete; American children typically are left relatively free to map out and wander through their own political environments.

In spite of its private, indirect, casual, and incomplete nature, the process of parental socialization effectively transmits some explicitly political orientations. Children usually acquire the political preferences and party loyalties of their parents, for example, although they fail to adopt all their parents' stands on policy questions. This pattern for transmitting partisan identification is shown in **Table 5.4**; most of the parents with an attachment to the Democratic Party (66 percent) also have "Democratic" children and a majority of the parents who are Republicans (51 percent) also produce "Republican" offspring. The pattern holds even for adults who think of themselves as "Independents."

The Role of Children.   In general, the parental socialization of youth produces both enduring and superficial results. From early childhood experiences, children do seem to acquire relatively enduring personal values. But, in the rest of their socialization process, children often connect their values to their political environments in their own, more idiosyncratic ways. In addition, through adolescent socialization, children usually acquire political feelings without

TABLE 5.4   Party identifications are transmitted from parent to child.

Party Identification Of Child	Party Identification Of Parent		
	Democrat	Republican	Independent
Democrat	66%	13%	29%
Republican	7	51	17
Independent	27	36	53
	100%	100%	99%

NOTE: The one total is less than 100% because of rounding in the subtotals.

SOURCE: From *The Political Character of Adolescence: The Influence of Families and Schools* by M. Kent Jennings and Richard C. Niemi. Copyright © 1974 by Princeton University Press. Table 2.2 adapted with permission of Princeton University Press.

FIGURE 5.2
When do children hear about religion, sex, and politics?

Question: In your opinion, at what age should parents begin to talk to children about politics? When the children are 3, 6, 11, 15, 18 years old or more—or shouldn't parents talk about politics at all? At what age should parents begin to give children sex education? At 3, 6, 11, 15, 18 years old or more —or shouldn't parents give them sex education at all? And how about a religious education? Should children be 3, 6, 11, 15, 18 years old or more—or shouldn't parents give them a religious education at all?

Talk to children about politics at age:

Eighteen or more 5%
Six years 18%
Fifteen years 25%
Eleven years 40%

Begin to give children sex education at age:

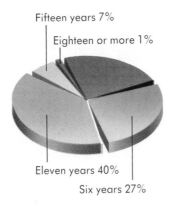

Fifteen years 7%
Eighteen or more 1%
Eleven years 40%
Six years 27%

Should give children a religious education at age:

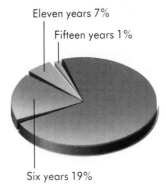

Eleven years 7%
Fifteen years 1%
Six years 19%

SOURCE: Survey by CBS News/*New York Times*, June 18–22, 1980. From *Public Opinion*, August/September 1980.

supporting facts, although those are gradually added afterwards. But this tendency to absorb parental values and attitudes does not mean that children are soft clay into which parents impress their own political orientations. While children do tend to mimic parental opinions on emotionally charged issues like school integration and prayer in public schools, children generally go their own way on most political issues, ranging from positions on civil liberties to personal levels of trust in governmental leaders and confidence in their own ability to exercise political influence.[16] In general, as the work of Robert Coles, a Harvard child psychiatrist, suggests, children play a very active role in the development of their own political and moral consciousness.[17]

The Roles of Religious Leaders and Schools.   Religious spokespersons and organizations, from Jesse Jackson and his Rainbow Coalition of racial minorities to Jerry Falwell and his Moral Majority of evangelical Christians also are

---

[16]M. Kent Jennings and Richard G. Niemi, *The Political Character of Adolescence* (Princeton, NJ: Princeton University Press, 1974).

[17]Robert Coles, *The Political Life of Children* (Boston: The Atlantic Monthly Press, 1986).

Jerry Falwell, leader of the Moral Majority.

increasingly active. Local elementary and secondary schools, the one well-accepted form of governmental involvement, too play a significant role. Although, as you probably know, high school civics courses have little effect on the acquisition of political attitudes. As an exception to this general rule, black students do seem to get more out of their high school civics course than do whites, according to Kenneth P. Langton and M. Kent Jennings.[18] Schools also provide significant opportunities for citizen training. As Gabriel Almond and Sidney Verba observed, for example, those who participate in school affairs as students are more likely to go on to participate in public affairs as citizens.[19]

The Role of Political Agents: The Media, Interest Groups, Political Parties, and Government Itself.

Post-adolescent political socialization is largely due to the media, interest groups, political parties, and, to a limited extent, governmental institutions. These are important socialization agents because they are national in scope and therefore tend to produce more widely shared political orientations. The modern mass media in particular (dealt with in detail in chapter 7) tend to homogenize political orientations. National news services, for example, focus the nation's political attention, as local newspapers all over the country increasingly practice "rip and paste journalism"—all reproducing nationally the same copy directly off their wire service. In spite of these nationalizing influences, however, distinctly regional and state subcultures persist.[20]

Interest groups also get into the act or, specifically, into editorial columns nationwide, by sending out "editorial memoranda" which lazy or harried editors may reprint as their own positions. Political parties too play a role, although an increasingly less important one, as their functions are taken over by the media, interest groups, and the personal organizations that form around candidates for elective office and officeholders. (These and other activities of political interest groups and political parties are discussed in chapter 6.) In addition, as we will see in chapters 11 through 14, governmental institutions also attempt to mold the public's expectations and behaviors, although the effort has to be subtle and it easily can backfire. Some governmental institutions have become quite skilled at it, however, as we will see in the presidency chapter's discussion of the Great White Publicity Machine. Finally, and often in spite of attempts to orchestrate public opinion, events intrude and have their own impacts on people's political orientations. These often are intense, sometimes catastrophic events, such as the exposure of official wrongdoing during the Watergate era or the societal trauma that accompanied school integration in Boston.[21]

---

[18]Kenneth P. Langton and M. Kent Jennings, "Political Socialization and the High School Civics Curriculum in the United States," *American Political Science Review* 62 (1968): 852–67.

[19]Almond and Verba, *Civic Culture*.

[20]See, for example, Daniel J. Elazar, *American Federalism: A View from the States* (New York: Thomas Y. Crowell, 1966). Also see Ira Sharkansky, "The Utility of Elazar's Political Culture: A Research Note," *Polity* 2 (1969): 66–83.

[21]See J. Anthony Lucas, *Common Ground* (New York: Alfred A. Knopf, 1985).

■ In his travels throughout America, Tocqueville was struck by the extent to which Americans did things for themselves, rather than wait for government to get involved. Although this is less true in many areas of contemporary life, it is still characteristic of the process by which Americans develop their psychological reactions to governmental institutions, policies, and politics.

The mostly private, indirect, casual, and incomplete process of political socialization often leaves Americans preoccupied with largely private concerns, at the expense of a deep regard for common, public problems. In addition, although they share underlying values, their reliance on many different socialization agents produces relatively pluralistic public opinions about specific governmental actions, policies, and politicians.

PUBLIC OPINION

> Do not do unto others as you would they
> should do unto you. Their tastes may not be
> the same.
> —*George Bernard Shaw*, Maxims
> for Revolutionaries

Because of a tendency to view things in terms of their personal relevance, Americans in general are more preoccupied with their private concerns than with society's common problems. In addition, because of the diverse conditions in which Americans find themselves and because of their different reactions to those conditions, public opinion tends to be pluralistic, split in many different directions. The private and pluralistic nature of public opinion exert enormous power over government, mostly by limiting what it may properly, or easily, do.

The Private Preoccupations of Americans

The American political culture, with its emphasis on individualism, liberty, and equality of opportunity makes us preoccupied with our private selves, secure in our optimism that human development is best realized while isolated from others and insulated from the state. The preoccupation has deep historical roots.

Private Concerns. Writing in Number 51 of the *Federalist Papers*, James Madison proclaimed: "Let the private interest of every individual be a sentinel over the public rights." The preoccupation, Tocqueville thought, was an unintended by-product of freedom. Since it liberated Americans from social roles and social obligations, freedom tended "to isolate them from one another, to concentrate each man's attention upon himself." The isolation also enjoys

"Today's topic is 'public awareness.'"

constitutional protection. As Supreme Court Justice Louis D. Brandeis put it: "The makers of the Constitution sought to protect Americans in their beliefs, their emotions, and their sensations. They conferred, as against the government, the right to be let alone . . . the most comprehensive of rights, and the right most valued by civilized man."[22] The preoccupation with private concerns has persisted throughout American history, as Andrew Hacker has pointed out: "America throws each of us on our own; we have always been less a nation than a congeries of individuals in continual competition."[23] The preoccupation endures and is clearly reflected in what Americans seem to care most about.

What Americans Really Care About. The preoccupation with private concerns is revealed by what Americans care about and know about. In general, Americans act as though they prefer private to public pleasures; for example, we spend more money on our personal stereos than we do on municipal symphonies, more on caring for our front lawns than on our cities' parks, more on hot tubs in our suburban back yards than on public pools in central cities. Indeed, some contemporary sociologists think Americans are retreating into increasingly private spheres of life, into modern manors, with the drawbridge up and the electronic alarm on.[24]

The evidence is more than impressionistic or speculative, however. Public opinion surveys, for example, document well the mostly private nature of American public opinion, as we show in the **Vantage Point**: Americans Mostly Care About Private Pleasures. In addition, most Americans are remarkably ignorant of public affairs, as the data in **Table 5.5** reveals. We also have anecdotal evidence; ask the person next to you the name of his or her senator in the state legislature. The conclusion is inescapable. For whatever reason, the American level of specific knowledge or concern about government is much to be modest about.

The private, apolitical quality of American public opinion also goes along with, and helps perpetuate, opposition to government's expanded role in both domestic and foreign affairs. We can illustrate and document this in various ways. While we value the fruits of our freedoms, we think poorly of the government that makes them possible. One American foreign correspondent, on returning to this country, was struck by this discrepancy: "While 62 percent of the public said that what made them proudest about this country was one or more of its freedoms, the theory of America was one thing and its government was another. When asked what they liked least, 16 percent mentioned government; 13 percent cited America's role in the world."[25] Moreover, Americans, once more trusting of government's capacity to do good in the wake of world-

---

[22]Quoted in *The New York Times*, 7 December 1982.

[23]Andrew Hacker, "Alexis de Tocqueville Was Here," *New York Times Book Review*, 13 June 1982, 7.

[24]See Richard Sennett, *The Fall of Public Man* (New York: Knopf, 1977).

[25]R. W. Apple, Jr., "New Stirrings of Patriotism," *The New York Times Magazine*, 11 December 1983, 47.

AMERICANS MOSTLY CARE ABOUT PRIVATE PLEASURES

It is hard to know what Americans really care about, and it is especially hard if you simply ask people directly. In one imaginative, indirect attempt, the Roper polling organization gave people a list of things that they expected people to daydream about. They asked them: Most people spend at least a small part of their waking hours daydreaming and thinking about different things. Some of those daydreams may be complete flights of fancy, others just simple, like a hungry person thinking about lunchtime. Here's a list of some things people might be expected to daydream about from time to time. Could you look it over and call off the things, if any, that you ever daydream or think about? Their responses, reported below, suggest that Americans are more concerned with private than public pleasures.

The Activity People Daydreamed About	Percent Identifying the Activity as Something They Daydreamed About (People could give as many daydreams as they wished.)
Traveling to different places around the world	53%
What your future life will be like	42
Being rich	41
Being smarter—understanding things better	41
Things that happened in the past	37
Having a better job	32
Having someone back in your life who was important to you in the past	30
Living in a different area in the world	28
Living in some past time	26
Living a completely different life than you do	24
Knowing a lot of different people that you don't know now	21
Being a great artist, musician or writer	20
Being famous	18
Becoming friends with a person or persons whom you admire but don't know	18
Being a great athlete	16
Being beautiful or handsome	13
Having great power and influence	12
Getting even with someone who has wronged you	12
Having a romance with a handsome or beautiful star	11
Being involved somehow with the media, TV, movies	10
Being elected to political office	6

SOURCE: Survey by the Roper Organization (Roper Report 79-3), February 10-24, 1979. Reported in *Public Opinion*, June/July 1979, p. 40.

TABLE 5.5 Many Americans are not well-informed about government.

Although Americans are better informed on some matters than others, large segments of the public are ignorant about some of the simplest aspects of politics and government. When asked factual questions, in different surveys at different points in time, the following percentages of the adults who were surveyed gave the incorrect answer:

Percentage Responding Incorrectly	Item
6%	Know the president's term is four years
11%	Can name governor of their home state
21%	Can name the current vice-president
30%	Can name their mayor
37%	Know China to be Communist
48%	Know that there are two U.S. senators from their state
62%	Know Russia is not a NATO member
66%	Can name the current secretary of state
70%	Know term of U.S. House member is two years
77%	Know which nations are involved in SALT

SOURCE: American Institute of Public Opinion (Gallup); Center for Political Studies; Lou Harris and Associates; National Opinion Research Center; CBS/NYT.

wide economic depression and military threat, now increasingly dislike big government, or at least say they do. This shift has been plotted from surveys conducted by Louis Harris, for example. **Figure 5.3** shows the turn-around in the percentages of respondents who *agree* with the statement, "The best government is the government that governs least."[26] This data, along with the other consequences of our preoccupation with private concerns, indicate the extent to which American public opinion continues to affirm our revolutionary legacy; government, we feel, is more enemy than savior.

The Pluralistic Quality of Public Opinion

Our political culture is open and dynamic, because of our lack of a feudal tradition, ongoing immigration, the relative dominance of the nuclear family and other private socializing agents, and our insistence on maintaining an autonomous sphere of action within which private individuals are free to judge the personal relevance of public policy. As a result, our public opinion is distinctively pluralistic.

---

[26]*Public Opinion*, (December/January) 1982, p. 36.

FIGURE 5.3
American public opinion is increasingly opposed to big government.

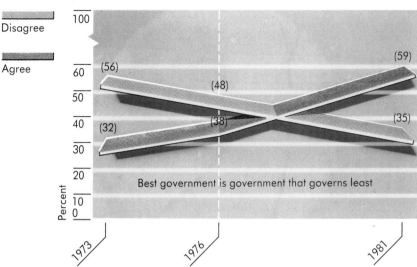

Question: Let me read you some statements some people have made about the way different levels of government should operate in this country. For each, tell me if you tend to agree or disagree? . . . The best government is the government that governs least.

SOURCE: Surveys by Louis Harris and Associates, latest that of February 19–22, 1981. From *Public Opinion*, December/January 1982, p. 36.

Pluralistic Public Opinion. To picture what it means to say that public opinion is pluralistic, think of society as a whole as though it were a huge orange. With a big knife, cleave it in two. Let that cleavage stand for one dimension, say sex, splitting the society into its male and female halves. Put the orange back together and cleave it again. Let this cleavage represent a ideological dimension, say the extent to which people favor governmental solutions to societal problems. Put the orange back together and visualize the way these two dimensions cut through our model of society and compare your image with the drawing in **Figure 5.4**. Note that the lines of cleavage are not identical; for example, it is *not* the case that all men are conservative and all women liberal. If that *were* true, that peculiar condition would represent a case of overlapping cleavage. Instead, these are **crosscutting cleavages**, cultural divisions that intersect, rather than overlap. This is generally true of public opinion in America; there are many cleavages and they tend to be crosscutting, scattering opinions in many different ways.

Crosscutting cleavages split public opinion in many ways, along the lines of wealth, religion, region, occupation, party affiliation, and willingness to support governmental spending on social programs, for example. The lines of cleavage are not perfectly crosscutting, however. For example, it is true that most blue collar workers are not wealthy and tend to vote Democratic. But it is not true that most blue collar workers are also southern Baptists. Thus, although there are many relationships between various demographic characteristics and politi-

FIGURE 5.4

American society is pluralistic, like a sphere with crosscutting—not overlapping—cleavages. When social cleavages crosscut, as they do here, it is *not* the case that all Republicans are white, male, and rich and it is *not* the case that all Democrats are black, female, and poor, for example.

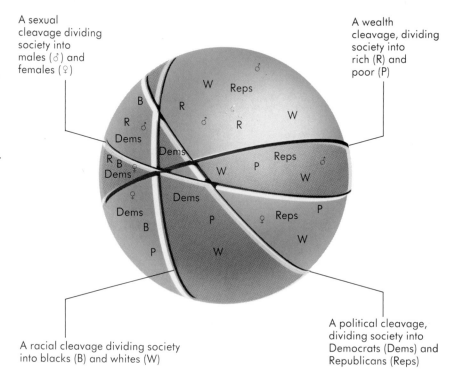

A sexual cleavage dividing society into males (♂) and females (♀)

A wealth cleavage, dividing society into rich (R) and poor (P)

A racial cleavage dividing society into blacks (B) and whites (W)

A political cleavage, dividing society into Democrats (Dems) and Republicans (Reps)

cal orientations, those relationships are not always strong and never are perfect. As a result, those who do fall on the same side of a line of cleavage have that in common, but they also differ from each other in many ways and often disagree with one another on what they believe to be government's proper role. Catholics, for example, have their faith in common, but wear both white and blue collars to work and do not all reach for the same lever in the voting booth.

Crosscutting, as opposed to overlapping, cleavages also seem to have become increasingly prominent in the past fifty years. When Franklin Delano Roosevelt first advanced the cause of social welfare and the corresponding social-welfare role of government, especially national government, social and political divisions were more deep and potentially more disruptive than is true today. In 1936–1937, occupational classes in particular split badly in their opinions about government's proper role. Most unskilled workers, for example, favored government ownership of the banks, governmental takeover of industry during war time, and legal limitations on the size of personal inheritances, whereas majorities of skilled and managerial workers were opposed to these views of an expanded federal governmental role.[27] By the 1980s, however, the expanded social welfare functions of government had won broad public accept-

[27]Evertt Carll Ladd, Jr. and Seymour Martin Lipset," Public Opinion and Public Policy," in Peter Duignan and Alvin Rabushka, eds., *The United States in the 1980s* (Stanford, Calif.: The Hoover Institution on War, Revolution and Peace, 1980), p. 49–84.

ance, especially as many of the benefits originally targeted to the poor spilled over into the laps of the middle class. Some even saw President Reagan as one who finally legitimized the basic commitments of the welfare state, since he only slowed down, and did not reverse, the rate of growth in most social welfare expenditures.[28]

The Absence of Political Ideology.   The pluralistic quality of American public opinion explains the absence of **political ideology**, a well-organized and coherent set of political attitudes and opinions about government's proper role. In a pluralistic society, public opinion is dispersed along many dimensions, not clumped about any one or two. American public opinion is exceptional in this regard; it is not cleaved either by a commitment to socioeconomic class or to coherent and dogmatically held political ideologies—unlike many Western democracies. Picture, for example, a single left-right dimension that we might use to characterize the nature and distribution of public opinion in America (or simply look at **Figure 5.5**).[29] This ideological continuum represents all the policy positions that people could take, between the extreme left "liberal" position that favors governmental intervention into all aspects of society to the extreme right "conservative" position that favors very little, if any, governmental intervention. But, when we try to sprinkle them along this continuum, few Americans stick on any of these points, since most of the public does not think of itself in these ideological terms and even profess ignorance of what the terms liberal and conservative mean. In some studies, for example, less than 12 percent of the American electorate are able to think in ideologically sophisticated terms, although there is some evidence that Americans are increasingly able to structure their political opinions in more coherent ways.[30] In the absence of ideological coherence, public opinion in American also is disorganized.

A disorganized public opinion is hard to follow—or lead. Indeed, policy makers get inconsistent rather than clear-cut signals from the American public.

---

[28]Ben J. Wattenberg, "The New Movement: How Ronald Reagan Ratified LBJ's Great Society, and Moved on to Other Important Items," *Public Opinion*, December/January (1982), p. 2ff.

[29]Figure 5.5. A Hypothetical Continuum of Liberal and Conservative Political Ideology.

[30]See, for example, Angus Campbell *et al.*, *The American Voter* (New York: Wiley, 1960). More current results, showing more coherence in political opinions, are found in David O. Sears *et al.*, "Self-Interest vs. Symbolic Politics in Policy Attitudes and Voting," *American Political Science Review* 74 (1980): 670–84. These two studies only skim the surface of a boiling debate.

FIGURE 5.5
A Hypothetical Continuum of Liberal and Conservative Political Ideology

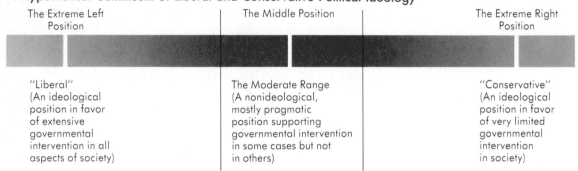

The Extreme Left Position	The Middle Position	The Extreme Right Position
"Liberal" (An ideological position in favor of extensive governmental intervention in all aspects of society)	The Moderate Range (A nonideological, mostly pragmatic position supporting governmental intervention in some cases but not in others)	"Conservative" (An ideological position in favor of very limited governmental intervention in society)

Americans, for example, often seem as though they want more done *for* them but they simultaneously do not want government to do more *to* them. In this regard, they often seem to want the benefits of an expanded governmental role in society, without the personal costs and constraints that would require. The inconsistencies of our disorganized public opinion fall out of various surveys. Americans, for example, dislike big government because of the threat it poses to a free people and simultaneously want it to do more because people are in need! This particular inconsistency has been shown in many public opinion surveys. The Harris Survey, for example, recently found that 53 percent of Americans feel that "big government is the biggest threat to the well-being of the country," while, simultaneously, 72 percent believe that "the federal government has a deep responsibility for seeing to it that the poor are taken care of, that no one goes hungry, and that every person achieves at least a minimum standard of living."[31]

■ Public opinion, as Tocqueville thought, is a very powerful force in the American democracy, one that shapes government's proper role in many ways. American public opinion—its private and pluralistic qualities—encourages people to favor nongovernmental solutions to the resource allocation problems we discussed in the Prologue. These qualities reinforce the desire to retain a personal sphere of action within which individuals are autonomous and into which government cannot intrude if it is to maintain the legitimacy we saw it. striving for in chapter 1. They reinforce commitments to maintaining liberty and to preserving an appropriate role for state and local governments, the sorts of commitments explored in chapters 2 and 3. Public opinion flourishes when people's civil liberties and civil rights enjoy the protections described in chapter 4. Public opinion increases the importance of interest groups and political parties as agencies that can both stimulate and express common sentiments, as we will see in chapter 6. Its private and pluralistic qualities,

---

[31]Quoted in *The Plain Dealer*, 23 March 1981.

however, leave public opinion quite susceptible to manipulation by politicians and the press, as chapter 7 suggests. It also means that most people will not rally to public causes; they must be rallied through an active process of agenda building of the sort described in chapter 9. These qualities also create potential problems for policy makers. In all of the major institutions of national government, as we see in chapters 11 through 14, governmental officials who wish to achieve ambitious goals must mobilize public opinion and convert it into influence over policy making.

In addition to these effects of public opinion, the political culture as a whole has its own effects on the determination of what government will do.

THE IMPACT OF POLITICAL CULTURE AND PUBLIC OPINION

> Public opinion stands out in the United States as the great source of power, the master of servants who tremble before it.
> —*James Bryce,* The American Commonwealth

The political culture and expressed public opinion have two major effects on the American political system: (1) they surround governmental institutions with expectations that both constrain and encourage certain tendencies and (2) they contribute to the stability of the system.

Expectations about Government's Proper Role

The political culture and expressed public opinions form a velvet noose around the neck of government. The political culture helps define the territory in which governmental involvement is appropriate; in this way, political culture sets limits or outer bounds on government's possible roles.[32] The noose also tugs gently at government, steering it in some policy directions rather than others; in this way, public opinion, the explicit expression of the underlying political culture, helps shape the specifics of public policy.[33] These effects are well illustrated in recent political history.

---

[32]See V. O. Key, Jr., *Public Opinion and American Democracy* (New York: Knopf, 1961); and Robert Weissberg, *Public Opinion and Popular Government* (Englewood Cliffs, NJ: Prentice-Hall, 1976).

[33]Path-breaking studies include Warren E. Miller and Donald E. Stokes, "Constituency Influence in Congress," in Angus Campbell *et al.*, eds., *Elections and the Political Order* (New York: John Wiley and Sons, 1966), pp. 351–73; Alan D. Monroe, "Consistency between Public Preferences and National Policy Decisions," *American Politics Quarterly* 7 (1979): 3–19; and Benjamin I. Page and Robert Y. Shapiro, "Effects of Public Opinion on Policy," *American Political Science Review* 77 (1983): 175–90.

The political culture is a source of expectations, demands, and supports that surround government. English poet Alexander Pope wrote, "Blessed is he who expects nothing, for he shall never be disappointed." By Pope's standard, most members of the American public would be in trouble because they have many expectations of what they want from government, they are demanding of those who are supposed to deliver it, and they are unforgiving of those who fail to do so.

During the 1930s, crushing economic depression at home and military aggression abroad helped transform our political expectations. Since then, no national political figure has maintained prominence without agreeing, at least tacitly, that government does have some basic responsibilities to maintain prosperity and deter aggression. In addition, increased public vigilance and involvement, exercised indirectly through the electoral process and more directly through special interest groups, have exerted what appears to be increasingly great influence over public policy. The Vietnam War, for example, occasioned an unprecedented involvement of the public in war making. Today, many liberals continue to demand that government try to cure all social ills, while many conservatives would reduce government's social welfare obligations.

Our political expectations bias policy making in favor of some values over others. The bias has a purpose: to protect personal liberties, those most central and enduring American political values. Accordingly, the culture is biased in favor of private, personal concerns versus public, societal ones; liberty versus equality; rights versus obligations. In general, we favor the Hamiltonian values of commerce over the Jeffersonian ones of agriculture, production over conservation, and competitive individualism over cooperative communalism. Since they bind a government that is concerned with its legitimacy and policy makers who are concerned with their re-electibility, these biases shunt policy initiatives and modifications in directions that reflect dominant values.

The private and pluralistic qualities of American public opinion constrain government's possible role in society. In addition to its preference for private solutions to social problems, public opinion distrusts public power and therefore, guards against the potential for abuse by fragmenting power and dispersing it throughout a decentralized federal system. The result has amazingly large consequences for policy making since it creates many opportunities for private persons and groups to attempt to exercise influence over the making of public policy. That, in turn, ensures that the policy-making process will be long, slow, gorged with opportunities for delay and obstruction, and unlikely to produce abrupt or radical change.

The political culture and the private and pluralistic qualities of public opinion weaken commitments to national purposes and detract from national unity. Our discussion of American political culture spun it around, examining its different aspects like the facets of a diamond. But do not carry the analogy too far; diamonds have a holistic quality to them, something that is more than the sum of individual carbon molecules. American political culture, however, is more fragmented. Not compressed by integrative pressures, its parts—and its peoples—are isolated from one another. Tocqueville saw this fragmentation and traced it to the American insistence on self-interest as the principle that should guide the affairs of individuals and that, unavoidably, makes it very difficult for this society to find a common purpose behind which all might unite. For this reason, Tocqueville feared that Americans could not be expected to act with a common unifying sense of national purpose and that America, therefore, might not realize her greatness as a nation.

Without going that far, we think it reasonable to conclude that the American political culture does deflect attention toward personal and away from common social concerns and to that extent, impairs the growth of a sense of national unity. As a result, it is politically difficult, except in times of national emergency, to mobilize public opinion behind broad national purposes—such as ending poverty, advancing civil rights, revitalizing industrial productivity, and maintaining military preparedness.

Contributions to System Stability

The political culture and expressed public opinions contribute in many ways to the stability of the political system. In some ways, however, underlying divisions in the culture threaten future disruptions.

Sources of Stability. The dominance of crosscutting cleavages makes the political culture a source of stability for the system as a whole. To understand why, consider what could happen if cleavages were not crosscutting, but overlapping. Imagine that all important cleavages *did* overlap. For example, imagine a society in which rich whites lived in the North and pushed for increased defense spending while poor blacks lived in the South where they worked to advance social welfare expenditures. What sort of a society do you think this would be? Would it resemble more a bunch of puppies or two packs of wolves? You can intuit the answer; the political significance of crosscutting cleavages is that they moderate social conflict and thereby, augment the stability of the prevailing system of government.

Sources of Instability. There are some disturbing exceptions to the general rule of crosscutting cleavages. To some extent, and increasingly some fear, cultural cleavages do overlap, threatening to divide the public into warring camps, each characterized by clashing constellations of opposing opinions. In particular, moving into the 1980s, cleavages coalesced along three major dimensions: sex, religion, and race.

One cleavage threatens a split between the sexes, with women showing signs of coalescing on a range of public issues including support for the Democratic party, opposition to increased defense spending, support for a freeze in levels of nuclear armaments, support for civil rights and affirmative action programs for women and racial minorities, and support for increased levels of governmental spending on social welfare programs. This particular set of overlapping cleavages, and the fear that it might deepen, caused great political concern during President Reagan's first years in office, as Republicans became increasingly worried that their inability to bridge this "gender gap" would cost them huge numbers of votes. Even among Republicans, women

THE POLSBY—WILDAVSKY DIALOGUE
CONTINUED . . .

AUTHOR: How would you characterize the American political culture?

WILDAVSKY: I don't think it's useful to characterize Americans as having a single political culture. My view is that you call the Establishment and nobody's ever home. You see it in the large organizations that have to have views on more than a few issues—trade unions, political parties, religious orders, the Executive Branch. These organizations are supposed to help integrate society by reconciling diverging viewpoints, but they are more divided, weaker, than they have been.

It used to be more true that there was a source of integration and compromise in our society—namely, a view that there is some hierarchy, a division of authority into different positions, such that all are worthy in their proper spheres and the separate parts sacrifice for the common good of society. This force of hierarchy is much weaker today.

In its place, there is more of a market-oriented or self-regulatory culture in which people, not so much reject it, but want to do without authority. For authority, they want to substitute bilateral bargaining agreements among consenting adults.

POLSBY: I think there are three categories; the market orientation and this hierarchial orientation which is more traditional. The hierarchial orientation emphasizes ascriptive norms, social rules of behavior based on such things as birth and deference.

WILDAVSKY: The third culture then is egalitarian or sectarian. These are people who are opposed to the ascriptiveness of hierarchies and they're opposed to the inequalities of the market. Those oriented toward egalitarianism want to diminish as many distinctions among people as possible, between whites and blacks, men and women, parents and children, old and young. But there is a conflict. Because they dislike and distrust hierarchial divisions of authority, egalitarians want group decisions arrived at without coercion, by virtually unanimous consent. But they advocate that the central government take on more and more activities of a basically redistributive nature. They advocate a larger, more redistributive government but they don't want to give it the kind of authority and respect that it would require.

POLSBY: I think the answer to the overall question is that we have a mixed culture in which there are at least these three forces and these forces challenge one another.

WILDAVSKY: America, like every other place, is a compound of different cultures. But what is distinctive about America is the belief that equality and liberty are compatible. Those who are market-oriented believe in equality of opportunity (so people can be different and gather unequal rewards) and those who believe in equality of condition (so as to diminish differences among people) have sometimes in American history come together under the extraordinary view that, if market competition were allowed to operate unfettered, then you would have an approximation of equality of condition.

> If you wanted to characterize political cultures globally as being either boundary maintainers or boundary erasers, I think the United States is a boundary eraser.
> —Polsby

POLSBY: I think that's right. If you wanted to characterize political cultures globally as being either boundary maintainers or boundary erasers, I think the United States is a boundary eraser. In the United States, the dominant values and ideologies are those which argue that differences among people differently situated ought to be lessened. That creates very powerful norms. For example, you can see it in something as simple as whether children are welcome in restaurants. You go to many places in Europe and it is still the case that they do not want children in restaurants. In the United States, to even say such a thing is regarded as against our fundamental mores. This phenomenon—that boundaries should be lessened—is actually a phenomenon more characteristic of nomadic than settled societies. I think it exists in the United States in part because we are a nation of immigrants. Because the great, central experience of our political culture has been taking in large numbers of people and making Americans out of them.

were much less likely to support President Reagan and his policies than were men; in one survey in the summer of 1983, for example, Republican women and men split 61 percent to 82 percent on whether Reagan should be the party's nominee in 1984 and 61 percent to 81 percent on whether Reagan had done a sufficiently good job of curbing inflation.[34] Reaganites were right to worry about the distance to the other side; Kathy Wilson, a Republican and head of the National Women's Political Caucus, had a remedy for the gender gap in 1983: "There is one thing President Reagan can do to help women and clean up his name with us . . . step down."[35]

Religion, and in particular a revival of religious fundamentalism, seem to some a second and potentially more serious cleavage. Moving out of the 1970s and into the 1980s, some Americans, sensing a weakening of societal support for the traditional American values of country, community, and family, coalesced in an effort to redirect the course of government. Although the items on their political agenda varied somewhat over time, the thrust of the religiously fundamental in politics was to decrease governmental involvement in what they viewed as "private" matters, including, for example, the decisions of school officials to allow prayer in public schools, and the hiring decisions of businesspersons. They had some statistical support; according to a survey conducted in 1981 by the firm of Yankelovich, Skelly and White, 70 percent of those polled believed that "government has become far too involved in areas of people's lives," 71 percent believed that "the Supreme Court and Congress have gone too far in keeping religious and moral values out of our lives," and 74 percent favored a constitutional amendment that would permit prayer in public schools.[36] Even in this instance, however, the overlapping cleavage around religious fundamentalism did not produce a coherent result.

Religious fundamentalism also was associated with an appeal for more governmental intervention—for example, in parental decisions about the provision of medical care to children born with severe birth defects. But budgetary and electoral pressures made more successful claims on the attention of the Reagan Administration, as the "social agenda" kept slipping off the President's desk through most of his first term. Nevertheless, what is interesting is the extent to which religious fundamentalism served as a rallying cry for previously more disorganized political opinions.

Race remains the deepest and most troubling cleavage—as it has throughout American history. (For the extent of the cleavage, see the **Vantage Point**: Differences of Opinion Between Blacks and Whites.) Tocqueville feared the consequences of slavery for the future of American democracy. Quoting his conversations, former President John Quincy Adams told him slavery ". . . is the root of almost all the troubles for the present and the future."[37] What keeps the racial cleavage so threatening is the extent to which this fault line coincides with those other cleavages that shape political opinions and behav-

---

[34]Quoted in *The New York Times*, 10 July 1983.

[35]Quoted in *The New York Times*, 10 July 1983.

[36]Quoted in *Time*, 1 June 1981, 12–13.

[37]Quoted in Richard Reeves, *American Journey: Traveling With Tocqueville in Search of "Democracy in America"* (New York: Simon and Schuster, 1982), p. 222.

VANTAGE POINT

DIFFERENCES OF OPINION BETWEEN BLACKS AND WHITES

*T*hroughout recent years, various polls have found many significant differences between the opinions of blacks and whites on a variety of public issues. Here are some of the more glaring differences, along with the year of the poll and the percent of blacks and whites who took the indicated position on the issue.

Opinion	Blacks	Whites
1. Favored pardon for Vietnam draft evaders and deserters (1977)	51%	30%
2. Favored use of the death penalty (1978)	46	72
3. Favored taking over oil companies to solve the energy problem (1979)	42	19
4. Believed federal policies of the 1960s made things better (1980)	51	28
5. Believed unemployment to be more important than inflation (1980)	60	37
6. Favored busing for school integration (1981)	41	13
7. Thought federal level of government most efficient (1981)	41	18
8. Felt food stamp spending should be reduced (1981)	17	55
9. Approved President Reagan's handling of his job (1981)	13	66

SOURCE: *The New York Times*, August 28, 1981.

ior—education, occupation, income, trust in government, confidence in the future, commitment to a sense of doing one's civic duty. When these lines of cleavage overlap, the greater is the reality of a permanent "underclass" of poor blacks who expect little from the established political system and who feel they owe it less than little political support in return. Moreover, in a society dedicated to human progress and sustained by beliefs in the American Dream and the magic of the marketplace, the persistence of apparently intractable problems only can erode the legitimacy of a governmental system that, as far as the needs of one segment of its people is concerned, seems resigned to permanent failure.

■ Tocqueville and Bryce may have exaggerated the influence of public opinion on the actions of governmental officials, policy makers, and politicians. The actual influence is probably less than they imagined, since Americans are so preoccupied with private concerns and since their opinions about public affairs are both superficial and disorganized. At a deeper level, however, the political culture does chart government's course by legitimizing certain conceptions of its proper role.

SUMMARY

In this chapter we sought to understand what Americans care about and what difference it makes for governmental institutions, policies, and politics. The effort took us back to Alexis de Tocqueville's search for insight on the relationship between political culture and democracy.

America's political culture consists of enduring, shared beliefs about government and about what it should—and should not—do. This culture emphasizes the importance of personal values, what we call the American triumvirate of values: individualism, liberty, and equality.

The political culture is transmitted by a process of political socialization. The agents of this socialization process are mostly private ones, especially other family members, although other more impersonal ones, especially the mass media, play an important role.

For the most part, Americans are more preoccupied with their private concerns than with society's common problems. In addition, since Americans live under many different conditions, public opinion tends to be pluralistic, scattered along many different dimensions.

Our political culture, its dominant values, and our private and pluralistic public opinion heavily influence governmental officials, the policies they make, and the political games they can play effectively.

Key Terms

political values	individualism
political culture	liberty
political socialization	equality
public opinion	crosscutting cleavages
political attitudes	political ideology
personal values	

Review and Reflection

1. Must the people believe certain things for democracy to endure? What would these be?

2. Define political culture.

3. After arriving in Paris for your spring break, you are accosted by a French snob: "Americans have no culture, political or otherwise." Defend yourself.

4. Identify and review the relevance of the American triumvirate of values.

5. Define political socialization.

6. How can it be true that Americans have common political values and wildly different political opinions?

7. Define public opinion.

8. What difference does it make that Americans are preoccupied with private concerns?

9. What difference does it make that American public opinion is pluralistic?

10. To what extent do you think that public opinion should determine government's role?

Supplemental Readings

It is very hard to understand what political culture is, the way it is transmitted, and the ways its expression influences governmental institutions, policies, and politics.

Reeves, for example, performs a useful service in updating Tocqueville. *Hagstrom* and *Pierce* have produced profiles of each state's distinctive political culture. The transmittal of political culture is demystified through the works of *Dawson, Easton, Dennis, Jennings,* and *Niemi*. The state of public opinion is discussed by *Erikson, et. al.* and by *Miller* and *Prewitt*. The effects of public opinion are detailed by *Welch*. Finally, if only for its value as a contrast, see *Bellamy*.

Bellamy, Edward. *Looking Backward, 2000–1887*. New York: Bantam Books, 1983.

Dawson, Richard, Kenneth Prewitt, and Karen Dawson. *Political Socialization*. 2nd ed. Boston: Little, Brown, 1977.

Easton, David, and Jack Dennis. *Children in the Political System*. New York: McGraw-Hill, 1969.

Erikson, Robert S., Norman G. Luttbeg, and Kent L. Tedin. *American Public Opinion: Its Origins, Content, and Impact*. 2nd ed. New York: John Wiley, 1980.

Greenstein, Fred I. *Children and Politics*. New Haven, Conn.: Yale University Press, 1965.

Hagstrom, Jerry, and Neal R. Peirce. *The Book of America: Inside 50 States Today*. New York: Warner Books, 1984.

Jennings, M. Kent, and Richard Niemi. *The Political Character of Adolescence: The Influence of Family and Schools*. Princeton, New Jersey: Princeton University Press, 1974.

Miller, Jon D., and Kenneth Prewitt. *The American People and Science Policy: The Role of Public Attitudes in the Policy Process*. New York: Pergamon, 1982.

Reeves, Richard. *American Journey: Traveling with Tocqueville in Search of "Democracy in America"*. New York: Simon and Schuster, 1982.

Welch, Susan. "The Impact of Urban Riots on Urban Expenditures," *American Journal of Political Science* 19 (1975): 741–60.

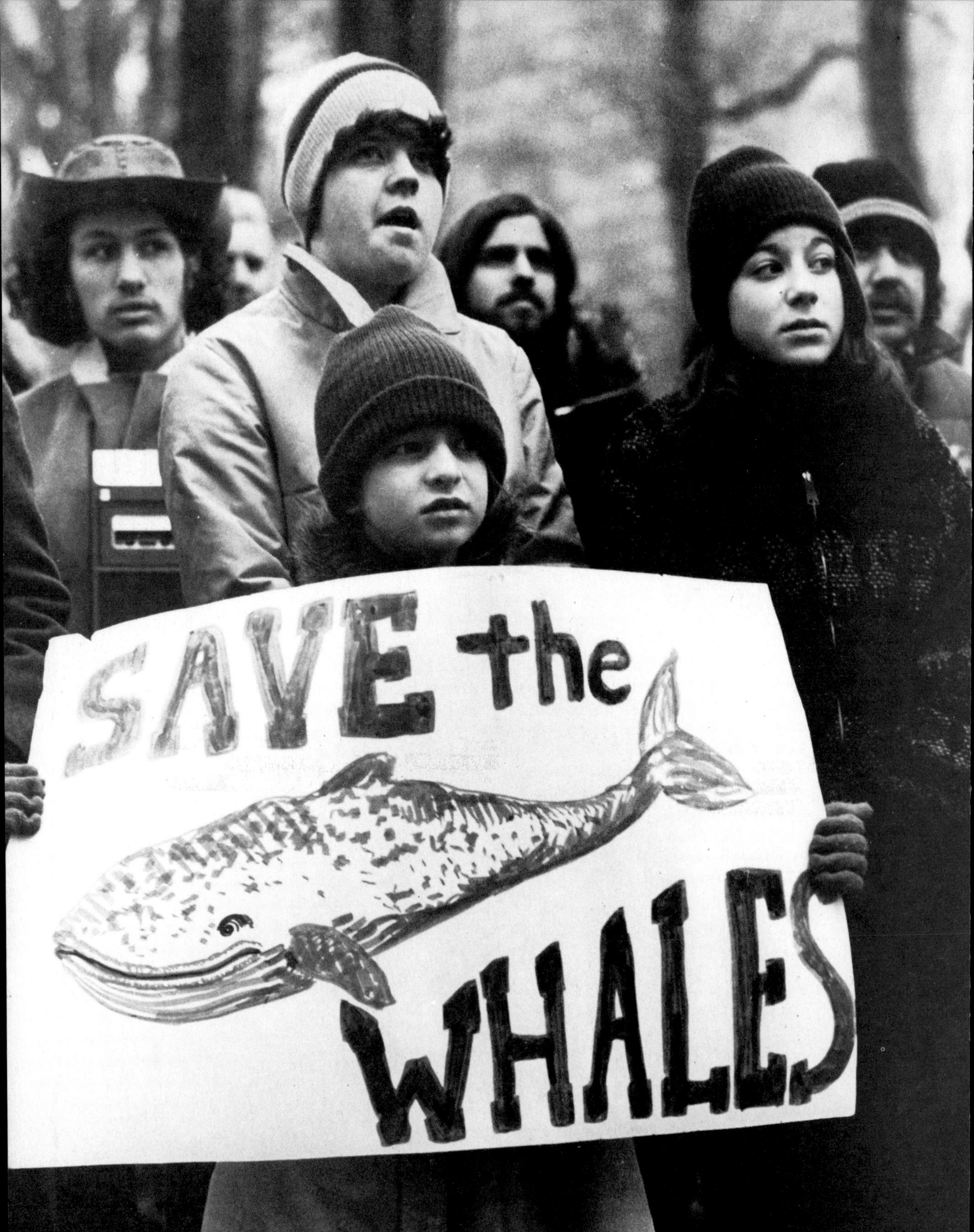
SAVE the
WHALES

CHAPTER SIX

POLITICAL PARTIES AND INTEREST GROUPS
DO WE NEED THEM?

*D*o we need political parties and political interest groups? It depends on what sort of a political system you want.

Do you want a political system in which there is somebody who can help carry your demands and complaints to governmental officials? Or somebody who can help those who are not millionaires run for elective office? Or somebody who can compensate for the tendency of members of Congress to fly off in many different directions? Or somebody who can intercede on your behalf when governmental officials become too oppressive? If these are the sorts of things you want out of your political system, then you do need political parties and political interest groups.

Moreover, political parties and political interest groups need each other. **Political parties** are loose coalitions of both principled and ambitious people who are organized for the purpose of winning elective office. To accomplish this goal, parties often depend heavily on **political interest groups**, usually tighter coalitions of people who are organized primarily for the purpose of influencing public policy. Each needs the other; parties need interest groups to win office and interest groups need parties to make policy. This does not mean, however, that political parties and political interest groups will always work together.

The following Case describes some of the events surrounding the breakdown in relations between the national Democratic party and its allied interest groups in 1968, as the party struggled toward its presidential nominating convention in Chicago. The Case focuses on one especially disruptive factor, the assassination of Robert Kennedy, and asks: Might the Democratic party have been different if Robert Kennedy had not been assassinated?

The answer reveals some interesting things about political parties and political interest groups, what they do, why they do it, and how they do it. It suggests that (1) the organizational lives of parties and interest groups are closely intertwined, (2) parties seek power, while interest groups are more interested in policy, and (3) parties and interest groups are supposed to offset, not augment, the centrifugal forces that otherwise threaten to fragment society.

Nobody won the election early this morning—certainly not the nation.
—*James Reston,* The New York
Times, *November 6, 1968*

The Case Might the Democratic party have been different if Robert Kennedy had not been assassinated?[1]

June 4, 1968. Los Angeles, California. The day had a special significance for Sirhan Beshara Sirhan. Tomorrow was the first anniversary of the Arab-Israeli war and, in Sirhan's twisted mind, vengeance was due. Sirhan had entered in his date book: "the necessity to assassinate Sen. Kennedy before June 5."

Robert Kennedy's fate would be the party's—and the nation's; his candidacy and his life, shattered in Los Angeles, symbolized a party—and a nation—torn asunder. Without Kennedy, the Democratic party's normally loose coalition would fall completely apart. Normally, Democratic voters would desert the ticket, and various political interest groups, usually allied to the Democratic party, would fail to provide its presidential nominee, Vice-President Hubert Humphrey, with adequate and timely support. The Democratic party would begin an agonizing and destructive period of self-appraisal and reform, and new interest groups, passionately committed to single purposes, would begin their effort to dominate the electoral process as parties once had. To compensate for the growing weakness of parties and to protect themselves from the growing strength of interest groups, ambitious politicians would accelerate their efforts to form their own organizations, ones loyal to them, not to any tradition or cause.

The beginning, in retrospect, was foreboding. Previously announcing his intention to support President Lyndon Johnson's bid for reelection, Kennedy had deeply disappointed his natural constituency, the liberal coalition of young social welfare activists who wanted more spending at home and less warfare abroad. Disaffected, this wing of the Democratic party rallied to Senator Eugene McCarthy's crusade against continuing American involvement in the war in Vietnam. But Kennedy's decision not to run made good political sense. Since there seemed no chance of denying a sitting president the renomination of his party, there was no point in trying, Kennedy must have thought. Kennedy, a skilled politician, did not believe in hopeless crusades for unreachable policy objectives, however principled. That meant nothing, unless you could win the office and command its power. The power was Johnson's; Johnson was king and Kennedy was wise enough to know that you never strike at the king—unless you are able to destroy him.

---

[1] The idea and much of the ending for this hypothetical account comes from Nelson W. Polsby, "What If Robert Kennedy Had Not Been Assassinated?" in Nelson W. Polsby, ed. *What If?: Explorations in Social Science Fiction* (Brattleboro, Vt.: The Lewis Publishing Company, 1982), pp. 144–52.

Senator Robert Kennedy campaigning in 1968.

Kennedy, however, soon jumped into the race for the party's presidential nomination, just after President Johnson was bloodied by Senator McCarthy in the New Hampshire primary. Sensing the erosion of his political support, President Johnson later announced that he would neither seek nor accept the nomination. The quest for the Democratic party's presidential nomination became a new three way race. Humphrey had to count on the party's traditional power brokers, other elected officials and the leaders of labor unions, to deliver the nomination. Kennedy had to count on his emotional appeal to the masses to convince the convention delegates that he and not Humphrey could go on to win the election. McCarthy had to hold on to his anti-war supporters, while hoping that a stalemated convention would turn to him.

Kennedy's strategy required a string of impressive victories in presidential primaries and by early June, it appeared clear that Kennedy had to win the California primary—or concede the nomination. As the California election results came in, the vote projections looked promising. (When all the votes were counted, Robert Kennedy won the California primary, but not very decisively, with 46 percent of the total Democratic vote over the 42 percent received by Senator Eugene McCarthy and the 12 percent received by a mixed slate that included supporters of both senators and of Hubert Humphrey.) The projected win was clear enough—the Kennedy forces had turned the corner. Robert Kennedy could claim both the California and South Dakota primaries, acknowledge the efforts of his supporters, command national press coverage, and hope to inspire enough enthusiasm to spill over into the New York primary on June 18. Buoyant before the jubilant crowd in the hotel ballroom, he offered unity to a splintered party and nation:

> I think we can end the divisions in the United States. What I think is quite clear is that we can work together in the last analysis.
>
> And that is what has been going on within the United States over a period of the last three years—the division, the violence, the disenchantment with our society, the division, whether it's between blacks and

whites, between the poor and the more affluent, between age groups, or in the war in Vietnam—that we can start to work together. . . .

So my thanks to all of you and it's on to Chicago and let's win there.[2]

It was a too brief moment of euphoria, purchased at too high a price.

As Kennedy left the podium, he turned left, heading through a short passage on his way to a meeting with the press. In the hallway, Sirhan waited. It was 12:13 A.M., Pacific daylight time.

What if Kennedy had not been assassinated?

It might have been different. The difference could have been felt in Chicago, in the future of the Democratic party, and in the future of the nation. To see this, let us construct a brief hypothetical scenario and through it, better understand the nature of political parties, political interest groups, and the relationships between the two.

Even if he had won the New York primary, as seemed likely, Robert Kennedy probably could not have overtaken Humphrey's delegate count. But some, most notably Nelson Polsby, believe that Kennedy, nevertheless "would have been a significant force for reconciliation within the Democratic party."[3] In general, Kennedy's presence on the ticket might have helped the Democratic party hold together its traditional coalition. The Kennedy forces, after all, did not represent, as did the McCarthy supporters, a force that was antagonistic toward the prevailing establishment within the party but what Polsby calls an "alternative establishment."[4] The Kennedy people therefore might have helped dampen the hostility toward the party that led some to denounce its candidate as the illegitimate product of illegitimate nomination procedures. Also, by protecting the legitimacy of the party's nomination process, Kennedy might have preserved those preferential arrangements with interest group leaders, drawn mostly from the ranks of elected office holders and organized labor and, thereby, better kept their loyalties and energies within the Democratic party. Most revealing for our purposes, Kennedy probably could have kept the Democratic party from self-destructing. Without him, winning the presidency did not seem important enough to hold together the disparate factions of the Democratic party, that patchwork coalition from the white southern conservative to the black northern liberal. If Kennedy had not been assassinated, the party and its relationships with political interest groups also might have been different in all the following ways.

- Traditionally Democratic segments of the electorate might not have deserted the ticket, as did the residents of large cities, youth, those with only grade school educations, manual workers, Roman Catholics, and Jews in the final days of the election campaign.[5]
- With Kennedy in Chicago, the anti-war, pro-social welfare Democratic followers might have defected from Eugene McCarthy and moderated their hostility toward the Democratic party's power structure.
- Broad segments of the American electorate might not have been alienated from the party by the image of the International Amphitheater, the site of the

[2] Quoted in *The New York Times*, 5 June 1968.

[3] Polsby, *What If?*, p. 150.

[4] *Ibid.*, p. 147.

[5] Gallup Poll results reported in *The New York Times*, 2 October 1968.

Democratic Convention in Chicago, as an armed camp, surrounded by seven-foot-high chain link fences, topped with barbed wire, and thousands of police, National Guardsmen, and federal agents, all braced, fearing the worst from an estimated 100,000 protesters.

- State Democratic party leaders and state-level candidates might not have had to run away from the head of the ticket, trying to protect themselves and other local candidates from the anticipated Nixon sweep.
- The financial support of business and labor interests for Humphrey's candidacy might have come sooner, in time to make a difference.
- The Democratic party might not have lost its capacity to unify its diverse constituencies behind a broad policy agenda.
- And, if the party had not withered, political interest groups might not have so quickly become so strident and so uncompromising in pressing their demands on policy makers.

Insights

It was not to be, of course. But still we can extract from this hypothetical Case some real insights about political parties, political interest groups, and their relationships.

Insight 1. *The organizational lives of political parties and political interest groups are closely intertwined.* Without the appeal that a Humphrey-Kennedy ticket might have offered, the Democratic party failed to rally traditional allies to its cause. Without a Democrat in the White House, many of those traditional allies lacked access to key policy makers and influence over policy choices. For the next four years at least, supporters of organized labor, advocates of increased social welfare spending, and civil rights activists, for example, dejectedly wandered the national corridors of power.

Insight 2. *Political parties seek power, while political interest groups are more interested in policy.* In theory, at least, those who lead political parties are supposed to do whatever they can to win office and therefore, the authority to govern, and those who lead interest groups are supposed to do whatever they can to make sure they can influence the policy actions of whoever wins office. The theory does not always work, however, as in 1968, when clear-headed pragmatism was shunted aside by intense personal ambitions and passionate policy commitments.

Insight 3. *Political parties and political interest groups are supposed to forge policy agreements, thereby offsetting the centrifugal forces that otherwise fragment society.* This did not work either in 1968, however. Moreover, since then political parties have gotten weaker, while some political interest groups, especially those deeply committed to single purposes, have become stronger. The combined effect makes government more vulnerable to the special claims of narrowly based interest groups and therefore, less able to command the respect and trust of the rest of the general populace.

To elaborate each of these insights, let us amplify our understanding of political parties, political interest groups, and their role in the American political system.

RELATIONSHIPS BETWEEN PARTIES AND INTEREST GROUPS

> To manage pressures is to govern; to let
> pressures run wild is to abdicate.
> —*E. E. Schattschneider,* Politics,
> Pressures and the Tariff

We have defined political parties and political interest groups in ways that suggest the nature of the relationship between the two. That is, (1) political parties are loose coalitions of both principled and ambitious people who are organized for the purpose of winning elective offices and (2) political interest groups are usually tighter coalitions of people who are organized primarily for the purpose of influencing public policy. Both parties and interest groups, therefore, need each other. Nevertheless, interest groups today often act as though they need parties less than parties need them.

The organizational lives of political parties and political interest groups can be intertwined in three major ways: (1) socially, as both are expressions of factiousness, (2) politically, as both are links between people and government, and (3) historically, as parties have evolved out of shifting alliances of interest groups.

Expressions of Factiousness

In any free society, people will split off into separate groups, many of which may have widely different views of government's proper role. People, in other words, will be factious and there are good reasons why this is so.

The Nature of Factiousness. The factious nature of humans created political problems for a democracy—problems dealt with early in the nation's history by the Founders. They suffered, for example, the opposing interests of patriots and Tories, the suspicions of states still dissatisfied with the resolution of border disagreements, the antagonisms of landholders and tenants, and—during the Constitutional Convention itself—the personal animosities fanned by "the self-righteous posturing of . . . egotists. . . ."[6]

The Founders wisely chose to cope with factiousness, rather than crush it, and therefore tried to design a system of government that could protect society against self-serving factions. They believed that the system of government they wrought in the new Constitution would do that—or at least they said so in their effort to persuade the voters of New York to vote for ratification. Writing in Number 10 of the *Federalist Papers*, Madison argued the thesis: "Among the

---

[6] Jack N. Rakove, *The Beginnings of National Politics* (New York: Alfred A. Knopf, 1979), p. 246.

POLITICAL PARTIES AND INTEREST GROUPS: DO WE NEED THEM?

numerous advantages promised by a well-constructed Union, none deserves to be more accurately developed than its tendency to break and control the violence of faction."[7]

Madison quite carefully and clearly defined his terms: "By a faction I understand a number of citizens, whether amounting to a majority or minority of the whole who are united and actuated by some common impulse of passion, or of interest, adverse to the rights of other citizens, or to the permanent and aggregate interests of the community." A **faction**, therefore, has three defining characteristics: (1) it consists of people who share some common interest; (2) the group actually does something to try to realize its objectives; and, (3) in trying to advance its interests, it may actually hurt the interests of other individuals, groups, or the society as a whole.

Under this definition, there are lots of groups, in a loose sense of the word, that are *not* factions—for example, air traffic controllers who do not stick together; students who are unhappy with their instructor but do nothing about it; women who suffer sexism silently; blacks resigned to second-class citizenship; the unemployed who do not register to vote. None of these categorical groups band together in an organized way to try to realize their common interests. Thus, under Madison's definition, such groups are *not* factions. But other groups are more aware, more active, and more demanding. Many categorical groups in contemporary American society really are factions—for example, people who milk cows and the public though governmental price supports, women who sit in the seats that used to be reserved for labor leaders at presidential nominating conventions; Vietnam war veterans who make the nation memorialize its dead; the physically handicapped who demand access to public facilities. All these, and many other groups, are factions; they know what they want and are determined to get it.

The Causes of Factiousness. Madison saw that there were two causes of factiousness: (1) the fallibility of human reason and (2) the freedom to exercise it. Instead of all uniting behind common conceptions of self-interest, different people—even those in identical circumstances—form different judgments about what is in their self-interest and what, if anything, they should do about it. In Madison's words: "As long as the reason of man continues fallible, and he is at liberty to exercise it, different opinions will be formed."[8] Regarding people's chances for acquiring infallible reason, no one, especially not Madison, was optimistic. Regarding the second condition—freedom—no one, especially not Madison, was ready to abandon the purposes of revolution by now arguing that people should not be free to exercise their own (fallible) reason. Liberty, the Founders believed, was essential to political life, and it could not be extinguished—even though "liberty is to faction what air is to fire."[9] The conclusion was, and is, inescapable; as long as people enjoy the

---

[7] *The Federalist Papers* (New York: New American Library, 1961), p. 77.

[8] *Ibid.*, p. 78.

[9] *Ibid.*, p. 78.

liberty to decide their self-interest for themselves, humans will be factious. Such factiousness can be politically disruptive, unless ways are found to accommodate it.

Linkages Between People and Government

Both political parties and political interest groups link people and their government in useful ways, although parties do it differently than interest groups.

Linkages Are Functional. A democracy has to find some way of tying together or linking the preferences of the people with the policies of their government. This is hard to accomplish and it is not going to happen naturally or spontaneously, especially in a society with many dispersed and different people who ignore politics and government. What is needed is somebody who will find out what the people want, try to pull together or aggregate the diverse policy demands of interest groups, watch closely enough to hold policy makers accountable for their actions and inactions, monitor and evaluate the success or failure of adopted policies, and then, after assessing the impact of policy on the problems of society, start all over again—by claiming anew the task of finding out what the people now want! In this society, political parties have traditionally performed all of these roles. In doing so, political parties are "linkage mechanisms," as V. O. Key taught, performing various functions that both shape and link popular preferences and public policies.[10] In this way, political parties integrate often diverse desires behind broad conceptions of government's proper role.

Parties and Groups Perform Different Functions. The functional view of political parties offers a clear-cut way of distinguishing them from political interest groups. While interest groups perform the more narrow function of **interest articulation**—expressing expectations of government—political parties are more inclusive organizations which perform the more inclusive function of **interest aggregation**—integrating demands into a broader set of policy proposals and actions. Both functions must be performed well if a democracy is to maintain its legitimacy. Both functions were performed well, for example, when both business and labor coalesced behind the legislation creating the social security system. Good articulation without aggregation, however, characterized the demand for affirmative action programs that gave women and blacks preferential treatment in hiring and promotion at the expense of others, at least as the others saw it. Effective interest articulation nudges government, altering its policy course. But effective interest aggregation forges political support for that course. Without aggregation, the gains of interest groups and the government that dispenses them can be seen as illegitimate.

---

[10] V. O. Key, Jr., *Public Opinion and American Democracy* (New York: Knopf, 1963).

Shifting Alliances

Throughout American history, political parties have endured as relatively stable coalitions of interest groups. Outside pressures, however, have produced evolutionary changes in their relationship.

Parties as Stable Coalitions of Interest Groups. There are many historical examples of political parties that illustrate their nature as relatively stable coalitions of diverse interests:

- the early Federalist party included banking and commercial interests, whereas the Democratic-Republican party of Jefferson appealed mostly to agrarian interests—small farmers, frontiersmen, and debtors in general;
- the Democratic party of Andrew Jackson appealed to the broad class of ordinary citizens, while, in reaction, bankers, commercial interests, and owners of large southern plantations rushed to the rival Whigs;
- the Republican party of 1854 coalesced around the issue of slavery, while it split the northern and southern halves of the Democratic party;
- Roosevelt's Democratic party dealt a New Deal sufficiently attractive to put together a grand coalition based in the rural South and the urban North, spanning the interests of industrial workers, immigrants, and blacks; and
- the New Deal also was sufficiently effective to lift normally "safe" Democratic supporters into middle-class life styles where they became more concerned with protecting their gains and more easily swayed by Republican campaign appeals.

In all these cases, interest groups and policy enthusiasts rallied behind ambitious office seekers and with the organizational assistance of party leaders and loyalists, formed a coalition.

Major Evolutionary Steps in the Relationship Between Parties and Groups. The evolving historical relationship between political parties and interest groups is a story of shifting alliances of factious coalitions. There have been nine major steps in the historical development of the relationship between parties and interest groups:

1. In the beginning, there was a premonition that political parties would emerge on the American scene, in spite of Washington's warning of "the baneful effects of the spirit of party." John Adams' presentiment that caused him to proclaim: "There is nothing I dread so much as the division of the Republic into two great parties, each under its leader."[11] But, as Madison had predicted in the *Federalist Papers*, the spirit of faction prevailed.
2. The first institutionalized expression of the spirit of faction emerged as Hamilton's Federalists and Jefferson's Democratic-Republicans.

---

[11] Quoted in Wilfred E. Binkley, *American Political Parties* (New York: Knopf, 1963), p. 19.

Partisanship surfaced early, as in this attack on Jefferson's worth as a successor to Washington and in this slur on the enemies of Thomas Jefferson and his Vice-President George Clinton.

3. Today's Democratic party lost its hyphenated half by the time Jackson was elected to the presidency in 1828, when opposition elements coalesced behind Henry Clay and Daniel Webster under the Whig standard.

4. Out of the ensuing competition, the two-party system became a well-established feature on the American political landscape. As Clinton Rossiter has written: "Out of the conflict of Democrats and Whigs emerged the American political system—complete with such features as two major parties, a sprinkle of third parties, national nominating conventions, state and local bosses, patronage, popular campaigning, and the Presidency as the focus of politics."[12]

5. The next major spurt in the evolution of the party system occurred when the Republican party was born in reaction to the passage of the Kansas-Nebraska Act of 1854 which permitted the westward expansion of slavery.

6. Ravaged as was the nation by the Civil War, the Democratic party did not recover competitive standing until around 1876 and only elected a Democrat twice—Grover Cleveland in 1884 and 1892.

7. Economic change also foreshadowed change in the appeal and composition of political parties. Between 1892 and 1912, for example, the rapid pace of industrialization produced wholesale classes of "winners" and "losers." The "winners," Eastern business and financial interests and urban industrial workers, for example, found happy refuge in the conservative fiscal policies

---

[12] Clinton Rossiter, *Parties and Politics in America* (New York: Cornell University Press, 1960), pp. 73–74.

POLITICAL PARTIES AND INTEREST GROUPS: DO WE NEED THEM?

Economic dissatisfaction fostered partisanship, as, for example, in William Jennings Bryan's campaign for President.

of the Republican party. Those who did less well under industrialization, small farmers, for example, vented their discontent through new minor parties and the Democratic party's populist candidate for president, William Jennings Bryan.

8. Except for Woodrow Wilson's two terms, Republican dominance continued until the Great Depression did to the Republican party what the Civil War had done to the Democratic. Starting in 1932, Franklin Delano Roosevelt began putting together the New Deal Democratic coalition that dominated presidential politics for the next twenty years, until the Republican party found a hero, Dwight D. Eisenhower, sufficiently popular to win over normally Democratic voters.

9. Since 1952, this has been the pattern of two-party competition at the presidential level: the Democrats struggle to hold together their increasingly factious majority coalition and the Republicans search for Democratic defectors. The former task has been difficult—too difficult for Hubert Humphrey in 1968, George McGovern in 1972, Jimmy Carter in 1980, and Walter Mondale in 1984.

In addition, sprinkled throughout this historical evolution, various minor parties have ridden momentary crests of passion strong enough to shake up the two major parties and make them accommodate pressing demands for policy change.

This brief historical overview suggests five major conclusions about the evolving relationship between parties and interest groups. First, the party system quickly emerged as a two-party system, with major parties tending to compete for the moderate middle majorities of the electorate. Second, the two-party system has been relatively stable, because our "winner-take-all" electoral system produces benefits only for the party with the winning plurality and, in the absence of a system of proportional representation, voters are reluctant to waste their vote on minor parties. Third, once in a while, a series of elections leads to a realignment of partisan loyalties, bringing about a reversal of majority-minority roles or the demise of one of the two major parties. Fourth, political parties have become increasingly less oligarchical and more openly democratic, although this is more true of the Democratic than Republican party. Fifth, as political parties have gotten weaker, interest groups and the mass media have become more powerful.

■ In 1968, social and political stresses fractured the uneasy alliances within the Democratic party. Since 1968, normally allied interest groups in both parties have increasingly gone their own way, increasing levels of factiousness, favoring interest articulation at the expense of aggregation, and generally, making the political system harder to govern. Today, political parties and political interest groups lead relatively independent organizational lives.

POLITICAL PARTIES

> I don't belong to any organized political
> party—I'm a Democrat.
> —*Will Rogers, American humorist*

In spite of the apparent truth and humor in Will Rogers' observation, American political parties have distinctive organizational characteristics and specific organizational components.

The Nature of Political Parties

We have defined political parties as loose coalitions of both principled and ambitious people organized for the purpose of winning elective office.

This definition accommodates many of the important insights that various experts have had about the nature of political parties. Leon Epstein, for example, suggests that parties be defined broadly as all "groups that provide the labels under which candidates seek election to governmental office."[13] This broad definition and its implied focus gets tightened up in Anthony Downs' definition of a party as a "team of men (and women) seeking to control the governing apparatus by gaining office in a duly constituted election."[14] Other definitions are as expansive as Epstein's, however, and add contextual richness to our view of parties. One early scholar, Charles Merriam, wrote that parties include group interests "which struggle to translate themselves into types of

---

[13] Leon D. Epstein, "Political Parties," in Fred I. Greenstein and Nelson W. Polsby, eds. *Handbook of Political Science*, vol. 4 (Reading, Mass.: Addison-Wesley Publishing Co., 1975), p. 230.

[14] Anthony Downs, *An Economic Theory of Democracy* (New York: Harper and Row, 1957), p. 25.

social control acting through the political process of government."[15] More recently, Gabriel Almond tried to capture the meaning of this process of translation by writing of parties as organizations that aggregate interests by converting the demands of interest groups into policy proposals.[16] But parties are not mere mechanical conduits. Rather, parties have their own distinctive character, rooted in their history and policy preferences, and may, as Carey McWilliams has argued, make deep claims "on our memories, our identities, and our hopes."[17] Finally, both of the central characteristics in our definition, the coalitional and the organizational, are reflected in Maurice Duverger's view of a political party as "a community with a particular structure."[18]

The Organizational Characteristics of Parties

Political parties have two main organizational characteristics: (1) they are highly decentralized and (2) they are coalitions.

Parties Are Decentralized. Political parties today are highly decentralized. They are *not* like large corporations with executives in a central headquarters making binding decisions about the operations of regional offices. Instead, parties are more like franchise operations, with certain standardized procedures, but decision-making power left to the local entrepreneurs. There is a good reason for the decentralized structure of parties; they are after particular elective offices, not offices in general. Therefore, unlike political parties in a parliamentarian system like Great Britain's, American political parties are not primarily focused on the task of winning a majority of the offices that are currently available. Instead, particular office seekers take the initiative for pulling together, around themselves, an organizational force that zeros in on the particular offices they want. This decentralized character of parties means that there are many different candidate-centered organizations parading under the national party label of "Democrat" or "Republican" and that each candidate-centered organization will tend to act independently of the other.

Candidates and elective office holders of the same political party have only weak incentives to cooperate with one another. Moreover, the reasons for this are relatively fixed, since they are rooted in the nature of the electoral system, as Joseph Schlesinger has shown. Professor Schlesinger once made a simple observation about relationships among electoral districts and then went on to draw from it profound implications for policy making.[19] He observed that most

15 Charles Merriam and Harold F. Gosnell, *The American Party System* (New York: Macmillan, 1929), p. 2.

16 Gabriel Almond and G. B. Powell, Jr., *Comparative Politics: System, Process, and Policy*, 2nd ed. (Boston: Little, Brown, 1978), pp. 198–205.

17 Wilson Carey McWilliams, "The Meaning of The Election," in Gerald Pomper et. al., *The Election of 1980: Reports and Interpretations* (Chatham, NJ: Chatham House, 1981), p. 178.

18 Maurice Duverger, *Political Parties*, rev. ed. (London: Butler and Tanner Ltd., 1959), p. xv.

19 Joseph A. Schlesinger, "Political Party Organization," in James G. March, ed. *Handbook of Organizations* (Chicago: Rand McNally, 1965), pp. 764–801. See also Joseph A. Schlesinger, *Ambition and Politics: Political Careers in the United States* (Chicago: Rand McNally, 1966).

FIGURE 6.1
Structural relationships
among electoral districts
and their consequences
for policy making

There are three types of structural relationships among electoral districts: distinct, enclave, and contiguous. Distinct districts have geographical boundaries that do not overlap. Most electoral districts, those for the U.S. House of Representatives, for example, are of this type. Enclaved districts are a part of a larger district, as is the case of the relationship between U.S. House and state-wide districts. Contiguous districts have identical geographical boundaries, gubernatorial and both U.S. Senate seats, for example. These three types are represented schematically.

Depending on the extent to which they share the same constituents, elected representatives who wish to keep their seats will be inclined to cooperate in all phases of the political process. In America, however, electoral districts are mostly distinct and, as a result, parties are less able to integrate the legislative activities of their members, since they must be attuned to their separate constituencies.

Distinct

Enclave

Contiguous

electoral districts (for state legislatures or for Congress) are geographically distinct from one another, not enclaved or contiguous (See **Figure 6.1**). From this simple structural characteristic, it follows: the nomination and election fates of one party's candidates are relatively independent of one another, the candidates of the same party will tend not to cooperate in the nomination and election stages of the political cycle, and, since each must legislate in a way to ensure their own re-election, office holders of the same party will tend to act independently of one another in the governing stage of the political process. In other words, political parties will find it hard to exercise centralized influence over the policy actions of office holders because they have to be attuned to the separate and often different concerns of a decentralized electoral system.

Political Parties Are Coalitions.   Political parties today are semi-loose coalitions of office seekers, party leaders and loyalists, interest groups, and policy enthusiasts. For example, going into the 1968 presidential nominating convention, the national Democratic party consisted of those seeking the presidency (Humphrey, McCarthy, and Kennedy, before his assassination), those whose careers in elective office had earned them stature as a party leader (Mayor Daley of Chicago, for example), those party loyalists who took care of the organizational machinery in between elections, representatives of various policy interests (labor, blacks, and so on), and those activists who were driven by particular policy causes (against the war, for social spending, and so on). By speaking of parties as coalitions, it should be made clear that parties are not homogeneous but rather peopled by different kinds of members who have related, but not identical, goals. It should also be stressed that parties are organizations with fluid lines of authority. (See **Figure 6.2**.) Therefore, you should expect that parties will have certain internal group dynamics; relations

Given their decentralized nature, this image of the party boss is a myth today.

POLITICAL PARTIES AND INTEREST GROUPS: DO WE NEED THEM?

FIGURE 6.2
The Formal and Informal Structure Of Political Parties

The formal structure of national political parties makes them appear as though they are quite hierarchical, with a clear-cut chain of command, as in the figure.

Informally, however, political parties look more like star-centered cliqués, with an office seeker at its center and clustered around, friends and neighbors, wealthy and/or powerful patrons, hired consultants, and advisors sent by a state or national party or campaign committee.

Moreover, there are many thousands of such informal organizations, each organized to pursue a particular elective office. To get a realistic image of a whole party, imagine thousands of informal organizations that look like the one below, all superimposed on the party's formal organizational structure.

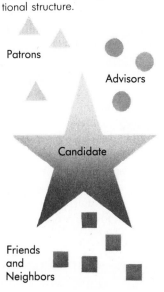

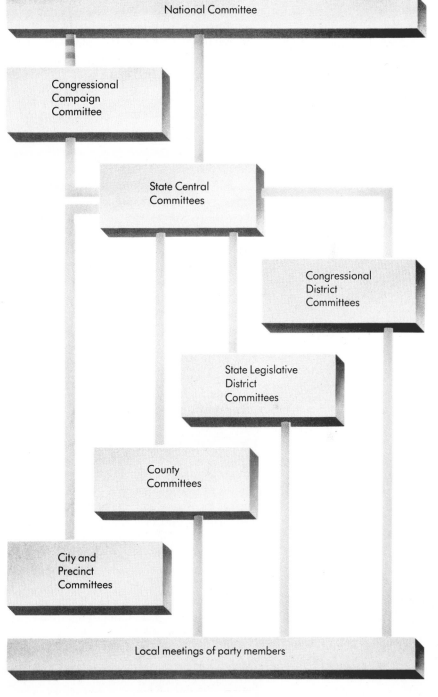

among normally allied party and interest group leaders will not always be harmonious. Because they have different goals, relationships among the party's constituent parts often become strained, although not as badly as they were between Vice-President Humphrey and anti-war activists in 1968 or between President Carter and labor leader Lane Kirkland (President of the AFL-CIO) during Carter's term, 1976–1980.

The Organizational Components of Parties

Political parties have *five main organizational characteristics*: goals, policy objectives, members, resources, activities, and tactics.

Goals. The two major political parties, the Democrats and the Republicans, are primarily interested in winning and holding elective office. If they are to be successful, parties must sell what people are buying. In 1984, for example, most Americans acted as though they preferred less government and more pride in their country and, not surprisingly, the presidential campaign of Ronald Reagan successfully sold it to them. Sometimes, however, one of the major parties may act as though principles are of primary importance. When this happens, the party abandons bland moderate positions and can lurch left, as the Democratic party did in nominating Senator George McGovern for President in 1972, or right, as the Republican party did in nominating Senator Barry Goldwater for President in 1964. In both cases, the party went down to disastrous defeat. In general, though, parties act as if they know that highly consistent or principled stands on issues are luxuries they can not afford.

Their high degree of opportunism makes the major parties different from other minor parties, ones that have been more principled and less enduring. Throughout American history, there have been *five types of minor parties* that have been active at the national level: (1) **ideological parties** that are organized around some coherent view of the proper relationship of government and society, such as the Marxist view taken by the Socialist Workers party; (2) **factional parties** that split off from a major party over some policy dispute, such as the American Independent party which split off from the Democrats in 1968, largely over civil rights issues; (3) **protest parties** that typically reflect regionally based dissatisfaction with economic conditions, such as the Populist party of 1892–1908; (4) **single-issue parties** that typically oppose a specific policy, as the Free Soil party of 1848–1852 opposed the spread of slavery or the Prohibition party which still opposes the sale of liquor; and (5) **media parties** that probably would not exist if television were less important, such as the National Unity Ticket, under which John B. Anderson ran for the presidency in 1980. (See **Figure 6.3**.)

Policy Objectives. To realize their primary goal, the major parties will do anything they can, even promise to adopt (or repeal) certain policies once in office. By adopting policy objectives, the major parties also differentiate themselves from one another and try to appeal to the party faithful. Therefore, the party platforms will express principled and contrasting points of view, as in the

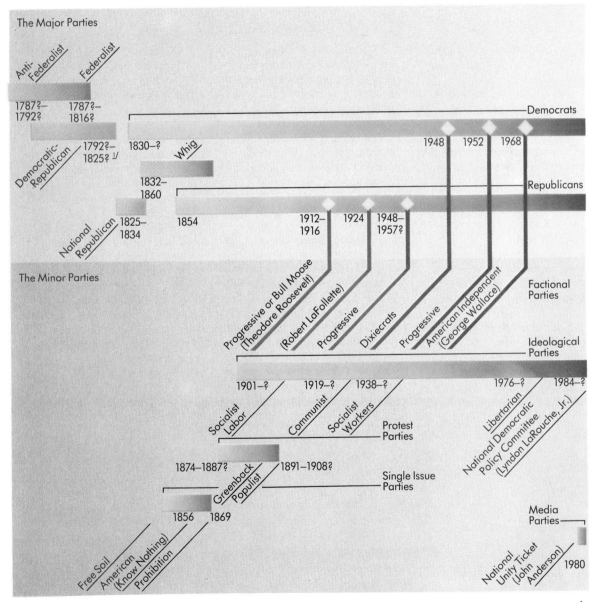

FIGURE 6.3 American Political Parties, 1789 to the Present, and Their Roots

The two major political parties, the Democrats and the Republicans, have deep historical roots. While factional parties share these, other minor parties are more deeply rooted in comprehensive ideologies, economic protest, and single issues. Other minor parties probably are media flashes. In addition, minor parties sometimes are huge star-centered cliqués, organized around its main candidate or spokesperson.

The Major Parties

Anti-Federalist
1787?–1792?

Federalist
1787?–1816?

Democrats

Democratic-Republican
1792?–1825? 1/

1830–?

Whig
1832–1860

Republicans

National Republican
1825–1834

1854

1948 1952 1968

The Minor Parties

Progressive or Bull Moose (Theodore Roosevelt)
1912–1916

(Robert LaFollette) Progressive
1924

Progressive
Dixiecrats
1948–1957?

Progressive

American Independent (George Wallace)

Factional Parties

Ideological Parties

Socialist Labor
1901–?

Communist
1919–?

Socialist Workers
1938–?

Libertarian
1976–?

National Democratic Policy Committee (Lyndon LaRouche, Jr.)
1984–?

Protest Parties

Greenback
1874–1887?

Populist
1891–1908?

Single Issue Parties

Free Soil
1856

American (Know Nothing)
1869

Prohibition

Media Parties

National Unity Ticket (John Anderson)
1980

[1] In some cases, historians disagree over precise dates. In other cases, minor parties may be moribund.

MAJOR POLICY DIFFERENCES IN THE DEMOCRATIC AND REPUBLICAN PARTY PLATFORMS, 1984

Selections from the Preamble to the 1984 Republican party platform:

The Republican party looks at our nation and sees a new dawn of the American spirit.

The Democratic party looks at our nation and sees the twilight of the American soul . . .

The Republican party's vision of America's future, the heart of our 1984 Platform, begins with a basic premise:

From freedom comes opportunity; from opportunity comes growth; from growth comes progress . . .

Selections from the Preamble to the 1984 Democratic party platform: A fundamental choice awaits America—a choice between two futures.

It is a choice between solving our problems and pretending they don't exist; between the spirit of community, and the corrosion of selfishness; between justice for all, and advantage for some; between social decency and Social Darwinism; between expanding opportunity and contracting horizons; between diplomacy and conflict; between arms control and an arms race; between leadership and alibis.

Selected differences on major policy issues:

1. Defense and Foreign Policy. Whereas the Republicans argued that increased defense spending would "keep the peace by keeping our country stronger than any potential adversary," the Democrats stressed the importance of reversing "the automatic militarization of foreign policy."

2. Economic Policy. Whereas the Republicans opposed any tax increase, the Democrats argued that the deficit required some increase in taxes.

3. The Conflict in Nicaragua. The Republicans promised support for those fighting against the Communist government in Nicaragua, while the Democrats called for a negotiated political settlement instead.

4. Women's Issues. The Republicans explicitly opposed abortion and the concept of equal pay for equal work, while the Democrats said they recognized "reproductive freedom as a fundamental human right," supported passage of the Equal Rights Amendment, and favored equal pay for equal work.

Vantage Point: Major policy differences in the Democratic and Republic party platforms, 1984.

Members. For all practical purposes, the members of a political party are those who consider themselves to be members. Members differ from one another, however, in the strength of their **party identification**, their psychological sense of attachment to the party, and in the extent to which they hold common policy objectives.

Most Americans report that they identify with one or the other of the two major parties, although more and more people consider themselves to be "Independent" voters who say they support whomever they consider to be the

TABLE 6.1   Party Identification Since 1937

Year	Republican	Democrat	Independent
		Percent choosing one of these:	
1937	34	50	16
—			
1952	34	41	25
—			
1960	30	47	23
1964	25	53	22
1968	27	46	27
1972	28	43	29
1976	23	47	30
1980	24	46	30
1984	31	40	29

SOURCE: Surveys reported in *Gallup Report*.

best person. In **Table 6.1**, for example, the percentage of Americans identifying with either the Republican or Democratic party has fallen from a high of 84 percent in 1937 to a low of 70 percent in 1980. Most of this falloff seems to have been at the expense of the Democrats; those identifying with the Democratic party shrank from a high of 50 percent in 1937 to a low of 40 percent in 1984.

Party members often differ among themselves, especially in their demographic characteristics and in their preferences for more or less government. To capture some of the differences within parties, let us compare **party delegates**, those who attend the party's national presidential nominating convention, with **party identifiers**, those who say that they consider themselves to be members of the same party.[20] In 1984, for example, Democratic delegates were better educated than Democratic identifiers (71 to 18 percent); richer (43 percent of delegates had incomes greater than $50,000 per year, whereas only 6 percent of identifiers did); and considered themselves more liberal (50 percent of delegates, as compared with only 27 percent of identifiers). At the same time, Republican delegates and identifiers were closer on all

---

[20] Data from CBS News Polls, *New York Times* Poll, and *Los Angeles Times* Poll, reported in Barbara Farah, "Delegate Polls: 1944 to 1984," *Public Opinion*, August 1984. Data on party identifiers from Harris Poll, November, 1984 election.

three measures: 67 percent of the delegates were college educated, as compared with 17 percent of the identifiers; only 25 percent of the delegates had incomes in excess of $50,000, as compared with 13 percent of the identifiers; and 60 percent of the delegates considered themselves conservative, closely mirroring the 56 percent of the identifiers who felt the same way. Such differences, especially the gap between the Democratic party faithful and their loosely allied followers, can endanger electoral success, as you will see in the next chapter's coverage of elections in America.

The members of the two major parties hold many different policy objectives, although they also share some common ones. Half-way through President Reagan's first term, for example, Republicans and Democrats split badly on spending for social programs and freezing nuclear weapons, but were rather close in favoring the death penalty and prayer in public schools. (See **Table 6.2.**)

Resources. Political parties provide candidates with money, labor, and expertise. Parties do this both directly, although their levels of contributions are limited by law, and indirectly. Through their indirect contributions, national political parties and party campaign organizations can be very helpful by, for example, steering potential donors toward particular candidates. National party campaign organizations also encourage others to contribute when they target a race as one they believe can be won. In addition, parties provide candidates with a base of popular support, party identifiers who, hopefully, can be converted into votes on election day.

Activities. Political parties are active throughout the full cycle of the political process—in nominations, campaigning, elections, and governing. In the nomination stage, political parties, especially party loyalists, often take a hands-off attitude, counting on the initiative of others who are trying to decide whether to run. In this way, the organizational core of the party can avoid becoming alienated from those who might surprisingly win the nomination or those who

TABLE 6.2   Selected policy differences (and similarities) between those who call themselves Democrats or Republicans.

	Democrats	Republicans
	Percent favoring	
Dramatic Differences		
1. Decrease social spending	24	49
2. Freeze nuclear weapons	54	32
Striking Similarities		
1. Keep the death penalty	70	79
2. Permit prayer in schools	74	77

SOURCE: *Gallup Reports*, No. 203 (August, 1982) and No. 206 (November, 1982).

might seek it again the next time. But this pattern is not uniformly true; relatively strong party organizations do get involved in the nomination process, trying to convince some people to run and working to discourage interparty strife.

"Metooism": The need to span the electorate forces parties to imitate each other.

The Democratic party tends to follow the hands-off model, as they did in the 1980 presidential primaries, first allowing the contenders to fight it out, often with great bitterness, before the nomination and then trying to unite the party's factions in subsequent battle against the Republicans. But Republicans tend to be a bit more orderly and by exercising a little more hierarchical influence over the care and feeding of potential nominees, have been able to develop more of a national pipeline of aspiring candidates for higher office—a bit like a "farm system" for a major league baseball team.

In the campaigning stage of the electoral process, political parties provide various kinds of resources to candidates who try to convert them into votes. Moving closer to election day, political parties and their workers do several other things: helping register voters, stimulating voter turnout on election day, transporting voters to the polls, assisting in the actual operation of the polling place, throwing victory parties and consoling losers. Finally, in the governing stage of the political process, state-wide and national party organizations sometimes engage in mostly halfhearted and pre-doomed efforts to get their elected office holders to work together in the making of public policy.

Tactics.   Although there are many variations, political parties rely on two main tactics: (1) appeal to as many potential voters as possible and (2) do whatever is necessary to turn potential into actual voters on election day. Both tactics are well-suited to the American electorate.

On an ideological continuum, ranging from an extreme left-hand position, favoring extensive governmental involvement, to an extreme right-hand position, favoring minimal governmental involvement, most Americans will be in the middle. More specifically, when asked to place themselves on such a continuum, only 2 percent say they are "extremely liberal," 9 percent are "liberal," 13 percent are "slightly liberal," a full 40 percent are "moderate," 20 percent are "slightly conservative," 13 percent are "conservative," and only 3 percent are "extremely conservative." (See **Figure 6.4**.) This distribution of potential voters dictates tactics. To win, political parties must use tactics that, hopefully, will span a majority of the actual votes cast. To do so, parties often adopt vague positions on issues or, if saddled with unambiguous and extreme party platforms, de-emphasize the platform during the campaign, as President Reagan did in 1984.

■ In spite of their long and continuing role, political parties live precarious organizational lives. To win elective office and the right to govern, they must successfully overcome fragmenting influences that threaten to tear them apart, as the Democratic party was torn apart during the 1968 race for the presidency. In recent years, this has become even more difficult, as political interest groups have become relatively more powerful and insistent.

FIGURE 6.4

Both the Democratic party (the donkey) and the Republican party (the elephant) try to win elective office through tactics that span a majority of the voters, even if that means adopting vague and overlapping positions on policy issues.

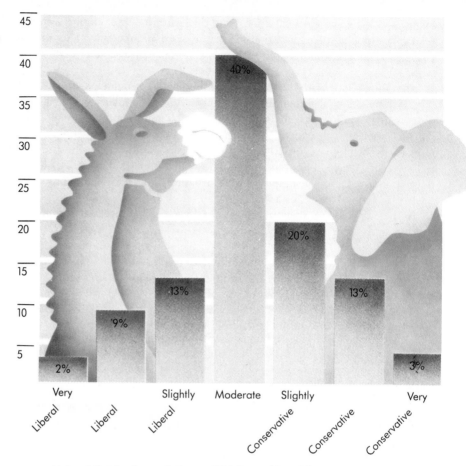

2%	9%	13%	40%	20%	13%	3%
Very Liberal	Liberal	Slightly Liberal	Moderate	Slightly Conservative	Conservative	Very Conservative

SOURCE: National Opinion Research Center, 1984 General Social Survey.

POLITICAL INTEREST GROUPS

> Sometimes in politics one must duel with skunks, but no one should be fool enough to allow the skunks to choose the weapons.
> —"Uncle" ("Dirty") Joe Cannon, a former Speaker of the United States House of Representatives

Ever since President Dwight Eisenhower used the occasion of his farewell address to complain about the influence of political interest groups over the making of defense policy, American presidents and many others have deplored

In a pluralistic society such as ours, there are many different channels through which people express their views of what government should, and should not, do. Some of these expressions are obviously political: writing a letter to a governmental official, contributing time and money to election campaigns, serving as a delegate at a political party's nominating convention, and voting, for examples.

We should recognize, however, that most forms of political participation are woven into the fabric of peoples' daily lives. Forms of political participation, therefore, are intimately related to all the other things that people do.

When people pay attention to election campaigns or contribute to social causes, they often are motivated by both principles and a simple desire to be a part of an exciting or entertaining event.

When people honor the sacrifices of veterans, they do so out of participation and simple respect or love.

When people vote, they also socialize and, perhaps, do a little business, especially in small towns and rural areas.

Before movies, TV, and rock concerts, electioneering was more than a way of matching preferences with policies—it was a major source of entertainment.

Visits to the Vietnam Memorial are a deeply moving experience, connecting the American people to their past and to one another.

Americans, and others around the free world, sometimes react personally to social problems, as through the concert to aid victims of starvation in Ethiopia.

Peaceful protests, such as this anti-Vietnam War candlelight vigil, often draw people who might otherwise not wish to participate.

The act of voting, especially in small towns and rural areas, becomes a social event, a part of the daily fabric of life.

National presidential nominating conventions still serve an important function, by firing up the troops who are needed to win the election.

Through rituals and visual symbols, such as this citizen swearing-in ceremony, Americans are socialized into civic obligations.

the strength and actions of these groups. Before assessing their role, however, let us understand the nature of political interest groups, their organizational characteristics, and their organizational components.

The Nature of Political Interest Groups

We have defined political interest groups as usually tight coalitions of like-minded people who are organized for the purpose of influencing public policy.

This definition incorporates David B. Truman's distinction between interest groups and *political* interest groups. An interest group, according to Truman, a pioneering scholar on the topic, consists of persons who share certain attitudes about themselves and the outside world.[21] Moreover, no interest group is able to pursue its common objectives as though the rest of society did not exist. Rather, all interest groups depend on other groups in society. For example, parents depend on teachers to teach something and auto workers depend on car dealers to sell something. Depending on other groups in society does not make interest groups political. To be political, an interest group must try to use government to get what it wants. In Truman's words: ". . . an interest group is a shared-attitude group that makes certain claims upon other groups in the society. If and when it makes its claims through or upon any of the institutions of government, it becomes a political interest group."[22] Thus, parents become a political interest group when they complain about bussing, for example, at school board meetings and auto workers do when they try to get a higher tariff on foreign cars. What is distinctive about a political interest group is that it attempts to use government to enforce its claims on others in society, as some religious fundamentalists would, for example, in requiring that Supreme Court nominees profess certain religious convictions.

The Organizational Characteristics of Groups

Throughout American history, political interest groups have assumed various organizational forms, since they have been very accommodating in responding to changing societal and political conditions and very enterprising in finding ways of advancing their policy goals.

Groups Are Accommodating. Political interest groups are the organized expression of certain kinds of underlying value conflicts. As new lines of cleavage form in the society, new interest groups often spring up to fight new political battles. In a pluralistic society, there are many potential cleavages: for example, between management and labor, between buyers and sellers, be-

---

[21] David B. Truman, *The Governmental Process: Political Interests and Public Opinion*, 2nd ed. (New York: Alfred A. Knopf, 1971).

[22] *Ibid.*, p. 37.

Political interest groups sometimes express the concerns of
the voiceless, as in this case.

Secretary of Transportation
Elizabeth Dole (right), supporting a minimum drinking age,
backed by Candy Lightner, a
leader of Mothers Against
Drunk Driving.

tween students and college faculty. Many of the conflicts that result from societal cleavages are worked out between the groups themselves, sometimes through face-to-face negotiation and most often, through the more impersonal mechanism called the private economic market. Thus, value conflicts can be resolved without government: for example, when management fires workers or when workers go elsewhere, when dissatisfied buyers switch rather than fight, when frustrated students change their majors from sociology to political science. But there are many cases of persistent value conflicts that have not been resolved without government. Without governmental intervention, for example, insurance companies were unwilling to give women the same annuity as men, auto companies did not recall defective cars, paper mills did not reduce pollution, and producers saw no reason to lower levels of sex and violence on television.

In addition, there are many underlying cleavages that are not easily expressed politically, because those that wish to do so lack the resources which are necessary to organize and press their demands on policy makers. Some potential interest groups are, in effect, blocked from entering the political process, just as large successful companies like IBM or General Motors block the entry of new firms into the marketplace. In general, however, political interest groups have been very accommodating in responding to and expressing evolving political concerns, and even disadvantaged interests sometimes find a sponsor.

Groups Are Enterprising.   Political interest groups also have been very enterprising in finding and creating new ways to press their claims on policy makers.

The historical development of interest groups reveals the ways in which they have evolved. David B. Truman gets credit for the observation: "The formation of associations tends to occur in waves."[23] The waves crested in the 1770s in demands for independence, before the Civil War over slavery, after the Civil War out of the grievances of farmers and trade unionists, in the 1880s and '90s on the basis of the newfound economic power of business, in the awakening of popular democracy after the turn of the century, and most recently, in the sense of empowerment that motivates racial minorities, women, consumers, environmentalists, and peace activists.

Recent growth in the number of interest groups has been explosive. The general growth of interest groups has paralleled expansion in the role of government at all levels and, within Congress, the dispersion of decision-making power throughout the body into more hands that more lobbyists were needed to hold. By one estimate, such factors helped account for a jump in the number of active Washington lobbyists from about 4000 in 1977 to a very roughly estimated 10 to 20,000 by 1982.[24] The general pattern of growth in the number of interest groups is repeated in the proliferation of **Political Action**

---

[23] *Ibid.*, p. 59.

[24] *The Washington Lobby* (Washington, D.C.: Congressional Quarterly Inc., 1982), p. 2.

FIGURE 6.5   Growth of Political Action Committees, 1974–1982

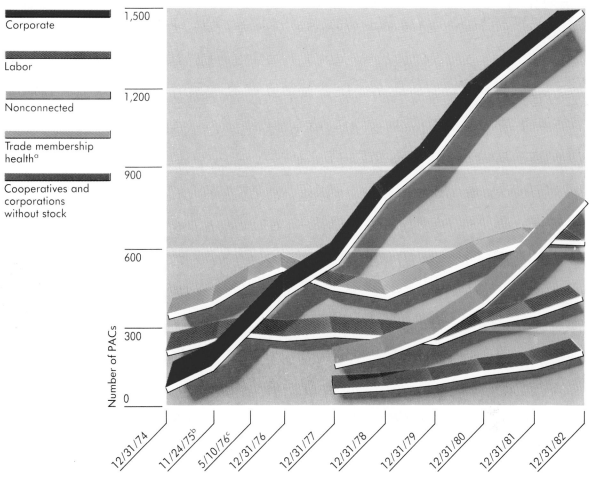

Corporate

Labor

Nonconnected

Trade membership
health[a]

Cooperatives and
corporations
without stock

1,500

1,200

900

600

300

0

Number of PACs

12/31/74   11/24/75[b]   5/10/76[c]   12/31/76   12/31/77   12/31/78   12/31/79   12/31/80   12/31/81   12/31/82

[a]Prior to 1977, this category includes all other PACs.
[b]Date of Federal Election Commission's "SunPAC" decision.
[c]Date FECA Amendments of 1976 were signed into law.
SOURCE: Federal Election Commission. From Jeffrey M. Berry, *The Interest Group Society*
(Boston: Little, Brown and Company, 1984), p. 161.

Committees (PACs), interest groups that try to achieve their policy objectives
by influencing the electoral process, either directly, through their own campaigns for or against particular candidates or indirectly, through cash campaign
contributions to particular candidates. The recent growth in the number of
PACs is plotted in **Figure 6.5**. The relative size of the PAC role in campaign
funding, measured as the share of congressional candidate campaign receipts
that come just from PACs, is shown in **Figure 6.6**.

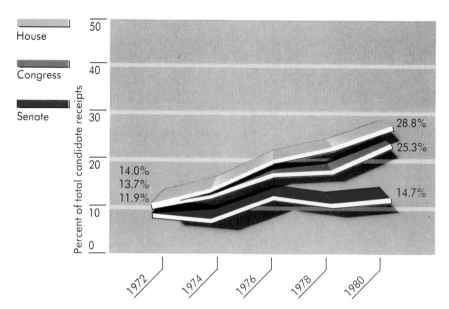

FIGURE 6.6
Share of Congressional Campaign Receipts Derived from PACs, 1972–1980

Political action committee contributions as a share of the total campaign receipts of House and Senate candidates in general elections.

House

Congress

Senate

Percent of total candidate receipts

50
40
30
20
10
0

14.0%
13.7%
11.9%

28.8%
25.3%
14.7%

1972 1974 1976 1978 1980

Note: Prior to the 1976 election, campaign spending data were compiled by Common Cause. The Common Cause studies in 1972 and 1974 covered shorter time periods than the FEC surveys. The FEC studies covered the 24 months through the end of the year in which the election was held.

SOURCE: Federal Election Commission 1976–80; Library of Congress publication by Joseph E. Cantor, 1972–74. From *The Washington Lobby* 4th ed. (Washington, D.C. Congressional Quarterly Inc., 1982), p. 45.

The evolution of interest groups reveals two sets of emerging patterns: those that reflect the operation of factors that directly impinge on individual decision making and those that reflect factors that operate at a broader, societal level. At the level of the individual, trying to decide whether or not to join others in a collective activity, shared attitudes are important, as Truman suggested; but, they are not always enough to overcome the disincentives that deter interest group formation. To overcome constraints, other ingredients must be present. As Mancur Olson hypothesized, group leaders sometimes are able to encourage and sustain individual commitments by providing selective benefits to those who join and work for the group.[25] For example, "citizen's lobbies," such as Common Cause, give things selectively to dues-paying members—newsletters, a chance to demonstrate leadership within their communities, and so on. Olson also focused attention on the motivating value of coercion as a device to raise the costs of inaction, as scabs often learn when they suffer verbal and sometimes worse abuse from striking union members.

[25] Mancur Olson, Jr., *The Logic of Collective Action: Public Goods and the Theory of Groups* (Cambridge, Mass.: Harvard University Press, 1965).

Other studies stress the importance of various non-economic inducements to group formation, including the motivating value of personal friendships.[26] Moreover, as Jack Walker has shown, groups often are able to reduce economic disincentives for their members by finding a financial angel—a wealthy patron, foundation or even governmental agency, to subsidize financially the formation and maintenance of the group.[27] In addition to these personal ones, societal forces too have been at work.

At a broader, societal level, there are eight major factors that contribute to the formation and evolution of interest groups in America: the nature of economic activity, the growth of government, regulatory policies, court decisions, technological advances, change in the role of political parties, the cost of running for elective office, and the supply of campaign resources from non-interest groups. The growth of the modern industrial system, for example, brought about a geographic concentration of workers and helped make them ripe for organizing, instilling new predispositions and political demands, as was seen in the growth of labor unions and in their increasingly assertive political role. The growth of federal government since the New Deal and, in particular, the mushrooming of welfare payments directly to individuals, created new clients who learned to expect and demand better benefits as, for instance, the aged have through such organizations as the National Association of Retired Persons.

In addition, the federal government's attempts to regulate various industries encouraged them to organize politically. In many cases, regulated indus-

---

[26] Terry M. Moe, *The Organization of Interests* (Chicago: University of Chicago Press, 1980); Terry M. Moe, "Toward a Broader Theory of Interest Groups," *Journal of Politics* 43 (1981): 531–43.

[27] Jack L. Walker, "The Origins and Maintenance of Interest Groups in America," *American Political Science Review* 77 (1983): 390–406.

tries came to dominate the governmental institutions that had been created to regulate them. This was shown, for example, in the successes of the railroads, bus and truck companies, and other transportation industries in "capturing" their regulatory agency, the Interstate Commerce Commission. New laws and interpretations of them by courts also provide new spawning grounds for interest groups. Consider the Supreme Court for a moment; in ruling on the constitutionality of the Federal Election Campaign Act of 1974, the Court gave great impetus to the formation of Political Action Committees when it found that the Congress could not prohibit the so-called "independent campaign expenditures" that interest groups make without consulting their favored candidate.[28] The Supreme Court also expanded the scope of Political Action Committees when it overturned efforts to keep PAC money out of public referenda elections that were held to decide on policy questions, not to elect policy makers.[29]

Technological advance also creates new methods of influence and organized interests are quick to exploit them. One computerized interest group leader, Richard A. Viguerie, used computer-based, direct-mail in 1980 to send out approximately 70 million letters to raise over $20 million for conservative congressional candidates. Interest groups also fill the political vacuum left by an historical decline in the strength of political parties. This leaves them less able to deliver the votes on election day that can protect those elected party members who would usually ignore the demands of organized interests. Tremendous rises in the cost of campaigning for elective office have increased the demand that candidates have for money and therefore, their receptivity to those who have it. Finally, there just is not a lot of campaign money supplied by non-interest groups; most Americans do not contribute enough money to election campaigns. As long as nomination and election campaigns are not adequately financed out of public funds, most office seekers will rely on the contributions of special interest groups.

By reacting to societal dissatisfactions and dislocations in the distribution of wealth and power, interest groups evolve and probably will continue to grow in number and influence. As they grow, it is certain that interest groups will find various ways of using the political process to press their claims on society. Some of these activities of interest groups will be in cooperation with political parties, as both work together to plow new pathways of political influence. Other interest group activities may conflict with the broader concerns of political parties, as interest groups try to plow parties under, gaining influence at their expense.

The Organizational Components of Groups

Political interest groups have the same *organizational components* as political parties: goals, policy objectives, members, resources, activities, and tactics.

---

[28] *Buckley* v. *Valeo*, 424 U.S. 1 (1976).

[29] *First National Bank of Boston* v. *Bellotti*, 435 U.S. 765 (1978).

Goals. Political interest groups are focused on their primary goal: to influence public policy in ways that favor the interests of their members. In a pluralistic society, however, there are many different and often competing policy objectives.

Policy Objectives. Since there are many different policy objectives, there are many different kinds of interest groups.

Maggie Kuhn, founder of the National Grey Panthers.

The *five major kinds of political interest groups* represent ideological, economic, citizen, minority group, and other governmental interests. Ideological interest groups, especially the more conservative ones, are today, the best financed and most active, as you can see in the **Vantage Point**: Money Talks. In general, however, ideological interest groups are both conservative and liberal. On the conservative side, for example, there is the National Conservative Political Action Committee (NCPAC) which targeted for electoral defeat six liberal Democratic senators in 1980 and helped dump four by running "anti" ads against them. On the liberal side, the National Committee for an Effective Congress (NCEC), for example, supports left-thinking, usually Democratic, congressional candidates. It has done this since its birth thirty-five years ago when Eleanor Roosevelt and other reform-minded Democrats used it to help elect Hubert Humphrey of Minnesota, Paul Douglas of Illinois, and Estes Kefauver of Tennessee, thus capturing the Senate in 1948.

Many other political interest groups are organized around economic interests: for example, the operators of fast food restaurants who lobby the Congress to exempt their teen-age employees from minimum-wage legislation; organized labor that refuses to see the right to strike struck from federal law; and milk producers who try to pump up federal price supports.

In addition, other political interest groups coalesce around the broader concerns of ordinary citizens, the felt needs of minority group members, and the self-interest of different levels and kinds of governments. Citizen groups, for example, typically focus on the need to reform government and policy-making procedures, as does Common Cause, for example, or on the need to remedy specific problems, as do various environmental action groups or many of the Ralph Nader task forces. Interest groups representing the various interests of minorities typically try to advance the civil and economic rights of the poor and usually aged, female, and black—the National Association for the Advancement of Colored People, the Children's Defense Fund, the National Welfare Rights Organization, the Lawyers Committee for Civil Rights Under Law, and the National Gray Panthers, for example.

Another category includes both state and local levels of government and many extremely active foreign governments. State and local governments, for example, often come to Washington seeking federal aid or relief from federal interference and typically close ranks behind one of their many lobbying organizations—the National Governors' Association, the National Council of Counties, the National League of Cities, the U.S. Conference of Mayors. This category, however, is dominated by foreign governments, many of which run extremely well-financed lobbying organizations, as you also can see in the

MONEY TALKS

Money is a terribly important resource for political interest groups. Some are better at amassing it than others, however.

One measure of the size of money's voice is provided by data on the expenditures of Political Action Committees. Here, for the 1983–1984 electoral season, are the top ten PACs, along with their total expenditures:

PAC	Expenditure
1. National Conservative PAC	$19,332,000
2. Fund for a Conservative Majority	5,451,498
3. National Congressional Club	5,222,378
4. Realtors PAC	3,874,782
5. National Rifle Association PAC	3,774,796
6. Republican Majority Fund	3,531,125
7. American Medical Association	3,513,763
8. Ruff PAC	3,499,272
9. Fund for a Democratic Majority	2,955,393
10. Citizens for the Republic	2,754,549

SOURCE: Federal Election Commission

Another measure of the role of money in policy making is what foreign governments report spending in their attempts to influence federal legislation. During 1984, these were the biggest spenders:

Country	Expenditure
1. Japan	$14,294,000
2. Canada	7,531,000
3. West Germany	6,362,000
4. Soviet Union	5,469,000
5. Ireland	5,438,000
6. Indonesia	5,290,000
7. Scotland	3,504,000
8. Korea	3,221,000
9. Saudi Arabia	3,209,000
10. France	3,204,000

SOURCE: United States Department of Justice

Vantage Point: Money Talks. In these cases, "registered agents" represent what foreign governments see as their national interests, as, for example, President Carter's brother Billy did representing the government of Libya, as Canada does, chafing under our acid rain, or as Japan does to keep American markets open to Japanese goods.

These categories capture the major interest groups, or lobbies, as they are sometimes called. But, be cautious of categorical labels. As David Truman first warned, categorical labels are apt enough, but one should not assume too much about them. All business groups are not the same, for example; on some issues, business groups may lobby for different points of view.[30]

---

[30] See Truman, *Governmental Process*, especially Chapter Three.

Members.   The members of political interest groups are its infantry, the ultimate source of its influence over the making of public policy. But membership characteristics often limit interest group influence, either because members are unaware of the need to act or are immobilized by competing pressures from various groups. When members are ill informed, a political interest group has to divert scarce resources away from the exercise of influence and spend them instead on educating and attempting to mobilize its own people. When they are pressured by competing attachments to other interest groups, members of interest groups will be either reluctant to act or, at least, will be reluctant to act forcefully.

This problem of competing interest group attachments was demonstrated in early 1986, for example, as Congress began its consideration of legislation that would have made it easier to purchase a hand gun through the mail. The National Rifle Association urged its members to support the legislation, but many of them also belonged to associations of law enforcement officials which attacked the legislation as a "cop-killer" bill. The members, caught in the middle and pressured by both sides, sat out the battle.

Richard Boyd, the president of the Fraternal Order of Police, organizing police officers who were about to lobby against congressional efforts to ease federal gun controls.

Resources.   The major resources of political interest groups are money and information. Political interest groups spend huge amounts of money, since all organizational purposes require money: attracting new members, renewing old memberships, educating members about upcoming legislative threats to their interests, mobilizing members in attempts to exert pressure on legislators, maintaining a professional staff, retaining outside expert advice, and conducting public relations campaigns.

Money surely is a necessary condition for interest group influence, since money buys access to policy makers. For example, in 1985, just as the Ways and Means Committee of the U.S. House of Representatives began to consider massive changes in the tax code, the committee's chairman, Dan Rostenkowski (D., Ill.) held a reception to raise contributions that he could spend on his own re-election campaign or give to his colleagues in the House for theirs. Those who attended got something for their $500 donations: a drink, something to munch on, and a little button saying "I did more than shake Rosty's hand" which they could wear the next time they went to see him. But, once access is obtained, an interest group must be able to draw on another important resource: information.

Information that is both accurate and detailed is a precious organizational resource. In addition to facts about problems and possible solutions, policy makers need several different kinds of information—explorations of long-term consequences, analyses of possible unintended effects, intelligence about the likely political fallout of alternative actions, insight on the likely support and opposition of fellow policy makers, assurances that people will comply with policies, and so on. Lacking good information and contextual analysis, most policy makers are heavily dependent on others and enterprising policy makers will use interest groups as auxiliary staff to gather and assess information.

In addition to the piece work contributions of individual lobbyists, some interests have geared up research operations or "think-tanks" to meet the informational and analysis needs of policy makers. Conservative interests, for example, help sustain the American Enterprise Institute (AEI), a Washington research organization whose staff argued for years the need to cut taxes, increase defense spending, and deregulate the economy. After the election of Ronald Reagan, the AEI supplied many of the people who tried to put these conservative ideas into practice including Reagan's first Chairman of the Council of Economic Advisers (Murray L. Weidenbaum), Ambassador to the United Nations (Jeane J. Kirkpatrick), member of the National Security Council (Roger Fontaine), and Undersecretary of Defense (Lawrence Korb). Throwing intellectual bricks from the other side of the street, organizations such as the Institute for Policy Studies argue the cause for human rights, against the arms race, and for expanded social welfare programs at home.

Activities.   We can begin to understand the activities of interest groups by thinking of them as communication channels that link demands from the environment to the policy-making processes of government. This view builds on Lester Milbrath's definition of lobbying as any "communication, by someone other than a citizen acting on his own behalf, directed to a governmental decision-maker with the hope of influencing his decision."[31] To this view, we would add that communication is a two-way process and the leaders of interest groups also are heavily involved in communicating with, and attempting to influence, their own membership.

Interest groups communicate with their members to socialize them and the general public about what can and should be expected from government. As "tutors" of political expectations, interest groups perform reality therapy on the public, helping ordinary citizens identify real options.[32] This sort of role, however, assumes that people have "instrumental" orientations toward government that make them want to find solutions to their problems, not simply "expressive" orientations that make them most interested in venting their anger.[33] Sometimes, of course, passion blinds and tutoring falls on deaf ears, as it did in Chicago in 1968. In other cases, interest groups show the indignant politically useful ways to vent their anger. In Iowa in 1980, for example, the Pro-Life Action Council channeled outrage over abortion, using it to help bury the liberal first-term Democratic Senator, John Culver.[34]

In communicating with policy makers, political interest groups try to shape the policy agenda. Their first task is to get the attention of policy makers. This is a more important function than it might initially seem, as most policy makers are preoccupied with two or three simultaneously ongoing projects and on the fringes of three or four more. To make things more complicated, several other people are also trying to get the policy maker's attention. Policy makers are just like everyone else; they have limited amounts of time, physical energy, and mental space. All of these are scarce commodities; policy makers are like rock stars after a concert, with everybody grabbing for a piece of clothing. In the consideration of the 1984 tax bill for example, large amounts of money were at stake as the Congress had before it proposals to eliminate various tax deductions; meanwhile the halls were lined with Washington lawyers all waiting to pounce on members. In this frantic environment, members of Congress focus at most on one of two major issues, and it is very, very difficult to get their attention for anything new.

To communicate policy recommendations effectively, political interest groups must be able to articulate policy problems and preferred solutions. This is a necessary function, since ours is a big, diverse country and policy makers are no more omniscient than the rest of us. Instead, policy makers, especially those in Washington, D.C., are distant from many of society's problems and

---

31 Lester W. Milbrath, *The Washington Lobbyists* (Chicago: Rand McNally, 1963), p. 8.

32 Nelson W. Polsby, *Consequences of Party Reform* (New York: Oxford University Press, 1983). See especially pages 131–56.

33 The distinction between lobbying that serves "instrumental" versus "expressive" purposes is made by Robert H. Salisbury, "An Exchange Theory of Interest Groups," *Midwest Journal of Political Science* 8 (1969): 1–32.

34 Marjorie Randon Hershey and Darrell M. West, "Single Issue Politics: Prolife Groups and the 1980 Senate Campaign," in Allan J. Cigler and Burdett A. Loomis, eds. *Interest Group Politics* (Washington, D.C.: CQ Press, 1983), pp. 31–59.

To attract attention and stimulate awareness, interest groups sometimes personalize policy problems, as environmental groups did in calling for the resignation of President Reagan's Secretary of the Interior, James Watt.

therefore depend on others to tell them what needs their attention. Interest groups are good at this. Martin Luther King, Jr., and other civil rights activists, for example, demonstrated graphically the problems of blacks in many parts of the country through marches, sit-ins and boycotts. More recently, environmental groups worked together to collect over one million names calling for the removal of James G. Watt, President Reagan's first Secretary of the Interior. Through their congressional testimony, interest groups try to convey an understanding of what unaddressed problems mean in human terms. There is a generic message: "Here is a problem, fix it my way!" If the advice is heeded and the policy adopted, the successful interest group can continue its watchdog role, by monitoring the policy and by feeding back information about its impact—thereby helping policy makers evaluate policy. In all these ways, interest groups perform intelligence functions, educating both the public and policy makers about government's possible and proper roles.

Tactics. In addition to their campaign tactics (dealt with in the elections section of chapter 7), political interest groups rely on a combination of what are called "inside" and "outside" lobbying tactics. Inside tactics are low-key and behind the scenes, and are used to put together the sort of coalition that is necessary to ensure favorable action. More confrontational and public outside tactics are designed to bring pressure to bear on policy makers, to command their attention and hopefully, their compliance. Outside tactics include, for example, the use of well-orchestrated letter writing campaigns or other attempts to direct grass-roots pressure and the use of litigation to bring about legal pressure.

Both inside and outside lobbying tactics are common. The classical inside

POLITICAL PARTIES AND INTEREST GROUPS: DO WE NEED THEM?

form of lobbying includes personal contacts and the presentation of testimony before legislative committees. In these efforts, the best "insiders" often are former legislators or administrators. Charls E. Walker, for example, a former Treasury Department deputy secretary and head of Ronald Reagan's tax advisory group in 1980, is a quintessential insider who would rather press the claims of his clients on the Reagan Administration than work within it.[35] That is great access if you can get it, but many interest groups do not have such great connections and instead have to rely more on "outsider" tactics to chastise policy makers for their actions and inactions. Outsiders often litigate, for example, taking policy makers to court to challenge their actions, as Common Cause did when Congress tried to restrict its access to reports of campaign contributions or as civil rights, consumer, and environmental advocacy groups often do to push governmental agencies.[36] Newer tactics of both inside and outside influence include using computers to evaluate alternative versions of pending legislation or to produce mass mailings in an attempt to stimulate grass-roots support for legislation.

■ As Madison observed in the *Federalist Papers* and as we saw in the events leading to the Democratic presidential nominating convention in 1968, people, and perhaps Americans especially, are factious, quick to assert their self-interests and to demand that government satisfy them. As long as political interest groups remain as accommodating and as enterprising as in the past, they will play important roles in the policy-making process.

THE PROPER ROLE OF PARTIES AND GROUPS

> Political parties created democracy
> and . . . modern democracy is unthinkable
> save in terms of parties.
> —*E. E. Schattschneider*, Party
> Government

Parties and interest groups have both desirable and undesirable effects on the American political system. It is important, therefore, that we sort out these two effects—before other Americans reform parties and regulate interest groups out of existence.

---

35 Elizabeth Drew, "Charlie," *The New Yorker* 53 (1978): 32–58. Reprinted in Allan J. Cigler and Burdett A. Loomis, eds. *Interest Group Politics* (Washington, D.C.: CQ Press, 1983), pp. 217–50.

36 For examples of the use of litigation tactics, see Stephen L. Wasby, "Interest Groups in Court," in Allan J. Cigler and Burdett A. Loomis, eds. *Interest Group Politics* (Washington, D.C.: CQ Press, 1983), pp. 251–74; and Karen O'Connor, *Women's Organizations Use of the Courts* (Lexington, Mass.: Lexington Books, 1980).

THE WILDAVSKY—POLSBY DIALOGUE CONTINUED . . .

AUTHOR: Let me raise a general issue. What are your views on the proper roles of interest groups, political parties, and the media?

POLSBY: I think it's important that people understand that their relations with the government and with political leaders are mediated, at least, by these three institutional complexes. There's a sense in which you use membership in a political party or membership in one or more interest groups or access to the news media as alternative ways of reaching leaders—and leaders use each of these as alternative ways of mobilizing followers.

WILDAVSKY: I think also that media elites are part of the egalitarian movement in this country. If you're talking about diminishing differences among people, or what role to take about the spread of Acquired Immune Deficiency Syndrome, or about the women's movement, and so on, I find consistently that the media are in favor of reducing such differences and far more so than the ordinary person. And, since the people in authority represent one of those differences, you have a constant building up of efforts to increase equality through government and constant denegration of those in government who have to do the job. Given that context, any President, not only Ronald Reagan, will find himself feeling that, if he allows the media to capture the public's attention, the results will be constantly negative. Therefore, the White House, over time, reaches out more and more with very large operations to send letters to people. Really millions of letters are going out. Reagan's radio bit is, however, another matter; in my opinion, the President is not all that persuasive.

POLSBY: Don't you think he's a Great Communicator?

WILDAVSKY: No. And the debate with Mondale in 1984 would tell you that. He's an excellent reader of a speech and he is also an excellent editor and writer of speeches (because I just saw a handwritten effort on his part). He is also a great setter of priorities, but it is easier for his opponents to claim that he somehow exudes persuasiveness.

AUTHOR: How do you account for Ronald Reagan's electoral victories in 1980 and 1984? And what do those reveal about the future of the Republican and Democratic parties?

POLSBY: My view is that the election of Ronald Reagan is the result of the disintegration of the Democratic Party. Internal conflicts hurt the Democratic Party and permitted the Republicans to elect a President when they did not have the allegiance of a majority of the American people. It's also the case that the message that Ronald Reagan has projected to the electorate has, for the most part, been empty of conflict and, simply, cheerful. This has played well among ordinary voters who are, on the whole, sick and tired of the Democratic party's internal conflicts.

WILDAVSKY: Listen to the rhetoric of the Democratic presidential nominating convention. By stressing the claims of those who have been left out of the system—women, blacks, Chicanos, the elderly—the single most important voting block in America—which is white males—has been led to understand, kind of subliminally and indirectly, that the Democratic Party is not for them. So, one reason I believe that the Democratic Party has had difficulty is that its desire to increase equality has lead to what I would call an elephantitis of the deprived. (Polsby: "Donkeyitis.")

POLSBY: I think people prefer their government to be managed by people who announce themselves to be in charge and don't seem to be squabbling. The Democrats have gone through twenty years of squabbling and this has given an enormous opportunity to Republicans, which they have used to win the presidency.

AUTHOR: What prescription would you write for the Democratic Party?

POLSBY: My prescription for the Democratic Party is perfectly straightforward. Since they have the allegiance of more people than any other political party, the Democrats should start representing those people and stop throwing away the election at the presidential level. That means they must reform their presidential nominating process.

AUTHOR: Didn't the Democratic Party initially reform their presidential nominating process to try to get more in touch with the people?

POLSBY: Yes, and I could tell you that people try to cure hiccoughs by soaking their heads in a bucket of water. You asked me to prescribe a cure, not to be a reporter of people's good intentions. Therefore, I must tell you that the reforms of the Democratic party, following 1968, in fact drove the Democratic Party further away from the opinions of most of the people. Those reforms gave the Democrats a presidential nomination process which was totally controlled by unrepresentative elites, those who participated heavily in primary elections and who were unable to represent the rank and file, who, in general, do not participate in primary elections.

The prescription I have is this. Delegates to the national presidential nominating convention should be representatives of state parties, rather than representatives of the faction of the state party

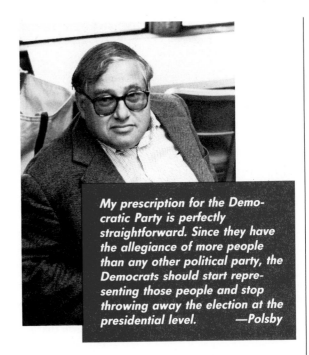

My prescription for the Democratic Party is perfectly straightforward. Since they have the allegiance of more people than any other political party, the Democrats should start representing those people and stop throwing away the election at the presidential level. **—Polsby**

which is allied with the candidate who won the most votes in the primary election. In other words, the Democrats have to get a broader spectrum of the members of the state party into the national convention. If a broader spectrum of rank and file sentiment is represented at the national convention, I think the Democratic Party will nominate more appealing and successful presidential candidates.

AUTHOR: Wouldn't that be a less democratic process?

POLSBY: It depends on what your political theory is. If your democratic theory is concerned with who actually participates and not how shallow the participation is, then, yes, it would be less democratic. If, however, one were to think about these issues of democratic theory more carefully, then a process that is more responsive to a wider range of rank and file views would be more democratic.

The Effects of Parties and Interest Groups

Political parties and political interest groups have ambiguous effects; they both act in ways that contribute to and detract from their own and the political system's legitimacy. They perform functions that are essential in a democratic system, especially one that values liberty so highly. But they do so under a cloud, haunted by constant suspicions of impropriety. In short, we could not govern without them, but it is difficult to govern with them. Whether one likes it or not, political parties and political interest groups are indispensable in American government.

Parties and interest groups act in ways that enhance the legitimacy of the political system by making it more representative and responsive. Ironically, however, the success of parties and groups in making the political system more representative and responsive invites suspicions about their own legitimacy.

Making the System More Representative. The Founders allowed for the possibility that the new government might get out of touch with the people. Accordingly, they saw the need for actions that might improve the fit between the government's policies and the people's preferences and thereby, improve the political system's legitimacy. The propriety of such actions was acknowledged by the First Amendment to the Constitution, prohibiting the Congress from making any law that abridged the right of the people "to petition the Government for a redress of grievances." But who would carry the complaints and make sure that policy makers paid attention? The Constitution, of course, was silent. But the democratic system had to find a way to give voice, and an *effective* voice, to the people. Somebody, somehow, had to take on the task of representing the people, of articulating their grievances, and of aggregating their demands in a way that facilitated a proper response by government. That task, the essential task of representation, fell to political parties and interest groups.

Raising Suspicions of Undo Influence. Political parties and political interest groups enhance government's representativeness by bringing about policy outcomes that benefit specific constituencies. Interest groups, in particular, are especially effective in biasing government and policy making, prompting actions that tend to favor the immediate, tangible interests of narrow but politically powerful interests.[37] But, leaning somewhat the other way, political parties, especially when they have to compete with one another, tend to advocate social welfare policies that appeal to the less-well-off. In one early assessment of this impact, V. O. Key, Jr. asserted that competitive parties were

---

[37] See the case study of highway policies in Ronald C. Kahn, "Political Change in America: Highway Politics and Reactive Policymaking," in J. David Greenstone, ed. *Public Values and Private Power in American Politics* (Chicago: University of Chicago Press, 1982), pp. 139–72.

"essential . . . for the promotion of a sustained program on behalf of the have-nots."[38]

In addition, political parties carry their own intellectual baggage into office and their ideological orientations do set priorities and shape policies. A significant consequence is that "the governing party is very much responsible for major macroeconomic outcomes—unemployment rates, inflation rates, income equalization, and the size and rate of expansion of the government budget."[39]

In general, however, political parties and interest groups work to protect the policy benefits they and their supporters enjoy from the status quo. Successful candidates for elective office know who helped them win and will try to protect the policy interests of their supporters. The irony, of course, is that the more successful they are, the more interest groups and parties attract suspicion and incite calls for their regulation and reform.

The Drive to Reform Parties and Regulate Groups

Their own successes and excesses raise suspicions about political parties and political interest groups, suspicions that they benefit at the public's expense. These suspicions, in turn, fuel the drive to reform parties and regulate groups.

Suspicions of undue influence on government and public policy, exercised by interest groups and parties is as deeply rooted as are the factions themselves. Most prominent among the warnings against them are those of departing Presidents. In a vein similar to George Washington's farewell warning against the evils of parties, President Eisenhower warned in 1960 against the pernicious effects of a particular coalition of interests—"the military-industrial complex"—and, more recently, a departing President Carter warned us about interest groups in general on the grounds that they are "a disturbing factor" that "tends to distort our purposes, because the national interest is not always the sum of all our single or special interests."[40]

Political parties and interest groups are most feared and most in need of regulation and reform when they undermine democratic government by co-opting public power. Out of their successes, parties and interest groups win power to make binding decisions that affect others in society, thus allowing private interests to act as though they were governmental agencies. This happens, for example, when political parties appoint public servants on the basis of partisan considerations, when state associations of doctors decide who can practice medicine within the state's borders, and when elected committees of local farmers decide what the federal government will do to help conserve the soil. Such instances pose dangers for a democracy, as Grant McConnell and

[38] V. O. Key, Jr., *Southern Politics* (New York: Alfred A. Knopf, 1949), p. 307.

[39] Edward R. Tufte, *Political Control of the Economy* (Princeton: Princeton University Press, 1978), p. 104.

[40] Quoted in *The Washington Lobby*, 4th ed. (Washington, D.C.: Congressional Quarterly Inc., 1982), p. 1.

Theodore J. Lowi have warned:[41] private groups, while insulated from public accountability and democratic control, can use public power to advance their own interests at the expense of the rest of society. Such a misuse of public authority, or even the appearance of misuse, some fear, can demoralize a democratic citizenry and delegitimize a democratic government.

The fear is strong enough to prompt efforts to regulate interest groups, and presumably because they are not beyond redemption, "reform" political parties. These regulatory and reform efforts have a long and continuing history in America. We can only note briefly here what others have detailed elsewhere; it is very hard to regulate interest groups, as long as they have intense interests and as long as society is unwilling to intrude on what people call liberty. In general, regulating interest groups is almost as difficult as getting a picture of the Loch Ness monster. Nevertheless, given the need to defend government's legitimacy and therefore its capacity to govern, the task of regulating interest groups and reforming parties is not so difficult as to cause most Americans to give up. For that matter, even interest groups and parties have an interest in curtailing their own excessive appetites, before they devour the host and the public's forbearance.

In conclusion, both political parties and interest groups have a proper role: to represent political concerns in a way that wins at least the attention of policy makers, and preferably their acquiescence. To perform this role, parties and groups shuttle back and forth between their own constituencies and policy makers. In the process, party and interest group leaders attempt to influence both policy makers and their own members. Both have constituencies to cultivate and both spend a lot of time trying to convince them how hard they are working. Indeed, the greatest impact of parties and interest group leaders may be the one they have on their own followers, raising their concern about impending policy losses and then convincing them how bad things would have been if their leaders had not been so politically astute and hard working. In the long run, however, political parties and interest groups must deliver real policy benefits, without appearing to corrupt the public interest, if they are to endure.

■ As we have seen in the years since 1968, political parties have gotten weaker and political interest groups stronger. Today, political interest groups are very good at providing particularistic benefits, while the major political parties find it harder to have a broad effect on the general policy directions of government. (For their effects on the policy-making process, minor political parties can be thought of as the suggestion boxes of American politics.) When they do have an impact, however, both parties and interest groups typically bring about marginal policy change, although some of the policy changes under President Reagan were a bit of an exception to this general rule.[42]

[41] Grant McConnell, *Private Power and American Democracy* (New York: Alfred A. Knopf, 1966); and Theodore J. Lowi, *The End of Liberalism: Ideology, Policy, and the Crisis of Public Authority* (New York: W. W. Norton, 1969).

[42] See Fred I. Greenstein, ed. *The Reagan Presidency: An Early Assessment* (Baltimore: The Johns Hopkins University Press, 1983).

SUMMARY

In any large and diverse society such as ours, there is a need for somebody to somehow link the preferences of people with the policy actions of governmental officials. Traditionally, that role has been performed by interest groups which express specific demands and by political parties which aggregate them into packages of proposals that could attract broad support.

Political parties are loose coalitions of both principled and ambitious people who are organized for the purpose of winning elective office. To reach this goal, parties depend heavily on alliances with political interest groups, usually tighter coalitions of people organized for the purpose of influencing public policy. The alliances, however, are uneasy and shifting, especially in recent years as interest groups have become more insistent and less compromising about realizing their narrow concerns.

Political parties and political interest groups have similar organizational problems: to realize their goals, they must carefully formulate policy objectives, attract and retain members, expand their resource base, perform certain activities, and design and execute tactics. In recent years, however, political interest groups have been more successful than political parties in solving their organizational problems.

Through their successes, both political parties and political interest groups are able to enhance the legitimacy of the political system as a whole by making it more representative and responsive to popular concerns. Ironically, their successes also raise suspicions of impropriety and fuel the drive to reform parties and regulate interest groups. The drive has popular appeal. Hopefully, it will be possible to control their excesses without reforming parties and regulating interest groups out of existence.

Key Terms

political party	protest party
political interest group	single-issue party
faction	media party
interest articulation	party identification
interest aggregation	party delegates
ideological party	party identifiers
factional party	Political Action Committee (PAC)

Review and Reflection

1. Define the terms political party and political interest group.

2. Describe the relationship between political parties and political interest groups.

3. Do we need political parties and political interest groups? Why?

4. In what ways are both political parties and political interest groups organizations?

5. If you, and people like you, do not give money to candidates who are running for elective office, where do you expect them to get it?

6. Describe the process by which political parties and political interest groups enhance the legitimacy of the political system, while eroding their own.

7. What do you believe to be the proper role of political parties? Interest groups?

Supplemental Readings

Much of the literature on parties and interest groups is concerned with their ability to improve the quality of political representation. Some studies, such as *Schattschneider*, lay down a basic understanding of the way representative linkages are forged. Most of the works on political parties provide a fairly gloomy assessment of their current role, as *Ranney* does, for example. While *Crotty* traces their decline, *Burnham* concludes it was inevitable and probably irreversible. Some, especially *Fleishman*, are optimistic about the future of political parties. Others, however, such as *Ceaser* and *Polsby*, believe that parties need to be more free of regulation if they are to survive. Some balance is provided by *Petrocik*, who believes that party coalitions are simply evolving, not disintegrating. Most of the literature on political interest groups is somewhat damning, tracing as it does the relationship between economic power and influence over public policy. It is real, of course, as *Drew* shows. But, as *Berry* and *McFarland* demonstrate, other interests also win access and influence, without showering policy makers with money.

Berry, Jeffery. *Lobbying for the People*. Princeton, NJ: Princeton University Press, 1977.

Burnham, Walter Dean. *The Current Crisis in American Politics*. New York: Oxford University Press, 1983.

Ceaser, James W. *Reforming the Reforms: A Critical Analysis of the Presidential Selection Process*. Cambridge, Mass.: Ballinger Publishing Company, 1982.

Crotty, William J. *American Parties in Decline*. 2nd ed. Boston: Little, Brown, and Co., 1984.

Drew, Elizabeth. "Charlie," in Allan J. Cigler and Burdett A. Loomis, eds. *Interest Group Politics*. Washington, D.C.: CQ Press, 1983. pp. 217–50.

Fleishman, Joel L., ed. *The Future of Political Parties: The Challenge of Governance*. Englewood Cliffs: Prentice-Hall, 1982.

McFarland, Andrew S. *Public Interest Lobbies: Decision Making on Energy*. Washington, D.C.: American Enterprise Institute for Public Policy Research, 1976.

Petrocik, John R. *Party Coalitions: Realignments and the Decline of the New Deal Party System.* Chicago: University of Chicago Press, 1981.

Polsby, Nelson W. *Consequences of Party Reform.* New York: Oxford University Press, 1983.

Ranney, Austin. *The Doctrine of Responsible Party Government: Its Origins and Present State.* Urbana, Ill.: The University of Illinois Press, 1962.

Schattschneider, E. E. *The Semisovereign People.* Hinsdale, Ill.: The Dryden Press, 1975.

CHAPTER SEVEN

THE MEDIA AND PARTICIPATION
THE PERMANENT CAMPAIGN

*D*oes it seem odd that George Washington did not have to work very hard to become President and Ronald Reagan spent twenty years running for the office? Or, if you judge by popular reactions, that President Carter was a failure and President Reagan a success? Or that Senator Walter D. Huddleston (D., Ky.) could start his 1984 re-election campaign fifty percentage points ahead of his opponent, Mitch McConnell, and lose by 5269 votes? All these things do seem strange, unless you understand the ways in which the mass media have transformed politics in America.

Whatever else they do, all political actors—government officials, policy makers, and politicians—must keep in touch with the people or, at least appear to do so. Their legitimacy—their right and their ability to act authoritatively—depends on it. Legitimacy, however, is hard to gain and easy to lose, and political actors must work very hard at it. Fortunately, for their sake if not for ours, astute political actors have a way of enhancing their own legitimacy; it's called the permanent campaign.

The **permanent campaign** is a process by which political actors win popular support by continuously monitoring public opinion and adjusting their media appeal. The process, therefore, requires quick and accurate public opinion polling and adroit use of the mass media to orchestrate popular reactions.

Permanent campaigns are difficult to run, as you will see in the following Case, the story of President Carter's failed re-election campaign in 1980. His failures may have revealed a few insights to President Reagan, as they do to us: (1) modern policy makers must maintain a permanent campaign to retain popular support and legitimacy; (2) policy makers use the media to market themselves and their policies; and (3) the permanent campaign complements, and may even be a substitute for, more traditional forms of political participation, such as voting and letter writing.

One of the fifty-three American hostages. This photo was taken only three days after their capture in 1979.

THE PERMANENT CAMPAIGN

It's all over—it's gone. The sky has fallen in. . . . All the people that have been waiting and holding out for some reason to vote Democratic have left us. . . . It's going to be a big Reagan victory. . . .

—*Pat Caddell, President Carter's pollster, the night before the 1980 presidential election*

The Case What President Carter's Failure Taught President Reagan[1]

President Carter's campaign headquarters, Washington, D.C. 7:00 P.M. November 3, 1980. Hamilton Jordan[2], Carter's White House Chief of Staff, and the others gathered at the campaign headquarters knew that the next day's election was lost; Jimmy Carter was about to become the first popularly elected President to fail to win re-election since Herbert Hoover lost to Franklin D. Roosevelt in 1932. Jordan knew for sure, because the last five minutes had nailed down the lid on Carter's electoral coffin; once again the three major television networks began their evening news broadcast with THE STORY.

The Story always begins the same way, Jordan must have thought—with its predictable and infuriating sense of unending tragedy. Tonight will be different, he must have hoped; surely the media will make the last day of campaigning the lead story. But it was the same again, only this time the numbered day reached its greatest and from his boss's point of view, its worst value; "Today," intoned television newsanchors, "is the 351st day of captivity for the American hostages in Iran." This lead was a classic understatement; it let the listener shout in his own mind the conclusion: "This is the 351st day that President Carter has failed to resolve the hostage crisis."

The bad got worse before the evening news was over that November 3. Before signing off, each of the three networks concluded their telecast with an in-depth review of the hostage crisis. For up to five minutes, the American viewing public was splattered with the seizure and ransacking of the American Embassy, photographs of blindfolded and stumbling hostages, the failed rescue mission, the story of the resignation in protest of Secretary of State Cyrus Vance, the continued and mounting outrage of Americans over their nation's impotence. In this manner, the media led Americans through the pride-wrenching year of the hostage crisis, brought them to an emotional brink, and invited them to push Carter off. Finally, blessedly, the news ended and at that moment they all knew.

---

[1] This account of the 1980 presidential election is based on: David Broder et al., *The Pursuit of the Presidency 1980* (New York: Berkley Books, 1980); Hamilton Jordan, *Crisis: The True Story of an Unforgettable Year in the White House* (New York: Berkley Books, 1982); Jonathan Moore, ed., *The Campaign for President: 1980 in Retrospect* (Cambridge, Mass.: Ballinger, 1981); and Gerald Pomper et al., *The Election of 1980: Reports and Interpretations* (Chatham, NJ: Chatham House, 1981).

[2] "Jordan" is pronounced Jur-dan.

Jordan subsequently recorded the reaction of Bob Strauss, the head of the Re-election Committee. Putting his hands over his face and shaking his head, Strauss said, "The news tonight was bad, bad, bad for us. We needed a lift tonight, an upbeat story, pictures of people clapping and smiling and a confident President shaking hands. . . . Instead we got this hostage stuff."[3] The impression was statistically sealed later that night, in the early morning hours of election day, when the President's pollster, Pat Caddell, called Jordan with the results of his latest survey. "It's going to be a big Reagan victory, Ham, in the range of eight to ten points. The hostage crisis symbolizes our impotence. Ronald Reagan's message is, 'Elect me and you won't have to take that anymore.'"[4] Thus, before a single voting booth opened, they all knew; the day and the office were lost.

The story had begun a year ago, on November 3, 1979, when Iranian militants overran the American Embassy in Tehran, the capital of Iran, and took hostage fifty-three Americans. Initially, the seizure worked to Carter's political advantage. Americans rallied behind their President who, in the name of duty, retreated into the White House and proceeded to implement his so-called "Rose Garden" re-election campaign strategy. Carter even looked presidential as he explained the reasons for abstaining from nomination politics:

> I, as President, have got to maintain the accurate image that we do have a crisis, which I will not ignore until those hostages are released. I want the American people to know it. I want the Iranians to know it. I want the hostages' families and the hostages to know it. I want the world to know that I am not going to resume business-as-usual as a partisan campaigner out on the campaign trail until our hostages are back here—free and at home.[5]

At first, the strategy worked; the President's standing in the polls doubled, and he did not have to waste his newly enhanced prestige competing with Senator Kennedy in the Democratic presidential primaries.[6] But then, President Carter's strategy began to fail, as he was unable to negotiate, or win through an aborted rescue mission, the release of the American hostages. The raising and dashing of hopes compounded the string of apparent American policy failures; a frustrated public turned on their President, who now seemed to be hiding in the Rose Garden.

After isolating himself from the people, the media was left free to interpret President Carter's foreign policy failure as a failure of character. Frustrated by the lack of campaign events to cover, the media took aim at the only thing visible: the Rose Garden strategy itself. Michael Gartner, for example, the president and editor of *The Des Moines Register*, reacted angrily to Carter's cancellation of the scheduled debate with Kennedy on the eve of Iowa's Democratic caucus: "The President says he can't come here because of Iran. Well, people see that as a transparent political situation, with the White House figuring we're too stupid to figure it out."[7] Attempting to satisfy the media with surrogates, Carter sent his

[3] Jordan, *Crisis*, p. 345.

[4] *Ibid.*, p. 346. Caddell's forecast was typically accurate; Reagan just beat the spread with 10.6 percentage points of the two-party vote.

[5] *Congressional Quarterly Weekly Report*, 38 (February 16, 1980), p. 410.

[6] Pomper, *The Election*, p. 99.

[7] Quoted in *The New York Times*, 3 January 1980.

President Carter's strategy for campaigning against Senator Edward Kennedy for the democratic presidential nomination in 1980 was not immune to criticism—or parody.

I cannot tolerate American citizens being held against their will. so, as in the past, I will put politics aside and remain in the White House until every last Kennedy delegate is released.

wife, his Vice-President, Walter Mondale, and his cabinet officials out on the campaign trail—where they were promptly ignored by the press: "I'd have to set my hair on fire to get on the news," Mondale moaned.[8] In one widely syndicated column entitled "President-in-Hiding," David Broder complained: ". . . it is Carter's interests—not the hostages' or the country's—that are being protected by his sequestered status."[9]

Events, not his own design, drew the President out. Only six days after announcing the cancellation of his failed attempt to rescue the American hostages, President Carter ended his self-imposed exile from the political process, declaring to a skeptical press that the country's foreign and domestic problems "are manageable enough now for me to leave the White House. . . ."[10] Emerging from the Rose Garden, President Carter, however, proceeded to lose the election, rather than make Ronald Reagan win it.

After emerging from his televised debate with John Anderson, the Republican-running-as-Independent, Reagan did not look as though he were an unstable warmonger. But the Carter campaign, in apparent desperation, turned ugly, with Carter directly attacking Reagan and conjuring up all sorts of horrors should he be elected. With unbecoming hyperbole, Carter hinted that the election of Reagan would turn loose the forces of racism: ". . . if I lose this election, Americans might be separate, black from white, Jew from Gentile, North from South, rural from urban."[11] Afterwards, Barbara Walters, the ABC newswoman,

---

[8] Jordan, *Crisis*, p. 322.

[9] *The Washington Post*, 3 February 1980, p. C7.

[10] Quoted in the *National Journal*, 10 May 1980.

[11] Quoted in Pomper, *The Election*, p. 80.

President Carter pitched a "blooper ball" when he cited his daughter, Amy, as someone who alerted him to the real issues of the 1980 election campaign.

led off a previously scheduled television interview with the "meanness question": "Mr. President, in recent days you have been characterized as mean, vindictive, hysterical, and on the point of desperation. . . ."[12] Then the polls picked up the public's perception of Carter's "meanness." The press reported the poll results and also began to characterize Carter's rhetoric as "mean" and "vindictive." Later, many in the press would conclude that Carter's attacks on Reagan undermined one of the President's strongest assets—"his reputation as a politician with a high sense of decency."[13]

Insights

The way in which President Carter lost his campaign for re-election may have taught Ronald Reagan something; as President, he surely acted as though he appreciated the following insights.

Insight 1. *Modern policy makers must maintain a permanent campaign to retain popular support and legitimacy.* When he retreated into his Rose Garden strategy, President Carter lost touch with the American people. He acted as though he believed that the Americans who rallied behind their President in a

---

[12] Jordan, *Crisis*, p. 330.
[13] *Congressional Quarterly Weekly Report*, (November 8, 1980), p. 3297.

trying moment would stay behind him as long as he needed them. He was wrong. The American people do not give away their trust; all policy makers, and perhaps especially Presidents, must earn it—day after day.

Insight 2. *Policy makers use the media to market themselves and their policies.* When he retreated into his Rose Garden strategy, President Carter lost the initiative in dealing with the media and therefore, the capacity to orchestrate popular support for himself and his policies. Moreover, after going on the defensive, the President became increasingly vulnerable to media attacks; unable to manipulate the media, it manipulated him.

Insight 3. *The permanent campaign complements, and may even substitute for, more traditional forms of political participation, such as voting and letter writing.* The American political system is founded on the belief that government is legitimate as long as it operates with the consent of the governed. Over time, we have experimented with different ways of deriving this consent, although, for the most part, the trend has been toward more direct forms of participation. Thus, we increasingly believe, government is legitimate only to the extent that the people effectively communicate their preferences through all the traditional forms of political participation: by, for example, following electoral campaigns, registering to vote, contributing time and money to election campaigns, voting in primary and general elections, and contacting policy makers. All of these forms of political participation are supposed to improve the fit between the people's preferences and the actions of their governmental officials. But this function, some argue, is performed perhaps better, by mass media techniques for responding to popular concerns and computer-assisted polling techniques for monitoring the impact of policy proposals and actions on popular support.

Television is gradually invading all aspects of government—including the Senate.

THE MEDIA AND PARTICIPATION: THE PERMANENT CAMPAIGN

Some go so far as to suggest we are entering a "media state."[14] If so, we should understand the nature of the media, the traditional forms of political participation, and the impact of the permanent campaign.

THE MEDIA

> Ancient Sparta was a military state. John Calvin's Geneva was a religious state. Mid-nineteenth century England was Europe's first industrial state, and the contemporary United States is the world's first media state.
> —Kevin Phillips, political commentator

The term **media**, plural of course, has come to mean the mass media, all those forms of communication between the society as a whole—the masses—and those political actors, let us call them elites, who seek to lead it, whether they do it as poorly as President Carter did or as successfully as President Reagan has.

The media are constantly transformed by technological change, perhaps more so than any other politically relevant institution in America. This means that there is some hard knowledge about them, some less well-substantiated insights, and a lot of uncertainty. In what follows, therefore, we are (1) quite certain of our discussion of the forms of mass media; (2) a little less certain of our characterization of the media's coverage of government, policies, and politics; and, (3) frankly, a little speculative in our discussion of the ways in which political actors seek to manage the media in their drive for popular support and legitimacy.

The Forms of Mass Media

Let us classify the various forms of media in two ways: categorically and analytically.

Categorical Types of Media. Categorically, media include television (network, local, and cable), radio (network and local), and all forms of print journalism: newspapers (and things in them, like editorials, polls, editorial cartoons, photographs, and even comic strips), magazines, the national news services, and books.

---

[14] See Kevin Phillips, "A Matter of Privilege," *Harpers*, January 1977, pp. 95–97.

"Don't you understand? This is life, this is what is happening. We can't switch to another channel."

Drawing by Day; © The New Yorker Magazine, Inc.

For many, television images are reality.

This categorical description of media follows that presented by Michael B. Grossman and Martha J. Kumar in their original study of the White House press corps, *Portraying the President.*[15] Consider the following major types of media: (1) television, (2) print journalism, (3) public opinion polls, (4) radio, and (5) a residual category of media bits and pieces.

Television. Television is so important that it seems as though today's political arena is about two feet square. (It's almost as though it is not real if it is not on TV.) This was especially true in the 1984 race for the Democratic presidential nomination, as candidates spent more time than ever before in more and more different televised debates than ever before. It was so striking that the *New York Times* editorialized: "Instead of just being one of the media that covers campaigns, television seems increasingly to be the forum in which the campaign takes place."[16]

Ever since Harry S. Truman was the first President to use television politically, network television has been the key conduit for political messages. In recent years, however, local television and independent cable operations have become more important. In 1984, for example, local television burst out of its role as a bit player in the presidential election drama. This was first seen in the Democratic primaries, as candidates flew around the country, timing their arrival to coincide with the local evening news, going live to local voters in upcoming primaries, often keeping waiting the television news teams of the more prestigious networks.

Print journalism. This is a crowded category, including newspapers with national distribution, such as the *New York Times*, *U.S.A. Today*, the *Washington Post*, the *Wall Street Journal*; large circulation regional daily newspapers, chains, and affiliated news services, such as the *Los Angeles Times* and the Knight newspapers; thousands of local newspapers around the country; newsmagazines with a broad, national circulation, such as *Time*, *Newsweek*, and *U.S. News and World Report*; and specialized newsmagazines with a more narrow circulation to elites, such as *Atlantic Monthly*, *New Republic*, *National Journal*, and *Business Week*; news services, like the United Press International (UPI) and the Associated Press (AP), that provide others with copy and other wire services that service specialized outlets, such as those fed by the Jewish Telegraphic Agency.

All of these news organizations feed on one another; what one picks up, others mimic. Sometimes, the cross-fertilization is planned, as between newspapers or television networks and polling organizations, such as the Gallup or Harris surveys. In these cases, a newspaper will commission (and pay for) a survey of what some sample of people think about some public issue. Everything is fair game: the preferences of Democrats among candidates for the presidential nomination; "trial heats" among different pairs of contenders; reactions to events and even reactions to news stories. The practice strikes

---

[15] Michael Baruch Grossman and Martha Joynt Kumar, *Portraying the President: The White House and the News Media* (Baltimore: The Johns Hopkins University Press, 1981).

[16] *New York Times*, 6 May 1984.

THE MEDIA AND PARTICIPATION: THE PERMANENT CAMPAIGN

Some believe that the media make news—and then cover themselves making it.

some as suspect, and when predictions turn out wrong, cynicism creeps in about polls—making people think that polls are nothing more than "A series of questions put to someone whom neither you, nor anyone you know, has ever met," as Mark Russell, a Washington-based comedian, has observed.[17] On the other hand, some political science researchers believe that the print media's use of survey research has enhanced their political influence. According to C. Anthony Broh, for example: "The media . . . are using polls in primary campaigns to evaluate the strength of and causes for a candidate's support—a role traditionally played by partisan insiders."[18]

In addition to news organizations, various newspeople fall into the print journalism category, including independent reporters who work for several small regional news organizations, photographers, editorial cartoonists, and comic strip artists.

There are two additional small groups of newspeople that have a significant effect on the content and tone of many newspapers, as well as on network television news stories: syndicated columnists and the reporters for national news services. Because of their prestige and influence, nationally syndicated columnists are the media's mandarins. Columnists, such as George Will, James Reston, David Broder, Meg Greenfield, Tom Wicker, Anthony Lewis, and Flora Lewis, write for one paper but are syndicated in many. Moreover, since other reporters admire and take cues from them, highly respected columnists have ripple effects that endure for weeks after an initial column. In a similar manner, the reporters for the major news services, because of their influence over other reporters, are leaders of a new kind of reporting, especially common in presidential election campaigns: pack journalism.[19] UPI and AP reporters ride point in the media army; by being the first to turn in a story, and because of their high regard, the stories and especially the leading introductory lines of

---

17 Mark Russell, *Presenting Mark Russell* (New York: Everest House, 1980), p. 63.

18 C. Anthony Broh, "Polls, Pols and Parties," *Journal of Politics*, 45 (1983): 736.

19 See Timothy Crouse, *The Boys on the Bus* (New York: Ballantine Books, 1974), for a highly entertaining exposé of pack journalism.

To get a jump on the news, the media often conduct their own polls.

wire stories *are* the content in hundreds of newspapers. These indirectly shape even the stories of reporters with major newspapers who do not want to try to explain to their editor why their lead differs from the wire lead.[20]

One final subcategory of print journalism deserves special mention: books, or newspaper serials that become books, which transform what Americans think of their society and what they want government to do about it. There have been only a few such blockbusters: examples include Harriet Beecher Stowe's damnation of slavery, *Uncle Tom's Cabin* (1852); Upton Sinclair's exposé of class exploitation and filth in the meat-packing industry, *The Jungle* (1906); and Ralph Nader's first salvo in what became the consumer movement, *Unsafe at Any Speed* (1971).

Polls. There are three major kinds of polling organizations: (1) commercial organizations that conduct public opinion surveys and marketing research for both political and nonpolitical clients, such as the Gallup Organization, the Roper Center for Public Opinion Research, and Louis Harris and Associates; (2) political pollsters who usually work either for liberal or conservative candidates, such as Patrick Caddell who worked for President Carter or Richard Wirthlin, President Reagan's pollster; and (3) media pollsters, survey research arms of electronic or print media, such as those attached to *The New York Times-CBS News*, *The Washington Post-ABC News*, or the *Los Angeles Times*.

Radio. Radio allows for fine tuning, as politicians exploit the tremendous number of different stations, many with their own specialized and homogeneous audience. In addition, radio is a much cheaper outlet for political campaign messages and even a more cost-effective one in some congressional districts, like those in Manhattan, where candidates can not afford television time. Radio also is a better outlet for allowing candidates to say more negative things about their opponents than television—without it backfiring, by making them look bad. Finally, some politicians simply come across better on radio. For example, those who heard on radio the first televised debate between John F. Kennedy and Richard M. Nixon in 1960 thought that Nixon won, whereas those who saw it on television judged Kennedy the winner.

Bits and pieces. Lastly, there is a residual category of media which include such things as computer-assisted mass mailings, computer-assisted telephone dialing banks, election campaign paraphernalia (bumper stickers, buttons, flyers, or songs), and even movies, such as "The China Syndrome," a sensationalization of the dangers of nuclear reactors.

This categorical listing could go on. Instead, let us stop and introduce an analytical distinction among forms of media.

Analytical Types of Media. Analytically, media are more or less free to decide what they cover and how they cover it.

Politicians exercise most control over the media when they buy airtime or space; with purchase comes control over content. That is the difference between positive and negative coverage. "To really get that positive message out," you have to use controlled media, said Dotty Lynch, the pollster for

---

[20] The point is made in Grossman and Kumar, *Portraying the President*.

THE MEDIA AND PARTICIPATION: THE PERMANENT CAMPAIGN

Senator Gary Hart during his run for the 1984 presidential nomination of the Democratic party, explaining her decision to purchase thirty minutes of air time one evening in the week before the 1984 New York primary.[21] This particular purchase was atypically long. Increasingly, political airtime is purchased in short (fifteen or thirty second) "spots."[22] Control also comes through regulating the flow of information to the media, or even blocking it, as President Reagan did during the American invasion of Grenada and as we will see in the discussion that follows, of techniques for managing the media.

Political candidates use radio to fine tune their media appeal.

Characteristics of Media Coverage

Even when uncontrolled, the media's coverage of government, policies, and politics has distinctive characteristics; it is superficial, personalized, conflictual, adversarial, and biased.

The Superficial Quality of Media Coverage.

The general indictment is that media coverage consists of superficial accounts of pseudo-issues; stories that focus more on politics than policy, and tend to highlight conflict and crisis more than cooperation and routine governing. Media coverage may be unavoidably superficial and increasingly homogenized; the business makes it so. Television programming and newspapers are not charitable concerns; reporters and editors adjust the focus and depth of their coverage to what they believe will sell.[23] The result is a little bit of everything but not much of anything. The indictment is especially true of television news; the entire evening network news seldom fills up one newspaper page. No wonder President Richard M. Nixon said: "Television is to news what bumper stickers are to philosophy." Moreover, coverage, especially newspaper coverage, is becoming increasingly homogenized, following a historical decline in the number of cities with competing daily newspapers and in the total number of newspapers in the country (down from over 2000 in 1900 to about 1700 in 1980 or, more strikingly, from 1 for every 35,000 Americans in 1900 to 1 for every 130,000 in 1980). The rest of the indictment is well made by Jeff Greenfield who charges, for example, that the media missed the real presidential campaign in 1980 because they focused on pseudo-issues—personalities, polls, predictions, and horse-race metaphors, not substantive issues as pedestrian as the economy, peace, or the arms race.[24]

The Personalized Quality of Media Coverage.

The media are preoccupied with the personalities of politicians and policy makers, especially with their warts and bloopers. Judging from the content of our mass media, you would

---

[21] Quoted in *The New York Times*, 30 March 1984, p. 11.

[22] See, for example, Edwin Diamond and Stephen Bates, *The Spot: The Rise of Political Advertising on Television* (Cambridge, Mass.: MIT Press, 1984).

[23] Ben H. Bagdikian, *The Media Monopoly* (Boston: Beacon Press, 1983).

[24] Jeff Greenfield, *The Real Campaign: How the Media Missed the Story of the 1980 Campaign* (New York: Summit Books, 1982).

The media focus more sharply on personalities than on policy issues.

think we were all voyeurs. The media tell us more than you would think we would want to know about the darkness of Ronald Reagan's hair, Senator Gary Hart's former name or true age, Senator William Proxmire's hair transplant, Jimmy Carter's stumble during a five kilometer run or the lust he told *Playboy* he had in his heart when looking at pretty women, or President Gerald Ford's physical and verbal stumbles. The preoccupation with personality is especially pronounced in coverage of the White House. As Martin Tolchin, a respected reporter for the *New York Times* who often covers the White House, has commented, "I have had stories on page one just because the President burped. I don't think they belong there at all."[25] Perhaps it is inevitable that the press will be preoccupied with personalities and that this will carry over into a tendency to personalize issues; many reporters simply lack the training to do otherwise. Some reporters assigned to the White House, for example, tend to be generalists who lack the technical expertise to inquire about or make sense out of complex policy issues and therefore focus on more easily understood things, like personalities and politics. Or, more sympathetically, reporters may have little choice, either because the person they are covering is not doing much or is not telling them much. In the meantime, these same reporters live under the gun of deadlines to meet and quotas to fill.

[25] Quoted in Grossman and Kumar, *Portraying the President*, p. 61.

The Conflictual Quality of Media Coverage. The media also focus more on conflict than cooperation and more on crises than routines. Philip Foisie, a *Washington Post* editor, confessed, "We have not developed the knack of identifying and writing regularly about problems before they become crises."[26] The media's shortcomings also are apparent to those who feel shortchanged by it. One of them, Jody Powell, President Carter's key aide and press advisor, used to repeat the old adage about newspaper columnists and editorial writers; they are "the kind of people who view the conflict from afar and then come down from the hills to shoot the wounded."

The Adversarial Quality of Media Coverage. The media properly values its independence from government and uses it to probe for social discontent and to criticize the performance of policy makers. As one of the press's best practitioners, the late H. L. Mencken said, the press is supposed to "comfort the afflicted and afflict the comfortable." This orientation forces the media into an adversarial relationship with those it covers.

The adversarial quality of media coverage has a long, if not glorious, history in American politics. Until his death in 1956, for example, Mencken, the iconoclastic journalist of the *Baltimore Sun*, prided himself on never having written a good word about any living President. William Loeb, the late owner and publisher of the *Manchester* (New Hampshire) *Union Leader* went further, calling President Eisenhower "a stinking hypocrite" and President John F. Kennedy "the No. 1 liar in the United States."[27]

The adversarial tradition continues today, although toned down a bit from Loeb's day. During the 1984 campaign for the presidency, for example, the press charged that Walter Mondale lacked the guts and determination to be President. (Later, when Mondale got worked up, they slammed him for looking like "an angry Bugs Bunny.") In a similar way, NBC's Roger Mudd went after Senator Gary Hart just after one of his wins in the 1984 Democratic presidential primaries: "You're really not a national candidate yet, are you? You're not in very good shape, are you, in Illinois or Michigan? Why do you imitate John Kennedy so much? Would you do your Teddy Kennedy imitation for me now?"[28]

The tendency toward pack journalism also can increase the media's adversarial stance toward governmental officials and politicians. The pack, for example, got especially vicious after Senator Edward Kennedy came off looking bad in a televised interview with Roger Mudd in 1980. Afterwards, the rest of the press picked the bones. "The press gang-up on Kennedy has been a herd attack, an obscene feast," wrote the publisher of the liberal periodical, the *Nation*; "Whoever thought of the metaphor first, it's true: reporters are like crows perched on a power line. When one of them flies down to investigate

---

26 Quoted in Stephen Hess, *The Washington Reporters* (Washington, D.C.: The Brookings Institution, 1981), p. 119.

27 Quoted in Loeb's orbituary in *The New York Times*, 14 September 1981.

28 Quoted in *Newsweek*, 26 March 1984, p. 59.

something, the flock follows. When one of them moves to another spot, the others follow. And when one of them returns to the power line to wait, so do the rest."[29] Meanwhile, other coverage suffers. Investigative reporting, for example, goes undone, public problems undiscovered, and governmental abuse unnoticed, although there are some notable exceptions, such as the *Wall Street Journal*'s early 1980s expose of "slave labor" camps in Louisiana or some of the stories on CBS's "Sixty Minutes."[30]

The Biased Quality of Media Coverage.

The media is biased whenever it adds its own interpretation to its coverage. Bias may come about either because of the political preferences of people in the media or because of commercial pressures to package the news.

There are some glaring cases of bias. In one instance, Walter Cronkite, the former long-reigning anchor of the CBS evening news, took sides when he editorialized against the war in Vietnam, arguing that the only "rational" solution was "to negotiate, not as victors, but as an honorable people who lived up to their pledge to defend democracy, and did the best they could."[31] In a more recent case of partisan journalism, George Will, the conservative columnist, first helped Reagan prepare for his televised debate with President Carter and then wrote about the event, praising Reagan for his performance.

In most cases, however, bias in the news is slight or, at worst, evens out. Although most reporters have liberal leanings and dislike some political leaders, most owners of newspapers favor conservative candidates and this ideological bias carries over to their editorial endorsements. These ideological biases evened out in the case of most reporters' *bête noire*, Richard Nixon, since he won an overwhelming majority of the editorial endorsements of newspapers around the country in his 1968 and 1972 campaigns for the presidency. In addition, even though many reporters and columnists, especially those who cover Washington, D.C., have liberal political leanings, or at least are perceived that way by members of the Washington press corps, it has yet to be shown that this attitude comes across on the printed page or over the air waves.[32]

Bias in media coverage may also be unavoidable because of (1) space limitations, (2) organizational incentives, and (3) the training and tastes of reporters.

Space limitations. There is a finite amount of news; there are limits to what fits in a newspaper or on a half-hour news program. The size of this "news hole" constrains what can be reported and forces someone to decide what is newsworthy. Reporters and editors decide on the basis of their standards of what is news and on the basis of their preferences about how it should be reported.

---

[29] Quoted, with credit for the crow metaphor given to the former senator and presidential aspirant, Eugene McCarthy, in Broder, *The Pursuit of the Presidency*, p. 44.

[30] See Axel Madsen, *60 Minutes: The Power and the Politics of America's Most Popular TV News Show* (New York: Dodd, Mead, 1984).

[31] Quoted in *U.S. News and World Report*, 21 February 1983.

[32] Hess, *Washington Reporters*.

Organizational incentives. The news media's organizational incentives force a concern with profits. If owners are denied what they view as a fair profit, they can put their time and money elsewhere. The news, therefore, must be marketable and that sometimes makes it a bit sensationalized.

The training and tastes of reporters. The training and tastes of reporters bias the news in other ways as well. Most reporters lack training or background in technical or complex policy questions. It is easier, therefore, for reporters to follow their personal tastes, usually their interests in politics, not policies, in personalities, not programs. Stephen Hess notes that Washington reporters, for example, are especially ignorant about energy and economics and not surprisingly, these policy areas get the worst coverage.[33] Knowing more about politics, and especially electoral politics, reporters cover it more and have more fun doing it.

All these characteristics of an uncontrolled media lead astute political actors to a conclusion: if you want to get your story out and get it out in a way that builds popular support and legitimacy, it is necessary to manage the media.

Managing the Media

To win elective office and to govern effectively, policy makers must have popular support. Policy makers, however, can not count on the free, uncontrolled media to generate popular support for them. Indeed, as we have seen, the characteristics of uncontrolled media coverage produce the opposite result; they erode personal popularity, limit political discretion, and weaken system legitimacy. To avoid this fate, policy makers who would govern must try to manage the media and its coverage of them and their policies. There are two basic techniques: (1) buy media coverage and (2) manipulate media coverage. Political actors must constantly evaluate and adjust both techniques if they are to be successful in creating favorable expectations and interpretations in the minds of both the public and the media.

The Purchase of Media Coverage. Political actors buy media coverage to create favorable images about themselves and their policies and to create negative ones about their opponents and their policies. The purchase of media coverage, especially the purchase of television airtime, has been extensive in presidential nominations and election contests for the last twenty years, has increased substantially in races for the United States Senate, and now, is becoming increasingly common in races for the U.S. House of Representatives.[34] The content of the purchased coverage is also becoming increasingly negative, prone to attack the alleged limitations of one's opponent.

In the 1984 senatorial race in Kentucky, for example, the challenger, Mitch McConnell, set out to exploit the perception that his opponent, the Democratic incumbent Walter "Dee" Huddleston spent too much time on the road,

---

[33] *Ibid.*

[34] Alan Ehrenhalt, "Technology, Strategy Bring New Campaign Era," *Congressional Quarterly Weekly Reports*, 7 December 1985, 2559–65.

giving speeches for lucrative fees, and too little time in Washington, D.C., representing his constituents. The negative ad showed a "detective" with a pack of bloodhounds searching for Senator Huddleston. After showing the hounds running past the United States Capitol, swimming pools, and other scenic locations, an off-camera voice said: "We can't find Dee. Maybe we ought to let him make speeches and switch to Mitch for senator."[35] In this case, the negative ad did not backfire; people apparently thought it was funny, not mean, and the people of Kentucky switched to Mitch, by 5269 votes. In this case, political advertising bought conversion, although, as Edwin Diamond and Stephen Bates point out, it usually works best to reinforce popular expectations and to keep the committed in line.[36]

The Manipulation of the Media.   Policy makers can manipulate even the uncontrolled media by exploiting the media's need for copy. Influence runs down, from government to the media, making them relatively more dependent on policy makers.[37] Usually, the manipulation is subtle, more like tuning a piano than banging a drum. President John F. Kennedy, for example, elected by an uncomfortably thin margin, put members of the press in situations where they almost could not help but produce favorable publicity for him. In one case, a group of editors and publishers of Tennessee newspapers was invited to the White House for a luncheon, under the ground rules that they could ask Kennedy any question but could not report his answers. Thus, they had little left to report but his personal manner ("charming," "polished," "sharp") or the lunch itself (some even printed a photograph of the invitation).[38] President Reagan also made good use of "backgrounder" meetings, off-the-record discussions with selected groups of columnists and reporters, to orchestrate favorable press coverage and thereby furrow the ground of public opinion in advance of a major speech.

These examples are instructive; in the American system of government, the presidency and those who pursue it exercise great influence over the media. Some think this also explains the organizational life of the presidency. In the words of a White House advisor: "Almost everything here is either a megaphone or a support mechanism for a megaphone."[39] Even presidential news conferences, especially televised ones, are controlled more and more, most notably by President Reagan who even had reporters sit in assigned seats, stroking them by calling on them by name. Candidates for the presidency work just as hard to manage the media's interpretation of their chances and progress. For example, in Jack Germond's and Jules Witcover's account of the pursuit of

---

[35] *Ibid.*, p. 2561.

[36] Diamond and Bates, *The Spot.*

[37] See Joseph C. Spear, *Presidents and the Press: The Nixon Legacy* (Cambridge, Mass.: The MIT Press, 1984) and Montague Kern, Patricia W. Levering, and Ralph B. Levering, *The Kennedy Crises: The Press, the Presidency, and Foreign Policy* (Chapel Hill: The University of North Carolina Press, 1983).

[38] Grossman and Kumar, *Portraying the President*, p. 164.

[39] *Ibid.*, p. 81.

the Democratic presidential nomination, campaign managers would anticipate events and consciously try to control what they called "the spin" the press put on events.[40]

The use of both controlled and uncontrolled media is becoming more sophisticated, largely because of technological advances in the science of opinion polling. These advances let media managers quickly evaluate the impact of their message and if necessary, quickly adjust it. The process is described in the **Vantage Point**: The Techniques of the Permanent Campaign.

■ President Carter's failure to manage the media left him vulnerable, unable to orchestrate popular support when he most needed it to deal with foreign policy crises, and to beat back competition in his own party for its presidential nomination. As a result, he lost his legitimacy and therefore it was only proper that he should lose his presidency.

The mass media are becoming the main devices through which governmental officials and aspirant governmental officials acquire and retain their legitimate right to make policy. Indeed, they may be becoming a substitute for more traditional forms of political participation.

POLITICAL PARTICIPATION

> For we are a great and special nation in that
> we regard the man who takes no part in
> public affairs not as easy going and sensible
> but as worthless and foul.
>> —Pericles, funeral oration on the
>> dead at Marathon

Even Pericles might be surprised at the inventiveness with which Americans have devised opportunities for participation in the life of this nation. These include both those where citizens must take some initiative, to register and to vote, for example, and those where policy makers take the initiative, by communicating through the mass media and by constant polling to evaluate and to adjust their impact on public opinion.

Political participation today spans many subjects: forms of political participation; levels of political participation; voting behavior; elections; the presidential nomination process; the national conventions; and the determinants of electoral success. All of these topics are treated next.

---

[40] Jack W. Germond and Jules Witcover, *Wake Us When It's Over: Presidential Politics of 1984* (New York: Macmillan, 1985).

THE TECHNIQUES OF THE PERMANENT CAMPAIGN

The process of permanent campaigning is a repetitious, continuing one that emphasizes quick reaction, not quiet reflection. One campaign consultant, Karl Stuble, for example, acknowledged the trend toward instant-response politics this way: "It's getting to be a microwave society."[1] Others, however, see the increased use of polls as just another reflection of a long-term trend toward greater direct representation.[2]

To run a permanent campaign, policy makers and their advisers:

1. *Poll the public.* The efforts sometimes are quite extensive. For example, in the first three and one-half years of the Reagan administration, his pollster, Richard B. Wirthlin, conducted surveys on an estimated 120 to 150 national issues.[3]

2. *Evaluate survey results.* By evaluating their own polls and other survey research findings, candidates and policy makers try to determine how the public perceives them and their policies. During President Reagan's first term, for example, his pollsters discovered that his so-called gender gap (his greater popularity among men than women) was largely due to the recession's especially hard impact on women who were the single heads of households. The President's advisers reasoned that the expected upturn in the economy would wipe out the gap, however, and they decided not to target new appeals to women.

3. *Decide what will alter public opinion.* More and more, campaign consultants seem to be deciding that negative messages about the opponent, rather than positive messages about the character or policies of their own candidate, most effectively alter public opinion. In one classic case of negative campaigning in the race in Kentucky for the U.S. Senate in 1984, for example, Mitch McConnell, the Republican challenger, implied that Walter D. Huddleston, the Democratic incumbent, spent too much time on the road, giving speeches for lucratic fees, and too little time in Congress, attending to the needs of his constituents. McConnell's television ads showed a "detective," aided by bloodhounds, failing to find his opponent. McConnell's message was explicit: "We can't find Dee. Maybe we ought to let him make speeches and switch to Mitch for senator."[4]

---

[1] Alan Ehrenhalt, "Technology, Strategy Bring New Campaign Era," *Congressional Quarterly Weekly Report* (December 7, 1985), p. 2561.

[2] C. Anthony Broh, "Polls, Pols and Parties," *The Journal of Politics* 45 (1983): 732–44.

[3] Dom Bonafede, "Campaign Pollsters—Candidates Won't Leave Home Without Them," *National Journal* (May 26, 1985): 1045.

[4] Ehrenhalt, p. 2565.

Forms of Political Participation

There are many ways ordinary people participate in politics, besides actually voting. Consider two major ways: those forms of political participation that have no direct connection with elections, nonelectoral forms, and the remainder, explicitly electoral forms of political participation. In addition, **electoral participation** is a composite, including behaviors that are associated with the act of voting—registering to vote (and sometimes re-registering),

Dotty Lynch, the pollster for Senator Gary Hart during the 1984 presidential nominating campaign.

Ed Lazarus and Mark Mellman, Democratic pollsters.

4. *Design a message.* Often the message is designed to counter a message put out by someone else or, in a campaign, by one's opponent. In the 1984 Illinois senatorial campaign, for example, Charles Percy, the Republican incumbent, tried to label Paul Simon, his Democratic opponent, as someone who would raise taxes: "If you think you're not paying enough taxes, Paul Simon's your man."[5] Simon quickly counterattacked with television commercials implying that

Senator Percy had become out-of-touch by drifting too far to the right and into alliances with such conservative figures as the Rev. Jerry Falwell.

5. *Communicate the message.* The best way, many agree, is through the controlled media, in purchased time or space.

6. *Poll the public again.* The key is to move quickly, whether one is trying to evaluate the impact of a new campaign tactic, an opponent's campaign tactic, a reaction to an opponent's campaign

tactic, or the impact of a reaction to a reaction (and so on). The device for moving quickly is a short-term tracking poll, questions put to a small sample of the public that try to measure changes in opinion. Moreover, recent technological advances have speeded up the process of polling, as for example, computers have been adapted to assist generating and dialing randomly selected telephone numbers.

7. *Evaluate survey results.*

[5] *Ibid.,* p. 2559.

arranging for time to register to vote (by getting off work or getting a babysitter), getting yourself to the voting site, and actually casting your vote—and other acts that are more closely associated with the electoral process as a whole. These include donating money to an election campaign (directly to a candidate or indirectly through a political action committee), committing your time and energy to campaigning, or working as a poll watcher or clerk on election day. **Nonelectoral forms of political activity** include paying attention to government—watching the President's State of the Union address on

Voting, one of the many forms of political participation.

TV; discussing with others governmental actions—what do you think of the deficit?; writing about public policy—through letters to friends and editors; joining with others in organized interest groups to press demands on government officials—either by a cash donation to your favorite cause or by donating your time or participating in a demonstration. In general, as all these examples show, there are many different electoral and nonelectoral forms of political participation.

Levels of Political Participation

Let us profile levels of participation this way: Picture an ice hockey match that has gotten out of control (with players off the bench, coaches, and a few fans joining in), spectators who are more or less engaged in what is going on in the ring, and those outside the hall who are not interested in these barbaric goings on. In the political arena, "Fighters" include, for example, those who make policy, those who protest against it, and those who help politicians run for office. "Spectators" include those who pay some kind of attention, vote regularly, and criticize fighters. And the uninvolved, let us call them "Cabbages," include those who do nothing; they do not vote, do not complain, and probably do not even love a Fourth of July parade! These three general levels of political participation are shown in **Table 7.1**, as well as specific actions at each level, and the frequency with which Americans engage in them. As you can see, there

TABLE 7.1   Levels of Political Participation

There is a hierarchy of political participation in America, characterized by three main levels: Fighters, Spectators, and the Cabbages. Each of these levels, along with rough frequencies showing the extent to which Americans engage in each, are given below:

Fighters (about 10 to 15 percent of the adult population)	Spectators (maybe as much as 70 percent of the adult population)	Cabbages do not vote and do not engage in any active form of political participation (22 percent)
run for office (3%)	join political parties (35%)	
join in protest demonstrations (3%)	work on political campaigns (26%)	
donate money to political campaigns (13%)	try to persuade others how to vote (28%)	
take initiative for forming groups to work on local problems (14%)	attend campaign rallies (19%)	
	work with others on local problems (30%)	
	contact policy makers about social problems (14%)	
	write letters to newspaper editors (9%)	
	vote regularly (63%)	
	keep informed about government (67%)	
	show patriotism by flying flag, attending parades, etc. (70%)	
	pay taxes (94%)	

SOURCE: Lester W. Milbrath and M. L. Goel, *Political Participation: How and Why Do People Get Involved in Politics?* 2nd ed. (Washington, D.C.: University Press of America, 1982), pp. 18–19.

are a few "Fighters" who show a high level of relatively intense forms of political participation; many, many "Spectators" who get involved, but less intensely; and fewer, but still many, "Cabbages" who can not be bothered.

Voting Behavior

Although there is no shortage of opportunities to vote in this country, there is a lot of nonvoting and many different explanations for it.

The Incidence of Nonvoting.   Although common in many elections, nonvoting is especially striking in presidential ones. The presidential election of 1980, for example, seems to have bored many. If you judge by whom they voted for, there were 35,481,435 Democrats, 43,899,248 Republicans, and 5,719,437 who cared enough to vote for the Independent candidate, John Anderson, even though he had no chance of winning—adding up to more than 85 million voters. But there also were about 70,000,000 Americans of voting age who preferred Nobody—making the No Party party, if only it were on the ballot, the biggest single political party.

The Explanation of Nonvoting.   It is useful to look at nonvoting over time, as a part of a trend. To do so, let us look at some figures on voter turnout in national elections. Voter turnout is graphed in **Figure 7.1** and illustrates the actual figures for each presidential and off-year congressional election. The trend is clear: since 1932, voter turnout in presidential elections rose to a high of 62.8 percent of the voting age population and then began to fall. This trend is reflected in the percentage of those voting for their congressional representative, although turnout falls off enormously in those "off-years" when the presidency is not contested. In general, a smaller and smaller percentage of the eligible electorate is actually coming out to vote.

Why? In general, people fail to vote when they conclude it is not worth the trouble; that is, when the perceived benefits of voting are less than the anticipated costs of lost time or income.[41] This view of voting[42] helps us understand the conditions under which people are more or less likely to vote. For example, the perceived benefits and therefore, the likelihood of voting will tend to increase with such things as the anticipated closeness of the election, the excitement that is generated by lots of campaigning, and higher levels of voter education that reflect a relatively greater capacity to see differences between candidates.[43] The perceived benefits and again the likelihood of voting, will fall, however, when prospective voters do not trust candidates to carry out their promises. On the other side of the scale, the perceived costs of voting and therefore the likelihood of nonvoting, go up when it is hard to get to the polls because they or their hours are not easily accessible. The perceived costs of voting go down and people are more likely to vote when voting has become habitual, as it has for the aged, or when it has become a routine, as it has for those with a strong sense of identification with a political party.

In general, much is known about the determinants of voting and nonvoting. But we should be careful not to overstate the case. Much is not known and there remains a bit of a puzzle for those who would seek to explain the nonvoting of so many. It really is a bit odd, especially when compared to voter participation rates in other western democracies that usually exceed 70 percent and sometimes reach 90 percent of the electorate in some Scandinavian countries. Since the high turnout of 1960, people have become more educated,

---

[41] For an excellent discussion of relevant studies that cast both light and doubt on explanations of voter turnout, see Samuel C. Patterson and Gregory A. Caldeira, "Getting Out the Vote: Participation in Gubernatorial Elections," *American Political Science Review*, 77 (1983): 675–89, especially pages 675–77.

[42] See Anthony Downs, *An Economic Theory of Democracy* (New York: Harper and Row, 1957).

[43] For research findings on the determinants of voting, see Paul A. Dawson and James E. Zinser, "Political Finance and Participation on Congressional Elections," *Annals of the American Academy of Political and Social Science*, 425 (1976): 59–73; Herbert B. Asher, *Presidential Elections and American Politics: Voters, Candidates, and Campaigns since 1952* (Homewood, Ill.: The Dorsey Press, 1976); Richard A. Brody, "The Puzzle of Political Participation in America," in Anthony King, ed., *The New American Political System* (Washington, D.C.: American Enterprise Institute for Public Policy Research, 1978), pp. 287–324; Raymond E. Wolfinger and Steven J. Rosenstone, *Who Votes?* (New Haven, Conn.: Yale University Press, 1980); Gary C. Jacobson, *The Politics of Congressional Elections* (Boston, Mass.: Little, Brown and Company, 1983).

THE MEDIA AND PARTICIPATION: THE PERMANENT CAMPAIGN

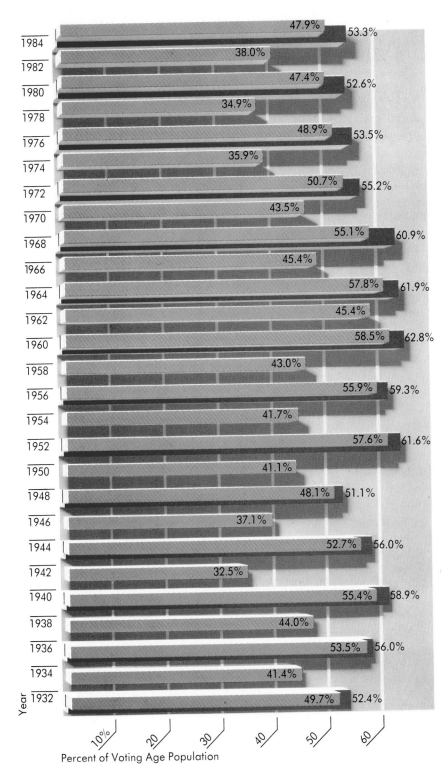

FIGURE 7.1
Falling Voter Turnout in Presidential and Congressional Elections, 1932–1984

[1] Percent of voting age population (VAP) who voted for President.

[2] Percent of VAP who also voted for Congressperson. Note the falloff in a presidential election year, such that not everyone who votes for President also votes for a member of Congress. Also note the falloff in turnout in non-presidential election years.

SOURCE: U.S. Bureau of the Census, *Statistical Abstract of the United States: 1986*, 106th ed. (Washington, D.C., 1985), Table 432, p. 255.

Voted for President

Voted for Congressperson

Year

Percent of Voting Age Population

Political Participation

253

and campaigns do seem more contested—or at least more campaign money is spent trying to stimulate voter interest. Nevertheless, turnout in presidential and off-year congressional elections has continued to fall.

The answer may lie in a number of different directions. Richard W. Boyd, for example, points out that there are many more opportunities to vote these days (in presidential primary elections, as well as in special cases of citizen initiative and referenda elections) and people simply are less likely to vote in any one election.[44] Richard Brody pursues a similar line of analysis in suggesting that people, in lieu of actually voting, are increasingly making use of substitutes, such as increased letter writing to their elected representatives and increased rates of joining and participating in the activities of organized interest groups.[45] In these views, the determinants of voting are not rooted in the apathetic or alienated mood of the electorate; such fears for the electorate's depressed psychological state appear overblown.[46]

In addition, currently low turnout may be temporary; some are guardedly optimistic that voter turnout will increase in the near future. The Census Bureau, for example, estimates that participation rates will pick up as the members of the baby boom generation of 1946–1964 (about 45 percent of the voting age population) gain increased experience with voting and as efforts continue to register the still large numbers of minorities who regularly do not vote.[47] They may be right, since once registered, over 80 percent of the electorate goes on to vote, at least in presidential elections.

Elections

In the United States, elections are frequent, but poorly attended—a little like church services. They are disparaged as manipulative entertainment, but are not as bad as they are made out to be. They are subject to the complaints of those who would reform them, but relatively unchanging over time; essential— (what if they gave an election and no one came?), but not quite as essential as we sometimes pretend—lots of people do not come and life goes on; covered by national laws and national political influences, but essentially fragmented and therefore open to local and often parochial concerns.

Elections also are misleadingly brief, since they occur on one day and usually last less than twelve hours. But the interval between the opening and closing of the voting booths does not span the entire election process; it starts much earlier as prospective candidates explore possible sources of financial support and lasts much later as winners and losers assess election results and begin to position themselves for the next launching. Once you see this broader

---

[44] Richard W. Boyd, "Decline of Voter Turnout: Structural Explanations," *American Politics Quarterly*, 9 (April 1981): 133–59; Richard W. Boyd, "Election Calendars and Voter Turnout," unpublished Paper delivered at the 1983 annual meeting of the Southern Political Science Association, Birmingham, Alabama, November 3–5, 1983.

[45] Brody, *The Puzzle of Political Participation*.

[46] *Ibid.*

[47] The prediction of the Census Bureau was reported in *The New York Times*, 22 November 1983.

context, it becomes clear that elections are brief events which interrupt campaigns. There are, however, many elections and many different types of elections, although this section focuses only on national and especially presidential elections.

The Presidential Nomination Process

Candidates for the presidency are nominated through primary elections or through party caucuses. **Primary elections** select either the candidates who will appear on the general election ballot or the delegates who will select the candidates at a political party's nominating convention. The form of presidential primary elections is decided by state governments, sometimes in consultation with national political leaders, and as you probably expect, there is a lot of diversity in them. Primaries differ in who can vote, for example. **Closed primaries**, used in most of the states, only let those who declare their party affiliation vote and only in their own party's nomination contest. **Open primaries**, used in fewer states, do not force partisan declarations and instead, let people vote in whatever nomination contest they want. Primaries that elect delegates also differ in the ways delegates are apportioned. In the case of the delegates elected to the 1984 Democratic presidential nominating convention, for example, some states allocated convention delegates in proportion to the percentage of the primary vote won by each candidate, while other states modified proportional representation by, for example, adding on a bonus number of delegates for each congressional district won by a candidate. The two major political parties differ in their nomination processes. In general, Democrats act as though they are forming circular firing squads during nomination contests, tearing each other apart before, hopefully, uniting in their attack on Republican candidates who typically march through the nomination process in neater, more orderly columns. But presidential primaries sometimes are only symbolic displays of popularity, so-called "beauty contests." In two such cases, Vermont and Texas, for example, the actual delegates to the nominating convention are chosen by a party **caucus**, an informal gathering of the party faithful.

Caucuses are compromises between the smoke-filled back rooms of yore and the free-wheeling primary elections of the 1960s and 1970s. Caucuses do allow a measure of broad voter participation, but mostly favor the loyal party follower who has the commitment, time, and money to participate. In the 1984 Democratic presidential primary in Texas, for example, you had to vote twice, once in the morning at the preference polls and later in the evening at the delegate election caucuses; of the 1.4 million who made it to the polls in the morning, 1.1 million called it quits before evening. Because of their bias toward hard-core partisans, nominating caucuses guard against the sort of wild swing that gave George Wallace a victory in the 1968 Michigan primary and in general, reduce voter turnout.

Caucuses, therefore, are a check on the democratic will of the people. In the words of Richard Cohen, a Washington Post columnist, "A caucus is to voter participation what cold water is to fighting dogs."[48] Primaries, in contrast, usually stimulate electoral participation, as they did in 1984 when about 17 million people voted in the twenty-four states that held primaries for the Democratic presidential nomination.

The major parties have experimented a bit with their mix of primaries and caucuses; the Democrats have been especially venturesome in seeking first to open up the presidential nomination process through primaries and, more recently, easing it shut through the practice of reserving delegate seats for party officials and through a greater reliance on caucuses.[49] The process of broadening participation in the Democratic party's presidential nomination process saw the number of primaries vary, from fourteen in 1960 (when only three or four were really important) to thirty-seven in 1980 and back to twenty-four in 1984. By 1984, most of the Democratic delegates still came from primaries, although almost 38 percent of the 3933 delegates to the Democratic presidential nominating convention were elected by caucuses. Not a trivial percentage, since these 1489 delegates represented about three-fourths of the 1967 needed to win the nomination.

The National Conventions

Since delegates to presidential nominating conventions are elected through primaries, the large number of elected delegates, often more or less bound to vote for a particular candidate, makes the actual nominating convention a less exciting affair. By the time the actual convention gets underway, it sometimes appears as though little is left to be decided, as in 1984 when the Democrats headed toward San Francisco, certain to nominate Walter Mondale. Network television, ever sensitive to what sells, cut back its coverage, leaving gavel-to-gavel coverage to the cable outfits.

Are presidential nominating conventions irrelevant anachronisms of an earlier age? This contemporary concern is a reflection of an enduring one. Americans always have had mixed, usually antagonistic, attitudes about nominating conventions. As H. L. Mencken so colorfully reported:

> There is something about a national convention that makes it as fascinating as a revival or a hanging. It is vulgar, it is ugly, it is stupid, it is tedious, it is hard upon both the higher cerebral centers and the gluteus maximus, and yet it is somehow charming. One sits through long sessions wishing heartily that all the delegates were dead and in hell—and then suddenly there comes a show so gaudy and hilarious, so melodramatic and obscene, so unimaginably exhilarating and preposterous that one lives a glorious year in an hour.[50]

---

[48] Quoted in *The Plain Dealer*, 14 May 1984.

[49] James W. Ceaser, *Reforming the Reforms: A Critical Analysis of the Presidential Selection Process* (Cambridge, Mass.: Ballinger Publishing Company, 1982).

[50] Quoted in The *Plain Dealer*, 14 July 1980.

John Chancellor in his press booth high above the 1984 Democratic convention floor.

In addition to what Mencken enjoyed, national nominating conventions have other virtues, sufficient to perpetuate their existence; most notably, they provide an occasion for forging consensus and building a coalition, hopefully strong enough to win power and hopefully united enough to know what to do with it. They also provide a point of demarcation, formally kicking off the general election campaign. In addition, the people who go to them seem to like them a lot.

Determinants of Electoral Success

There is no sure-fire recipe that will guarantee electoral success. In all good electoral recipes, however, there are three kinds of ingredients: characteristics of the political system as a whole (election and voter registration laws and procedures, the performance of the economy), characteristics of the electorate (especially their attachment to a political party), and characteristics of candidates and their campaigns (timing, incumbency, money, skill, image, rhetoric, issues, race, sex). Fortunately, there are many fine connoisseurs of what works well in campaigns, including Gary Jacobson, Edie Goldenberg, and Michael Traugott at the congressional level and at the presidential level, Nelson Polsby, Aaron Wildavsky, James David Barber, and Herbert Asher.[51] Because of them,

---

51 Gary C. Jacobson, *The Politics of Congressional Elections* (Boston: Little, Brown, 1983); Edie Goldenberg and Michael Traugott, *Campaigning for Congress* (Washington, D.C.: CQ Press, 1984); Nelson W. Polsby and Aaron Wildavsky, *Presidential Elections: Strategies of American Electoral Politics*, 6th ed. (New York: Charles Scribner's Sons, 1984); James David Barber, *The Pulse of Politics: Electing Presidents in the Media Age* (New York: W. W. Norton, 1980); Herbert Asher, *Presidential Elections and American Politics: Voters, Candidates, and Campaign Strategies Since 1952* (Homewood, Ill.: The Dorsey Press, 1976).

there is something to be said about the first two categories of determinants and a lot to be said about the effect of candidates and campaigns on election results.

Characteristics of the Political System.   Election and voter registration laws and procedures used to cut more deeply into election outcomes, before national legislation and court action reduced the impact of local discriminating practices. Our laws and procedures, however, do reflect that hybrid public-private mix that is so characteristically American. Consider some of the curious offspring. Elections are obviously public phenomena, but we leave much of their financing in private hands. The airwaves belong to the public, but candidates for public office have to buy access from private for-profit businesses. Although government, specifically state governments, formally register prospective voters, responsibility for actually getting American citizens registered to vote is in private hands, unlike the situation in other western democracies, such as Canada, where the state assumes responsibility for registering eligible electors. In the United States, private citizens themselves and private organizations—nonpartisan organizations like the League of Women Voters, more partisan interest groups like labor unions, or decidedly partisan political parties—take the initiative for encouraging and assisting voter registration, especially ones that tilt toward them. Election procedures can have partisan effects. For example, even how long the polls are open makes a difference,

Senate pages (center) carry boxes containing Electoral College ballots through Statuary Hall in the Capitol. These ballots were counted at the opening of Congress in 1937.

THE MEDIA AND PARTICIPATION: THE PERMANENT CAMPAIGN

since America tends to vote Republican until 5 P.M., when working men and women begin to pile up mostly Democratic votes.

The performance of the economy as a whole, especially levels of unemployment and inflation, affect electoral outcomes. Generally, good times help, and poor times hurt incumbents. This is not lost on incumbents in national government who try to put the best possible election-day face on leading economic indicators. Generally, however, the economy is too big and too complex to be easily manipulated for political gain by national policy makers.[52]

The continued existence of the electoral college also has its own effects, as discussed in the **Vantage Point**: The Impact of the Electoral College on Campaign Strategy.

Characteristics of the Electorate. Characteristics of voters do, of course, affect electoral outcomes. At the national level, the **party identification**, the partisan attachment of voters for one political party or the other is often cited as a major determinant of electoral outcomes, and has been ever since the first systematic studies of voting in this country in the early 1960s.[53] Since then, however, the impact of partnership seems to be waning, as psychological ties loosen and as people become more concerned with what office holders deliver.[54] This may account for the increased importance of candidate and campaign characteristics, especially incumbency.

Characteristics of Candidates. There are a number of characteristics of candidates and their campaigns that affect electoral outcomes: (1) incumbency; (2) timing; (3) money; (4) image; (5) rhetoric; (6) race; (7) sex; and (8) luck.

Incumbency. Incumbency has several advantages, even though it has been a two-edged sword in recent presidential contests. In general, incumbency is a plus, unless you are unfortunate enough to be one incumbent running against another, as sometimes happens after a census when congressional seats are reapportioned to adjust for changes in population. The general finding for congressional elections is well-summarized by Gary Jacobson: "Typically, more than 90 percent of the candidates are incumbents, and more than 90 percent of them win."[55] Incumbency, however, is a more useful resource in House than in Senate elections. At the presidential level in 1984, President Reagan was

---

52 See, for example, Edward R. Tufte, *Political Control of the Economy* (Princeton: Princeton University Press, 1978) and Morris P. Fiorina, "Short- and Long-Term Effects of Economic Conditions on Individual Voting Decisions," in D. A. Hibbs and H. Fassbender, eds., *Contemporary Political Economy* (Amsterdam: North Holland, 1981), pp. 73–100.

53 See Angus Campbell, Philip E. Converse, Warren E. Miller, and Donald E. Stokes, *The American Voter* (New York: Wiley, 1960). See especially chapter 6. For more recent work, see Norman H. Nie, Sidney Verba, and John R. Petrocik, *The Changing American Voter* (Cambridge, Mass.: Harvard University Press, 1976).

54 See, for example, Samuel Popkin, John W. Gorman, Charles Phillips, and Jeffrey A. Smith, "Comment: What Have You Done for Me Lately? Toward an Investment Theory of Voting," *American Political Science Review* 70 (1976): 779–805.

55 Jacobson, *Congressional Elections*, p. 26.

THE IMPACT OF THE ELECTORAL COLLEGE ON CAMPAIGN STRAGEGY

*T*oday, the electoral college is a bit of an anachronism, something that always seems in need of reform if not outright abolition. Nevertheless, it still has great relevance, especially for those who devise presidential campaign strategies.

Somewhat distrustful of direct democracy, the Founders wrote into the Constitution an indirect method of electing the President and the Vice-President.

Article II, Section 1 of the U.S. Constitution specifies that the President and the Vice-President shall be chosen by "Electors," with each state having a number equal to their number of U.S. senators plus their number of U.S. representatives.

The contemporary operations of the electoral college are proscribed by the Twelfth Amendment.

The Twelfth Amendment, for example, specifies that electors meet in their respective states, vote separately for President and Vice-President, send their ballots to the president of the U.S. Senate, that the president of the Senate open them in front of all members of Congress, and so on.

Clearly, this is an unnecessarily cumbersome process in an age of instant communications. Nevertheless, the electoral college exists and has a tremendous impact on presidential campaigning.

Since the votes of the electoral college are the only ones that determine the presidential election, a successful presidential candidate must have a strategy for putting together a majority—270 votes— or have a strategy for preventing the opposing candidate from doing so.

Going into the presidential election campaign of 1984, here is how some of President Reagan's campaign advisors calculated: (1) the Mondale-Ferraro ticket appealed primarily to the Northeast, thereby conceding the South[1] with its 158 electoral votes and the West[2] with its 111 electoral votes (for 269 electoral votes, or only one short of majority); (2) the only way Mondale could win was to sweep the Rust Belt, the heavily industrialized states of the Northeast and Midwest, and get lucky elsewhere; and (3) to make sure Mondale could not win, the Reagan campaign only had to lock up one of the Rust Belt states. Following this strategy, the Reagan campaign concentrated resources on its target state, Ohio, and ensured Mondale's defeat. In the words of Roger Stone, President

[1]The South includes the eleven states of the Confederacy: Alabama, Arkansas, Florida, Georgia, Louisiana, South Carolina, Mississippi, North Carolina, Tennessee, Texas, and Virginia, plus Kentucky and Missouri.

[2]The West includes: Alaska, Arizona, California, Colorado, Hawaii, Idaho, New Mexico, Nevada, North Dakota, Montana, Oregon, Utah, and Washington.

enormously resourceful in capitalizing on the advantages of incumbency, although it was a bit of an electoral burden for Presidents Carter and Ford.

Incumbency, in presidential nominations, is a formidable advantage. President Chester Alan Arthur, (1881–1885), for example, was the last sitting President to be denied his party's renomination. In presidential elections, however, incumbency can be a handicap, especially when your opponent tries to lay blame at your door for national calamities, as Carter was made to suffer for the Iranian hostage situation. Public antipathy toward government has

Current Electoral College Votes

The basic building blocks of the 1984 Reagan re-election campaign:

The South	=	158 electoral votes
The West	=	111 electoral votes
plus Ohio	=	23 electoral votes
Total	=	292 electoral votes

Reagan's campaign coordinator for the Northeast:

> In essence, by picking off Ohio and putting as much resources in there as we did, we really were trying to construct a hole card just in case Mondale drew to an inside straight. If there'd been any chance of Mondale sweeping the industrial Northeast and the Midwest, we had one hold card there that we knew he couldn't get. And there we could deny him the 270 if this thing ever became tight.[3]

In such ways, the electoral college has continuing relevance: it creates and rewards geopolitics.

---

[3] Quoted in Jack W. Germond and Jules Witcover, *Wake Us When It's Over* (New York: Macmillan, 1985), p. 467.

increased in recent years, nurtured by those challengers who seek to become part of it, and incumbency has become like nitroglycerin, a potential liability that needs careful handling.

Most recently, President Reagan showed remarkable dexterity in distancing himself from the down-side of incumbency, often appearing to step out of the role of President while commenting critically on other Washington politicians or even on the members of his executive branch. Reagan, for example, often said what a pleasure it was to be leaving town, as he headed usually to the West

Coast. In a specific illustration of his ability to avoid blame, word was carefully leaked to reporters that Reagan had "burst in on a meeting of his own staff, as if unexpectedly, to instruct them sternly to get to the bottom of the charges about purloined Carter strategy papers."[56] His skillful use of incumbency, in claiming credit and avoiding blame, frustrated Democratic campaign strategists, leading one, Chris Matthews, to comment, "It's amazing. Ronald Reagan's mastery of incumbency is in escaping its heat, posing as a kind of commentator who happens to live on Pennsylvania Avenue."[57] As Reagan's performance suggests, even incumbents need great timing, money, the ability to cultivate images, rhetorical appeal, and sensitivity toward issues that move people.

Timing. Timing considerations dominate all phases of the campaign, and candidates work hard on it. The timing behind fund raising, for example, is crucial, especially if you can raise lots of "early bird" money, even in advance of the filing deadline if possible. That is a good way of discouraging potentially strong candidates from running against you—in your own primary or in the general election. The lesson of the example can be expressed more cogently, "The best time to beat someone is before they decide to run." Once the campaign begins, tactics have to be made, revised, and sometimes abandoned quickly, in reaction to your opponent. During this phase, campaigning is not like playing chess with someone who can not move; opponents do react and do launch their own initiatives. This means that good campaigning is going to be hit-and-run fighting, not siege-laying. This is especially true of electronic campaigning. Tony Schwartz, for example, the creator of the infamous "daisy spot" for President Johnson's re-election campaign in 1964, described the role of timing in television campaigning this way, "At its best, TV campaigning is guerrilla warfare. You need to be highly reactive, whereas in a regular advertising campaign you just lay out a schedule and follow it."[58]

Reactive campaigning, quick strategic adjustments that are made on the basis of the opponent's campaign, permeates the electoral process. The boxing metaphor is useful; campaigning does require jabs, fancy footwork, feints, and especially good counter-punching, even though candidates sometimes brutalize themselves with self-inflicted wounds—as Senator Roger Jepsen (R., Iowa) did in visiting a health club that met sexual needs. Astute candidates exploit opportunities, as Ronald Reagan did in 1980 when George Bush, then an opponent for the party's presidential nomination tried to keep other candidates out of a press conference. Grabbing the mike, Reagan declared, "I paid for this microphone," in a way that made him look presidential, Bush petty, and the other candidates merely appreciative. The reactiveness of campaigning also is seen in the ways candidates spend money. Candidates, as they choose among alternative campaign expenditures, seem to watch and emulate their opponent. In one study of election campaigns for the U.S. House of Representatives, Paul Dawson and James Zinser discovered that one of the best predictors of one

---

56 *The New York Times*, 18 September 1983, p. E 5.
57 *Ibid.*
58 Quoted in the *National Journal*, 1 March 1980, p. 348.

THE MEDIA AND PARTICIPATION: THE PERMANENT CAMPAIGN

"Ten, nine, eight, seven . . .   *six, five, four, three . . .*   *two, one . . .*

These are the stakes. To make a world in which all of God's children can live . . .   *or to go into the dark. We must either love each other or we must die . . .*   *The stakes are too high for you to stay home."*

Television campaign spots are effective—and controversial.

candidate's level of campaign spending on media was the amount of money being spent by the opponent.[59] As a result, media campaigning in congressional elections closely resembles an arms race—one that sometimes gets out of control, as for example, in the 1984 North Carolina Senate race when Governor James Hunt and Senator Jesse Helms peaked out at about $12 million each. Reactiveness also is illustrated by the case of televised campaign debates.

Money. Money is an essential ingredient in a successful election campaign, especially for challengers who need to offset the advantages of incumbency.[60] It used to be said that, "Money is the mother's milk of politics." There is still a lot of truth in that saying, but money increasingly seems to be the surrogate mother of electoral success, as party organizations wither and as the cost of campaigning mushrooms. Today, it seems generally true that ". . . because no one knows what works in a campaign, money is spent beyond the point of diminishing returns."[61] Escalating levels of campaign expenditures raise diverse concerns. One is that candidates will be sold like soap, through mass

[59] Paul A. Dawson and James E. Zinser, "Broadcast Expenditures and Electoral Outcomes in the 1970 Congressional Elections," *Public Opinion Quarterly* 35 (1971): 398–402.

[60] Herbert E. Alexander, *Financing Politics: Money, Elections, and Political Reform* (Washington, D.C.: CQ Press, 1984).

[61] Stimson Bullitt, *To Be a Politician* (Garden City: Doubleday, 1961), p. 72.

marketing appeals.[62] High levels of campaign spending also invariably lead to suspicions of undue influence and stimulate interest in making all federal elections totally dependent on public funds, in an attempt to sever the link between the money of those who want special favors and public policy. On the other hand, anybody who purports to represent significant numbers of people ought to be able to attract significant support, including financial support. Moreover, even though it is clear that money translates into votes, it is not clear that money alone wins elections.

You can not win elective office without money; fortunately, however, the flip side is not true. Just spending a lot of money will *not* necessarily get you elected, as John Connally learned, when he spent $12 million to win one convention delegate in 1980. Although it is true that all congressional candidates spent $300,000,000 dollars seeking election in 1982, it is also true that about 64,514,000 people voted in those elections. If we think about it in terms of how much was spent communicating with and sometimes transporting each voter, then what we have here is an expenditure of about $4.65 per voter. Also, the impact of political advertising is not as great as some fear; media consultants, for example, know they can sell soap—it is politicians they have trouble selling.

In addition, some believe that "money buys influence over policy."[63] This concern is overstated. No one has proven a systematic relationship between campaign contributions and policy choices, although there are many isolated cases and enough free-floating suspicions to erode confidence in the integrity of the policy-making process. In general, money by itself is neither decisive or intrinsically corruptive; it depends on how wisely or how profanely it is used— and those are matters of skill and ethics.

Image. Successful campaigns create a favorable image for themselves and a negative one for opponents. It is your opponent's negative image that will turn off, or away, more votes than you probably can win through trying to cultivate a positive image for yourself. Reagan knew this in 1980 and effectively latched on to a line that crystallized free-floating negative feelings about President Carter; "Are you better off than you were four years ago?" Reagan jabbed throughout the campaign. Not forgetting his lesson, Reagan showed throughout his first four years a remarkable ability to walk away unscratched from controversies and bad press that focused on some of his advisers and policies. So remarkably did Reagan avoid blame, his became known as the stickless or "Teflon" presidency.

In image making, appearances tend to count more than reality. The race for the 1984 Democratic presidential nomination, for example, was a test of who could be stuck with the most negative image: John Glenn, "the emotionless space celebrity," Walter Mondale, "a mere tool of special interests" who lacked "fire in his belly," Gary Hart, "the unknown, and maybe identityless technician," and Alan Cranston who some thought looked like E.T.'s grandfather.

The view from Moscow of the corrosive role of money in American policy making.

---

[62] The alarm was first sounded by Joe McGinnis. See *The Selling of the President* (New York: Funk & Wagnalls, 1972).

[63] Elizabeth Drew, *Politics and Money: The New Road to Corruption*, 2nd ed., (New York: Macmillan, 1984).

THE MEDIA AND PARTICIPATION: THE PERMANENT CAMPAIGN

President Gerald Ford was also a target of press abuse. As a member of the University of Michigan varsity football team, Ford had demonstrated considerable athletic prowess. Still, the press managed to find enough instances of him stumbling to portray him as clumsy. It got so bad, it was news when Ford did not fall down! Equally unfairly, the late Democratic Senator from Washington, Henry "Scoop" Jackson, was characterized as so dull that he once gave a fireside chat and the fire went out. America's macho culture deals harshly with any male candidate who appears less than manly, as some thought Mondale did in 1984. Even back in 1948, Thomas Dewey was picked on by the press when after declaring his candidacy for the 1948 Republican presidential nomination, he was characterized as having "thrown his diaper into the ring."

All these examples show how hard it is to come up with a positive image. This difficulty led David Garth, John Anderson's media consultant, to suggest facetiously we assume, that the ideal running mate for Anderson would be the Jedi Master of Star Wars fame, Yoda. Garth explained, Yoda was "the perfect candidate for the '80s: a credible outsider with magical powers."[64]

Rhetoric. Rhetorical skill is indispensable in massaging issues and in manipulating one's image. Nevertheless, a lot of campaign rhetoric is pretty insipid. Apparently fearing that "words are made for eating," candidates keep their campaign rhetoric bland. There are rare exceptions; the Reverend Jesse Jackson was one. In 1984, running for the Democratic presidential nomination, Jackson invigorated campaign rhetoric, his candidacy, and his party.

Race and Sex. Finally, the candidate's race and sex hurt at the polls, suppressing the likelihood of electoral success, although this is increasingly less true. As **Tables 7.2** and **7.3** show, more blacks and women are winning elective office. The gains of blacks are closely tied to increased black registration. Women also are winning more offices and getting elected on their own right, rather than as the widows of incumbents—a trend that Geraldine Ferraro's nomination probably accelerated.[65] Race and sex still suppress success, however. Some losers do not take it too well. Maureen Reagan, for example, after being defeated in her attempt to run for the U.S. Senate said, "I will feel equality has arrived when we can elect to office women who are as incompetent as some of the men who are already there."[66]

Luck. Most of the luck in campaigning is somebody else's bad luck which rebounds to your advantage. It is the bad luck that Edmund Muskie had in 1968 when he gave an emotional speech outdoors in New Hampshire and the snow that melted on his face made it look like he was crying; the bad luck that the Democratic party's 1972 nominee, George McGovern, had when no one checked out his vice-presidential nominee's history of electro-shock treatments; and the bad luck of Senator Edward Kennedy when he could not come up with a good reason for wanting to be President during a nationally televised interview in 1980.

Having generalized about elections and the determinants of success, we

---

64 Quoted in Ellis Weiner, "On the Campaign Stump with Yoda," *New York Times Magazine.*

65 Irwin N. Gertzog, "Changing Patterns of Female Recruitment to the House of Representatives," *Legislative Studies Quarterly* 4 (1979): 429–45.

66 Quoted in *Life*, January 1983, p. 31.

TABLE 7.2 Race matters less, as the number of elected black officials grows.

YEAR	Number of Elected Black Officials
1975	3,503
1977	4,311
1979	4,584
1981	5,014

SOURCE: U.S. Bureau of the Census. *Statistical Abstract of The United States: 1984.* 104th Ed. (Washington, D.C.: U.S. Government Printing Office, 1983), p. 261.

TABLE 7.3 Sex slips, as the number of elected women officials grows.

YEAR	Number of Elected Women Officials
1975	7,089
1977	11,392
1979	14,353
1980	16,083
1981	16,585

SOURCE: U.S. Bureau of the Census. *Statistical Abstract of The United States: 1984.* 104th Ed. (Washington, D.C.: U.S. Government Printing Office, 1983), p. 262.

should return to our original caveat. When we make generalizations about presidential or congressional elections, for example, these are supposed to hold for all cases, as though we were talking about only one kind of thing. But even a presidential election really is fifty separate elections for the electoral votes of fifty different states. National elections, "in general," are not terribly national, but more local in their appeal. Once we allow for the possibility that local tastes and preferences will determine election outcomes, then there may be all kinds of idiosyncratic reasons why a particular person won in a particular district on a particular day. In the 1982 congressional elections, for example, the Democratic candidate, John Wilson won the seat from Texas's 18th district. We are sure that this race got included with others in several computer analyses of the determinants of electoral success, showing the statistical impact of party, money, and so on. The only reservation we would make in this case is that John Wilson was dead, having died of cancer forty-five days before the election. There were peculiar reasons for his electoral success. By electing Wilson, local Democrats were to get a special election called and vote for a live Democrat, thereby keeping the uncontested Republican from what would have been a full term. The case illustrates the general point; generalizations about elections and campaigns are like campaign promises—made to be broken.

■ Election campaigns, as President Carter learned, are full of often very unpleasant surprises which, once they occur, are very difficult to handle. At best, one can only prepare for the worst by laying, ahead of time, a foundation of popular support and legitimacy. As more and more policy makers learn this lesson, their permanent campaigns are having more pronounced effects on the American political system.

THE ROLE OF THE MEDIA AND POLITICAL PARTICIPATION

> When we lost Channel 4, we were in trouble. And the worst part was when Channel 9 went off the air just as President Marcos was about to take the oath. We lost all the initiative then.
>
> > —Colonel Deleon, an officer in the palace guard of President Ferdinand Marcos, after he fled the Philippines in 1986

The modern mass media shape forms and patterns of political participation. In addition, both influence the American political system in many ways.

The Functions of the Media

Since Douglass Cater first labeled it "the fourth branch of government," the media have been studied more and better understood.[67] Although Americans differ in their views of their *proper* role, the media do perform three broad functions within the political system: (1) the media protect liberty by serving as permanent, critical watchdogs of those who exercise public and private power; (2) they are instruments of popular rule; and (3) they provide policy makers with a mechanism through which they can attempt to exercise mass persuasion.

The Media's Role as Critic. The media are a permanent critic of those who exercise public and private power. One of its best practitioners, the late H. L. Mencken, had a way of summing up the press's role in a democracy; the press were supposed to "comfort the afflicted and afflict the comfortable." In this, its adversarial role, the media lay bare the workings of government to that great antiseptic—sunshine. This is an appropriate, and constitutionally well-protected role for the media, although they do not always perform it well or fairly. To protect this role the Supreme Court has ruled that government can not rely on **prior restraint**, court orders that prevent publication of stories it deems damaging.[68] Because of their effectiveness as a critic, some suggest that the media have become the permanent Out Party. This was true, for example, in the controversy over the ethics of one of Ronald Reagan's national security advisors, Richard Allen. The mass media served as a surrogate opposition force, and Allen responded as though he knew whose concerns he had to assuage, making the rounds from one news show to another, pleading his case.

But there is a difference between a critic and a scold; sometimes the media, because of their tendency to distort through exaggeration and dramatization, go too far. By amplifying the worst in American politics, while ignoring the best and the routine functioning of government, the news media encourage cynicism. By portraying compromise and trades as corruption, not as useful ways of circumventing conflict in a pluralistic society, the media make it harder to settle value conflicts harmoniously. By overreacting, often first one way and then the other, as they did in their excessively favorable coverage of candidate Carter and subsequent excessively negative coverage of President Carter, the news media contribute to the muddled state of public awareness of public issues.

The media may not be as powerful as other political institutions—not as powerful as the presidency, for example. Although the media are not totally immune from penalty for incorrect and damaging reporting, you probably can not find another political institution that is simultaneously as powerful and as unaccountable. If the media are the guardians of democracy, there simply is no one visible and powerful enough to guard the guardians. Their non-accounta-

---

[67] Douglass Cater, *The Fourth Branch of Government*, Special ed. (New York: Random House, 1977).

[68] The definitive ruling against "prior restraint" came in the Pentagon Papers case, *New York Times* v. *United States*, 403 U.S. 713 (1971).

Bob Woodard (left) and Carl Bernstein. Their investigation into the Watergate break-in helped to legitimize public concerns over presidential behavior.

bility can also make their mistakes worse, since those with power and no need to answer for its exercise often tend to misuse it. The best available antidote for an abusive and biased media is your now-heightened sensitivity to their failings. So, remember, things are never quite as bad (or as good) as the news media make them out to be.

The Media's Role in Popular Rule. The media also function as instruments of popular rule, by their role in agenda building and by helping hold policy makers accountable for what they do about public problems. In agenda building, the media help define objects of public regard and help nurture public expectations. This agenda-setting role was first seen by Walter Lippmann,[69] a highly respected newspaper columnist, and later confirmed by political scientists. Shanto Iyengar, Mark D. Peters, and Donald R. Kinder, for example, in an ingenious experiment, simulated television news broadcasts to show that, as the media paid more attention to a particular policy issue, members of the viewing audience became more personally concerned about the problem.[70] In addition to shaping the public's perception of issues and politicians, the media also legitimize public concerns. A whole basket of consumer issues was legitimized, for example, when Ralph Nader, identified as "Consumer Crusader," appeared on the cover of *Newsweek* magazine in 1966. Since the media are mostly reactive, however, they can not *create* government's policy-making agenda in the absence of some minimal or floor level of public interest and concern. Nevertheless, some think that the media, by focusing on bad news, try to make government more interventionistic. This, for example, seemed to motivate President Ronald Reagan when he complained, "Is it news that some fellow out in South Succotash has just been laid off, that he should be interviewed nationwide?"[71]

The media's value as an instrument of popular rule is heightened by helping hold policy makers accountable for their actions (and non-actions). Research also has shown, for example, that as they become more concerned about a policy area, people base their overall evaluation of the policy maker on his or her apparent success in dealing with what they believe to be important problems. In this way, the mass media "prime" the evaluative pumps of the public, altering the evaluative standards they use to judge policy makers.[72] Having helped set the standards, the media feed those mills with the most critical grist they can find. No wonder policy makers are impressed by the adage, "Never argue with people who buy ink by the barrel." Even Presidents are more accountable than they used to be; televised news conferences make

[69] Walter Lippmann, *Public Opinion* (New York: Harcourt, Brace, 1922). See also, for a more current overview of findings, Donald L. Shaw and Maxwell E. McCombs, *The Emergence of American Political Issues: The Agenda-Setting Function of the Press* (St. Paul: West Publishing, 1977).

[70] Shanto Iyengar, Mark D. Peters, and Donald R. Kinder, "Experimental Demonstrations of the 'Not-So-Minimal' Consequences of Television News Programs," *American Political Science Review*, 76 (1982): 848–58.

[71] Quoted in *Life*, January 1983.

[72] *Ibid.*

them so. "Up to the Eisenhower years, a parliamentary democrat could say that American leadership lacked the spirited accountability demanded of Prime Ministers facing hostile questioning in the House of Commons. Came our new press conference tradition, and that accountability gap was closed."[73] That tradition, however, weakened in President Reagan's tenure as he did not often submit to news conferences and was quite adept at using the media to affect the public.

The Media's Role in Mass Persuasion.   The media are a mechanism, available to policy makers, for mass persuasion. Newspapers have always been available for this purpose. The first major political use of newspapers came just after the Constitutional Convention. As a part of the campaign to win New York's ratification of the new Constitution, Alexander Hamilton recruited John Jay and James Madison to help write a series of articles. The articles, printed in four of the state's five newspapers, tried to persuade voters to elect pro-ratification delegates to the upcoming convention—held in Poughkeepsie, of all places. These articles, appearing under the pseudonym, "Publicus," were widely read and debated. They, however, did not have much immediate impact, since most of the delegates elected were opposed to ratification. Nevertheless, the assembled papers (what we now call *The Federalist Papers*) had a broader impact in the ratification debates of other states and, because of their interpretation of the meaning and intent of the Constitution, on the minds and policy directions of the nation's leaders.

Today, mass persuasion is exercised most often through television and most effectively by the President, thereby expanding the potential influence of the presidency over the political system as a whole. Moreover, although they peak just before and just after elections, policy makers today make almost constant use of the media as an instrument of mass persuasion.

The Consequences of Political Participation

The American public, as was discussed above, is a bit sloth-like; large parts of the public do not spontaneously initiate political demands and are slow to react, either to social problems or to the proposals of policy makers. This fact has three major consequences for the American political system: (1) American policy makers enjoy enormous discretion, (2) policy making in America is an elite, not a mass, phenomenon, and (3) public policies often are made without broad-based public support. In addition, particular forms of participation, especially electoral forms, have additional effects.

The Discretion of Policy Makers.   The American public also has much it could be persuaded about, although their inattentiveness makes it hard to reach them. A politically uninvolved public, while raising their uncertainty and

---

[73] Quoted in *The New York Times*, 20 September 1981.

THE POLSBY—WILDAVSKY DIALOGUE CONTINUED . . .

AUTHOR: Let's think out loud about the Presidential election of 1988. Who are the nominees? What's the campaign like? What's the outcome?

POLSBY: We can predict several things. Since both parties will have non-incumbents running (in the presidential election of 1988), both parties will require nomination processes which are extraordinarily dependent upon the ways in which primary electorates are organized—which means who runs in which states and which states have the early primaries.

WILDAVSKY: Let us suppose that the current relative prosperity continues and is even enhanced somewhat. So there's relatively low interest rates (no higher than today or even lower), unemployment might go down (say from 7 percent to 6 percent), and the dollar stays where it is (or goes a little lower), thereby reviving exports, and inflation does not ignite again. Then, a Republican candidate should have an immense advantage.

POLSBY: Wait, an incumbent should have a great advantage.

WILDAVSKY: Yes, an incumbent, but, even so, I think that this would mean to most people that whatever Republicans stand for (in an economic sense) is working and, therefore, most people will be less anxious to rock the boat. Well, what would change that? A bitter internal struggle within the Republican Party or the nomination of a candidate who turns out not to be able to do well when the spotlight of publicity is on him. And it could be that there would

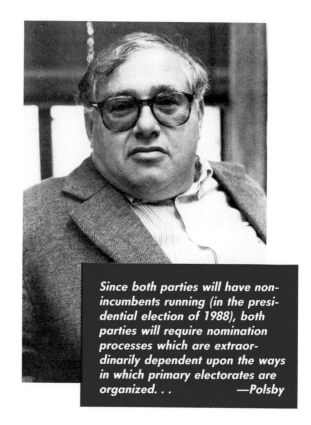

Since both parties will have non-incumbents running (in the presidential election of 1988), both parties will require nomination processes which are extraordinarily dependent upon the ways in which primary electorates are organized. . . —Polsby

be some Republican error. But I think it is their election to lose.

POLSBY: Now, it isn't just a Presidential election in 1988; there are also elections for the House and the Senate. And, if we're right in thinking that benign general economic circumstances help incumbents, it might very well help a whole bunch of incumbent Democrats to get reelected.

. . .it's truly unlikely that any Republican presidential candidate would have Reagan's popular appeal or his superb strategic sense.
—Wildavsky

WILDAVSKY: Let me just summarize my whole agreement with Nelson by saying that it would not be unreasonable for the electorate to conclude that divided control of Congress gives them, more or less, exactly what they want—and that would leave us where we are today. My caveat would be that it's truly unlikely that any Republican presidential candidate would have Reagan's popular appeal or his superb strategic sense.

POLSBY: I think there is an important historic change underlying this which is very important to emphasize. Up until fifteen years ago, the idea of the Republican Party as the party of the Great Depression still had enormous resonance with the American voters. This meant that when they were thinking about their pocket books, people would shy away from voting for a Republican for President.

Now, I think, and I have seen some public opinion data on this, that curse has been lifted and when people think about their pocket book they do not automatically vote against the Republican candidate.

WILDAVSKY: Indeed, if they were once considered the Party of Prosperity, the Democrats also were considered the Party of War, rightly or wrongly, because of the association between Democratic Presidents and war. Reagan's rhetoric, however, opened him to the charge that the Republicans had become the Party of War. If that happens, we could have exactly reversed roles; the Republicans would be the Party of Prosperity and War and the Democrats would be the Party of Depression and Peace.

apprehension, also grants policy makers fairly broad discretion to do what they think should be done. Most congressional districts, for example, have one or two "killer" issues on which any representative who wants to stay in office must vote the "right" way—water for agriculture in Colorado, import quotas on foreign automobiles in Michigan, federal subsidies for agricultural crops in Nebraska. But after the obligatory nod to key district issues, many congresspersons pretty much can go their own way, riding their favorite hobby horse of the moment—Senator William Proxmire (D., Wis.) giving "Golden Fleece" awards to dramatize waste of tax dollars, or Senator Lowell Weicker (R., Conn.) fighting against a constitutional amendment that would have allowed prayer in public schools.

Policy makers exercise discretionary policy-making authority while casting an apprehensive eye over their shoulder, however. The apprehensive eye is focused on that mass of the potential electorate that is momentarily quiescent. Policy makers have to remember that this mass, if stimulated, could affect the electoral process, disrupting routines and deseating incumbents. The concern is justified; the politically uninvolved, when stimulated sufficiently to enter the electoral arena, behave differently, more on the extremes of the political spectrum, than like those who participate routinely.

In 1968, for example, many of the over nine million who voted for George Wallace for President, the former racial segregationist running as an Independent, had not voted before, or had done so only irregularly. In 1980, as another illustration, Right-to-Lifers, sticking leaflets on cars in church parking lots picturing an unborn human fetus with the caption, "This little feller needs your help," provoked an emotional reaction strong enough to defeat some normally "safe" members of Congress. Such events have a big impact on elected officials who are perhaps more impressed than they should be by what may be isolated election returns, and therefore more apprehensive than they really need to be.

The Elitist Nature of Policy Making.   The existence of a large segment of the potential electorate that is relatively passive also means that policy making will be an elite, not a mass, phenomenon. Governing therefore requires that elected elites (the President and members of Congress, for example) negotiate among themselves, that both negotiate with non-elected elites who represent organized interests (the presidents of the Chamber of Commerce as well as the Communication Workers of America, for example), *and* that non-elected elites negotiate among themselves as they put together a deal that government can ratify (the representatives of public and parochial education that President Lyndon Johnson locked in a room until they could agree on an appropriate federal role in education, for example). Moreover, there is no good substitute for elite bargaining and negotiation; President Carter, for example, failed miserably when he tried to go over the heads of various elites, appealing directly for public support of his policies.

The public, however, can be provoked. When it is, it charges into the corridors of policy making, mimicking the Merrill Lynch bull. The public, in other words, behaves like other participants in the policy-making process—it too is more likely to be reactive than proactive. Moreover, as was the case in the 1980 presidential election, the public tends to react negatively—against the past actions of policy makers. In this way, the American electorate shows some ability to criticize past policy actions—what political scientists are beginning to call "retrospective voting."[74] The electorate, however, has much more trouble relating to the future visions of policy makers and therefore is reluctant to line up behind them.

The Lack of Popular Support for Policy. Because the American electorate behaves as it does, it is difficult to build a broad-based social consensus about what government should do. The electorate's tendency to react negatively denigrates policy actions much more than it signals a willingness to rally behind broad public purposes. There is an immediate result. After an election, new policy makers have trouble claiming plausibly that they have a mandate to do anything drastic. (Although that will not keep them from trying to claim a mandate or from trying to create the illusion of one, as President Reagan skillfully did in his administration.) The lack of an electoral mandate, in turn, means that elected policy makers usually will attempt only marginal, incremental, non-radical changes in public policy. (Although Reagan is again an exception in what he was able to accomplish, especially during his first year in office.)

In addition to these effects of various forms of political participation, elections have their own effects. In particular, elections (1) create a sense of public purpose and (2) enhance the legitimacy of the political system.

Elections Signal National Purpose. Elections provide some semblance of public purpose for an otherwise weak and fragmented political order. This effect comes about through something of a contrivance. In this country, elective offices are won through a winner-take-all system, as opposed to a system of proportional representation that would reward even minority parties with a few seats in a legislative body, for example. This electoral arrangement therefore encourages candidates and political parties to be inclusive, to accommodate as many supporters as possible within a broad policy agenda. In the process, sharp differences are blunted, controversies are muted, and policy objectives are defined in general terms. Moreover, these things must happen to put together a coalition big enough to win office.

Elections Enhance Government's Legitimacy. Elections enhance the apparent legitimacy and thereby the stability of the existing system of government. Appearances count, remember, and the appearance of even a somewhat-informed electorate, freely participating in a richly variegated electoral process, helps substantiate the claim of rule by the people. The appearance is more

---

[74] See Morris P. Fiorina, *Retrospective Voting in American National Elections* (New Haven, Conn.: Yale University Press, 1981).

than a facade; popular democracy *is* more likely when both the rulers and the ruled believe it works and when both act as though the consent of the governed has been derived through the electoral process.

■ It is hard to underestimate the impact of the mass media—or to estimate it correctly. Because the media are so heavily impacted by technological change and because those changes are occurring so rapidly, the media's effects are both significant and in flux. In some ways, the media offer hope that Americans will participate more effectively in political and policy-making processes. In other ways, however, the media only serve as an inadequate substitute for the more traditional forms of political participation it has shunted aside.

SUMMARY

The mass media have come to play an increasingly important role in the American political system, largely because policy makers try to enlist them in a permanent campaign to win popular approval for themselves and their policies.

The mass media have many forms and perform many valuable functions within the political system. Still, the media are criticized for superficial coverage that focuses more on politics than policy, more on conflict and crisis than cooperation and routines. Moreover, the news media are biased, with a tilt toward exaggeration and the dramatic, if not the ideological or partisan. The bias is inevitable, since the tastes and preferences of owners and undertrained reporters rule decisions about what will go into limited space.

While political participation is more than voting, most forms of participation have few activists. Voting participation is like other forms, however; it is a function of perceived costs and benefits. Although those who turn out to vote are representative of the adult population, a politically passive public, more reactive than forward-looking, presents policy makers with peculiar problems.

Elections also should be seen as relatively brief events which interrupt the permanent campaign. During the relatively brief election campaign, candidates try to convert political resources into electoral support, although there are no sure-fire recipes. Lots of things make a difference: incumbency, partisan attachments, money, skill, image, rhetoric, issues, race, sex—and luck.

While elections do not provide policy makers a straight-forward agenda for action, they do contribute to the formation of coalitions behind broad public purposes and provide the electorate with an opportunity to ratify past policy actions. In these ways, elections enhance the desirability, legitimacy, and stability of the existing political system. As Justice Learned Hand said: "Even though counting heads is not an ideal way to govern, at least it is better than breaking them."[75]

---

[75] Speech, March 8, 1932, cited in *Bartlett's*.

Key Terms

permanent campaign
media
electoral participation
nonelectoral forms of political
   activity
primary elections

closed primaries
open primaries
caucus
party identification
reactive campaigning
prior restraint

Review and Reflection

1. What is the permanent campaign?

2. How would you characterize the media's coverage of government and politics?

3. What are some of the ways in which candidates and policy makers try to influence the media's coverage of government and politics?

4. What are some of the electoral and nonelectoral forms of political participation?

5. How would you characterize the nature of political participation in America?

6. Why do so many people fail to vote?

7. Describe the process by which presidential candidates are selected.

8. What are the determinants of electoral success?

9. What is the impact of political participation on the political system?

10. What is the role of the media in the American political system? What do you think it *should* be?

Suggested Readings

Since so many of the linkages between the American people and their governmental institutions are mediated by the mass media, it is essential that we understand as much as we can about those who control, or try to control, it.

The media, however, have proven resistant to scrutiny. *Halberstam*, however, was one of the first to get behind the scenes in his informal study of *Time*, CBS, the *Washington Post*, and the *Los Angeles Times*. *Grauer* focuses more narrowly, on twelve of America's most popular and influential newspaper columnists: Jack Anderson, Russell Baker, Erma Bombeck, Jimmy Breslin, David Broder, William F. Buckley, Jr., Ellen Goodman, James J. Kilpatrick, Carl T. Rowen, Mike Royko, and George F. Will. *Madsen* goes further inside, in his book on CBS's popular "Sixty Minutes." Shooting from the outside, President Carter's press secretary, *Powell* charges that the press would rather make stories interesting than accurate. With greater balance, *Deaken*, a veteran member of the White House press corps, entertainingly recounts the endless disputes between the presidency and the press.

Others, *Spear* and *Grossman and Kumar*, for example, focus on the attempts of the presidency to manipulate the press or on the use of particular media techniques, as *Diamond and Bates* do, for example.

Some works are more concerned with overall characteristics of political participation (*Milbrath and Goel*), with sorting out determinants of voting behavior (*Neimi and Weisberg*), or with understanding of what works in election campaigns (*Goldenberg and Traugott, Jacobson*, and *Polsby and Wildavsky*).

Deaken, James. *Straight Stuff: The Reporters, the White House and the Truth*. New York: Morrow, 1984.

Diamond, Edwin, and Stephen Bates. *The Spot: The Rise of Political Advertising on Television*. Cambridge, Mass.: MIT Press, 1984.

Goldenberg, Edie, and Michael Traugott. *Campaigning for Congress*. Washington, D.C.: CQ Press, 1984.

Grauer, Neil A. *Wits and Sages*. Baltimore, Md.: The Johns Hopkins University Press, 1984.

Grossman, Michael Baruch, and Martha Joynt Kumar. *Portraying the President: The White House and the News Media*. Baltimore: The Johns Hopkins University Press, 1981.

Halberstam, David. *The Powers That Be*. New York: Dell, 1980.

Jacobson, Gary C. *The Politics of Congressional Elections*. Boston: Little, Brown and Company, 1983.

Madsen, Axel. *60 Minutes: The Power and the Politics of America's Most Popular TV News Show*. New York: Dodd, Mead, 1984.

Milbrath, Lester W., and M. L. Goel. *Political Participation: How and Why Do People Get Involved in Politics?* 2nd ed. Washington, D.C.: University Press of America, 1982.

Neimi, Richard G., and Herbert F. Weisberg. *Controversies in Voting Behavior*. Washington, D.C.: CQ Press, 1984.

Polsby, Nelson, and Aaron Wildavsky. *Presidential Elections*, 6th ed. New York: Charles Scribner's Sons, 1984.

Powell, Jody. *The Other Side of the Coin*. New York: William Morrow and Co., 1984.

Spear, Joseph C. *Presidents and the Press: The Nixon Legacy*. Cambridge, Mass.: The MIT Press, 1984.

PART THREE

PUBLIC POLICY:
ORGANIZATIONS, PROCESSES, GOALS

"Governments tend not to solve problems, only to re-arrange them."
—Ronald Reagan, as Governor of California

CHAPTER EIGHT

POLICY ORGANIZATIONS— AND EDUCATION

*W*ho makes public policy?

The answer, in a formal sense, is governmental officials. But they usually act in concert with many others, including people and groups outside of government.

The answer, in an informal sense, is all who work to realize a policy goal. These people are scattered around, in different governmental agencies and in various private groups. Moreover, these people often have different motivations. Sometimes, however, they form a **policy organization***, a set of public and private actors who work together to shape government's role.*

The following Case introduces a very human problem and describes what some people did to bring about a governmental solution for it. The problem was adult illiteracy, and for some, the solution was a regular program for determining whether or not learning was taking place before it was too late. The Case focuses on only a specific problem and a specific policy to deal with it, however. To place the Case in a historical context, the chapter also describes a variety of educational policies and the social goals they are meant to realize.

The Case and the historical context suggest some insights about those who make public policy in America: (1) public policy comes about because of the combined effects of governmental officials and nongovernmental actors; and (2) if they are to realize their goals, the members of a policy organization must convert resources into influence.

EDUCATION POLICY

> . . . you can't conquer the world in a pair of
> gym shoes.   —Kevin Ross

The Case   Making Sure Californians Can Read and Write

Kevin Ross had a problem. Long after he was supposed to know how to read and write, he could not. Some, quite properly, found ways to help him. But Mr. Ross also dramatized a larger societal problem: adult illiteracy. Others began pushing government to do something to prevent its occurrence.[1]

After four years at Creighton University in Nebraska, Kevin Ross went back to the eighth grade[2] at Chicago's Westside Preparatory School. His new teachers made the diagnosis. With a reading proficiency of a seventh grader, Kevin could read —a little. But he had more trouble speaking, with the language proficiency of a fourth grader. After only one year of remedial work, however, Kevin graduated from the Westside Preparatory School, reading at the level of a college sophomore. He had been an inspiration to his classmates and he planned to be to others. Entering Roosevelt University in Chicago, Kevin majored in education and resolved that he would find a way to break through the pretense behind which functional illiterates, and those who produce them, hide.

The problem of adult illiteracy is bigger than Kevin, of course. He was, after all, the product of a certain kind of educational system, one that did not ensure that pupils would learn to read and to write. To deal with this broader problem, some have banded together to advocate specific governmental remedies, public policies to assess pupil proficiency. One of the first and most successful efforts came in California.

The development of California's pupil proficiency policy came in three major stages. Initially, state law only specified the goal of pupil proficiency, without providing either for the means for reaching it or for penalties for failing to do so. Later, on March 10, 1976, Gary K. Hart, a state representative from Santa Barbara County, introduced a bill that added some teeth to the state's pupil proficiency law. Hart's bill put a new hurdle on the high school graduation stage; students who lacked proficiency in basic skills would not receive a high school diploma. The third major stage of policy making occurred after the bill was passed, but before it went into effect four years later, in June of 1980.

Senator Hart and other supporters of proficiency testing wanted to make sure that the new policy would work.[3] They therefore tried to anticipate problems that might come up when the policy was implemented, and worked to circumvent

---

[1] We want to thank Joseph W. Gurtis, Jr., Professor of Physical Education at Oberlin College, for suggesting this case. Most of the background material for the Kevin Ross story is drawn from press accounts.

[2] See *The New York Times*, 26 May 1983.

[3] The background material on education policy in California and the conceptual framework on policy organizations is adapted from Arnold J. Meltsner and Christopher Bellavita, *The Policy Organization* (Beverly Hills, Calif.: Sage Publications, 1983).

involved, the members of policy organizations must first convince one another, garner sufficient resources from their environment, and convert their resources into influence over the making of public policy. As we will better understand after our examination of the conversion of resources into influence, that is difficult. To get a sense of exactly how difficult, see the **Vantage Point**: Creating a Policy Organization.

■ Policy organizations occupy a very special place in the policy-making process, since they alter the course of the policy debate and the direction of public policies.[21] You can anticipate seeing lots of policy organizations in the chapters ahead; they are to policy making what carbon molecules are to organic chemistry. In the institutions chapters of Part IV, for example, you can view each institution—Congress, for example, acting as though it were a policy organization. In addition, as we will see in the two policy evaluation chapters of Part V, policy organizations can form out of different parts of institutions—particular congressional committees, for example—and other political actors in pursuing a policy goal, such as promoting the welfare of the people or providing for the defense of the nation.

ORGANIZATIONAL DYNAMICS

> Do it to them before they do it to you.
> —Sergeant Yablonski

Policy organizations live a bittersweet existence. They are the agents of change in public policy, making it hopefully more responsive to democratic sentiments and social aspirations. But to carry out their mission, policy organizations must cope with an often hostile environment that makes excessive demands, imposes disabling constraints, and grants sometimes only meager resources and stingy supports. Yet there are problems to solve, allocative decisions that must be made in any social system. If the private market is not doing the job, it falls to policy organizations. Whether or not they are successful depends on the ways they interact with their multiple environments.

Multiple Environments

Policy organizations are tied to four major environments, although not all are equally supportive or equally hostile. The **cultural environment** contains broad public expectations of government's proper role. In the case of the

---

[21] Karl Deutsch, *The Nerves of Government: Models of Political Communication and Control* (New York: Free Press, 1966).

proficiency policy organization, for example, a potentially hostile opposition to the involvement of the state government in local educational concerns was blunted by emphasizing a return to the basic three "Rs."

The **institutional environment** includes all those public and private organizations that must agree before any policy change takes effect. In the case of the proficiency policy organization, passage of the new law required the formal agreement of the California legislature and the state Department of Education. In addition, the effective implementation of proficiency testing required the agreement and active support of other groups, including formal bodies like the Association of California School Administrators and informal ones, like collections of concerned parents and teachers.

The **political environment** includes all those who stand to win or lose from some policy change. What is important, of course, is their *own* calculation of whether they are about to become winners or losers, because that is what will determine their level of support or opposition. The proficiency policy organization cultivated many winners, the entrepreneurs who championed the cause, the politicians who rode the band wagon, the educators who helped kids and their own reputations, the consultants who made some money, and of course the pupils themselves.

The **policy environment** includes all the other policy organizations that are pursuing their own goals and unavoidably competing with one another for scarce commodities—the attention of policy-making officials, space in the mass media, the vocal support of institutional actors, and so on. In the case of the proficiency policy organization, a relatively low public profile helped avoid what could have been draining battles over scarce resources and entangling alliances that could have blurred goals and sapped organizational strength.

Environmental Interactions

Policy organizations are relatively open to and dependent on their environments—on lots of them and for many different things.[22] The proficiency policy organization, for example, interacted with its environments in many ways. The organization reached out to teachers and others who were looking for something that could be used to improve instruction. The organization (1) fostered in them the belief that proficiency testing would be a useful tool, (2) drew on their advice and energies, (3) met some of their demands, and (4) encouraged them to generate more. The organization then pointed to their escalated demands as evidence that the policy and the organization that supported it were justified. Through these interactions, the proficiency policy organization both stimulated and then met demands, provided and gained resources, and generated sufficient support to overcome obstacles to its goal. In general, the successful policy organization must find ways of using environmental inputs to overcome environmental obstacles.

---

[22] David Easton, *A Systems Analysis of Political Life* (Chicago, Ill.: University of Chicago Press, 1979).

Environmental Inputs

A policy organization is dependent on its environments for three kinds of inputs: resources, supports, and demands. Resources are whatever an organization can convert into policy influence. In the words of Meltsner and Bellavita, "resources are the raw material of power."[23] Resources, in the case of the proficiency organization, included expertise about testing and the legislative process; personal attributes of commitment and trust; the attributes of official positions, such as authority and credibility; and so on.

Supports are more diffuse and intangible, often consisting of a widely shared sense that the organization enjoys public support and is exercising its loose mandate in a responsible manner. Educational policy organizations usually enjoy a lot of diffuse support, generated by the popular association between their policy goals and other social values.

Demands are much more specific, since many in the organization and its broader environment know their self-interest and are not shy in insisting on it. In the proficiency organization, for example, the personal incentives of parents, teachers, educators, and politicians led them to make fairly specific demands of the policy organization. In return for meeting their demands, for satisfying their conception of the public, or their personal well-being, the policy organization received their support and was able to convert it into policy effectiveness. Some policy organizations and the governmental institutions at their center are remarkably adept at doing this, as was especially true in Philip Selznick's study of the Tennessee Valley Authority (TVA), the governing authority for the area's system of water control and electrical power generation.[24] In general, however, most policy organizations find that environmental demands exceed environmental supports.[25]

Environmental Constraints

The environments that surround policy organizations also impose constraints, barriers to goal realization. From earlier chapters, you know quite a bit about the many ways environmental influences constrain policy making.

- Popular expectations constrain what government may properly do. Democratic governments, in particular, nagged by doubts of their legitimacy and sensitive to political expressions of dissatisfaction, are pushed to try to resolve discrepancies between the system's policies and popular preferences (chapter 1).
- Throughout their history, Americans have sought to protect hallowed ground: their personal liberty. This primordial concern is reflected in the many constitutional constraints that limit and check the powers of the federal government and its branches (chapter 2).

---

23 Meltsner and Bellavita, *The Policy Organization*, p. 151.

24 Philip Selznick, *TVA and the Grass Roots* (New York: Harper and Row, 1966). (First published in 1949.)

25 See, for example, Arnold J. Meltsner, *The Politics of City Revenue* (Berkeley, Calif.: University of California Press, 1971).

- Each level of government is further constrained by other levels. In a federal system of divided national and state responsibilities, political actors, driven either by personal ambition, a vision of the public's welfare, or both, will find and create many opportunities for blocking policy initiatives, thereby forcing others to take them and their interests into account (chapter 3).
- Policy organizations are further constrained by this country's pervasive concern with guarding against arbitrary governmental interference with civil liberties and by desires to promote civil rights (chapter 4).
- Policy organizations also are constrained by the need to deal with a schizophrenic public, one that is difficult to arouse but, if aroused, is exceedingly hard to appease (chapter 5). Our private preoccupations and pluralistic political culture both liberate and constrain policy choices. The culture allows policy actors freedom of movement but makes them wary of an abyss, the possible perception that they have betrayed the public's trust.
- The competing demands of interest groups, and to some extent the competing claims of the members of those coalitions that make up political parties, further constrain policy organizations (chapter 6).
- To some extent, the media and the various forms of political participation can be used to overcome some of the constraints on policy organizations. As we saw in chapter 7, some policy makers are quite skillful in advancing their policy goals by using the media to cultivate political support and by using various forms of political participation to express that support.

Converting Resources Into Influence

Policy organizations in a democracy must successfully juggle resources, supports, demands, and constraints.[26] When they do so, they are more likely to elicit the agreement of those whose behavior they are trying to alter. With voluntary acceptance of policy, compliance is straight forward—and cheap. Without the acceptance of both elites and relevant publics, policies can be made and implemented only by force. This is too costly; however, the use of force robs government of its legitimacy.

Policy makers, however, are selectively attentive to an **organizational set**, those parts of their environment that can do the most to aid, or block, the realization of policy goals.[27] Within the Environmental Protection Agency, for example, officials worry less about the press corps as a whole than they do about *The New York Times* and *Washington Post* reporters who regularly track environmental issues; campaign contributors worry about Common Cause and Ralph Nader and certain reporters, such as Adam Clymer of *The New York Times*. Congressional policy makers also are more susceptible to some environmental influences than others. John Ferejohn, in his book, *Pork Barrel Politics*

---

26 See Jeffrey Pfeffer, *Power in Organizations* (Marshfield, Mass.: Pitman Publishing Corp., Inc., 1981).

27 William M. Even, "The Organization-Set: Toward a Theory of Interorganizational Relations," in James D. Thompson, ed., *Approaches to Organizational Design* (Pittsburgh, PA.: University of Pittsburgh Press, 1966), pp. 173–91. See also Richard H. Hall, *Organizations: Structure and Process* (Englewood Cliffs, NJ: Prentice-Hall, 1982). See especially chapter 10.

tells a classic tale.[28] A well-placed ranking member of Congress once helped pass a bill that raised the height of the levees, holding back the waters of the Mississippi River—but only on his district's side. When the Mississippi rose the next spring, his district stayed dry, as the water flooded the banks on the other side of the river. (You do not know whether to laugh or cry.) In the general case, it often is true; policy makers are captives of their own, often limited, horizons.

Governments, of course, are not totally dependent on public favor. Governments do not have to be loved, or even liked, to be effective. Indeed, if this were true, the endemic American antipathy toward government often would frustrate its advances. Instead, governments can win, and often win cheaply, public acceptance. All they have to do is find, or create, policies that both advance the public welfare and coincide with what people view as their own self-interests. Energy shortages during the 1970s provide confirming examples. To cope with energy shortages in 1974, for example, the citizens of Los Angeles did conserve electricity and did cut back on driving—just as official policy makers wanted them to. But it did not matter whether or not the people were politically supportive or distrustful of government. In this case, the public interest in conserving energy and private incentives in saving money coincided in ways that enhanced compliance—even though distrusting residents thought the government was exaggerating the severity of the energy crisis.[29] In this instance you can see a hint of what we will argue is the noble task of policy makers: seek that which simultaneously advances public and private interests.

When policy makers in a democratic system try to advance the public interest, but without convincing the people that the cause also advances their own personal interests, then government is about to take a long walk on a short plank. At any time, of course, governmental policies may get too far out in front of, or too far behind, popular preferences. When they do, as when President Reagan appeared to push for tax reform before there was a strong public demand for it, that velvet noose of public opinion jerks tightly. If they fail to anticipate and are unable to influence such shifts of public opinion, political and governmental organizations will lose legitimacy. Facing that harsh environment, organizations and institutions must adapt—or die.[30]

■ This discussion of organizational dynamics has been useful. If, that is, it has made you suspect that the interactions between policy organizations and their environments affect the way government behaves and what policies get made—or unmade. Hold on to this hunch; it will prove true when you turn to your study of the major institutions of American national government and the policy organizations that cluster around them (chapters 11 through 14).

---

28 John A. Ferejohn, *Pork Barrel Politics: Rivers and Harbors Legislation, 1947–1968* (Stanford, Calif.: Stanford University Press, 1974), p. 57.

29 David O. Sears, Tom R. Tyler, Jack Citrin, Donald Kinder, "System Support and Public Reactions to the Energy Crisis," *American Journal of Political Science* 22 (1978): 56–82.

30 James Sundquist, "The Crisis of Competence in Our National Government," *Political Science Quarterly* 95 (1980): 183–208.

SUMMARY

The idea of a policy organization is useful because it identifies those who make public policy and explains how they do it.

A policy organization is the set of governmental and nongovernmental actors who work together to realize a particular policy goal. This organization ties together the various parts of an otherwise fragmented political system.

A policy organization has certain components: members, goals, and tasks. Members are those who regularly interact over policy goals. Goals are the preferred futures they seek. Tasks are what has to be done to get there.

All policy organizations have a dynamic life. To be successful in overcoming environmental obstacles, the policy organization must respond to demands, convert resources into influence, and build on the support it receives in exchange for the services it provides.

Key Terms

policy organization	management tasks
political members	cultural environment
entrepreneurial members	institutional environment
technical members	political environment
goal displacement	policy environment
policy tasks	organizational set
research tasks	

Review and Reflection

1. What is a policy organization?

2. Why are policy organizations important?

3. What are the three major components of policy organizations?

4. Should we view a single government agency as a policy organization?

5. To be successful, what must a policy organization do?

6. Why was the policy organization that worked to establish the policy of proficiency testing successful?

7. Do you think it proper that nongovernmental actors get so heavily involved in the making of public policy? Why or why not?

Supplemental Readings

The literature on policy organizations falls into two categories: (1) theories of organizational behavior and (2) case studies of policy organizations at work.

In the theoretical category and in addition to those works cited in the body of the chapter, three pioneering works stand out: *Easton*'s adaption of systems

POLICY ORGANIZATIONS—AND EDUCATION

theory to the study of what we call (post Easton) political systems; *Deutsch's* application of cybernetics theory to the study of political communication; and *Lowi's* analysis of the reasons why private groups are able to dominate policy making in America.

In the case study category, most works emphasize the problems that attend efforts to make policy. *Allison* tries to explain some of the difficulties that President John F. Kennedy suffered as he tried to deal with the Cuban missile crisis. *Bauer et al.* show why it is hard to form a single policy organization to revise trade policies. *Berry* describes never-ending battles over the drafting of certain administrative regulations. *Janis* describes the ways in which delusional thinking distorts small group decision making. *Mazmanian and Nienabar* show the way one policy organization moved to expand its membership, by building in public participation. *Neustadt and Fineberg* explain the failures of the policy organization that pushed mass innoculation against the threat of a swine flu pandemic. And *Tuchman* dissects, in exhausting detail, the wooden-headed pursuit of foolish policies. On the other hand, for a more positive case, see *Rettig's* account of one person's heroic efforts to put together a policy organization devoted to the cure of cancer.

Allison, Graham T. *Essence of Decision: Explaining the Cuban Missile Crisis*. Boston: Little, Brown, 1971.

Bauer, R., I. Pool, and L. A. Dexter. *American Business and Public Policy: The Politics of Foreign Trade*. 2nd ed. Chicago: Aldine-Atherton, 1972.

Berry, Jeffrey M. *Feeding Hungry People: Rulemaking in the Food Stamp Program*. New Brunswick, NJ: Rutgers University Press, 1984.

Deutsch, Karl. *The Nerves of Government: Models of Political Communication and Control*. Chicago: University of Chicago Press, 1979. (First published in 1966).

Easton, David. *A Systems Analysis of Political Life*. New York: John Wiley & Sons, 1965.

Janis, Irving Lester. *Groupthink: Psychological Studies of Policy Decisions and Fiascos*. 2nd ed. Palo Alto, California: Houghton Mifflin, 1983.

Lowi, Theodore J. *The End of Liberalism*. Rev. ed. New York: W.W. Norton, 1979.

Mazmanian, Daniel and Jeanne Nienaber. *Can Organizations Change: Environmental Protection, Citizen Participation, and the Army Corps of Engineers*. Washington, D.C.: The Brooking's Institution, 1979.

Neustadt, Richard E. and Harvey V. Fineberg, M.D. *The Epidemic that Never Was: Policy-Making and the Swine Flu Scare*. New York: Random House, 1983.

Rettig, Robert. *Cancer Crusade*. Princeton, NJ: Princeton University Press, 1977.

Tuchman, Barbara. *The March of Folly*. New York: Ballantine, 1985.

CHAPTER NINE

POLICY PROCESSES— AND CIVIL RIGHTS

How is policy made?

It often seems as though policy is made very cautiously—if at all. This tendency toward inaction is maddening—but understandable.

Governmental officials, like the rest of us, are reluctant to trade the comforts of the status quo for the uncertainties of the future. Not knowing for sure whether they should act, whether their actions will be successful, or whether they will be blamed or praised for their actions, governmental officials tend to do what they have always done.

The following Case describes a crucial event in the evolution of civil rights policy: the campaign of civil disobedience in Birmingham, Alabama. For blacks and the nation, the campaign was useful because it dramatized the evils of segregation and helped bring about policy change. For us, the Case is useful because it suggests two fundamental insights about the way in which policy is made.

First, before governmental officials give up the comforts of the status quo, they have to be pushed. This can happen through **agenda building**, a process that defines the problem, legitimizes it as a proper matter of public concern, specifies alternative policies, and prods government into accepting responsibility for seeking a solution.

Second, to cope with the uncertainties of policy change, governmental officials rely on **incrementalism**, a reactive strategy of decision making which leads them to prefer marginal change, to search for remedies, not cures, and to define good policy as that which wins popular approval.

CIVIL RIGHTS POLICY

> Perhaps it is easy for those of you who have never felt the stinging darts of segregation to say, "Wait."
>
> —The Reverend Martin Luther King, Jr., Letter from the Birmingham City Jail

The Case Marching for Civil Rights in Birmingham

Early spring, 1963, Birmingham, Alabama. It was an astounding time—astounding that conditions for blacks were so bad, the barriers to change so large, and the chances of overcoming them so small.

Reverend Martin Luther King, Jr., believed that Birmingham was the most segregated city in the South. "Jim Crow signs" in the windows of local merchants made it clear what blacks could not do, where they could not eat, drink, shop, or work, except in menial jobs. Birmingham, for Reverend King, had a special significance: desegregate it and you could desegregate the South.

Reverend King believed in nonviolent forms of protest which forced people and the nation to confront the reality and the evil of segregation. Many cautioned, however, that the time was not yet ripe, the nation not yet ready. Most notably, President John F. Kennedy and his brother, Robert, the Attorney General, urged delay. Nevertheless, the Reverend King and his followers marched, persisted in the face of snarling dogs, and continued in violation of a court order against them. It was his violation of the court order that led to his arrest on Good Friday, April the twelfth and his incarceration in the Birmingham city jail.

The reaction to Reverend King's arrest threatened to stall the civil rights movement. For many Southern whites who had hoped for peaceful change, King's strategy of confrontation seemed inflamatory and therefore counterproductive. This view was expressed by eight prominent clergymen, in a letter published in the local newspaper. Their letter, in calling continued demonstrations "unwise and untimely," raised doubts, especially within the moderate white community. Their letter, if unanswered, offered too much comfort to those who preferred inaction to continued protest. To regain the initiative, King, still in jail, writing first in the margins of old newspapers and then on scraps of paper given him by a black trustee, drafted a response.

The Reverend King's response, the "Letter from Birmingham Jail," provided the rationale for continued action:

> Perhaps it is easy for those who have never felt the stinging darts of segregation to say, "Wait." But when you have seen vicious mobs lynch your mothers and fathers at will and drown your sisters and brothers at whim; when you have seen hate-filled policemen curse, kick and even kill your black brothers and sisters; when you see the vast majority of your

Newspaper photographs such as this one, made it hard for people to conclude that blacks were the problem in Birmingham.

twenty million Negro brothers smothering in an airtight cage of poverty in the midst of an affluent society; when you suddenly find your tongue twisted and your speech stammering as you seek to explain to your six-year-old daughter why she can't go to the public amusement park that has just been advertised on television, and see tears welling up in her eyes when she is told that Funtown is closed to colored children, and see ominous clouds of inferiority beginning to distort her personality by developing an unconscious bitterness toward white people; when you have to concoct an answer for a five-year-old son who is asking: "Daddy, why do white people treat colored people so mean?"; when you take a cross-country drive and find it necessary to sleep night after night in the uncomfortable corners of your automobile because no motel will accept you; when you are humiliated day in and day out by nagging signs reading "white" and "colored"; when your first name becomes "boy" (however old you are) and your last name becomes "John," and your wife and mother are never given the respected title "Mrs."; when you are harried by day and haunted by night by the fact that you are a Negro, living constantly at tiptoe stance, never quite knowing what to expect next, and are plagued with inner fears and outer resentments; when you are forever fighting a degenerating sense of "nobodiness"—then you will understand why we find it difficult to wait. There comes a time when the cup of endurance runs over, and men are no longer willing to be plunged into the abyss of despair. I hope, sirs, you can understand our legitimate and unavoidable impatience.

Yours for the cause of Peace and Brotherhood,
(signed) Martin Luther King, Jr.[1]

---

[1] Martin Luther King, Jr., *Why We Can't Wait* (New York: Harper and Row, 1963, 1964), pp. 83–84.

With this rationale, the marches against injustice continued and blacks continued to suffer at the hands of local authorities. The injustice and the suffering was graphically displayed on the front pages of the nation's newspapers. The images drove home King's message: "Injustice anywhere is injustice everywhere."

In spite of obstacles, significant progress would soon come. Within a year, the federal government would accept responsibility for ensuring the civil rights of all Americans and codify that acceptance by passing the Civil Rights Act of 1964. In general, the Act prohibited discrimination on the basis of race, color, religion, national origin, and in the case of employment only, sex. Its specific provisions (1) outlawed arbitrary discrimination in voter registration; (2) banned discrimination in public accommodations; (3) authorized the federal government to use the courts to end racial segregation in public schools; (4) expanded the life and the authority of the Civil Rights Commission; (5) authorized the withholding of federal funds from discriminatory programs; (6) provided for equal opportunity in employment; and (7) established a Community Relations Service to help resolve complaints about violations of civil rights.

Insights

Martin Luther King's actions and his letter justifying them suggest two major insights about the process by which public policy is made.

In 1954, Rosa Parks' decision not to relinquish her seat on a Montgomery, Alabama, bus sparked the beginnings of the Civil Rights movement.

Insight 1. *Policy making follows agenda building.* In Birmingham and in the nation, governmental officials were very reluctant to do anything other than defend the status quo. Martin Luther King, Jr., and others, through their words and deeds, had to push governmental officials, both in Birmingham and in Washington, D.C., to act favorably. In this case and in general, governmental officials act in response to agenda building, the process through which people and events (a) define the problem, (b) legitimize it as a public concern, (c) specify alternative policy responses to the problem, and (d) pressure government into accepting responsibility for solving the problem.

Insight 2. *Governmental officials usually act as though they believe in incrementalism.* Governmental officials try to avoid making comprehensive or radical changes in the status quo; the future is too uncertain, the potential costs of moving quickly are too great. Whenever possible, therefore, they will act as though they are relying on a strategy of incrementalism, a set of tactics by which they (a) try to make marginal changes in policies, (b) look for policy alternatives that will remedy, but not necessarily solve, problems, and (c) tend to define good policies as those that win popular approval. In the making of civil rights policy, governmental officials in Birmingham and in the rest of the nation had relied on incrementalism for years, actually for over a hundred years. By 1964, however, the nation concluded that it could not inch toward equality and took a bold step by passing a comprehensive Civil Rights Act. Nevertheless, this comprehensive policy only occurred after a long and arduous journey to Birmingham.

POLICY PROCESSES—AND CIVIL RIGHTS

Historical Background: The Montgomery Experience

In Birmingham, Dr. King successfully shaped the agendas of governmental officials and forced them into making policies that they, at least, found radical. In large part, Dr. King's success was due to his persuasive powers and his political skills. Neither had come quickly, or cheaply. Both had been earned and honed earlier, in Montgomery, Alabama.[2]

Martin Luther King, Jr., was installed as the twentieth pastor of the Dexter Avenue Church in Montgomery, Alabama on October 31, 1954. From that position he would quickly move to the forefront of what became the successful effort to desegregate public transport in Montgomery.

In 1955, the municipal buses in the city of Montgomery segregated passengers by race, directing blacks to the rear of the bus and requiring that they relinquish their seats to any white who had none. The requirement, common throughout much of the South, was generally followed. But not on December 1, 1954. That day, one black passenger, Rosa Parks, returning home tired after a long day's work as a seamstress, simply refused to relinquish her seat to a white man. She continued to refuse after being ordered to by the bus driver. After the bus driver ordered her off the bus, she refused him that as well. For her actions, Rosa Parks was arrested by the Montgomery police and removed from the bus.

It was a spark that inflamed the black population of Montgomery, drawing them together as never before. Still, they had few resources, little with which they could pressure municipal officials. But they did have the right to refuse to ride on segregated buses and the will to exercise it. In this way, they hoped, fewer riders and fewer revenues would convey the message; for their own economic well-being, the city's buses must be desegregated.

The Montgomery bus boycott was on. By December 5, an organization, the Montgomery Improvement Association, was formed to coordinate the effort, to direct protest marches to dramatize the struggle, and to create a car-pooling system as an alternative means of transportation. The Association would continue this effort for the next full year, under the leadership of its first president, the Reverend Martin Luther King, Jr.

Nineteen hundred and fifty-six was a year full of the conflict and tension Dr. King would later recall from the Birmingham city jail. In January of that year, his home in Montgomery was bombed; in February, Dr. King was among those indicted with conspiring to hinder the operation of a business without "just or legal cause"; and by October, the city's legal department had begun efforts to block the continued operation of car pools.

Meanwhile, the marches continued, the pressures mounted, and inexorably the case worked its way through the courts. Eventually, on November 13, the United States Supreme Court reaffirmed a lower court decision, declaring unconstitutional Alabama's segregation of municipal buses. To further the implementation of the decision, federal marshals, on December 20, served

---

[2] See, for its historical value, Stephen B. Oates, *Let the Trumpet Sound: The Life of Martin Luther King, Jr* (New York: Harper and Row, 1982).

officials of the city and its bus company with injunctions that threatened them with jail, if they refused to integrate the buses.

The Montgomery bus boycott was over. Martin Luther King, Jr., had emerged as a major civil rights leader. More importantly, he had learned how to shape the agenda of governmental officials and how to make them move in nonincremental ways.

■ During Reverend King's life and since, most of the change in civil rights policy has not come about spontaneously or at the initiative of federal or state or local governmental officials. Policy change, rather, has come about in response to the efforts of others to shape the policy agenda.

THE POLICY-MAKING PROCESS: AN OVERVIEW

> You cannot govern nations without a mailed fist and an iron will.
> —*Benito Mussolini, Italian dictator*

> To rule is not so much a question of the heavy hand as the firm seat.
> —*José Ortega y Gasset,*
> *Spanish philosopher*

There is a world of difference between the views of Mussolini and Ortega y Gasset. Let us take a quick glimpse at these two extreme views of policy making and then explore the depths in-between.

Many things are implied in Mussolini's view. For example, he presumes that there is some single leader who knows what policies should be made and with the iron strength of his convictions, imposes these policies on the rest of society. The implications make sense—if the presumptions were true. If they were true, there would be no need for hesitation or consultation, and it would be irresponsible for the leader not to impose his iron will.

On the other extreme, Ortega y Gasset portrays policy makers as much more patient and passive, more inclined to wait for events rather than direct them. The passive policy maker does not know what is right and therefore lacks the conviction to act. The two extremes do not give us much of a choice: both are too idealized, too far removed from reality. Most policy making falls between these two idealized extremes. The middle ground, as is often true, is more messy—and interesting.

Most policy makers, even those who know what goals they prefer, struggle to cope with forces over which they have little control and of which they have too little comprehension. Wise policy makers are those who know this and view

Policy makers confront highly uncertain futures, as President Reagan does here at the beginning of his first term as President.

reality with respectful awe. "If you can keep your head when all about you are losing theirs, you don't understand the situation," goes the parody of one of the lines in Rudyard Kipling's poem, "If." The parody touches on an essential truth about the situation that confronts policy makers: uncertainty.

Policy makers confront highly uncertain situations, where both policy options and their likely consequences often are obscure. Confronting highly uncertain choices, policy makers simply do not know (and often can not find out) the answers to compelling questions: "Will the policy work? Will people think it is the correct policy?" Peering into an uncertain future, policy makers must have some sense of apprehension, even dread—the kind of feeling you get from Oliphant's cartoon of Ronald Reagan (above), at the beginning of his first term as President.

To see what they have to cope with, get uncomfortably settled inside the shoes of policy makers. The choice situation they face is more than uncertain. It also is filled with great danger, the potentially disastrous consequences of being wrong. Imagine, for example, that you were President Carter, trying to cope with the problem of Americans held hostage in Iran, or Ronald Reagan, trying to cope with the problem of international terrorism sponsored by Libya's Moammar Khadafy.

Assume you were presented with only two feasible courses of action: (1) meet the demands of the terrorists and (2) launch a military raid to deter future acts of terrorism. To choose between these, you probably would like more information—about whether the terrorists, if their demands were met, would stop being terrorists and about the chances that a raid would be successful. Unfortunately, there is not any more information. You have to choose now, on the basis of too little information and too much uncertainty.

Policy making is like passing in football; three things can happen—and two of them are bad. In football, the two bad outcomes of an attempted pass are, of course, an incompletion and an interception. In policy making, the two bad consequences are failure to get the intended consequences and the occurrence of undesirable unintended consequences. Since both are possible and portend possible disaster, the wise policy maker, like the smart quarterback, acts prudently.

■ The prudent policy maker, wise enough to know that the future is uncertain and filled with danger, gropes tentatively. The prudent policy maker also needs policy-making aids. There are two major ones, each discussed next: the stages of agenda building and the tactics of incremental decision making.

THE STAGES OF AGENDA BUILDING

> There can be no rain without lightning and
> thunder.　　　　　　　—*Frederick Douglass,*
> 　　　　　　　　　　　*black abolitionist*

Governmental officials, especially ones in a democratic system, tend to react to problems and policies that are pushed upon them. That situation is created by a process of agenda building. The four major stages of the process are: (1) define the problem; (2) legitimize it as a proper subject of governmental concern; (3) specify policy alternatives; and (4) convince governmental officials to accept responsibility for dealing with the problem.[3]

Defining the Problem

This first stage of agenda building is crucial, because the way in which the problem is defined often determines whether or not the process will continue. In Birmingham, for example, it was crucial that the concerns of blacks *not* be defined as a temporary problem, one that would go away if ignored. In other cases, it is crucial that problems not be defined as inevitable and beyond human control, as, for example, oscillating periods of economic boom and bust once were. In this first stage, therefore, those who would shape government's agenda must make the case that there is a problem, that it will not go away by itself, and that it is susceptible to remediation.

　　Problems are defined through political activities, especially those that produce conflict.

Political Activity.　There is nothing natural or inevitable about the way in which people come to see a certain situation as a problem, a harmful condition that should not, and need not, exist. Rather, this is a political process, one in

---

[3] See John W. Kingdon, *Agendas, Alternatives, and Public Policies* (Boston: Little, Brown, 1984).

which some use words and deeds in an attempt to shape the way in which people perceive a problem and what, if anything, they are willing to do about it.

Through political rhetoric and political deeds, those who would define a problem must convince others that something is broken. It is a necessary objective, since most people, just like their governmental officials, tend to prefer the status quo and distrust change. This preference is captured in the political wisdom: "If it's not broken, don't fix it." The objective, in other words, is to convince people that something is "broken." In Birmingham, for example, the organizers of the bus boycott tried to convince municipal officials that the segregated bus system was "broken," no longer economically viable. In many other cases, those who try to expand government's role try to convince others that the private economic market is broken, that it is failing to produce what people want or to do so at a price people can afford. On the other hand, however, there are an increasing number of cases, where those who would reduce government's role are trying to convince others that government is broken, that it is both interfering with the proper operation of the private market and failing to deliver what people want as efficiently as they want it.

"After all, we've only been here a little over four years."

Conflict. To convince people that there is a problem that they should do something about, agenda builders seek to create internal, psychological conflict. Social psychologists refer to this kind of conflict as **cognitive dissonance**, a psychological state of tension produced by the discrepancy between (a) a person's perception of the way things are and (b) the person's belief about the way things should be.[4] Since this state of tension is unpleasant, the theory holds, individuals will try to resolve it, either by: (a) changing their perception of the way things are, (b) changing their belief about the way things should be, or (c) joining in a political effort to actually change the way things are.

To bring about the obviously preferred third result, there are many things agenda builders can do. Here are some examples, drawn from the case of civil rights and elsewhere, of things that have happened, either by design or otherwise, which have defined problems in ways that helped build a policy agenda:

- In Montgomery, the arrest of a woman for her failure to give her seat to a man made segregation appear less tenable.
- In Birmingham, putting people in situations where they were attacked by police dogs made it clear that the problem was repression.
- Documenting the cost of hammers and toilet seats for the armed forces made it hard to be in favor of increased defense spending.
- Stories, whether apocryphal or not, about people on welfare driving Cadillacs, erode public support for governmental spending on social services.
- Publicity about millionaires who pay no income taxes increases pressure for tax reform.

---

4 See, for example, Leon Festinger, *A Theory of Cognitive Dissonance* (Stanford, Calif.: Stanford University Press, 1957) and S. J. Kantola, "Cognitive Dissonance and Energy Conservation," *Journal of Applied Psychology* 69 (1984): 416–21.

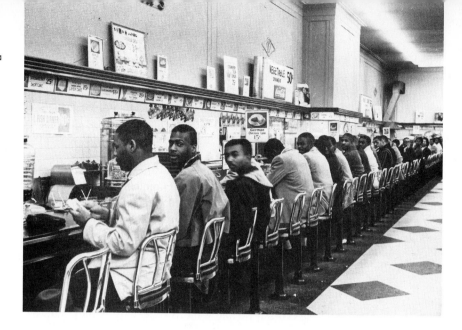

Scenes such as this one, of a sit-in at a lunch counter in 1963, proved to be effective tactics in the fight over civil rights.

In all these and countless other ways, splashed across the pages of your daily newspaper, some people try to convince others that something is broken, that it can be fixed, and that they should do something about it (or at least support those who try).

The definition of the problem can determine the course of the political process. Defining the problem is like drawing the battlelines in war; if you can do it, you win. This is what Schattschneider had in mind when he wrote: "He who determines what politics is about runs the country. . . .[5] Sometimes, this has been done skillfully:

- During his campaign for the presidency in 1960, John F. Kennedy spoke of the millions who went to bed hungry every night. His handling of the issue was masterful, since people ended up debating how many millions went to bed hungry, not whether it was healthy to do so;
- As he tried to reduce social spending in his first administration, President Ronald Reagan masterfully answered critics of his proposed cuts in food stamps by distilling the debate "to a bare question: . . . Is anyone going to starve?"[6];
- As he tried to move mass transit subsidies off the national policy-making agenda, President Reagan asked rhetorically, "Does the rest of the nation care if someone in Los Angeles is five minutes late to work?"

[5] E. E. Schattschneider, *The Semisovereign People: A Realist's View of Democracy in America* (Hinsdale, Ill.: The Dryden Press, 1975), p. 68.

[6] *The New York Times*, 12 June 1981.

POLICY PROCESSES—AND CIVIL RIGHTS

Legitimizing the Problem

Before government will act, problems must be transformed into things that people believe are public concerns that government should do something about. Transforming them is, again, a political activity which involves the creative use of conflict.

Political Activity. There is no objective or logical distinction between problems that are private and problems that are public. Rather, the distinction is a subjective one, made on the basis of people's subjective beliefs. Moreover, as John Stuart Mill has written, there is no hard and fast line between private and public problems.[7] Rather, the division is a fluid one, a "fence on wheels," to use his analogy. Mill's example helps to make the point. Consider the drunkard: Is he an appropriate object of public concern? It depends, Mill suggests, on whether he is hurting anyone else. For example, does he spend his paycheck on drink, rather than food for his family? Does he drive his daughter to despair? Does he later require kidney dialysis treatments, subsidized at the public's expense? If the answer to any of these questions is "yes," then the drunkard falls over the line and becomes a public concern.

People, left to their own devices, may come to see a problem as a public concern. Those who would increase government's role, as well as those who would reduce it, try not to leave such things to chance. Instead, both types of agenda builders, usually through the use of political symbols, try to persuade others of the "publicness," or "privateness," of some problem.[8] There have been many attempts:

The 1963 March on Washington proved to be a dramatic moment that symbolized the cause of civil rights as a public as well as a national problem.

- After his arrest in Birmingham, the Reverend Martin Luther King, Jr., stayed in jail, rather than post bail to be released. Thereby he kept the story of his arrest in the news, provoked a concern with his welfare, and focused attention on efforts of President Kennedy's administration to ensure his safety while in jail.
- During the March on Washington, the mass meeting on the mall in front of the Lincoln Memorial symbolized the cause of civil rights as a public, indeed, a national problem.
- Poor education and crime, some argue, is a problem better dealt with by parents, than by government.[9]
- Sometimes the message is subtle. During his State of the Union Addresses, for example, President Reagan often introduced private citizens, not governmental bureaucrats, as "heroes" who had made some special contribution or who had achieved some special accomplishment.

---

[7] John Stuart Mill, *On Liberty* (New York: Penguin, 1982).

[8] See Murray Edelman, *Politics as Symbolic Action: Mass Arousal and Quiescence* (Chicago: Markham, 1971).

[9] See, for example, Daniel Patrick Moynihan, *Family and Nation* (San Diego: Harcourt Brace, 1986).

- In general, every demonstration and every political message on a roadside billboard or television set is an attempt to create public awareness of problems.

Conflict. The creation and manipulation of conflict is central to the task of legitimizing a problem as a public concern, or delegitimizing a current public concern as one better dealt with privately. Conflict works because it is contagious. As E. E. Schattschneider wrote: "Nothing attracts a crowd so quickly as a fight."[10] Agenda builders, of course, try to recruit more supporters than opponents. (The point, after all, is to win, not get bloody.) This is why Dr. King had to respond as he did to the clergymen who questioned the wisdom and timing of the demonstrations in Birmingham; they, and he, were trying to broaden the conflict in ways that would aid their cause. To be used successfully, therefore, conflict must mobilize people selectively, bringing in more and stronger allies than opponents.

Specifying Policy Alternatives

Those who would shape the policy agenda must take the additional step of identifying and evaluating alternative policy responses to the problem. Their goal, after all, is not just action, but action in the service of some policy goal. (See the discussion in chapter 8 of the goals of policy organizations.)

By this stage in the process of agenda building, many possible policy responses have been winnowed out by earlier stages. This was true, for example, in all the following cases:

- By the time Dr. King drafted his letter from the Birmingham jail, he and his followers had acted in ways that eliminated, as a viable alternative, continued acceptance of segregated buses.[11]
- By the time the head of the federal government's Center for Disease Control went to President Ford and advised him of the threat of a swine flu pandemic, there was no viable policy option other than mass innoculation.[12]
- If people believe that Senator Ted Kennedy's personal character disqualifies him from serving as President, there is very little he can do to advance his candidacy.
- If people believe that government is the problem, not the solution, very few who hope to win or retain elective office will propose new programs. In other cases, however, there is a need to generate, sort out, and evaluate policy options.

---

[10] Schattschneider, *The Semisovereign People*, p. 1.

[11] See, for its discussion of the role of irreversible actions in negotiations, Thomas C. Schelling, *The Strategy of Conflict* (Cambridge, Mass.: Harvard University Press, 1960).

[12] See Richard E. Neustadt and Harvey V. Fineberg, M. D. *The Epidemic that Never Was: Policy-Making and the Swine Flu Scare* (New York: Random House, 1983).

The press and political cartoonists often try to define the issue. In this case, the issue, Oliphant insists, is personal character.

In these cases, both agenda builders and governmental officials often rely on the techniques of incremental decision making (to be described in the next section of this chapter).

Establishing Government's Responsibility

Agenda building may move successfully through its first three stages and stall at this, its last stage. It will stall, unless agenda builders successfully: (a) get the attention of governmental officials and (b) convince them that it is proper for them to act. Although this is difficult, agenda builders often get help from intermediary political agents, as in the **Vantage Point**: The Media as an Agenda Builder.

Getting the Attention of Governmental Officials. Government often seems like an old mule that has to be hit with a two-by-four to get its attention. For the most part, government's attention is so hard to get because governmental officials are preoccupied with their current agendas and the problems that are already on them. At the beginning of the Birmingham crisis, for example, both President Kennedy and his brother, Robert, were preoccupied with foreign policy problems in Cuba, Western Europe, and Southeast Asia and with congressional opposition to a proposed tax cut to stimulate the economy. Their agenda already crowded, they understandably urged Dr. King to delay. It is generally true; since governmental officials already are preoccupied with pressing problems, it is very hard to get their attention for new ones.

Government's agenda is almost consumed by **routine issues**, matters that come before policy makers on a regular cycle. There are many reasons why this is so. The Constitution, for example, requires the President to report on the State of the Union and, preparing to do so will preoccupy many for several months before it is due. Also, most new statutes are enacted with expiration dates that dictate Congress' schedule a number of years hence. In addition, the

THE MEDIA AS AN AGENDA BUILDER

*T*oday, the subject of child abuse is firmly on the agenda of federal, state, and local governmental officials.

Child abuse moved on to the public agenda relatively recently and primarily because of the power of the press.

One study, for example, found that the first mass media article did not occur until *Time* magazine published an article in July of 1962. By 1967, sixteen articles had been published in mass circulation magazines and over one hundred and thirty had been published in the professional journals of health care professionals, lawyers, and academic researchers. Also by 1967, all fifty states had adopted at least a law requiring health officials to report suspected cases of child abuse. Mass media coverage fell off and then began to rise rapidly in the mid-1970s (see Figures 1 and 2).

FIGURE 1
Mass Media Coverage Of Child Abuse and Neglect

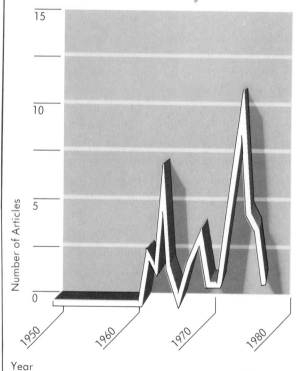

FIGURE 2
Professional Media Coverage Of Child Abuse and Neglect

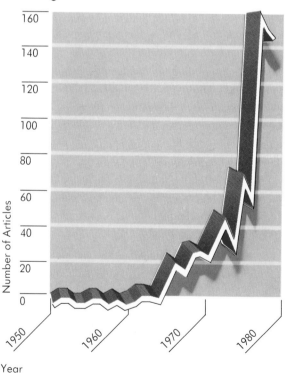

SOURCE: Barbara J. Nelson and Thomas Lindenfeld, "Setting the Agenda: The Case of Child Abuse," in Judith V. May and Aaron B. Wildavsky, pp. 28, 29 in *The Policy Cycle.* Copyright © 1978 by Sage Publications, Inc. Reprinted by permission.

electoral cycle helps set the congressional agenda, as candidates often crank up their re-election campaigns by introducing new bills, including ones that have no chance of enactment. In general, as Jack Walker has shown in his study of the United States Senate, governmental officials are inclined to attend to matters that are mandatory, not optional.[13]

Convincing Governmental Officials That They May Properly Act. Agenda building will not be complete, and agenda builders will not be successful, unless someone, somehow, convinces governmental officials that they may properly take the policy course which is being pressed upon them.

Governmental officials, especially ones in democratic systems, must maintain legitimacy, for them, their policies, and their offices. They, therefore, often act as though they adhere to the advice of the late Richard Daley, the Democratic mayor of Chicago: "Don't make no waves and don't back no losers." To assure them that they are not about to, agenda builders must convince governmental officials and the public of three things: (1) government has the capacity to act; (2) the cost of governmental action is low (or hidden); and (3) the proposed action is consistent with dominant social values.

Meeting these conditions can be tricky. The question of government's capacity to act can be in doubt, for example, as it was before the development of an economic doctrine that increased confidence in the government's capacity to fine-tune the economy and as it was when Presidents Carter and Reagan moved to deregulate many aspects of the economy. (See the discussion of economic policy making in chapter 10.)

The likely costs of governmental involvement also can make governmental officials reluctant to accept responsibility for a problem. These costs, however, usually are low (sometimes underestimated) in the initial stages of governmental involvement. For example, in the early days of environmental protection, low perceived costs facilitated the rapid growth of an expansive federal role. As real costs, both to the public treasury and to those employed in polluting industries became more visible, however, the pace of progress slowed.[14]

Finally, governmental officials are quicker to accept responsibility for a new policy course when they and, they believe, most of the public, are convinced that it is consistent with dominant cultural values. Sometimes this can be done by linking the new policy to an established principle, as, in the 1930s, Social Security was sold to the American people as though it were a form of insurance[15] and as, in the 1960s, Medicare (a radically new federal responsibility) was sold as "just another application of the 'time-tested' Social Security principle."[16] In the long run, however, the lack of a real social consensus is disabling.

---

[13] Jack L. Walker, "Setting the Agenda in the U.S. Senate," *British Journal of Political Science* 7 (1977): 423–45.

[14] Anthony Downs, "Up and Down with Ecology—the 'Issue-Attention' Cycle," *Public Interest* 32 (1972): 38–50.

[15] See Katie Louchheim, ed., *The Making of the New Deal: The Insiders Speak* (Cambridge, Mass.: Harvard University Press, 1983).

[16] James L. Sundquist, *Politics and Policy: The Eisenhower, Kennedy, and Johnson Years* (Washington, D.C.: The Brookings Institution, 1968), p. 393.

One eminent political scientist, Samuel Beer, speculated, for example, that many of the new social programs of President Johnson's Great Society would not long endure, because the President had not successfully transformed popular beliefs about government's proper role.[17]

This description of the dynamics of agenda building has tended to cast the process as one of moving things off the personal agendas of private citizens and on to the public agendas of governmental decision makers. It often works this way. But, it also works the other way, as some try to bring about **privatization**, a process of reducing government's role in society by moving matters back into the private sector. Moreover, both efforts occur simultaneously, although one usually tends to dominate the other. As Albert Hirschman, a politically perceptive economist, has written, the American political system seems to swing back and forth between "periods of utter privatization to total absorption in public causes. . . ." In general, Hirschman concludes: "Western societies appear to be condemned to long periods of privatization during which they live through an impoverishing 'atrophy of public meanings,' followed by spasmodic outbursts of 'publicness' that are hardly likely to be constructive."[18]

■Governmental officials in democratic political systems, no less than angels, are reluctant to rush into highly uncertain situations and risk losing their precious legitimacy. Rather, they prefer to wait on others and on events to build the positive case for action, whether that means a bigger or a smaller role for government.

Agenda building is the process through which the case is made. It consists of four stages in which actions define a problem, legitimize it as a proper matter for governmental concern, specify alternative policy responses to the problem, and convince governmental officials to accept responsibility for dealing with the problem.

"Dealing with the problem," seldom means "solving it," however.

---

[17] See Samuel Beer, "In Search of a New Public Philosophy," in Anthony King, ed., *The New American Political System* (Washington, D.C.: The American Enterprise Institute, 1978), pp. 5–44.

[18] Albert O. Hirschman, *Shifting Involvements: Private Interest and Public Action* (Princeton, NJ: Princeton University Press, 1982). See especially pp. 132–34.

THE TACTICS OF INCREMENTAL DECISION MAKING

> . . . it is better to be a little wrong and a little
> late than to be too right too quickly.
> —*David Halberstam,* The Powers
> That Be

The Reactiveness of Decision Making

Governmental officials cope with an uncertain and dangerous environment by waiting on it, hoping the situation will become more clear. In doing so, the policy maker is risk-adverse. Thomas Jefferson had a more simple way of saying it: "Delay is preferable to error." In waiting, the prudent policy maker knows that the current situation is, at least momentarily, secure. Moreover, waiting is cheap; no resources are expended fighting unknown demons. The policy maker at rest, therefore, tends to stay at rest, that is, until pushed to move by a successful process of agenda building.

Policy makers who react to events know that the demand for policy change must come from the bottom, from outside the policy organization—or, at least, must be made to appear that way. There is no good alternative to being reactive, even though policy makers may be inclined to try to anticipate problems. There is no good alternative because policy makers lack the organizational resources to charge off against problems that no one is complaining about—yet. Recall the foolishness of Don Quixote, ill-equipped and under-staffed, tilting at windmills. That image, if suffered upon a policy maker who gets too far in front of public opinion, spells disaster.

The prudent *and* enterprising policy maker, however, can be both reactive and a little proactive, by applying the wisdom embedded in Chairman Mao's theory of revolution: "Two steps forward, one backward." Policy makers with the vision to anticipate future problems can move forward, if they are resourceful enough to cultivate sufficient public support and astute enough to amass sufficient political power. Ronald Reagan, for example, was resourceful enough to translate his apparent election mandate into enough momentum to pass a comprehensive program of budget cuts in his first year in office. Even during his second term, President Reagan was able to govern as though the issueless campaign of 1984 settled fundamental policy disputes. In general, leaders, especially those who have the skill to shape and control their own agenda, appear to outsiders as those who can organize a parade and then leap to its front.

Time and again the pattern repeats itself; policy making is a largely reactive process, with occasional dashes of proactiveness. For example, many of those members of Congress who advocate gun control will step back from the barricades when they see one of their colleagues go down to electoral defeat, after being targeted by the National Rifle Association. A politically astute President can expand his influence over the executive branch, after he senses and helps cultivate public antipathy toward the bureaucracy. Mothers and high school students can organize and exert political pressure to get policy makers to toughen and enforce drunk driving laws, but, unfortunately, too often only after some personal tragedy. Those charged with worrying about national security will look for new naval bases, but usually only after our sometime allies close their ports to American ships carrying nuclear weapons, as New Zealand did in 1984. In all these cases, and in general, governmental policy makers tend to wait on and react to public demands for action, although they sometimes try to orchestrate demands.

The reactiveness of policy making helps explain why it is so hard to get government to deal with future problems, especially those whose effects have yet to be felt dramatically. It is even hard to get policy makers to do a lot about possibly horrendous future problems, like the prospect of a nuclear holocaust, the depletion of the ozone layer, or the crumbling urban infrastructure of water and transportation systems. Policy makers, for better but often for worse, tend to react to wheels that have already squeaked, not ones yet heard.

Eventually, however, agenda-building processes may force governmental officials to react before they are absolutely sure they know what will be both correct and popular. At that point, they, and all policy makers, rely on certain tactics for coping with uncertainty and danger. Ideally, one might think that policy makers would behave rationally; that is, they would identify all possible ways of solving some problem, systematically evaluate the likely effects of different policies, and then choose that policy that would best solve the problem. As a practical matter, however, the lack of time and information does not permit such a comprehensive approach. At best, policy makers exercise highly constrained, or what psychologist Herbert Simon calls "bounded," rationality.[19] Policy makers with bounded rationality cope with danger by groping through it, by relying on incremental decision-making tactics.[20]

There are three main tactics of incremental decision making. These are behavioral imperatives and instructions to policy makers:

- Prefer marginal to comprehensive policy change. (And pay attention to the consequences of little steps, so you know whether to proceed.)
- Search for policies that will remedy problems; do not waste time looking for ones that will cure, or solve, problems. (Remember, policy making is an ongoing process and you will get another chance to respond to the problem.)
- Desire those remedies that can win popular approval, especially the approval of those most directly affected by the problem. (You often need their agreement to get the policy passed and implemented.)

---

[19] Herbert A. Simon, *Models of Man* (New York: Wiley, 1966), pp. 198–200.

[20] The early descriptions of incrementalism are found in Charles E. Lindblom, "The Science of 'Muddling Through'," *Public Administration Review* 19 (1959): 79–88. See also Lindblom's short monograph *The Policy Making Process* (Englewood Cliffs, NJ, 1968). Since then the literature has mushroomed, exposing the dangers of incrementalism, exceptions to it, and alternative ways of making public policy.

The Preference for Marginal Change

The incremental policy maker will try to make **marginal changes** in policy, customary and small, rather than radical or large ones. This tactic recognizes that: (a) policy is made through a process, not as a result of any single action and (b) small steps can generate **feedback**, useful information about consequences that can be used to adjust policy.

The preference for marginal change is reflected in many contemporary instances: Supreme Court decisions that modify the due process rights of criminal defendants; Justice Department proposals to weaken the requirements of affirmative action programs; Interior Department proposals to sell public lands; legislated changes in the warning labels on cigarettes; and in most cuts in federal spending on social welfare. The preference for marginal change is also demonstrated in the frustration and gridlock that attends attempts to make fundamental shifts in policy, as for example, in President Reagan's initial attempts to bring about comprehensive tax reform in the mid-1980s. The preference of marginal change is even present in cases where, on first glance, it appears not to be, as illustrated, for example, in the **Vantage Point**: Has There Been a Radical Increase in Defense Spending?

The Search for Remedies, Not Cures

The incremental policy maker searches for remedies, whatever lessens social discomforts and the political pressure they generate. Seeking only remedies, policy makers are open to whatever promises relief, however slight. Being open, policy makers will be more willing to act, even to experiment, as many around Franklin Roosevelt were at the beginning of what came to be called the New Deal.[21]

The political justification of the search for remedies is compelling. Policy makers are under pressure to make uncertain and dangerous choices. Simultaneously, they are armed only with limited power, supported by an often fragile public consensus, and under constant attack by politically ambitious adversaries. The prudent policy maker, therefore, can not afford to settle into an arm chair to discern the best possible policy. The pressure is to act, to do something, however tentative. Real life policy makers, therefore, seek improvements that promise some relief, even if those policy actions do not solve the underlying problem.

This tactic of remedial policy making asserts itself throughout American history and into ongoing policy disputes. Needing the political support of the abolitionists, Lincoln sought half a remedy, the Confiscation Act as the Case at the beginning of chapter 1 showed. Unable to decide, once and for all, the proper line between the authority of the national government and that of the states, we use the judicial system to render case-by-case remedies for the issues of nuclear waste disposal, the permissible length of trucks, the appropriate pay

---

21 Louchheim, *The Making of the New Deal.*

HAS THERE BEEN A RADICAL INCREASE IN DEFENSE SPENDING?

One way of measuring policy change is to look at the amount of money that is spent on something and the way that changes over time. Consider the policy changes that are made in the federal budget for defense. The table, for example, shows federal budget outlays for national defense over the administrations of the last four Presidents, Nixon, Ford, Carter, and Reagan. At first glance, it does appear as though this nation has been embarked on a fairly rapid program of building up its defense forces—if you look just at the total dollars spent in Column 1. That column shows that national defense expenditures grew from $76.6 billion in 1972 to more than $187 billion in 1982. But a part of

this increase is due to inflation. Once you correct for the effects of inflation, the apparently radical policy change largely disappears. This is shown in Column 2, "Constant (1972) Dollars." In this column, defense spending increases, in real dollars, from $76.6 billion in 1972 to $81.7 billion in 1982. Admittedly, $5,100,000,000, the increase, is a big number, but hardly a radical change in spending.

To see the real change in levels of defense spending over time, examine the figures in Column 3, "Annual Percent Change, in Constant (1972) Dollars." Column 3 shows that real change has occurred in relatively small steps, ranging between a change of an

8.6 percent decrease in 1973 to a 6.9 percent increase in 1982. Indeed, if you look at real defense expenditures expressed as a percentage of the total Gross National Product (in Column 4), it becomes increasingly clear that change in levels of defense spending occurs in small, marginal steps.

This conclusion about defense spending is generally true of other policy areas. Even policy goals that sound radical (land a man on the moon, eradicate smallpox, put a naval blockade around Cuba) are reached, if they are reached at all, as the result of a series of small, manageable steps, over what is often a long, drawn-out process.[1]

---

[1] For a different view, see Paul R. Schulman, "Nonincremental Policymaking: Notes toward an Alternative Paradigm," *American Political Science Review* 69 (1975): 1354–70 and his book, *Large Scale Policy Making* (Westport, Conn.: Greenwood Press, Inc. 1980).

levels of municipal employees. Fully aware that they are not going to solve all the health problems of rural America, concerned policy makers nevertheless push ahead with policies that encourage the outward flow of new doctors. Even if the Congress and no state legislature know what to do about the problem, a state judge in New Jersey may hold liable a defendant who served alcohol to a drunk who then drove and hurt someone. In all these cases, and in the ones in the headlines of your morning paper, incremental policy makers are trying to make a real problem a little less bad.

Incremental policy makers are also justified in seeking remedies, not cures,

Changes in Defense Spending, 1972–1982

Year	National Defense Outlays			
	Column 1 Total (billions)	Column 2 Constant (1972) Dollars (billions)	Column 3 Annual Percent Change, in Constant (1972) Dollars (percent)	Column 4 Real Change, in Constant (1972) Dollars, as a Percen- age of GNP (percent)
1972	76.6	76.6	x	x
1973	74.5	70.0	−8.6	6.0
1974	77.8	68.4	−2.3	5.6
1975	85.6	68.7	.4	5.8
1976	89.4	67.1	−2.3	5.5
1977	97.5	67.8	1.0	5.2
1978	105.2	68.0	.3	5.0
1979	117.7	70.6	3.8	5.0
1980	135.9	72.7	3.0	5.3
1981	159.8	76.4	5.1	5.6
1982	187.4	81.7	6.9	6.2

SOURCE: U.S. Bureau of the Census, *Statistical Abstract of the United States: 1984*, 104th ed., (Washington, D.C., 1983), Table No. 551, p. 343.

because they know that no problem ever goes away completely. Therefore, they will, if they do not lose their job in the meanwhile, be around tomorrow to try again. This means that policy making will be an ongoing, iterative process.

Lane Kirkland, the President of the AFL-CIO, once said: "In a democracy, there's no last shot." The saying helps us remember that policy making is not like most board games. Board games have an end-rule; when you get all the little pies in your Trivial Pursuit piece or checkmate the opponent's king, the game is over. But policy making is a never-ending process, one without an end-rule or an end-game.

Incremental policy makers are comforted by the knowledge that policy making is an ongoing process. If it were a one-shot, all-or-nothing affair, policy

The distribution of free food. This public policy works well because it is acceptable to those people who are involved in adopting, implementing, and living under the policy.

makers would be under incredible stress to get it right the first time, because there would be no second chance. But with an ongoing process, policy makers can relax a little and try something, anything that looks plausible. (It's more like fishing for perch than hunting for Moby Dick.) It often works that way. This society, for example, does not know how to abolish poverty and has never really tried, in spite of campaign rhetoric. Instead, federal anti-poverty policy has been more experimental, trying one thing, government-run job training programs, for example, and then another, tax cuts to spur private businesses to invest and thereby create real jobs. Buoyed by the knowledge that they will get another chance, policy makers can try out policies, get some feedback on what seems to be working, adjust their policies, and try again.

The ongoing process of policy making is well suited to this political system. Without a clear division between the public and the private spheres of authority, social strain is relieved when what are seen as imbalances can be continuously adjusted. Since there is only a fluid line of demarcation between appropriate federal and state responsibilities, it is appropriate that battles over federalism too are subject to continuous adjustment. Since the legitimacy of public policy ultimately rests on a fickle basis, the shifting sentiments of the public, the continuous nature of policy making means opportunities to improve the fit between public policies and popular preferences. For members of Congress, the ongoing search for partial remedies is an unavoidable decision-making tactic, one intimately tied to Congress' many opportunities to reshape legislation. For the President, the ongoingness of policy making means facing a string of opportunities to exercise influence—and an unforgiving gauntlet that can wear him down. For the Supreme Court, the use of judicial review is an example of an ongoing process that is rooted in both constitutional and statutory law. In general, many of the characteristics of American political processes and governmental structures reinforce the continuous quality of policy making.

The ongoingness of policy making is also a prominent feature in our political history and in current policy cases. Lincoln's war policy, for example, had to be good enough to endure the constant bickering of his cabinet. Chief Justice John Marshall's decisions, elevating the role of the Supreme Court, also had to endure both scrutiny and strife. Long-smoldering disputes between the rights of criminal defendants and the rights of society can not be extinguished by any one judicial decision. The standards of ethical election campaigning are not etched in stone, and need to be continuously re-defined to retain public confidence. New information and competing demands can change the value people place on equal health care and their willingness to support national health insurance.

Finally, policies can have unintended, adverse consequences. If, for example, we learn that a policy to save seals is attracting man-eating sharks off the coast of California, we can adjust the policy. In such a case, and in general, the ongoing pattern of policy making is both dominant and useful.

The Desire for Popular Approval

It is a truism that policy makers look for what they hope will be "good" policies. But what is "good?" More precisely, what is the standard that policy makers apply to the options before them? There are, of course, many different standards that policy makers *might* use: standards of political feasibility, economic efficiency, legality, ideological correctness, or ethical purity. While perhaps drawing on some or even all of these standards, the incremental policy maker is primarily concerned with selecting those policies that can win acceptance—especially the acceptance of the people who are going to be involved in adopting, implementing, and living under the policy. Consider, for example, the way this standard entered into the making of one of this nation's policies to fight hunger: the distribution of surplus food. This policy was adopted, and is continued, because it is acceptable to many relevant groups: big city liberal congresspersons whose constituents are hungry; rural conservative representatives whose farmers produce too much; voluntary social welfare agencies that help out with the distribution; the recipients themselves who line up and consume the food. In this case, and in so many others, public policies work as well as they do because they are acceptable to relevant constituencies. Indeed, in a political system that distrusts, and therefore limits public power, there is no better and still viable criterion than the standard of public acceptability.

This discussion does not mean, of course, that incremental policy-making tactics are without faults. They are not. In particular, incremental policy-making tactics: (a) are slow, often excruciatingly and maddeningly so; (b) lead to a terribly inefficient process; and (c) are potentially, ruinous, especially if they ignore future problems whose costs mount catastrophically.

■ Wise enough to recognize their own fallibility and politically conscious of their need to maintain legitimacy, democratic policy makers tend to rely on incremental decision-making tactics. In general, they will (1) prefer to make marginal, not comprehensive, changes in policy; (2) search for policy alternatives that remedy problems, rather than try to solve them; and (3) try to adopt policies that offer some promise of popular approval.

SUMMARY

In the case of civil rights policy, the process by which policy is made is biased in favor of small, marginal changes in policy that, at best, provide slight remedy for problems, but seldom a cure.

Most nonincremental changes in policy occur only after the sustained efforts of others to shape the policy agendas and to convince governmental officials that a proposed policy course will enhance their legitimacy.

The policy agenda is built in stages, through efforts that define the problem, legitimize it as a proper object of public concern, specify alternative policy responses, and establish government's responsibility to do something about it.

Once they begin dealing with a problem, governmental decision makers will tend to act incrementally. Doing so means they will tend to react to problems, rather than exercise their own initiative; prefer marginal to comprehensive policy changes; search for policies that remedy problems, even if they do not cure them; and be inclined to embrace policy proposals that are likely to win popular approval, especially the approval of those who will be affected.

In general, these characteristics of the policy-making process also imply that it will tend to be slow, inefficient, and unresponsive to future problems that are anticipated but not yet felt.

Key Terms

agenda building   privatization
incrementalism   marginal changes
cognitive dissonance   feedback
routine issues

Review and Reflection

1. How is policy made?

2. How do you account for the policy successes of Martin Luther King, Jr.?

3. What are the effects of uncertainty on the predispositions and behavior of governmental officials?

4. What are the stages of agenda building?

5. What are the tactics of incremental decision making?

6. On balance, do you think the advantages of incremental decision making outweigh its disadvantages?

7. Do you think government moves too quickly or too slowly in response to problems? Why?

Supplemental Readings

Much of the interesting literature on policy-making processes include both a theoretical framework and a substantive focus on real cases. This is true, for example, of the excellent texts by *Cobb and Elder*, and *Kingdon*. Other works trace the policy-making process further than we do in this chapter. *Nakamura and Smallwood*, for example, follow the process through implementation and evaluation.

The theoretical focus is a little less strong in works that have complicated case studies to relate. This, for example, is true of *Derthick's* study of the development of Social Security, *Erbring, Goldenberg, and Miller's* study of the press, *Lewis's* analysis of the careers of Hyman Rickover, J. Edgar Hoover, and Robert Moses, *Provine's* study of the Supreme Court, and *Redman's* entertaining study of Congress.

The theoretical focus is most strong in what must be viewed as the classics in the field: *Bachrach and Baratz's* analysis of what keeps some issues off the policy agenda, *Downs'* insights on why issues rise and fall on the agenda, and *Schattschneider's* enduring treatment of issue formation.

Bachrach, Peter and Morton Baratz. *Power and Poverty*. New York: Oxford University Press, 1970.

Cobb, Roger W., and Charles D. Elder. *Participation in American Politics: The Dynamics of Agenda-Building*. Boston, Mass.: Allyn and Bacon, 1972, 1983.

Derthick, Martha. *Policymaking for Social Security*. Washington, D.C.: The Brookings Institution, 1979.

Downs, Anthony. "Up and Down with Ecology—The 'Issue-Attention' Cycle." *Public Interest* 32 (1972): 38–50.

Erbring, Lutz, Edie N. Goldenberg, and Arthur H. Miller. "Front-Page News and Real-World Cues." *American Journal of Political Science* 24 (1980): 16–49.

Gerston, Larry N. *Making Public Policy: From Conflict to Resolution*. Glenview, Ill.: Scott, Foresman, 1983.

Kingdon, John W. *Agendas, Alternatives, and Public Policies*. Boston, Mass.: Little, Brown, 1984.

Nakamura, Robert T., and Frank Smallwood. *The Politics of Policy Implementation*. New York: St. Martin's, 1980.

Provine, Doris Marie. *Case Selection in the United States Supreme Court*. Chicago, Ill.: University of Chicago Press, 1980.

Redman, Eric. *The Dance of Legislation*. New York: Simon & Schuster, 1974.

Schattschneider, E. E. *The Semisovereign People: A Realist's View of Democracy in America*. Hinsdale, Ill.: The Dryden Press, 1975.

CHAPTER TEN

POLICY GOALS—AND THE ECONOMY

Y ou owe Uncle Sam about $8,333.33. That is your share of the total amount of money the federal government owes; that is, the national debt divided by the number of people in the country (as of 1986).

It took about 200 years for the United States to acquire a national debt of one trillion dollars. Between 1981 and 1986, however, the national debt grew from one to two trillion dollars. The growth came in increments, the result of a pattern of annual federal budget deficits, each one larger than the one preceding it, until by 1986, some saw annual deficits of $200 billion stretching into the future as far as the eye could see.

The prospect of continuous deficits and crushing debt evoked haunting memories of economic collapse and depression; created a conviction, on a scale unprecedented in American history, that the economic future was less bright than the present; threatened to consign the poor to a permanent underclass; and occasioned a political flurry of finger-pointing and blame-laying.

The following Case sheds some light on two of the basic economic questions of our time: (1) How did the national debt get so large? and (2) Does it matter? The answers suggest some broader insights about the relationship between federal deficits, the national debt, the federal government, and the economy. First, deficits and therefore the debt have grown as the federal government has assumed greater responsibilities for the economy. Second, deficits and the burden of the national debt may hinder the realization of various economic goals. Third, deficits and the national debt are the result of a variety of economic policies.

POLITICS AND ECONOMICS

> Politics dominates economics.
> —Robert M. Solow, former Presi-
> dent of the American Economic
> Association

The Case   The National Debt

To fight and win the Second World War, the United States went into debt. Rather than raise taxes to pay as it fought, the United States borrowed the money, promising to pay it off in the future, with future taxes. As a result, the United States ended the war owing over $260 billion, up from about $50 billion in 1940, just before entering the war. Since the end of WW II, the total national debt has continued to grow and today amounts to about $2 trillion—almost eight times larger than it was in 1945.

The national debt has grown in increments, specific additions that resulted from annual budget deficits, each year's difference between revenues and expenditures. As **Table 10.1** shows, there have been some federal budget surpluses in the years since 1945. For the most part, however, the federal government has ended each year in the red and has to borrow to make up the difference. Throughout the 1950s and 1960s, each year's addition to the total national debt was relatively small, ranging between a deficit of 1.6 billion in 1965 to what was then a whoppingly large deficit of over $25 billion in 1968. In the 1970s, however, some annual deficits topped $73 billion. Finally, in the 1980s, annual additions to the national debt began to grow alarmingly, starting with annual deficits of over $80 billion in 1980 and 1981 and ending with annual deficits of $200 billion as far as computers could reliably project. By 1986, all these annual deficits had helped push the total outstanding national debt to over $2 trillion.

It would be a mistake to think that each year's deficit and the total national debt are natural phenomena, like the beginning of the Ice Age or the ending of dinosaurs. They are not. Rather, deficits and debts are human inventions, the product of: (1) a belief in the value of counter-cyclical spending; (2) political pressures; and mostly (3) a reliance on supply-side economics.

The Belief in Counter-Cyclical Spending. Americans used to believe that governmental spending should be cyclical; that levels of governmental spending should follow levels of economic activity. Thus, if the economy was going strong, more revenue would flow into the coffers of government, and it would have more to spend. Similarly, if the economy was in a slowdown, government's revenues would fall, and it should not spend money it did not have. So strongly did Americans subscribe to this view that both President Herbert Hoover and initially, President Franklin Roosevelt argued in favor of the need to balance the federal budget during the Great Depression.

The cyclical theory of governmental spending had one glaring weakness, of course. It meant that government was not supposed to spend money when there was the greatest need for it to do so. The glaring weakness was not, by itself,

TABLE 10.1 Federal Deficits (Surpluses) and the National Debt

Year	Federal Deficit (Surpluses) (in billions of dollars)	Total National Debt[1] (in billions of dollars)
1940	3.1	50.7
1945	47.5	260.1
1950	3.1	256.9
1955	3.0	274.4
1960	(.3)	290.9
1965	1.6	323.2
1970	2.8	382.6
1975	45.2	544.1
1976	73.7	631.9
1977	53.6	709.1
1978	60.0	780.4
1979	40.2	833.8
1980	73.8	914.3
1981	78.9	1,003.9
1982	127.9	1,147.0
1983	207.8	1,381.9
1984	185.3	1,576.7
1985	222.2	1,841.1
1986	180.0	2,074.2

[1] Total National Debt is known technically as the "Outstanding Gross Federal Debt."
SOURCE: The data for years 1940 through 1975 is drawn from U.S. Bureau of the Census, *Statistical Abstract of the United States: 1984.* 104th ed. (Washington, D.C., 1983), p. 315. The data for years 1976 through 1986 is drawn from *Economic Report of the President* (Washington, D.C.: GPO, 1985), pp. 316–17.

enough to justify reversing the pattern. That reversal awaited the popular acceptance of a new theoretical justification: Keynesian economics.

Counter-cyclical governmental spending was justified by **Keynesian economics.** John Maynard Keynes, a British economist, provided the justification in his book *The General Theory of Employment, Interest, and Money,* first published in 1936. In it, Keynes argued that government could reverse an economic slowdown by spending money itself and by encouraging private persons to spend money, thereby putting people back to work to produce what was demanded. Thus, when the economy (and governmental revenues) fell, the government should increase spending (even though that would mean a deficit) or cut taxes so that private persons could increase their spending (even though that too would mean a deficit). Governmental spending, in other words, should be counter-cyclical: (1) increasing when the economy slowed down, even if that meant a deficit and (2) decreasing after economic activity picked back up, so that the deficit could be wiped out. The first half of the theory made deficits defensible; the second half was easy to forget.

Political Pressures. No longer inhibited by a belief that deficits were morally reprehensible, ambitious politicians soon discovered the secret to electoral success: take from as few, as surreptitiously as possible, and give to the many, as dramatically as possible. Since the end of the Second World War, many policy makers have followed the advice, with a resulting enormous growth in social welfare policies and expenditures. (For the full story, see chapter 15.) Over these years, liberal, typically Democratic, members of Congress and Democratic Presidents have differed from conservative, typically Republican members and Presidents: while liberals favored domestic spending, conservatives favored spending on national defense. On one thing most agreed, however: few elected policy makers wanted to increase taxes to pay for either expanded social welfare obligations or increased defense spending.

There were exceptions, of course; politicians who tried to argue the need to raise revenues to match America's commitments at home and abroad. As the national debt and each year's deficit grew larger, however, it became harder and harder to make this argument. By 1984, it seemed impossible. Walter Mondale tried, for example, in his 1984 presidential election campaign against President Ronald Reagan. Mr. Mondale tried most candidly in his acceptance speech:

> Here is the truth about the future. We are living on borrowed time and borrowed money. These deficits hike interest rates, clobber exports, stunt investments, kill jobs, undermine growth, cheat our kids and shrink our future . . . I mean business. By the end of my first term, I will cut the deficit by two-thirds. Let's tell the truth. Mr. Reagan will raise taxes. So will I. He won't tell you. I just did.[1]

Mondale's message, of course, was greeted with glee in Republican circles but was overwhelmingly rejected by an electorate that was quick to slay the bearer of unpleasant economic advice.

In addition, the political makeup and organizational structure of Congress encourages members to increase expenditures, but not taxes, as we will see in chapter 12.[2] Members are elected (and re-elected) on the basis of their ability to deliver tangible benefits to their own district today and not on the basis of ability

---

[1] Quoted in Jack W. Germond and Jules Witcover, *Wake Us When It's Over: Presidential Politics of 1984* (New York: Macmillan Publishing Co., 1985), pp. 408–409.

[2] See Allen Schick, "The Distributive Congress," in Allen Schick, ed., *Making Economic Policy in Congress* (Washington, D.C.: American Enterprise Institute, 1983), pp. 257–73.

"Here it is under stampede . . . *stand in front of cow and say* **NO!**"

to do that which might benefit the entire country tomorrow. Thus, most members will pay more attention to local constituents and to well-organized special interest groups, whether that means higher farm subsidies or higher Social Security payments, than they do to national considerations, such as deficit reduction. Moreover, Congress is organized in ways that nurture these electoral incentives. The existence of many committees and subcommittees, for example, provide many possible launching pads for new programs and many different battlegrounds for fighting attempts to cut back pet programs.

Reliance on Supply-Side Economics.   A reliance on supply-side economic theory has, quite unintentionally, increased federal deficits and therefore, the national debt. In brief, **supply-side economic theory** holds that government, by cutting taxes, can encourage people to invest in productive enterprises that, in turn, create new jobs, decrease unemployment, and thereby increase personal income and with it governmental revenues. With President Reagan's endorsement, the theory was used in 1981 to justify enactment of three annual 10 percent tax cuts. The tax cuts went through, of course. The overall rate of federal spending did not fall, however, and in President Reagan's first term and one-half, annual deficits and the total national debt soared, as **Table 10.1** shows.

Insights

These partial explanations for the growth of annual deficits and the national debt suggest four basic insights about the behavior of the national government as it goes about trying to make economic policy.

Insight 1. *The federal deficit is a product of both economics and politics.* There are competing economic ideas about the proper relationship of government to the economy and about what policies will achieve desired goals without compiling huge deficits. This task is made even more difficult by the existence of many different economic policy makers, some of whom are politically responsive to different constituencies.

Insight 2. *The federal deficit may endanger desired economic policy goals.* When the federal government incurs a deficit, it does realize some economic goals. In the short run, for example, increased spending on social services can reduce levels of poverty. But incurring a deficit may hurt the chances of realizing other goals. In the long run, for example, government's need to borrow might reduce the amount of money that is otherwise available to be invested in new businesses and therefore slow down economic growth.

Insight 3. *There are various economic policies that can be used to reach desired economic goals.* Some of these attempt to alter the operation of the economy as a whole; others attempt to alter the behavior of individual economic actors.

■ The growth of deficits and the national debt also has been a by-product of the willingness of the federal government to take on responsibility for the economy without developing both the will and the capacity to make sound economic policy. For more information on this topic, see the **Vantage Point**: Putting the Federal Deficit and the National Debt in Perspective.

GOVERNMENT AND THE ECONOMY

> Practical men, who believe themselves to be quite exempt from any intellectual influences, are usually the slaves of some defunct economist. . . . It is ideas, not vested interests, which are dangerous for good or evil.
> —*John Maynard Keynes,* The General Theory of Employment, Interest, and Money

The growth of budget deficits and the national debt has followed the expansion of government's responsibilities for regulating the economy. This expansion was not an inevitable result of any laws of history. Rather, ideas about the proper relation between government and the economy have fueled the expansion of federal responsibilities and the ascendency of federal economic policy makers.

Federal Responsibilities

Since the Founding, there have been three main historical periods, each dominated by a particular view of the proper relationship between government, especially the federal government, and the economy. During the initial and longest period, the spirit of capitalism held sway and effectively constrained what people believed government might properly do. After the Great Depression, Americans moved closer to a form of statism which justified a more expansive role for government. More recently, there are some pressures for a kind of corporatism in which more cooperative relationships among government, business and labor might help America compete in the global economy.

The Spirit of Capitalism. In eighteenth century Europe, national governments followed the dictates of **mercantilism**, a doctrine that justified governmental regulation of all aspects of the economy. The result was the stifling of personal initiative and economic development. Smoldering sentiments for change eventually found new champions, advancing new doctrines.

Adam Smith's *The Wealth of Nations* (1776) justified and popularized **capitalism**, the view that private persons should own society's resources and that economic competition should be the force (the "invisible hand") that dictated what use was made of them. In such a capitalistic economic system, government had only a limited role. Other than using its authority to make sure that people lived up to the contracts they entered into, the state was supposed to follow a **laissez-faire** approach, leaving alone what was viewed as well enough.

The nature of capitalism became more clear with the historical growth of its opposite, **socialism**, an economic system in which the state, in the name of the people, owns all of society's resources and decides, presumably in the service of the people, what use will be made of them. Interestingly, the appeal of socialism grew in response to what some viewed as the evils of capitalism, just as it grew in response to what were seen as the evils of mercantilism.

The practice of capitalism did not exclude government, however. Even in the early days, many found good reasons to make of government more than a neutral referee on economic playgrounds. Alexander Hamilton, for example, in his *Report on Manufactures* argued that the national government should play an indirect role in the development of a strong economy, by protecting fledgling industries from foreign competition. Others, even including Thomas Jefferson, also found good reasons for the state to acquire land and to help develop it in ways that strengthened the economy and therefore the nation. These attempts were not without constitutional footing, since Article I, section 8 of the Constitution empowered Congress to "provide for the . . . general Welfare of the United States." In addition, the attempts were not made without controversy, however, as Americans struggled politically over their interpretations of that constitutional directive.

Capitalistic ideals, ironically, inspired attempts to expand governmental involvement in what had been largely private decisions about the uses of

PUTTING THE FEDERAL DEFICIT AND THE NATIONAL DEBT IN PERSPECTIVE

The figures of Table 10.1, on the annual deficit and the total national debt should be put in perspective.

The Deficit. The annual deficit is, of course, how much money the federal government has to borrow to make up the difference between how much it spends and how much it takes in. But it is much more alarming if the federal government has to borrow 90 percent of what it spends rather than 10 percent. Therefore, the size of the federal deficit should be expressed as a percentage of total federal expenditures, as it is in the following Table.

Viewed as a percentage of total federal expenditures, the federal deficit today is much lower than it was after fighting the Great Depression and World War II. On

The Federal Deficit as a Percentage of Total Federal Expenditures

Year	The Deficit (Surplus) as a Percentage of Expenditures	Year	The Deficit (Surplus) as a Percentage of Expenditures
1940	32.6%	1978	13.1
1945	51.2	1979	8.0
1950	7.3	1980	12.5
1955	4.4	1981	11.6
1960	(.3)	1982	17.2
1965	1.4	1983	25.7
1970	1.4	1984	21.8
1975	13.9	1985	23.2
1976	19.8	1986	18.9
1977	13.1		

the other hand, it is much higher than it was in the period of relative calm after WW II and before the increase in the price of oil. Today, one out of every four or five dollars spent by the federal government is borrowed.

The Debt. The total national debt is, of course the sum of all the money borrowed and still

societal resources. The competitive ideal, for example, argued that the economic system worked best when people were free to decide for themselves what they wanted and what they were willing to pay for it. This was not true when businesses acted as monopolies, with the power to set prices. With the growth of monopolies, the discrepancy between capitalistic ideals and practices was too glaring and helped precipitate the drive to reform capitalism.

The belief in capitalism, thus justified governmental intervention into the economy, when it was necessary to restore and maintain economic competition. This justification sustained some early attempts to improve the fit between capitalist theory and economic realities: the Sherman Act of 1890, the Clayton Act of 1914, and the Federal Trade Commission Act of 1914. This justification remains strong. In 1975, for example, the Supreme Court held that

owed by the federal government. But it is more alarming if the national debt has been growing faster or slower than the economy as a whole. Therefore, the federal debt should be expressed as a share of the Gross National Product, the value of all goods and services produced by the economy in a given year. The graphs in the following Figure show both the growth of the federal debt and the debt as a percentage of GNP.

Except for the years since 1981, the national debt has grown more slowly than the economy as a whole. Indeed, the total debt was almost as large as the GNP in 1950. Since 1950, the national debt, expressed as a percentage of GNP, consistently fell, until it started back up in 1981.

The Federal Debt and Its Relationship to GNP

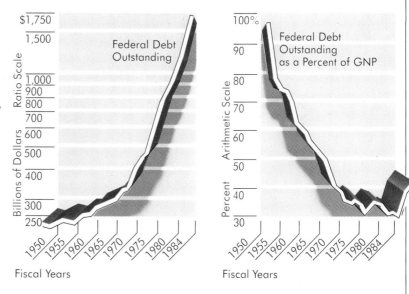

SOURCES: U.S. Department of the Treasury; The Conference Board.

lawyers violated federal anti-price-fixing laws when they set minimum fees for their services.[3] In general, the spirit of capitalism is an enduring source of support for the view that some forms of governmental intervention into the economy are proper.

Today, ours is a **mixed economy** which relies primarily on capitalistic forces, while allowing for a governmental role in the regulation of most economic activities and in the production and distribution of some goods and services. It got that way in response to instances of market failure (described in the Prologue) and because of the appeal of two other kinds of ideas about the proper relationship of government to the economy: statism and corporatism.

---

[3] *Goldfarb* v. *Virginia State Bar*, 421 U.S. 773.

"The rising of the usurpers, and the sinking of the liberties of the people."

Monolopies and trusts frustrated both economic competition and democratic principles.

Statism. **Statism** is a doctrine that would have the central government do more than merely remedy the defects of capitalism; it holds that government should have primary responsibility for the allocation of societal resources and the re-allocation of personal wealth. Statism, therefore, is like socialism, except it does not directly challenge private ownership of property. Statist approaches to economic policy making are, however, hostile towards both business and labor and distrustful of market forces. Under a statist approach, governmental officials believe that they know best what people and society need and are quick to act on their own judgment, rather than wait for political preferences to filter their way through governmental channels. Statist approaches, therefore, tend to be elitist and pro-active, rather than democratic and reactive. As such, statism is not likely to become a dominant ideology, although it has been quite influential from time to time.

In recent times, statist approaches to economic policy making are most pronounced in the federal government's attempts to correct for market failures. (As discussed in the Prologue, the free market fails when it does not produce what people want, or it produces what people do not want.) Today, one of the most visible and serious forms of market failure is environmental pollution, whether it enters the air, as sulfur dioxide does from the soft coal that is burned in Ohio, or the water, as illegally dumped toxic chemicals do all over the country. In many instances, enough people have become concerned enough about environmental pollution to demand governmental action. In many other instances, however, the people who stand to lose the most simply are not yet around, politically aware, or politically active; they are the unborn, the young, and the ignorant. Who is to speak for these voiceless constituencies? Somebody should and statism justifies giving government the task. Indeed, especially in the 1970s, the federal government radically expanded its responsibility for regulating many different forms of pollution far beyond what one would have predicted just by looking at the strength of the environmental lobby. The policies promised a cleaner environment, a goal many could support. But the policies also carried a price tag, one that many began, rightly or wrongly, to see as lost jobs. As people anticipated and, in some cases, experienced the costs of environmental protection, political support cooled and intense opposition heated up.[4] In general, statist approaches to environmental protection, although surely needed, hindered their own long-term acceptance, because they provoked political opposition that was more intense and persistent than the political support they generated and enjoyed.

Economic policies also will be short-lived if they are fundamentally hostile toward both business and labor. Since they often are, statist economic policies tend to produce adversaries who will react and press their grievances upon government, as long as they are able to do so. In one Great Society program, for example, the attempt to promote affirmative action policies in promotions and dismissals, at the expense of the seniority rights of workers, quickly split the traditional alliance between labor unions and civil rights organizations. When they have such effects, statist policies are self-defeating, especially if

---

[4] Anthony Downs, "Up and Down with Ecology—the 'Issue-Attention' Cycle," *Public Interest* 32 (1972): 38–50.

In the Love Canal case, citizen involvement led to government involvement, by first evacuating the citizens and then by trying to clean up the toxic wastes throughout the town.

they alienate powerful constituencies, without simultaneously generating equally powerful new ones. Some non-economic Great Society programs also are instructive. For example, the attempt to rely on mandatory busing as the main device to bring about racial integration of the schools, alienated many whites without whom schools could never be integrated, while failing to convince many blacks that their children were better off because of the experience.[5] Thus, in both economic and non-economic spheres, those who have laudable goals but no, or only a weak, constituency may adopt a statist approach to policy making. In some cases, there may be no alternative to getting ahead of public opinion. But, unless, policy makers also exercise sufficient leadership to fill in the gap with a new constituency, statist policies will be attacked and, in disrepute, will crumble.

The statist policies of the Great Society, in other words, gave big government a bad name; direct attempts of the federal government to regulate economic activities were discredited. The need for some kind of strong governmental role remained, however. Moving into the mid-1980s, some became increasingly attracted to what they believed was a middle way, an approach to policy making that would produce something between a laissez-faire and a state-run economy.

Corporatism.   What we and others call **corporatism** is a doctrine which holds that the state should assume substantial responsibility, along with private business and organized labor, for the development of a strong economy.[6] In its most highly developed form, corporatism underlies the economy of Japan, and is credited by some as the reason for that country's rapid growth and current economic health. In this form, corporatism justifies a high degree of govern-

---

[5] See, for example, Anthony J. Lukas, *Common Ground: A Turbulent Decade in the Lives of Three American Families* (New York: Alfred A. Knopf, 1985).

[6] See, for example, Robert B. Reich, *The Next American Frontier* (New York: Times Books, 1983).

Government and labor sometimes agree upon affirmative action policies, as in the case of the Cleveland firefighters.

mental intervention, one that is inconsistent with the value that most Americans place on personal liberty.

Although not sold under the name of corporatism, the belief in the desirability of national economic planning has had a strong influence on the evolving relationship between government and the economy. The belief has gained in favor in times of **depression**, technically defined as a period of falling economic growth. During the Great Depression, for example, the economic slowdown pushed unemployment to perhaps 25 percent sidelining many who were willing to work, at almost any price. In this case, capitalistic market forces failed to respond to the availability of cheap labor and the failure helped prompt the call for an expanded governmental role.

During the New Deal, the federal government assumed responsibilities for altering economic relationships, especially the relationship between business and labor. Through a series of statutes, the federal government redefined the conditions of employment, saying, for example, that children could not be employed, that there was a limit to the number of hours people could be required to work, and that employees have a right to organize and bargain collectively over wages and working conditions. Subsequently, additional expansions in the federal role came to include safety on the job (under the Occupational Safety and Health Act of 1970) and protections of one's pension (under the Pension Reform Act of 1974).

Since the New Deal, national economic planning has accelerated, although, according to Robert Kuttner, a public commentator on economic issues, we often do not recognize it or acknowledge it as such. For example, the federal government helps plan the future course of the economy: (1) through a tax code that makes some kinds of investments more attractive than others; (2) when the Justice Department approves some, but not all, corporate mergers; (3) when the President and the Defense Department get committed to the development of a weapons system requiring a new technology, such as President Reagan's Stategic Defensive Initiative; and (4) when Congress legislates certain kinds of financial

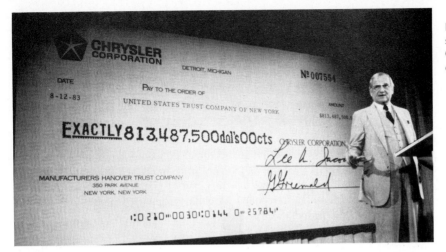

Lee Iacocca, with the last installment on the Chrysler Corporation's federally guaranteed loan.

subsidies to different industries or agricultural products.[7] In all these examples, the actions of the federal government alter the operation of market forces and thereby help direct the nation toward particular economic goals.

More recently, the nation's difficulty in competing in the world economy has sparked interest in the need to develop an **industrial policy**, a way of revitalizing companies that manufacture goods, as opposed to those that provide services. As most use the term, an industrial policy would require new relationships among government, business, and labor, ones that are less adversarial and more cooperative. Some have embraced this essentially corporatist policy as the best way for the nation to regain economic strength.[8] Others, however, suggest that an industrial policy will postpone economic change and development, as essential resources are used to shore up ailing and outmoded industries, not to start up newer, more productive ones. Thus, the proponents of an industrial policy would view the federal government's guarantee of loans to the Chrysler Corporation, arranged with organized labor's support, as a success story. Skeptics, however, would point out that Chrysler sold more cars while protected from vigorous Japanese competition and would urge the nation to end its flirtation with "lemon socialism." In addition, professional economists warn that it is very hard, perhaps impossible, to know whether or not a nation should commit its resources to one form of production over another.[9]

The debate over corporatism, and among it and more purely capitalistic or statist approaches to economic policy making continues to rage. This battle, like so many others, will be fought out politically. As it is, new ideas and new policy-making agencies will form.

---

[7] Robert Kuttner, *The Economic Illusion: False Choices between Prosperity and Social Justice* (Boston: Houghton Mifflin, 1984), p. 90.

[8] Felix Rohatyn, "Time for a Change," *The New York Review* (August 18, 1983).

[9] See, for example, Charles L. Schultz, "Industrial Policy: A Dissent," *Brookings Review* (Fall, 1983), pp. 3–13.

Federal Economic Policy Makers

There are many different official and unofficial economic policy makers whose interactions help determine economic policy. Some of the key ones include the President, the Council of Economic Advisors, the Board of Governors of the Federal Reserve System, the Office of Management and Budget, and Congress and, in particular, some of its specialized committees.

The President.   The President and whoever he views as his key advisors on the economy are by far the most important official source of influence over economic policy. It has not always been so. Prior to passage of the Budget and Accounting Act of 1921, the heads of cabinet departments and individual federal agencies bypassed the President and took their policy proposals and budget requests directly to Congress. The 1921 Act, however, obligated the President to prepare and present a comprehensive federal budget. The President, thereby, was placed in a position of influence by virtue of his ability to coordinate the actions of different federal agencies and to control the flow of information to Congress.

For assistance, Presidents turn to advisors. In his second term, President Reagan, for example, tended to rely on what the press referred to as the "Big Six" for help in making economic policy. Two of the six were cabinet officers: Treasury Secretary James A. Baker III and Secretary of State George P. Shultz. Two more resided at the White House: Donald T. Regan, the President's chief of staff, and Alfred H. Kingdon, one of Mr. Regan's top aides. The other two were Richard G. Darmen, a key aide to Secretary Baker and Paul A. Volcker, the chairman of the Board of Governors of the Federal Reserve System. By

relying on these advisors, President Reagan was able to shift control over the making of economic policy away from most cabinet officers, who tended to represent certain constituencies, and toward a newly formed Economic Policy Council, which was able to develop and help articulate a clearer economic policy.[10]

Council of Economic Advisors (CEA).   The Employment Act of 1946 formally made the federal government responsible for maintaining economic stability, so that the nation would, hopefully, no longer have to suffer through the ups and downs of the business cycle. The Act also created the Council of Economic Advisors as a new agency within the Executive Office and directed it "to maintain employment, production, and purchasing power." Finally, the Act required the President to make an annual report to Congress on the state of the economy and to include in it the recommendations of his Council. By law, the 1946 Act forced the advice of professional economists on the President. In practice, Presidents have allowed the Council to exercise more or less influence, depending on whether it was saying what they wanted to hear. In President Reagan's first term, for example, the then Chairman of the Council, Martin Feldstein, got too out-of-step with the White House position on the importance of the federal deficit and was isolated from the presidential policy-making circle.

Board of Governors of the Federal Reserve System.   The Federal Reserve System, or the "Fed" as it is commonly called, controls the supply of money and thereby sets monetary policy. To assure the Fed some degree of independence from political pressure, members of the Board of Governors are appointed to non-overlapping fourteen-year terms by the President, with the Senate's confirmation.

Office of Management and Budget (OMB).   Created by Executive Order in 1970 as a replacement for the Bureau of the Budget, the Office of Management and Budget participates in the making of economic policy through its role in developing the federal budget and, more recently, in serving as a clearinghouse for regulations that affect both business and labor.

Congress.   Congress as a whole and especially some of its more specialized committees play an important role in the making of economic policies. In particular, those committees that control taxing and spending (the Senate Finance Committee and the House Ways and Means Committee) can exercise substantial influence over some economic policies, as they did, for example, over tax reform in 1986.

In addition to these key economic policy makers, many other parts of the executive and legislative branches of the national government play more minor

---

10 See Peter T. Kilborn, "How the Big Six Steer the Economy," *The New York Times*, 17 November 1985, F1.

roles, through, for example, the adoption of regulations, decisions to prosecute antitrust cases, and provision of tax breaks to special interest groups.

These various policy makers exercise important, but probably not decisive, influence over the economy.[11] Their influence, like that of most policy makers, is heavily constrained in ways that limit its quality and effectiveness. Quality suffers whenever economic advice is ignored for political considerations, as when members of Congress ignore economic arguments against protectionism to save the jobs of workers in their own constituencies. Effectiveness suffers because, for better or worse, what our economy does is still mostly the result of market forces, the largely private decisions of many buyers and many sellers. In addition, both the quality and the effectiveness of government's attempts to influence the economy are constrained by the lack of unambiguous scientific knowledge about ways of manipulating the economy. As one presidential advisor complained: "If the nation's economists were laid end to end, they would point in all directions."

■ The competition among different ideas about the proper relationship of government to the economy and among different actors complicates the making of economic policy. In addition, the existence of multiple and sometimes conflicting economic goals makes the policy process invariably political.

ECONOMIC GOALS

> America must get to work. . . . The
> Republican program for solving economic
> problems is based on growth and produc-
> tivity.
>
> —*President Ronald Reagan*

Throughout our history, the national government has pursued four main economic goals: growth, stability, efficiency, and equality. Moreover, each of these goals has been successfully pursued, although some more than others. (In addition, these economic goals may not be mutually compatible. Economic efficiency and growth, for example, often make the distribution of income less equal, at least in the short run.) Nevertheless, moving into the 1980s, projected federal deficits and the size of the national debt made these goals appear more distant and intensified the political debate over what would have to be done to ensure continued economic success.

---

[11] Edward R. Tufte, *Political Control of the Economy* (Princeton, NJ: Princeton University Press, 1980).

The completion of the transcontinental railroad—an investment in the nation's future made possible by huge grants of federal land.

Economic Growth

The national government has always tried to encourage economic growth. Sometimes the attempt was rather indirect, as in the early days of the republic when tariffs were used to encourage the production and consumption of American goods, by making foreign ones relatively more expensive and therefore less competitive. Somewhat later, the national government moved more forcefully and directly to foster economic growth, primarily through territorial expansion, by helping create a financial system that made money available for investment, by improving land and water transportation systems, and by helping educate and train a work force that had the skills to adapt to a rapidly changing economy.

There are many factors that account for the economy's capacity for continued growth. One of the clearest determinants is the amount of money that is saved and therefore, potentially available for investment in new industries and new jobs. In general, countries that have a higher savings rate also have a higher growth rate, as **Figure 10.1** shows. There are many reasons for the United States' relatively lower level of savings and growth, including some that

FIGURE 10.1
The Relation Between Savings and Growth
Savings rate vs. growth for the 21 major O.E.C.D. countries, averages for 1960-70

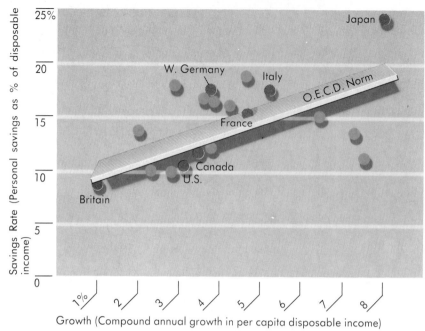

Savings Rate (Personal savings as % of disposable income)

Growth (Compound annual growth in per capita disposable income)

SOURCE: The New York Times, November 3, 1985.

are beyond government's control, such as personal habits. Nevertheless, it is quite clear that continuing deficits and mounting interest payments on the nation's debt force government to borrow money that might otherwise be available for investment purposes. As Franco Modigliani, the 1985 winner of the Nobel Prize in Economics, has said: "the deficit does in fact 'crowd out' private production investments."[12] To the extent that this is so, deficits and the national debt endanger long-term prospects for economic growth.

Economic Stability.   After suffering the trauma of the Great Depression, Americans became more intolerant of wild economic swings and more insistent that government do something to smooth out the business cycle. The political demands for economic stability became even more intense after economists began to advertise the availability of techniques for managing the economy and after politicians began to pledge their willingness to employ them, as we will see in the section on economic policies.

Economic Efficiency.   As we saw in the Prologue, a society may choose to use its resources in many different ways. Land, for example, may be used for amusement parks, open green spaces, chemical factories, or any of an almost

---

[12] Quoted in *The New York Times*, 3 November 1985.

limitless variety of other purposes. Almost all purposes make some people better off and other people less well off, at least as they see and define it. Since this is true, how should resources be used? In a manner that is most economically efficient, economists would argue, whereby they mean that there is no alternative use that would (1) make somebody better off without (2) making somebody else worse off. **Economic efficiency**, thus defined, is very difficult to visualize or to achieve, however.

In practice, the goal of economic efficiency is worked toward indirectly, by trying to avoid economic inefficiency. This is more practical, since economic inefficiency is easier to see and therefore avoid. Economic inefficiency exists whenever resources are wasted, that is, whenever they are allocated in ways that do not increase human happiness. There are many clear-cut examples: money is wasted when it is spent on fake diets or unnecessary or unsuccessful surgery; water and land is wasted when it is contaminated by chemical spills. In these examples, resources are not being used in ways that make either individuals or society better off.

Throughout our history, government has attempted to improve the operation of the private market to make it more economically efficient. (These attempts can be described as specific economic policies, as they are later, or as generic types of policies, as they are here.) To do this, governments may rely on two types of policies: inducements and sanctions.

Policy inducements are ways of encouraging certain economic behaviors by rewarding them. The federal government, for example, encourages personal savings by insuring deposits, provides tax breaks to encourage certain kinds of investments, helps people buy homes by not taxing their mortgage interest payments, encourages farmers to grow less by paying them to let their land lie fallow, and so on.

Policy sanctions are ways of discouraging certain economic behaviors by punishing them. The federal government does this, for example, by taxing the interest earned on personal savings, by abolishing tax breaks, by limiting the number of homes on which interest payments are tax exempt, and by encouraging farmers to get out of the business of farming by restricting financial credit, and so on.

Through American history, the national government has used both policy inducements and policy sanctions in an attempt to realize the goal of economic efficiency. Over time, the mix between inducements and sanctions has varied considerably, however. Throughout most of the 1960s and 1970s, the federal government relied heavily on regulations to reduce what were seen as economically inefficient behaviors, including, for example, stricter testing requirements before new drugs could be put on the market, more demanding mileage requirements for new automobiles, a requirement that funeral directors provide itemized lists of their services, more stringent safety regulations covering workers in textile mills and coal mines, and so on. Moving through the late 1970s and into the early 1980s, some blamed worsening economic conditions on excessive governmental regulation, however. Some, especially the conser-

An instance of policy sanctions. Through financial credit restrictions, this farmer has been forced to sell his farm.

vative supporters of President Reagan, believed that fewer regulations would enhance both economic efficiency and economic growth; others were doubtful.

Economic Equality. **Economic equality** exists when the wealth of a society is uniformly distributed over the entire population. A similar, but weaker, condition of economic equality exists when family income (excluding inherited wealth) is uniformly distributed among all families. In this weaker case, the distribution of family income would be perfectly equitable if 10 percent of the families received 10 percent of the family income, 20 percent of the families received 20 percent of the family income, and so on. (If this relationship were to hold for all families, the relationship between the cumulative percentage of income and the cumulative percentage of families could be represented by the straight line in **Figure 10.2**.)

The desire for some kind of economic equality has been a compelling policy goal throughout American history.[13] As Nelson Polsby notes in the exchange with Aaron Wildavsky on page 354, ours is a political system that tends to erase, rather than perpetuate, boundaries among people, including differences in wealth or, more narrowly, income.

There has been some historical progress toward a more equal distribution of income in America. This has come about primarily through two economic policies: the income tax and transfer payments. After it came into being with the adoption of the Sixteenth Amendment in 1913, the federal income tax

As this cartoon suggests, some doubted that fewer regulations would make U.S. industry more productive and competitive.

FLY FREE AT LAST, O MAJESTIC AMERICAN EAGLE.... NOBLE MONARCH OF THE AIR!

[13] See Kenneth E. Boulding, "The Pursuit of Equality," in James D. Smith, ed., *The Personal Distribution of Income and Wealth* (New York: National Bureau of Economic Research, 1975), pp. 11–28.

FIGURE 10.2
Comparison of the Distribution of Family Income Before and After Individual Taxes and Transfers, All Families, 1966

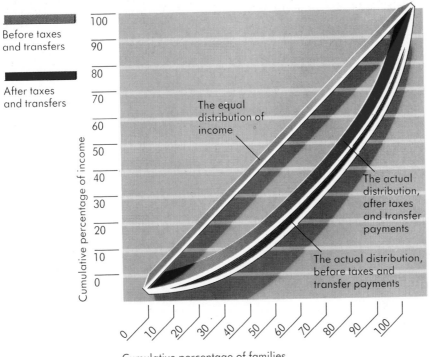

tended to be mildly **progressive**, taxing people on the basis of their ability to pay. (Sales taxes, in contrast, are called **regressive**, because everybody pays the same tax on $60 worth of groceries, whether they are rich or poor.) The federal income tax thereby generates revenue that is available for redistribution, from the haves to the have nots. The actual redistribution occurs as a **transfer payment**, a direct payment from the government to a private person which is made as a matter of law. Today, transfer payments include Social Security payments (by far the largest), workmen's compensation (unemployment), public assistance (welfare), and veterans' disability payments and pensions. In their combined effect, these transfer payments alter the distribution of income, making it slightly more equal (the broken line in Figure 10.2) than it would be otherwise (the lower curve in Figure 10.2).

The pursuit of economic equality is difficult. As Kenneth Boulding has noted, the quarry sometimes seems as elusive as a herd of unicorns.[14] In addition, the attempt to redistribute wealth may engender political opposition

---

[14] *Ibid.*, p. 25.

TABLE 10.2 Reversing the Redistribution of Income

Although the 1981 and 1982 changes in federal tax laws increased everyone's income somewhat, increases in Social Security taxes and inflation-caused bracket-creep left those with less income worse off.

Income Category (in thousands)	Column 1 Income Gain From 1981 and 1982 Tax Laws (in dollars)	Column 2 Income Loss From Increases in Social Security Taxes and Inflation (in dollars)	Column 3 Net Loss (−) or Gain (+) (in dollars)
Below $10	$ 58	$ 153	$ − 95
10–20	387	573	− 186
20–30	882	1,020	− 138
30–40	1,465	1,587	− 122
40–50	2,210	2,346	− 136
50–75	3,305	3,407	− 102
75–100	5,258	4,855	+ 403
100–200	8,284	5,979	+ 2,269
Above 200	24,982	7,579	+ 17,403

SOURCE: Thomas Byrne Edsall, *The New Politics of Inequality* (New York: W. W. Norton and Company, 1984), p. 205.

among the ranks of those groups which, historically, have been most effective in pressing their claims upon the system. There, of course, is no necessary reason why wealthy people might not believe that their heavier tax burden helps buy something they want, such as a more just or a more peaceful society. But, if they do not believe that, and if political leaders do not socialize them to that point of view, then those who believe they have an excessive tax burden will demand redress. There is some indication that they began to do so, even before 1980, and that they became increasingly vocal and effective during the presidency of Ronald Reagan.

Recently, the drive for economic equality has stalled and, some findings suggest, reversed itself. The reversal started after passage of the 1981 and 1982 federal tax cuts. Because of these tax cuts, persons in every income group saved something over the period of 1980 to 1984. The savings, shown in Column 1 of **Table 10.2**, amounted to $58 for persons in the lowest income category and to $24,982 for persons in the highest income category. For some, however, these savings evaporated because of (1) legislated increases in Social Security contributions and because (2) inflation pushed them into a higher tax bracket. Both of these factors brought about the tax *increases* for all income groups that appear in Column 2 of **Table 10.2**. Some fared better than others, however.

As Column 3 reveals, those in the higher income categories ended up better off, while those in the lower categories ended up worse off—exactly the opposite of what a policy of income redistribution would try to accomplish. Simultaneously over the years 1980 to 1984, the Reagan Administration also cut many of the benefits that go to those in lower income categories: unemployment, welfare, food stamps, school lunches, and so on. The combined effect of the net tax loss and the loss of federal benefits led Thomas Edsall, a Capitol Hill reporter for the *Washington Post*, to conclude: ". . . the first four years of the 1980s have produced a regressive redistribution within federal tax and spending policies."[15]

■ The national government has consistently pursued the economic goals of growth, stability, efficiency, and equality. Some goals, however, have been pursued more vigorously than others. Historically, the national and most other levels of government have acted as though they have been most concerned with economic growth and increasingly, with economic stability. An important, but second-order, priority has been to realize economic efficiency, primarily by maintaining competive forces within the private market. Finally, the goal of economic equality remains a compelling symbol in American political life, one that has helped bring about a modest degree of income redistribution.

These goals are ambitious and difficult to achieve. Whether or not they are realized will depend on the use that is made of a variety of different economic policies.

ECONOMIC POLICIES

> The San Andreas fault of the Reagan Administration is the failure to match tax cuts with spending cuts. Who's to blame? Why, there's enough blame to go all the way up and down Pennsylvania Avenue.
>
> —Murray L. Weidenbaum, Chairman of the Council of Economic Advisors (1981–1982)

Federal deficits and the national debt are the result of the interplay of a variety of economic policies. This section considers four major types: fiscal policies, monetary policies, regulatory policies, and trade policies.

---

[15] Thomas Byrne Edsall, *The New Politics of Inequality* (New York: W. W. Norton and Company, 1984), p. 206.

THE WILDAVSKY—POLSBY DIALOGUE CONTINUED . . .

AUTHOR: Could we move on to the national policy-making process in general and the budget process in particular?

WILDAVSKY: I think the budget process strongly exemplifies a growing dissensus among political elite. Do we have a basic, underlying agreement on how to deal with the deficit? Will the surface froth of disagreement between two elderly Irishmen, Reagan and O'Neill, disappear when they leave the scene? Or do we have a growing dissensus among the major portions of our political officialdom that is covered over by a surface froth of agreement? Let's take a look at the evidence here. It is getting more and more difficult to pass a budget or pass it on time. The latest figures I saw suggested that the House of Representatives spends 50 percent of its time on taxing and spending and the Senate about two-thirds. Yet, all this time simply results in more disagreement. The Gramm-Rudman Act, which everybody says is stupid (and is dumb) is testimony to the inability of Congress to agree.*

I'd like to give you one indicator of this, which to me is very meaningful. The budgetary base is the expectation among participants that policies will, more or less, be continued as they have been in the past few years, with only the exception of a few new or contested programs. So, when you can't agree on time on an annual budget, you fall back to the base, and simply adopt continuing resolutions, where you fold in everything and just carry it on. During the Reagan Administration, this has become a major form of budgeting.

But now, not only don't we agree on the annual budget, on time, we also don't agree on the starting time. Does the budget process start when Congress receives the President's budget? "No," Congress says; it's dead on arrival. Does it start with a congressional budget? No, they can't agree on that either.

In addition, the participants in the budget process do not agree, program by program, on what the numbers are. There's a new unit in the Office of Management and Budget, people called bill trackers. What they do is go around, at every stage of the congressional budget process, and issue complaints—complaints that congressional claims of budget savings are false.

Well, here we have a situation where, just as the classical literature describes, the major indicator of dissensus is failure to agree on a budget. We used to laugh at the French because they had the practice of twelveths, where, when they couldn't agree, they would vote one twelveth, one month, of the budget. We now do them twelve times better. Our expressions of our failure to agree, our continuing resolutions, run hundreds and hundreds of pages.

POLSBY: There are four main elements when you're considering the budget. Any real attempt to address the budget problem has to deal with the four in relation to one another. There are taxes and how big taxes are. There is the deficit and how big it gets. There are entitlements, which is to say, Social Security and related benefits. And there's the defense budget. These are the four big manipulable items. The political game is to attempt to make one or more of these unmanipulable and, thereby, get it

---

* See the description of the Gramm-Rudman budget-balancing act in chapter 12.

out of the game. Gramm-Rudman takes the deficit out of the game. That's its purpose; to make the size of the deficit unnegotiable. Entitlements are taken out of the game frequently by political promises made during campaigns. Ronald Reagan wanted to take defense spending and taxes out of the game. You begin to see the political context of Gramm-Rudman very rapidly. The reason for Gramm-Rudman was this. It was the only one of the four, that is to say, deficits, left on the table. The passage of Gramm-Rudman pulled the size of the deficit off the table. The reason they had to pull deficits off the table is to get the other three back on the table. So the question is what happens when all four are off the table and you can't bargain

. . .the fundamental problem with President Reagan is that he is uninterested in and incapable of substantive political leadership. . . —Polsby

I think the budget process strongly exemplifies a growing dissensus among political elites. —Wildavsky

about them. You have to go back to work at getting them back on the table again. That's the point at which you have to have real substantive, no baloney, political leadership. Now, we're going to have a little partisan conversation, Aaron. My view is [that] the fundamental problem with President Reagan is that he is uninterested in and incapable of substantive political leadership which, in effect, would put all four elements of a deal back on the table and start some real, substantive hard bargaining. It is not the case that he doesn't have such people in his administration, however. The Secretary of the Treasury (James Baker) is good at this kind of game, but, at the moment, and this is a very long moment, the President does not seem capable of this sort of game.

Fiscal Policies

Fiscal policies are attempts to realize economic goals through governmental spending, taxing, and borrowing. Traditionally, federal rates of spending and taxation were changed in an attempt to alter **demand**, the amount of goods and services people are willing and able to buy (and sell) at a particular price. When the economy is not growing fast enough and policy makers believe that unemployment is unacceptably high, government can act as a consumer, increasing its purchases and thereby increasing demand and causing producers to step up output. In addition, a similar result can be obtained by cutting taxes, especially when consumers and producers go out and spend their tax savings. In these cases, increased government spending and decreased federal taxation are **demand-side fiscal techniques**, ones that are primarily concerned with increasing consumption.

In contrast, some believe that fiscal policies can and should be used as supply-side techniques that increase work effort, personal saving, and economic investment. Supply-side economics evolved in reaction to what some viewed as excessively high taxes that, they believed, robbed people of the incentive to make more money, because so much of it would be lost through taxation. Credit for the insight generally goes to the economist Arthur Laffer. His famous Laffer curve, which some think was first drawn on the back of a cocktail napkin, appears as **Figure 10.3**.[16] The curve expresses a hypothetical relationship between various tax rates and the total revenues raised by each rate. The curve makes an argument: (1) at high tax rates, say point Z_2, people lose the incentive to work, so they do not, the level of economic activity falls, and with it, total tax revenue goes down; (2) when the tax rate is lowered to some point, say L, work incentives, economic activity, and tax revenues go up; and (3) when the tax rate reaches some optimal level, say r_B, work incentives, economic activity, and tax revenues are at their theoretically greatest levels. The curve and the theory behind it had intuitive appeal, enough to justify the tax cuts of 1981 and 1982. Economists differ in their interpretation of the results, however. While some believe they had the intended supply-side effects, other economists argue that the tax cuts only increased consumer demand, in a manner typical of demand-side economics. The argument confirms a basic premise. Through their various actions, economic policy makers surely have a fiscal result, even if it is less clear that they act with a coherent, well-tested, and confirmed fiscal policy.

In addition, there are two specialized types of fiscal policy: fiscal subsidies and tax preferences.

Fiscal Subsidies and Tax Preferences.

These policies are attempts to encourage certain economic behaviors by making them less costly (or more rewarding). A **fiscal subsidy** does so directly, by compensating producers for their efforts. For example, agricultural subsidies guarantee farmers that they can earn certain prices for their crops, whether or not anyone wants them. As you

---

[16] According to some, Mr. Laffer drew his curve during lunch with an aide to President Ford. See Jude Wanniski, *The Way the World Works* (New York: Simon and Schuster, 1978), p. 97.

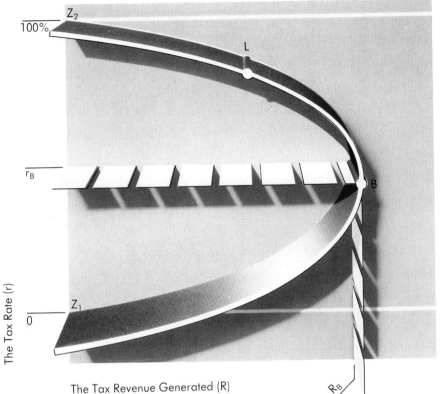

According to this Laffer curve, the greatest amount of revenue (R_B) would be generated at a point B, where the tax rate = r_B. To see why this is true, consider what happens when you move either up the curve, toward point Z_2 or down the curve, toward point Z_1. At Z_2, for example, the tax rate is 100% of income, no one would work, and therefore, there is no income to tax. At Z_1, on the other hand, a zero tax rate, not surprisingly, produces zero revenue. (Economists differ over the shape of this curve.)

might suspect, agricultural subsidies keep prices high, even though they result in overproduction. This often seems wasteful to those who would prefer lower prices, although the defenders of the practice argue that subsidies keep many producers in business and thereby, help guarantee the long-term health of American agriculture. The argument in favor of agricultural subsidies often carries the day, primarily because of the political clout of those who make it, the strategic placement of their representatives in Congress, and because it is so effectively reinforced by dominant cultural values that celebrate rural virtues.

Tax preferences are provisions built into the law that reduce certain tax liabilities. Since a reduced liability means that somebody pays fewer taxes than they would otherwise and since this means that the government collects fewer tax revenues than it would otherwise, tax preferences create tax expenditures, i.e., lost revenue. In theory, tax preferences are ways that government can lower the cost of some economic activity, thereby making it more profitable and more likely. There are many such activities that a society may want to encourage, including for example, charitable contributions, employment training, daytime care for the children of working parents, business investments in more productive equipment, and so on. In part because they are so desirable and so easy to hide in the tax law, tax preferences have mushroomed in recent

TABLE 10.3 Lost Revenue Through Selected Tax Preferences

Tax Preference	Year			
	1982	1983	1984	1985
	(millions of dollars of lost revenue)			
Credits and deductions on political contributions	$ 180	$ 190	n.a.	n.a.
Parental personal income tax exemption for students aged 19 or over	1,070	995	$ 1,060	$ 1,120
Benefits given to Armed Forces personnel	2,250	2,200	1,825	1,960
Cost of oil and gas exploration	3,430	1,520	1,415	2,030
Deductibility of charitable contributions	9,675	9,090	12,885	14,135
Deductibility of interest on consumer credit	10,825	10,765	12,680	14,625
Exclusion of employer contributions for medical insurance premiums and medical care	16,365	18,645	19,145	21,245
Deductibility of mortgage interest on owner-occupied homes	23,305	25,065	22,735	24,925
Deductibility of state and local taxes	27,520	28,825	29,715	32,245
Exclusion of contributions to pension plans	48,115	53,455	56,450	57,840
Total revenue lost from these selected tax preferences	142,735	150,750	157,910	170,125[1]

[1] That's $170,125,000,000!

NOTES: n.a.: Not available in either the 1985 or 1986 Statistical Abstract because they were less than $300 million. A "deduction" reduces the amount of the income on which one owes tax. A "credit" is a dollar for dollar reduction in taxes owed. An "exclusion" is a dollar for dollar reduction in the amount of income on which one owes income tax.

SOURCE: For the years 1982 and 1983, U.S. Bureau of the Census, *Statistical Abstract of the United States: 1984*, 104th ed., (Washington, D.C., 1983), Table 509, p. 321. For the years 1984 and 1985, U.S. Bureau of the Census, *Statistical Abstract of the United States: 1986*, 106th ed., (Washington, D.C., 1985), Table 498, p. 310.

years, as **Table 10.3** reveals. The proliferation of tax preferences, sometimes for purposes with little if any redeeming social value, reduces revenues (thereby making deficit reduction harder) and reduces public confidence in the fairness of the tax code (thereby making full compliance less likely.) Moving

POLICY GOALS—AND THE ECONOMY

into the mid-1960s, both effects increased pressure for tax reform that would eliminate many tax preferences and thereby, generate more tax revenue, so that overall tax rates could go down.[17]

Monetary Policies

Monetary policies are attempts to realize economic goals by changing the rate of growth of the supply of money that is in circulation. Whereas fiscal policies are made primarily by the President and Congress, monetary policies are made primarily by the Board of Governors of the Federal Reserve System. Before looking at the techniques for doing so, it is important to realize that the Fed does not "create" money, in the sense that it prints new bills and coins new coins. Rather, the Fed acts in ways that increase the supply of money that operates in the economy. It can do this because some people deposit their money in banks and do not immediately go out and spend it all. For example, say somebody rich deposits a million dollars but, in the short run, only spends half of it. Theoretically, the other half, $500,000, is still sitting in the bank. In practice, however, the bank may lend some portion of that $500,000 to somebody else for some other purpose—thereby effectively increasing the amount of money in circulation. What can the Fed do to have this result?

The Fed can increase the supply of money that is in circulation through a variety of techniques. For example, through *open market operations* it can buy government bonds that people hold, giving them cash in exchange which they then deposit in banks, thereby making some portion of that deposit available for loans. The Fed also can increase the supply of money by lowering the *reserve requirement*, the share of their deposits which banks have to keep on deposit at the regional Federal Reserve Bank. As the reserve requirement is lowered, banks get to keep a greater share of their deposits, and therefore have more money to loan. In either event, the resulting increase in the supply of money means that there is more of it to spend and to invest in hopefully productive enterprises.

Some, **monetarists**, such as Milton Friedman, an economist at the Hoover Institution, argue that the rate of growth of the money supply is the main, if not the sole, determinant of economic growth. Whether or not they agree with this view, the President and members of Congress have become increasingly concerned with the actions of the Fed and increasingly vigorous in their attempts to influence it. Their ability to do so is constrained by the long and staggered terms of the members of the Fed's Board of Governors. In recent years, the Fed has become more politically responsive, however, primarily because of a congressional resolution, passed in 1975, requiring the Fed to make reports to the House and the Senate.[18]

---

[17] See, for example, Neal Pierce, "Tax Reform Proposal Exposes Subsidies," *Public Administration Times*, 1 May 1985.

[18] See also Nathaniel Beck, "Presidential Influence on the Federal Reserve in the 1970s," *American Journal of Political Science* 26 (1982): 415–45.

Fiscal and monetary policies belong in a class of what are called **macroeconomic policies**, because they are attempts to alter the performance of the economy as a whole. In contrast, we next turn to **microeconomic policies**, attempts to alter the behavior of individual economic actors: firms, consumers, and those who own resources.[19]

Regulatory Policies

Regulatory policies try to alter the behavior of producers by setting minimum standards for their products, by prescribing working conditions, by pricing regulations, and by outright prohibitions on the production of some commodities. As chapter 13 describes it, the federal bureaucracy is the main source of regulatory guidance. Through its activities, for example, minimum standards have been set on the gasoline consumption of automobiles, workers in textile mills must wear a breathing apparatus that cuts down the inhalation of fibers, and food with too many microscopic rodent hairs may not be sold.

Regulatory policies discourage certain economic behaviors by making them more costly, initially for producers and, in some cases, for consumers as well. In theory, those who make the regulations are supposed to undertake a **cost-benefit analysis** to determine whether or not regulatory costs are matched or exceeded by some benefit to consumers or to society as a whole. For example, if electrical generating plants are required to burn "cleaner" and more expensive coal, the cost of doing so should be less than the benefit derived by those downwind. In practice, however, people, even economists, disagree about what should be included in these calculations and about how costs and benefits should be measured. For example, if an American burner of dirty coal emits sulfur dioxide through a smokestack tall enough to cause acid rain in Canada, or even Sweden, should the damage it causes be included in our calculation of costs and benefits? In the absence of scientific agreement, we do what we do best; we fight over the issue politically. As the smokestack example suggests, the political conflict sometimes spills over international borders.

Trade Policies

Many economists believe that, in theory, the best trade policy is no policy at all. If all the nations of the world had no trade policy, some economists argue, then (1) producers would be free to produce whatever people wanted and as much of it as they wanted and (2) consumers would be free to find the best quality at the lowest price. In practice, however, some countries may be more efficient producers than other countries, and thereby, may be able to drive some countries' producers out of business. Such an outcome may be politically unacceptable, especially to the representative of the district where the ineffi-

---

[19] See, for example, Edwin Mansfield, *Microeconomics: Theory and Applications*, 5th ed. (New York: W. W. Norton, 1985).

cient producer and the producer's workers (the representative's constituents) are located.

Although there are many examples, consider the case of automobile imports. Japan, for example, seems to be an extremely efficient producer of automobiles. The American demand for them, over comparable but more expensive American cars, tends to lower domestic sales, the employment of automobile workers, and the payroll taxes earned by cities with automobile plants. In reaction to this felt, or anticipated result, Congress has considered a variety of trade policies, ones that either impose a tariff on imported cars or that require that a certain percentage of the imported car's parts be made in America. In this case, and in general, restrictions on international trade make a few better off, while making many others, both domestic consumers and foreign producers and their workers, for example, worse off. On the other hand, some argue that trade restrictions are only meant as a short-term bargaining lever, used to encourage other countries to lower their restrictions on our exports. This argument and the more general political demand for a better trade policy is becoming increasingly compelling, since in 1985, the trade deficit, the gap between what the United States buys from foreign countries and what it sells to them, hit $148.5 billion, an all-time high.

■Policy makers pursue economic goals on a slippery path, often hampered by the lack of unambiguous scientific knowledge and by the presence of strong political pressures. The stumbles eventually show up, as for example, a low rate of economic growth, inflation, recession, waste, trade deficits, and continued poverty. As they become more visible, perhaps economists will know more and will become better able to explain it to economic policy makers. Even then, however, the ears of economic policy makers may be too attuned to political soundings.[20]

SUMMARY

Throughout their history, Americans have expected different things of the economy and have been more or less demanding that government make sure they were provided. In response, the federal government has assumed greater and greater responsibility for the making of economic policy, although it has been less vigorous in acquiring and exercising economic wisdom. In addition, the American people have not proven themselves willing to sacrifice today for the sake of their own, and their children's, economic future.

Today, the lack of economic wisdom and the insistence on consumption over investment has helped produce twin deficits in the federal budget and in foreign trade. Both loom and threaten today's and tomorrow's economic well-being. In the face of these twin threats, economic policy makers may try to continue to muddle through as they have in the past, postponing calamity but not preventing it. Indeed, given the state of knowledge and the pervasiveness of politics, it may be unreasonable to expect more.

On the other hand, we hope that, by now, you have concluded that matters of economic policy are not inaccessible. You can understand the way the economy works and what government might do to try to make it work better.

Key Terms

Keynesian economics	economic equality
supply-side economic theory	progressive tax
mercantilism	regressive tax
capitalism	transfer payment
laissez-faire	fiscal policies
socialism	demand
mixed economy	demand-side fiscal techniques
statism	fiscal subsidy
corporatism	tax preferences
depression	monetarists
industrial policy	macroeconomic policies
economic efficiency	microeconomic policies
policy inducements	cost-benefit analysis
policy sanctions	

---

[20] See, for example, Herbert Stein, *Presidential Economics: The Making of Economic Policy from Roosevelt to Reagan and beyond* (New York: Simon and Schuster, 1985).

Review and Reflection

1. Why are the federal deficit and the national debt so large?

2. Differentiate capitalism, statism, and corporatism.

3. What are the main goals that the economy can move toward? Do you believe that some of these goals are more important than others? If so, which ones and why?

4. What are the macroeconomic and microeconomic policies which the government can use to attempt to influence economic activity?

5. What do you believe should be the proper relationship between the federal government and the economy?

Supplemental Readings

To supplement the reading you will do in the additional economics course we hope you take next semester, consider the following. You should find all of these accessible and interesting.

See, for example, the discussion between *Friedman* and *Heller* on the relative merits of monetary and fiscal economic policies.

Gilder, for example, was one of the first to argue for the supply-side economics that was embraced, at least rhetorically, by the Reagan Administration. The administration's track-record is well-described by *Roberts* and roundly criticized by *Kuttner*.

For a somewhat more comprehensive consideration of the actual relationship between government and the economy, see *Tufte*. For more focused examinations of specific kinds of economic policies, see *Carson, Wilson* and *Woolley*. Additional, insider insights are available in *Stein*.

Finally, join the debate about the evolving relationship among government, business, and labor, as you can by reading *Reich*.

Carson, Robert B. *Economic Issues Today: Alternative Approaches*. 3rd ed. New York: St. Martin's Press, 1983.

Friedman, Milton, and Walter K. Heller. *Monetary vs. Fiscal Policy*. New York: Norton, 1969.

Gilder, George. *Wealth and Poverty*. New York: Basic Books, 1981.

Kuttner, Robert. *The Economic Illusion: False Choices between Prosperity and Social Justice*. Boston: Houghton Mifflin, 1984.

Reich, Robert. *The Next American Frontier*. New York: Times Books, 1983.

Roberts, Paul Craig. *The Supply Side Revolution: An Insider's Account of Policymaking in Washington*. Cambridge, Mass.: Harvard University Press, 1984.

Stein, Herbert. *Presidential Economics*. New York: Simon and Schuster, 1984.

Tufte, Edward R. *Political Control of the Economy*. Princeton, NJ: Princeton University Press, 1980.

Wilson, James Q., ed. *The Politics of Regulation*. New York: Basic Books, 1980.

Woolley, John. *Monetary Politics*. New York: Cambridge University Press, 1984.

PART FOUR

GOVERNMENTAL INSTITUTIONS

"There are not enough jails, not enough policemen, not enough courts, to enforce a law not supported by the people."
—*Senator Hubert Humphrey (D., Minn.), 1965*

CHAPTER ELEVEN

THE PRESIDENCY
THE PERSONIFICATION OF POWER

We are not very fair to our Presidents. We expect a great deal from them, and we erect barriers to the realization of those expectations.

We demand of Presidents that they properly administer the operations of the federal government. But we decentralize power throughout the executive branch and protect, both legally and politically, many of its employees from presidential influence.

We demand of Presidents that they lead their political party into both electoral and legislative battles. But we defend an electoral system that encourages the members of the President's party in Congress to be more attuned to local than national considerations and to be more concerned with their own re-election than with enactment of their President's program.

We demand of Presidents that they set the nation's policy course and that they get out in front to lead. But we are slow to follow and quick to criticize.

Pressured to achieve in spite of disabling constraints, American Presidents seek to expand their formal powers, mobilize their organizational and staff supports, and create and exercise informal political power.

Even then, there is no guarantee, of course, that a President will be successful. The political system may be impervious to presidential leadership, too frozen by political gridlock, as those driven by their own narrow self-interests each block one another, thereby frustrating both their own goals and the common good.

The following Case presents an exception to this gloomy diagnosis—perhaps a turning point in the evolution of the American presidency. In 1981, President Reagan enjoyed enormous success in getting Congress to pass his first budget and his recommended tax cuts. The President's success suggests three insights. First, the modern presidency is a very human place, a product both of its occupant and its organizational structure. Second, the President must simultaneously try to govern, make policy, and exercise political leadership. Third, to achieve these goals, the President needs to expand the office's formal power and create and exercise personal political power.

THE NATURE OF THE PRESIDENCY

> . . . being a President is like riding a tiger. A
> man has to keep on riding or be swallowed.
> —*Harry S. Truman*

The Case   The Battle of the Budget, Part I

The nation was ungovernable, the job impossible, they said. "This is my kind of script," the President must have thought, as he rode the tiger well.

When Reagan came to office in 1981, the nation did seem ungovernable, the presidency an impossible burden. Recent history argued the case. Not since Dwight David Eisenhower had a popularly elected President completed a second term. In recent memory, all occupants had left with their reputations in rags. The instant histories were cruel: Lyndon Johnson, savaged in the press and the streets as a war monger; Richard Nixon, driven from office under the threat of impeachment; Gerald Ford affably stumbling out of office; and Jimmy Carter, seen as intense and inept. All had entered the White House riding high; all had been consumed by the job. Prudence cautioned a defensive posture. So Reagan attacked, first rhetorically and then through actions.

In his campaign for the presidency, Ronald Reagan promised a "celebration" of the traditional American values of "individualism, liberty, hard work, production, morality, religion and patriotism . . ."[1] The values would be restored to their proper place, by reversing the modern trend toward big, paternalistic government. The Reagan campaign thereby promised an attack on the very foundations of the modern welfare state: the assumptions of what the federal government should do for its citizens.

Taking office in 1981, Ronald Reagan could have believed he was poorly equipped to launch a frontal attack on the welfare state. Surely, most Washington insiders thought, the interlocking alliances of congressional committees, governmental agencies, and organized special interest groups were strong enough to blunt the Reagan assault.[2] After all, people had voted mostly against President Carter, not for anything that Reagan proposed. If there was a rightward drift in the country, toward Ronald Reagan's more conservative positions on public policy issues, it was not apparent in the public opinion surveys of the time. Nevertheless, in spite of his lack of obvious resources and allies, Ronald Reagan mounted his campaign to reverse the course of the federal government, turning it away from its expanding social welfare responsibilities. Believing that to be more difficult than talking an alcoholic out of his bottle, the cynics celebrated.

---

[1] Robert Dallek, *Ronald Reagan: The Politics of Symbolism* (Cambridge, Mass,: Harvard University Press, 1984), p. 7.

[2] This view of the meaning of the 1980 presidential election follows that which appears in Fred I. Greenstein, "The Need for an Early Appraisal of the Reagan Presidency," in Fred I. Greenstein, ed., *The Reagan Presidency: An Early Appraisal* (Baltimore: The Johns Hopkins University Press, 1983), pp. 1–20.

The cynics might have been right, had not President Reagan had the daring to claim a mandate, the ability to transform personal popularity into presidential influence, and a strategy for breaking gridlock in the national policy-making process. He simply asserted his mandate to change the course of the federal government, while mobilizing public opinion in support of his assertion. The Democrats in Congress, demoralized in defeat and disarmed by Reagan's engaging personal manner and ability to orchestrate popular support, acquiesced. The opportunity ripe, Reagan struck quickly on both sides of the federal ledger: revenues and expenditures.

The Reagan assault had a theoretical justification: **supply-side economics**. Whatever its scientific value, the theory was seductive: by reducing federal taxes, government would encourage investment in productive enterprises, thereby stimulating economic growth and increasing future tax revenues. Meanwhile, a healthy, growing economy would reduce unemployment, raise personal income, and lower the need for social welfare expenditures. By embracing the theory, one could claim that leaving more money in the pockets of the already rich was good for society. In theory, less was more; reducing governmental revenues would stimulate private business investments and the benefits of the resulting economic growth would trickle down through the rest of society. Thus shielded from criticism, representatives of both parties and of special interest groups were encouraged to pile on their own tax cuts, in what David Stockman, Reagan's former Budget Director, later acknowledged was "an obscene feast."[3] The theory also justified budget cuts, ones that were quickly and smoothly implemented in a manner that defied conventional political wisdom.

The Reagan assault on the welfare state, many assumed, would be blunted by all the steps of the traditional **budget-making process**: (1) the President's comprehensive budget would be broken down into specific legislative proposals, (2) separate proposals would be parceled out to separate congressional committees, (3) each proposal might be broken down further and the pieces parceled out to congressional subcommittees, (4) the members and the administrative staff of subcommittees might refuse to act or, if they did act, alter the original proposal before sending it back to the full committee, (5) the members and the staff of the full committee also could make their own changes in the subcommittee's version of the proposal before deciding whether or not to report it out for consideration and possible action by the members of the entire House and Senate, (6) if one of the President's proposals passed both chambers, it might do so in a different form, and (7) a conference committee, composed of some of the members of both houses, would have a chance to reconsider the two versions and try to resolve the differences, before reporting their agreement back to both chambers for a final vote. Past experience with this legislative labyrinth sustained the suspicion: there would be many opportunities for undoing the President's budget. There might have, except for Reagan's ability to manipulate the process.

By latching on to one piece of the budget-making process, Reagan was able to dominate the whole thing. In earlier legislation,[4] Congress had said it would try to keep expenditures in line with revenues. The device for doing so was the **reconciliation process**, the congressional budget-making procedure through

---

[3] See William Greider, "The Education of David Stockman," *The Atlantic*, December 1981, vol. 248 no. 6, pp. 27–54.

[4] The Budget Impoundment and Control Act of 1974.

which committees could be instructed to go back and pare down initial budgetary commitments. Through the reconciliation process, it was hoped, the sum of all federal expenditures would be brought in line with anticipated revenues and acceptable deficits. By moving the reconciliation step forward in the budget cycle, before individual committees acted, the Reagan administration made members of Congress declare themselves in advance on an overall expenditure ceiling and therefore on an entire package of budget cuts. The members of Congress, especially some of the more conservative Democrats who defected from the party position, thus were able to vote in favor of reducing the size of government. At the same time, they were able to claim that they really did not want to vote against anybody's pet program, but had to because the process buried it deep inside this legislative bundle. The political logic was unassailable and President Reagan's momentum was unstoppable. On the same day, in August 1981, President Reagan signed two acts, simultaneously cutting federal revenues and expenditures.

Within seven months of his first inaugural, Ronald Reagan had confounded the cynics. He could claim, sincerely and credibly, that he had slowed the growth of the federal government's social welfare responsibilities, begun the largest military buildup in peacetime, renewed public confidence in the institutions of government, and restored faith in traditional American values. Crowned with these accomplishments, Reagan sailed through his first term, parlaying success into success, and strolled through his re-election campaign, easily parrying aside Mondale's weak rhetorical thrusts.

Insights

As President, especially in his first term, Ronald Reagan re-wrote the script, assigned roles, choreographed moves, and told the audience when to applaud. Turning the truism on its head, he showed that good theater can be great politics. And he revealed a lot about the nature of the presidency.

Insight 1. *The modern presidency is a very human place, a product of both its occupant and its organizational structure.* The institutional arrangements surrounding President Reagan had not changed much since President Carter's time. Only the occupant had changed, bringing with him a new manner and a new approach for meeting the multiple challenges of the office. Those differences, however, made all the difference in the President's ability to realize his goals.

Insight 2. *The President must govern, make policy, and exercise political leadership.* Modern Presidents must work toward all three goals simultaneously, or at least appear to do so. They must (1) govern, by overseeing the administration of the executive branch, (2) make policy, primarily by seizing control of the policy agenda, and (3) exercise political leadership, by redefining the issues before the country and the way people debate those issues. Today, it is not enough to govern; no one worked harder at the task of governance than President Carter. It was not enough, however, as he found himself ensnared by the policy-making process and without political clout or allies. President Reagan, in contrast, was not known for working hard at the nitty-gritty of governance. President Reagan, however, was successful because he dominated the nation's policy agenda and the nation's political debate.

Insight 3. *To achieve his various goals, the President needs more than the formal powers of the office.* The presidency, as an institution, is equipped with considerable formal powers (which we shall soon enumerate). The formal powers are not enough, however. To have any chance of success, the President must (1) expand the formal powers of the office and (2) create and exercise additional, informal political power. To elaborate each of these insights, the rest of this chapter describes (1) the organization of the presidency, (2) its goals, and (3) ways Presidents try to realize them.

■ As a practical matter, the President declares all wars, both foreign and domestic. Indeed, the failure to declare war on society's problems can erode the President's popular support. Presidents must successfully wage war, however, and that means rallying and arming the troops. In this effort, the President is both empowered and constrained by the organizational structure of the office.

THE ORGANIZATION OF THE PRESIDENCY

> The office of the President is such a bastard-ized thing, half royalty and half democracy, that nobody knows whether to genuflect or spit.
>
> —*attributed to Jimmy Breslin, the Pulitizer prizewinning newspaper columnist*

After their experiences with a monarchy, the Founders had no intention of kneeling to a President. Although some, Alexander Hamilton, for example, hoped that Presidents would be able to expand their formal powers through the force of their personality and their political leadership skills, the Constitution only vaguely defined the formal structure and duties of the office. Over time, however, the organizational presidency has become much more expansive and dynamic.

Organizational Structure

The organizational structure of the presidency is described by its members, the formal qualifications for the office, the limitations on length of tenure, and provisions for removing a sitting President. (See **Table 11.1**.)

TABLE 11.1 The Presidents of the United States

Year	President	Party	Vote	Percentage of Popular Vote	Electoral Vote
1789	George Washington	no designation			69
1792	George Washington	no designation			132
1796	John Adams	Federalist			71
1800	Thomas Jefferson	Democratic-Republican			73
1804	Thomas Jefferson	Democratic-Republican			162
1808	James Madison	Democratic-Republican			122
1812	James Madison	Democratic-Republican			128
1816	James Monroe	Democratic-Republican			183
1820	James Monroe	Democratic-Republican			231
1824	John Quincy Adams	Democratic-Republican	108,740	30.5	84
1828	Andrew Jackson	Democratic	647,286	56.0	178
1832	Andrew Jackson	Democratic	687,502	55.0	219
1836	Martin Van Buren	Democratic	765,483	50.9	170
1840	William H. Harrison	Whig	1,274,624	53.1	234
1841	John Tyler[1]	Whig			
1844	James K. Polk	Democratic	1,338,464	49.6	170
1848	Zachary Taylor	Whig	1,360,967	47.4	163
1850	Millard Fillmore[2]	Whig			
1852	Franklin Pierce	Democratic	1,601,117	50.9	254
1856	James Buchanan	Democratic	1,832,955	45.3	174
1860	Abraham Lincoln	Republican	1,865,593	39.8	180
1864	Abraham Lincoln	Republican	2,206,938	55.0	212
1865	Andrew Johnson[1]	Democratic			
1868	Ulysses S. Grant	Republican	3,013,421	52.7	214
1872	Ulysses S. Grant	Republican	3,596,745	55.6	286
1876	Rutherford B. Hayes	Republican	4,036,572	48.0	185
1880	James A. Garfield	Republican	4,453,295	48.5	214
1881	Chester A. Arthur[1]	Republican			
1884	Grover Cleveland	Democratic	4,879,507	48.5	219
1888	Benjamin Harrison	Republican	5,447,129	47.9	233
1892	Grover Cleveland	Democratic	5,555,426	46.1	277
1896	William McKinley	Republican	7,102,246	51.1	271

Year	President	Party	Vote	Percentage of Popular Vote	Electoral Vote
1900	William McKinley	Republican	7,218,491	51.7	292
1901	Theodore Roosevelt[1]	Republican			
1904	Theodore Roosevelt	Republican	7,628,461	57.4	336
1908	William H. Taft	Republican	7,675,320	51.6	321
1912	Woodrow Wilson	Democratic	6,296,547	41.9	435
1916	Woodrow Wilson	Democratic	9,127,695	49.4	277
1920	Warren G. Harding	Republican	16,143,407	60.4	404
1923	Calvin Coolidge[1]	Republican			
1924	Calvin Coolidge	Republican	15,718,211	54.0	382
1928	Herbert C. Hoover	Republican	21,391,993	58.2	444
1932	Franklin D. Roosevelt	Democratic	22,809,638	57.4	472
1936	Franklin D. Roosevelt	Democratic	27,752,869	60.8	523
1940	Franklin D. Roosevelt	Democratic	27,307,819	54.8	449
1944	Franklin D. Roosevelt	Democratic	25,606,585	53.5	432
1945	Harry S. Truman[1]	Democratic			
1948	Harry S. Truman	Democratic	24,105,812	49.5	303
1952	Dwight D. Eisenhower	Republican	33,936,234	55.1	442
1956	Dwight D. Eisenhower	Republican	35,590,472	57.6	457
1960	John F. Kennedy	Democratic	34,227,096	49.9	303
1963	Lyndon B. Johnson[1]	Democratic			
1964	Lyndon B. Johnson	Democratic	43,126,506	61.1	486
1968	Richard M. Nixon	Republican	31,785,480	43.4	301
1972	Richard M. Nixon	Republican	47,169,905	60.7	520
1974	Gerald R. Ford[2]	Republican			
1976	Jimmy Carter	Democratic	40,827,394	50.0	297
1980	Ronald Reagan	Republican	43,899,248	50.8	489
1984	Ronald Reagan	Republican	54,281,858	52.9	529

[1] Succeeded to Presidency upon death of the incumbent.

[2] Succeeded to Presidency upon resignation of the incumbent.

MEMORY AID: When Aunt Jessie made my Aunt Jackie's burns hurt terribly, Polk's tailor's file pierced Buchanan. Lincoln, Johnson, Grant, hey Garfield, aren't (you going to) Cleveland (with) Harrison? Cleveland? The kingly Roosevelt (supported), Taft. Wilson's 14 points were hard to understand, but Coolidge stayed cool after whom hovered Hoover. Roosevelt stayed true. I like Ike. Ken I see Johnson's nix on Ford or the cart before Reagan?

Members. While there is only one President, the presidency, as a governmental institution, includes many others: the Vice-President, others in the line of succession, those on the White House staff, other staff persons who are a part of the Executive Office of the President, past Presidents, and even the President's spouse.

Only few have been President of the United States, a fact that facilitates memorization and research, while limiting the confidence one can have in generalizations about the presidency. Vice-Presidents are even harder to remember, and most of them, in spite of the fact that thirteen out of forty-one have gone on to become President, have had few good things to say about the office. Behind the Vice-President, the succession to the presidency is determined either by the Twenty-Fifth Amendment to the Constitution or by the Succession Act of 1947. When the Vice-President assumes the presidency (following the President's death or resignation), the Amendment requires that the new President nominate a new Vice-President, who takes office if confirmed by a majority of both houses of Congress. When there is no Vice-President, however, the 1947 Act specifies the line of succession: (1) the Speaker of the House of Representatives, (2) the president of the Senate, and, (3) beginning with the Secretary of State, the cabinet officers.

In a formal sense, the presidency also includes those who are a part of the Executive Office of the President and its various subdivisions. As **Table 11.2** indicates, the Executive Office of the President is a huge bureaucracy, although it is a small part of the executive branch as a whole (described in chapter 13: The Bureaucracy). Within the Executive Office, the staff of the White House Office are the most important, because of their proximity to power. The White House staff also has become quite large, although both President Carter and Reagan reduced it somewhat.

In an informal sense, the presidency also includes past Presidents, and even the President's spouse. Many incumbents have drawn on former Presidents, sometimes for advice, as President Reagan drew on Richard Nixon for campaign advice, and often for their symbolic, unifying appeal in times of difficulty, as President Kennedy did, in calling on Dwight Eisenhower after the failure of the American-sponsored invasion of Cuba. Now that former Presidents seem to feel increasingly free to criticize their successor, they may be less available for these roles in the future, however. Spouses, on the other hand, are unfailingly loyal and active. While a few, most notably Eleanor Roosevelt, and to some extent Nancy Reagan, have been quite visibly active in their devotion to social causes, most have been more influential behind the scenes.

Formal Qualifications. There are few formal qualifications for becoming President, other than the constitutional requirements that one must be at least thirty-five years old, a "natural born" citizen, and a resident of the United States for at least fourteen years. Informal qualifications have more to do with electability, however, as discussed in chapter 7. In addition to the obvious historical bias toward white males, future candidates might have to be unemployed, so they can run for the office full-time.

TABLE 11.2 The Executive Office of the President

A President who would take charge of the executive branch faces a formidable array of offices and bureaucrats.

The numbers suggest how formidable it would be.

As of 1980, the entire executive branch of the federal government was occupied by over 2.7 million bureaucrats, not counting the 2.1 million people on active duty in the Armed Forces. Even if you object that no one expects the President to take charge of the entire executive branch, the task is still impossibly huge.

A subset of the executive branch, the Executive Office of the President, included, as of 1980, all the following components, each with its own sizable staff.

Components	Staff Size
The White House Office	366
The Office of Management and Budget (OMB)	612
The National Security Council	60
The Council of Economic Advisors	40
The Council on Environmental Quality	12
Various other parts of the Executive Office	506
TOTAL number of positions in the Executive Office of the President	1596

SOURCE: U.S. Bureau of the Census, *Statistical Abstract of the United States: 1984*, 104th ed., (Washington, D.C., 1983), p. 336.

Tenure.   Although the Founders limited a term to four years, they placed no restriction on the number of terms a President could serve. President Washington, however, quickly set a precedent by not seeking a third term, even though he probably could have won it easily. The tradition continued until it was twice broken by Franklin Roosevelt (in 1940 and in 1944). After almost twenty consecutive years of Democratic Presidents, the adoption of a Republican-inspired constitutional amendment (the Twenty-second) imposed the current two-term limit. Some people, apparently fearing that even two terms is too much, argue for a new constitutional amendment that would limit the President to one, usually, six-year term. The fear and the effort, while especially strong under unpopular Presidents (in the late 1960s and early 1970s, for example), evaporate under popular ones. As a practical matter, it is not a serious issue, however, as we suggest in the **Vantage Point**: Should There Be a Single Six-Year Presidential Term?

Removal.   The removal of a sitting President is an extraordinary step, twice attempted but never successful: (1) when President Andrew Johnson was impeached by the House of Representatives but found innocent by the Senate and (2) when the House was preparing to impeach President Richard Nixon before he resigned. Even the remote possibility of removal, however, makes Presidents concerned about their legitimacy and active in their efforts to maintain and if possible increase it. (For one way of doing so, see chapter 7's **Vantage Point**: The Techniques of the Permanent Campaign.)

Organizational Dynamics

The organizational dynamics of the presidency consist primarily of interactions within the White House and between it and those in its more distant environ-

Eleanor Roosevelt was one presidential spouse who was visibly active in her devotion to several social causes.

SHOULD THERE BE A SINGLE SIX-YEAR PRESIDENTIAL TERM?

Those who favor a constitutional amendment to create a single, six-year term for President probably are overreacting to what they believe to be the need for it and probably are undercalculating the impact of this idea on the President's ability to realize his goals.

The perceived need for a single term seems to be based on the perception that Presidents who serve two terms become despots, out-of-touch and unaccountable. The perception, however, conflicts with some basic facts about the tenure of Presidents.

It is not the case, although it may be the perception, that most Presidents in fact serve two full, or almost full, terms. This was the norm in the early days, when five out of our first seven Presidents did serve two full terms. In recent memory, however, only Dwight Eisenhower was in office the full eight years. Over all, of the forty different men who have served as President, the average length of time in office is about five years.

The history suggests a conclusion: If you want to be in favor of a single, six-year term, do not do it because you think people serve too long under the current system.

ments. (Some of these, and their proximity to the White House, are shown in **Figure 11.1**.) These environments create the **institutionalized presidency**, the set of relatively permanent expectations that are imposed on any President.

Presidents differ in their ability to cope with environmental expectations. James David Barber, a political scientist with a special interest in the presidency, has suggested that Presidents tend to be either active or positive in their approach to the job and either positive or negative in their own feelings about it.[5] Active-positive Presidents seem to do better and be more favorably evaluated than passive-negative ones.

Presidents also differ in the kind of control they try to exercise over their immediate, administrative environment. Some, President Reagan for example, have seemed to prefer more formal lines of authority, while others, most notably Franklin Roosevelt, have encouraged more informality among their staff. Although more formal lines of authority may cover it up, internal staff relations often seem quite conflictual, however. Infighting among the President's staff, over policy turf and access, was quite visible in Franklin Roosevelt's administrations and while not terribly visible, quite intense under Ronald Reagan, according to David Stockman.[6]

---

[5] James David Barber. *Presidential Character* (Englewood Cliffs, NJ: Prentice-Hall, 1977).

[6] David Stockman, *The Triumph of Politics: Why the Reagan Revolution Failed* (New York: Harper and Row, 1986).

FIGURE 11.1   The President is surrounded by many federal offices and related policy organizations.

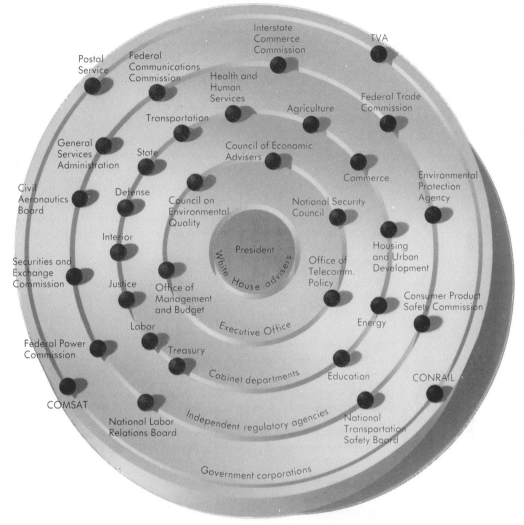

Interstate Commerce Commission

TVA

Postal Service

Federal Communications Commission

Health and Human Services

Agriculture

Federal Trade Commission

Transportation

General Services Administration

State

Council of Economic Advisers

Commerce

Environmental Protection Agency

Civil Aeronautics Board

Defense

Council on Environmental Quality

National Security Council

Interior

President

White House advisers

Office of Telecomm. Policy

Housing and Urban Development

Securities and Exchange Commission

Justice

Office of Management and Budget

Executive Office

Energy

Consumer Product Safety Commission

Labor

Treasury

Cabinet departments

Education

CONRAIL

Federal Power Commission

COMSAT

National Labor Relations Board

Independent regulatory agencies

National Transportation Safety Board

Government corporations

SOURCE: From *The American Presidency* by Benjamin I. Page and Mark P. Petracca. Copyright © 1983 by McGraw-Hill, Inc. Reprinted by permission.

■ The organizational structure of the presidency only vaguely defines the job and the qualifications of those who can do it well. The dynamics of the presidency, however, seem to favor Presidents who enjoy trying hard to accomplish something and who are willing to surround themselves with a strong, if contentious, staff.

THE GOALS OF THE PRESIDENCY

> The Presidency is not merely an admin-
> istrative office. . . . It is preeminently a place
> of moral leadership.
>
> —*Franklin D. Roosevelt*

We have great expectations about the presidency. Consider the many hats we expect the President to wear, rapidly switching them like some quick change artist. The President simultaneously is the chief administrator of the entire federal government, the chief diplomat and foreign policy spokesman, the Commander-in-Chief of the Armed Forces, the head of his political party, the key legislative leader, and the shaper of public opinion.[7] Under each of these hats, American Presidents are expected to act out different roles. Because we demand it, they must try—or suffer for our disappointment.

Presidents have their own reasons for trying to meet popular expectations. They, just like the rest of us, have values, desired ends they want to realize. They are driven by their personal values, their desires for power, prestige, and sometimes profit. Presidents also have political values, especially a desire for re-election. Perhaps more nobly, Presidents also have policy values, visions of the good society they would like to see realized.

These two things, popular expectations and presidential incentives, converge. To meet popular expectations, while advancing their own personal, political, and policy concerns, Presidents must pursue various goals and pursue them simultaneously. In particular, Presidents must try to achieve:

- *governance goals*, ones that require administering the operations of the executive branch, even though the President is not in charge of all its employees;
- *policy goals*, ones that require that the President try to set the nation's policy agenda; and
- *political goals*, ones that require winning the heart of the people.

Governance Goals

Modern Presidents must try to administer the executive branch, even though there are formidable obstacles in the way.

The Task of Governance. During his presidency, James Polk wrote: "I prefer to supervise the whole operations of the government myself . . . and

---

[7] The enumeration of presidential roles follows Louis W. Koenig, *The Chief Executive*, rev. ed. (New York: Harcourt, Brace and World, 1968).

 AS YOUR PRESENT PRESIDENT IT IS INCUMBENT UPON ME TO PLAY A VARIETY OF ROLES IN THE COURSE OF A SINGLE DAY.

 POLICEMAN TO THE WORLD.

 SOCIAL WORKER TO THE POOR.

 LOVER OF PEACE.

 SEEKER OF CONSENSUS.

 EDUCATOR.

 CIVIL RIGHTS LEADER.

 AT THE CLOSE OF DAY WHAT A RELIEF IT IS TO BE ABLE TO SIT IN MY PAJAMAS—

 AND JUST BE MYSELF.

this makes my duties very great."[8] It is a good thing James Polk is not President today; the job would kill him. But modern Presidents sometimes do try to administer too much. President Jimmy Carter, for example, often tried to take direct administrative control of everything, even going so far as to schedule use of the White House tennis courts.

The American people and their political traditions make Presidents try to gain control of the executive branch of the federal government. We personalize government, making the President symbolize the entire executive branch of the federal government and demanding that he carry its responsibilities on his shoulders. This mental residue of our upbringing is constantly confirmed. Our ritual for transferring power legitimizes the popular image and expectation. In the oath of office, the President vows: "I will faithfully execute the office of the President of the United States, and will, to the best of my abilities, preserve, protect, and defend the Constitution of the United States." Our electoral system also reinforces the image and the expectation, since the winner-take-all method of allocating a state's electoral votes magnifies the extent of the President's victory. The press perpetuates the illusion, as reporters feel free to ask any question in a presidential news conference, and we insist on being shocked if the President does not know all the answers. Historical experiences also deepen our convictions; Franklin Roosevelt lifted us out of depression, Dwight Eisenhower kept the peace, Lyndon Johnson committed the federal government to a war on poverty, Ronald Reagan convinced us he would tame the federal bureaucracy. In all these ways, the constitutionally rooted expectation of presidential government is reinforced—by history, the press, the electoral process, public opinion, presidential candidates, and Presidents themselves.

Obstacles to Governance. The goal of governance is blocked by four main obstacles: (1) the executive branch is huge; (2) it is factious, full of value conflicts; (3) many federal bureaucrats have legal protections against presidential pressure; and (4) many of the bureaucracy's functions have strong political support.

---

[8] Quoted in Richard F. Fenno, Jr. *The President's Cabinet* (Cambridge, Mass.: Harvard University Press, 1959), p. 217.

The goal of governance is difficult to realize because the executive branch of the federal government is so huge as to be almost totally beyond the President's reach. It is so huge that American Presidents are no more able to rule the executive branch than the czars were able to rule Russia. "Not I but 10,000 clerks rule Russia," Nicholas I moaned. American Presidents have more reason to complain, because they face a much more imposing array of bureaucratic offices and personnel, as **Table 11.2** on p. 375 reveals.

The executive branch is also difficult to govern because it is a factious place, full of the same kinds of pluralistic values and value disputes that roar through the rest of society. Even members of the Executive Office of the President bring with them their own personal ambitions and political values, although some presidential administrations try hard to screen their appointees.

President Richard Nixon, for example, suspected that his policy goals were subverted by unsympathetic federal civil servants who had been initially appointed under Democratic Presidents.[9] Intent upon trying to direct the bureaucracy, Nixon tried to extend his control through presidential appointments. His efforts, however, often were frustrated by appointees who became socialized by the very agencies they were supposed to subdue. As John Ehrlichman, one of Nixon's closest advisors, confessed: "We only see them at the White House Christmas party. [After that] they go off and marry the natives."[10]

President Reagan tried harder to make sure that his political appointees were both loyal to him and ideologically committed to his policy goals. As Laurence E. Lynn, Jr., concluded in his study of some of the appointees in the first Reagan administration, "President Reagan helped his cause by choosing appointees who shared his vision. . . ."[11] Ronald Reagan's preference for "like-minded subordinates" was especially pronounced among the White House staff, John H. Kessel discovered.[12] In addition, Reagan successfully pushed his politically loyal appointees further down into the normally nonpartisan ranks of the federal civil service, according to Edie N. Goldenberg.[13]

The statutory protections many federal bureaucrats enjoy further complicate the President's job of controlling the executive branch, as do the various independent commissions (discussed in chapter 13). Believing that the implementation of public policy should be an apolitical process, reformers of the

---

[9] President Nixon's adversarial relationships with the senior civil service were rooted in real policy disagreements. As Joel D. Aberbach and Bert A. Rockman put it: " . . . even paranoids have enemies." See Joel D. Aberbach and Bert A. Rockman, "Clashing Beliefs within the Executive Branch," *American Political Science Review* 70 (1976): 456–69.

[10] Quoted in Richard P. Nathan, *The Plot that Failed* (New York: Wiley, 1975), p. 40.

[11] Lawrence E. Lynn, Jr. "The Reagan Administration and the Renitent Bureaucracy," p. 370, in Lester M. Salamon and Michael S. Lund, eds., *The Reagan Presidency and the Governing of America* (Washington, D. C.: The Urban Institute Press, 1985), pp. 339–70.

[12] John H. Kessel, "The Structures of the Reagan White House," *American Journal of Political Science* 28 (1984): 231–58.

[13] Edie N. Goldenberg, "The Permanent Government in an Era of Retrenchment and Redirection," in Salamon and Lund, *The Reagan Presidency*, pp. 381–404.

THE PRESIDENCY: THE PERSONIFICATION OF POWER

Progressive era worked to expand the number of appointments that were made on the basis of merit, instead of on the basis of personal relationships (**nepotism**) or political loyalty (**patronage**). Historically, the reformers' cause was aided by successive presidential administrations, as each sought to build statutory protections around the political appointments they had just made. Over time, these statutory protections were reinforced by a public and press who bought and resold the notion that implementation was apolitical and by the civil servants themselves, who used their growing strength to shore up their statutory protections.

The President also finds it hard to take charge of the executive branch because it is politically well-protected. The federal bureaucracy grew in response to political pressures, some of which were orchestrated by active Presidents, members of Congress, and federal bureaucrats themselves. As federal responsibilities and programs for meeting them grew, so too did the number of bureaucratic agencies and bureaucrats. Federal programs, in turn, turned many citizens into clients, some of whom organized themselves into political networks of support for the expanded federal roles and for those who carry them out. These **iron triangles**, political support networks involving bureaucratic agencies, congressional authorizing committees, and organized special interest groups, provide political insulation and make it hard for a President who wishes to do anything other than expand existing programs.

For all these and other yet-to-be recounted reasons, Presidents who would pursue the goal of taking charge of the executive branch can not just order bureaucrats around. In general, Presidents, at best, can influence, not control, the executive branch. There are, however, exceptions, examples of swiftly executed presidential commands: President Truman firing a disobedient general, President Reagan firing striking air traffic controllers. In Truman's case, he fired General Douglass MacArthur after the general publicly challenged the President's policy for fighting a limited war in Korea. In Truman's own words: "I fired him because he wouldn't respect the authority of the President. . . . I didn't fire him because he was a dumb son of a bitch, although he was, but that's not against the law for generals."[14] In Reagan's case, the air traffic controllers were in violation of their oath not to strike. Their political sin, however, was poor timing. They went out on strike for higher pay and, they maintained, for improvements that would make flying safer. But they did so early in Reagan's first term, when he was riding high on his mandate to cut back on federal expenditures and perhaps anxious for a chance to flex his political muscles. Even worse for the air traffic controllers, they struck at a time when airline companies were financially hard-pressed and looking for an excuse to cut back flight schedules, because (before deregulation) they were committed to too many unprofitable flights. In spite of these two examples of the President's ability to command compliance, presidential influence over the

---

14 Quoted in Merle Miller, *Plain Speaking: An Oral Biography of Harry S. Truman* (New York: Greenwich House, distributed by Crown, 1985), p. 308.

Early in his first term, President Reagan probably could have gotten away with firing Santa's elves, had they gone on strike.

executive branch is usually heavily constrained.[15] To govern effectively, therefore, Presidents must develop more subtle forms of influence. (To further your understanding of constraints on the President's ability to command, see the **Vantage Point**: The Nature of Presidential Power.)

Policy Goals

To have any chance at all to realize policy goals, the President must try to set the nation's agenda.[16] To help, there are some useful devices. Most importantly, however, any President who would control the nation's agenda must first learn to control his own.

The Demand for Policy Leadership.   The presidency has been elevated to a premier place in the policy-making process by the Constitution and history. The Constitution ensures that the President is provided with a stage and an opportunity, by mandating what has become the State of the Union Message: "He shall from time to time give to the Congress information of the state of the Union, and recommend to their consideration such measures as he shall judge necessary and expedient. . . ." (Article II, Section 3)

In spite of this constitutionally mandated opportunity, only Presidents in the modern era have actively tried to shape the nation's policy agenda. As Richard Neustadt discovered, it was not until the Second World War that the

---

[15] See Thomas E. Cronin, "'Everybody Believes in Democracy Until He Gets to the White House . . .': An Examination of White House Departmental Relations," *Law and Contemporary Problems* 35 (1970): 573–625 and Hugh Heclo and Lester M. Salamon, eds., *The Illusion of Presidential Government* (Boulder, Colo.: Westview Press, 1981).

[16] See Paul Light, *The President's Agenda: Domestic Policy Choice from Kennedy to Carter* (with Notes on Ronald Reagan) (Baltimore: Johns Hopkins University Press, 1983).

THE NATURE OF PRESIDENTIAL POWER

*P*residential power has been defined by Richard Neustadt as the power to persuade. This definition implies what presidential power is not and when it is most precarious.

Presidential power is not the ability to order people around, as President Truman knew, but feared his successor did not. After learning of Dwight David Eisenhower's election as his successor, President Truman thought Eisenhower would not understand the fragmented and unresponsive nature of the federal bureaucracy. Figuring Ike would assume that the bureau-

cracy was just like the army, Truman predicted of Ike: "He'll sit there and he'll say, 'Do this! Do that!' *And nothing will happen.* Poor Ike—it won't be a bit like the army."[1]

This definition of presidential power also suggests that it is most precarious when it appears most strong. Somehow, we mistakenly assume that the President's power is at its peak when he is throwing his weight around, a Truman firing MacArthur, an Eisenhower using troops to integrate a high school, a Kennedy bullying steel companies into rolling back price

increases. But stop and ask yourself why, if the President really were so powerful, would he have to go to such lengths to get his way? The answer is he would not have to and therefore such demonstrations do not necessarily signal strength. Rather, when Presidents act forcefully, it usually is because they have exhausted their more subtle and typically more successful forms of persuasion. Moreover, acting forcefully can deplete the President's power base and thereby make his situation even more precarious.

[1] Quoted in Richard E. Neustadt, *Presidential Power* (New York: Wiley, 1980), p. 9. For an argument that Truman was wrong, see Fred I. Greenstein, *The Hidden-Hand Presidency: Eisenhower as Leader* (New York: Basic Books, 1982).

President formulated and sent to the Congress his own package of policy proposals.[17] But even the Founders expected much of the office, as Alexander Hamilton made clear in the *Federalist Papers*:

> Energy in the executive is a leading character in the definition of good government. It is essential to the protection of the community against foreign attacks; it is not less essential to the steady administration of the laws; . . . to the security of liberty against the enterprises and assaults of ambition, of faction, and of anarchy.[18]

[17] Richard E. Neustadt, "Presidency and Legislation: Planning the President's Program," *American Political Science Review* 49 (1955): 980–1021.

[18] *The Federalist Papers*, with an introduction by Clinton Rossiter (New York: New American Library, 1961), p. 423.

Note Hamilton's implied connection between the prominence of the presidency and policy making; the President would make policy in a certain manner, i.e., steadily or efficiently we would probably say today, and the presidency is the likely source of policies that both preserve national security and protect civil liberties. Moreover, the evolution of the office has magnified its promise and its powers. This was seldom planned; promise and powers grew out of presidential responses to conflicts. As Alan Wolfe put it: "The American Presidency has been a product of practice, not theory. Concrete struggles between economic and political forces have been responsible for shaping it, not maxims from Montesquieu."[19]

Devices for Policy Leadership. American Presidents try to shape the nation's policy agenda through three main devices: (1) words, (2) other symbols, and (3) events. When used effectively, these devices alter people's perceptions of the President's and the federal government's proper role.

Presidential rhetoric helps shape the nation's policy agenda. It is as though American Presidents appreciate the political wisdom attributed to Nikita Khrushchev, a former head of the U.S.S.R.: "A seductive slogan is the most powerful political instrument."[20] Through their rhetoric, Presidents exercise policy leadership by articulating, and if possible personalizing, attractive visions of the future. Indeed, President Franklin Roosevelt thought that "One of the chief obligations of the Presidency is to think about the future."[21] Especially successful Presidents also have a sixth sense to know what the American people yearn for.[22] In spite of his administration's failures to deliver on civil rights for blacks, President Franklin Roosevelt, for example, "swelled hope in the formerly disheartened. A belief that 'we are on our way' took root in the Negro community."[23] In contrast and without success, President Ford often tripped over his own words and President Carter failed to convey any vision of an attractive future. The failure was acknowledged by Carter's Chief of Staff, Hamilton Jordan: "My most basic regret is that in doing so many things, we never clearly fixed in the public mind a sense of our priorities."[24] President Reagan, especially in his first term, excelled at the use of rhetoric to build support for a short list of his policies and to deflect criticisms of their shortcomings. As the Chairman of the House Budget Committee, William H. Gray 3d

---

[19] Alan Wolfe, "Presidential Power and the Crisis Of Modernization," in Thomas E. Cronin, ed. *Rethinking the Presidency* (Boston: Little, Brown, 1982), p. 141.

[20] Quoted in Arkady Shevchenko, *Breaking With Moscow* (New York: Knopf, 1985), pp. 101–102.

[21] Quoted in Arthur Bernon Tourtellot, *The Presidents on the Presidency* (New York: Russell & Russell, 1970).

[22] Otis L. Graham and Meghan Robinson Wander, eds., *Franklin D. Roosevelt: His Life and Times— An Encyclopedic View* (Boston: G. K. Hall, 1985).

[23] Harvard Sitkoff, "Negros," in Graham and Wander, *Roosevelt*, p. 283.

[24] Quoted in James Ceaser, "The Theory of Governance of the Reagan Administration," in Lester M. Salamon and Michael S. Lund, eds., *The Reagan Presidency and the Governing of America* (Washington, D. C.: The Urban Institute Press, 1985), p. 62.

(D., Pa.), begrudgingly acknowledged: "Finally we've got a preacher who can preach."[25]

Presidents also shape the nation's policy agenda through the creation and manipulation of political symbols. Symbols, especially ones that activate dominant cultural values, alter public assumptions of what is both politically proper and posssible. The technique is best illustrated by those who were its masters. President Franklin Roosevelt, for example, used his First Hundred Days to restructure public expectations: "The effect on the country was like a stiff shot of bourbon on an empty stomach. Drooping spirits began to revive, a new spirit of optimism began to build, and there was a flurry of business activity even before the emergency recovery measures could possibly begin to be felt."[26] President Ronald Reagan was just as adept. In his first inaugural address, President Reagan identified the enemy: " . . . government is not the solution to our problem; it is the problem . . . ." And Reagan did battle, compiling a string of apparent victories: expenditure and tax cuts, the appointment of a female but conservative Supreme Court Justice, and the firing of federal employees who violated their oath not to strike, for example. Although largely symbolic, Robert Dallek has argued, Reagan's victories were meaningful.[27] By appearing to restore traditional values, Reagan increased both the self-esteem of Americans and the gratitude they showered on him at the polls. The symbolic effect, in addition, was buttressed by events.

In addition, Presidents shape the nation's policy agenda through the creation and manipulation of events. During the battle of the budget in 1985, for example, the crushing reality of $200 billion in deficits dominated the policy-making process. In the shadow of looming deficits, liberals folded away plans for new federal policies and congresspersons facing re-election scrambled to avoid blame for the feared economic downturn. You do not have to agree with the allegations of some, that the deficit was deliberately created as a brake on federal spending, to accept the conclusion: events, especially ones that alter beliefs about government's proper role, shape the nation's policy agenda.

FDR's use of the fireside chat proved to be an effective means of articulating and personalizing attractive visions of the future.

Altering Public Perceptions.

When used effectively, these various devices shape the nation's policy agenda by altering public perceptions. History illustrates the lesson. Just after his inaugural, and before he had any definite sense of his policy course, Franklin Roosevelt convened a special session of Congress and took to the airwaves in the first of his "fireside chats"; he had to appear as though he knew what to do and was determined to do it. Going further, Roosevelt reinforced the appearance of decisive action by ordering the nation's banks closed for a "bank holiday," even though many of them already had been closed by the actions of state governments. In any successful effort to shape

---

25 Quoted in *The New York Times*, 4 July 1985.

26 George Wolfskill, *Happy Days Are Here Again* (New York: Holt, Rhinehart, 1974), p. 27.

27 Robert Dallek, *Ronald Reagan: The Politics of Symbolism* (Cambridge, Mass.: Harvard University Press, 1984).

public perceptions, Presidents use all the tools: words, symbols, and events. What is crucial is knowing when to use which tool.

Public perceptions are effectively altered by good timing and the proper sequencing of events. There is a saying in Washington that when a new President is elected, desk drawers fly open all over Georgetown. The saying conveys the insight that there is no such thing as a new policy. Rather, there are many policy proposals lying around, incubating, waiting for the right time to hatch. The Washington, D.C. neighborhood of Georgetown, an upscale home of presidential advisors-in-waiting, is one incubation chamber; Congress and all its committees is a second; the file cabinets of the federal bureaucracy a third. Policy proposals might be kept warm in all these places, but it is the President who can best help them break out of their shell. Presidents prepare the way subtly, sometimes directly with words but more often indirectly, by manipulating public perceptions of problems and possible solutions.

The process was played out perfectly in Franklin Roosevelt's administration, as he and his advisors tried to pave the way for a massive redistribution of income from young workers to unemployed older Americans. Realizing that "a nation has to be educated to the point where reforms can be assimilated naturally, without dangerous spasms of indigestion,"[28] the Roosevelt Administration carefully cultivated public opinion. By selling the Social Security program under the well-understood and accepted banner of "insurance," not the radical notion of "income redistribution," Roosevelt sought to "clothe the apparently unorthodox in the garb of familiarity."[29]

The President's Need for Self-Control.

Presidents who would successfully shape the nation's policy agenda must learn to control their own.[30] Ronald Reagan, for example, did this very well in his first term. One astute political observer, Hugh Heclo, describes the first term success this way: "By drastically narrowing his priorities to a few economic road signs, the President appeared to rise above the prevailing policy congestion. In place of ambiguity and trade-offs appeared simplicity and decisions. . . . By drastically limiting White House priorities, the President seems to rise above the confusion and squabbling of a congested policy environment."[31]

In contrast, President Reagan's loss of control early in his second term's agenda was acknowledged even by those friendly to the Administration: "There's a lack of coherence and I think people on the Hill sense there's no overall game plan, that the Administration hasn't come to grips as they did in the first Administration with the need for Congress to have an ordered priority."[32] The failure to control his own agenda starts a President down a

---

[28] Elmer E. Cornwell, Jr., *Presidential Leadership of Public Opinion* (Bloomington: Indiana Unversity Press, 1965), p. 118.

[29] *Ibid.*, p. 129.

[30] Arnold J. Meltsner, "Memorandum to Ronald Reagan: Advice on Politics and Governance," in Arnold J. Meltsner, ed. *Politics and the Oval Office*, pp. 3–9.

[31] Hugh Heclo, "One Executive Branch or Many," in Anthony King, ed., *Both Ends of the Avenue* (Washington, D. C.: American Enterprise Institute, 1983), p. 47.

[32] Quoted in *The New York Times*, 28 February 1985.

THE PRESIDENCY: THE PERSONIFICATION OF POWER

slippery slope, as Reagan began to discover in 1985 before taking corrective action. In general, however, Presidents who fail to control their agenda become reactive and defensive, as they try to cope with the demands of others who are in control of theirs. Presidents who become reactive and defensive erode their power base and therefore their capacity to lead.

Political Goals

Traditionally, Presidents have tried to win the heart of their party. Today, however, Presidents tend to bypass the parties and go directly for the people's heart.

The colorful Lyn Nofziger, Ronald Reagan's "Hit Man."

Winning the Support of the Party. In theory, presidential aspirants must win the heart of their party if they are to capture its nomination and govern effectively. This is especially hard to do, since Presidents should not appear too political. The deception is necessary, because of the American ambivalence about their Presidents and politics: we admire Presidents but distrust politicians. The ambivalence is one of our cultural fantasies, deeply rooted in our historical experience. Ever since George Washington, many of us have esteemed Presidents who seemed above party, celebrating them as statesmen and disparaging the others as mere politicians.[33] Harry S. Truman did not share this view. "A statesman is a politician who's been dead 10 or 15 years," he often said. Understandably, Presidents often adopt what one presidential scholar, Richard Pious, calls a "lofty nonpartisan pose."[34] Appearing apolitical can work to the President's advantage, increasing his ability to mobilize public opinion and manipulate other politicians, as Fred Greenstein thinks was true of President Eisenhower.[35]

In practice, however, presidential aspirants win their party's nomination by creating their own candidate-centered organizations. This has been the practice ever since Dwight Eisenhower, the political novice, defeated Robert Taft, "Mr. Republican," for the party's presidential nomination in 1952.[36] More recently, Jimmy Carter's method of seeking the Democratic party's nomination in 1976 made him "perhaps the most 'outsider' of all 'outsiders' in the history of presidential politics."[37] Also in 1976, Ronald Reagan almost beat Gerald Ford, a sitting President, out of the Republican party's presidential nomination. Once in office, sitting Presidents can gain control of their national party organization, by making it over in their image. Doing so also creates a personal army for the President, one to enlist in legislative battles. Under President Reagan, for

[33] See, for example, Ralph Ketcham, *Presidents Above Party: The First American Presidency, 1789–1829* (Chapel Hill, University of North Carolina Press, 1984).

[34] Richard M. Pious, *The American Presidency* (New York: Basic Books, 1979), p. 123.

[35] Greenstein, *The Hidden-Hand Presidency.*

[36] Austin Ranney, "Political Parties: Reform and Decline," in Anthony King, ed., *The New American Political System* (Washington, D.C. American Enterprise Institute for Public Policy Research, 1978), p. 240.

[37] The story of the Carter campaign is well-told by Jules Witcover, *Marathon: The Pursuit of the Presidency, 1972–1976* (New York: Viking Press, 1977).

example, one of his special assistants, Lyn Nofziger, had the job of running the Republican National Committee. That meant Nofziger could get the Committee to do things that the White House could not do legally, such as organize grass-roots lobbying to pressure members of Congress into supporting the president's legislative program.

Winning the Support of the People.   As they try to govern and make policy, Presidents rely only tentatively on their political party and instead appeal directly to the people.

Political parties are no longer the vital or cohesive force they once were, as chapter 6 showed.[38] People no longer identify with them the way they used to; the growth of presidential primaries has weakened the ability of political parties to gain control of their own nomination process; parties have been eclipsed by the increased prominence of special interest groups as financiers of presidential campaigns; few congressional candidates try to cling to the President's electoral coattails; and party leaders in Congress have a tough time enforcing party loyalty on all but the most overriding legislative votes. Knowing all these things, Presidents have adapted to changing political realities by trying to make direct appeals to the American people.

To mobilize political support, Presidents appeal over the heads of members of their own party, hoping to capture in their own person and rhetoric the hopes and fears of the masses.[39] They self-consciously encourage us in the identification:[40]

> Theodore Roosevelt: "No man is fit to hold the position of President of the United States at all unless as President he feels that he represents no party but the people as a whole."
> Franklin Roosevelt: "No man can occupy the Office of the President without realizing that he is President of all the people."

The encouragement is deliberate and perhaps unavoidable, for any President who is committed to more than incremental policy change and who, therefore, must try to find a public appeal that can overcome the decentralized and fragmented nature of American politics. As presidential scholar Louis Koenig has put it: "The lack of an effective national party institution forces the President into a heavy dependence upon his personal skills as party leader."[41]

■ By now, it is quite clear that the President has ambitious governance, policy, and political goals and that the American people are very demanding that these goals be met.

What is less clear is whether these goals can be realized.

---

[38] See also Martin P. Wattenberg, *The Decline of American Political Parties, 1952–1980* (Cambridge, Mass.: Harvard University Press, 1984).

[39] See Samuel Kernell, *Going Public: New Strategies of Presidential Leadership* (Washington, D.C.: CQ Press, 1986).

[40] Quoted in Pious, *The American Presidency*, p. 123.

[41] Louis Koenig, *The Chief Executive* (New York: Harcourt, Brace and World, 1968), rev. ed., p. 87.

WAYS OF ACHIEVING PRESIDENTIAL GOALS

> This is at once the most powerful office in the world—and among the most severely constrained by law and custom.
> —*President Jimmy Carter's farewell address*

President Carter may have learned the lesson too late. To reach his goals, a President must overcome constraints, expand formal powers, and create and exercise informal, political powers.

Overcoming Constraints

The President confronts many constraints, things that limit his ability to realize his goals. President Carter, in his farewell address, voiced his frustration with the contraints he suffered. Some of his suffering was unavoidable; however, it is an intrinsic part of the American political system.[42] Rather than complain, a President who would try to achieve his goals must expand his formal powers and create and exercise political power.

Sources of Constraint.   The constraints on presidential actions come from a variety of sources: the Constitution, federalism, civil liberties, public opinion,

---

[42] James MacGregor Burns, *The Power To Lead: The Crisis of the American Presidency* (New York: Simon and Schuster, 1984).

'Okay, bring in the new guy . . .'

interest groups, political parties, the electoral system, the mass media, presidential policy preferences and actions, the policy-making process, and all the other institutions of the national government.

These constraints are not accidental. The presidency, just like the other branches of the federal government, should be constrained, the Founders reasoned. They believed that liberty was best protected when the government's authority was parceled out among different agencies, each of which might check the other. James Madison, writing in *Federalist No. 51*, stated the case: "In framing a government which is to be administered by men over men, the great difficulty lies in this: you must first enable the government to control the governed; and in the next place oblige it to control itself."[43]

The Founders also believed that the public interest was served by making it very hard for majoritarian factions to impose their will on the rest of society. In this way, Madison, for example, hoped, " . . . a coalition of a majority of the whole society could seldom take place on any other principles than those of justice and the general good. . . . "[44] The Founders sent contemporary Presidents clear messages: "Yes, you will find it hard to realize your goals. We purposefully have imposed constraints on your office, so that you can not too easily extinguish the liberty of the people. We know this also makes it hard for you to realize your goals. But, if your goals are worthwhile, truly in the public's interest, then you should be able to realize them, in spite of the obstacles." Given the importance and desirability of constraints, it is not surprising that so many were written into the Constitution.

The Constitution. The Constitution constrains the President in many ways: by limiting each term of office to four years (Article II, Section 1); by limiting the total number of terms to two (the Twenty-Second Amendment); by making the exercise of many of the President's powers contingent upon the agreement of other branches (under Article II, Section 2, for example, the President's power to negotiate treaties and appoint Supreme Court justices and ambassadors is contingent upon the agreement of the U.S. Senate); by giving other powers, legislative and judicial ones, for example, to other branches; and by providing for removal from office, after impeachment and conviction (Article II, Section 4).

Federalism. The American tradition of federalism further constrains the President, by making all the fifty states important players in the policy-making process. Federalism serves as both a political rallying cry and as a judicial doctrine which advocates and justifies an important policy-making role for states, as chapter 3 described. The cry and the doctrine throw up additional obstacles to any President who might prefer to act unilaterally, without state support. In most cases, state-imposed obstacles have only inhibited presiden-

---

[43] *The Federalist Papers*, introduction by Clinton Rossiter (New York: New American Library, 1961), p. 322.

[44] *Ibid.*, p. 325.

Presidents as Boys. These are photos of several past Presidents when they were boys. Can you name them? For help, see the answers below.

A

B

C

D

E

F

G

A. Dwight D. Eisenhower, age 16, in 1907.
B. Herbert Hoover, age 3, in 1877.
C. Lyndon B. Johnson, age 5, in 1913.
D. John F. Kennedy, age 8, in 1925.
E. Harry S. Truman, age 15, in 1899.
F. Franklin D. Roosevelt, age 11, in 1893.
G. Gerald R. Ford, age 12, in 1926.

391

'They're all out taking polls to see which way you want to be led'

Presidents who rely too heavily on public opinion polls handcuff their leadership potential.

tial initiatives, however. Some of these rear guard actions include the now abandoned attempt of New York City to block the transport of nuclear materials through Manhattan; the attempts of states to ban trucks with tandem trailers from their highways; the heel dragging of states that tried to keep their interstate highway funds without stopping the flow of alcoholic beverages to those under the age of twenty-one; the opposition of various high taxation states to presidential tax proposals that would eliminate the deductibility of state and local taxes. In all these and other, yet to surface, controversies, federalism pushes additional contenders into the President's policy domains and arms them with various devices for frustrating presidential initiatives.

Civil Liberties. The American tradition of respect for civil liberties, sanctified by the Constitution and the Bill of Rights and codified by statute and judicial decisions, further constrains Presidents. Civil liberties constrain Presidents by narrowing the field of available options. Because of civil libertarian concerns, Presidents have to be less heavy-handed than they might otherwise be, as, for example, they try to ensure the personal loyalty of civil servants, prevent politically embarrassing leaks, gain access to the confidential notes of reporters, or block the immigration of illegal aliens.

Public Opinion. Public opinion and its roots in the American political culture also complicate life, especially for any President who wishes to lead. The American public is largely apathetic about public problems, especially ones that appear off in the future, with yet unfelt adverse effects, as many members of Congress, for example, found out in trying to mobilize public concern over the federal deficit. Our political culture also encourages our preoccupation with the pursuit of private pleasures and not civic virtues, as President Johnson, for example, found out in trying to put together a coalition for grand social purposes, such as a war on poverty.[45] Because of its apathetic and private nature, Presidents who wait passively on public opinion woo disaster. As Hugh Sidey, the Washington editor of *Time* and a commentator on the presidency puts it: " . . . the Chief Executive who reads the domestic polls every night for political guidance is apt to be paralyzed each morning."[46] In general, Presidents who rely too passively on public opinion polls handcuff their leadership potential—unless it is a public opinion they have molded.

Political Interest Groups. Political interest groups, often well-funded and well-organized, also are quick to ambush any President who wanders into their special pastures, especially the ones subsidized by federal funds. In recent years, for example, special interest groups, with the support of their congressional allies, have frustrated presidential attempts to cut back agricultural price supports, to pull the plug on economically wasteful water projects, to slow down the growth of Social Security cost-of-living increases, to break the scoops

---

[45] See Albert O. Hirschman, *Economics and Philosophy* 1 (1985): 7–21.

[46] *Time*, 23 November 1981, p. 16.

of retired members of the Armed Services who double-dip into Social Security retirement benefits—to list just a few examples. The problem has been endemic; almost all Presidents have complained about it. Surrounded by so many vigilant and potentially vengeful sacred cows, Presidents are easily gored.

Political Parties. Political parties too constrain Presidents. Presidents, and citizens, often expect the opposition party to do this. It is the President's own party that inflicts the most damaging blows, however. It happens because of intra-party conflict, sometimes over matters of principle and always because of personal ambition. The rivalry constrains policy options. In 1960, for example, the young John F. Kennedy was jockeying for position in the race for his party's presidential nomination. It was no time to offend those in the party who took a hard line on the Russian threat and the need for military preparedness—the party's cold war warrior wing. All of Kennedy's competitors were linked in the public mind with a weapon: "Scoop Jackson (the Senator from Washington) had the Polaris (submarine), and Lyndon had Space, and Symington (the Senator from Missouri) had the B-52 . . . Kennedy . . . needed a weapon."[47] His options limited, Kennedy shored up his stance as a hard-liner on national security by latching on to his own arms policy—modernization of the infantry.

In addition, Presidents sometimes open themselves up to damage from other members of their own party, as President Carter did when he let Vice-President Mondale set up his office within the West Wing of the White House. This, according to Griffin B. Bell, Carter's friend and Attorney General, was a crucial error. It let Mondale develop his own power base within the White House, one that he and his liberal advisors used to crowd Carter's agenda with their own issues, thereby reinforcing the public's perception that Carter lacked a clear policy direction.[48] Especially during the battle of the budget in 1985, President Reagan too suffered real policy blows from Republican members of Congress who were concerned about their own electoral future and in particular from Robert Dole (R., Kan.), the Senate leader of the Republican majority. All Presidents learn the lesson: one's political party is full of unreliable and potentially hurtful allies.

The Electoral System. The electoral system heaps additional constraints on Presidents. Because it is decentralized, the electoral system encourages members of Congress to be attuned to local, and not necessarily national, concerns. Not surprisingly, members of Congress can not be expected to follow the President's legislative initiatives, if doing so will endanger their seat. In the first two years of Reagan's second administration, for example, Republican senators were increasingly independent of Reagan's policy leadership, after two of their colleagues had lost their Senate seats during the Reagan landslide in 1984 and since they felt as though the President had abandoned them on the issue of Social Security increases during the 1985 battle of the budget. The electoral

---

47 David Halberstam, *The Best and the Brightest* (New York: Penguin Books, 1983), p. 31.

48 Griffin B. Bell, *Taking Care of the Law* (New York: William Morrow and Company, 1982).

THE POLSBY—WILDAVSKY DIALOGUE
CONTINUED . . .

AUTHOR: What is your assessment of the Reagan Presidency?

WILDAVSKY: My disagreement with Nelson is that what he calls substantive leadership is exactly, in my opinion, what Reagan provides—only to such a pronounced degree that it is difficult to recognize. For President Reagan to behave like Nelson Polsby, whatever image that might conjure to the mind, would mean that he abandon every reason for being in public life, give up his lifelong views on proper public policy, and say that compromise on any basis was better than his own policies. But the President's idea of a terrific policy is to let people keep their own money. His view is that, if you leave the system as it is and allow the normal process of bargaining to go on, the result is going to be a higher level of taxing and spending, as it was all the time before he came into office. Therefore, he has been determined not to act like a pseudo-Walter Mondale, which Nelson's prescription would have him do, but as a person who believes that we should have a strong defense, and a strong economy to bolster that defense. This, in his view, requires that the public sector take less and leave more for the private sector. Therefore, the President, who we all recognize is not addicted to preemptive surrender, is holding back, because if he puts back everything on the table he will have lost.

[Author's Note: If you need to refresh your memory on "the table" and what was taken off it, review Nelson Polsby's comments about the impact of Gramm-Rudman on the budget process on p. 355.]

POLSBY: Let me just respond to a little bit of this. It seems to me that we do not have a political system which is terribly well-geared to realizing the lifelong wishes of Presidents who refuse to discuss public policy with members of Congress. The Constitution just isn't written that way. The Constitution demands that the President and Congress reach agreements on these things even when their fondest, lifelong hopes do not argue this way. So, the notion that the President wishes to go down in history as a man who doesn't like to compromise, and discuss, and all the rest of it, simply runs counter to the demands of our Constitution. Since he compaigned for the job, it seems to me that, therefore, he had better start trying to do the job.

WILDAVSKY: Well, Paul, I'm going to try again to give your readers a sense of how President Reagan and his people might look at this. If you take a look from the President's point of view, he is often asked to compromise endlessly, to give up some tax increases and get spending cuts in return. This, in fact, was the policy reluctantly followed by Reagan in 1982 and a bit in 1983. But he wakes up and says, look, the tax increases are here, but the spending cuts, in fact, did not materialize nearly to the same degree. Enough, he says, of this phony compromise.

AUTHOR: Let's focus this a little. Is Ronald Reagan a great President?

POLSBY: I believe very much in making this system work and the more responsibility you have the more obligated you are, the more responsible you are, to make the system work. And I feel that Reagan has systematically taken the view that it's in his interest

foreign policy. The problem, in my opinion, is that he does not have a doctrine. He knows that what he wants in defense is more. But, what the more is for, he has not yet succeeded in spelling out. Secretary of Defense Weinberger says, well, any time we go in, we want all the support we need, and you never give up until we win. I wouldn't give my mother that and the people are not going to give any administration that.

> *It seems to me that we do not have a political system which is terribly well-geared to realizing the lifelong wishes of Presidents who refuse to discuss public policy with members of Congress.*
> **—Polsby**

to make the system appear not to work and to exploit that politically. I think that's bad civic education and bad government.

WILDAVSKY: If a number of things last, then he will at least be rated a very powerful President.

Reagan has made a marked difference as to how the Presidency operates. Remember that, before Ronald Reagan, there was a series of discredited Presidents. People were talking about the ritual destruction of the presidency. President Reagan has shown how it's possible to run the presidency without necessarily becoming wholly discredited. Some people say, then, that, inadvertantly, President Reagan has elevated the office in a way the Democrats in the future will find useful. The President's weakness resides largely in defense and

> *For President Reagan to behave like Nelson Polsby, whatever image that might conjure up to the mind, would mean that he abandon every reason for being in public life, give up his lifelong views on proper public policy, and say that compromise on any basis was better than his own policies.*
> **—Wildavsky**

system also permits "split-ticket" voting, an increasingly common practice that forces a President to deal with a Congress in which the other party controls at least one of the two chambers. Finally, even party control of Congress does not ensure congressional followership, as John F. Kennedy learned.

The Mass Media.   The mass media further constrain the President.[49] The adversarial relationship often produces hostile coverage. One who suffered at the hands of the White House press corps, David R. Gergen, President Reagan's Director of Communications, described the relationship this way; "Wonderful fun—the fox and the hounds, and frequently they corner you."[50] Coping with hostile coverage throws the President off his game plan, as he is forced to react to negative press.

The problem was especially severe during the presidency of Jimmy Carter, according to Lloyd N. Cutler, a consummate Washington insider and counsel to President Carter. Once out of office, Cutler spoke of what he termed "the galvanizing effect" that the evening news had on the White House, especially after it ran a story strongly criticizing the President or his policies. Then, Cutler said, everything stopped and whatever people were working on was put aside to formulate a response—to avoid a rerun of the story the next night or a follow-up story to the effect that the President's failure to react indicated that his advisors were undecided and he did not know what to do.[51]

The President.   The President is an additional constraint on his own freedom of maneuver. Because of their policy preferences, words, and actions, Presidents can tie their own hands *and* paint themselves into corners. The adverse effects often are unanticipated or unavoidable. President Johnson, for example, pushed his anti-poverty program through Congress "but drove millions of middle class whites into the GOP."[52] In a different case, President Carter's decision to admit the former Shah of Iran to the United States precipitated the takeover of the American Embassy in Tehran, a crisis that dominated the rest of his term of office. In a similar way, President Reagan's 1984 campaign pledge not to raise taxes constrained his subsequent budgetary decisions.

Presidents, of course, must know the grief they cause themselves, although few have described it as profanely as Lyndon Johnson, torn between his Vietnam War policy and his Great Society social welfare programs: "I knew from the start that I was bound to be crucified either way I moved. If I left the woman I really loved—the Great Society—in order to get involved with that bitch of a war . . . then I would lose everything at home."[53]

---

[49] See, for example, a veteran's account of his twenty-five years in the White House Press corps: James Deakin, *Straight Stuff: The Reporters, the White House and the Truth* (New York: Morrow, 1984).

[50] Quoted in *The New York Times*, 12 December 1982.

[51] *The New York Times*, 7 July 1983.

[52] Mark I. Gelfand, "The War on Poverty," in Robert A. Devine, ed., *Exploring The Johnson Years* (Austin: University of Texas Press, 1981), p. 129.

[53] Quoted in Doris Kearns, *Lyndon Johnson and the American Dream* (New York: Harper and Row, 1976), p. 251.

Nothing better symbolizes the adversarial nature of the relationship between the mass media and the presidency than this cartoon. *The Washington Post*, because of its role in digging up the Watergate story, here gets credit for the political demise of Richard Nixon.

Presidents and their advisors also are sources of constraint.

The Political System. As though all these constraints were not binding enough, the President is also constrained by the policy-making process itself and by all the other institutions of the national government. The process, for example, constrains because its fragmented nature provides many opportunities for delay; Congress constrains because its members and committees push their own agendas for their own reasons; the federal bureaucracy frustrates because it often is too deeply immersed in its own routines; and federal courts sometimes strike down presidential initiatives as unconstitutional excesses.

The President, however, is more constrained in some policy areas than others. Success in policy making, as in boxing, depends on which ring you climb into, according to Robert J. Spitzer's study of the arenas of presidential power.[54] The President, for example, is relatively unconstrained in the making of the nation's foreign policy. Relatively unconstrained, but not totally, as Jesse Jackson revealed, practicing "citizen diplomacy," in going to Syria in January 1984 to obtain the release of Lieutenant Robert O. Goodman, Jr., a downed Navy flyer. Still, the President is less constrained in the making of foreign than any other kind of policy. In general, presidential policy-making success depends heavily on who else climbs into the policy arena. In recent years, for example, Presidents have found the policy organization that protects domestic cigarette producers more formidable than the one that tries to protect domestic shoemakers.

In almost every way, constraints limit the President's capacity for independent action and impose entangling dependencies on him. The dependencies force the President into accommodations and compromises—unless he real-

[54] Robert J. Spitzer, *The Presidency and Public Policy: The Four Arenas of Presidential Power* (University, Alabama: The University of Alabama Press, 1983).

Jesse Jackson practiced "citizen diplomacy," in his role in the release of downed Navy flier, Lieutenant Robert Goodman, Jr.

izes that some constraints are variable and that he can weaken, if not break, their hold. Not all do. According to James David Barber, only those Presidents who view their political environments as malleable tend to be active and assertive.[55] Presidents who believe they have options try to (1) expand their formal powers and (2) create and exercise informal political power.

Expanding Formal Powers

The President is at least as strong as the Constitution makes him. To realize his multiple goals, that is not strong enough, however. Most Presidents, therefore, have sought to expand their formal powers.

Abraham Lincoln's response to his Cabinet, after learning of their opposition to the Emancipation Proclamation, bridged the gap between the President's paper and real powers: "One Aye, Seven Nays. The Ayes have it," he said. Lincoln knew that a President can not accept, as given and unalterable, the contraints on the office. Instead, the President must find ways to overcome or circumvent constraints. One way to do that is to expand the formal powers of the presidency.

The President's Formal Powers.   The President's formal powers have evolved out of both the Constitution and statutes. By drawing on these formal resources, the President is able to exercise various powers:

---

[55] James David Barber, *The Presidential Character.*

THE PRESIDENCY: THE PERSONIFICATION OF POWER

- the power to make appointments, the initiative in making budget proposals, " . . . the power to speak or listen as a representative of the nation";[56]
- the claimed right to exercise whatever "war powers" are necessary to protect the nation;
- special "emergency powers";
- the right to enter into "executive agreements" with the leaders of foreign nations;
- the right to issue "executive orders," carrying the force of law, to implement previous laws;
- the right to grant pardons, the right to veto acts of Congress;
- the right to exercise a "pocket veto" by which an act of Congress dies during an adjournment (but not a recess);
- the power to establish (or break) diplomatic relations with foreign governments;
- the power to dismiss those he appoints;
- the prerogative to insist that agencies of the executive branch clear with his office all legislative proposals before they are submitted to Congress and all proposed regulations before they are issued for public comment.

The President's power to act can establish his claim to additional powers, however. In the first few weeks of the Civil War, for example, President Lincoln acted as though he had certain power—and therefore he did. After raising and equipping an army, sending federal troops to arrest some members of the Maryland legislature, blocking southern ports, and suspending civil liberties, Lincoln declared: "I felt that measures otherwise unconstitutional might become lawful by becoming indispensable to the preservation of the Constitution through preservation of the nation. Right or wrong, I assumed this ground and now avow it."[57]

The Evolution of Formal Powers.   Many of these constitutional and statutory powers have evolved over time, sometimes pushed by events and by assertive Presidents into extraconstitutional and extralegal dimensions and sometimes trimmed back, once the precipitating event had passed or some other branch found the political courage to contest the felt abuse of power. This evolution in the formal powers of the presidency has occurred along five main branches: (1) executive agreements, (2) executive orders, (3) executive privilege, (4) impoundments, and (5) war powers.

Executive agreements. Presidents have expanded their formal powers through the use of executive agreements. President Franklin Roosevelt, for example, took an expansive view of the office and relied heavily on **executive agreements**, international understandings between the President and the head of a foreign nation which do not require senatorial approval but which can be nullified by congressional action and ignored by future Presidents. When

---

56 *United States* v. *Curtiss-Wright Export Corp.*, 299 U.S. 304 (1936).

57 Quoted in Arthur Bernon Tourtellot, *The Presidents on the Presidency* (Garden City, New York: Doubleday, 1964), p. 311.

Roosevelt agreed with Winston Churchill to trade fifty American destroyers for the use of British air bases in the Western hemisphere, an executive agreement became a substitute for legislation. Through this trade, Roosevelt was able to help Great Britain in the war against Germany—when he probably could not have gotten the deal through Congress.

Executive Orders. Presidents also have used their administrative responsibilities to expand their formal powers. Over time, as the tasks of governmental regulation have become more technical and complex, Congress has expanded the President's right to issue **executive orders**, administrative regulations that serve as guidelines for the implementation of policy and that have the force of law, once they are published in the *Federal Register*. Relying on them as though they too were a substitute for formal legislation, modern Presidents have used executive orders to establish the Executive Office of the President, to classify secret material, to slow down enforcement of affirmative action requirements for firms doing business with the federal government, and to authorize the use of lie detectors to check for leaks of classified information. In some cases, presidential excesses have been ruled unconstitutional by the Supreme Court, as was President Truman's executive order to seize the nation's steel mills, after they were struck by labor unions during the Korean War,[58] and as was President Reagan's attempt to make racially segregated private schools exempt from federal income taxes.

Executive Privilege. Presidents also have simply asserted claims to additional formal powers. Throughout American history, for example, Presidents have asserted, expanded, and usually defended successfully their claim of **executive privilege**, the right of the President (and those he gives it to) to refuse to appear before congressional committees or provide them with requested information. The claim, however, as Thomas Cronin points out, lacks constitutional backing: "The Founding Fathers did not intend that the President should decide what information Congress and the American people need to know. They were aware of the maxim that he who controls the flow of information rules our destinies."[59] The expansion of the privilege was checked in 1974, however, after the Supreme Court ruled that President Nixon had to turn over the "Watergate" tape recordings because they allegedly contained information that was necessary for criminal trials.[60] In more recent years, Congress has curtailed the use of the privilege by the President's aides, as in 1982 when the House of Representatives voted a contempt citation against Anne M. Burford, President Reagan's head of the Environmental Protection Agency (EPA), for her refusal to supply information on the alleged failures of the EPA to clean up toxic wastes.

Impoundments. Presidents also have used their control over spending to expand their formal powers. To increase their formal budget-making powers,

---

[58] Truman's seizure of the steel mills was ruled unconstitutional in *Youngstown Sheet and Tube Co.* v. *Sawyer*, 343 U.S. 579 (1952).

[59] Cronin, *Rethinking the Presidency*, p. 194.

[60] *U.S.* v. *Nixon*, 418 U.S. 683 (1974).

American Presidents exercise impressive war powers, as President Reagan did in the 1983 invasion of Grenada.

for example, modern Presidents have made extensive use of **impoundment**, "the extraconstitutional power . . . (that) . . . allows the executive to refuse to spend funds that have been appropriated by Congress."[61] Sometimes there are good reasons for impounding appropriated money, as when the need has passed or when slowing down the rate of expenditure might be more efficient, for example. But the power is subject to abuse, as when Presidents use impoundments to kill programs, because they do not have the votes in Congress to block passage or to prevent an override of their veto or because the despised program was buried inside some more comprehensive and acceptable bundle of legislation. In an attempt to check such abuses, Congress passed the *Budget and Impoundment Control Act of 1974*. The Act, however, has been a weak rein on a strong horse. President Reagan, for example, has been especially inventive in finding ways around the Act: "Through a series of mechanisms, such as failing to report impoundments, reprogramming funds without congressional actions, and misclassifying impoundments, the (Reagan) administration has been able to pursue its own objectives."[62]

War Powers. Presidents also have argued that military necessity dictated expansion of their formal powers. In fighting the war in Vietnam, for example, both President Johnson and President Nixon made extensive use of **war**

---

[61] Cronin, *Rethinking . . .*, p. 195.

[62] Representative Norman Y. Mineta (D., Cal.), quoted in Bob Tate, "Impoundment: An Old Dispute Resurfaces," *Congressional Quarterly Weekly Reports*—40:16 (April 17, 1982): p. 854.

powers, their claimed prerogative to do what they believed necessary to protect this nation. These prerogatives are judgment calls and others may conclude that a President has gone too far, as Congress did, for example, in passing the *War Powers Resolution of 1973*. The Resolution, however, was only a joint resolution passed over President Nixon's veto, and imposed statutory constraints on the President's War Powers.[63] In practice, the President's exercise of his war powers can be constrained only by a determined and unified Congress. So far, Congress has not been willing to back up constraints implicit in the War Powers Resolution. President Gerald Ford, for example, pointed out that the Resolution is only as constraining as the President lets it be: "The United States was involved in six military crises during my presidency. . . . In none of those instances did I believe the War Powers Resolution applied."[64]

The Line-Item Veto.   In addition, Presidents continue to try to stretch their constitutional and statutory powers. In recent years, for example, some sought to add an item veto to the powers of the presidency. The **item**, or **line-item**, **veto**, for example, would let the President veto selective parts of appropriation bills, while signing the rest into law. President Reagan, for example, repeatedly called for this new power, arguing it was necessary to cut the budget deficit. If granted, the item veto would increase presidential influence over the budget-making process and probably presidential dominance of the entire congressional process.

Through all these devices, American Presidents have sought to expand their formal powers and thereby increase their ability to reach their goals of governance, political leadership, and policy making. Even these expansions have not been sufficient, however, and either because of necessity or political convenience, Presidents also have sought to create and then exercise political powers as well.

Creating and Exercising Political Power

Over the course of American history, there has been an impressive expansion of the formal powers of the presidency. These formal powers, however, only buy the President into the policy-making game; they do not make him the key player. President Carter, for example, had the same formal powers as President Reagan—but Carter was not a key player and Reagan was. It is like poker, all the players know the rules and all get the same number of cards. But some win more than others. It is the same in the policy-making game. Some Presidents do better than others—the ones with an edge.

Through the enactment of his taxing and spending policies in 1981, President Reagan created and exercised new political powers. Through those pol-

---

[63] Robert Scigliano, "The War Powers Resolution and the War Powers," in Joseph M. Bessette and Jeffrey Tulis, eds., *The Presidency in the Constitutional Order* (Baton Rouge, Louisiana: Louisiana State University Press, 1981), pp. 115–153.

[64] Quoted in *Inquiry*, 26 June 1978.

icies, the President was able to redefine political reality by letting the federal deficit grow to the point where people worried more about reducing the deficit than they did about meeting the needs of the poor, for example. According to Daniel Patrick Moynihan, the Democratic senator from New York: "The policy was the Administration's deliberate decision to create deficits for strategic, political purposes. . . . The strategy was to induce a deficit and use that as grounds for dismantling . . . a fair amount of the social legislation of the preceding 50 years."[65] In this way, President Reagan's policies altered both economic conditions and people's perceptions of what government should do about them.

As a result of his legislative successes in 1981, President Reagan created for himself new power which he proceeded to use to advance his policy agenda. From 1981 on, policy makers and the public assumed that the assault on the welfare state was serious. They reacted accordingly. Some jumped on the personnel carrier, others prepared to fight a protracted war of attrition. But almost everyone ended up playing the game that Reagan had created. Whether they wanted to or not, other policy makers had to react to the prevailing presumption: the social welfare role of the federal government would shrink. As David Stockman put it in 1985, surveying his four and one-half years as Budget Director, "There have been some fairly fundamental attitudinal changes. Nobody is starting new spending programs. Nobody is proposing that every problem can be solved with another federal effort."[66]

Future Presidents may not be as successful as President Reagan in creating and exercising political power. Whether or not they are will depend on the use they make of the key sources of political power: image, timing, and persuasion.

Image. Presidents create power by cultivating the image of power. The popular image is all-important. Both philosophers and politicos know it, although not all can apply the lesson. Thomas Hobbes, the philosopher, thought that the reputation of power was power. Patrick H. Caddell, Jimmy Carter's pollster and campaign advisor, put it somewhat differently, in a pre-inaugural memo to his boss: "Too many good people have been beaten because they tried to substitute substance for style."[67] Unlike the Carter White House, the Reagan Administration both knew the lesson and knew how to apply it. Indeed, Reagan's early success in creating and selling his image prompted Judy Woodruff, a former NBC correspondent, to complain: "Reagan White House policy sometimes seems to have more in common with a Procter and Gamble's approach to marketing a new toothpaste than with customary presidential decision-making."[68] For Reagan, personal popularity was a downpayment on

---

[65] Daniel Patrick Moynihan, "Reagan's Inflate-the-Deficit Game," *The New York Times*, 21 July 1985, p. E 21.

[66] Quoted in *The New York Times*, 22 April 1985.

[67] Quoted in James T. Wooten, "Pre-Inaugural Memo Urged Carter to Stress Style over Substance," *The New York Times*, 4 May 1977, p. 1.

[68] Judy Woodruff (with Kathleen Maxa), *This Is Judy Woodruff at the White House* (Reading, Mass.: Addison-Wesley, 1982), p. 133.

presidential influence. Each successful exercise of presidential influence added to the President's power base, his capacity to exercise more influence.

Presidents try to cultivate images that expand their informal powers. Modern Presidents understand the importance of their image and work hard to shape a useful one. What is a useful image? Writing in the early 1500s, Niccolo Machiavelli attempted to define for his prince, Lorenzo the Magnificient, the best image: "He should seem to be all mercy, faith, integrity, humanity, and religion. . . . Everybody sees what you appear to be, but few feel what you are, and those few will not dare to oppose themselves to the many, who have the majesty of the state to defend them. . . ."[69]

Most modern Presidents have stumbled in their pursuit of this ideal, although some have come closer than others. Franklin D. Roosevelt, for example, created a buoyant, optimistic image when it was most needed. "Meeting him," said Winston Churchill, "was like opening a bottle of champagne."[70] The image was not accidental. Trying to convince the country that it could recover from its own crippling disease, the Great Depression, Franklin Roosevelt purposefully misled the nation about the severity of his own disease, as Hugh Gregory Gallagher points out in *FDR's Splendid Deception*.[71] Jimmy Carter also understood the importance of image, although he created one that eroded, rather than expanded, his personal power. Picture Jimmy Carter, flying into Washington for the first time as the President of the United States. See him coming down the ramp of Air Force 1—carrying his own suitcase. A touching, but politically stupid, symbol. Having lowered himself to the level of the people, he would never rise above them or, more importantly, he would never be able to inspire them to rise above their own narrow self-interests. In contrast, Ronald Reagan fashioned an enormously attractive image, one that enjoyed wide-spread popular appeal: "Ronald Reagan is a mood that seeped through the land like the beguiling scent of honeysuckle on a soft Georgia night. Millions have been soothed and seduced."[72] Reagan's image was so popular that the American public simply was not interested in hearing about his verbal slips or the transgressions of his staff. In begrudging admiration for his ability to disassociate his positive image from the often harsh criticisms of his policies and of some of his appointees, Congresswoman Patricia Schroeder (D., Colo.) dubbed his the "Teflon Presidency." These examples suggest a general lesson. A President's personal image is political capital, a resource that can be converted into political power.

By cultivating their popular image, modern Presidents personalize the presidency and encourage people to think of them as though they were the government, the source of all solutions to society's problems. This, what Theodore Lowi calls the **plebiscitary presidency**, is a Faustian bargain a

---

[69] Niccolo Machiavelli, *The Prince* (New York: New American Library, 1952), p. 94.

[70] Quoted in *The New York Times*, 30 January 1982.

[71] Hugh Gregory Gallagher, *FDR's Splendid Deception* (New York: Dodd, Mead, 1985).

[72] *Time*, 27 August 1984, p. 22.

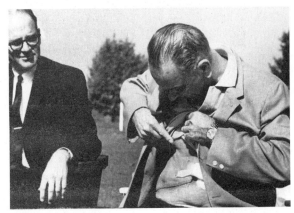

Jimmy Carter hurt his own image when he decided to appear no better than anyone else, as he carried his own luggage and walked the length of his inaugural parade. Carter's mistake, however, was not as damaging as one made by President Johnson, when he listened to Bill Moyers, his press advisor, showed the press the scar from his gall bladder operation, and uncorked the ink for the cartoonists' pens.

President strikes with the American people.[73] The plebiscitary leader is a charismatic figure, one with whom the people easily bond. This was true of Lyndon Johnson, for most of his career. Robert Caro, in his biography of Johnson, freezes a brief moment during one of Johnson's congressional campaign rallies:

> The people before him were, many of them, people he had seen for the first time only a few minutes before. But as a result of his brief conversations with them, he could attach to their faces not only names but circumstances of their lives—and, in so doing, could make them feel that their destiny was linked to Roosevelt's destiny, and to Lyndon Johnson's.[74]

In exchange for their political support, plebiscitary Presidents relinquish their fallibility; they will suffer ridicule and loss of power if they fail to meet the public's inflated expectations. Unfortunately, the damage is more than personal; the office and the political system as a whole also suffer. As James MacGregor Burns points out: "Plebiscitary leadership is classically short-run, unstable, ineffective, irresponsible."[75]

Modern Presidents try to cultivate a favorable image by manipulating the mass media. Franklin Roosevelt was the first modern President to see the need and to master the techniques. Roosevelt learned from the mistakes of his

---

[73] Theodore J. Lowi, *The Personal President: Power Invested, Power Unfilled* (New York: Vintage, 1983), p. 416.

[74] Robert A. Caro, *The Years of Lyndon Johnson: The Path to Power* (New York: Vintage, 1983), p. 416.

[75] James MacGregor Burns, *The Power to Lead: The Crisis of the American Presidency*, (New York: Simon and Schuster, 1984), p. 159.

predecessor, Herbert Hoover. As the Depression grew worse, so too did Hoover's. Turning inward, Hoover isolated himself from the press and the people, leaving them free to draw their own conclusions about the country and its leader. Roosevelt set out to control the press, through charm if possible, and if not through intimidation. Usually, the charm was enough. For example, when asked by Roosevelt why he had stopped attending presidential press conferences, Arthur Krock, an influential columnist, replied: "Because, I can't keep my objectivity when I'm close to you and watching you in action. You charm me so much that when I go back to write a comment on the proceedings, I can't keep it in balance."[76] Sometimes, however, charm did not work, and Roosevelt would browbeat and harass reporters, once going so far as to present an Iron Cross to a reporter who had written a story friendly to Germany. [77] President John F. Kennedy also excelled at the task, enhancing his image while using it to manipulate televised press conferences: " . . . he was so good, so smart, so fresh, so intuitive, as he manipulated from the very first with a powerful new weapon without seeming to manipulate. That was his real skill. Manipulation au naturel."[78] As President, Ronald Reagan continued the tradition and imposed new order on televised press conferences by having reporters sit in assigned seats, thereby letting him call everyone, even strangers, by their first name—"a piece of flattery that feeds the ego of the obscure correspondent as well as making the President seem all-knowing."[79] The examples reinforce the general point: a positive image is never thrust on Presidents—it is deliberately and carefully cultivated.

Timing. A President's understanding of the importance of timing and his ability to sequence events also contribute to his informal powers. Good timing, for example, can catch swings of public opinion and build momentum behind the President's policies. Reagan and those around him had instinctively great timing. After the assassination attempt, for example, Reagan's personal popularity shot up and he moved to exploit it. In his first televised appearance after the attempt, before a joint session of Congress, Reagan focused the nation's attention on the centerpiece of his first term, his economic program, and pushed for its enactment. Reagan's ability to sequence events properly also contributed to his policy successes and to the political capital he earned from them. Confronting his first major crisis, the threatened strike of the air traffic controllers, for example, the Reagan administration gradually escalated its rhetoric, waiting for the controllers to walk out. In this way, the controllers appeared petulant, not the President, and the President's eventual ultimatum to end the strike or be fired looked more reasonable than it would have at first.

---

[76] Arthur Krock, *Memoirs: Intimate Recollections of Twelve American Presidents from Theodore Roosevelt to Richard Nixon* (London: Cassell, 1968), p. 180.

[77] Timothy Crouse, *The Boys on the Bus* (New York: Ballantine Books, 1975).

[78] David Halberstam, *The Powers That Be* (New York: Dell, 1984), p. 325.

[79] Robert D. Hershey, Jr., "Taming of the News Conference," in *The New York Times*, 24 May 1984, p. 12.

THE PRESIDENCY: THE PERSONIFICATION OF POWER

Later, in 1986, the United States conducted its air strike against Libya only after a gradual media campaign had publically established Libyan responsibility for terrorist acts against Americans in West Germany. In President Reagan's case and in general, good timing and good sequencing can increase a President's informal powers and stretch out their value.

A presidential term also has its own rhythm, an electoral governance cycle, which creates some openings while slamming shut others. Because of this cycle, Presidents who would realize their goals have less time than they think and fewer good opportunities than they might imagine. There is what Hedrick Smith, a *New York Times* journalist, calls "the life cycle of the modern American Presidency": " . . . flashy freshman beginnings, followed by sophomore slump, with some third-year recovery or dazzling achievement, like Richard Nixon's opening to China or Jimmy Carter's Camp David accords."[80]

In addition, second terms close in on Presidents; they are " . . . afflicted with a kind of political Alzheimer's disease, a progressive and incurable loss of potency leading sooner or later to terminal lame duckery."[81] The symptoms have varied in different administrations. President Johnson, embroiled in controversy over the Vietnam War, had to take himself out of the race for his party's nomination; Nixon, under the threat of impeachment, had to resign; and even Ike, the last President to serve two full terms, was crippled in the first year of his second term, when Congress approved only 37 percent of his legislative requests (as compared with 73 percent in the first year of his first term). Going into his second term, even Ronald Reagan had some difficulty, especially when he failed to control his agenda and tried to push simultaneously for budget cuts and tax reform. Throughout history, the pattern repeats, as second term Presidents try to do too much, just when other policy makers are least likely to follow.

The 1978 Camp David summit negotiations between Egypt and Israel was one of the highlights of Jimmy Carter's presidency. Shown here are the late Anwar Sadat (left), President Carter and Menachem Begin (right).

---

[80] Quoted in *The New York Times*, 10 January 1982.

[81] Morton M. Kondracke, Washington Bureau Chief of *Newsweek* magazine, quoted in *Newsweek*, 10 June 1985, p. 23.

Persuasion. To increase their power and its efficacy, modern Presidents must persuade both (1) elites and (2) the masses. There are different techniques for the two targets, although gains with one usually translate into gains with the other.

1. Elite persuasion. Presidents are most successful in persuading elites when they discover their needs and when they are willing to meet them. Presidents discover the needs of others through their staff and through their ability to read people, or simply by asking. President Reagan, for example, sometimes ended his lobbying calls to members of Congress with the invitation: "What can I do to help you make up your mind?"[82]

    When convinced it is important to win the support of another player, Presidents accommodate others in whatever way they can, through granting or withholding support on legislation or through the granting of more personal favors, such as a weekend at the President's Camp David Retreat, or even presidential cuff links. In this, Presidents are "jugglers of motives."[83] At its worst, this form of persuasion is little more than crass deal making, backscratching that leaves only a few better off, as when dairy producers win bigger milk subsidies in exchange for their campaign donations and political support. At its best, this form of persuasion also serves society, as when federal spending on interstate highways creates jobs, fattens pocketbooks, enriches campaign coffers *and* helps develop the nation's infrastructure in a manner that fosters economic growth. In a pluralistic democracy where people seldom rally around common public purposes, it usually is necessary to persuade people by linking their private wants with broader public purposes.

    Elite persuasion is essential to the task of creating and exercising presidential power, although it is seldom a visible or obvious process. Indeed, when the President's power is most visible, it is most weak, as is made clear by the **Vantage Point:** The Nature of Presidential Power.

2. Mass persuasion. Presidents attempt to persuade the masses through what is becoming a permanent campaign (described in detail in chapter 7).[84] In the permanent campaign, the White House commissions its own surveys of public opinion and uses the results to gauge public support for alternative policies. Moreover, the effort is ongoing, as polling operations are kept in the field, looking for popular support that might be nursed along with additional rhetoric and gauging the public's response to presidential actions. The practice has a premise: presidential power is scarce and easily eroded. Politically astute Presidents, therefore, rely on their permanent campaign to help them find policy fights they can win—or fights that increase their power, even if they lose them.

---

[82] Quoted in *The New York Times*, 26 July 1985, p. 8.

[83] James Deakin, a former White House correspondent for the *St. Louis Post-Dispatch*, quoted in *The New York Times*, 28 February 1983.

[84] See also Sidney Blumenthal, *The Permanent Campaign*, rev. ed. (New York: Simon and Schuster, 1982).

Permanent campaigning also is essential if a President is to avoid policy fights that deplete his powers. President Reagan's polling operations, for example, showed that the issues of cutbacks in federal funding of abortions and Social Security pensions were political losers, fights that promised a net loss of political support. While paying lip service to such causes, President Reagan focused his attentions and powers elsewhere. It is not necessarily his fault; Presidents have to sell what people are willing to buy, although Presidents who would lead try to influence *what* people are willing to buy. There is no feasible alternative. In the permanent campaign—and in general—politics drives policy making.

■ To overcome the formidable obstacles that block the realization of their goals, Presidents must expand their formal powers and find ways to create and exercise informal, political power.

SUMMARY

The popular expectations that surround the presidency mean that its occupant must govern, by administering the operations of the executive branch, make policy, primarily by seizing control of the nation's agenda, and demonstrate political leadership, by persuading both other policy-making elites and the mass public.

In his attempt to realize these goals, the President is constrained by the Constitution, federalism, civil liberties, public opinion, interest groups, political parties, the electoral system, the mass media, his own preferences and actions, the policy-making process as a whole, and all the other institutions of the national government.

To overcome these obstacles, Presidents try to: (1) expand their formal powers, as they have through the use of executive agreements, executive orders, executive privilege, budgetary impoundments, and war powers and (2) create and exercise informal, political power, especially by building a favorable image and through good timing and effective persuasion.

Key Terms

supply-side economics
budget-making process
reconciliation process
institutionalized presidency
nepotism
patronage
iron triangles
executive agreements

executive orders
executive privilege
impoundment
war powers
item or line-item veto
plebiscitary presidency
presidential power

Review and Reflection

1. Do you think Ronald Reagan will be judged a great President? Why or why not?

2. What are the major goals of the presidency?

3. What constrains the President's ability to realize these goals?

4. What can a President do to overcome these constraints?

5. Do you think it is proper for the President to expand the office's formal powers or to try to create and exercise additional political power?

Supplemental Readings

The literature divides easily into three major categories: textbooks, case studies, and analyses that usually integrate a number of cases within some overall theme.

The classic, authoritative textbooks are *Corwin* and *Koenig*.

Some of the most fascinating case studies are those written by *Caro, Dallek, Donovan, Greenstein,* and *Wills*.

In the still fascinating but more analytical category are *Barber, Burns, Kernell, Kessel, Leuchtenburg, Lynn and Whitman, Neustadt,* and *Wayne*.

Barber, James David. *The Presidential Character: Predicting Performance in the White House.* Englewood Cliffs, NJ: Prentice-Hall, 1977.

Burns, James MacGregor. *The Power To Lead: The Crisis of the American Presidency.* New York: Simon and Schuster, 1984.

Caro, Robert. *The Years of Lyndon Johnson: The Path To Power.* New York: Vintage, 1981.

Corwin, Edward S. *The President: Office and Powers, 1787–1984.* 5th rev. ed. New York: New York University Press, 1984.

Dallek, Robert. *Ronald Reagan: The Politics of Symbolism.* Cambridge, Mass.: Harvard University Press, 1984.

Donovan, Robert J. *Conflict and Crisis: The Presidency of Harry S. Truman, 1945–1948.* New York: W. W. Norton, 1977.

———. *Tumultuous Years: The Presidency of Harry S. Truman, 1949–1953.* New York: W. W. Norton, 1982.

Greenstein, Fred I. *The Hidden-Hand Presidency: Eisenhower as Leader.* New York: Basic Books, 1982.

Kernell, Samuel. *Going Public: New Strategies of Presidential Leadership.* Washington, D. C.: CQ Press, 1986.

Kessel, John H. *The Domestic Presidency: Decision-Making in the White House*. North Scituate, Mass.: Duxbury Press, 1975.

Koenig, Louis W. *The Chief Executive*. 4th ed. New York: Harcourt Brace Jovanovich, 1981.

Leuchtenburg, William E. *In The Shadow of FDR: From Harry Truman to Ronald Reagan*. Ithaca, New York: Cornell University Press, 1985.

Lynn, Laurence E., Jr., and David deF Whitman. *The President As Policymaker: Jimmy Carter and Welfare Reform*. Philadelphia: Temple University Press, 1981.

Neustadt, Richard E. *Presidential Power: The Politics of Leadership from FDR to Carter*. New York: John Wiley and Sons, 1980.

Wayne, Stephen J. *The Road to the White House: The Politics of Presidential Elections*. 2nd ed. New York: St. Martin's Press, 1983.

Wills, Garry. *Nixon Agonistes: The Crisis of the Self-Made Man*. New York: Mentor, 1979.

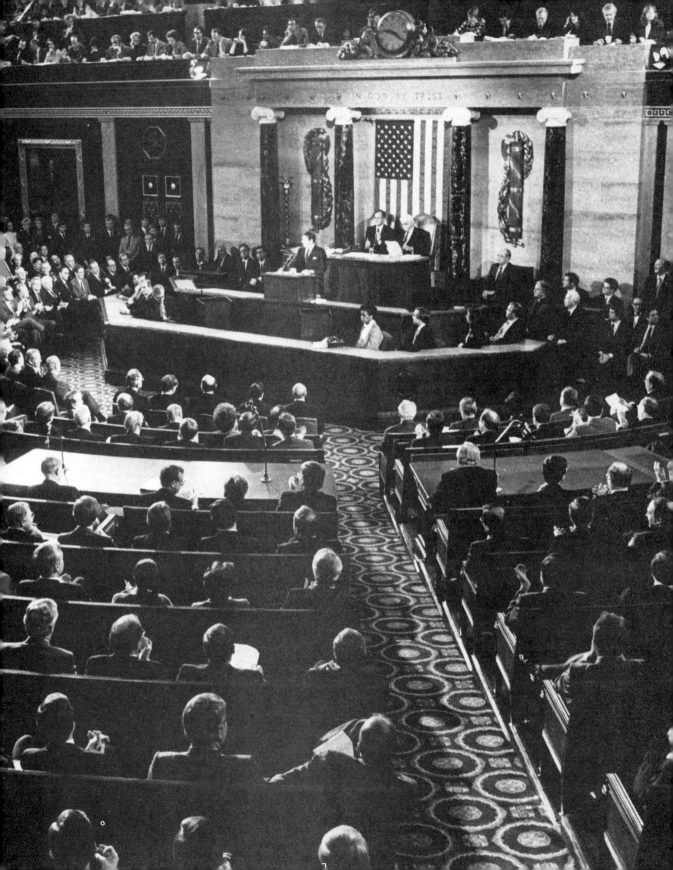

CHAPTER TWELVE

THE CONGRESS
CAN IT GET ITS ACTS TOGETHER?

*I*f you are like most Americans, you probably think more highly of your representative in Congress than of the institution as a whole.

There are good reasons why the whole of Congress seem less desirable than its parts. Indeed, this result is not an accident. Rather, it is the product of constitutional design, historical evolution, and Congress' ongoing efforts to cope with the demands of its many political environments.

Individual members of Congress do some things well, but not others. They, for example, do a good job of realizing their political goals in ways that keep their constituents happy. But their individual efforts often detract from the institution's ability to make policy and to oversee its implementation.

The following Case on one of Congress' continuing struggles with the federal budget is an opportunity for sorting through these impressions and the possible explanations for them. The Case also leads to one dominant insight: Congress is organized in ways that favor the realization of political, over governance and policy-making, goals.

There are exceptions to this insight, of course, instances when the institution does a good or even heroic job of making policy or making sure that policies are faithfully administered. But, the reality always intrudes and shapes almost everything that goes on in Congress: institutional goals will not be performed at the expense of the political careers of the members of the institution. That may help explain why members can advance their own careers, while the institution loses both esteem in the eyes of the public and power in competition with the presidency.

THE NATURE OF CONGRESS

> As a unified and ruthless body, there is virtually no way a Congress can be outmatched by a President. But Congress, of course, is seldom a unified body. Seldom, too, has it been a ruthless body.
> —*President Richard M. Nixon*

Representative William Gray
(D., Pa.)

The Case   The Battle of the Budget, Part II

Late summer, 1985. In the beginning, the participants in the federal budget-making process all seemed committed to reducing expenditures, even though that would provoke angry reactions from constituents and powerful special interest groups. They also acted as though they were committed to maintaining a united front, so that no one participant or group of participants would be totally exposed. As long as the consensus and the coalition held, no one had to accept all the blame.

The commitment and the consensus made Representative Gray's job feasible. William H. Gray III, the Democratic Representative from Philadelphia's largely black Second Congressional District, was in his fourth term in the United States House of Representatives.

As the Chairman of the Budget Committee, Representative Gray knew he had no choice. He had to join the battle of the budget and try to roll back, temporarily at least, the threat posed by the federal deficit.

The battle was unavoidable; others had made it so. For too many years, the members of previous Congresses had done the popular thing, adding new federal programs, expanding others, refusing to raise taxes to pay for it all. They had been able to do all this and claim the credit for it, because they had counted on inflation to increase revenues by kicking taxpayers into higher tax brackets and because they had been willing to have the federal government go into debt to pay for it all. Thus, the role of the federal government grew, as it acquired new and more costly responsibilities for the economic and social well-being of Americans.

The day of reckoning might never have come, if only the growth in government had been matched by a growing public awareness and acceptance that it was a good thing. But that broad base of public support never materialized. It was true that every client group liked its own benefit; the dairy farmers lapped up dairy subsidies and welfare mothers warmed to the prospect of liberalized payments to dependent children. But neither liked the other nor acknowledged the legitimacy of their need. Over time, the irony compounded itself; the federal social welfare role became bigger, more costly, more heavily depended upon, less respected, and more funded out of future, not current, revenues.

The President's legislative successes had worsened the problem. (The story was told in the brief Case beginning chapter 11.) The President had been extraordinarily successful in cutting taxes but not as successful in cutting expenditures. Now, in January of 1985, the President remained steadfast in his opposition to a tax increase. Meanwhile, the huge federal deficit was locked over Washington like a permanent high pressure area. The deficit now dominated the policy-making process; everything else had been pushed off the agenda. The deficit's domination was shown in the questions people did not ask. Even such traditional liberals as the Speaker of the House, Tip O'Neill (D., Mass.), acknowledged, "there are many areas where the Federal Government can save money without hurting the needy."[1] In general, no one asked whether the deficit had to be cut. Rather, everyone asked how much it had to be cut.

As the chair of the House Budget Committee, Representative Gray was supposed to put together an overall budget for the federal government, one that showed the total amount of money that could be spent next year, how it could be spent, and the relationship between total revenues and total expenditures. Under the House rules and past practice, his committee would hammer out an agreement and bring a budget resolution to the floor of the House for debate and hopefully adoption. Meanwhile, the Budget Committee in the Senate would be going through similar steps.

Representative Gray fully expected that the Senate budget resolution probably would be different, however, since Republicans held the majority there. But he and others were acting as though they believed that they would be able to negotiate the differences in a conference committee and then take the compromise back to be ratified in their respective chambers. If all this happened, the budget resolution would bring order to the legislative process, because the Congress would have committed itself to live within certain budgetary guidelines. It was not going to be easy, however.

To reduce the federal deficit without increasing taxes, the blood had to flow. Representative Gray wanted to make sure that it was not the blood of people he cared about—the poor, the ill, the undernourished, and the poorly housed residents of his district. In addition, his Democratic colleagues in the House shared some of these concerns and had their own political and policy interests to defend. As far as they were concerned, the cuts had to come from some place other than domestic spending on social services.

The majority of the members of Gray's committee and in the House as a whole favored large cuts in military spending. The military budget seemed bloated to many and its supporters were on the defensive, fielding stories of military waste and fraud. But the cuts had to be made quietly, behind a united front, since many of the Democrats in the House feared the campaign charge that they were "soft" on defense. For a while, at least, the coalition held.

With bipartisan support of its members, the House Budget Committee developed a budget resolution that committed Congress to reduce the projected deficit by $56 billion. It did it by freezing the military budget at its 1985 level (a real decrease, because of inflation), while leaving intact the previously scheduled cost-of-living increases in Social Security payments. Meanwhile, the Senate Budget Committee had come up with an equally large reduction, but through different cuts. The Senate budget resolution was a mirror image, increasing the military budget so that it kept even with inflation, while decreasing the real level of Social Security payments. Thus, the battle lines were drawn, although the House seemed in a superior position.

In its negotiations with the House, the Senate started off in an inferior position, since twenty-two Republican Senators were due to come up for re-election in

---

[1] *The New York Times*, 2 February 1985.

1986, and they feared the electoral wrath of the nation's 36 million Social Security recipients. Those twenty-two, especially the sixteen first termers who rode in on the President's coattails in 1980, were nervous about tinkering with Social Security—or any other federal aid program.

Nevertheless, the majority leader, Robert Dole, (R., Kansas) held the Senate coalition together. Gradually, however, its members (and others it turned out) began to feel the mounting political opposition to their proposed Social Security cuts. In addition, their anxieties grew, especially after the Democratic Congressional Campaign Committee, for example, mailed out a new bumper sticker, "Save Social Security Again—Vote Democratic." On the other hand, the Senate and House Republicans took comfort from having the President on their side. No wonder they reacted so badly when President Reagan abandoned them.

Unexpectedly, the President announced that he was not in favor of freezing scheduled cost-of-living increases in Social Security payments. With that announcement, the Republicans in Congress were left out on a limb, one that they had gone out on only because of the President's earlier support for a freeze. They now felt exposed and vulnerable. Their reaction was swift and intense. In his news conference on July 12, Senator Dole accused the President and both parties in the House of "surrendering to the deficit." Dole's words, however, were a tepid reflection of the anger of other Senate Republicans. Warren B. Rudman (R., N.H.), one of those who voted for the Social Security cut despite his upcoming 1986 re-election bid obviously was upset when he said, "I just think people feel they flew a kamikaze mission and ended up in flames and got nothing for it."[2] Senator Charles Grassley (R., Iowa) could not have gone much further than he did, saying, "It would be better if the President sticks behind us rather than Tip O'Neill. I feel if the President can't support us he ought to keep his mouth shut."[3] At that moment, the budget-making process died, as the Senate backed off from its attempt to cut Social Security, as the House continued to refuse to cut other expenditures, and as the President continued to refuse to raise taxes.

The deficit, of course, did not die. And neither did the congressional fear of being blamed for it die. What the participants in the budget process did was create an alternative. Reunited by their common political need, they passed the **Gramm-Rudman Act**, which mandated automatic, across-the-board cuts in spending. (See Nelson Polsby's analysis of the politics of Gramm-Rudman on page 354.) Under the act's provisions, budget cuts would be made and the blood would flow, but, hopefully it would not be the blood of members of the Congress. After all, they could say, the cuts were the law's fault, not theirs.

Insights

This story of one of a string of failures in the federal budget-making process reveals a lot about Congress, its goals, and the ways it tries to realize them. We next consider one broad insight and its implications. (For other insights, see the **Vantage Point**: David Stockman's View of the Federal Budget-Making Process.)

---

[2] *The New York Times*, 12 July 1985.

[3] *Ibid.*

Congress is organized in ways that tend to encourage its members to pursue political, and not necessarily governance and policy, goals. Because of the way Congress is organized and because of the way it functions, many different and often competing interests flow quite freely into the congressional process and the members must respond to them. As a result, the members of Congress are under constant pressure to fight political and therefore interminable battles. The battles are interminable because the issues are. Do more nuclear missiles make us safer? Should the federal government guarantee that older Americans can maintain their standard of living, no matter what the rate of inflation? Are the unemployed entitled to thirty-two or fifty-two weeks of compensation? Are corporations paying their fair share of taxes? Should federal subsidies be used to guarantee the income of farmers?

The political controversies forced on Congress are issues without final answers, so objective that all could embrace them without dispute. There is no objective way of determining, for example, whether this society should let 100 or 1000 farmers go bankrupt next year. In the absence of an objective rule, members of Congress, just like the rest of us, fight it out politically.

As you will see, the organization of Congress encourages and rewards this political focus; it does not facilitate or reward an equally strong focus on the making or administering of policy.

■ Congress does a very good job of reflecting society's political disputes. This, of course, does not mean that Congress, necessarily, will (1) be able to adopt policies that resolve those disputes or, if it did, (2) be able to oversee the implementation of these policies. (Indeed, it will turn out that Congress is well-equipped to represent societal conflicts, but poorly equipped to resolve them or to monitor the attempt to resolve them.)

THE ORGANIZATION OF CONGRESS

> The (congressional) system is complicated, fragmented and messy—and was intended to be. That's what this place is for. It's a forum of tugging and hauling and fighting.
> —John Brademas, the former Democratic representative from Indiana and Majority Whip in the House of Representatives

Organizational Structure

The contemporary organizational characteristics of Congress are a product of its constitutional design and its historical evolution.

DAVID STOCKMAN'S VIEW OF THE FEDERAL BUDGET-MAKING PROCESS

*I*n an interview published in 1981[1] that could only increase the sales of the book he would later write[2], David A. Stockman, President Reagan's first Director of the Office of Management and Budget (OMB), gave his views of the federal budget-making process. (For an overview of the formal stages of the budget process, see the Figure.) Later, after he had left government for an extremely lucrative position as an investment banker with the Wall Street firm of Salomon Brothers, Mr. Stockman elaborated his views of the budget process.

In early 1981, after assuming his post, David Stockman sharpened his ax and put together a budget that included $41.4 billion in cuts, including, for example, reductions in minimum Social Security benefits, Medicaid, food stamps, federal aid to education, federal job training programs, federal subsidies for businesses engaged in international trade, milk-price supports, and defense spending. The resulting budget, President Reagan's first, sailed through Congress, its passage assured by the combination of Ronald Reagan's personal popu-

larity and David Stockman's apparent expertise.

In late 1981, however, after less than a year as the Director of the OMB, David Stockman confessed that his expertise was less than it appeared to be. In commenting on previous estimates of anticipated expenditures and revenues that eventually determined the size of the federal deficit, Stockman confessed: "None of us really understands what's going on with all these numbers."[3] The phrase stood out in the text of the interview, was picked up by the news media, and resulted in a reprimand from President Reagan (Stockman's celebrated trip to the "woodshed").

In 1986, after four years as the Director of the OMB, David Stockman had become even more cynical about the budget process and more pessimistic about the future of the country. Indeed, Stockman had concluded that the Reagan revolution, which he had hoped would roll back the welfare state, had failed. As he wrote in *The Triumph of Politics*:

> . . . no significant welfare state premise had changed. The giant Social Security en-

Stockman's "trip to the woodshed" also resulted in some editorial cartoons, such as this one.

titlement is unchanged: UDAG (the Urban Development Action Grants Program) still builds its hotels; the cattle ranches still get cheap federal grass on which to graze their cattle. From top to bottom, the welfare state budget rolls along much as before.[4]

The failure, Stockman believed, ultimately, was the responsibility of Republican politicians, their constituents, and special interest groups. In Stockman's own words:

> In the end, it was up to them (GOP politicians) to decide; it was they who had been elected by the American people to struggle with such choices. In the process, they heard from the squeaky wheels and interest groups; they heard from the local voters and grass roots constituencies.
>
> They decided when all was said and done to ratify the American welfare state as it had evolved by 1980. They decided not to roll back history.[5]

[1] William Greider, "The Education of David Stockman," *Atlantic* 248 (1981): 27–54.

[2] David A. Stockman, *The Triumph of Politics: Why the Reagan Revolution Failed* (New York: Harper & Row, 1986).

[3] Greider, "The Education of . . .", p. 38.

[4] Stockman, *The Triumph . . .*, pp. 401–402.

[5] *Ibid.*, p. 402.

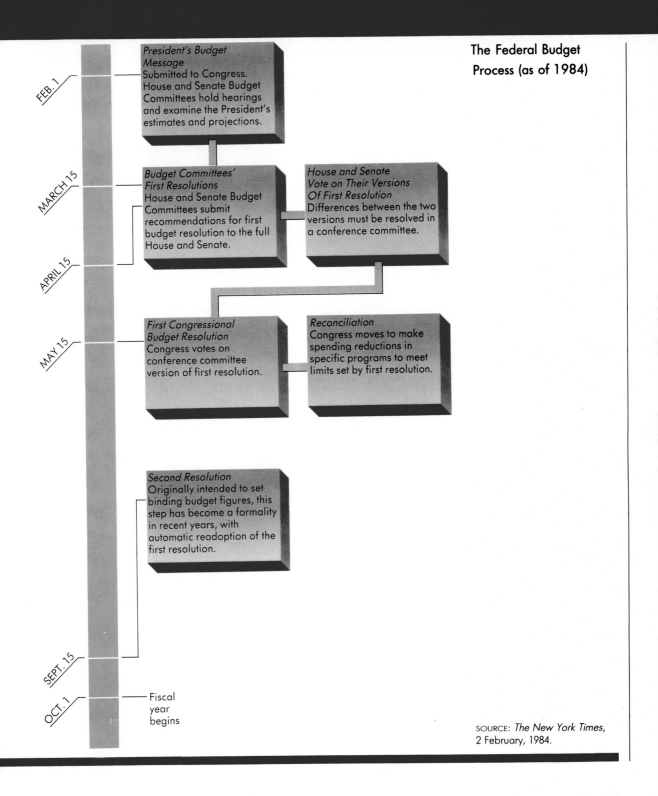

The Federal Budget Process (as of 1984)

FEB. 1

President's Budget Message
Submitted to Congress. House and Senate Budget Committees hold hearings and examine the President's estimates and projections.

MARCH 15

Budget Committees' First Resolutions
House and Senate Budget Committees submit recommendations for first budget resolution to the full House and Senate.

House and Senate Vote on Their Versions Of First Resolution
Differences between the two versions must be resolved in a conference committee.

APRIL 15

MAY 15

First Congressional Budget Resolution
Congress votes on conference committee version of first resolution.

Reconciliation
Congress moves to make spending reductions in specific programs to meet limits set by first resolution.

Second Resolution
Originally intended to set binding budget figures, this step has become a formality in recent years, with automatic readoption of the first resolution.

SEPT. 15

OCT. 1

Fiscal year begins

SOURCE: *The New York Times*, 2 February, 1984.

Constitutional Design. The Founders made it clear that they viewed Congress as the center of authority, the primary policy-making institution in the new national government.[4] "In republican government, the legislative authority necessarily predominates," James Madison had written in No. 51 of the *Federalist Papers*.[5] Indeed, the Founders' view of Congress was an extension of their assumption that the national government's authority would be exercised mostly through the making of laws, especially laws that raised revenue. Since lawmaking was the main instrument of governmental authority, it was essential that the legislative power be kept somewhat responsive to popular sentiments and therefore, hopefully, restrained. Seeing the institution, and especially the House of Representatives, as "the people's branch," the Founders thought Congress would be mostly in touch with popular sentiments and therefore least likely to abuse the right to make law.

Given their conception, their expectations, and their distrust of executive authority, it made sense for the Founders to write the Constitution as they did: let Congress house the major instrument of government's authority, the right to legislate. The Constitution's Article I began with the legislative power and with a description of the branch that would exercise it. Indeed, the Constitution devoted most of its text to this topic, much less to a discussion of presidential power, and even less to a discussion of judicial power. (Turn to the copy of the Constitution at the back of the book, to compare the amount of space devoted to each branch and its power, in Articles I, II, and III.) Article I's discussion of legislative powers thereby established the constitutional foundations for Congress' future role.

In the early days of the Republic, the national government acted as the Founders thought it would, mostly through the adoption of relatively few laws. Most of these could be easily implemented, without the exertion of a lot of presidential or judicial authority. As Theodore Lowi has written in his classic work, *The End of Liberalism*, "the first century was one of government dominated by Congress and virtually self-executing laws."[6] "Fishbait" Miller, a Democratic doorkeeper of the House of Representatives, put it another way: "In the early days, the Congress didn't spend in a whole year what is now spent in one hour."[7] Self-executing laws worked; congressional subsidies to private entrepreneurs and businesses did help develop the nation's economy. Lowi provides more detail on the congressional role: "Between 1795 and 1887, the

---

[4] For the Founders' hopes and fears for the new Congress, see Max Farrand, *The Framing of the Constitution of the United States* (New Haven, Conn.: Yale University Press, 1913). For historical material on the early Congress, see James S. Young, *The Washington Community, 1800–1828* (New York: Columbia University Press, 1966).

[5] Clinton Rossiter, *The Federalist Papers* (New York: New American Library, 1961), p. 322.

[6] Theodore J. Lowi, *The End of Liberalism: Ideology, Policy, and the Crisis of Public Authority* (New York: W. W. Norton, 1969), p. 128. See also Grant McConnell, *Private Power and American Democracy* (New York: Knopf, 1986).

[7] William Mosely Miller, *Fishbait: The Memoirs of the Congressional Doorkeeper* (New York: Warner Books, 1977), p. 280.

key Federal policies were tariffs, internal improvements, land sales and land grants, development of a merchant fleet and coastal shipping, the post offices, patents and copyrights, and research on how the private sector was doing."[8] Since self-implementing laws needed few bureaucrats to implement them and occasioned few court challenges, Congress, for the nation's first century, was the first among theoretically equal branches of government.

Historical Evolution.   The basic form of Congress, its organizational structure and internal decision-making procedures, still follows the design of Article I: (1) two houses; (2) Representatives serving two-year terms in the House and Senators serving six-year terms in the Senate; (3) representation in the House proportional to population and equal among all states in the Senate; (4) minimum age and residency requirements for election; (5) bills for raising revenue must start in the House before the Senate can react to them; (6) bills must complete a certain obstacle course before they become law or are vetoed by the President; and (7) both houses are still in charge of deciding who is entitled to be a member of the body and what rules they must follow while they are there.

The modern Congress, however, does show many refinements in both its structure and decision-making procedures.[9] Most of these refinements came in the 19th century, as the membership of Congress and the strength of political parties grew, and in the 20th century, following marked increases in the congressional work load. These developments dictated change in both form and function. The House of Representatives, for example, came under particularly strong pressure to find ways of limiting floor debate and regulating the flow of business on to the floor.

A bit like the hemlines on skirts, public confidence in Congress and its policy-making power have moved up and down over time. (See **Table 12.1**.) The movement is a result of two processes. First, there has been a process of interinstitutional conflict, between the President and the Congress, with varying patterns of relative dominance and submission. Second, there is a process of intrainstitutional conflict, as one chamber seeks the upper hand over the other. Both processes are well-illustrated in American history.

The Era of Presidential Dominance. In the beginning, the Congress was effectively dominated by the executive branch. Alexander Hamilton, for example, George Washington's Secretary of the Treasury, personally pressed his plan for economic development on Congress. So hard and successfully did he push that Jefferson would complain to Washington that Hamilton's "system flowed from principles adverse to liberty, and was calculated to undermine and demolish the republic, by creating an influence of his department over the

---

[8] Lowi, *End of Liberalism*, p. 128.

[9] The history of the two houses of Congress is well-told in George B. Galloway, *History of the House of Representatives* (New York: Crowell, 1962) and George H. Haynes, *The Senate of the United States, 2 vols.* (Boston: Houghton Mifflin, 1938).

TABLE 12.1 Public Confidence in Congress

Since 1973, the Gallup Poll has asked Americans how much confidence they had in the Congress, as well as other governmental and nongovernmental institutions. The percentage of people responding a "great deal" of confidence or "quite a lot" of confidence in each institution are as follows:

	1985	1984	1983	1981	1979	1977	1975	1973
Church or Organized Religion	66%	64%	62%	64%	65%	64%	68%	66%
Military	61	58	53	50	54	57	58	NA
U.S. Supreme Court	56	51	42	46	45	46	49	44
Banks and Banking	51	51	51	46	60	NA	NA	NA
Public Schools	48	47	39	42	53	54	NA	58
Congress	**39**	**29**	**28**	**29**	**34**	**40**	**40**	**42**
Newspapers	35	34	38	35	51	NA	NA	39
Big Business	31	29	28	20	32	33	34	26
Television	29	25	25	25	38	NA	NA	37
Organized Labor	28	30	26	28	36	39	38	30

NA: Question not asked in that year

SOURCE: The Gallup Poll, 14 July 1985

members of the legislature."[10] The election of one of Jefferson's allies, James Madison, brought a quick end to executive supremacy over Congress, however. Madison, the strong behind-the-scenes leader in the Constitutional Convention, lost control of his party's members in Congress. Emboldened, they pushed him into war with England and, under the Speakership of Henry Clay, took effective control of the House and used it to overshadow the presidencies of Madison, Monroe, and John Quincy Adams.

Meanwhile, the Senate too grew in influence, soon outstripping the House. The Senate's smaller size and its constitutional roles in presidential appointments and in treaty making provided opportunities to advance the prestige of Senators and thereby the Senate. In the Senate, for example, the Missouri Compromise was fashioned to cap the expansion of slavery. In the Senate, the relatively even split of pro- and anti-states fueled the great debates over slavery before the outbreak of the Civil War in 1861. It was an age of giants—Daniel Webster, Henry Clay (seeking a bigger stage in the Senate), and John C. Calhoun—and the Senate's supremacy soared, eclipsing both the presidency

[10] Paul Leicester Ford, ed., *The Writings of Thomas Jefferson*, vol. 6 (New York: G. P. Putnam's, 1895), p. 102.

THE CONGRESS: CAN IT GET ITS ACTS TOGETHER?

Henry Clay addresses the Senate to plead for the passage of the Compromise of 1850.

and the House of Representatives. The contrast in the apparent prestige of the Senate and its members, in comparison to that enjoyed by "the other body," was striking.

The contrast between the House and the Senate did not escape Alexis de Tocqueville. In *Democracy in America*, Tocqueville would write:

> When one enters the House of Representatives . . . one is struck by the vulgar demeanor of that great assembly. One can often look in vain for a single famous man. . . . A couple of paces away is the entrance to the Senate, whose narrow precincts contain a large proportion of the famous men of America. . . . Every word uttered in this assembly would add luster to the greatest parliamentary debates in Europe.[11]

Although the power and the prestige of the presidency soon expanded, under the press of military necessary and the grease of President Lincoln's political skills, this was an aberration, soon reversed.

---

11 Alexis de Tocqueville, *Democracy in America*, ed. J. P. Mayer, trans. George Lawrence (Garden City, New York: Doubleday & Company, 1969), pp. 200–201.

The Era of Congressional Government. Too badly suppressed under President Lincoln, members of Congress rode roughshod over his successors and over the South during the Reconstruction. Extending to the end of the century, the norm was "congressional government," in Woodrow Wilson's famous phrase. So effectively did Congress expand its power and consolidate its gains in standing committees that Wilson would later write: "the business of the President, occasionally great, is usually not much above routine. Most of the time it is mere administration, mere obedience of directions from the masters of policy, the Standing Committees (of Congress)."[12] But it also was a period of party bosses and patronage, not intellectual giants and stirring debate. The Congress, increasingly dominated by special interest groups, tumbled into popular disrepute, only to be salvaged somewhat by the adoption in 1913, of the 17th Amendment to the Constitution, providing for the popular election of U.S. senators.

The Era of Oscillating Fortunes. Since the turn of the century, the fortunes of Congress and the President have oscillated. Turning inward when countering strong Presidents (Theodore Roosevelt, Woodrow Wilson, Franklin Roosevelt, Lyndon Johnson, and Richard Nixon, for example), Congress tends its own store, often groping for new ways to conduct its business, trying to enhance its policy-making role. The House and the Senate are likely to be engaged in their own tug-of-war, each seeking to buttress its own power, often at the expense of the other.

Following such battles, Congress, or at least one branch of the Congress, often seems better able to reassert its claim for a strong policy-making role. For example, congressional subservience to the presidency became humiliatingly clear under the presidency of Richard Nixon. Partly in reaction, the Congress passed the *War Powers Act of 1973* in an attempt to curb the President's ability to fight a limited war without congressional approval, and the *Budget and Impoundment Control Act of 1974* in an attempt to challenge the President's dominance in budget making. These efforts have not stemmed the flow of power down Pennsylvania Avenue, although they have redraped some of the trappings of power around Congress. The causes of the loss of congressional power simply run too deep.

The Modern Era. The modern era in the history of presidential-executive relations is a product of its past. Beginning in the late 1880s, Congress began to wrestle with the increasingly complicated chore of trying to regulate the commercial activities of a growing economy. Rather than involve itself in what would have been a very difficult and mostly politically thankless task of designing detailed programs and closely regulating their implementation, Congress simply gave this task, and the power to carry it out, to the federal bureaucracy. Theodore Lowi makes this argument, dates the turning point,

---

[12] Woodrow Wilson, *Congressional Government* (New York: Meridian Books, 1956), p. 170. Quoted in Roger H. Davidson and Walter J. Oleszek, *Congress and Its Members* (Washington, D.C.: Congressional Quarterly Press, 1981), p. 38.

and names the occasion: 1887 and the passage of the *Interstate Commerce Act*.[13]

The Interstate Commerce Act established an independent regulatory body, the Interstate Commerce Commission, and charged it with the task of regulating all forms of commercial activity within the United States, including, for example, the setting of railroad rates and the granting of approval for gas and oil line routes. To carry out such responsibilities, Congress gave the Commission the right to act as legislature, chief executive, and judiciary. Specifically, the Commission was given the authority to make rules, implement them, and settle disputes over their interpretation. Since 1887, necessity and political pressure have accelerated the delegation of congressional authority and the growth of the administrative state. Effective policy-making authority, in both domestic and especially foreign policy matters, is increasingly concentrated in the White House.

It will be hard for Congress to reclaim a central role in policy making, because of the enormity of the regulatory chores, the outstanding grants of delegated authority, and the political clout of interest groups and their defenders within the executive branch. For all their posturing about presidential excesses, many members probably do not want Congress to have a more central role in policy making. From their point of view, the Congress functions well because it allows them to claim credit for new programs, while avoiding responsibility and blame for previously enacted ones that do not work.[14] Since the current arrangement serves the political interests of its members, Congress, for the foreseeable future at least, probably will remain relatively subordinate to the presidency in policy making and mostly on the defensive, reacting to presidential policy initiatives.

"The Senatorial Round-House"

In 1887, the Interstate Commerce Commission was created. This cartoon shows the dismay the American railroads felt towards the powers Congress gave the Commission.

Contemporary Organizational Characteristics

There are a large number of "nuts and bolts" that make up the contemporary Congress, as **Table 12.2** reveals. This section, however, focuses primarily on five major organizational characteristics: membership, size, leadership, committees, and staff.

Membership Characteristics.   Congress is a very human institution, and its members and their characteristics are very important determinants of what Congress does. Who are these people? There are many different ways of describing them. We use three: (1) the formal, constitutional requirements for membership; (2) popular images; and (3) objective characteristics.

At a formal level, the members of Congress are those who meet the three constitutional requirements: age, citizenship, and residency. In addition, Congress can exercise control over its own membership, by refusing to seat a newly

---

[13] See Lowi, *End of Liberalism*. See especially pp. 128–56.

[14] David R. Mayhew, *Congress: The Electoral Connection* (New Haven: Yale University Press, 1974).

TABLE 12.2 The "Nuts and Bolts" of Congress

Chambers (2) SENATE, HOUSE OF REP
Members (539)
    House Members, with Votes (435)
    House Members, without Votes (5)[1]
    Senate Members (100) 2/STATE
Official "Leaders" (11)
Standing Committees (43)[2]
Subcommittees and "Task Forces"[3] (242)
Chairpersons of Committees and Subcommittees (281)
Personal and Committee Staff Persons (16,000+)
Special, Select, and Joint Committees (approx. 20)
Congressional Support Agencies (4)
Major Buildings (10)
Number of People on the Capitol Hill Payroll (40,000+)

[1] Five members of the House—from the District of Columbia, Guam, American Samoa, Puerto Rico, and the Virgin Islands—can not vote but may speak on the floor, serve on committees, and are permitted to vote in party caucuses.

[2] As of 1985, according to Randall B. Ripley, "Committees and Subcommittees of the 99th Congress," *Congressional Quarterly Special Report* (Washington, D.C.: Congressional Quarterly, Inc., 1985), p. 162.

[3] Some committees have "task forces," instead of subcommittees.

---

elected member or by expelling a member. In general, Congress is reluctant to exercise these prerogatives. A squabbling Congress makes itself look too preoccupied with narrow partisan concerns and too inattentive to broader social problems. Such a Congress loses public confidence and, in the competition with other institutions of government, the chance to play an important role in the policy-making process.

At a subjective level, members of Congress have been fair game for popular stereotypes, which tend toward comic exaggeration, while capturing a bit of the truth:

> "535 high-school class presidents with a few prom queens thrown in."
> —"Fishbait" Miller[15]

> " . . . there is no distinctly native American criminal class except Congress."
> —Mark Twain

> "People who promise to build a bridge even if there is no river."

In their surface characteristics—their age, occupation, religion, gender, race—members of Congress look very different from most of us, as you can see from the data in **Table 12.3**.

On these and other surface characterictics, the members of Congress are not representative of the population of the country. The makeup of Congress seriously underrepresents all the following: youth, blue collar workers, the

---

[15] William Mosely Miller, *Fishbait*, p. 13.

THE CONGRESS: CAN IT GET ITS ACTS TOGETHER?

TABLE 12.3 Members of Congress Are Objectively Different from the Rest of Us

	Members of Congress	Most Americans
Age	49.2 years (average)	30.6 years (median)
Occupation[1]		
Lawyers	47.3%	.51%
Bankers and Businesspersons	30.3%	21.6%[1]
Farmers	6.9%	2.9%
Religion[2]		
Protestant	58.6%	33.0%
Catholic	25.8%	22.1%
Jewish	6.2%	2.6%
Gender		
Males	80.4%	48.7%
Race		
White	96.8%	85.6%

[1] The estimate of "bankers and businesspersons" in the civilian labor force includes all those the *Statistical Abstract* lists as managers and professionals, excluding medical and health professionals.

[2] The religious makeup of Congress is reflected in the self-reports of members. The religious composition of the country is based on church membership figures, which probably underestimate the number of people who feel they belong.

SOURCE: The characteristics of "the average member of Congress" are for members of the 97th Congress, which began on January 5, 1981. Information is drawn from the *Guide to Congress*, 3rd ed. (Washington, D.C.: Congressional Quarterly, Inc., 1982). The characteristics of "the average American" are drawn from the U.S. Bureau of the Census, *Statistical Abstract of the United States: 1984*, 104th ed. (Washington, D.C., 1983).

unemployed, women, blacks, and, in general, the poor. It remains to be seen, however, whether members, in spite of these differences, represent either the will or the interests of their constituencies.

Size Characteristics. **Bicameralism**, the product of the Constitutional Convention's Great Compromise, divides Congress into two chambers of greatly unequal size. The size difference between the Senate and the House of Representatives has also grown over time. As the House grew larger, the relatively smaller number of Senators gave each one greater public visibility and a forum for a potentially large policy-making role.

Senators even today tend to be policy generalists, focusing on broad public policy issues, while their relatively more obsure counterparts in the House tend to specialize on the details of legislation and on oversight of the executive branch. Representatives, perhaps a little jealous, tend to denigrate Senators for their oratorical displays and love to refer to the Senate as "the cave of the winds." Seeing themselves as "workhorses," Representatives tend to dismiss Senators as "show horses." Senators, in contrast, often disdainfully look down on the narrow preoccupations of rabble-rousing Representatives, some of whom actually presume to speak to them in less than reverential tones, and disparagingly refer to the House as "the other body."

These differences in public prominence, policy-making influence, and work styles affect the internal dynamics of the two bodies as well. The interpersonal relations among Senators, for example, are governed by a rule of **comity**, the hallmark of which is mutual courtesy and deference. Among Representatives, however, interpersonal relations are more openly conflictual and verbal exchanges can be more abusive.

Largely because of their size difference, the House and the Senate also have developed different ways of conducting their business. "Conducting business" means finding a way of deciding what will be done, when it will be done, and how it will be done. Because of its size and because of large differences in the status of its members, the House has to rely on much more formal and hierarchical mechanisms for conducting its business. The Senate, in contrast, is a much more informal body and can rely on mutual agreements to conduct its business. These ways of conducting business imply other important structural differences. In the House, for example, "leaders" are much more important than they are in the Senate.

Leadership Characteristics. There are eleven "official" leaders in Congress, although the Constitution mentions only three: the Speaker of the House, the President (or presiding officer) of the Senate (the Vice-President of the United States), and the **President pro tempore** of the Senate who acts in the absence of the Vice-President. The Constitution's Article I also gives the two houses the power to choose other officials, however. This they do, voting along party lines.

The key officials of Congress are party leaders. In the House, the majority party elects one of its own as **Speaker**. In addition to their constitutionally mandated officials, both the House and the Senate have four main party leaders: the **majority leader**, the **majority whip** (the majority leader's second in command), the **minority leader**, and his lieutenant, the **minority whip**.

Congressional leaders hold weak reins, since their power is seriously constrained. Lacking the power to command or to enforce party loyalty, congressional leaders rely on their personal skills of persuasion. This is especially true in the informal collegial Senate than it is in the more tightly run House, where party leaders act more forcefully in their attempts to keep members in line, especially on key votes. Even in the House, however, party leaders will not try to force someone to vote against their district, especially if they believe it could hurt them at the polls.

By the force of their personality and the skills of their vocation, some formal congressional officials are able to exercise some degree of leadership. For

Congressional Leaders Are Party Leaders

When the 99th Congress convened in January of 1985, one of its first tasks was to elect its leaders: the Speaker of the House, the majority and minority party leaders and the whips in both the House and the Senate. Here is who was chosen:

House Leaders

Speaker	Majority Leader	Majority Whip	Minority Leader	Minority Whip

Thomas P. O'Neill, Jr. (D., Mass.)	James C. Wright, Jr. (D., Texas)	Thomas S. Foley, (D., Wash.)	Robert H. Michel, (R., Ill.)	Trent Lott, (R., Miss.)

Senate Leaders

Majority Leader	Majority Whip	Minority Leader	Minority Whip

Robert Dole, (R., Kan.)	Alan K. Simpson, (R., Wyo.)	Robert C. Byrd, (D., W. Va.)	Alan Cranston, (D., Cal.)

Note: These photographs tend to confirm a theory of power advanced by Professor Joel Schwartz: "Powerful people have bushy eyebrows."

many of the years before his retirement in 1986, Thomas P. ("Tip") O'Neill, for example, epitomized congressional leadership. His own words reveal the subtlety of influence.

> You know, you ask me what are my powers and my authority around here? The power to recognize on the floor; little odds and ends—like men get pride out of the prestige of handling the Committee of the Whole, being named Speaker for the day; those little trips that come along—like those trips to China, trips to Russia . . . plus the fact that

there is a certain aura and respect that goes with the Speaker's office. He does have the power to be able to pick up the telephone and call people. . . . Rare is the occasion when a man has a personal fund-raiser or being personally honored that I don't show up at it. . . . I'm always accessible . . . it shows the warm hand of friendship.[16]

Here, O'Neill, as Speaker, portrays a soft, but not spineless, manner. Make no mistake, the "warm hand of friendship" can become a velvet fist. As a leader, he used both finesse and force, a powerful combination that led a long-time colleague, Richard Bolling, to say of O'Neill:

He's an Irish politician. No table pounder. He puts an arm around your shoulders and says he needs you. . . . When he's going somewhere he's like a tank, a kind tank.[17]

Even O'Neill, however, in his final years before retirement, sometimes seemed unable to bridge the gap between the more patient members of his generation and more petulant newcomers. It is possible for gifted members to exercise personal influence, but most influence over policy is exercised not by individuals, but by and through congressional committees.[18]

Characteristics of the Committee System. Congressional government is government by committees. It has always been so, although the total number of committees and subcommittees is greater today than it used to be. Throughout most of the 1980s, for example, there were more than 250 different committees or subcommittees in the Congress. Committees and subcommittees help the Congress deal with a work load and a federal bureaucracy that otherwise would overwhelm it. Indeed, the proliferation of committees and subcommittees has come about in response to environmental pressures: from attentive publics and organized interest groups who press complex demands on members; from an expanded federal bureaucracy quick to go its own way if unchecked; from Presidents who implement laws with minimal regard for congressional intent.

In addition to these outside stimuli, members of Congress have their own reasons to favor committee proliferation. With proliferation, there are more committee and subcommittee chairmanship (or ranking minority member) positions to hold, more committee and subcommittee staff to hire, more opportunities to attract publicity, more leverage over bills, and therefore more political resources which members need if they are to advance their own careers and even policy goals they believe in. For all these reasons, Woodrow

---

[16] Michael J. Malbin, "House Democrats Are Playing with a Strong Leadership Lineup," *National Journal* (June 18, 1977): 942.

[17] Richard Bolling, quoted in Richard L. Lyons, "A Powerful Speaker," *Washington Post*, 3 April 1977.

[18] For an in-depth examination of leadership, see Robert L. Peabody, *Leadership in Congress* (Boston: Little, Brown, 1976).

One of the many special committees that Congress sets up to examine, for a limited time, a particular situation. Here, members of House Science and Technology Committee inspect debris from the space shuttle Challenger at the Kennedy Space Center in Florida.

Wilson's insight is still valid: "Congress in its committee-rooms is Congress at work."[19]

There are four major kinds of committees in Congress: (1) standing, (2) select or special, (3) joint, and (4) conference.

1. **Standing committees** are the main substantive committees of Congress, because they focus on the substance of social problems and proposed policy remedies. They are an enduring feature of the institutional Congress, existing from one Congress to the next, with relatively stable memberships and fixed jurisdictions that define what should come before them. Both chambers have comparable committees, although the names sometimes vary. There are some exceptions, however. Most notably, only the House has a **Rules Committee**, the device it uses to regulate the outflow of committee bills on to the floor for debate and action.

2. **Select or special committees** are ones that are set up for a limited period to examine a particular problem. An especially famous one was the Senate Select Committee on Presidential Campaign Activities which investigated the set of campaign abuses collectively known as Watergate back in the

---

[19] Woodrow Wilson, *Congressional Government* (New York: Meridian Books, 1956), p. 69. (The original was published in 1885.)

early 1970s. One, as yet enduring, exception to the temporary rule is the House's Permanent Select Committee on Intelligence. Nevertheless, select or special committees investigate but lack the authority to propose legislative remedies; they are a little like carpenters with heavy hammers and no nails, able to make a lot of noise without building anything.

3. **Joint committees** are those the Congress relies on to minimize noise and further constructive action. They consist of members of both bodies and are designed to coordinate decision making on broad national concerns, such as the Joint Committee on Taxation and the Joint Economic Committee. Since most legislation passes through separate, not joint, committees, certain problems might be solved by the last kind of committee.

4. **Conference committees** are like joint committees, except they are more ad hoc affairs, convened for the sole purpose of trying to work out differences. Conference committees come about because each chamber can pass different versions of the same bill. When that happens, there simply is no one bill that has passed both bodies. To resolve the differences between the two versions, each chamber will appoint concerned members to a conference committee. The bill that emerges from the conference committee still must go back to each chamber and in its new form, pass again, however.

All committees have a head, a chairperson who can exercise great influence over the committee's affairs. Since the chair is so important, there has to be some "good" mechanism for selecting chairpersons. For a Congress that is supposed to be grappling with value conflicts in the outside world, it is "good" to keep its own internal conflict as low as possible. But anything valuable of which there are not enough to go around—like chairmanships—is likely to be fought over. The device Congress uses to circumvent what might otherwise be disabling internal conflict is a relatively simple rule: the chair of a committee is the person who has been on it the longest (as long as they are a member of the majority party). This is the rule of committee seniority or **seniority rule**.

In general, the seniority rule has worked well to deinstitutionalize conflict, but at a price. Historically, the price has been higher when the rule was adhered to blindly, producing committee chairs who sometimes were too old or too out of touch with the majority of their party. The resulting chairpersons made Congress seem decrepit, the party leadership obstructionist, and in general gave the seniority system a bad name, "the senility system." Partly in reaction to the bad press they were giving themselves, the Democrats in Congress, then the majority party in both chambers, began to move away from a strict reliance on the rule of seniority, and in other ways as well, began to weaken the powers of committee chairs. The trend since then has been to democratize committee operations as chairpersons "defer to the other members of the committee; (and as) much of the committee's work . . . devolved onto subcommittees, often chaired by junior, even freshman, congressmen and senators."[20]

How the congressional seniority system is sometimes viewed by political cartoonists.

'I DON'T KNOW WHY THEY WANT
TO GET RID OF US. I SAID,
I DON'T KNOW WHY THEY WANT
TO GET RID OF US! I SAID
I DON'T KNOW WHY

---

[20] Anthony King, "Introduction," in Anthony King, ed., *The New American Political System* (Washington, D.C.: American Enterprise Institute for Public Policy Research), p. 2.

THE CONGRESS: CAN IT GET ITS ACTS TOGETHER?

A nation's postage stamps are prominent symbols of its political culture, representing past achievements and heroic causes. Stamps, thus, have been used to legitimize valued policy goals and to commemorate their realization. In the following pictorial essay, we have used stamps of different eras as the centerpieces for illustrating some of these policy goals and events: education, conservation, civil rights, and historical signings.

EDUCATION

America is distinguished by its ongoing commitment to adult education (above).
In this 1767 engraving (right) of Harvard University, the artist, Paul Revere, captured a symbol of educational excellence.

CONSERVATION

Concern about the environment helped transform a strip-mine area in Pennsylvania into a Boy Scout campground.

This hand-colored 1920s drawing shows that extreme images of success and failure can reinforce commitments to policy goals.

CIVIL RIGHTS

The 1865 painting at left symbolizes Lincoln's emancipation of the slaves and shows that art can celebrate policy goals.

The 1963 March on Washington (above) dramatized the commitment to the cause of civil rights.

The 1983 March on Washington (left) focused attention on civil rights gains and unmet social needs.

SIGNINGS

The Treaty of Versailles, signed in the Hall of Mirrors in 1919, signaled the end of World War I.

In 1945, the formal Japanese surrender, ending World War II, came aboard the USS Missouri in Tokyo Bay, a setting which symbolized the achievement of America's military might.

The ceremony surrounding President Lyndon Johnson's signing of the Civil Rights Act of 1964 added to the historic accomplishment.

Staff Characteristics.   Congressional staff persons, both those on the personal staff of a member and those formally assigned to committees and subcommittees, have become more numerous and influential in the modern era. Most staff persons perform key intelligence functions and thereby extend the intellectual reach of members. Few staff persons are mere political hacks, simply getting their fill from the public larder. Members who have any kind of goals simply can not afford to so stupidly indulge their campaign workers.

The proliferation of congressional staff has additional consequences. More staff, for instance, means more points of access, more potentially influential policy actors who can be, and sometimes should be, influenced. More and more lobbyists will queue up to try to influence them. Instead of doing the bidding of the lobbyist, however, the smart staff person finds ways to use lobbyists as though they were auxiliary staff persons, sending them out to reconnoiter the opposition, to float trial balloons in a search for allies, to negotiate tentative compromises that do not prematurely lock in their boss, and so on.

The growth of congressional staffs, especially the growth of a politically astute and ambitious staff, has other effects on Congress' role. It makes Congress less of a reactive body, more interested in initiating the search for problems (before a dissatisfied public forces them upon Congress), and more determined to dream up possible cures for what insiders think ails society. As Senator Robert Dole (R., Kan.) puts it: "There's more staff around here than we need. They're all nice people. But the more staff you have, the more ideas you have, and most of them cost money. I haven't had many staff people come in with ideas to save money. It's always some new program to get their boss out front."[21] Whether one believes in less or more government, however, the policy initiatives generated by an expanded staff balance Congress' typically more reactive nature.

Organizational Dynamics

The modern Congress has become highly institutionalized and badly fragmented; both characteristics have extensive consequences for Congress' ability to realize its goals.

Institutionalization.   The contemporary Congress is highly *institutionalized*. This means that Congress has developed relatively permanent ways of conducting its business. These decision-making devices include established rules and procedures, a finely grained division of labor, the growth of policy specialization with decentralized units, and an increased stability in the membership of the body.[22]

© 1978 by NEA, Inc.   JIM BERRY ©NEA

"Look! One of the senators is briefing his staff."

---

21 Quoted in *The New York Times*, 9 May 1985.

22 Nelson W. Polsby, "Institutionalization in the U.S. House of Representatives," *American Political Science Review* 62 (1968): 144–68. See also Douglas H. Price, "The Congressional Career—Then and Now," in Nelson W. Polsby, ed., *Congressional Behavior* (New York: Random House, 1971), pp. 14–27.

The institutionalization of congressional power has both desirable and adverse consequences. Roger Davidson and Walter Oleszek sum up the defense:

Institutionalization enables Congress to cope with its contemporary work load. Division of labor, primarily through standing committees, permits the two houses to process a wide variety of issues at the same time. In tandem with staff resources, this specialization allows Congress to compete with the executive branch in assembling information and applying expertise to given problems. Division of labor also serves the personal and political diversity of Congress. At the same time, careerism encourages legislators to develop skills and expertise in specific issues. Procedures and traditions can contain conflict and channel the political energies that converge upon the lawmaking process.[23]

Institutionalization, thus, consists of strategies that Congress uses to cope with the complexities and demands that others put upon it. It is, to some extent, a defensive maneuver, an inward turning that can help the institution marshal its resources and its resolve. But, like any form of introversion, institutionalization can cut Congress off from its environments and the nurturing they provide. In this way, institutionalization carries with it the danger that Congress can become too isolated from the people, too preoccupied with servicing the personal and political needs of its members, too rigid and unable to respond adequately to pressing societal problems, and too uninterested in overseeing the implementation of its laws.

Fragmentation. The contemporary Congress is badly fragmented. *Fragmentation* means that the power to make decisions is fractured and decentralized, dispersed throughout the Congress and placed in the relatively autonomous hands of many different committees and persons.[24]

The fragmentation of congressional power also has both desirable and adverse consequences. On the plus side, fragmentation does help keep Congress open to the diverse sentiments of many constituencies and thus more representative than it might be otherwise. By spreading decision-making power around, fragmentation makes it harder for a majority coalition to impose its will, and in the process, erects a barrier to the feared tyranny of the majority that might extinguish individual liberty. Fragmentation serves the interests of those who like the status quo, because it is difficult for the advocates of any new cause to amass enough power to bring about radical change. On the minus side, fragmentation means that Congress will be more likely to adopt inconsistent policies and that it will not work very hard to oversee the bureaucratic implementation of policy. In addition, any body that pays little attention to the impact of inconsistent policies looks irresponsible and lacks clout in the policymaking process.

Finally, fragmentation has two other less obviously positive or negative

---

[23] Roger H. Davidson and Walter J. Oleszek, *Congress and Its Members* (Washington, D.C.: Congressional Quarterly Press, 1981), p. 47.

[24] See Randall Ripley, *Congress: Process and Policy* (New York: Norton, 1983), especially pp. 4–41.

THE CONGRESS: CAN IT GET ITS ACTS TOGETHER?

consequences. Fragmentation makes some kinds of policies more likely than others. In particular, Congress is predisposed to adopt **distributive policies**, ones that promote private activities, such as attending college or buying homes, through governmental subsidies, such as guaranteed loans and the deductibility of home mortgage payments. In contrast, Congress is not well-designed to move through **redistributive policies**, such as massive tax reform, which reallocate costs and benefits over the whole society. Fragmentation also makes it most likely that distributive policies will come about because of bargains and compromises, not because of fundamental agreement on principles.

■ The failed attempt at budget making, described in the beginning of this chapter, illustrates some of the effects of the two major characteristics of the contemporary Congress, the institutionalization and fragmentation of internal decision-making power. Although more stable as an institution and more well-equipped with specialized knowledge about problems, the contemporary Congress is a less powerful actor in the policy-making process—less powerful than it has been at some moments in history and surely less powerful than most contemporary Presidents.[25] What is more troubling is the possibility that Congress' policy-making and governance roles have plateaued. Whereas its concern with these roles varied historically between highs and lows, the contemporary Congress seems mostly preoccupied with realizing the political goals of its individual members.

THE GOALS OF CONGRESS

> If members were ever legislators and statesmen, they have more and more taken on the characteristics of constituency ombudsmen and grant brokers.　　—David Stockman

Congress, just like the presidency, works toward governance, policy, and political goals.[26] Even more than the presidency, however, the contemporary Congress tends to specialize in the realization of political, over governance and policy, goals. Moreover, Congress tends to focus on a particular aspect of each of these goals.

---

[25] See Samuel P. Huntington, "Congressional Responses to the Twentieth Century," in David B. Truman, ed., *The Congress and America's Future*, 2nd ed. (Englewood Cliffs, NJ: Prentice-Hall, 1973), pp. 6–38.

[26] For discussions of the multiple goals of members of Congress, see Richard F. Fenno, *Home Style: Representatives in Their Districts* (Boston: Little, Brown, 1978); Steven S. Smith and Christopher J. Deering, *Committees in Congress* (Washington, DC: CQ Press, 1984); and David E. Price, "Congressional Committees in the Policy Process," in Lawrence C. Dodd and Bruce I. Oppenheimer, eds., *Congress Reconsidered*, 3rd ed. (Washington, DC: CQ Press, 1985), pp. 161–88.

In general, Congress tries to realize:

- *governance goals*, with a focus on overseeing implementation and breaking bottlenecks;
- *policy goals* with a focus on the making of law;
- *political goals*, with a focus on the representation of political interests and on the realization of personal political ambitions.

Governance Goals

Congress finds it hard to participate in the governance process, except on an occasional and narrow basis.

The Task of Oversight. Congressional **oversight**, activities that gather and evaluate information on the implementation of public policy, is typically exercised by committees, although individual members have become self-appointed watchdogs of bureaucratic wrongdoing, as Senator William Proxmire (D., Wis.) has. In theory, any agency or program is subject to at least four reviews, often on an annual basis: two each in the Senate and the House, before both authorizing and appropriations committees (and often their subcommittees as well). In this way, Congress' control over funding is what buys them the opportunity to evaluate both laws and bureaucrats.

There are many circumstances that encourage members to perform their congressional oversight role. Randall Ripley summarizes well the research:

> Oversight is promoted by the existence of autonomous subcommittees; ample committee staffs; perceptions of partisan advantage on the part of the majority party members; perceptions that service to constituents can be enhanced . . . (by) committees that are highly prestigious (and productive) . . . (and when) a committee is considering major revisions in policy.[27]

Ripley further notes that, historically, these conditions held in reviews of federal housing policy but were generally absent in the field of civil rights. More recently, congressional oversight seems strong on such matters as defense spending and relatively weak on federal enforcement of civil rights policies. In addition, congressional oversight occurs on a less systematic basis through congressional **casework**, the favors that members do for constituents. These favors often require some intervention into the administrative process, to cut, for example, red tape that is holding up a Social Security check or a passport.

In general, however, congressional oversight is a haphazard process of reacting to "fire alarms," rather than a more preventive process of maintaining regular "police patrols," in the graphic language of Mathew McCubbins and

---

[27] Randall Ripley, *Congress*, pp. 376–77.

Thomas Schwartz.[28] Members of Congress know, better than anyone else, that most constituents do not know or care about congressional oversight. There are, of course, exceptions: big, splashy investigations that cultivate a member's heroic image. But, for the most part, oversight is grunt work, requiring the kind of slow, plodding attention to detail that wins many enemies and little applause. Oversight, in other words, takes too much time and produces too little payoff for most members, especially those who are trying to rally a largely inattentive and apathetic electorate to their side or behind some new policy proposal.

Obstacles to Oversight.   Congress' capacity to participation in governance is also heavily constrained by the complexity of the administrative process, its lack of expertise, and the dominance of other, more realizable and rewarding goals. The administration of law is a very complex and technical matter, as chapter 13's focus on the bureaucracy reveals. It is true that, over time, some members are able to build up considerable expertise in a particular policy area, as Senator Russell Long (D., La.) did on the subject of taxes, or as Representative William Ford did on the subject of federal aid to education. In addition, there has been a growth of professional staff on Capitol Hill. Because of their expertise and memory, staff enhance congressional participation in governance. In general, however, governance tasks are slighted, because Congress is better equipped to pursue other goals and because its members have more reasons to do so.

Policy Goals

The process of making law tends to be both routine in terms of what is on the agenda and disorderly in terms of how a bill is passed. The factors that determine how members vote necessarily impose some order.

What Is on the Agenda?   When a new Congress convenes in January, it sees pretty much what it saw before: the same problems, the same solutions. A new Congress does what it does best: what it did before. This means that, for the most part, Congress' and the nation's agenda is already set, like the pretuned channels on a new TV. Given its crowded agenda, most of the attention and effort of most of the members will be focused on the routines of lawmaking and on the possibility of making tiny, marginal adjustments in existing policies.[29] This means, therefore, that (1) new agenda items are rare, (2) most agenda items move slowly, and (3) agenda change is unlikely.

First, it is hard to get a new problem on Congress', or the nation's, agenda. It usually happens only as the result of some extraordinary event or because of

---

28 Mathew D. McCubbins and Thomas Schwartz, "Congressional Oversight Overlooked: Police Patrols versus Fire Alarms," *American Journal of Political Science* 28 (1984): 165–79.

29 Jack L. Walker, "Setting the Agenda in the U.S. Senate: A Theory of Problem Selection," *British Journal of Political Science* 7 (1977): 423–45.

somebody's extraordinary persistence. Congress, for example, became more concerned with the accounting practices of the military after discovering that the Pentagon had paid hundreds of dollars for hammers, wrenches, and toilet seats. Similarly, Congress became more concerned with the problems of underdeveloped countries after Haitian bodies washed up on Miami beaches and after illegal Mexican immigration crested our southwestern border. Sometimes members of Congress themselves take the initiative and call attention to a problem in a way that precipitates policy making, as Senator Paula Hawkins (R., Fla.) did when she spoke of having been sexually abused as a child. Other times, the initiative lies outside of Congress, as it did, for example, in the tenaciousness of a policy entrepreneur, Dr. Abe Bergman, who helped push through Congress a program to encourage new M.D.s to practice where they were most needed—in poor, rural areas of the country.[30] As a result of such events and pressures, new items do inch onto the policy agenda, in the process often displacing old problems that have lost their appeal, usually because they have proved too intractable, too costly, or too divisive—like poverty, national health insurance, and abortion.

Second, even after it makes it on the congressional agenda, it is very difficult to move a new policy through the lawmaking process. Once on the agenda, most new proposals go through a period of policy incubation, as the problem is more and better studied, as the word filters out that some change is in the air, as those likely to be affected form their reactions, as policy proposals are formulated and trial balloons floated, and as Congress waits, weighing reactions and assessing the political consequences of policy change. Reluctant to operate blind on the body politic, members of Congress will talk long and listen hard before adopting policy changes, especially ones that cut deep into personal values and pocketbooks. Delay, therefore, is functional, because it gives Congress a chance to see if a proposed policy change will be perceived as legitimate. If the ducks do not line up, Congress will shrink from action, as it did when no social consensus formed behind President Carter's energy conservation proposals, for example. In the absence of social consensus, most members of Congress demur when offered a key role in the policy-making process. As a result, policy proposals often linger in their own political purgatory.

Third, agenda change is unlikely. Policy change occurs when immigration quotas are raised, when revenue sharing programs are cut, when new weapons systems are authorized. Once in a while, however, there is an **agenda change**, the focus of congressional attention on some new problem or policy. Agenda change, as Barbara Sinclair has shown, has happened a number of times in American history: in the expansion of the domestic responsibilities of the federal government during the Great Depression; in the expansion of the nation's international responsibilities, from Europe in the early 1930s to Korea

---

[30] The story of the creation of the National Health Service Corps is told in Eric Redman, *The Dance of Legislation* (New York: Simon and Schuster, 1973).

in the early 1950s; in the assault of President Reagan on the size of the federal budget and the depth of the federal tax bite.[31]

Agenda changes usually occur only after some major change in the political environment, the makeup of Congress, or both. During the early 1960s, for example, a social conscience grown too disgusted with violations of the rights of black Americans sustained the agenda change symbolized by the Civil Rights Act of 1964. In a similar manner, the growth of a social conscience sickened at the sight of environmental degradation demanded a shift toward the more environmentally conscious legislation of the 1970s. The historical record, Sinclair finds, supports the conclusion: "Significant change in the political agenda usually can be traced to a change in the broader, politically relevant environment."[32]

How a Bill Is Passed.   Describing the process by which a bill becomes a law is a little like going to childbirth classes; it makes giving birth seem a whole lot neater than it really is. Here is a step-by-step description of the general process by which a bill becomes a law. (For a less orderly representation, see **Figure 12.1**, What Can Happen to a Bill: Most Roads Lead to Oblivion.)

Step 1. Introduction. A **bill**, a draft of a proposed law, may originate in either the House or the Senate, with two important exceptions. (Bills for raising and spending money must start in the House, although the Senate can add its own amendments.)

Step 2. Referral. The bill is referred to the appropriate committee, the one that has jurisdiction over the subject of the bill. (When a bill includes many subjects, touching on the jurisdictions of different committees, it is simultaneously referred to all appropriate committees or it is broken down into specific pieces and the pieces are referred to the appropriate committees.) Once in a committee, the bill is usually referred again, to a subcommittee of the committee.

Step 3. Hearings. Usually at the subcommittee level, hearings are held, the bill is modified ("marked-up"), voted on, sent back to the full committee, where more hearings may be held, the bill may be marked up some more, and again voted on.

Step 4. The Route to the Floor. The House uses a comparatively formal process for getting a bill on a calendar, a schedule that determines when the bill will be voted on. The House Rules Committee determines when and how the bill can be dealt with on the floor (for example, whether or not amendments will be permitted, how much time will be allotted for debate, and so on.) An informal process, only requiring the consent of key actors, is used in the Senate.

---

31 Barbara Sinclair, "Agenda, Policy, and Alignment Change from Coolidge to Reagan," in Lawrence C. Dodd and Bruce I. Oppenheimer, eds., *Congress Reconsidered*, 3rd ed. (Washington, D.C.: Congressional Quarterly Press, 1985), pp. 291–314.

32 Sinclair, "Agenda, Policy, and Alignment Change . . .", p. 312.

Step 5. Floor Action. The bill must receive a majority of votes in both the House and the Senate before it is sent to the President. (If the House and the Senate pass different versions of the same bill, they each send some members to a conference committee to hammer out one common version. The common version, if it is different than the one already passed, must then be passed again.)

Step 6. Presidential Action. The President may approve the bill, veto it, or "pocket-veto" it (fail to return it to the chamber from which it came, within ten days while the Congress is in session).

Step 7. Congressional Override. If vetoed, a bill can still become a law, if it can repass both the House and the Senate by a two-thirds vote.

Most of the time, this is only one-half the story, however. This, for example, may be just an authorization process, the method for creating a new policy or program. But most policies and programs need to be funded and therefore also must go through a subsequent **appropriations process**, the method for authorizing expenditures.

The process by which a bill becomes a law is interesting for what it reveals about American government, policy making, and politics. Lawmaking is a process that:

- is long and tortuous, as one would expect in a decentralized and fragmented decision-making body like the U.S. Congress.
- requires the agreement of those who represent many different points of view, as is appropriate in a pluralistic society which distrusts those who think that they have a lock on the truth.
- is full of stumbling blocks that frustrate proposals to increase the extent to which the federal government intrudes into what some view as the concerns of state and local governments, as you should expect in a federal system.
- makes members act timidly, as they should if they are concerned that their laws look legitimate and that their careers look worthy of continuance.
- most importantly, is driven more by political calculations than by any objective evaluation of the merits of alternative proposals, as is unavoidable in a society that does not agree on government's proper role.

How Members Decide to Vote. When it comes time to vote, members of Congress do not roll around like loose cannons on the deck. Rather, they tend to vote in ways that have been explained scientifically.[33] Because of the ease of obtaining data, most research has focused on **roll-call votes**, the recorded floor votes of individual members. While this is not an exact science, it has furthered our understanding of why members vote the way they do.

---

[33] There is a huge amount of literature on the determinants of members' voting decisions, including Herbert B. Asher and Herbert F. Weisburg, "Voting Change in Congress: Some Dynamic Perspectives on an Evolutionary Process," *American Journal of Political Science* 22 (1978): 391–425; Aage Clausen, *How Congressmen Decide: A Policy Focus* (New York: St. Martin's, 1973); John W. Kingdon, *Congressmen's Voting Decisions*, 2nd ed. (New York: Harper and Row, 1981); Donald R. Matthews and James A. Stimson, *Yeas and Nays: Normal Decision-Making in the U.S. House of Representatives* (New York: Wiley, 1975).

FIGURE 12.1 What Can Happen to a Bill: Most Roads Lead to Oblivion

TABLE 12.4 Party-Line Voting

Percent of all recorded votes on which a majority of Republicans voted one way and a majority of Democrats voted the other.

Year	House	Senate
1985	61%	50%
1984	47	40
1983	56	44
1982	36	43
1981	37	48
1980	38	46
1979	47	47
1978	33	45
1977	42	42
1976	36	37

SOURCE: *Congressional Quarterly Weekly Report*, January 11, 1986, p. 87.

The major determinants of members' voting decisions include: their political party and its leadership, their state delegation, the members of the committee reporting the bill, presidential pressure, constituency, the closeness of the next election, whether or not they are in their first term, informal groups, staff members, interest group cues, and even personal conscience. Of all these, and in spite of the general decline in the role of political parties, knowing a member's party affiliation is still the most reliable predictor of his or her voting behavior.

Members often exhibit **party-line voting**, when a majority of one party votes one way, and a majority of the other party votes the other way. The frequency of party-line voting in recent congresses is given in **Table 12.4**. As the Table shows, party-line voting is quite common, a little more so in the House than the more independent-minded Senate and especially more so in recent years.

In the modern era, party-line voting has been more common on some kinds of issues—more on domestic than foreign policies issues and more on social welfare matters than on questions of civil liberties.[34] As we have seen in the continuing battle of the budget, members of the House and the Senate are under strong pressure to remain faithful to the party's position on fiscal policies, those concerned with spending and taxing. In the 99th Congress (1984–1986), tax reform became a watershed issue, as both parties attempted

[34] Aage R. Clausen, *How Congressmen Decide* (New York: St. Martin's, 1973).

to shape their public images as "responsible," "fair," and "compassionate." Such issues can provoke a sense that all members of a party share a common fate. To some extent, all party members are better off when their party is better off, especially when it becomes the majority party. Because with majority status goes committee chairmanships, more staff, the ability to set the legislative agenda, and various other real and psychological benefits. This sense of a common fate, therefore, does counteract somewhat the stronger centrifugal forces that fragment the party's sense of legislative purpose.

Political Goals

In the Case at the beginning of this chapter, Congress did attempt to make policy, specifically, a comprehensive budget for the federal government. Their attempt failed, however, because of the dominance of other concerns. In this case and in general, the members are preoccupied with political goals, specifically, with representing political interests and with realizing their political ambitions.

The Representation of Political Interests. Congress does an excellent job of representing most political concerns because it is so open to its institutions and political environments.

First, the other major components of the federal government—the presidency, the bureaucracy, and the federal courts—heavily influence Congress. Depending on his personality and his legislative skills, the President can be the most influential of these.[35] The bureaucracy and its allies also can be very effective in communicating their policy preferences. Sometimes, for example, bureaucratic agencies and special interest groups form **subgovernments**, effective alliances to advance their common interests.[36] The views of federal courts and specifically of the Supreme Court also can be reflected in what Congress does, or is kept from doing, as when the Supreme Court overturns law as unconstitutional.

Second, the members of Congress depend on a variety of political environments and therefore are careful to respond to their political concerns. In particular, members tend to represent the views of their constituency and dominant interest groups, whether or not they are located primarily within their electoral district.

Not all constituency concerns are terribly important, however. In most districts, there are only one or two issues that command the member's attention and action. These are *killer issues* on which the member must not be caught voting the wrong way. The identity of these issues varies, of course,

---

[35] On the evolving relationship between Congress and the President, see James L. Sundquist, *The Decline and Resurgence of Congress* (Washington, DC: The Brookings Institution, 1981).

[36] See, for example, the sugar subgovernment described in Douglass Cater, *Power in Washington* (New York: Random House, 1964).

from Social Security in the districts of Dade County around Miami, Florida, to water in the districts running down the San Joaquin Valley in California.

Interest groups are also important sources of political cues for members. Interest groups, as we saw in chapter 6, are important because they command resources that members find relevant; policy expertise, political support, and campaign revenues. Members, however, can not become so dependent on special interest groups that they sacrifice their political futures.

The Realization of Political Ambitions. Most of the members who are there want to stay in Congress and many who are there aspire to higher office, the Senate or the presidency, for example. In general, the desire to realize these political ambitions is very strong and often explains much of what members of Congress do.

■ Congress is biased toward political goals and away from governance and policy goals. The task of governance is an extremely difficult one, especially for members who need to be concerned with more visibly pressing concerns. Also, in spite of their posturing about presidential excesses, many members of Congress may not wish responsibility for a greater policy-making role. From their point of view, the President's domination of policy making allows members to claim credit for policies that work and avoid blame for those that do not.[37] Finally, as we are about to see, the organizational arrangement of Congress and members' ability to work within it, makes the realization of political goals easier.

WAYS OF ACHIEVING CONGRESSIONAL GOALS

> Congress is not easy to lead, or to speak for. Like the nation from which it springs, it is pluralistic and diverse, a distillate of the strengths and weaknesses, the virtues and faults of the electorate it serves.
> —Jim Wright (D., Texas)

To realize any of their goals, members of Congress must find ways of overcoming constraints, ways to expand Congress' formal powers, and ways of creating and exercising informal, political power.

Overcoming Constraints

Congress' ability to realize its various goals is hindered by outside, environmental constraints and by inside, institutional constraints.

---

[37] See David R. Mayhew, *Congress: The Electoral Connection* (New York: Yale University Press, 1974).

Environmental Constraints.   Once in a while, Congress is able to shut itself off from its various environments. If they are to take action, members sometimes need to wall themselves off from the army of lawyers, representing special interest groups, who line the halls of Congress. During consideration of tax reform, in 1985 through 1986, for example, members tended to retreat inside their own mental bunkers so they could focus on a few key issues and avoid a stalemate that would favor already entrenched interests. In other rare cases, debates and votes on matters of national security, for example, members are able to act as though their discretion is unconstrained.

In general, however, members must try to cope simultaneously with the demands of their multiple environments. Some of the most constraining demands come from the other major institutions of the federal government.

The President, for example, may try to act as the chief legislative leader, as President Reagan successfully did on matters of vital concern to him. Confronting a popular and skilled President, Congress' ability to cope often requires it to delay, as Congress often did in President Reagan's second term, on matters of tax reform, military aid to those fighting communism in Central America, and budget policy, as we saw in the Case at the beginning of this chapter.

In dealing with the rest of the executive branch, Congress may try to use its control over appropriations to lever out of the bureaucracy the information it needs to help govern and to make policy. In recent years, this back door into governance and policy has been closed by the ability of the Office of Management and Budget to centralize and dominate the budget requests coming from individual agencies.

Congress can attempt to cope with constraints imposed by the federal court system and the Supreme Court in particular in four major ways:

1. To block appointments and anticipated decisions, Congress can alter the size of the Court, something it has done six times in American history.
2. To keep the Court from ruling the "wrong" way, Congress also can exercise its constitutional authority to change the Court's appellate jurisdiction, thereby limiting what cases can be appealed from lower courts.
3. To overturn the impact of a Court ruling, Congress, in concert with the states, can change the Constitution by amending it. It did this, for example, in 1909 to create the federal income tax and in 1971 to lower the voting age to eighteen for all, not just federal, elections.
4. To frustrate the Court's (and the President's) ability to make policy, Congress can exercise its constitutional authority, under Article II, Section 2, and withhold its "advice and consent" on the President's nominations for membership on the Supreme Court or for appointment as its Chief Justice.

Institutional Constraints. Many of the constraints on Congress' ability to realize its goals, especially its policy goals, are the unintended by-product of its own internal, institutional characteristics, in particular, its highly fragmented and its highly representative nature.

Fragmentation of congressional decision-making authority means that there is no one person or group who can speak authoritatively for Congress as an institution. In this way, Congress itself constrains its governance and policy-making roles. This side-effect, of course, is intensified when one party controls one house and the other party controls the other.

Congress' relative success in realizing its political goal of representation constrains its ability to realize other goals. The result is a product of a pluralistic and factious society. Moreover, existing political cleavages may be made worse by more and better information. As Charles Mosher, the late representative from Ohio observed: the more informed members become, the more divided they are.[38]

In addition, many political interests are not well or fully represented and the ongoing democratization of the policy-making process also can only make representation more faithful—and more contentious in ways that may detract from Congress' ability to govern or make policy.

Expanding Formal Powers

The Constitution made Congress a heavyweight contender, with considerable formal powers—the ability to make jarring jabs and if necessary to throw a knockout punch. Congress' jabs are its enumerated, formal powers; the knock-out punch, its expanded, implied powers.

After outlining the way Congress was to be organized, members selected, and bills enacted into law, Article I, Section 8, provided a formal description of the legislative powers of Congress. The Section described the formal powers of Congress in two ways.

First, Article I, Section 8 listed a large number of specific powers. The elements in this list are called *enumerated powers*, or sometimes, explicit powers. Some of the most important of these are control over raising government's income (its revenues) and its expenditures, the authority to say when we are at war and to make people fight in them, control over all forms of commercial activity between states and with foreign nations, and the power to create federal courts that would be subordinate to the Supreme Court. Section 8 could have stopped here, after enumerating what Congress could do. If it had, the proper role of Congress would have been completely unambiguous, nothing more than the sum of its enumerated powers. But the Constitution did not stop there. Rather, it went on, providing a way Congress could expand its authority, by stretching its enumerated powers.

Second, Article I, Section 8, also implied that Congress could do more than just exercise its enumerated powers. Section 8 did this with its last sentence, a clause that said Congress could do whatever it wanted to carry out its own enumerated powers or any of the other powers that were lodged anywhere else in the national government. The language is striking:

---

[38] Charles A. Mosher, "Somber Reflections on Congress by a Retiring Member," *Science* (December 26, 1975).

To make all laws which shall be necessary and proper for carrying into execution the foregoing powers, and all other powers vested by this Constitution in the Government of the United States, or in any Department or Office thereof.

This, the *elastic* or *necessary and proper clause*, established what would become over time a tremendously important resource for the expansion of congressional power. Armed with this formal authority, Congress would be more flexible in exercising its enumerated powers and more able to respond to new, unanticipated problems.

Creating and Exercising Political Power

If they are to have any realistic chance of achieving anything other than the most narrow of personal goals, members of Congress have to do more than expand the formal powers of the institution. They also must find ways of creating additional political powers for themselves and ways of mobilizing that power behind larger goals. Doing this, of course, is a constant and uphill battle. There are, however, a number of steps they can take in the right direction:

- To minimize the outside constraints of an intrusive press, members of Congress can operate removed from public view.
- To expand their freedom to act as they see fit on some policy matters, members of Congress can attempt to buy themselves room to maneuver, by meeting constituency demands on killer issues and through effective casework.
- To decrease their susceptibility to electoral pressures, members of Congress can try to transform their incumbency (and its associated resources of visibility and campaign contributions) into a safe seat, as Gary Jacobson reports most have.[39]
- To compensate for the disadvantages they suffer in dealing with those more expert than they (the executive branch and lobbyists, for example), Congress has created and members may draw on the more professionalized staff and on congressional support agencies. In particular, these are the Congressional Research Service of the Library of Congress, the General Accounting Office, the Office of Technology Assessment, and the Congressional Budget Office.
- To counter the President's effort to win the heart of the people, members of Congress too can try to cultivate an attractive popular image, whether that requires them to do battle with the bureaucracy, to bait foreign devils, or to actually do a good job of legislating.

In many ways, members of Congress are able to create the sort of power that can be used to improve their image, even if it is not used to further

---

[39] Gary C. Jacobson, *The Politics of Congressional Elections* (Boston: Little, Brown and Company, 1983).

Members of Congress try to stay in touch with their constituents as often as possible. Here, Claudine Schneider, a Congresswoman from Rhode Island meets with two constituents who tape an interview with her for home consumption.

Congress' ability to meet its larger goals. Morris Fiorina, for example, showed that members, quite independently of what they did in Congress, spent a lot of time back home in their district, cultivating personal attachments and weaving them into their own political support structure.[40] This finding also helps resolve the apparent inconsistency that Americans love their own member of Congress but are less positive about the institution as a whole.

■ Over time, Congress and its members have been quite resourceful in finding ways to realize governance, policy, and political goals. Nevertheless, there is also the danger that this resourcefulness will be directed toward meeting the more narrow personal and political goals of members and away from the governance and policy goals of the institution. In late 1968, Nelson Polsby warned that Congress, as it became more institutionalized, might turn inward

---

[40] Morris P. Fiorina, *Congress, Keystone of the Washington Establishment* (New Haven: Yale University Press, 1977).

and focus on meeting the needs of its members "at the expense of external (societal) demands."[41] More than any strong President, any entrenched bureaucracy, or any assertive Supreme Court, the turning inward and the preoccupation with creature comforts, if unchecked, will effectively erode Congress' proper role in the American governmental system.

SUMMARY

The Congress and its members, like the President, wrestle with governance, policy, and political goals. In the case of Congress, there are important differences, however, both in the nature of its goals and in its ability to realize them.

Congress defines each of its goals differently than the President. For Congress, governance means trying to oversee the implementation of laws and breaking bottlenecks when they develop, policy making means crafting laws, and playing politics means representing both the broad political concerns of society and the more narrow personal concerns of the membership of the body.

Congress, unlike the contemporary President, finds it hard to advance each of its goals simultaneously. For Congress, the two main political goals of representing societal concerns and advancing members' ambitions often detract from the institution's ability to govern and to make policy.

Congress' record of mixed success in realizing its goals may help explain why many people love their representative in Congress but think much less highly of the institution as a whole. Unfortunately, that view of the body may further weaken its future capabilities and performance.

Key Terms

Gramm-Rudman Act
bicameralism
comity
President pro tempore
Speaker
majority leader
majority whip
minority leader
minority whip
standing committees
Rules Committee
Select or special committees
joint committees

conference committees
seniority rule
distributive policies
redistributive policies
oversight
casework
agenda change
bill
appropriations process
roll-call votes
party-line voting
subgovernments

---

41 Nelson W. Polsby, "The Institutionalization of the U.S. House of Representatives," *American Political Science Review* 62 (March 1968): 144–68. See especially p. 166.

Review and Reflection

1. Why is Congress usually on the defensive, typically blocking presidential initiatives?

2. What are the major goals of Congress and its members?

3. What constrains the realization of these goals?

4. What, if anything, can Congress or its members do to overcome these constraints?

5. President Reagan has been very successful in translating his personal popularity into legislative support for his policies. Do you think it might be possible for members of Congress to translate their personal popularity into greater public support for Congress as a whole? Why or why not?

6. Do you think Congress will ever perform a more important governance or policy-making role than it does today? Why or why not?

Supplemental Readings

The ranks of political scientists are full of Congress-watchers who love to study the institution and have written some wonderful books about it. A sampling of these include the works by *Fenno, Mann* and *Ornstein, Sundquist,* and *Maass.*

Political scientists and political journalists also have produced some fine biographies and legislative histories (case studies that give a blow-by-blow account of the sometimes successful congressional struggles to pass legislation). Some of these include *Drew* (on former Senator John Culver); *Whalen* and *Whalen* (on passage of the 1964 Civil Rights Act); *Redman* (on passage of a bill to encourage medical doctors to serve rural areas).

For up-to-date information on your (and every other) member of Congress, see *Barone* and *Ujifusa.*

Barone, Michael, and Grant Ujifusa. *The Almanac of American Politics.* Washington, D.C.: National Journal, 1986. (updated every two years)

Drew, Elizabeth. *Senator.* New York: Simon and Schuster, 1979.

Fenno, Richard F., Jr. *Home Style.* Boston: Little, Brown, 1978.

Maass, Arthur. *Congress and the Common Good.* New York: Basic Books, 1984.

Mann, Thomas E., and Norman Ornstein, eds. *The New Congress.* Washington, D.C.: American Enterprise Institute, 1981.

Redman, Eric. *The Dance of Legislation.* New York: Simon and Schuster, 1973.

Sundquist, James L. *The Decline and Resurgence of Congress*. Washington, D.C.: The Brookings Institution, 1981.

Whalen, Charles, and Barbara Whalen. *The Longest Debate: A Legislative History of the 1964 Civil Rights Act*. City: Seven Locks Press, 1985.

CHAPTER THIRTEEN

THE BUREAUCRACY
LIFE IN THE TRENCHES

*I*magine what an automobile could do without a transmission; that is about what government can do without bureaucracy.

The bureaucracy is needed to translate policy intentions into policy outcomes and to do so in a way that people perceive as legitimate. To do both, bureaucracies must have certain characteristics. According to Max Weber, the German sociologist, a **bureaucracy**, has (1) people with the authority to get the job done, (2) experts who apply their knowledge to particular problems, (3) procedures for all members to follow, and (4) rules for making decisions.

Bureaucratic organizations, therefore, must be able to take often loosely worded laws, figure out what they mean, design some way of administering them, keep track of their effects, and make the necessary and proper adjustments. Unfortunately, bureaucracies also have characteristics that often limit their ability to do these things successfully.

The following Case is drawn from a study of what went wrong when a federal agency, the Center for Disease Control, designed and implemented a program to protect Americans against a feared outbreak of swine flu. The Case suggests three insights. First, bureaucratic errors can produce disastrous policies. Second, the federal bureaucracy does much more than merely implement law. Third, federal bureaucrats can try too hard to overcome things that are meant to constrain them.

THE NATURE OF THE BUREAUCRACY

> Implementation is not only something to be
> done after decision, it is as much or more a
> thing to think about before decision, right
> along with substance. Of this there was but
> little in the swine flu case.
>
> —*Professor Richard E. Neustadt*
> *and Harvey V. Fineberg, M.D.,*
> *The Epidemic That Never Was:*
> *Policy-Making and the Swine*
> *Flu Affair*

The Case   The Costs of Trying Too Hard

Atlanta, Georgia, 1976. The Center for Disease Control. Doctor David J. Sencer
only wanted to do good by protecting as many Americans as possible from the
feared outbreak of a swine flu epidemic.[1] In the beginning, the threat seemed
real and the bureaucracy's response appropriate. In the end, the epidemic never
materialized, a $135 million congressional appropriation was wasted, the side
effects of the swine flu vaccine left a few Americans dead and many others
paralyzed, liability claims were pressed on the federal government by survivors
and the heirs of victims, and the involved federal agencies and their bureaucrats
were discredited. Moreover, all these, the costs of trying too hard, were avoida-
ble, some believe.[2]

The swine flu had not appeared since 1918, when a worldwide pandemic had
killed an estimated 20 million people, including 500,000 Americans. Moreover,
since the interval had been so long, few Americans under the age of fifty had built
up any natural protective agents, "antigens," against this form of influenza. The
potential for disaster therefore loomed in the thoughts and actions of Dr. Sencer
and others.

Dr. Sencer quickly defined the problem and designed the policy to solve it.
Instead of moving slowly, through a more open and inclusive process of consultation with others who may have had different views, Dr. Sencer wrote a
memo to his superiors in which he described the threat of a swine flu pandemic,
outlined the argument against excluding any part of the population, and "rolled
the felt need to do 'something' into one decision: manufacture, planning, immu-
nizing and surveillance all together, and tied the whole to . . . (a) deadline . . . two weeks away."[3] At that point, his superiors, including President Ford,
had little choice. They had to agree or turn down the recommendation and run

---

[1] This case is drawn from Richard E. Neustadt and Harvey Fineberg, *The Epidemic That Never
Was: Policy-Making and the Swine Flu Affair* (New York: Random House/Vantage Books, 1983).

[2] *Ibid.*

[3] *Ibid*, p. 31.

the risk that the pandemic would hit, Sencer's recommendations would be leaked to the press, and they would suffer inestimable political damage.

In retrospect, it would appear to those who analyzed the whole affair as though Dr. Sencer's policy assumed too much and guarded against too little. For example, it assumed the worst about the problem (it could kill millions) and it assumed the best about the proposed solution (the entire population of the United States could be inoculated without serious adverse side effects). The assumptions may have been unavoidable. The failure to build in checks on them was not, however.

The policy for dealing with the threat of a swine flu pandemic was grievously flawed, because it failed to allow for the discovery of error and to provide for ways of adjusting to it. Policies, including this one, are not implemented all at once, but rather over time, in a step-by-step manner. The implementation process, therefore, automatically provides many opportunities for gathering information that can be used to re-examine the policy and the assumptions behind it.

Tragically, in this case, those who advocated the policy also pushed its implementation and they either failed to seek out information that may have slowed them down or acted in ways that prevented such information from surfacing. For example, in the words of Neustadt and Fineberg:

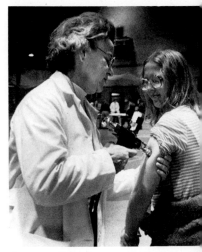

A nurse administers a swine flu vaccine.

> In immediate terms, Sencer gained a tactical advantage by attaching to the manufacturing decision, with its short deadline, the less tightly constrained decision to inoculate. But this deprived him of strategic opportunities to think through consequences of the likely case, the case of no pandemic. And it squeezed down to two weeks the time available for everyone from him through Ford to probe mass immunization before they embraced it.[4]

Instead, but perhaps for the most noble of purposes, the process rushed ahead—toward its own demise.

In the end, the failure to anticipate unintended and undesirable implementation problems doomed the success of the policy and the credibility of those who had pushed it.

Insights

Insight 1. *The federal bureaucracy is staffed with people whose values and commitments shape policy.* Sometimes bureaucrats are motivated by narrow personal or partisan considerations. More often, however, they simply are performing their duty—as they interpret it. That allows for both commitment and initiative, ingredients that can both enhance bureaucratic performance and, as in the case of the swine flu affair, detract from it.

Insight 2. *Although it is primarily concerned with governance tasks, the federal bureaucracy is intimately involved in making policy and in advancing political interests.* The federal bureaucracy is primarily concerned with administering the

---

[4] *Ibid.*, p. 124.

laws that others develop. Doing so, however, invariably forces its involvement into both policy and political concerns. Indeed, on highly complex or technical matters, the bureaucracy can become the main source of policy, as the Center for Disease Control did in the swine flu case.

Insight 3. *In the attempt to realize its various goals, the federal bureaucracy may bypass constraints in undesirable and self-destructive ways.* The federal bureaucracy, just like every other governmental institution is constrained by a variety of forces. It too chafes under these constraints and sometimes tries to ignore or evade them, as Dr. Sencer appears to have done, perhaps inadvertently, by the way he defined the problem and designed the remedy.

■ Federal bureaucrats do not have to be thought of as faceless and mindless autotrons. They are real people—dedicated to public service, deeply committed to the specific goals of their agency, and very resourceful in advancing what they believe to be the public interest. Indeed, sometimes the federal bureaucracy is quite successful, as for example, it was in implementing the Voting Rights Act of 1965. (See the **Vantage Point**: The Impact of the Voting Rights Act of 1965.) All that, unfortunately, does not mean they will be successful. Oftentimes, however, the federal bureaucracy will fail to realize its goals, especially if it ignores democratic traditions and processes.

THE ORGANIZATION OF THE FEDERAL BUREAUCRACY

> I naively viewed the executive branch as some monolithic being. One of my first surprises was that it is just as Balkanized as the legislative branch, only that it's much more beneath the surface and much less discernible.
>
> —*Richard S. Schweiker, former Congressman, Senator, and Secretary of Health and Human Services*

To begin understanding its nature, think about what the federal bureaucracy is not—and why it is not that way. For example, the federal bureaucracy is not small, since this is a society in which the federal government has many important roles to play. The federal bureaucracy is not the whole bureaucracy, since this is a federal, not a unitary, government. The federal bureaucracy is not full of people who are terribly responsive to presidential leadership, since they enjoy both legal and political protections. The federal bureaucracy can not capriciously order the rest of us around, since it is heavily constrained both by

THE IMPACT OF THE VOTING RIGHTS ACT OF 1965

*T*he implementation of the Voting Rights Act of 1965 increased black voter registration and the number of black officeholders.

The middle column shows black voter registration figures for eleven southern states[1] from 1960 to 1981.

The increased black voter registration figures in the South and elsewhere soon began to show up in the increased numbers of blacks running for and winning elective office throughout the United States. (See the right column.)

Over the period from 1970 to 1981, the figures indicate the number of blacks winning elective office in Congress, state legislatures, city and county government, in law enforcement (as judges and sheriffs, for example), and in education (on state university boards of regents and on local school boards, for example).

Black Voter Registration	
1960	1,463,000
1966	2,689,000
1970	3,357,000
1976	4,149,000
1980	4,254,000
1982	4,302,000

Black Officeholders	
1970	1,472
1972	2,264
1974	2,991
1976	3,979
1978	4,503
1980	4,890
(1982)	(5,115)

[1] The eleven states are Alabama, Arkansas, Florida, Georgia, Louisiana, Mississippi, North Carolina, South Carolina, Tennessee, Texas, and Virginia.

SOURCE: U.S. Bureau of the Census, *Statistical Abstract of the United States: 1984*, 104th ed. (Washington, D.C., 1983), p. 261.

laws and political pressures. Different parts of the federal bureaucracy often fail to act in concert, because they are torn apart by centrifugal, fragmenting forces. The federal bureaucracy often fails to achieve its goals, because it often lacks the resources to get the job done.

Characteristics of the Federal Bureaucracy

The organizational character of the federal bureaucracy is shaped by its size, methods of administration, staff, internal fragmentation, and inefficiency.

Size. How big is the federal bureaucracy? It is smaller than you might imagine, bigger than it looks, and maybe even shrinking a little.

The federal bureaucracy is smaller than you might imagine—considering the size of the federal budget, the size of the combined bureaucracies of state and local governments, and the size of the country. In the 1980s, for example, there were about 2.8 million federal bureaucrats (not counting members of the armed forces). But, at the same time, the federal government also had a budget of $728 billion dollars (not counting dollars spent on defense). To put these numbers in perspective, the federal government employed about 2.5 percent of the work force and had a budget equal to about 24 percent of the Gross National Product. Or compare the 2.8 million federal bureaucrats with the over 13 million state and local bureaucrats in 1982; just three states combined—New York, California, and New Jersey—had more bureaucrats than the national government as a whole. Finally, with 2.8 million federal bureaucrats and about 229.9 million people in the country, there is one federal bureaucrat for every 82 people—not quite enough to put one under every bed.

The federal bureaucracy is bigger than it looks, however, since it draws heavily on the administrative services of nonfederal bureaucrats, private contractors, voluntary not-for-profit organizations, businesspersons, and other private citizens. It is not as though all those state and local bureaucrats are minding their own business; many are administering federal programs according to federal regulations. The federal bureaucracy also augments its staff by contracting with private business for all kinds of things, ranging from chemical research to aerial shots of the Capitol. Other volunteers come forward to swell the effective size of the federal bureaucracy, for example, the Salvation Army that passes out surplus cheese and the Red Cross that passes out disaster relief.

Through law and regulations that have the force of law, the federal government also turns lots of people into informal bureaucrats—businesspersons who have to monitor and report their own pollution, university financial aid officers who compute the size of your Guaranteed Student Loan, and private citizens like you and me who fill out our own tax returns. There are a lot of these "informal federal servants," maybe as many as three for every federal bureaucrat, according to one estimate.[5] Once you add in all these people, the effective size of the federal bureaucracy becomes much larger.

The federal bureaucracy also may have started getting a little smaller in the early 1980s. Although the bottom line has not been totalled up yet, some sketchy evidence is available. In a few cases, whole agencies have been abolished, as was the fate of the Civil Aeronautics Board, the agency regulating commercial airlines, for example. In most cases, staff sizes shrunk less dramatically, mostly through attrition, as senior bureaucrats retired or simply got discouraged by multi-year freezes on salary increases. Shrinkage through attrition seemed especially severe in agencies with regulatory missions not well supported by the Reagan administration, such as the Food and Drug Administration.

Methods of Administration. The federal bureaucracy administers its programs in both a direct and an indirect fashion. It directly administers, for example, when it hires its own rangers to patrol national parks, its own doctors to staff veterans' hospitals, or its own clerks to process income tax returns. For the most part, however, the federal bureaucracy administers things indirectly,

---

[5] *National Journal*, 5 May 1979, p. 730.

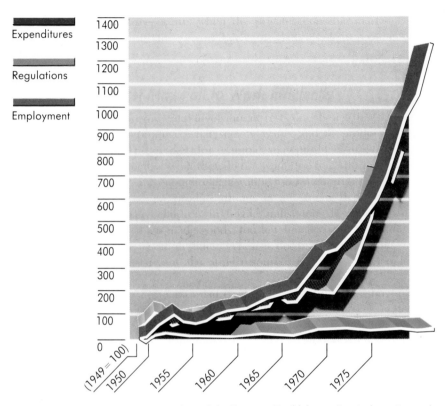

Expenditures

Regulations

Employment

FIGURE 13.1
Since WWII, federal reg-
ulations and expenditures
have grown rapidly, as
the number of bureau-
crats has stayed about
the same.

SOURCE: Hugh Heclo, "Issue Networks and the Executive Establishment," in Anthony King, ed., *The New American Political System* (Washington, D.C.: American Enterprise Institute, 1978), p. 90.

with the help of state and local bureaucrats and with the often begrudging assistance of private persons. In both cases, the federal bureaucracy brings about their cooperation with both a carrot—the promise of federal funds—and a stick—penalties for failure to follow federal regulations. Ever since the 1950s, while the number of bureaucrats stayed about the same, the federal bureaucracy has made increased use of both of these instruments of indirect administration, federal expenditures and federal regulations, as **Figure 13.1** shows.

Staff.   Those who staff the federal bureaucracy are hired on the basis of partisan political considerations or the merit principle.

The federal bureaucracy is staffed in two major ways; through political appointments and through what are supposed to be nonpartisan appointments made on the basis of merit. For the most part, the "top" jobs go to political appointees. According to one estimate, there are a couple of thousand of these, extending from the cabinet level on down, through undersecretaries, and assistant secretaries, all the way to the level of bureau chief.[6] These political appointments are "plums" the President gets to dispense. (For a sampling of some of these jobs, see the **Vantage Point**: Presidential Plums.) In making them, the President tries to expand both his image and his influence; his image is enhanced by appointing people who reflect the characteristics and preferences of his supporters and his influence is increased, theoretically, at least, by appointing people who are sympathetic and therefore, hopefully, responsive to his policy directions.

In practice, however, the President's political appointees often fail to deliver. Sometimes this happens because their own subordinates, by virtue of their expertise and staying power, frustrate their nominal bosses or convert them to the agency's, not the President's, point of view. Other times, political appointees fail to deliver for their President because they do not stay around very long; their transience (an average of twenty-two months on the job for assistant and undersecretaries) has led one scholar to refer to them as "a government of strangers."[7] Their departure may weaken presidential influence, but it also gives the President another chance to refurbish his image through a new appointment.

There is no absolutely clear-cut dividing line between what are supposed to be political and what are supposed to be nonpolitical, or at least, nonpartisan, jobs in the federal bureaucracy. The ambiguity reflects our cultural ambivalence towards bureaucracy; we believe that politics should not influence the administration of the laws but we also hold the President politically accountable when he fails to get his policies implemented. Different Presidents have coped with the ambiguity in different ways.

President Carter, for example, tried to separate politics from administration with a new law that split the old Civil Service Commission (CSC) into two parts: the **Office of Personnel Management (OPM)** and the **Merit System Protection Board (MSPB)**. The OPM, the agency that does most of the hiring, was to juggle both considerations of political loyalty and objective merit. Once hired, however, federal employees were to be protected from political pressure and retribution by the MSPB.

The Reagan administration took more of a hands-on approach to staffing the federal bureaucracy and in some cases made political appointments further down than ever before into the ranks of the traditionally protected civil service. Even President Reagan, however, was frustrated in his attempt to make the federal bureaucracy more responsive to all parts of his agenda, especially by the Defense Department. Its Secretary, Casper Weinberger, was especially skillful in blunting the attempts of Reagan's first budget director, David Stockman, to cut defense spending, for example. It is a fine line presidential appointees tread; to run their departments, they must be in tune with their subordinates. To keep their job and the President's ear, they need to follow, or

---

[6] Hugh M. Heclo, *A Government of Strangers* (Washington, D.C.: The Brookings Institution, 1977), p. 94.

[7] *Ibid.*, p. 103.

PRESIDENTIAL PLUMS

*T*he President has a great deal of influence over the staffing of key positions in the federal bureaucracy. For many of these, the President can simply appoint whomever he chooses, although for others, the President needs to get the advice and consent of the Senate of the United States.

Positions (and salaries)[1] that can be filled through presidential appointment include:

Counselor to the President	up to $ 72,600
Assistant to the President for National Security Affairs	up to $72,600
Deputy Assistant to the President and Director of Speechwriting	up to $71,100
Architect of the Capitol	$71,100
Chairman, U.S. Holocaust Memorial Council	$ 254.56 (per diem)[2]
Alternate Federal Member of the Delaware River Basin Commission	$66,400
Members of the Pennsylvania Avenue Development Corporation	$ 254.56 (per diem)
Chairman, President's Committee on Employment of the Handicapped	none
Chairman, American Battle Monuments Commission	none

Positions (and salaries) that can be filled by the President, with the advice and consent of the Senate include:

Cabinet Secretaries	$83,300
Judges, U.S. Court of Appeals	$80,400
Director of the Central Intelligence Agency	$72,600
Chairman of the Council of Economic Advisers	$72,600
Director of the Office of Management and Budget	$72,600
Chairman, Board of Governors of the Federal Reserve System	$72,600
Director of the Office of Science and Technology Policy	$72,600
Administrator, National Aeronautics and Space Administration	$72,600

---

[1] Salary figures are for 1984.

[2] Per diem (daily) salary rates are for part-time positions that usually meet infrequently.

SOURCE: Committee on Government Affairs, United States Senate, *Policy and Supporting Positions* (98th Congress, 2d Session, 31 December 1984).

even better, anticipate, his policy desires. If they tilt the wrong way, the President has a dilemma: "Will my image and influence shrink if I fail to replace a rogue appointee? Can I get rid of him or her without bleeding politically? Is there someone else whose appointment would help me recoup my political losses?"

Since neither the public nor policy makers know for sure how political the federal bureaucracy should be, we do what we do best; we fight out the issue politically. The political fight is an ongoing one, as you can see in the evolution of the merit principle.

In the beginning, everyone simply wanted the "best" people to serve; not surprisingly, the "best" people under the Federalists turned out to be other wealthy Federalists and under the Jeffersonian Republicans, other wealthy Jeffersonian Republicans. Later, President Jackson used the principle to clean out what he saw as an unresponsive federal bureaucracy, and President Lincoln used it to consolidate his shaky hold on the Republican party. Thus, the **spoils system**, under which those victorious in elections rewarded their supporters with appointed positions, was firmly established.

Eventually, the corruption and inefficiency of the spoils system hastened its demise. Public outrage, progressive reformers, and incumbents who wished to protect the appointments they had just made joined in support of what became the **Civil Service Reform (Pendleton) Act of 1883**. The act tried to reduce **patronage**, the practice of filling governmental positions primarily on the basis of political considerations. In its place, the new Civil Service Commission was to follow a **merit principle**, under which positions were to be filled primarily through a system of competitive examinations.

Later, new growth in the size of the federal bureaucracy, under the New Deal and wartime programs of Franklin Roosevelt, brought more opportunities for filling the federal bureaucracy with the politically faithful. As the political

Casper Weinberger presents a report on Soviet defense buildup in order to justify an increase in defense spending.

THE BUREAUCRACY: LIFE IN THE TRENCHES

HALT! Sentinel Hayes: "You can't come in here, Gentlemen, with that Flag!"

tide swung away from liberal Democrats, however, Congress tried to limit the political, and especially the electoral, activities of this new army of federal bureaucrats, through passage of the **Political Activities (Hatch) Act of 1939**. Since then, the conflict between patronage and merit principles has continued, with no one side dominant. In the second administration of President Nixon, for example, the White House tried hard to politicize what they saw (probably correctly) as a federal bureaucracy heavily staffed with the politically liberal holdovers of previous Democratic administrations. Not defenseless, the bureaucracy fought back, often leaking to its allies in Congress and the press, information that politically damaged the Nixon administration and thereby weakened its will and capacity to fight on.[8]

Internal Fragmentation.   The federal bureaucracy, just like the rest of society, is a pretty factious place, full of competing values and their advocates. In one case, for example, the Department of Transportation had to defend its record of protecting the rights of the physically handicapped before another federal

---

[8] Richard Nathan, *The Plot That Failed: Nixon and the Administrative Presidency* (New York: Wiley, 1975).

agency, the Civil Rights Commission. In other cases, where it takes more than one agency to implement a policy, different parts of the federal bureaucracy fail to act in concert. In its efforts to clean up toxic wastes in the early 1980s, for example, the Environmental Protection Agency identified those who, it believed, violated the law and then referred those cases to the Justice Department, for prosecution. The Justice Department, however, did not always agree and sometimes failed to press formal charges. In this case, the federal bureaucracy was immobilized by a failure to agree on either the problem (did a violation of federal law occur?) or the solution (was it more important to punish the offender or to end the practice that brought the charge?). On this matter and on many others, there often are serious internal disagreements over what the problem is and what the law requires.

The fragmented structure of the federal bureaucracy creates opportunities for the acquisition and exercise of power. It is not the case that each federal agency commands its own well-fenced pastures; rather, it is as though many different agencies all want to graze, hunt, or plow the same open rangeland. In the words of Richard Neustadt, an astute observer and former insider, "Like our governmental structure as a whole, the executive establishment consists of separated institutions sharing powers. The president heads one of these; cabinet officers, agency administrators, and military commanders head others. Below the departmental level, virtually independent bureau chiefs head many more."[9] The bureaucracy's fragmentation also affects the way it does business, by making it more complicated and usually more inefficient.

Inefficiency.   How inefficient is the federal bureaucracy? The bad news is that the federal bureaucracy is not terribly efficient; the good news is that it is not supposed to be. There is no shortage of examples of the federal bureaucracy's inefficiency; in one case, the Food and Drug Administration (FDA) had to write regulations governing the percentage of peanut butter that was supposed to be made from peanuts—as opposed to solid vegetable fat. But, being a bureaucracy, the FDA had procedures to follow, hearings to conduct, preliminary findings to issue, hearings to consider objections to preliminary regulations, and so on—and on. Representatives of the peanut butter industry exploited every opportunity to press its case. Eventually, after a very sticky and not very efficient process, the FDA did adopt a regulation—twelve years after it first proposed one.[10]

It is hard to argue that bureaucratic inefficiency is desirable. It is waste, a squandering of social resources which, therefore, are not available for unmet social needs. As such, bureaucratic inefficiency should be rooted out, as President Reagan's Grace Commission concluded. In addition, policy makers themselves abhor bureaucratic inefficiency, because it erodes public support for public policies and for those who administer them.

---

[9] Richard E. Neustadt, *Presidential Power: The Politics of Leadership from FDR to Carter* (New York: Wiley, 1980), p. 39.

[10] Joseph C. Goulden, *The Superlawyers: The Small and Powerful World of the Great Washington Law Firms* (New York: Weybright and Talley, 1971, 1972), pp. 186–87.

Bureaucratic inefficiency knows no national boundaries, this cartoon from the Soviet Union suggests.

KROKODIL, Moscow

For example, after the disastrous explosion of the space shuttle Challenger in 1986, public exposure of bureaucratic waste and mismanagement eroded confidence in the National Aeronautics and Space Administration (NASA) and support for space exploration. As the investigation into the loss of the Challenger proceeded, it appeared as though the space shuttles cost much more than was promised by NASA, carried less than was expected, flew less often than was predicted, and, therefore cost much more than NASA had led Congress and the public to believe. (For some of the details, see **Figure 13.2**: NASA's failure to deliver on its promises.) The subsequent loss of public support was made clear in congressional hearings, newspaper editorials, and editorial cartoons.

Efficiency, however, is only one of the things that Americans value and expect of their governmental institutions. Moreover, efficiency often is not the most highly valued thing. Other qualities, such as fairness, effectiveness, and responsiveness often are more important. Indeed, excessive efficiency, speed at all costs, can be a bad idea, as it was when the federal government's Center for Disease Control tried too hard to inoculate Americans against the swine flu virus.

Finally, the inefficiency of the federal bureaucracy should be compared against other ones. On first glance, it is not obvious that the federal bureaucracy is more inefficient than the administrations of most colleges and univer-

FIGURE 13.2   NASA's Failures to Deliver on Its Promises

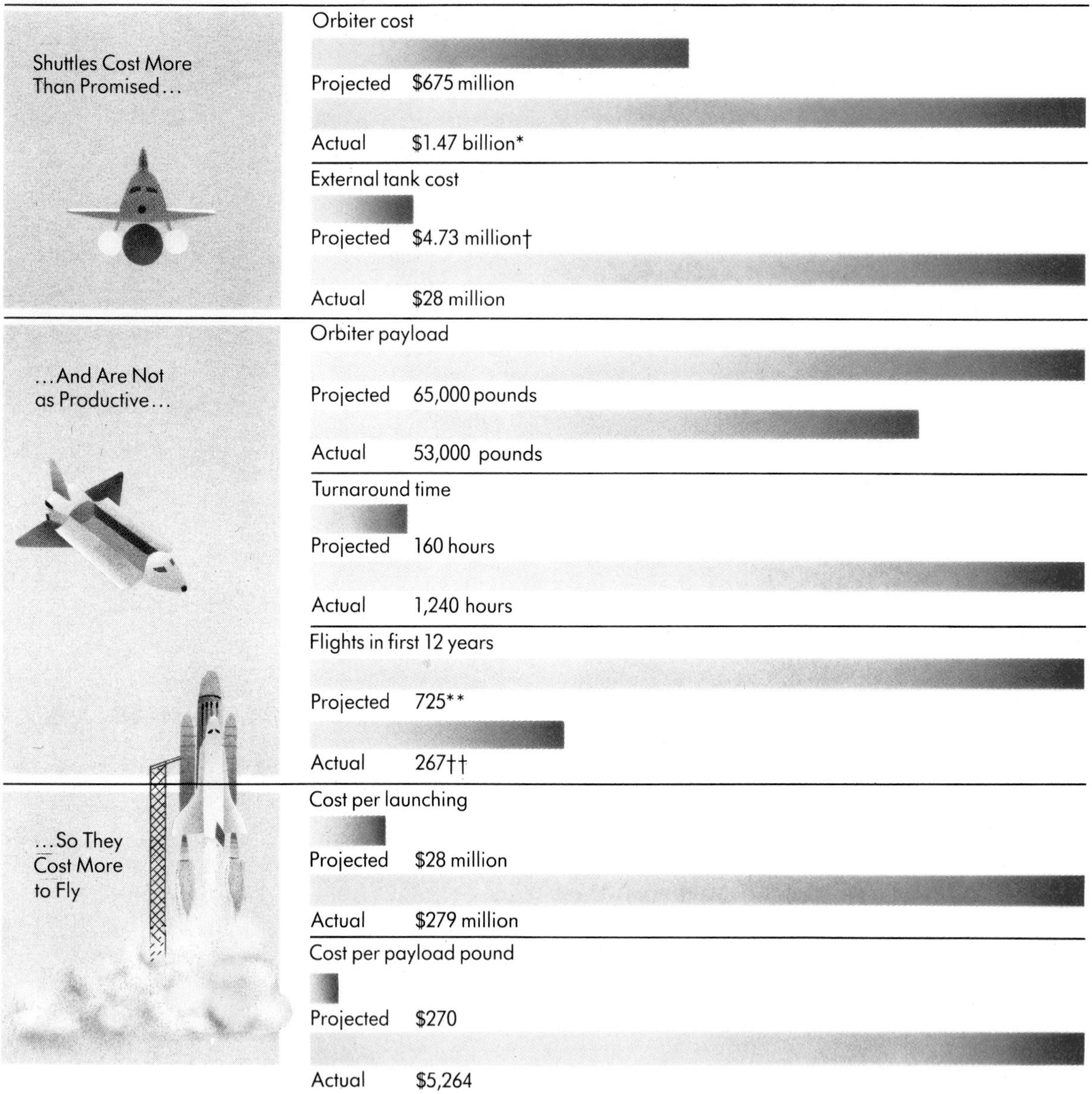

Shuttles Cost More Than Promised...

Orbiter cost

Projected $675 million

Actual $1.47 billion*

External tank cost

Projected $4.73 million†

Actual $28 million

...And Are Not as Productive...

Orbiter payload

Projected   65,000 pounds

Actual   53,000 pounds

Turnaround time

Projected   160 hours

Actual   1,240 hours

Flights in first 12 years

Projected   725**

Actual   267††

...So They Cost More to Fly

Cost per launching

Projected $28 million

Actual $279 million

Cost per payload pound

Projected $270

Actual $5,264

*Average cost of Challenger, Discovery and Atlantis.
† 1974 projection.
**1973 projection.
††Before Challenger accident.

NASA projections from 1972, except where noted, compared with actual figures.
All costs are in 1986 dollars.

sities, for example. In addition, the federal bureaucracy may be less inefficient than the administrative structures of private businesses, some researchers suggest.[11]

In spite of these caveats, it is hard to defend bureaucratic inefficiency, and politically it is easy and useful to attack it, as politicians often do. None do it more skillfully, and profitably, than Ronald Reagan. Moreover, as President, Reagan fought bureaucratic inefficiency and simultaneously advanced his policy agenda, by centralizing in the **Office of Management and Budget (OMB)** a process that required all federal agencies to clear proposed regulations before they could be issued. OMB, in turn, used this preclearance process to monitor and reduce the adoption of administrative regulations.

Components of the Federal Bureaucracy

The organizational structure of the federal bureaucracy is a bit overwhelming, or at least it must have seemed to William Gibbs McAdoo, President Woodrow Wilson's Secretary of the Treasury:

> I was like a sea captain who finds himself on the deck of a ship that he has never seen before. I did not know the mechanism of my ship; I did not know my officers—even by sight—and I had no acquaintance with the crew.[12]

To help it become less confusing, consider the following discussion.

The **federal bureaucracy** consists of four major components: cabinet departments, independent executive agencies, government corporations, and independent regulatory commissions. (**Figure 13.3** provides an overview of the entire bureaucratic structure of the federal government.)

Cabinet Departments. **Cabinet departments** are the main administrative units of the federal bureaucracy, with significant responsibilities over broad areas of the public policy. Today, there are thirteen cabinet departments, each headed by a Secretary who is nominated by the President and confirmed by the Senate. (The head of the Justice Department, however, is called the Attorney General.)

Congress originally created only three departments (State, Treasury, and War) and two offices (Attorney General and Postmaster General). By calling them together, President Washington created the first cabinet, making it clear that it was only an advisory body. Since then, the number of departments and the size of the cabinet have grown in response to pressures to expand government's role. Over time, some departments have come, others have gone, some have been renamed, and one has been divided in two. Today's thirteen

---

11 See Mark Green and John F. Berry, *The Challenge of Hidden Profits: Reducing Corporate Bureaucracy and Waste* (New York: Morrow, 1985).

12 In Richard F. Fenno, Jr., *The President's Cabinet* (Cambridge, Mass.: Harvard University Press, 1959), p. 225.

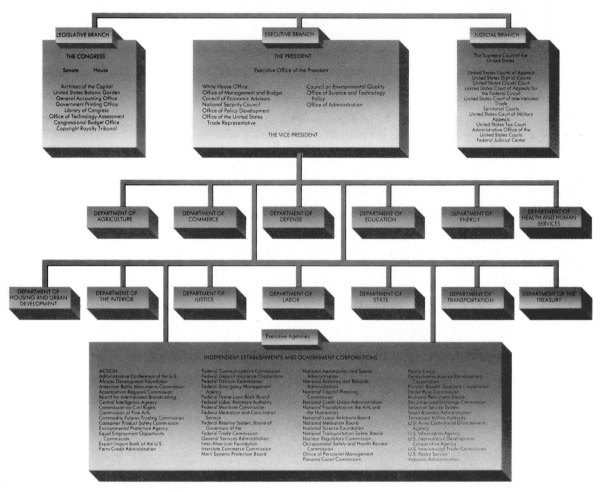

FIGURE 13.3   The Bureaucratic Structure of the Federal Government

SOURCE: Adapted from the U.S. Government Manual, 1985–86, p. 827.

departments are shown in **Table 13.1**, along with their dates of creation, numbers of employees, and budgets.

Cabinet departments are curious mixtures of administrative, policy-making, and political functions. As administrative units, departments are supposed to implement laws that fall under their jurisdiction. As policy makers, however, they often are expected to help design ways of serving the interests of a particular constituency, as the Department of Commerce is supposed to serve the interests of business and the Department of Agriculture is expected to look out for the concerns of farmers, for example. With their appointed heads, departments are supposed to be responsive to presidential leadership. As you might imagine, and as Secretary McAdoo laments, carrying out all these functions equally well can be very difficult.

THE BUREAUCRACY: LIFE IN THE TRENCHES

TABLE 13.1   Cabinet Departments

Department	Created	Civilian Employees (as of 1984)	Budget (as of 1984, in billions)
State	1789	24,706	$ 2.4
Treasury	1789	130,654	148.3
Defense (previously War)	1789	1,043,784	240.4
Justice	1789	61,398	3.2
Interior	1849	78,661	4.9
Agriculture[1]	1889	118,809	37.5
Commerce	1913	43,540	1.9
Labor	1913	18,320	24.5
Health and Human Services (previously Health, Education, and Welfare)	1953	144,240	292.3
Housing and Urban Development	1965	12,393	16.5
Transportation	1966	62,781	23.9
Energy	1977	16,976	10.6
Education	1979	5,349	15.5

NOTE: With dates of creation to show when the federal government accepted a new major role and employment and budget figures to show the prominence of their current role.

[1] Although created in 1862, Agriculture was not a part of the Cabinet until 1889.

SOURCE: U.S. Bureau of the Census, *Statistical Abstract of the United States: 1986,* 106th ed., (Washington D.C., 1985), Table 531, p. 325 and Table 499, p. 311.

Independent Executive Agencies.   There are over fifty independent agencies of the federal government, each headed by a "director" or "administrator," who also is appointed by the President and confirmed by the Senate. **Independent executive agencies**, like cabinet departments, are headed by someone who reports directly to the President but, unlike departments, executive agencies usually perform more narrowly defined functions (environmental protection, the peaceful exploration of space, or caring for veterans). Nevertheless, in addition to their administrative functions, executive agencies also get involved in policy making and are more or less open to political and particularly presidential, pressure. Examples of independent executive agencies include the Central Intelligence Agency, the National Science Foundation, and the U.S. Arms Control and Disarmament Agency. All the independent executive agencies appear in the lower half of **Figure 13.3**.

Government Corporations. **Government corporations** are public entities that perform business-like activities (delivering the mail, generating and distributing electricity in the Tennessee Valley, running passenger or freight trains, or insuring bank deposits). Other examples of governmental corporations are the Federal Deposit Insurance Corporation and the Pennsylvania Avenue Development Corporation. These are a lot like independent executive agencies, but a few steps away from policy and political considerations and a few steps toward more purely administrative chores. These, too, are listed in **Figure 13.3**, along with the independent executive agencies.

Independent Regulatory Commissions. Even further removed from political considerations, **independent regulatory commissions** are supposed to regulate various economic activities, not serve the interests of those who engage in them. Their members, although appointed by the President and confirmed by the Senate, enjoy some political independence, since they serve fixed terms and can not be fired by the President, unless he is prepared to defend such an action and take the heat for it. Some of the more important regulatory commissions are identified in **Table 13.2**, along a time line giving their date of creation (and, sometimes, demise).

■ This overview of the organizational structure of the federal bureaucracy makes it clear that it is many different things, not one uniform thing.

While continuing to allow for internal variations, it is now time to begin thinking about *what* goes on within the federal bureaucracy and *why* it happens as it does.

THE GOALS OF THE BUREAUCRACY

> Bureaucrats themselves have now become a central force in the policy process: in the identification of proposals, the weighing of alternatives, and the resolution of conflict.
> —*Professor Francis E. Rourke,*
> Bureaucratic Power in National Politics

In the swine flu case and in general, bureaucrats often work towards multiple goals.[13] In particular, the federal bureaucracy acts as though it has:

- *governance goals*, realized through following administrative routines, enforcing the law, and providing goods and services;

---

[13] Joel D. Aberbach, Robert D. Putnam, and Bert A. Rockman, *Bureaucrats and Politicians in Western Democracies* (Cambridge, Mass: Harvard University Press, 1981).

TABLE 13.2 Independent Regulatory Commissions, with their current
names, dates of creation (and demise).

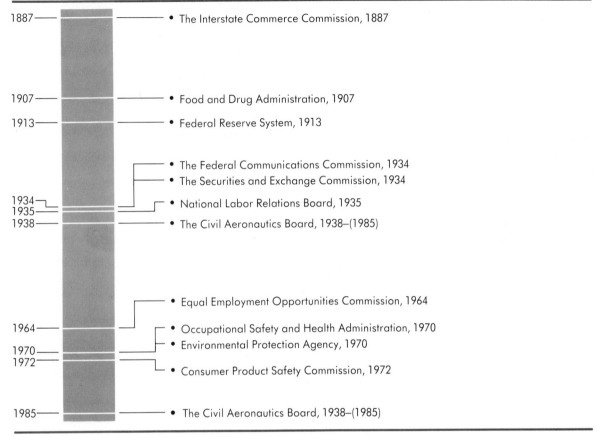

- *policy goals*, realized by interpreting the law, promoting organized interests, and regulating economic activity; and
- *political goals*, realized by representing political concerns, enhancing its own organizational powers, and furthering personal values and ambitions.

Governance Goals

In its classic, "textbook" role, the federal bureaucracy is primarily concerned with the goal of governance. "Governance," unfortunately, has a mundane ring to it. As one recent study concludes: "Politicians articulate society's dreams, and bureaucrats help bring them gingerly to earth."[14] Governance, however, is anything but mundane. Bringing the politician's dreams to earth requires the performance of various tasks: (1) following administrative routines; (2) enforcing the law; and (3) providing goods and services.

---

[14] *Ibid.*, p. 262.

Following Administrative Routines.

There are those who believe that the bureaucracy can, and should, administer the law without making policy or playing politics. Woodrow Wilson, for example, in his prepresidential career as a political scientist, claimed, "Administration lies outside the proper sphere of politics."[15] Without testing the general validity of Wilson's claim, there are some governance tasks that are primarily administrative. Without making meaningful policy choices and without getting involved in political conflicts, there are bureaucrats who put out forest fires, collect payroll withholding taxes, and sail Coast Guard icebreakers, for example. In these, and in many other cases, the law can be administered in ways that do not entail new policy choices and do not engage ongoing political conflicts.

Bureaucrats can administer the law in a straightforward manner, without making policy choices or playing politics, only when policy goals and procedures for realizing them have been clearly thought through and clearly laid out. When both these things are true, the federal bureaucracy only has to set up and follow **administrative routines**, regularized and repetitive tasks that can be handled impersonally, according to objective criteria.[16]

Enforcing the Law.

It is especially important that the federal bureaucracy try to avoid policy making and politics as it goes about enforcing laws that can take away, or infringe on, personal liberty. There are two reasons why this is desirable: (1) Americans act as though they believe that personal liberty is the most precious of all political values and, therefore, (2) the political system seriously endangers its own legitimacy when it lets the enforcement of criminal laws, for example, be contaminated by either policy or political considerations.

Enforcing the law, however, can not be totally a routine matter. Law enforcement agencies, even the Federal Bureau of Investigation, also are constrained by scarce resources. Since they do not have as much time, money, or staff as they would like, law enforcement officials must make choices among alternative ways of using the resources they do have. Making these choices is a matter of judgment in which competing considerations are weighed on imprecise, human scales.

The Antitrust Division of the Justice Department, for example, is responsible for enforcing the Sherman Antitrust Act.[17] The act makes it a federal crime to monopolize, or even try to monopolize, *most* commercial activities in the United States. While lots of people are trying lots of things to maximize profits, which of these things will be investigated for possible violations of the antitrust law? Of the investigated possible violations, which ones are worth prosecuting? Facing these choices, even the most professional staff attorney will find it necessary to weigh policy considerations, and sometimes will find it hard not to weigh political ones, as Suzanne Weaver shows in her study of the Antitrust Division.[18]

---

[15] *Ibid.*, p. 4.

[16] See Ira Sharkansky, *The Routines of Politics* (New York: Van Nostrand Reinhold, 1970).

[17] (15 U.S.C. secs. 1–7, Supp. I 1975).

[18] Suzanne Weaver, *Decision to Prosecute: Organization and Public Policy in the Antitrust Division* (Cambridge, Mass.: MIT Press, 1977).

Providing Goods and Services.   Some kinds of policies lend themselves to straightforward administration—ones that entail providing goods and services. There are many of these: making direct payments to individuals (Social Security checks to older Americans, Medicare and Medicaid payments to doctors and hospitals, for example); providing sick veterans with a hospital bed and treatment; delivering most of the mail; generating and distributing electricity (as the TVA does, for example); lifting commercial satellites into orbit (as NASA does, for example); letting contracts for the construction of military hardware. Even the provision of such goods and services can not be made completely automatic, in a manner that excludes policy and political considerations, however. For example, it probably was not an accident that NASA decided to construct its new, expensive main control center in President Lyndon Johnson's home state of Texas.

Policy Goals

The federal bureaucracy pursues policy goals by (1) interpreting the law, (2) promoting the interests of organized interest groups, and (3) regulating economic activity.

Interpreting the Law.   The federal bureaucracy often finds it necessary to interpret the law. There are four main reasons for this: (1) since it is not omniscient, Congress can not anticipate and legislate for all possible contingencies; (2) since it may not have thought through the social problem or the proposed policy, Congress may adopt badly designed and vague, but symbolically appealing, policies, but fail to consider the procedures for implementing them;[19] (3) since it sometimes lacks political courage, Congress may purposefully leave tough policy choices to the bureaucracy; and (4) since it needs to conserve its capacity to make fundamental policy choices on a wide range of issues, Congress must avoid getting bogged down in too much detail. Whatever the reason, the result is the same; the bureaucracy is given many chances to interpret the law and therefore to make meaningful choices among policy alternatives, while weighing political considerations.

In all the following situations, the actions (and nonactions) of Congress made bureaucratic interpretation unavoidable:

- Unable to anticipate every contingency, Congress simply provided that the U.S. tax code would allow for the deductibility of medical expenses, but left to Internal Revenue Service agents the task of deciding whether people could deduct the cost of cosmetic surgery.
- Unable to resist its symbolic appeal, Congress built into the War on Poverty legislation a requirement that citizens themselves should be involved, "to the greatest extent possible," in designing and carrying out community action projects but did not spell out what that entailed.[20]

---

[19] See Eugene Bardach, *The Implementation Game* (Cambridge, Mass.: MIT Press, 1977), pp. 250–51.

[20] See Daniel Patrick Moynihan, *Maximum Feasible Misunderstanding: Community Action in the War on Poverty* (New York: The Free Press, 1969).

- Not courageous (or stupid) enough to get in the middle of businesspersons who were going to complain about the cost of safety and representatives of labor who were going to object to attempts to place a dollar value on human life, Congress simply instructed the Occupational Safety and Health Administration (OSHA) to provide for the vague goal of "safety in the workplace."
- After tying itself in knots, while trying to keep U.S. foreign aid money from being spent, even indirectly, on abortions in China, the Senate simply shelved the whole matter, thereby dumping the problem in the lap of the head of the Agency for International Development.

In all these cases, either because Congress was not able to or did not want to, bureaucrats had to decide what the law really meant.

All these factors have a logic that is difficult to refute: it does seem inevitable that the federal bureaucracy will interpret the law. The Supreme Court also has acknowledged the inevitability: "Delegation by Congress has long been recognized as necessary in order that the exertion of legislative power does not become a futility," (as apparently, the Court thought it would, if Congress had to try to draft highly specific rules and regulations for all possible contingencies).[21] Nevertheless, Congress sometimes may go too far in delegating its constitutional duty and thereby erode the legitimacy of the law, as Theodore Lowi has argued forcefully.[22] In addition, members of Congress sometimes are irresponsible; especially when people object to the bureaucracy's exercise of authority, run to a member of Congress to complain, and he or she "lends a sympathetic ear, piously denounces the evils of bureaucracy, intervenes in the latter's decisions, and rides a grateful electorate to ever more impressive electoral showings."[23]

Promoting Organized Interests. Throughout American history, organized interest groups have pressed their claims on the national government, often demanding that Congress establish a new federal agency for the expressed purpose of looking after the group's special interests. This dynamic has brought us a large number of client agencies, parts of the federal bureaucracy that are supposed to promote the interests of particular groups. The Department of Agriculture, for example, is in the business of aiding the cause of farmers, not consumers and not migrant workers. Similarly, the Department of Commerce focuses on business concerns, while the Department of Labor is selectively attuned to things that organized labor cares about. In addition, once a new federal agency is established, it often maintains close working relationships

---

[21] *Sunshine Anthracite Coal Co.* v. *Adkins* 310 U.S. 381, 398 (1940). Also, *Opp Cotton Mills* v. *Administrator of Wage and Hour Division*, 312 U.S. 126 (1941).

[22] Theodore J. Lowi, *The End of Liberalism: Ideology, Policy, and the Crisis of Public Authority* (New York: W. W. Norton, 1969).

[23] Morris P. Fiorina, *Congress: Keystone of the Washington Establishment* (New Haven: Yale University Press, 1977), p. 49.

with both the congressional committee that recommended its creation and representatives of the organized interests it is supposed to serve. Such three-way relationships are often referred to as **iron triangles**, thus suggesting how durable they tend to be over time.

The federal bureaucracy promotes well-organized interests by two main routes: (1) it is ordered to, by law; and (2) it is coopted into doing so, usually by those it is supposed to serve or regulate. Client agencies, such as Commerce, Labor, and Agriculture, for example, carry explicit statutory mandates. Regulatory agencies, such as the Food and Drug Administration and the Interstate Commerce Commission, often end up looking as though they have been captured by those they are supposed to regulate. In some cases, it does appear as though regulatory agencies are biased towards the interests of the regulated industry; in other cases, however, the apparent bias may be the less conspiratorial result of the absence of competing political pressures.

The Food and Drug Administration, for example, sometimes acts as though it is more concerned with the image and profits of food producers than with the concerns of consumers who, typically, are not well-organized enough to bring effective pressure to bear. To see the ease with which the bias can come about, consider the case of the coarse hot dog. Producers find it cheaper, and therefore potentially more profitable to use machines, not people, to debone the meat they put into hot dogs. It is efficient, but not precise; little chunks of bone get mixed up with the meat. Instead of hiring people to pick out the pieces of bone, producers would rather use other machines to grind everything up more finely. The technology precipitated a policy choice for the FDA: what information, if any, should consumers be given about their hot dogs? Should they simply be told that the meat was mechanically deboned—and leave the rest to their imagination? Or, should they be told that their hot dogs had very fine pieces of bone mixed in? Given your understanding of the biases of client agencies, guess what it says on the package of hot dogs at your corner grocer?

Sometimes, when they find themselves promoting competing and well-organized interests, federal agencies have to try to reconcile conflicting ones. The Agriculture Department, for example, is supposed to promote agricultural interests. But whose? The interests of well-organized large farmers (typically represented by the American Farm Bureau Federation, AFBF), or the interests of also well-organized small farmers, who are better represented within the ranks of the National Farmers' Union? In such a situation, accommodations must be reached.

In general, the federal bureaucracy is big and diverse enough to do a good job of accommodating many of the society's important political interests, especially those of well-organized interest groups. In contrast, as Samuel Huntington has observed, the United States Congress does a better job of serving as "the representative of unorganized interests of individuals."[24]

Regulating Economic Activity. Federal regulations are the primary means through which the bureaucracy makes policy. These regulations are issued by all parts of the federal bureaucracy, not just the independent regulatory commissions. Their use, moreover, jumped in the early 1970s, partly because of increased demands for consumer protection, occupational safety, and environmental protection.

The increase in the regulatory policies of the federal government also reflected a belief that, in many areas of economic activity, the private market was not working, or was not working as efficiently as it was supposed to. Some correctly argued that the market did not, and could not, work if there were some things that people wanted, but no one selling them. For example, consider the people in upstate New York who would rather have clean air, than air laden with sulfur dioxide, and neutral, not acidic rain. There simply is no private market where these people could go to buy what they wish to buy. Therefore, if they are to be provided, government must produce such public goods. In this case, the federal government could produce clear air and non-acidic rain for New York through federal regulations governing what comes out of smokestacks in Ohio, for example.

In different situations, the argument for federal regulation rested on a belief that, while the private market might be working, in the sense that there were some people producing what other people wanted to buy, the market was not working as efficiently as possible.

For example, consider again the mechanically deboned meat in hot dogs. It is possible that the label on the hot dogs in your grocery store make no mention of this unappetizing deboning process. In that event, assume that you, blissfully ignorant of this process, buy $40 worth of hot dogs per month. Is the hot dog market working? Absolutely. Is it working efficiently? Well, that depends; it depends on how many dollars worth of hot dogs you would buy if you knew about the deboning and the ground up pieces of bone. If that number is less than $40, then the difference—the amount you are spending out of ignorance—is called waste. Any degree of waste is evidence that the market is not working efficiently. In such a situation, the advocates of regulation argued, government can improve the operation of the market (i.e., reduce waste) by

---

[24] Samuel P. Huntington, "Congressional Responses to the Twentieth Century," in David B. Truman, ed., *The Congress and America's Future* (Englewood Cliffs, NJ: Prentice-Hall, 1965), p. 30.

requiring producers to provide potential consumers with more and better information—such as explicit labels on hot dogs. In the short run, the argument for more federal regulation picked up momentum, because most people (consumers, for example) only saw its benefits, not its costs.

Over time, however, the drive for more regulation soon peaked, as more people began to believe that the benefits, even of environmental protection, were not worth the economic costs of lower productivity, higher unemployment, and lost wages.[25] By the late 1970s, the implicit benefit-cost calculation left increased federal regulation unappealing and some, encouraged by critical economic analyses of regulation[26] and goaded by a revitalized conservative movement, began to define governmental intervention in the economy as the cause, not the cure, of its difficulties.

Eventually, and surely by the early 1980s, the federal government embraced **deregulation**, a return to the principles of free-market economics which deemphasized government's role. In the rush, many regulations have been abolished, the rate of growth of new ones has been slowed drastically (partly because of a new procedure, under President Reagan, requiring that proposed regulations must be cleared by the Office of Management and Budget before they are issued, even in a tentative form), and whole regulatory agencies have been abolished, most notably, the Civil Aeronautics Board (CAB). In lieu of regulations and the bureaucrats who make and enforce them, people acted as though they were more willing to count on the private market

25 Anthony Downs, "Up and Down with Ecology—the 'Issue-Attention' Cycle," *Public Interest* 32 (1972): 38–50.

26 Charles L. Schultze, *The Public Use of the Private Interest* (Washington, D.C.: The Brookings Institution, 1977).

A Marine plays "Evening Colors" at a ceremony to mark the demise of the Civil Aeronautics Board.

to deal with its own problems. No one, however, could be sure it would and, moving into the late 1980s, some began to worry about and debate the costs of deregulation.[27] In the case of airline deregulation, for example, controversy focused on what some argued was a bitter by-product: an increase in air traffic accidents and deaths. While some refuted the claim, most of the public remained relatively inattentive, apparently not inclined to demand a return to more federal regulation.

There are valid arguments against some forms of federal regulations, especially ones that obviously favor producers and which may interfere with the operation of market forces. Both conditions seemed present in the case of the CAB, for example. As subsequent events proved, CAB regulations had locked out new companies which were able to offer cheaper fares. Fueled by such successes in the early 1980s, many people leaned toward **privatization**, letting the private sector perform public responsibilities. The movement was infectious; some states began to get out of the prison business, for example, by contracting with private businesses that thought they could run prisons more cheaply than the state.[28] It was hard to know where to stop, until the cost of deregulation and privatization began to pile up, in the form of such incidents as airline accidents, leaky toxic waste dumps, and contaminated ground water.

Political Goals

The federal bureaucracy pursues political goals by (1) representing political concerns, (2) enhancing its own organizational power, and (3) furthering the political values and ambitions of its members.[29]

Representing Political Concerns. The federal bureaucracy performs a political function by actively representing a diverse array of political concerns. Some scholars, such as Peter Woll, go so far as to suggest that the federal bureaucracy is, in general, more representative than Congress and especially more representative of national, as opposed to local, concerns.[30] Because of the expertise they bring to their tasks and because of their relatively greater tenure in office, federal bureaucrats are more able to provide ongoing representation of the political concerns of particular interest groups, as the Department of Labor has for labor unions and as the Social Security Administration has for older Americans.

The federal bureaucracy also tends to serve a function of **passive representation**, staffing the bureaucracy to reflect the characteristics of the American people as a whole. Those who advocate the federal bureaucracy's

---

[27] Susan J. Tolchin and Martin Tolchin, *Dismantling America: The Rush to Deregulate* (New York: Oxford University Press, 1983).

[28] See E. S. Silvas, *Privatizing the Public Sector: How to Shrink Government* (Chatham, NJ: Chatham House Publishing, 1982).

[29] See Robert T. Nakamura and Frank Smallwood, *The Politics of Policy Implementation* (New York: St. Martin's, 1980).

[30] Peter Woll, *American Bureaucracy* (New York: W. W. Norton, 1977).

affirmative obligation to promote equal access to public service do not equate access with effective representation, however. Even if women or blacks, for example, were well-represented at all levels of the federal bureaucracy, that, by itself, would not mean that the bureaucracy's actions would be more responsive to their political concerns. Nevertheless, it is argued by Frederick Mosher, for one, that the absence of even passive representativeness shouts too loudly; it immediately raises doubts of the bureaucracy's legitimacy.[31]

In more general ways, the federal bureaucracy is unavoidably political; it is a part of, and open to, its many political environments. Moreover, to carry out its governance and policy goals, the federal bureaucracy must interact with all the political actors in these environments: presidential appointees, members of Congress, representatives of organized interests groups, state and local governmental officials and their Washington representatives.

Enhancing Organizational Power. The process of political socialization (discussed in chapter 5) continues after people leave their parents' homes and after they become a part of some organization. In their case, federal bureaucrats often are socialized into a strong identification with their agency's mission and will become increasingly committed to furthering it. Furthering the cause typically means bureaucratic growth—more staff, a bigger budget, more authority, more discretion, and less interference.

Bureaucracies tend to grow, not shrink; they are, however, far from immortal.[32] Some theorists suggest that bureaucracies have their own growth dynamic; just as business firms are driven to maximize profits, bureaucracies are driven to maximize the size of their budget.[33] The theory may capture some of the reasoning behind the more superficial, but equally driving, motto that some attribute to the Army Corp of Engineers. Known for its dogged commitment to water projects, dredging here, damming there, and straightening streams everywhere, the Corps lives up to its informal motto: "dig we will 'cause dig we must."[34] In addition, encouragements for growth come from outside the bureaucracy, from clients and members of Congress, for example, who stand to benefit from expanded bureaucratic missions.

Furthering Political Values and Ambitions. Federal bureaucrats, just like the rest of us, have their own political values and personal ambitions. If they are any good, however, and many are, they will try to keep these private. As a result, it is difficult to obtain a documentation on these more private characteristics of public servants. As one of the best, Jim T. Tozzi, a member of the OMB under President Reagan, revealed: "I don't want to leave fingerprints."[35]

---

31 Frederick C. Mosher, *Democracy and the Public Service* (New York: Oxford University Press, 1968).

32 Herbert Kaufman, *Are Government Agencies Immortal?* (Washington, D.C.: The Brookings Institution, 1976).

33 W. Niskanen, *Bureaucracy and Representative Government* (Chicago: Aldine-Atherton, 1971).

34 See John A. Ferejohn, *Pork Barrel Politics: Rivers and Harbors Legislation, 1947–1968* (Stanford, Calif.: Stanford University Press, 1974).

35 Quoted in *The Journal*, 30 August 1981.

■ As was true of the Center for Disease Control, the federal bureaucracy does more than administer the law; it also makes policy and tries to serve various political interests. Performing these multiple goals can be very difficult, however, since they sometimes conflict with one another and since the bureaucracy's ability to realize goals is heavily constrained.

WAYS OF ACHIEVING BUREAUCRATIC GOALS

> Implementation is the continuation of policy-making by other means.
> —*Professor Eugene Bardach,*
> The Implementation Game

There is one thing more impressive than the federal bureaucracy's multiple goals: what it does to try to overcome its constraints.

Overcoming Constraints

The federal bureaucracy is constrained by general characteristics of the American political system and by specific characteristics of national governmental institutions.

In many ways, the American political system provides an environment that hinders the bureaucracy's ability to realize its goals.

- Most efforts to realize bureaucratic goals require some alteration of the way society uses its resources, but most resource allocation decisions are made outside the bureaucracy's reach, by private individuals.
- All efforts to realize bureaucratic goals require the use of the authoritative decision-making power of the state, but our constitutional framework limits government's authority and our political culture distrusts its exercise.
- The federal system of government also blunts bureaucratic efforts by imposing the need to coordinate the actions of many only loosely integrated levels of government.
- A strong tradition of protection of civil liberties and civil rights further limits what bureaucracies can do.
- Bureaucracies also find it difficult to develop broad-based public support for their mission, since this is a pluralistic political culture, where people tend to organize themselves around narrowly focused interests, while drifting away from appeals that try to span group differences.
- Finally, a bureaucracy will find it difficult to realize any broad public purpose in a culture that is preoccupied with private pleasures. As though all these barriers were not imposing enough, the federal bureaucracy is also

locked into a set of institutional constraints, stemming from (1) the bureaucracy itself, (2) the President, (3) Congress, and (4) the judicial system.

Bureaucratic Constraints. The federal bureaucracy is full of self-imposed constraints. Indeed, the defining characteristics of the bureaucracy, the sources of its capacity to achieve goals, can also block their realization. Specialization of function breeds expertise, but it also increases the number of specialists who need to be consulted and who, therefore, have opportunities to block action. Hierarchy places in the hands of some the authority to act, but also encourages what may be excessive caution. Objective rules and impersonal routines minimize the impact of subjective preferences, but also encourage bureaucratic indifference. Most importantly, the highly fragmented nature of the federal bureaucracy often breeds confusion and delay.

Presidential Constraints. The federal bureaucracy is constrained by any President who tries to make it responsive to his policy leadership. In recent years, Republican Presidents, specifically Reagan and Nixon, have tried to bend the bureaucracy to their will. Their very different experiences illustrate the President's ability to constrain the bureaucracy and the bureaucracy's capacity to resist.

President Reagan did to the federal bureaucracy what the tank did to trench warfare in World War I; he broke through static lines and changed the face of the battlefield. Through a variety of devices, ranging from outright abolition of agencies, such as the Community Services Agency, to more subtle techniques, such as leaving job openings vacant, Reagan successfully hamstrung the bureaucracy's capacity to carry out what it defined as its mission. A federal bureaucracy under presidential attack is not defenseless, of course; sometimes it can inflict damaging wounds on a President it sees as too intrusive. Under President Nixon, for example, the highly adversarial relationship between the White House and parts of the federal bureaucracy was "guerrilla warfare," according to one insider and political analyst.[36]

Congressional Constraints. Through a wide variety of devices, Congress also constrains the federal bureaucracy, especially on distributive policy matters that affect members' districts. Congress, for example, is especially likely to impose constraints on **congressional agencies**, those whose actions have significant effects on members' constituencies and therefore on their reelection prospects. This is especially true of the cabinet departments of Agriculture and Interior and other agencies, including the Army Corps of Engineers, the Small Business Administration, and the Veterans' Administration.

The devices used by Congress to constrain the bureaucracy include confirmation hearings, legislated mandates, agency appropriations, congressional oversight, and congressional investigations. In recent years, however, the major device has been the legislative veto. In general terms, a **legislative veto** is a

---

[36] Harold Seidman, *Politics, Position, and Power: The Dynamics of Federal Organization,* 2nd ed. (New York: Oxford University Press, 1975), p. 108.

As this cartoon suggests, it is hard for the President to impose his will on the federal bureaucracy.

This is the President! Throw out your rubber stamps . . . I have you surrounded!

requirement, written into a law, that some of the bureaucratic decisions required by the law can not go into effect until Congress has had a chance (x days) to veto them. In recent years, Congress has used legislative vetoes to block presidential actions, especially proposed foreign sales of military weapons. Presidents, understandably, believe that the threat of a congressional veto undermines their foreign policy-making role. They will fight hard and often successfully, against it, as President Reagan did, for example, in beating back an attempt to block his proposed sale of the airborne radar system, AWACS, to Saudi Arabia.

Moreover, recent action by the Supreme Court has attacked the constitutionality of the legislative veto and may have weakened its effectiveness as a constraint on the federal bureaucracy. In 1983, the Supreme Court ruled that everything which passes Congress must go to the President for his signature or veto. Therefore, legislative vetoes that do not require the President's signature are unconstitutional. The decision appears to have a firm basis in constitutional law. But, as a matter of administrative necessity, Congress does need some way of keeping a rein on the bureaucracy and, until it comes up with a better one, it probably will continue to rely on legislative vetoes (as it has). As long as the continued use of legislative vetoes goes unchallenged, the Supreme Court probably will continue to ignore the practice.

Judicial Constraints. The federal bureaucracy is heavily bound by a number of legal and judicial constraints. These include the Administrative Procedure

Act that guarantees a hearing to people likely to be affected by bureaucratic regulations, civil service laws that protect employees against unreasonable discipline and dismissal, and the Freedom of Information Act which provides public access to records of internal deliberations. In addition, the federal bureaucracy is constrained by a number of laws regulating internal accounting and hiring practices; environmental protection laws that, for example, require the completion and filing of environmental impact statements on proposed projects; sunshine laws, such as the Government in the Sunshine Act of 1976, which require that many federal agencies conduct their business publicly; and sunset laws that set expiration dates on some bureaucratic activities, unless Congress formally re-authorizes them.

Some laws constrain those who would constrain the bureaucracy, however. The President, for example, may not fire people he has appointed to regulatory commissions, as the Supreme Court ruled in 1935, in *Humphrey's Executor* v. *United States*.[37] (It is Humphrey's "executor" because Humphrey died shortly after President Roosevelt fired him; it was the executor of his estate who wanted Humphrey's back pay.) In general, the Supreme Court has ruled that most federal employees can not be fired without the protections of due process.[38] On the other hand, while they are quick to constrain the bureaucracy's failure to follow certain procedures, courts are reluctant to intervene on substantive matters, especially ones involved in the making of regulatory policy.[39]

Expanding Formal Powers

The federal bureaucracy can succumb to its various constraints. Or, it can try to expand whatever formal powers it has—and find, or invent, additional informal ones, as well.[40]

The federal bureaucracy seeks to expand its formal powers (1) through bureaucratic imperialism, (2) by exploiting its expertise, and (3) by exercising discretion.

Bureaucratic Imperialism. Agencies act as though they are motivated by a territorial imperative, a drive to expand and defend their own domain. The objective, as in political and economic forms of imperialism, is greater control over relevant resources. For a bureaucratic agency, the imperialistic ideal is self-sustaining power, the capacity to be master of its own fate.

This imperialistic ideal is hard to approach. Few federal agencies have come as close, in recent years, as the Federal Bureau of Investigation (FBI). For years after its creation, the FBI suffered under its deservedly poor reputa-

---

[37] *Humphrey's Executor* v. *United States*, 295 U.S. 602 (1935).

[38] *Arnett* v. *Kennedy*, 416 U.S. 134 (1974).

[39] *Railroad Commission of Texas* v. *Rowan and Nichols Oil Co.*, 311 U.S. 570 (1941).

[40] See, for its treatment of the sources of bureaucratic power, Francis E. Rourke, *Bureaucracy, Politics, and Public Policy*, 3rd ed. (Boston: Little, Brown and Company, 1984).

Marie Ragghianti. Her act of "whistle-blowing" eventually forced then-Governor of Tennessee, Ray Blanton, out of office.

tion, until the appointment of J. Edgar Hoover in 1924. Over the next fifteen years, Hoover cultivated his image of personal integrity and political independence, while simultaneously professionalizing the FBI's staff, recruiting people on the basis of job-related qualifications, not political connections, and rewarding them on the basis of dedication and accomplishment. By the early 1930s, the FBI had established itself as a politically clean crime-fighting machine, ready to take on new challenges. Its opportunity came in Hoover's much publicized campaign against the antiheroes of the Depression, John Dillinger, "Pretty Boy" Floyd, "Ma" Barker, Bonnie and Clyde Barrow, and others who helped Hoover fill the public eye. By the end of the 1930s, "Hoover had established himself and the FBI as national figures. . . . (H)is nominal superiors in the Justice Department began to lose their grip on Hoover. . . . His agency was sealed off from public scrutiny . . . (the FBI had become) one of the most powerful public agencies in the history of the United States."[41] Imperialism, however, can make bureaucrats too powerful and too inclined to misuse that power, as, for example, Hoover did in spying on civil rights activists, most notably the Reverend Martin Luther King, Jr.

Exploiting Expertise.   Through various forms of imperialism, federal bureaucracies expand their domain. But to exercise effective influence over its domain, a federal bureaucracy also must acquire and exploit expertise.

For the bureaucracy, expertise is the ultimate resource. According to Max Weber: "The absolute monarch is powerless opposite the superior knowledge of the bureaucratic expert."[42] To expand their formal powers, therefore, federal bureaucracies will seek to develop and to protect their own reservoirs of information. There are, obviously, different kinds of useful information. The FBI, for example, was able to expand and to exploit its centralized storehouse of fingerprints. In more recent years, the Office of Management and Budget (OMB) became more powerful because of its Director's comprehensive and unrivaled command over the details of the federal budget.

Expertise can be used by bureaucrats against their own bureaucracy, however. Whatever the cause, either because they sincerely believe that the agency is moving counter to its mission or for less noble reasons, a member of an agency can turn their expertise against its practices. To frustrate what they see as improper or undesirable, "whistle-blowers," for example, can leak surreptitiously or can go public with damaging or embarrassing information. Moreover, it is easy to leak, since the media are selectively attuned to scandal. "Whistle-blowing," however, is not entirely costless, since civil service laws afford little protection against retaliation. The federal bureaucracy would prefer to wash its dirty linen behind closed doors, something it tries to do by maintaining toll-free "hot lines" to encourage internal reporting of fraud or abuse.

---

[41] Eugene Lewis, *Public Entrepreneurship: Toward a Theory of Bureaucratic Political Power* (Bloomington, Ind.: Indiana University Press, 1980), pp. 122–23.

[42] Quoted in H. H. Gerth and C. Wright Mills, *From Max Weber: Essays in Sociology* (New York: Oxford University Press, 1953), p. 234.

Exercising Discretion. There are, of course, many ways in which a federal bureaucrat may exercise discretionary decision-making authority. This can be done, for example, by changing the rate of spending, exercising the right to refer matters for criminal prosecution, or altering enforcement efforts. Given the opportunity, however, federal bureaucrats tend to exercise discretion in ways that increase and protect their power base.

Unfortunately for them, but not necessarily for the rest of us, many federal bureaucrats exercise discretion in ways that erode their power base. In recent memory, no federal servant exceeded James Watts' number of self-inflicted wounds. Time and again, the Secretary of the Interior would exercise his discretion in a manner that appeared capricious, by, for example, letting it look as though he was trying to keep the Beach Boys from performing on the Washington Mall because they were not moral enough. Ultimately, Watts' misuses of discretion hastened his downfall; power, he may have learned, like virtue, is easier to lose than acquire.

Creating and Exercising Political Power

In addition to their formal powers, federal bureaucracies that would overcome constraints and realize goals also try to create and exercise political power. There are three major ways of doing this: (1) by cultivating constituencies; (2) through power brokering, and (3) through various strategies for converting environmental resources into institutional power.

Cultivating Constituencies. A bureaucratic agency's image counts as much as anyone's; they often try hard to improve it, by cultivating wide-spread popular support. The desired image is one of legitimacy, the view that the agency's role is both proper and desirable. The image can be cultivated well or poorly. The Defense Department, for example, once advertised its virtues too blatantly; a television documentary, "The Selling of the Pentagon," badly discredited the campaign. In other cases, the effort is more subtle and more substantive. Sometimes, for example, an agency will try to cultivate "grass-roots" support through **cooptation**, the inclusion of representatives of the public or concerned groups in its internal deliberations, as Philip Selznick showed in his study of the Tennessee Valley Authority[43] and as Daniel Mazmanian and Jeanne Nienaber found in their research on the Army Corps of Engineers.[44] In these ways, federal bureaucrats massage the masses, shore up their political foundations, and generate popular support for their mission.

---

[43] Philip Selznick, *TVA and the Grass Roots: A Sociology of Formal Organization* (New York: Harper and Row, 1966).

[44] Daniel Mazmanian and Jeanne Nienaber, *Can Organizations Change?: Environmental Protection, Citizen Participation, and the Corps of Engineers* (Washington, D.C.: The Brookings Institution, 1979). See also John E. Chubb, *Interest Groups and the Bureaucracy: The Politics of Energy* (Stanford, Calif.: Stanford University Press, 1983).

THE WILDAVSKY—POLSBY DIALOGUE CONTINUED . . .

AUTHOR: What about Congress' role? What does it do well? What does it do poorly?

POLSBY: I think the most important thing people have to remember about Congress is that all these are elected officials and, collectively, they have considerable legitimacy in our political system—a fact that is sometimes not appreciated by people who are president-centric. You simply have to remember that the reason Congress often fails to come to agreements is because there are genuine disagreements in the political system about how things should be done or what should be done. Congress is a very influential arena in which these disagreements are battled out. Congress is not meant to be efficient in the sense of taking one particular line of action and pursuing it relentlessly. The efficiency of Congress comes in mirroring the diverse sentiments of a very diverse political system.

WILDAVSKY: Congress is both asking more divisive questions and depriving itself of the moderating mechanisms it used to have. In the old days, they were so worried about conflict, they diffused, they fragmented, they never confronted anything, they ran away from the whole business. Now they confront so there's more disagreement.

POLSBY: I wonder about that. I think, in fact, they're less inclined to do that than any other part of our political system.

AUTHOR: Less inclined to create conflicts?

POLSBY: That's right. They contain and moderate a lot of conflict. After all, there is a lot of disagreement in Congress; Congress embodies conflict. And

when they come to any kind of a conclusion it's quite unusual. They do a lot of stalemating and fight a lot of guerilla warfare against the President. That's normal in our system, in my view for Congress to be the reluctant partner in changing public policy.

AUTHOR: What would you have students see as the strengths and weaknesses of bureaucracy, especially the bureaucracy of the federal government?

POLSBY: Well, in the first place, I don't see any reason to draw a distinction between the efficiency of the Social Security Administration, let's say, and the efficiency of the Sears Roebuck Company or the efficiency of the General Motors Company. And if

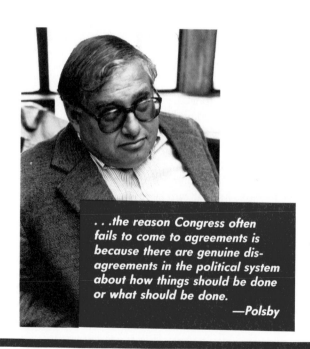

. . .the reason Congress often fails to come to agreements is because there are genuine disagreements in the political system about how things should be done or what should be done.

—Polsby

I think it exceptionally unfortunate that Jimmy Carter campaigned against the government as a Democrat. Who do you expect will carry out your policies? And, indeed, how can Reagan make a distinction between the defense bureaucrats, who're supposedly all right, and the domestic ones who are not?
                                                                    —Wildavsky

you believe that General Motors never made a lemon then you believe that the U.S. bureaucracy never makes mistakes.

In fact, given the size and scope of the governmental bureaucracies, they're pretty efficient. There are some screw ups, but not a lot. And there's some corruption, but not a lot.

Something else rather more interesting is true of our bureaucracies; they are changing their fundamental functions. The fundamental functions fifty years ago were to provide direct services of various kinds. Today, their fundamental functions are far more likely to be to write regulations and then to let contracts so that contractors (private entrepreneurs, states, localities and non-profit organizations, such as universities) perform the primary functions.

WILDAVSKY: I think one of the failures of the Reagan Administration has been not giving adequate support to the federal bureaucracy. It is perfectly appropriate for an administration advertised as believing in limited government to do what it can to reduce the size of that domestic government. But,

for people who claim to support American institutions and who wish citizens to have respect for authority, for these people to denegrate the major forms of authority in America, which is our bureaucracy, our public service, is a major mistake. I think also that the quality of government in our country has something to do with the adequacy of reward. It has never been very great in the public service. But the Reagan Administration, joined by Congress everytime it wants an easy expenditure cut, chooses the public service. I think that is unfortunate; they would do better to take opportunities to build up the status of that service than to tear it down. I think it exceptionally unfortunate that Jimmy Carter campaigned against the government as a Democrat. Who do you expect will carry out your policies? And, indeed, how can Reagan make a distinction between the defense bureaucrats, who're supposedly all right, and the domestic ones who are not?

Power Brokering. To create and exercise political power, bureaucracies must do more than generate diffuse public support for general goals. In addition, bureaucratic agencies need to generate more active support for specific policy proposals. They try to get it through **power brokering**, the exchange of tangible benefits for active political support.[45] The practice, moreover, reaches throughout the society, into different pockets of power. Many federal agencies, for example, run congressional liaison operations to service the ego and constituent needs of members of Congress, either through free overseas travel or through delivering benefits, such as public works projects, to a member's district. Deals also can be struck by threatening to withhold benefits. When members of Congress talk of reducing the federal subsidy to Amtrak, for example, its officials find reason to announce possible cutbacks in lines that seem "to run through the districts of critical members of the Appropriations and Commerce committees."[46] In other cases, federal agencies practice power brokering with politically well-organized interest groups, as, for example, the Veterans' Administration often does with Vietnam Vets, supporting their policy aims, while counting on their continued support for the Administration's various goals. In such ways, bureaucracies give whatever they can to get what they need. To accomplish their goals, they need political power. To get it, bureaucracies should be willing to provide whatever it takes—other than their own power.

Converting Resources into Power. The federal bureaucracy, like other institutions of American government, is buffeted by conflicting expectations of its proper role. We both demand that it realize many goals and distrust its efforts to do so. In this hostile environment, it is not surprising that federal bureaucracies try to find or invent additional resources and convert them into political power. They must, if they are to have any chance of overcoming the fragmentation of governmental institutions and therefore of public power.

Federal bureaucracies, however, often fail to acquire enough power to realize their goals. Ironically, they usually fail because they try to do too much. The lesson can be drawn from many disasters. By overreaching, in his attempt to control the rest of the executive branch, President Nixon, for example, hastened his own demise. By overreaching, in its attempt to regulate all aspects of the workplace, even the required shape of toilet seats, the Occupational Safety and Health Administration embarrassed its own supporters.[47] By overreaching, in his attempt to dominate all public works projects in and around New York, Robert Moses lost quality control—and power.[48] In all these and other cases, the lust for power was its own corrective.

---

[45] For a related view, see Robert H. Salisbury, "An Exchange Theory of Interest Groups," *Midwest Journal of Political Science* 13 (1969): 1–32.

[46] Morris Fiorina, *Congress: Keystone of the Washington Establishment*, p. 78.

[47] Timothy B. Clark, "What's All the Uproar Over OSHA's 'Nit-picking' Rules?," *National Journal*, 7 October 1978, pp. 1594–95.

[48] See Robert A. Caro, *The Power Broker: Robert Moses and the Fall of New York* (New York: Vintage Books, 1974), especially Part VII.

Finally, even when bureaucracies succeed, the price may be too high. Intent upon success, bureaucracies may give away too much. As Theodore Lowi showed in *The End of Liberalism*,[49] federal agencies have become increasingly dependent on the continued support of powerful special interest groups. As a result, federal agencies are powerful only as long as they service the interests of their clients. When this happens, as it does too often Lowi believes, the bureaucracy gives away its most precious resource: its capacity to chart its own course and to achieve justice for all Americans.

■ Most federal bureaucracies are heavily constrained and therefore limited in their ability to realize their goals. The constraints are purposeful, however; they protect other values of concern to people and guard against the premature adoption of a policy that may turn out to be undesirable or even disastrous.

The bureaucracy, however, is not passive in the face of constraints and, in various ways, tries to overcome these obstacles and achieve its various goals. Sometimes its success in doing so can bring about successful implementation and greater power for the bureaucracy. More often and as was true in the case of the Center for Disease Control's drive to immunize the country, bureaucratic efforts to circumvent constraints produce results that are undesirable, both for a bureaucracy that values its legitimacy and for a society that values democratic traditions and procedures.

SUMMARY

Much of what the federal government does is determined in the trenches of the federal bureaucracy. That is why it is important to know the following.

The federal bureaucracy is huge, with almost three million civilian employees; tends to administer programs indirectly, by relying on state and local governmental officials, voluntary associations, and private persons; is staffed at the bottom, mostly by civil service appointees and at the top, mostly by political appointees; is badly fragmented by the same kinds of value conflicts that roar through the rest of society; and, finally, is not terribly efficient, but it is not meant to be.

The major structural components of the federal bureaucracy are Cabinet departments (Defense, for example), independent executive agencies (the Veterans' Administration, for example), Government corporations (the Tennessee Valley Authority, for example), and independent regulatory commissions (the Environmental Protection Agency, for example).

The federal bureaucracy strives to achieve three kinds of goals: governance goals (following administrative routines, enforcing the law, and providing goods and services to various clients); policy goals (interpreting the law,

---

[49] Theodore Lowi, *The End of Liberalism*.

promoting organized interests, and regulating economic activity); and political goals (representing political concerns, enhancing its own organizational power, and furthering the political values and ambitions of individual bureaucrats).

Various obstacles stand in the way of the federal bureaucracy's attempt to realize its various goals. These constraints stem from the general nature of the political system and from specific characteristics of the bureaucracy itself, the presidency, Congress, and the judicial system.

To overcome these constraints and have any chance of realizing its goals, the bureaucracy needs to expand its formal powers and find ways of creating and using additional, political power. It tries to expand its formal powers through imperialistic expansion, by exploiting its expertise, and by exercising its discretion selectively. It tries to create and exercise its political power by cultivating broad, public constituencies, by exchanging services for support, and in general by converting various resources into institutional influence.

Key Terms

bureaucracy
Office of Personnel Management
Merit System Protection Board
spoils system
Civil Service Reform (Pendleton) Act of 1883
patronage
merit principle
Political Activities (Hatch) Act of 1939
Office of Management and Budget
federal bureaucracy
Cabinet departments

independent executive agencies
government corporations
independent regulatory commissions
administrative routines
iron triangles
deregulation
privatization
passive representation
congressional agencies
legislative veto
cooptation
power brokering

Review and Reflection

1. Describe the organizational characteristics of the federal bureaucracy.

2. In what ways do the following components of the federal bureaucracy differ from one another: cabinet departments, independent executive agencies, government corporations, and independent regulatory commissions?

3. Why is the federal bureaucracy simply unable to administer the law, without making policy or playing politics?

4. What constrains federal bureaucrats as they try to realize their various goals?

5. What can bureaucrats do to realize their goals?

6. What do you think is the proper role of the federal bureaucracy in the American system of government?

Supplemental Readings

The literature on the federal bureaucracy is as varied as its subject.

Good overviews can be found in *Edwards, Nakamura and Smallwood*, and *Rourke*.

For excellent case studies of particular policy areas, take a look at *Bardach* (on the implementation of a policy to protect the civil liberties of those alleged to be mentally ill), *Chubb* (on energy policy), and *Halperin* (on foreign policy).

For topical information, see current issues of the *National Journal* and the slightly more sensationalized *Washington Monthly*.

For lasting insights, it is hard to beat *Downs* or *Pressman and Wildavsky*.

Finally, since some are trying to slow down, or even reverse, the growth of the federal bureaucracy, it would be useful to consider *Tolchin and Tolchin* on the costs of deregulation and *Schultze* on the search for non-coercive alternatives to regulations.

Bardach, Eugene. *The Implementation Game: What Happens after a Bill Becomes a Law*. Cambridge, Mass.: The MIT Press, 1977.

Chubb, John E. *Interest Groups and the Bureaucracy: The Politics of Energy*. Stanford, Calif.: Stanford University Press, 1983.

Downs, Anthony. *Inside Bureaucracy*. Boston: Little, Brown, 1967.

Edwards, George C., III. *Implementing Public Policy*. Washington, D.C.: CQ Press, 1980.

Halperin, Morton H. *Bureaucratic Politics and Foreign Policy*. Washington, D.C.: Brookings Institution, 1974.

Nakamura, Robert T., and Frank Smallwood. *The Politics of Policy Implementation*. New York: St. Martin's, 1980.

The *National Journal*, a Washington, D.C. based periodical that covers the federal bureaucracy as well as the *Congressional Quarterly Weekly Report* which covers Congress.

Pressman, Jeffrey L., and Aaron Wildavsky. *Implementation*. 3rd ed. Berkeley, Calif.: University of California Press, 1984.

Tolchin, Susan J., and Martin Tolchin. *Dismantling America: The Rush to Deregulate*. Boston: Houghton Mifflin Company, 1983.

Washington Monthly.

Rourke, Francis E. *Bureaucracy, Politics, and Public Policy*. 3rd ed. Boston: Little, Brown, 1984.

Schultze, Charles L. *The Public Use of the Private Interest*. Washington, D.C.: The Brookings Institution, 1977.

CHAPTER FOURTEEN

THE COURTS
LIFTING THE CURTAIN ON JUDICIAL BEHAVIOR

*T*he robes on judges and the curtains on judicial proceedings obscure the highly personal nature of judges and shield from public view the role of courts in making policy and in resolving political conflict. Moreover, it may be essential that these characteristics and these roles be kept out of the public eye.

Courts and the Supreme Court in particular, more so than any other governmental institution, have a tenuous grip on their own legitimacy. For the other institutions, especially the presidency and Congress, legitimacy requires a close fit between their actions and the preferences of the people. The legitimacy of courts rests on less firm and more abstract footing, however. For courts in general, legitimacy requires a close fit between their actions and what is believed to be the intent of the law. For the Supreme Court in particular, legitimacy requires a close fit between their actions and what is believed to be the intent of the Founders, as expressed in the Constitution.

Given the nature of their legitimacy, it is more than appropriate that other governmental institutions alter their actions so as to move closer to public opinion. That is not true of courts. Given the nature of their legitimacy, it is generally thought to be inappropriate that courts alter their actions so as to move closer to the wishes of other policy makers or the desires of the people. Nevertheless, they do, while trying to cling to their legitimacy.

The following Case lifts the curtain to expose the inner workings of the Supreme Court, as they were revealed in a book by Bob Woodward and Scott Armstrong, The Brethren: Inside the Supreme Court. The account, although perhaps sensationalized, suggests three insights. First, the Supreme Court is a very human institution whose decisions are shaped both by legal doctrine and by personal preferences. Second, in spite of its image, the Supreme Court does more than administer justice; it also makes policy and selectively advances political values. Third, the Supreme Court acts like other governmental institutions. Constrained in its ability to realize its various goals, the Court expands its formal powers and seeks to create and exercise informal, political ones as well.

THE NATURE OF THE SUPREME COURT

> Judicial decision making involves, at bottom,
> a choice between competing values by falli-
> ble, pragmatic, and at times nonrational men
> in a highly complex process in a very human
> setting.
>
> —Nina Totenberg, a former
> Supreme Court law clerk
> (writing before the appoint-
> ment of Associate Justice
> Sandra Day O'Connor)

The Case   The Brethren Brouhaha

Why all the fuss? It was only a book, after all. Surely the Supreme Court was strong enough to survive this account of its inner workings. Nevertheless, the reactions were hot and typically hostile.

The Brethren, by Bob Woodward, of *Watergate* fame, and Scott Armstrong, purported to be an insiders' account of the term-by-term workings of the Supreme Court of the United States from 1969 to 1975, the first seven years of Warren E. Burger's service as chief justice.[1] The author's method of gathering and reporting information helped make the book both appealing and, to some, appalling. They described their approach in the book's introduction:

> Most of the information in this book is based on interviews with more than two hundred people, including several Justices, more than 170 former (Supreme Court) law clerks, and several dozen former employees of the Court. Chief Justice Warren E. Burger declined to assist us in any way. Virtually all the interviews were conducted "on background," meaning that the identity of the source will be kept confidential.[2]

The approach promised revelations, at a price. The public would see the inner workings of one of the most hallowed and secret of American governmental institutions. The price would be its loss of mystery, and, some argued, the trust broken by those who agreed to be interviewed.

With their fast-paced, breathless, gossipy reporting, uncluttered with either quotation marks or serious documentation, Woodward and Armstrong raised the curtain on the deliberative processes that lead to Supreme Court decisions, exposing its human and highly political nature.

The book's prepublication hype sampled the forthcoming revelations:

---

[1] Bob Woodward and Scott Armstrong, *The Brethren: Inside the Supreme Court* (New York: Avon, 1979).

[2] *Ibid.*, p. xiv.

The Brethern, by Bob Woodward (the mouse on the right) and Scott Armstrong, left the Supreme Court justices with little to hide behind.

- When badly outnumbered, Chief Justice Burger sometimes voted against his own beliefs, just so he would be in the majority and therefore able to get the credit for writing the majority's opinion.
- Chief Justice Burger, apparently motivated by partisan political considerations, slowed down the release of the Court's decision upholding a woman's right to an abortion, until after President Nixon's re-election and inaugural.
- Many of the clerks had their own ideas about what "their" justice should do and tried to push him in that direction.
- As they saw more of the work of Chief Justice Burger, the Court's law clerks narrowed their debate—was he evil or stupid? The prepublication hype worked; within days of its publication, *The Brethren* moved to the top of *The New York Times* best-sellers' list.

While its revelations titillated many, *The Brethren* appalled others: . . . a "failure," said *The New York Times*; a "travesty," intoned *The New York Review of Books*; a "trivial, vulgar and stupid book," blasted *The New Republic*. . . .[3] Others, however, saw both redeeming virtue and apparent validity in *The Brethren*. Drawing on his own experience in California's Supreme Court, Robert M. Kaus, for example, wrote of *The Brethren*: "For all its obvious flaws, it reveals more of what there is left to know about how an entire branch of government works . . . than just about any single book you could name."[4]

---

[3] Quoted in Robert M. Kaus, "They Were Wrong About *The Brethren*," *The Washington Monthly*, March, 1981, 32–40.

[4] *The Washington Monthly*, March 1981, p. 32.

BOB WOODWARD, MODERN DAY MUCKRAKER

Bob Woodward, age twenty-nine, was still in his first year as a reporter with *The Washington Post* when he was assigned to cover the break-in, on June 17, 1972, at the Democratic National Committee's headquarters in the Washington, D.C. office-apartment complex, Watergate.[1]

For the next two years, Woodward and a colleague at the *Post*, Carl Bernstein, pursued what became the story of the attempt to coverup the break-in, eventually producing a staggering string of scoops: tracing the money used to finance the break-in to the (Republican) Committee to Re-elect the President, implicating key aides in the Nixon White House with illegal attempts to disrupt the presidential campaign of the Democratic nominee (George McGovern), linking the FBI and the CIA with the coverup, exposing the Republican party's receipt and attempts to "launder" illegal campaign contributions, and documenting attempts to use the IRS to harass Nixon's political enemies. These and other revelations would fuel the drive to impeach President Richard Nixon, precipitating his resignation on August 9, 1974.

Woodward and Bernstein's account of their investigation, *All the President's Men*,[2] published in 1976, revealed some of their techniques but concealed the identify of their key source, dubbed "Deep Throat." The movie, *All the President's Men*, was released the same year. With Robert Redford portraying Woodward, the film further romanticized the press and apparently stimulated a flood of applications to journalism schools.

Woodward and Bernstein completed their coverage of the Watergate affair with a gripping, almost hour-by-hour account of Nixon's last few months in office, *The Final Days*[3] It, too, like *The Brethren*, relied on anonymous sources and an omniscient third-person observer tone to heighten the drama. It, too, was attacked as irresponsible and praised as an important contribution to contemporary political history.

Moving up the corporate ladder, Woodward became a managing editor at *The Washington Post*, before taking a year's leave of absence to complete *The Brethren*. Taking the unpaid leave was not a problem, apparently; Woodward and Armstrong had received a $350,000 advance on anticipated royalties.

---

[1] See Leonard Downie, *The New Muckrakers* (Washington, D.C.: New Republic Books, 1976).

[2] Bob Woodward and Carl Bernstein, *All the President's Men* (New York: Simon and Schuster, 1974).

[3] Bob Woodward and Carl Bernstein, *The Final Days* (New York: Simon and Schuster, 1976).

In addition, other accounts supported some of *The Brethren*'s observations. In his posthumously published biography, Justice William O. Douglas, for example, substantiated *The Brethren*'s account of an improper attempt to lobby two sitting justices about a pending case.[5]

Between the extremes of very negative and quite favorable reactions to *The Brethren*, there was little middle ground. Eventually, however, the brouhaha blew over. With its passage, the Supreme Court seemed strong enough to survive the exposé and the attending controversy. As former Justice Arthur Goldberg put it:

---

[5] William O. Douglas, *The Court Years: 1939–1975* (New York: Random House, 1980).

" . . . if the court can survive the *Dred Scott* case, which helped start the Civil War, it can survive *The Brethren.*"[6]

Nevertheless, *The Brethren* was not the first, and it will not be the last, account of the inner workings of the Supreme Court.[7] Indeed, the justices themselves are increasingly making public statements, through published interviews and their own speeches.[8] Even Warren Burger, the justice who once wrestled with television reporters to keep them from broadcasting a speech he was about to give, eventually appeared on ABC's late night news show, "Nightline."

Americans, therefore, will continue to learn more about the Supreme Court and will continue to be shocked, because their expectations about the Supreme Court are often out of touch with what it really does. As Bruce Allen Murphy, author of *The Brandeis/Frankfurter Connection: The Secret Political Activities of Two Supreme Court Justices*[9], put it: "The public believes that once Supreme Court justices don the judicial gown, they divest themselves from all instincts for politics and become secluded monks. But that image is unrealistic—and it has always been so."[10] By entertaining the following insights, you can become more realistic about what the Supreme Court does and why it does it.

Insights

Insight 1. *The Supreme Court is a very human institution whose decisions are shaped both by legal doctrine and by the personal preferences of the justices.* Whether as a result of the process of becoming a judge or because of a sincere belief in the propriety of doing so, Supreme Court justices do rely on preexisting rules of law. In addition, they often act as though they have personal views of what is just.

Insight 2. *Although it is mostly concerned with governance tasks, the Supreme Court also works to realize policy and political goals.* The Supreme Court (1) governs, primarily by administering justice, (2) makes policy, primarily by interpreting the law, and (3) acts politically, primarily to ensure the protection of individual's rights.

Insight 3. *The Supreme Court, constrained in its ability to achieve its goals, tries to expand its formal powers and create additional political ones as well.* The Supreme Court, just like other governmental institutions, must struggle to achieve its goals. It must struggle because the goals are difficult to realize, in some ways they are inconsistent, the barriers to their realization are high, and the resources

---

[6] Quoted in *Time*, 10 March 1980, p. 49.

[7] See, for example, Bernard Schwartz, *Super Chief: Earl Warren and His Supreme Court—A Judicial Biography* (New York: New York University Press, 1983).

[8] See, for example, John A. Jenkins, "A Candid Talk with Justice Blackmun," *The New York Times Magazine*, 20 February 1983, pp. 20ff, and John A. Jenkins, "The Partisan: A Talk with Justice Rehnquist," *The New York Times Magazine*, 3 March 1985, pp. 28ff.

[9] Bruce Allen Murphy, *The Brandeis/Frankfurter Connection: The Secret Political Activities of Two Supreme Court Justices* (New York: Oxford University Press, 1982).

[10] Quoted in *US News and World Report*, 19 April 1982, p. 101.

available for the effort are few. Confronting such a difficult environment, the Court can accept failure or it can (1) enhance its strength as an institution and (2) enlarge its role in all stages of the policy process.

■ Supreme Court justices, like the rest of us, are a part of a relatively pluralistic and factious society and will act as though they are, whether or not anyone leaks it to a reporter like Bob Woodward.

THE ORGANIZATION OF FEDERAL COURTS

> To understand how judges, lawyers, and litigants operate, it is necessary to become acquainted with the labyrinthine environment in which they work.
> —*Professor Herbert Jacob, Justice in America*

The federal court system has three main levels: the Supreme Court of the United States, a second tier of circuit courts that only hear appeals, and a third tier of district courts that mostly hold trials. There also are specialized federal courts that hear issues pertaining to reorganization of the nation's railroads, appeals of military court-martials, claims against the U.S. government, international trade disputes, cases involving U.S. territories and insular possessions, federal tax disputes, and bankruptcy proceedings.

There is no nationwide or unified system of nonfederal courts. Instead, there are many different state systems and many states with different kinds of local courts. Because of their tremendous diversity, this chapter considers state courts only as sources of cases that can be appealed to federal courts.

Characteristics of the Supreme Court

The organizational character of the Supreme Court (often referred to simply as "the Court") is shaped by the nature of its justices, the way cases come before it, the way the Court disposes of cases, its ability to acquire legitimacy through restraint or activism, and its history.

Who Are Supreme Court Justices?   Both the Constitution and statutory law are silent on the subject of the qualifications of federal judges, including the Supreme Court's. Over time, however, they have looked pretty much the same. The slightly more than one hundred appointees to the United States Supreme Court have been mostly of the same political party as the President who nominated them; mostly lawyers engaged in private practice or in sitting as a

The United States Supreme Court. Back row from left: John Paul Stevens, Lewis Powell, William Rehnquist, and Sandra O'Conner. Front row from left: Thurgood Marshall, William Brennan, Warren Burger (who retired in June, 1986), Byron White, and Harry Blackmun.

federal or state judge; overwhelmingly white, male Protestants; mostly over the age of fifty; and college educated.[11]

There are some notable exceptions to this general pattern, however. Neither John Marshall nor Earl Warren, for example, had any experience as a judge before becoming chief justice of the Supreme Court. Thurgood Marshall, in 1967, became the only black and Sandra Day O'Connor, in 1981, became the only woman ever to sit on the Supreme Court. Louis Brandeis, in 1916, became the first Jewish justice and Antonin Scalie, in 1986, became the first justice on the Court of Italian descent. The Court's loosely defined "Jewish" seat was last held by Abe Fortas who resigned in 1969. In their personal characteristics, their values and their temperament, the justices have been more different, ranging from the slightly iconoclastic to the staid.

The Way Cases Come to the Supreme Court. The cases that reach the Supreme Court involve either civil or criminal law, are brought by certain parties, fall within the Court's jurisdiction, and are heard because enough justices want to hear them.

The Supreme Court's cases involve either **civil laws** that define the rights and obligations between private persons (whether or not your university sup-

11 See *Congressional Quarterly's Guide to Government, Spring, 1983* (Washington, D.C.: Congressional Quarterly Inc., 1982), pp. 108–109. See also C. Neal Tate, "Personal Attribute Models of the Voting Behavior of U.S. Supreme Court Justices," *American Political Science Review* 75 (1981): 355–67.

plies the meals you pay for) or **criminal laws** that prohibit private acts against society (whether or not you murdered someone).

Cases are brought by **litigants** (the plaintiff who brought the suit or the defendant against whom it was filed) or by **appellants**, if the case comes on appeal. In civil law cases, the litigants usually are private persons, although the government may get involved, on either side. (When the government is involved in a civil case, it usually is as a plaintiff, although it is becoming increasingly easy for private persons to challenge the decisions of the federal bureaucracy, thereby making the government a defendant in civil cases.) In criminal cases, the government, representing the public, always is the plaintiff.

There are three kinds of cases that fall within the Supreme Court's **jurisdiction**, its formal authority to decide a certain kind of case. Some, very few, cases fall within the Court's **original jurisdiction**, its right to act as a trial court on a case that no other court has heard—or, for that matter, will hear. Most cases, however, fall under the Court's **appellate jurisdiction**, its right to hear cases on appeal, either from other federal courts or from state courts.

As a practical matter, cases make it to the Supreme Court because they involve issues on which the justices wish to rule. Over time, Congress has cut back on the kinds of cases that the Supreme Court *must* hear, either because they fall under its original jurisdiction or because there is some formal right to an appeal. This means that today, most cases come to the Supreme Court because it grants a request (from either side of a case) for a ***writ of certiorari***, a written order to a lower court to deliver, for the Supreme Court's review, all or part of the case.

The Way the Supreme Court Disposes of Cases. The Court disposes of cases in the following manner. Initially, to rule on a request for *a writ of certiorari*, justices review summaries (prepared by their law clerks) before meeting privately among themselves. During their private conference, justices vote whether or not to grant the request (*grant cert*). Assuming all nine justices attend, it takes four affirmative votes for the Court to agree to hear the case.

Once a case is accepted for review, the Court invites the submission of additional materials (*briefs*). Once the briefs are in hand, most of the cases under review are subsequently disposed of in another conference, without additional oral argument (this outcome is called a *per curiam* decision). In a few cases, however, the justices schedule oral argumentation before the full Court (and whoever comes to watch these public sessions).

During oral argumentation, each side has a fixed amount of time and is often interrupted by the justices' questions. Afterwards, again in private conference, the justices discuss the case and, prodded by the chief justice, try to move to a decision. If all justices reach the same conclusion, the result is announced, with or without explanation. If the justices split and if the chief justice is in the majority, he assigns the task of writing the majority decision to whomever he wishes (the members of the minority are free to write individual opinions or to join together, completely or partially, in a minority opinion).

After the conference, drafts of written opinions are then circulated among the justices and they decide whether to join with someone else's opinion or to write their own. Finally, before the decision is issued publicly, the justices decide whether or not to release all or just part of their written opinions.

The Supreme Court's Ability to Acquire Legitimacy. Most governmental institutions acquire legitimacy by acting in ways that improve the fit between public policies and popular preferences. The Supreme Court, for the most part, bases its legitimacy on widely shared beliefs that it is relying on legal doctrines to determine the cases that come before it. Nevertheless, the Court may appear to be adhering more or less closely to legal principles.

The Supreme Court may attempt to gain legitimacy through the exercise of **judicial restraint**. This requires that the justices: (1) define the Constitution narrowly, relying more on what it says than on what they think it means; (2) tend to defer to the decisions of Congress, trusting more to its interpretation of the people's will than their own interpretation of the intent of the Founders; and (3) are reluctant to overturn others' decisions, except when they clearly violate the Constitution or run counter to either **statutory law**, ones passed by Congress, or **case law**, the previous decisions of judges. Instead of following their own interpretations, justices who exercise restraint are more inclined to follow the principle of ***stare decisis***, letting the precedents set in prior cases apply to subsequent cases.

On the other hand, the Supreme Court may attempt to gain legitimacy by acting according to the doctrine of **judicial activism**. When they take this route, the justices: (1) broadly define the Constitution, stretching its original

After a decision on a Court case has been reached, copies of each new opinion are released immediately to the press and the general public.

intent to better fit current circumstances; (2) are less deferential toward popular will, as expressed in acts of Congress; and (3) do not hesitate to overturn either laws or lower court decisions, when they believe them wrong. When justices act in these ways, the doctrine of judicial activism maintains that the Supreme Court will increase its legitimacy.

There clearly is no stable solution to the Supreme Court's need to struggle to maintain its legitimacy; it is both made and eroded by action and inaction. In the absence of stability, you should expect to see the Court varying its role over time, sometimes quick and sometimes slow to intervene in various disputes.

The History of the Supreme Court.   Since there have been so few chief justices and since some of them so firmly set the course of the Supreme Court, historical periods in the life of the Court often are known by the identity of the chief justice sitting at the time. We will discuss several of these historical periods next. (See **Table 14.1** for information on the full set of chief justices.)

TABLE 14.1   Chief Justices of the United States Supreme Court

Chief Justice	President Who Nominated	Years of Appointment	Years of Service as Chief Justice
John Jay[1]	Washington	1789	6
John Rutledge[2]	Washington	1795	< 1
Oliver Ellsworth[1]	Washington	1796	4
John Marshall	Adams	1801	34
Roger B. Taney	Jackson	1835	28
Salmon P. Chase	Lincoln	1864	8
Morrison R. Waite	Grant	1874	14
Melville W. Fuller	Cleveland	1888	22
Edward D. White	Taft	1910	10
William H. Taft[1]	Harding	1921	8
Charles E. Hughes[1]	Hoover	1930	11
Harlan F. Stone	Roosevelt	1941	1
Fred M. Vinson	Truman	1946	18
Earl Warren[1]	Eisenhower	1954	15
Warren E. Burger[1]	Nixon	1969	17
William H. Rhenquist	Reagan	1986	—

[1] Ended service as Chief Justice by retiring.
[2] Although Rutledge was sworn in as Chief Justice on August 12, 1795, the Senate rejected him four months later.

Early in its history, the Supreme Court had little legitimacy to preserve. It was the **Marshall Court** (1801–1835) that changed this. Drawing on his own vigorous nature and his vision of the needs of a growing economy, Chief Justice John Marshall raised the Court to prominence as a coequal branch of the national government, as described in detail in chapter 3. Through two key cases, the Marshall Court established the principle of **judicial review**, holding that the courts have the duty and the right to declare unconstitutional and therefore invalid executive and legislative actions,[12] and the principle of **national supremacy**, holding that the laws of the federal government were supreme over state laws.[13]

The activism of the Marshall years was followed by the passiveness of the **Taney Court** (1836–1864). Under Chief Justice Roger Taney, the Court resisted the attempts of Congress to deal with the issue of slavery, ruling that it could not extend the rights and privileges of citizenship to blacks and it could not prohibit slavery in the western territories.[14]

The Pre-Warren Court (1865–1952), in the period between the Civil War and the chief judgeship of Earl Warren, maintained its isolation from contemporary political currents, now resisting the efforts of those who sought to limit the growing economic power of business. The Court's pattern of inaction had a legacy. "By the middle of the nineteenth century, the legal system had been reshaped to the advantage of men of commerce and industry at the expense of farmers, workers, consumers, and other less powerful groups within society."[15] Moreover, the Court also restrained other national governmental institutions, frustrating their ability to deal with social conflicts.

The confrontation was inevitable and came in the 1930s. President Franklin Roosevelt, pushed by the nation's despair, sought to expand the federal government's role, assuming massive, new responsibilities for the welfare of the nation and its people. Roosevelt's incursions into nonfederal matters clearly exceeded what had been traditionally viewed as proper. Seeking to protect the status quo ante, the division of winners and losers that existed before Roosevelt, the Supreme Court sought to blunt new forms of federal interventionism. In one case, for example, the Supreme Court ruled that the federal government did not have the authority to regulate local businesses that did not engage in interstate commerce.[16] In reaction, Roosevelt proposed that Congress exercise its constitutional right, by expanding the size of the Supreme Court. He could then exercise his constitutional right to appoint additional, and hopefully more sympathetic, justices. But Roosevelt moved too far, intruding on what many saw as the Court's proper sphere of autonomy. The message, nevertheless, got through; two justices found good reason to stop voting against New Deal legislation and another found the idea of retirement irresistible.

Chief Justice Roger Taney.

---

12 *Marbury* v. *Madison* 5 U.S. 137 (1803).

13 *McCulloch* v. *Maryland* 17 U.S. 316 (1819).

14 *Dred Scott* v. *Sanford* 60 U.S. 393, 454 (1857).

15 Morton J. Horwitz, *The Transformation of American Law, 1780–1860* (Cambridge, Mass.: Harvard University Press, 1977), pp. 253–54.

16 *Schechter Poultry Corporation* v. *United States* 295 U.S. 495 (1935).

A political cartoonist's view, from 1937, of Franklin Roosevelt and his Court packing plan.

Chief Justice Earl Warren.

The **Warren Court** (1953–1969) best illustrates the principles of judicial activism. Chief Justice Earl Warren encouraged the Court to ask a simple question of issues before it: "What was fair?" Over the course of his tenure, much was found unfair and changed. In the process, the Supreme Court expanded and protected the rights of many kinds of persons who, previously, had been poorly protected by the political and legal system. Many of the expansions came in the areas of criminal and civil rights: (1) even indigent persons were entitled to an attorney during criminal proceedings, the Court ruled in *Gideon* v. *Wainwright*; (2) those suspected of crimes had a right to remain silent before seeing their lawyer, the Court decided in *Miranda* v. *Arizona*; and (3) the rights of black students were violated by the perpetuation of separate schools, no matter how good some believed them to be, the Court concluded in *Brown* v. *Board of Education of Topeka, Kansas*. Through these

THE COURTS: LIFTING THE CURTAIN ON JUDICIAL BEHAVIOR

and many other decisions, the Warren Court extended the scope of personal rights and committed the federal government to protecting them. (See chapter 4 for detail on these cases.) The exercise produced both bickering and back-lash.

The **Burger Court** (1970-1986) many thought, would retreat behind the doctrine of judicial restraint and in the process, undermine the Warren Court's expansion of personal rights. Those who thought this, for the most part, have been disappointed.[17] Under Chief Justice Warren Burger, one of the four justices President Nixon appointed, the Supreme Court only trimmed some of the rights of criminal defendants. In other areas, the Burger Court enlarged the scope of personal rights, by, for example, finding a constitutional foundation for a woman's right to privacy that permits her to have an abortion as late as the first trimester, by continuing to rule that forced busing is an appropriate remedy for school segregation, and by ruling that welfare recipients are entitled to a hearing, before a state can cut off their benefits, for example. In all these and other ways, the Burger Court has struggled to accommodate conflicting expectations of its proper role. Chief Justice Burger retired in June of 1986.

Chief Justice Warren Burger.

Components of the Federal Judiciary

Below the level of the United States Supreme Court, are the two tiers of federal courts: district courts and circuit courts.

Federal District Courts.   Every state has at least one **federal district court**. These courts, created by Congress, serve as trial courts over matters on which they have original jurisdiction (review of decisions of the federal bureaucracy, for example) and as courts that hear appeals (from the U.S. Bankruptcy Court, for example).

Federal Circuit Courts.   By act of Congress, there is also a second tier of **federal circuit courts**, consisting of thirteen Courts of Appeals (one for each of eleven geographically defined judicial circuits, plus one for the District of Columbia and one for the Federal Circuit as a whole). Federal circuit courts only hear appeals, from district courts or, in the case of the Court of Appeals for the Federal Circuit, from certain specialized courts (federal ones that hear disputes pertaining to U.S. territories and insular possessions, for example). (See **Figure 14.1**.)

The full-blown organization chart for the entire federal judiciary is shown in **Figure 14.2**. Parallel to it, there are fifty-one other nonfederal court systems, one for each of the states and one for the District of Columbia.

■ The Supreme Court's characteristics are shaped by its justices, its role in reacting to cases that are brought before it, the very private way in which it decides cases, and its historical patterns of judicial activism and restraint.

17 Vincent Blasi, *The Burger Court: The Counter-Revolution That Wasn't* (New Haven, Conn.: Yale University Press, 1983).

FIGURE 14.1 Geographical Boundaries of Federal Circuit Courts

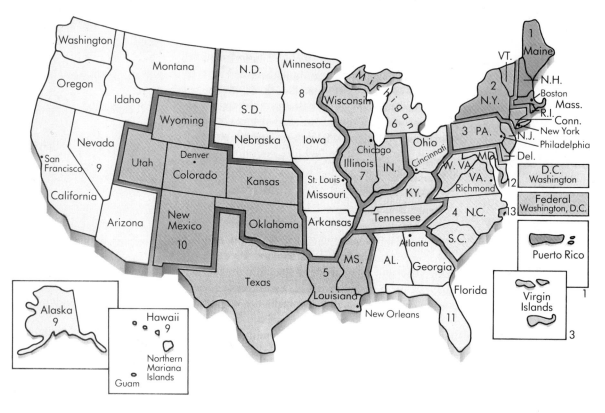

THE GOALS OF THE SUPREME COURT

Faithfulness to the "original intent" of the framers of the Constitution . . . "is the only legitimate basis for constitutional decision," and "is essential to prevent courts from invading the proper domain of democratic government."
—Judge Robert H. Bork, Federal Appeals Court, Washington, D.C.

As Woodward and Armstrong showed and in spite of the views of Judge Bork, the Supreme Court, like the other major institutions of national government, works toward more than one goal. In its traditional role, the Court is concerned primarily with:

FIGURE 14.2 The Organizational Structure of the Federal Court System

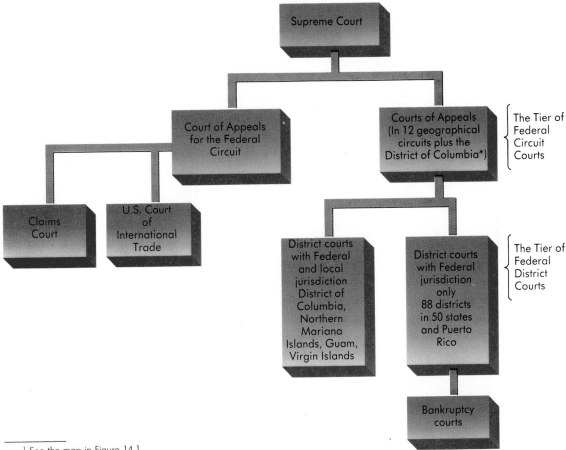

¹ See the map in Figure 14.1.

- *governance goals*—exercising judicial power; balancing the powers of other institutions of national, state, and local government; and administering the federal system of justice. The Supreme Court also increasingly performs various:
- *policy goals*—interpreting the Constitution and statutory law; protecting individual rights; and regulating the operations of the private economic system.

  In the course of working toward these governance and policy goals, the Supreme Court unavoidably acts out:
- *political goals*—altering the distribution of power within the society; developing its own institutional power base; and selectively furthering both political values and personal ambitions.

Governance Goals

The Supreme Court contributes to governance by exercising its judicial power; by trying to adjust the power relationship between the President and Congress (and between them and itself) and to balance the various power relationships among national, state, and local levels of government; and by working to administer the federal court system as a whole.

Exercising Judicial Power. At the time of the Founding, the term "judicial power" apparently did not need elaboration; it surely did not get any in the Constitution. Article III, Section 2 only mentions the term before going on to describe when the Court can exercise it. In general, the Supreme Court's judicial powers extend to two kinds of cases: (1) those that raise some federal question because they involve the Constitition, treaties, or federal statutes, including admiralty and maritime laws and (2) those that involve any kind of a dispute between certain litigants (anytime the United States is involved, whenever one state sues another, whenever a citizen of one state sues another state or any of its citizens, and whenever a citizen of a state sues a foreign government). In all such cases, the Supreme Court may exercise its judicial power. But will it?

For it to exercise its judicial power, the Supreme Court must decide that the dispute properly falls within its jurisdiction. This determination is critical. As Chief Justice Salmon P. Chase explained in 1869: "Without jurisdiction the court cannot proceed at all in any cause. *Jurisdiction* is the power to declare the law, and when it ceases to exist, the only function remaining to the Court is that of announcing the fact and dismissing the cause."[18] The determination is straightforward; whenever it concludes that a dispute raises some "federal question," the Court rules that the case falls within its jurisdiction.

Once it accepts jurisdiction, the Supreme Court is ready to exercise its judicial power. The Court does this primarily by determining whether or not the laws passed by Congress or by the states violate the U.S. Constitution. Laws that do are deemed unconstitutional and are set aside, as null and void. As **Table 14.2** reveals, the Supreme Court has found unconstitutional slightly more than one hundred acts of Congress and over a thousand state laws and local ordinances.

Balancing Institutional Powers. Many of the Supreme Court's key decisions have molded the powers of other branches of the national government, the powers of state governments, and power relationships among the branches of the national government and between them and the state governments. In recent years, there have been two especially notable Court decisions, one limiting the powers of the presidency and one that tried to cut back congressional poaching on the executive branch's sphere of influence.

---

[18] Quoted in *Guide to the U.S. Supreme Court* (Washington, D.C.: Congressional Quarterly Inc., 1979), p. 256.

TABLE 14.2 The Supreme Court's historical record of declaring unconstitutional provisions in federal laws and in state laws and local ordinances.

Period	Number of Federal Laws Ruled Unconstitutional	Number of State Laws and Local Ordinances Ruled Unconstitutional
1790–1799	0	0
1800–1809	1	1
1810–1819	0	7
1820–1829	0	8
1830–1839	0	3
1840–1849	0	9
1850–1859	1	7
1860–1869	4	23
1870–1879	8	37
1880–1889	4	45
1890–1899	5	36
1900–1909	9	40
1910–1919	5	118
1920–1929	15	139
1930–1939	13	93
1940–1949	2	58
1950–1959	4	68
1960–1969	16	140
1970–1979	19	193
1980–1983	8	63
TOTAL	114	1,088

SOURCE: Lawrence Baum, *The Supreme Court*, 2nd ed. (Washington, D.C.: CQ Press, 1985), pp. 171, 173.

In the 1974 case, *United States* v. *Nixon*,[19] the Supreme Court refused to acknowledge President Nixon's claim that he could withhold information that a judge deemed necessary for a criminal trial. The information, including tape recordings of conversations between President Nixon and his aides, revealed

_____
[19] *United States* v. *Nixon* 418 U.S. 683 (1974).

the extent of the White House cover-up of the Watergate break-in. Its Court-ordered release defined one of the limits on a President's power and precipitated Nixon's resignation from office.

In a case in 1983, *Immigration and Naturalization Service* v. *Chadha*,[20] the Court ruled unconstitutional Congress' use of a "legislative veto," the practice of requiring that federal agencies clear proposed regulations with Congress before they take effect. Finally, the Supreme Court also has imposed many limitations on what states can do to their own citizens. Ever since it declared that federal laws were supreme over state laws, in *McCulloch* v. *Maryland*, the Supreme Court has rolled back various state power claims, over such diverse matters as contractual obligations, immigration and the rights of aliens, the rights of women, the regulation of pornography, and the conduct of state courts.

In addition, the Court is the head referee of the power relationships: (1) between the federal, state, and local levels of government and (2) among the branches of the federal government, even when one branch tries to give away its formal authority, as Congress did under the Gramm-Rudman Act.

Administering Justice.   The chief justice of the Supreme Court also joins with other federal judges in the work of the *Judicial Conference of the United States*. The Judicial Conference is, by law, the administrative body charged with overseeing the operation of the entire federal judicial system, trying to make it work more fairly and efficiently. The Conference's main contributions are made through the studies it conducts and the recommendations it forwards to Congress. In recent years, some of these have resulted in changes in rules of evidence and in rules governing the practice of plea bargaining. During his tenure as Chief Justice, Warren Burger has been especially interested in finding some administrative solution to the problem of the Supreme Court's mounting work load. For example, the number of cases the Supreme Court was asked to review increased from 1,463 in 1953 to 5,311 in 1983. Fearing that an overworked Court produced inferior decisions, Chief Justice Burger argued, for example, in favor of a new national court of appeals to hear some of the cases that, otherwise, would go to the Supreme Court. Others, however, thought that the Chief Justice was exaggerating the problem and favored simpler administrative reforms.

Policy Goals

Like it or not, the Supreme Court makes public policy.[21] It does so because its decisions alter the way in which society uses its resources. The Court accomplishes its policy goals by interpreting the law, by protecting individual rights, and by regulating the private economy.

---

[20] *Immigration and Naturalization Service* v. *Chadha* 462 U.S. 919 (1983).

[21] Robert A. Dahl, "Decision-making in a Democracy: The Role of the Supreme Court as a National Policy Maker," *Journal of Public Law* 6 (1957): 279–95.

Left: A political cartoon on the overworked Supreme Court. Here, the opinion is that not all were impressed by Chief Justice Burger's complaint that the Supreme Court was overworked. Right: A historical political cartoon on the same problem.

Interpreting the Law.   Most words are a little vague, inviting disputes over what they really mean. The words of the Constitution and those in statutory laws are no exception. Some institutions of government must resolve such disputes. In this political system, that institution is the Supreme Court. As Chief Justice John Marshall said: "It is fundamentally the duty of the Court to say what the law is."

Over its history, the Court often has said what the law is. By determining that "separate" necessarily meant "unequal," the Supreme Court outlawed segregated public schools. By determining that a woman's right to "privacy" covered her womb, the Court blocked some states' attempts to limit abortions. By determining that the right to be secure in one's home meant secure from listening devices, the Court restricted police practices. By *not* viewing executions as "cruel and unusual," the Court allowed capital punishment to continue. In all these ways, the Court, by interpreting the law, has protected the rights of individual persons.

Protecting Individual Rights.   The Supreme Court, more so than any other institution of American government, acts in ways that expand and protect the rights enjoyed by individual persons. It is a little odd, but true. The Court, the least democratic institution of American government, is the most protective of democratic rights, especially the right to personal liberty.[22]

The Constitution was intended to protect the liberty of the people against the biggest threat to it—government. The main defense, the Founders thought, would be the Fifth Amendment's guarantee that no one would be deprived of "life, liberty, or property" with the due process of law. While the phrase can be interpreted different ways, **due process of law** usually means

22 See Herbert Jacob, *Justice in America: Courts, Lawyers, and the Judicial Process*, 4th ed. (Boston: Little, Brown, 1984).

that people have procedural rights against arbitrary governmental actions.

The Supreme Court has used the due process shield to expand the domain of protected personal rights and to defend that expanded domain. Over time, for example, the Court has ruled that public schools may not summarily dismiss students, without giving them a chance to defend themselves against accusations and states may not try, without a jury, any case that could send someone to jail for more than six months. But even due process rights are limited; for example, in competing for a share of their father's inheritance, illegitimate children have fewer due process rights than do legitimate offspring.

Regulating Economic Activity.   This political system does not leave the private economic market alone; it is regulated in many ways by many different governmental agencies.

Throughout its history, the decisions of the Supreme Court have had many indirect effects on the economic system. The Court's largest indirect effect has come through its support of Congress' expansive exercise of its *commerce power*, the right to regulate such diverse economic activities as working conditions, child labor practices, labor unions, monopolistic business practices, and racial discrimination in interstate transportation. In these and many other instances, the Supreme Court's indirect regulation generally has promoted the growth of a national, highly industrialized economy.

In all these ways, the Supreme Court contributes to the realization of policy goals. Like all other policy decisions, the judgments of the Court often alter the use that is made of society's resources, whether, for example, endangered species are protected in the wild or young children are protected in the workplace.

Political Goals

The Supreme Court pursues political goals whenever it acts in ways that affect the distribution of power within the political system. It does this, for example, by ensuring political participation rights, by enhancing its own institutional power, and by selectively furthering certain political values and even the personal ambitions of its members.

Political Participation Rights.   The Supreme Court ensures political participation rights when it protects the right to vote, the value of the vote, and the freedom of people to do more than vote. It took many amendments to the Constitution to establish a federal right to vote. The promise of the Fourteenth and Fifteenth Amendments was insufficient; it was not fulfilled until the civil rights movement of the 1960s and the Voting Rights Act of 1965. Since then, however, the Supreme Court has worked to ensure that expanded participation rights are not eroded by state actions. Since upholding the enactment of the Voting Rights Act,[23] the Court has ruled that states may not use literacy tests to abridge the right to vote, that political parties and their primary election

---

[23] *South Carolina v. Katzenbach* 383 U.S. 301 (1966).

contests may not be run as though they were private, white-only clubs, and that the Twenty-fourth Amendment's prohibition of poll taxes is constitutional. Some restrictions on the right to vote remain, however; convicted, unpardoned felons, for example, can be barred from voting.

Historically, state legislatures have drawn district lines so as to dilute the value of urban, as compared with rural, votes and the value of black, as compared with white, votes. In reaction, the Supreme Court has resisted attempts to dilute the value of people's votes. For example, in 1960, the Court ruled that a city could not have voting lines drawn to exclude blacks from the city limits; two years later, in the famous case, *Baker* v. *Carr*, the Court recognized its obligation to hear challenges to improper or malapportioned districts; subsequently, the Court moved to a more precise definition of equality—"one man, one vote," it ruled in *Gray* v. *Sanders*. In all these and additional ways, the Court has tried to ensure that people have more than a right to vote; they also are entitled to an *equal* right.

Finally, the Supreme Court has also tried to ensure the right to do more than vote. People, for example, should also have rights to run for office and to exert political pressure on those who win. To ensure these rights, the Court has outlawed large filing fees that discourage the poor from running for office, overturned congressional prohibitions that limit the amount that noncandidates can spend during election campaigns, and has thrown out lots of laws that attempt to restrict or penalize membership in the Communist party.

Organizational Power. While working to promote its various governance and policy goals and to expand the political rights of private citizens, the Supreme Court has not been oblivious to its own organizational needs. Foremost among these is the need to cultivate and protect its own power base.

It is very hard for the Supreme Court to enhance its organizational power, since it rests on such a subjective and often fickle base. Ultimately, the Court has power only when the people believe that it is behaving properly and when other institutions—political parties, the media, the President, and Congress, for example—act in ways that reinforce and magnify that perception of legitimacy. Because it is both essential and ephemeral, the Supreme Court must work very hard to cultivate its power base, as we will see next.

Political Values and Ambitions. Finally, it is important that we do not romanticize the Court; these are people on the bench, not gods or angels. You, therefore, should expect that justices will have political values that they would like to see codified in the law, although some may exercise more personal restraint than others. Justice Potter Stewart (1959–1981), for example, worked very hard to suppress his political tendencies. In other cases, as recent scholarship reveals, Supreme Court justices have gone to great lengths to advance their political values, as for example, both Louis Brandeis and Felix Frankfurter did, according to Bruce Allen Murphy's biography.[24]

Most Supreme Court justices are quite distant from electoral politics,

---

[24] Bruce Allen Murphy, *The Brandeis/Frankfurter Connection.*

however. Justice John Marshall Harlan (1955–1971), for example, refused to vote in presidential elections or to applaud during the President's State of the Union Message, for fear of looking political. Nevertheless, electoral ambition bites in strange places; some, for example, believe that Sandra Day O'Connor's presence on a Republican presidential ticket would make it irresistible.

■ Looking back over its many governance, policy, and political goals, it is clear that the Supreme Court has a lot to do. What remains to be seen is what blocks goal realization and what, if anything, the Court can do to overcome these obstacles.

WAYS OF ACHIEVING JUDICIAL GOALS

> The Court doesn't work at all in the logical way people think it works. But it does work.
> —Bernard Schwartz, law professor, legal scholar, and biographer of Chief Justice Earl Warren

Although Supreme Court justices exercise their personal discretion, as *The Brethren* revealed, the Supreme Court, just like every other institution of American national government, is constrained. It is constrained by judicial forces (the Constitution, law, and its own procedures, for example), by other national governmental institutions (especially the President and Congress), and by various parts of the broader political environment (especially public opinion and certain kinds of national elections).

The Court can accommodate these constraints in various ways. It can, for example, defer to them, as it has through much of its history, especially under Chief Justice Roger Taney, in the years leading up to the Civil War. Alternatively, the Court can assert itself, by trying to overcome these constraints, as it did under Chief Justice Earl Warren.

What, in fact, will the Court do? It depends—on how intent the justices are on achieving their various goals—and on what skill they bring to the effort.

Overcoming Constraints

If it is to reach its various governance goals, the Supreme Court must try to overcome (or circumvent) constraints that are imposed by the President, Congress, the judicial process, and by the political environment.

Presidential Constraints.   The President really only has one major opportunity to constrain the behavior of Supreme Court justices—before they take their seat. Since justices are appointed for life (subject only to a loose constitutional requirement of "good behavior") and since most retire or die only after long service, Presidents try to select their nominees carefully. While many factors enter into the President's decision, including the need to pay off political obligations and the desire to capitalize on the nomination's symbolic appeal, Presidents try to select nominees who share their conception of government's proper role. Presidents have a tough time figuring this out, however; even if a nominee has one, the prior judicial record does not necessarily predict future behavior. Even interviewing them does not help much; few go out of their way to emphasize their policy disagreements with the President.

For the most part, Presidents who fail to get the kind of Court they want accept the outcome, although not without a little bitterness. President Dwight Eisenhower, for example, revealed his disappointment with the way two of his five Supreme Court appointees worked out; when asked if he made any mistakes as President, Eisenhower responded, "Yes, two, and they are both sitting on the Supreme Court."[25] Other Presidents try to influence justices after they have been appointed, although the attempts are guarded and indirect. Under President Reagan, for example, his Attorney General, Edwin Meese, publicly pressed the Administration's claim that the Court was continuing to drift away from a strict construction of the Constitution.

In making their nominations, even Presidents are not totally unfettered, however. Some, like Richard Nixon, have acted quite unilaterally, failing to clear prospective nominees either with members of Congress or with other relevant opinion leaders. In Nixon's case, the results were disastrous, as two, back-to-back nominations, Clement Haynsworth, Jr., and G. Harold Carswell, went down to defeat in the Senate. Partly in reaction, Nixon and subsequent Presidents broadened the extent to which others, including the American Bar Association, were consulted before the nomination was made.

Congressional Constraints.   Congress is a little better armed than the President to constrain the Supreme Court and for that matter the entire federal court system. Most of Congress' weapons, however, are either too weak or too powerful. Some of its potential weapons include the Senate's power to reject presidential nominees to the Supreme Court, its constitutional role in removal of a sitting justice, its constitutional right to increase the size of the Court and allow for changes in its composition, and its ability to overturn a Court decision by amending the Constitution and making constitutional what the Court had said was not. These four, however, are relatively ineffectual weapons, infrequently and clumsily wielded by Congress. On only nineteen occasions has the Senate actually rejected a Supreme Court nominee, although the threat of rejection has lead to the withdrawal of a nomination, as it did when allegations

---

[25] President Eisenhower reportedly meant Chief Justice Earl Warren and Associate Justice William Brennan.

of impropriety led President Lyndon Johnson to withdraw his nomination of Abe Fortas for Chief Justice in 1968. It is also pretty hard for Congress to wield its formal power to remove a sitting justice; only once, in the case of Samuel Chase in 1804, has the House impeached a sitting justice and he was subsequently acquitted by the Senate. Tradition and the transparency of the attempt also limit Congress' (or the President's) exercise of rights to expand the size and therefore alter the composition of the Court. Similarly, the extraordinariness of amending the Constitution also narrows this route, although it was taken in passing the Thirteenth, Fourteenth, and Fifteenth Amendments to reverse the effects of the *Dred Scott* decision, which had declared that blacks were not citizens.

Congress can try to impose more effective constraints over the Court by doing what it does best: passing laws, either laws that shore up some statutory foundation or laws that change the jurisdiction of the courts leading up to the Supreme Court. The former tactic is especially useful when the Court tries to reverse policy trends or when it and lower federal courts consistently fail to act in a way that is seen as legitimate.

In one recent case, *Grove City College* v. *Bell*, for example, the Supreme Court overturned a federal policy that required colleges to prove they were not discriminating against women on the grounds that there was no specific statutory authorization for it, even though every other institution of national government had been acting as though there was. The reaction was intense, as Congress moved to try to codify its policy understanding in a new law, *The Civil Rights Restoration Act of 1985*.

Congress also can attempt to constrain the Court by altering the jurisdiction of other federal courts. By keeping some matters out of lower federal courts, Congress can effectively prevent their appeal to the Supreme Court and thereby keep it from issuing (what it finds to be) noxious rulings. This, too, would be an extraordinary step. Understandably, it becomes most appealing when those who feel very intensely about a cause also believe they are consistently frustrated by a Court that appears totally unresponsive to them. Such political pressures do not well up often, but, in recent years, they have, over opposition to the use of court-ordered busing to eliminate racial segregation, court-permitted abortions, and court-prohibited prayer in public schools. This route, thus far, has mostly only symbolic appeal, however. In practice, it is so extraordinary and so out of step with the American tradition of an independent judiciary as to be largely an anachronism. Before it would be taken, a politically savvy Court probably would find some better way to accommodate such intense pressure.[26]

Judicial Constraints.   The Supreme Court is effectively constrained, however, by the federal judicial system as a whole and by the Court's own nature.

The judicial system constrains the Court because it makes it a wholly

---

[26] See Carl Bent Swisher, *American Constitutional Development*, 2nd ed. (Cambridge, Mass.: Houghton Mifflin Co., The Riverside Press, 1954), p. 331.

THE COURTS: LIFTING THE CURTAIN ON JUDICIAL BEHAVIOR

The legitimacy of the Supreme Court does come under attack from political cartoonists from time to time. Here, the feeling is that the Court spoon feeds criminals much to the dismay of Congress.

"Come now—there is no such thing as a bad boy. . . ."

reactive institution, one that is unable to show any initiative in taking up a problem before events (and litigants) push it up, through the appeals process. Moreover, the appeals process is time-consuming and costly; its inaccessibility further limits opportunities for the Court to intervene in social disputes. The judicial system also has produced a rich record of cases and precedents that justices are reluctant to ignore.

The nature of the Supreme Court further constrains the potentially interventionist role it can play. Most notably, the Court's relatively small size necessarily reduces its potential work load and especially the number of significant cases, requiring oral argument, long conferences, and extensive bargaining.

Environmental Constraints.   Ironically, perhaps the most effective constraint on the Court is the most tenuous and informal: that imposed by public opinon.

Since it commands no police force to impose its will, the Supreme Court's power ultimately rests on the popular conviction that it is a legitimate body, behaving properly. The Court's legitimacy has been sorely tested throughout American history, especially when it lagged too far behind shifts in popular opinion, as in the drift into the Civil War, or when it rushed a little ahead of a sustaining social consensus, as in its expansions of private, and especially defendant's, rights under Chief Justice Earl Warren. In both cases, the lack of fit between popular preferences and the actions of the Court strained its legitimacy and thereby threatened to erode its power.

Such threats to the Court's legitimacy are especially severe in times when the electorate adopts more than marginally different policy preferences. There are times, admittedly rare, when the electorates' preferences for more or less government shift abruptly, producing immediate replacement of elected policy makers and long-term shifts in policy direction. After such elections, (or *critical elections* as mentioned in chapter 7), the Supreme Court is well-advised to adjust its policy course and actually does so, according to a study by Richard Funston.[27]

The Supreme Court is relatively unconstrained by the mass media, however. It is really a little surprising, given the journalistic glee with which the media criticize most politicians and public servants. But, in their treatment of the judges of higher level courts, most reporters are relatively deferential. It may be that reporters who cover the courts, and especially the Supreme Court, consciously protect their legitimacy. There also, however, are less subjective and speculative factors that help account for the inability of the media to better cover and constrain the Court.

The Court's work schedule and internal rules, for example, make it a difficult beat to cover; after the Court accepts a case, it may be months before a decision is announced, usually without advance word and always with no explanation other than the official court opinion(s). The Court also is an unrewarding beat, especially for those with regular news quotas to fill. After long dry spells, the Supreme Court gushes forth many decisions at the end of its term. Finally, Supreme Court procedures purposefully make it more mysterious and less of a "media event."

This array of constraints is imposing. They, however, have not frustrated the ability of American courts and especially the Supreme Court to realize their goals. The Court's success, however, is largely due to the skills of some of its justices: their skills in expanding their formal powers and their skills in creating and exercising political power.

Expanding Formal Powers

There are three major forms of judicial power: the right of judicial review, the power to issue writs, and the contempt power. All have expanded over the course of American history.

Judicial Review.   As we saw in chapter 2, the Supreme Court, under Chief Justice John Marshall, quickly fashioned a key formal power; the Court's right of judicial review. Armed with this power to declare unconstitutional the actions of Congress, the Executive, and the states, the Court, would compete henceforth as a coequal branch of government.

The Power to Issue Writs.   **Writs** are formal, written court orders, directing someone to carry out its rulings. Under authority granted them by the *Judiciary Act of 1789*, federal courts issue a variety of writs. The most important is the ***writ of habeas corpus***. This writ tells governmental authorities, say, those that are holding someone in custody, that they must justify their actions. The

---

[27] Richard Funston, "The Supreme Court and Critical Elections," *American Political Science Review* 69 (1975): 795–811.

writ of habeas corpus is therefore the first line of defense against governmental impropriety and the primary device for protecting personal liberty. In the course of its history, the Supreme Court's use of the writ of habeas corpus has reformed federal and state criminal procedures. As a result, liberals would argue, we all are more secure in our liberties, better protected against illegal governmental intrusions. On the other side, conservatives would argue that the "reforms" of criminal procedure have made us less secure in our homes, less well protected against court-coddled criminals. Who is right? What is the proper use of the writ of habeas corpus? We are sure we do not know. But no one else does either—that is why there is politics.

The Contempt Power. Never argue with people who wear long black robes. If you do, you can be found in **contempt**, a judge's ruling that you failed to follow its decision in a civil proceeding or that you interfered in some way with a criminal proceeding. In either event, a contempt citation is handed down and carried out summarily (without trial). Those cited are quickly sent off to jail, as *The New York Times* reporter, Myron Farber was in the case beginning chapter 4, for his refusal to turn over his notes in a criminal trial. Most of the expansive uses of the contempt power have come from judges below the level of the Supreme Court. Indeed, ever since 1821, the Supreme Court has tried to regulate the use of the contempt power and in recent years has argued that its use may not ignore due process rights.

These and other expansions of formal powers could not have occurred and surely could not have been sustained, if it were not for the skills with which judges have created and exercised political power, however.

Creating and Exercising Political Power

The Supreme Court creates and exercises political power in two locales: backstage and onstage. Through backstage preparations, individual justices try to create and exercise their own personal power over one another. Through onstage performances, justices try to persuade both various elites and the masses. They have a lofty perch and a presumption that they will be successful. But, if they should fail, they can always retreat behind that ultimate curtain of judicial respectability, the doctrine of *stare decisis*, until they find better ways and more propitious times for converting resources into power.

Backstage Preparations. Life behind the scenes at the Supreme Court is pretty factious, if we accept the accounts in *The Brethren*—or many of the other accounts that have leaked out, some of them provided by justices themselves. Where there are factions, we expect many different kinds of political maneuvers.

Since decisions are by majority vote, we, for example, expect that justices will try to build coalitions, by using the major devices that are available to them, the opinions they draft, and often redraft, trying to expand or preserve preliminary coalitions.

Courts are, and must be, concerned about their popular image.

Since the membership of the Court is relatively stable, we also expect that informal rules of comity will prevail and when they are breached, individual justices then will act in more independent and unpredictable ways. Rules of comity, in addition, should moderate opinions, as justices will be reluctant to alienate those who they might need as future allies. Comity also has a conservative bias; decisions will tend to be marginally, not radically, different from earlier ones.

Onstage Performances.   It is hard for the Supreme Court to be effective onstage; they are playing to two, very different, audiences. While onstage, the Court must persuade them both: other elites and the masses.

When they issue their decisions and opinions, the Court tries to persuade various elites: other judges, whose behavior on the bench they hope to modify; lawyers, who will be encouraged to bring certain suits and discouraged from bringing others; the President and members of his Cabinet who, hopefully, will not challenge publicly the propriety of the Court's decision; current and aspiring members of Congress who, hopefully, will resist the temptation to dump tough decisions on justices and then criticize them for whatever they do. As though that is not a tough enough audience, the Court, simultaneously, must appeal to the masses.

Since its ultimate power rests on its perceived legitimacy, the Court must be concerned with shaping mass perceptions. Since the perceptions of legitimacy may be weak and tentative, the Court will try to protect its power base and therefore its future capacity to exercise power. When it does so, we expect to see the Court striving to achieve unanimity on important, controversial decisions, and we expect to see individual justices being very concerned with appearances, by, for example, joining with the majority, whenever possible; rallying behind the majority opinion in significant cases; and adhering to a norm of institutional loyalty.

Converting Resources Into Power.   The Supreme Court, like the other institutions of national government, can not realize its various goals without converting resources into political power.

The Court can draw on some potentially useful resources: its apparent legitimacy, its mantle of remoteness from mere politics, its image of intellectual rigor and personal integrity, its considerable control over timing and therefore its ability to exploit events. When the Court draws on these resources and efficiently converts them into political power, two remarkable things happen: first, other elites defer to the Court's prestige and second, its sources of power are replenished.

■ *The Brethren* probably overstated the extent to which Supreme Court justices are able to exercise their unfettered, personal discretion. In fact, the Court seems heavily constrained by tradition and by other governmental institutions. Nevertheless, the Court has been remarkably successful in achieving its various goals, largely through its ability to maintain its image of impartiality.

SUMMARY

In spite of efforts to obscure it and procedures that imply quite the opposite, courts and perhaps especially the Supreme Court are very human places.

The Supreme Court's actions are shaped by the character of its justices, its willingness to accept jurisdiction over a dispute, the way it disposes of cases before it, and its attempts to maintain legitimacy, either by exercising judicial restraint or judicial activism.

The Supreme Court strives toward more than one goal, although this provokes more controversy than it does in the cases of other institutions. In its traditional role, the Court is concerned primarily with governance goals: exercising its constitutionally mandated judicial power; balancing powers among the branches of the national government and between the national government and state and local governments; and participating in the administration of the federal court system. In its increasingly prominent and controversial role, the Court also is concerned with policy goals: interpreting constitutional and statutory laws; trying to protect the rights of individual persons; and regulating economic relations in the private market. In its most controversial role, the Court also pursues political goals: by altering the distribution of power within society; by developing its own institutional power base; and by selectively furthering political values and personal ambitions.

Because its power base is so fragile, the Supreme Court must be especially careful in the ways it copes with its various constraints, especially its need to maintain legitimacy in the eyes of the public. In addition, the Court is constrained by the President's appointment power, various congressional prerogatives, and by the Court's own limited capacity to hear cases.

Because of the importance of its goals and the hindrance of its constraints, Supreme Court justices need to be very adept in expanding their formal powers and in finding ways to create and exercise political power. Over the course of American history, the Court has expanded primarily its power of judicial review and its power to issue a *writ of habeas corpus*. Especially in the modern era, the justices of the Court have created and exercised political power primarily through backstage intrigues, through their onstage appearance, and in general, by their ability to convert various resources into a level of legitimacy that helps the Court maintain its stature as a coequal branch of the national government.

Key Terms

civil laws	*stare decisis*
criminal laws	judicial activism
litigants	judicial review
appellants	national supremacy
jurisdiction	federal district courts
original jurisdiction	federal circuit courts
appellate jurisdiction	due process of law
writ of certiorari	writ
judicial restraint	*writ of habeas corpus*
statutory law	contempt
case law	

Review and Reflection

1. Describe the organizational structure of the federal judiciary.

2. In what ways do characteristics of the Supreme Court influence the ways it does business?

3. In addition to its various governance responsibilities, does the Supreme Court also get involved in policy making and in attempting to settle political conflicts? Why?

4. What constrains the Supreme Court as it tries to realize its various goals?

5. What can the Supreme Court do to try to realize its various goals?

6. Do you think that the Supreme Court, in recent years, has "invaded" the proper domain of democratic government?

Supplemental Readings

The literature on courts and the Supreme Court in particular falls neatly into four major categories.

First, there are a number of general, synthetic works: *Jacob* provides an excellent overview of the court system; *Posner* examines the administrative problems of the Federal courts; *Rhode and Speath* focus on the way the Supreme Court makes decisions; and *Wasby* focuses on the impact of those decisions.

Second, there are a number of excellent case studies that either examine landmark decisions or continuing controversies. These include, for example, *Casper* on civil liberties, *Kluger's* analysis of the Brown decision, *Lewis's* account of the appeal of an indigent, *O'Connor's* exposition of the legal strategies of women's organizations, and *Sorauf* on the separation of church and state.

Third, it is useful to examine closely the relationships between the Supreme Court and the other institutions of national government, as *Schmidhauser and Berg* and as *Scigliano* do, for example.

Fourth, biographies and autobiographies help expose the very human nature of justices. Especially illuminating works include *Douglas, Hirsch, Murphy,* and *Schwartz.*

Casper, Jonathan D. *Lawyers before the Warren Court: Civil Liberties and Civil Rights, 1957–66.* Urbana: University of Illinois Press, 1972.

Douglas, William O. *The Court Years 1939–1975: The Autobiography of William O. Douglas.* New York: Random House, 1980.

Hirsch, H. N. *The Enigma of Felix Frankfurter.* New York: Basic Books, 1981.

Jacob, Herbert. *Justice in America: Courts, Lawyers and the Judicial Process.* 4th ed. Boston: Little, Brown, 1984.

Kluger, Richard. *Simple Justice: The History of Brown v. Board of Education and Black America's Struggle for Equality.* New York: Alfred A. Knopf, 1976.

Lewis, Anthony. *Gideon's Trumpet.* New York: Random House, 1964.

Murphy, Bruce Allen. *The Brandeis/Frankfurter Connection: The Secret Political Activities of Two Supreme Court Justices.* New York: Oxford University Press, 1982.

O'Connor, Karen. *Women's Organizations' Use of the Courts.* Lexington, Mass.: Lexington Books, 1980.

Posner, Richard A. *The Federal Courts: Crisis and Reform.* Cambridge, Mass.: Harvard University Press, 1985.

Rhode, David W., and Harold J. Speath. *Supreme Court Decision Making.* San Francisco: W. H. Freeman & Co., 1976.

Schmidhauser, John R., and Larry L. Berg. *The Supreme Court and Congress: Conflict and Interaction, 1954–1968.* New York: Free Press, 1972.

Schwartz, Bernard. *Super Chief: Earl Warren and His Supreme Court—A Judicial Biography*. New York: New York University Press, 1983.

Sciliano, Robert. *The Supreme Court and the Presidency*. New York: Free Press, 1971.

Sorauf, Frank J. *The Wall of Separation: The Constitutional Politics of Church and State*. Princeton: Princeton University Press, 1976.

Wasby, Stephen L. *The Impact of the Supreme Court: Some Perspectives*. Homewood, Ill.: Dorsey Press, 1970.

PART FIVE

POLICY EVALUATION

"Every country has the government it deserves."
—Joseph de Maistre, French political philosopher, 1811

525

CHAPTER FIFTEEN

SOCIAL WELFARE
ARE MOST AMERICANS BETTER OFF?

If thirty years is a generation, we are in one and you are in another. Let us assume that we were born in 1940 and you were born in 1970. Is your generation better off than ours? If so, by how much? How did you get that way? Are your children also likely to be better off in thirty years, or worse off, than you are now?

The social welfare of a nation is measured by the well-being of its people. In this nation, almost all measures show that most Americans are better off, although some are much better off than others while certain kinds of people are becoming worse off.

This chapter opens with a focus on those who are becoming worse off, unmarried teenage mothers and the broader class of female-headed families. This Case suggests three basic insights. First, in spite of massive increases in social welfare expenditures over the last thirty years, poverty remains a harsh reality for millions of Americans. Second, in general, however, social welfare policies have been modestly successful in improving the lot of most Americans. Third, social welfare policies are made through highly political processes.

SOCIAL WELFARE

> Birth control pills? I'd heard of them. People
> tell me they make your hair fall out.
> —*An anonymous teenage mother*

A pregnant fifteen-year-old in
Brooklyn, New York.

The Case   The Feminization of Poverty

In 1982, Phyliss was about to join the ranks of those who were becoming worse off, in spite of federal social welfare policies that tried to help them.[1] In fact, some argued, the federal programs made it worse.

Although we call her Phyliss, her name was not as important as her age and her condition; she was between fifteen and nineteen years of age, unmarried, and pregnant. A large number of young women in Phyliss' age group and condition planned on obtaining a legal abortion; over 450,000 did in 1982. Phyliss, however, was going to have her baby, just as over 270,000 other unwed teenagers did the same year.

Since Phyliss is a composite of national statistics, we know a few other things about her and about the other adolescents in her condition:

- She will probably drop out of high school and never return.
- She is almost equally likely to be white as black.
- She is vulnerable to serious health risks throughout her pregnancy.
- If she delivers a live child, she probably will keep her baby, as do over 90 percent of the unwed teenage mothers.
- The baby probably will have a low birth weight, usually an indication of subsequent medical problems and high infant mortality.
- She and her baby probably will live with her parents.
- She may have another baby out of wedlock within the next two years, as do 40 percent of girls like her.
- She is unlikely to be able to find a job and probably will go on welfare.
- Her child, as compared with those who are born to post-adolescents, is more likely to suffer medical problems and developmental difficulties.
- She and her child are about to become what the demographers call a *female-headed family*, one with no spouse present.
- Many people, especially those who are poor, tend to believe that she and young women like her became pregnant so they can go on welfare, as shown in the data in the **Vantage Point**: The Public's View of the Poor.

---

[1] Phyliss is a composite who represents a demographic group: pregnant and unmarried girls below the age of nineteen. The data for this case study is drawn from Lewayne D. Gilchrist and Steven Paul Schinke, "Teenage Pregnancy and Public Policy," *Social Science Review* (June, 1983): 305–22; U.S. Bureau of the Census, *Statistical Abstract of the United States: 1985* 105th ed. (Washington, D.C., 1984); Select Committee on Children, Youth, and Families, United States House of Representatives, *Teen Parents and their Children: Issues and Programs* (Washington, D.C.: GPO, 1984); Select Committee on Children, Youth, and Families, United States House of Representatives, *Teen Pregnancy: What is Being Done? A State-by-State Look* (Washington, D.C.: GPO, 1986); and Ruth Sidel, *Women and Children Last: The Plight of Poor Women in Affluent America* (New York: Viking, 1986).

THE PUBLIC'S VIEW OF THE POOR

*I*n April of 1985, the *Los Angeles Times* interviewed a sample of over 2500 persons to determine their views of the poor. To analyze the responses, the sample was split into those who fell below the federal government's poverty line and those who did not. In addition, the respondents were grouped by sex and race.

To get a quick overview of the views of most people, without regard to their own condition, see the entries in Column 11 where, in their responses to Question 1, for example, almost 60 percent of the national sample thought that welfare benefits encouraged dependency.

To see the ways the poor and the non-poor view those in poverty, compare the entries in Column 5 with those in Column 10. In most cases, what is most striking is the closeness of views. In their responses to Question 6, for example, 60 percent of the poor thought that welfare encouraged husbands to flee, as did 61 percent of the non-poor.

To compare the views of different subgroups that are in poverty with those that are out of it, match up the relevant columns. The responses of blacks living in poverty are reported in Column 1, while the responses of blacks not living in poverty are reported in Column 6. In their responses to Question 1, for example, these two subgroups differed dramatically in their view of the effectiveness of welfare programs.

Public View of the Poor

| | Respondents in Poverty | | | | | Respondents Not in Poverty | | | | | |
| | Black | White | Men | Women | Total | Black | White | Men | Women | Total | National |
	1	2	3	4	5	Column 6	7	8	9	10	11
1. Welfare benefits give poor people a chance to stand on own two feet and get started again, or make poor people dependent and encourage them to stay poor											
Get started again	43%	27%	41%	25%	31%	19%	15%	15%	17%	16%	19%
Neither (vol.)	19	7	3	13	9	11	13	12	11	11	11
Encourage people to stay poor	31	45	36	48	43	58	60	59	64	61	59
Don't know	5	21	18	14	16	11	12	14	7	11	11
2. Most poor people are lazy, or most are hard-working											
Lazy	22	15	18	25	22	16	27	26	27	26	25
Hard-working	69	61	50	63	58	62	46	51	46	48	50
Don't know	7	16	23	10	15	21	26	22	26	24	23

	Respondents in Poverty					Respondents Not in Poverty					
	Black	White	Men	Women	Total	Black	White	Men	Women	Total	National
						Column					
	1	2	3	4	5	6	7	8	9	10	11
3. Most poor people have been poor for a long time and will probably remain that way, or most move into poverty and then out of it in a relatively brief period of time											
Remain poor	46	68	63	47	53	50	81	68	79	73	71
Out in brief time	39	23	26	45	38	42	13	24	14	19	21
Don't know	13	8	10	8	8	8	6	7	7	7	7
4. On average, poor people have less education, more difficulty holding jobs, and live in worse conditions than other people. These differences are mainly because poor people have less in-born ability to get ahead											
Yes	28	33	29	32	31	30	29	25	33	29	29
No	62	54	63	58	60	67	61	69	57	63	62
Don't know	10	10	8	8	8	3	9	5	10	7	8
5. Most poor people prefer to stay on welfare, or most would rather earn their own living											
Prefer welfare	6	19	20	20	20	18	25	23	28	25	25
Earn their own living	79	73	61	73	68	78	60	59	65	62	63
Don't know	15	5	17	5	10	4	15	18	7	13	12
6. Some people think welfare encourages husbands to avoid family responsibilities because it's easier for wives											

Phyliss and adolescents like her are a part of a growing national problem: the **feminization of poverty**, the tendency of the ranks of the poor to be filled with female-headed families. Increasingly, millions of single women and their children are trapped in poverty, put there by more liberal sexual mores, ignorance about contraception, the lack of employment opportunity, and a divorce rate that is now twice what it was at the end of World War II. Together, these social forces have greatly expanded the number of female-headed families. In recent years, female-headed families have become more numerous, and especially among blacks, more typical. For example, between 1960 and 1983, the number of female-headed families increased from 4.5 million over 9 million. Simultaneously, the percentage of female-headed white families increased over 12 percent and

SOCIAL WELFARE: ARE MOST AMERICANS BETTER OFF?

	Respondents in Poverty					Respondents Not in Poverty					
	Black	White	Men	Women	Total	Black	White	Men	Women	Total	National
						Column					
	1	2	3	4	5	6	7	8	9	10	11

to get aid for children if father has left. This happens almost always, often, seldom, or almost never

	Black	White	Men	Women	Total	Black	White	Men	Women	Total	National
Often	28	65	67	55	60	48	64	54	68	61	61
Seldom	59	28	27	35	32	40	31	40	28	34	33
Don't know	13	7	6	10	8	12	5	6	4	5	6

7. Poor young women have babies so they can collect welfare: almost always, often, seldom, or almost never

	Black	White	Men	Women	Total	Black	White	Men	Women	Total	National
Often	58	59	54	70	64	51	45	39	49	44	48
Seldom	32	24	29	20	23	45	50	56	47	51	46
Don't know	10	17	17	10	13	4	5	5	4	5	6

8. We are coddling the poor— poor people live well on welfare—or they can hardly get by on what the government gives them

	Black	White	Men	Women	Total	Black	White	Men	Women	Total	National
Coddling	8	32	38	19	26	2	25	19	27	23	23
Hardly get by	82	63	45	76	64	79	66	71	64	68	68
Don't know	8	5	15	5	9	19	8	8	9	8	8

9. Anti-poverty programs have almost always, often, seldom, or almost never worked

	Black	White	Men	Women	Total	Black	White	Men	Women	Total	National
Often	25	35	31	31	31	60	27	32	34	33	32
Seldom	55	58	50	59	56	35	64	63	55	59	58
Don't know	20	7	19	10	13	5	9	5	11	8	10

SOURCE: The data is drawn from I. A. Lewis and William Schneider, "Hard Times: The Public on Poverty," *Public Opinion* (June/July 1985): 6–7.

the percentage of female-headed black families increased by almost 42 percent. Meanwhile their number is growing. Indeed, before it was disbanded by the Reagan administration, the National Advisory Council on Economic Opportunity observed that: "All other things being equal, if the proportion of poor in female-headed households were to continue to increase at the same rate as it did from 1967 to 1978, the poverty population would be composed solely of women and their children before the year 2000."[2]

Female-headed families are poor, perhaps intractably so. In 1982, for exam-

---

[2] Quoted in Barbara Ehrenreich and Francis Fox Piver, "The Feminization of Poverty," *Dissent* (Spring, 1984), p. 162.

Many single parents have to pay for their food with food stamps.

ple, families headed by unmarried mothers had an average annual income of about $12,000. Families headed by divorced women did somewhat better, with their average income of $15,000. In contrast, the average income of families headed by unmarried fathers was over $21,000, and the average income of those headed by divorced males was over $24,000. At the other end of the income scale, families with both parents present did much better: their annual income topped $30,000 in 1982.

Although the total number of people in poverty declined from 1959 to 1979, it has started back up in recent years.[3] In 1959, for example, there were almost 40 million poor persons, as compared to about 25 million in 1979. Moreover, this decline came about even though the total population of the United States in 1980 was about 50 percent larger than it was in 1959. In 1982, however, the total number of poor persons was back up to over 34 million.

Since 1959, the number of poor persons in female-headed families has grown dramatically. In 1959, for example, female-headed families contributed about 10 million persons to the ranks of the poor. By 1982, this number was over 16 million, an increase of over 56 percent. Moreover, it did not appear as though this growth rate was going to slow down, in spite of a number of federal social welfare policies.

Teenage pregnancy and the associated problem of the feminization of poverty have been attacked by the federal government in three ways: with counseling, money, and food.

Counseling. In 1981, Congress passed and President Reagan signed the Public Health Service Act. One portion of the Act, Title XX, created an Office of Adolescent Pregnancy Programs which was authorized to spend up to $90

---

[3] "People in poverty" are those below the federal government's official poverty line, a number that is about three times the cost of an adequate but minimal diet. The number, moreover, is adjusted annually, to compensate for changes in the cost of food.

SOCIAL WELFARE: ARE MOST AMERICANS BETTER OFF?

A mother consults a nutritionist from the federal Women, Infants, and Children (WIC) supplementary food coupon program, in Boston, Massachusetts.

million on programs that would counsel teenagers about the risks of pregnancy and for those who did have babies, about the possibility of putting their child up for adoption. Successful implementation rested in private hands, however, since it required that adolescents seek advice about how to prevent pregnancy before it was too late. That was something that most were unwilling to do. One study, for example, reported that only one out of five sought birth control advice before sexual intercourse, although black adolescents were much more likely to do so than were white ones.[4] Nevertheless, political support for the program remained high, uniting such strange bedfellows as Jeremiah Denton, the conservative Republican senator from Alabama and Edward Kennedy, the liberal Democratic senator from Massachusetts.

Money.   Most of the money that goes to unwed mothers comes from one federal program: Aid to Families with Dependent Children (AFDC). This program was created as part of the Social Security Act of 1935. Originally, AFDC was intended to help keep children in private homes, with a single, usually widowed, parent or grandparent. Eventually, however, it expanded to the point where it was a major public welfare program, providing an average of $320 per month to about 3.7 million families in 1983 (for a total federal expenditure of about 8.2 billion dollars).

Food.   Food, vouchers to buy certain foods, and information about nutrition is targeted toward pregnant women and the infants of poorly nourished women through a relatively new and successful program, the Special Supplemental Food Program for Women, Infants, and Children (WIC). Started in 1974, with about 344,000 participants and an annual budget of less than $90 million, WIC had grown to the point where, in 1984, it had over 3 million participants and an

---

4 Cited in *The New York Times*, 29 October 1982.

annual budget of over 1.3 billion dollars. Part of the support for the WIC program is rooted in the belief that it works: the children born to mothers who are in the program tend to weigh more at birth and therefore tend to be healthier. Additional support comes from the program's symbolic appeal among members of Congress. After all, in the words of Robert E. Leard, the program's administrator: "What Congressman wants to go home and say he voted against pregnant women and children."[5]

Some argue that recent changes in the federal government's social welfare policies have made the poor less, not more, well off. Charles Murray, for example, in his controversial work, *Losing Ground: American Social Policy 1950–1980*,[6] argues that the poor, inadvertently, have been encouraged to remain on welfare, rather than get a job, by (1) liberal levels of welfare; (2) the end to the requirement that the male spouse can not live with the welfare mother; (3) less restrictive rules covering the amount of income that can be kept, without an offsetting reduction in welfare payments; (4) the poor changing their attitude toward welfare, now tending to see it as a civil right, not a political handout; and (5) by women actually choosing to have and to keep an illegitimate baby in order to become eligible for various cash and non-cash welfare benefits. In response, various critics have attacked Murray's use of statistics as misleading and have shown quite convincingly that higher welfare benefits do not lead to higher rates of illegitimacy, although they do seem to lead to higher divorce rates.[7] Although the relative merits of these views are still being sorted out, some points seem irrefutable.

In spite of, if not because of, federal social welfare policies, the poor, in increasing numbers, are still with us. Indeed, beginning in the 1970s and throughout the 1980s, more and more people began to speak of **structural poverty**, a permanent condition in our economy, rather than one that might be resolved through economic growth, job training, and personal initiative. Whatever the overall validity of the structural view of poverty, it did seem increasingly clear that unwed mothers and their children tended to fall through some rather large holes in the social safety net.

Insights

This brief glimpse is not enough to absorb the full impact of a life of poverty on those who live it. This view, however, might further understanding about some of the remaining obstacles to ongoing attempts to enhance the welfare of most Americans.

Insight 1. *In spite of massive increases in social welfare spending, poverty remains.* There is no denying the massive increases in social welfare spending, especially through federally directed programs, over the last four decades.

[5] Quoted in Jonathan Rauch, "Women and Children's Food Program is 'Off Limits' to Reagan Budget Cutback," *National Journal*, 17 November 1984, p. 2198.

[6] Charles Murray, *Losing Ground: American Social Policy 1950–1980* (New York: Basic Books, 1984).

[7] See, for example, the analysis presented in Christopher Jencks, "How Poor are the Poor?", *The New York Review*, 9 May 1985, pp. 41–49.

SOCIAL WELFARE: ARE MOST AMERICANS BETTER OFF?

Nevertheless, it is equally hard to deny the continued existence of hard-core pockets of poverty that have proven very resistent to remedy, either by government or through the charitable efforts of private persons and organizations.

Insight 2. *In general, however, social welfare policies have been modestly successful.* On most measures of human welfare, most Americans are much better off than they used to be, although this is much more true of whites than it is of blacks.

Insight 3. *Social welfare policies are made through highly political processes.* The issue of whether or not society decides to use its resources to improve the lot of the poor, or to target its efforts towards certain poor persons rather than others, is a political matter. In general, the political process for making social welfare policies is a distinctive one, heavily influenced by political principles, the political environment, and by governmental institutions.

To elaborate these insights, the rest of this chapter examines historical improvements in the lives of most Americans and the determinants of the social welfare policies that helped bring about those improvements.

■ It is ironic and tragic that some people have slipped even deeper into poverty, while others—most Americans—have enjoyed unprecedented improvements in the quality of their lives.

SOCIAL WELFARE POLICIES

> I see one-third of a nation ill-housed, ill-clad,
> ill-nourished.
> —*President Franklin Roosevelt,*
> *1937*

Are Most Americans Better Off?

The obvious, and correct, answer is yes. But by how much? How did they get that way? Are they to become more so in the future? To start the search for the answers, first go back in time and place, to January 20, 1937, Washington, D.C.

During his second inaugural address, President Roosevelt amplified his assessment of the American condition:

I see millions of families trying to live on incomes so meager that the pall of disaster hangs over them day by day.

I see millions whose daily lives in city and on farm continue under conditions labeled indecent by a so-called polite society half a century ago.

I see millions denied education, recreation, and the opportunity to better their lot and the lot of their children.

Living conditions during the Depression. Left: While his children wait in their baby carriage, a Cleveland, Ohio father is given his ration of potatoes. Right: A shantytown or "Hooverville." This was one way people critized President Hoover for not providing adequate housing during the Depression.

> I see millions lacking the means to buy the products of farm and factory and by their poverty denying work and productiveness to many other millions.

The President's rhetoric created a powerful image. But, exactly how bad was it and how much better has it become?

To compare levels of social welfare in the 1940s with the 1980s, consider the following aspects of American life: housing, infant mortality and maternal deaths, education, and poverty.

Housing. The quality of a nation's housing can be measured in various ways. By any measure, the quality of housing has improved since FDR's second inaugural, as is revealed by data on the percentage of people who owned, rather than rented, the house in which they lived. (See **Table 15.1**.)

Infant Mortality and Maternal Deaths. This is obviously a terribly subjective measure of whether or not most Americans are better off. But most people would agree that the number of deaths of children under the age of one back in 1940, over 43 per 1000 for whites and over 72 per 1000 for blacks, were indecent. In addition, most people would deplore, as indecent, the 1940 maternal death rate for white women (about 320 per 100,000 deliveries), and be totally shocked at the rate for black women (over 780 per 100,000 deliveries).

Education. Opportunity to do well is often intangible and elusive. The lack of opportunity, however, can be documented dramatically, as measured in terms of either education or poverty. These measures provided a more ambiguous answer to our question about improvements in American living conditions. On the one hand, the educational level of Americans has risen dramatically over the last forty years. For example, the percentage of persons graduating from high school rose from 24.5 percent in 1940 to over 72 percent in 1983. This 50

TABLE 15.1 Measures of Improvement in the American Quality of Life

Quality of Life Measure[1]	Year					
	1940	1950	1960	1970	1980	1983
Housing, owner-occupied (in percent) White	45.7	57.0	64.4	65.4	67.8	67.7
Black	23.6	34.9	38.4	42.1	44.2	46.2
Infant mortality (deaths per 1,000 live births) White	43.2	26.8	22.9	17.8	11.0	na
Black	72.9	43.9	44.3	32.6	21.4	na
Maternal deaths (per 100,000 live births) White	319.8	61.1	26.0	14.4	6.7	na
Black	781.7	223.0	103.6	88.3	21.5	na
High School graduates (in percent) Of all persons over age of 25	24.5	34.3	41.1	52.3	66.5	72.1
Of black persons over age of 25	7.3	12.9	20.1	31.4	51.2	56.8
Below poverty level[2] (in percent) White	na	na	17.8	9.9	10.2	12.1
Black	na	na	47.0	33.5	32.5	35.7

[1] Some of these measures were suggested by Nelson Polsby, "The Role of Government in Providing for the General Welfare," in Robert E. Cleary, ed., *The Role of Government in the United States: Practice and Theory* (New York: University Press of America, 1985), p. 102–15.

[2] People are classified as above or below the poverty level solely on the basis of cash income. The classification, therefore, does not reflect non-cash benefits, such as food stamps or subsidized public housing. (Due to the lack of data, the percentage of blacks below the poverty level in 1960 was estimated from data in the *Statistical Abstract*.)

SOURCE: U.S. Bureau of the Census, *Statistical Abstract of the United States: 1985*, 105th ed. (Washington, D.C., 1984), Tables 108, 213, 758, and 1315. na: Not Available

percentage point gain held for blacks as well, although their high school completion rate started and ended up deplorably low, as compared to the rate for whites. Greater educational opportunity has not provided a sure route out of poverty, however.

Poverty. If we take President Roosevelt's words to mean that one-third of all Americans lived in poverty in 1937 and use a subsequent statistical invention, the "official poverty line," to identify those living in poverty in later periods, then that percentage shrunk to about 20 percent in 1960 and to about 6 percent in the 1970s. By the 1980s, however, the percentage of Americans living in poverty was back up above 10 percent. Thus, in spite of dramatic reductions in poverty, as late as 1983, one out of ten white Americans still lived in poverty, as did more than one out of three blacks.

In general, then, are Americans much better off? The answer has to be a qualified, "Yes." Yes, they are, especially if they are white and, as we saw at the beginning of this chapter, not the female head of a family or her children.

How Did They Get That Way?

Dramatic gains in at least the material quality of American life have come about in the last generation mostly because of (1) sustained economic growth, (2) a steady increase in governmental spending, and (3) a substantial re-allocation of federal dollars away from defense and toward social welfare spending. (See **Table 15.2**.)

Economic Growth. There has been sustained economic growth since the end of the Second World War. Moreover, controlling for the effects of inflation shows this to be real growth that expands the economy, creates jobs, and reduces unemployment. Such growth serves social welfare purposes.

Expanded Government. While the economy was growing, most levels of government were growing faster, thereby absorbing an increasingly large share of the Gross National Product. As the data of Column 2 in **Table 15.2** show, spending by all levels of government added up to about one-third of the GNP in 1970. Over the period 1970 to 1983, governmental spending as a percentage of GNP steadily expanded one-half a percentage point a year. That is not a trivial increase; in the three trillion dollar economy we had in 1983, for example, one-half a percentage point added up to 15 billion dollars! By 1982, all levels of government combined were spending over 40 percent of the Gross National Product, a considerable sum of money that was available to do many things, including support a variety of antipoverty programs, such as those in **Table 15.3**.

The Domestic-Defense Reversal. An historical event occurred between the presidential inaugurals of John F. Kennedy and Lyndon B. Johnson: the percentage of the federal budget that was spent on nondefense items became larger than the percentage spent on defense. The reversal became a rout under President Richard M. Nixon; between 1970 and 1974, nondefense spending went from about 58 percent to about 70 percent of the federal budget, while defense spending fell from about 42 percent to 30 percent. That massive re-allocation of dollars from defense to domestic programs radically altered federal priorities, although the event is generally ignored by historians and liberal critics of President Nixon, according to Senator Daniel Patrick Moynihan (D., N.Y.).[8] Since 1974, domestic spending has continued to eat into the defense budget, although some of President Johnson's Great Society programs gradually withered and died, such as a system of cash grants to community organizations of the poor that were made under the Office of

---

[8] Senator Moynihan's views are expressed in *The New York Times*, 17 May 1985.

SOCIAL WELFARE: ARE MOST AMERICANS BETTER OFF?

TABLE 15.2 Growth in the Economy, Governmental Spending, and Domestic Versus Defense Spending by the Federal Government, 1965 to 1984

Year	Column 1 Economic Growth (annual percent increase, from prior year, in Gross National Product)[1]	Column 2 Governmental Spending[2] (as a percentage of GNP)	Column 3 Domestic Federal Spending (as a percentage of total federal spending)
1970	3.2	33.2	58.2
—			
—			
—			
1975	− 1.2	36.2	73.3
1976	5.4	36.4	75.4
1977	5.5	35.6	75.7
1978	5.0	34.4	76.7
1979	2.8	34.4	76.3
1980	− .3	36.4	76.8
1981	2.5	37.5	76.0
1982	−2.1	40.1	74.6
1983	3.7	35.7	74.0
1984	6.8	na	73.3

[1] This is a real rate of economic growth, corrected for the effects of inflation. (The Gross National Product is the dollar value of all the goods and services sold in a given year, including the dollar value of all new construction.)

[2] "Government Spending" includes all the expenditures of the federal government plus all the expenditures of all state and local government. The percentage was calculated by using constant (1972) dollars for both the expenditures and the GNP.

na State and local expenditures not available.

SOURCE: U.S. Bureau of the Census, *Statistical Abstract of the United States: 1986*, 105th ed. (Washington, D.C., 1985), Tables 720, 441, 491, and 718.

Economic Opportunity. Other ambitious attempts never got off the ground, such as assistance to poor neighborhoods provided under the Model Cities Program.

Over the last forty years, the federal government has woven a **social safety net**, a set of social welfare policies that are designed to protect people against a sudden and personally catastrophic loss of income. Many of these programs are also called **entitlements**, because they provide benefits to all who meet the eligibility requirements that are written into the law. Although people differ on

TABLE 15.3   Key Anti-Poverty Programs, 1980

Listed below are the chief elements in the *federal* effort to combat poverty among people of working age in 1980. They included both cash payments and "in-kind" transfers. "Cost" refers to federal share. Not shown: programs focused on the disabled or the elderly and subsidies that are not "means-tested." In 1980, the "public-aid" category of the U.S. budget accounted for 11 percent of federal nondefense spending, or $49.2 billion.

Program	Eligibility	Cost	Recipients	Benefits
Aid to Families with Dependent Children (AFDC)—1935	"Need" defined by each state. In all states, eligible families included those with one parent absent owing to death, desertion, divorce, incapacitation, or incarceration. Half of states aided two-parent families with father out of work.	$ 6.9 billion.	3.6 million families (monthly avg.).	Average monthly payment per family: $275.96.
Food Stamp Program—1964	Households with net income (i.e., income after certain deductions) at or below federal poverty line.	$ 9.1 billion.	21.1 million individuals (monthly avg.).	Coupons distributed on basis of need and redeemable in exchange for food *only*. Average value of coupons per recipient per month: $34.35.
Medicaid—1965	In most states, recipients of AFDC or Supplemental Security Income automatically qualified for Medicaid; 31 states also provided for the "medically needy," whose medical bills offset excess income.	$14.1 billion.	21.6 million individuals.	Covers most medical expenses.
Comprehensive Employment and Training Act—1973 (expired 1983)	Varied. In general, the unemployed, underemployed, economically disadvantaged.	$ 8.9 billion.	4 million individuals	Job training in classroom or workplace; allowance paid for in-class time and minimum wage (at least) for on-the-job instruction. Provided public-sector jobs and support (e.g., daycare, transportation).
Housing Programs: 1) Low-Rent Public Housing—1937; 2) Rent Supplement Program—1965; 3) Home Ownership Assistance—1968; 4) Interest Reduction Payments—1968; 5) Lower Income Rental Assistance Program—1974	In general, income could not exceed a certain percentage (usually 80 percent) of median income for the area.	$ 5.4 billion.	3.1 million households.	Ceiling placed on proportion of income (e.g., 25 percent) spent on housing. Average yearly benefits: 1) $1,843 per household; 2) $1,577 per household; 3) $504 per household; 4) $1,732 per household; 5) $2,051 per household.

SOURCE: "The War on Poverty: 1965-1980," by Charles Murray. From *The Wilson Quarterly*, Autumn 1984, p. 130. Reprinted by permission.

SOCIAL WELFARE: ARE MOST AMERICANS BETTER OFF?

what should be included in the category, social safety net programs typically are defined to include (1) Social Security payments to the elderly; (2) additional payments made to the elderly poor (Supplemental Security Income); (3) basic unemployment benefits; (4) Aid to Families with Dependent Children (AFDC); (5) payments to disabled veterans; (6) food stamps, food, and nutritional information; (7) health care for the poor (Medicaid); (8) low-income housing assistance, and (9) low-income energy assistance.

Beginning in 1981, President Ronald Reagan began to slow down the rate of growth in social welfare spending. Even then, however, total federal spending on most antipoverty programs (listed in **Table 15.3**) increased, although there were real cuts in selected programs. Today, the social safety net is still mostly in place, although some of its holes are larger than they used to be, especially those that fail to cushion the economic hardship of female-headed families and their children and those that fail to catch many of those who are hopelessly dependent on others for their livelihood.[9] In addition, many of the holes in the social safety net would have been considerably larger, if Congress had acquiesced to all of the proposals of the Reagan Administration.[10]

An example of a social safety net program in use. Here a nurse-practitioner examines a baby at an inner-city medical clinic.

Will Americans Be Better Off in the Future?

The answer to this question is that it depends. It depends, for example, on all the following.

The National Debt. As chapter 10 pointed out, there is some concern that the federal government's need to borrow money makes less of it available for investment in things that can bring about economic growth. To the extent that this is true and we do not tap other sources, from foreign nations, for example, the next generation of adult Americans (you and your peers, mostly) will be worse off.

Infrastructure Repair. The future well-being of Americans also depends on the ability of states and cities to maintain their **infrastructure**, those things, such as roads and water and sewage systems, without which economic growth is impossible.

A Trainable Work Force. America's future well-being also depends on the availability of a work force that can be trained and retrained, as economic tasks change. Since a trainable work force is a generally well-educated citizenry, America's future well-being depends on the continued willingness of federal policy makers and local voters to invest in the education of both children and adults.

---

9 According to one prominant policy analyst, Richard Nathan, as he is quoted in the *Wall Street Journal*, 14 June 1983.

10 See Timothy M. Smeeding, "Is the Safety Net Still In Place?", in D. Lee Bawden, ed., *The Social Contract Revisited: Aims and Outcomes of President Reagan's Social Welfare Policy* (Washington, D.C.: The Urban Institute Press, 1984), pp. 69–120.

ONE VIEW OF CURRENT OBLIGATIONS TO FUTURE GENERATIONS

Just before his retirement from public life in 1986, Thomas P. O'Neill Jr., the Democratic Representative from Massachusetts and Speaker of the House of Representatives, spoke of what he believed past generations of Americans had done for current ones and of what the current generation should do for the next one.

. . . Today, there is a new conventional wisdom. Very often, you hear successful people talk about the "good old days." Their message is always the same: how good things were generations ago, when there was less Government responsibility and fewer programs, when people were left free to take care of themselves. But the conventional wisdom of 1986 is . . . wrong.

. . . Like most simple ideas, the . . . conventional wisdom has a great deal of appeal. It promises a life that is less complicated, where there is less Government, less red tape and hardly any taxes whatever. But, like most simple ideas, it ignores not only reality but our own national history.

I began my public life in 1936 on the slogan of "work and wages." I remain convinced that our greatest goal is to give the average family the opportunity to earn an income, to own a home, to educate their children and to have some security in their later years. That is still the American dream and it is still worth fighting for.

Today, there are those who argue that the way to achieve this dream is to go it alone. The new morality says that the young should forget about the old, the healthy should ignore the sick, the wealthy should forget the poor. . . .

I believe it is wrong for the people who have made it up the ladder to pull up the ladder behind them. . . .

SOURCE: These selections are taken from Thomas P. O'Neill Jr., "When Government Was a Friend in Need," *New York Times*, 16 May 1986, p. 27.

The Removal of Artificial Barriers. An efficient economy produces the best products at the lowest possible price, and does it (1) without regard to the sex or race of prospective workers and (2) without recourse to high tariffs. The future well-being of Americans, therefore, depends on (1) their willingness to end at least employment-related forms of sexual and racial discrimination and (2) their capacity to compete in the world economy.

Domestic and International Peace. America's well-being depends on government's ability to maintain domestic peace and tranquility, so that people will be confident enough about the future to invest in it. Similarly, maintaining international peace is necessary if society's resources are not to be wasted or destroyed.

In addition, whether or not the next generation of Americans will be better off than yours depends in large measure on the way in which your generation sorts out its obligations to the next. The issue is live and pushed upon you by many. Some, those who expressed the conventional wisdom of the 1980s, ignored or downplayed your obligations. Others, however, expressed a different view, as Thomas P. O'Neill, Jr. (D., Mass.), the Speaker of the House of Representatives, did just before he retired in 1986. (For his view, see the **Vantage Point**: One View of Current Obligations to Future Generations.)

■ As compared with their lot at the time of President Roosevelt's second inaugural, most Americans are much better off today. There are, however, some important qualifications and exceptions. The social welfare gains of most whites, for example, have far exceeded those of most blacks and many, such as those in female-headed families, remain trapped in poverty.

These social welfare gains have been brought about through an expansion in the roles of all levels of government, through the federal government's tendency to favor domestic over defense spending, and perhaps, most importantly, by a sustained pattern of vigorous economic growth.

Whether or not Americans will continue to be better off in the future is an open question. In large measure, the future well-being of Americans depends on the way they handle problems, only some of which can be identified today. The future well-being of Americans, in other words, is in their (your) own hands.

DOMESTIC POLICIES

> The spirit of liberty . . . is the spirit which is
> not too sure it is always right.
> —*Judge Learned Hand*

Anti-poverty policy and domestic policy in general is shaped by (1) our historical foundations, (2) the various parts of our political environment, (3) the various characteristics of the policy-making process, and (4) characteristics of the major institutions of the national government.

Historical Foundations

Our historical foundations consist of a number of enduring principles that continue to influence the domestic policies of this country: (1) the belief that government's legitimate right to rule requires a close fit between its policies and the people's preferences; (2) the belief that a written Constitution constrains the improper exercise of governmental authority; (3) continuing support for a federal system of government in which different levels of government maintain some proper role in policy making; and (4) an enduring commitment that the civil liberties of people should be protected from government and a deep, but more tenuous, belief that government should act to guarantee the civil rights of minorities.

Legitimacy. In a democracy, government has a limited right to make policies and to demand compliance with them. The right is constrained by the need to act in a manner that is generally perceived as legitimate, that is, consistent with the preferences of the people. (See chapter 1 for a fuller discussion of the need for legitimacy.)

American government, therefore, has a limited capacity to act and domestic policy makers are constrained by the need to maintain their legitimacy. Thus, except under unusual circumstances, the American political system will tend to not take the initiative for identifying and solving social problems, such as those associated with female-headed families, chronic unemployment among blacks, the contamination of water, or even the loss of endangered species. Instead, the American political system will tend to wait on and then respond to widespread or intense public demands. This means that government will be more reactive than proactive.

There are exceptions, of course, relatively rare moments when some parts of the political system or some policy makers appear to have struck out on their own, intent upon remedying some old problem or avoiding some new one. For example, some congressional policy makers, such as Representative Henry Waxman (D., Cal.), have tried to regulate pollutants in automobile emissions and others, such as President Lyndon Johnson, have tried to move forcefully in the attempt to eradicate poverty. In both cases, these policy makers, because of their own initiative and ambition, moved further and faster than public opinion. Thus, policy makers sometimes are willing to crawl out on a limb—they just do not want to stay out there, all by themselves, too long.

Policy makers who take the initiative must act, quickly and effectively, to shore up their position by mobilizing supportive public opinion. To do so, they may draw on their own leadership abilities or on other things—luck, intense policy entrepreneurs, supportive interest groups, or friendly journalists. President Johnson, for example, used his considerable powers of behind-the-scenes persuasion to enlist in his war on poverty civil rights organizations, religious organizations, local and state political leaders, members of Congress, and some of the more liberal members of the press.

Although they can help bring about change, personal initiative and elite persuasion can not perpetuate significant changes in domestic policy. The perpetuation of change requires broad-based public support of the kind, for example, that President Johnson's War on Poverty never enjoyed. In this case, most of society never concluded that the poor had a right to a better standard of living and that it was the obligation of the federal government to provide it. Thus, many of President Johnson's antipoverty policies had a fragile foundation, one that was easily eroded by the discrepancy between excessively high expectations and mounting evidence of program failure.

President Lyndon Johnson and his wife, Lady Bird, dramatized their concern for the poor, by visiting unemployed workers in Kentucky.

The need to appear legitimate also extends to the process of making public policy. Thus, we tend to insist that only elected officials make policy, that they do so in a public manner, and that they act only on the basis of good evidence or sound argumentation. In recent times, the effect of this insistence and the need to maintain at least the appearance of legitimacy has helped bring about more open committee meetings in Congress, disclosure rules that require policy makers to declare their assets, and registration and reporting requirements that require lobbyists to make known some of their activities. All these ways of opening up the policy-making process are driven by a desire to expose and eliminate any contrivance that might distort the translation of popular preferences into policy and thereby, erode the system's legitimacy.

Constitutionalism. The principle of constitutionalism (as we saw in chapter 2) holds that the proper role of government is constrained by a written contract or constitution. Moreover, the Constitution is supreme over ordinary laws and those who make and administer them, because, the Founders believed, the Constitution embodied natural or fundamental law.

The principle of constitutionalism, therefore, provides policy makers with a directive that is simultaneously clear and ambiguous: Do nothing that violates natural law. The directive is clear enough, although, throughout their history, Americans have disagreed over what it meant. As is the practice in democracies, they have fought over their differing interpretations, usually, but not always, in a peaceful, political manner, not a violent, military one.

In an attempt to act in accordance with the principle of constitutionalism, or to reverse actions that were seen to violate it, Americans, for example, have fought over whether or not an employer can adopt a program of affirmative action to compensate minority employees for the legacy of past discrimination; whether or not women and men should get comparable pay for comparable work or comparable pensions for comparable contributions; whether or not welfare recipients can be removed from the rolls without a hearing, and so on.

Federalism. As the discussion in chapter 3 tried to make clear, federalism is a way of distributing governmental authority among national, state, and local levels of government. Thus, under a federal system, everyone agrees that each level of government has some proper role to play in the making of domestic policy. They disagree, however, over which level should do what.

The disagreement over the appropriate roles of different levels of government is reflected in a number of ongoing political controversies:

- Even if it is in the national interest to do so, should states be able to block the burial of nuclear wastes within their borders?
- Although they and their citizens may find it cheaper to do so, can one state's electrical generating plants burn soft, dirty coal that pollutes the air and water of other states downwind?
- Should the national government allow states to maintain their own welfare system, when that means some states will provide much more generous allowances than others, thereby encouraging the poor to migrate and increase the tax burden of some?

In these and many other cases, the existence of a federal form of government encourages different governments to devise different policy responses to domestic problems and to contest the courses of action each chooses.

Civil Liberties and Civil Rights. As they were defined in chapter 4, *civil liberties* are guarantees that government will not interfere arbitrarily with people, their property, or their opinions and *civil rights* are guarantees that government will protect people against discrimination, either by other persons or by some other part of government. Thus, respect for civil liberties and civil rights both constrain and direct the making of domestic policy.

The belief that civil liberties should be protected constrains domestic policy making. Policies that impinge on people's civil liberties or appear to do so face an uphill fight, as have recent proposals, made in the name of national security, to subject members of the executive branch to lie detector tests. Similarly, existing policies that appear to impinge on civil liberties are susceptible to challenge and reversal, as was the policy that prohibited welfare payments to female-headed families in which a spouse was present.

The belief that civil rights should be guaranteed encourages governments to protect minorities from discrimination and raises doubts about their legitimacy should they fail to do so. In recent history, the belief has been strong enough to sustain successful assaults on voting procedures that dilute the voting rights of blacks and on administrative practices that fail to provide the mentally handi-capped with an appropriate education. In the future, the strength of the nation's commitment to the cause of civil rights will continue to be tested on new battle grounds, as, for example, the physically handicapped become more demanding about their rights of access to public facilities and as nonsmokers become more intolerant of those who pollute their air. In these cases, modern society has thrown together many different kinds of people who often infringe on others. It does not matter whether or not societal change produces more infringements or a greater personal intolerance of them. In either event, the cause of civil rights will continue to feed ongoing political controversies and attempts to cope with them through the making of domestic policy.

A concern with protecting the civil liberties of some often frustrates the political objec-tives of others, as non-smokers learned while gasping for breath.

The Political Environment

The political environment consists of a number of sources of demands and supports that help mold the behavior of domestic policy makers. These en-vironmental inputs come from (1) the political culture, (2) organized political interest groups and political parties, and (3) the mass media and various forms of political participation.

The Political Culture.   As it was described in chapter 5, the American political culture provides domestic policy makers with ambiguous cues. On the one hand, policy makers might conclude that they can exercise considerable per-sonal discretion in identifying problems and in deciding what should be done about them, since so many in the public are so inattentive to so many policy matters. On the other hand, many Americans dislike and distrust government and can quickly arouse themselves to oppose policies which they see as personally restrictive or oppressive.

This somewhat schizophrenic quality of public opinion in America influ-ences the behavior of those who would make policy. Sometimes it expands the discretion they can exercise in certain policy disputes, while contracting what they can exercise in others. Some policy makers navigate these shoals ex-tremely well. The late Senator J. William Fulbright (D., Ark.), for example, exercised tremendous discretion and influence over the making of foreign policy, while forced to hew closely to a strict segregationist stance on civil rights matters. Sometimes policy makers cope with the schizophrenic quality of American public opinion by a form of misrepresentation, usually by wrapping the policies they want to advance in terms they believe to be acceptable to the public at large. This can work, at least in the short run, as it did when advisors to President Roosevelt decided to sell income redistribution (Social Security payments to elderly retirees that were financed with the wages of young workers) as though it was just another form of insurance. In the longer run, however (or hopefully), attempts to mislead the people will be exposed, through the probing and challenge of ambitious politicians and journalists, if not through the greater awareness of a better-educated citizenry.

THE POLSBY—WILDAVSKY DIALOGUE CONTINUED . . .

AUTHOR: How would you evaluate the political system's performance in providing for the social and economic welfare of its people, say since the New Deal?

WILDAVSKY: Let's take both an absolute and a relative point of view. If we ask about classes of people, men, women, blacks, whites, and so on, then we would say that virtually all classes are better off than they were at any comparable period in our history. The one possible exception to this is children in single-parent families. When Robert Dahl wrote *Who Governs,** he emphasized the importance to the democratic life of preventing the cumulation of inequalities. If we look at relative inequalities, we see, on the one hand, that they are pretty much either a little less or a little more, depending on how they're calculated. But, if we ask whether they cumulate, that is, whether some people are getting richer and others are getting poorer, it's false. That is to say, the poorest people in the population at the end of the Second World War were almost entirely elderly. Through governmental programs and other mechanisms that has changed. Whoever it is that is poor now, two things can be said about them. They're people who had it worse earlier, and, secondly, they're not all the same people who were poor earlier. So, if you came at this with a different question, namely, not what is the change over time, but, what is the relative

resource position or life chances of people, then you would have to say that, although American society is today characterized by substantial inequality of resources, they have not grown larger, they have been dispersed, there is a lot of downward, as well as upward, mobility, and the sense of the U.S. as an opportunity society, exemplified by waves of recent immigrants, remains largely unimpaired, with one exception. In my opinion, racial differences are the single most important problem in American political life, dwarfing everything else by large magnitudes, except, possibly, nuclear war. And, because poverty is not distributed evenly racially, and because many of the poorest children are disproportionately black, this creates far greater difficulties for us than if we had the same proportion of poor people but they were more evenly distributed in the population.

POLSBY: Well, when you ask a question about whether people are better off, I'm trying to think of dimensions—welfare, health, education, basic political freedoms, freedom of expression, freedom of assembly, access to variety of life, things like that. I can't think of a measure on which you can't show that, on average, people are better off. With respect to the least well off, roughly the young, the old, the black and the poor, I think you're also going to show that they're better off. It's not the same thing as claiming there are no problems, however.

It's also the case that the government is not the sole actor here. We're a rich country with a rich economy. Now, there's a very complex relationship between governmental activity and economic ac-

---

*Robert A. Dahl, *Who Governs? Democracy and Power in an American City* (New Haven: Yale University Press, 1961).

548

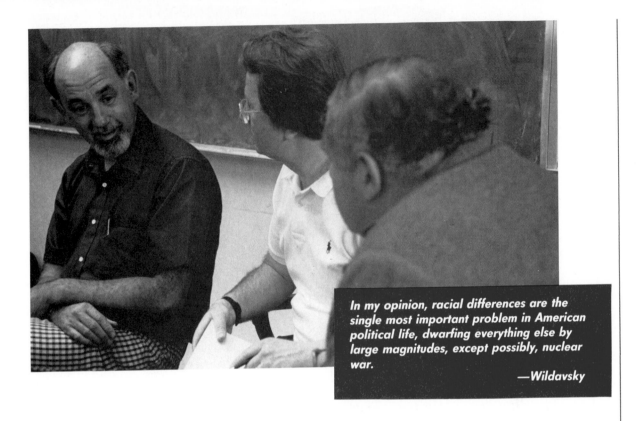

In my opinion, racial differences are the single most important problem in American political life, dwarfing everything else by large magnitudes, except possibly, nuclear war.

—Wildavsky

tivity. The tradition in this country is for the government to guarantee conditions of political stability so that economic investment is profitable. There are a lot of places where economic investment is shied away from, because political stability is uncertain and, for example, contracts can't be enforced. A long period of internal political stability and the absolutely confident expectation of continued political stability are economic tools of paramount importance. And we've had both.

In addition to that, it's been the American political tradition for the government to make very sizable investments in ways that frequently are not counted as governmental economic activity. Universal public education, for example, has been a significant economic tool. It means that you have a labor force which is highly reprogrammable. And that increases our capability not merely to create new jobs but of having a labor force which can flow into new jobs.

Political Interest Groups and Political Parties. In theory, political interest groups and political parties can work together in the making of domestic policy: interest groups are supposed to identify and articulate demands for specific policy changes and political parties are supposed to accommodate many such groups and their demands and organize them in support of a broader, more comprehensive domestic program. As chapter 6 showed, however, in practice, political interest groups have become more willing and able to press their demands in a much more strident, intense, and uncompromising manner, just as political parties became less able to integrate those groups and their demands behind a common agenda. The result has been a domestic policy-making process in which narrow interests seem quite adept at getting what they want, whether it is more money for nursing mothers or for stealth bombers, and no one seems to speak for the common good. Thus, although more, but selectively, responsive, the domestic policy-making process has become less representative of any sense of the broader, public interest. To the extent this is both true and widely believed, the process is illegitimate.

More recently, political parties, especially the Democratic party, and some governmental institutions, especially the Congress of the United States, have made some attempts to regain influence over the making of domestic policy. Some elements of the Democratic party, for example, have tried to cut back the influence of special interest groups by giving elected politicians more control over the organizational life of the party and especially, over the process of nominating its presidential candidate. In an even more spectacular display of organizational vitality, the members and committees of Congress appeared able to reform the nation's tax code, in 1986, even though that meant offending some powerful special interest groups.

Mass Media and Political Participation. Both the mass media and the various traditional forms of political participation strongly influence the course of domestic policy making. (See chapter 7.)

The mass media, all those forms of communication which governing elites try to use to influence public opinion, have come to play an increasingly strong, some would say dominant, role in the making of domestic policy. When it is unconstrained, the media are an effective critic of governmental officials and their policy actions. The media, however, through exaggeration and dramatization, often distort events, amplify the worst in American politics, ignore the regular operations of government, encourage popular cynicism, and erode the perception of legitimacy. In addition, the media have become a strong force in determining what goes on or through the nation's policy agenda—strong enough to cause some to suggest that the media represent the permanent party-out-of-power.

Meanwhile, those running for elective office and their consultants have become more active and skilled in using mass media marketing techniques to sell themselves and their policies to the American people. Indeed, the use of public opinion polling techniques, to tap public opinion, coupled with well-crafted mass media messages, today amounts to an ongoing or permanent campaign that makes traditional election contests seem relatively unimportant.

SOCIAL WELFARE: ARE MOST AMERICANS BETTER OFF?

The Policy Process

The policy process, as it was described in the three chapters of Part III, is really many different policy processes, each with its own (1) policy organization, (2) stages through which issues get on agendas and techniques by which policy makers deal with them, and (3) broad policy goals and ways of reaching them.

Policy Organizations. The concept of a policy organization was described in chapter 8 and was used to explain the making of education policy. Beyond this particular policy domain, however, the concept can be used to visualize and understand all those who regularly interact over the making of any policy, whether domestic or foreign.

A policy organization is a set of public and private actors who work together to shape what they view as government's proper role. In the recent course of the making of domestic policy, there have been many policy organizations.

In an attempt to advance the civil rights of blacks, a policy organization of black activists, black and white religious organizations, liberal whites and mostly-white organizations, such as the American Civil Liberties Union, largely Jewish groups, such as the Anti-Defamation League, and many elected officeholders closed ranks behind what became a string of civil rights policies throughout the mid-and late-1960s.

In an attempt to provide for a greater degree of consumer and environmental protection, activists such as Ralph Nader, a mass media that got good copy, and elected officeholders who were motivated both by principle and political expediency successfully advanced their common cause in the 1970s.

In an attempt to shrink the federal government's role in the economy and reduce its social welfare obligations, conservative spokespersons, such as economist Arthur Laffer, right-wing think tanks, such as the Heritage Foundation, and charismatic politicians, such as President Ronald Reagan and Representative Jack Kemp (R., N.Y.), acted as though they were a common policy organization. Working together, they were very successful through most of the 1980s in cutting taxes and popular expectations of what government should do, even if they were considerably less successful in their handling of the national debt.

In all these cases and in many ways (some of which have not yet been invented), people with common concerns, although perhaps different motives, combine their resources to overcome obstacles to policy making.

Policy Processes. Policy processes, as they were described in the study of civil rights policy in chapter 9, require the completion of certain stages of agenda building and the application of certain decision-making techniques.

Policy making starts with agenda building, a process in which the problem is defined, people come to believe that it is a matter of public concern, policy alternatives are identified and evaluated, and finally, governmental officials come to accept responsibility for dealing with the problem. Knowing this, you might think (correctly) that it is a little foolish for some to go directly to policy makers and demand that they solve a problem, without first laying the groundwork by following the earlier stages of agenda building. Knowing this might

The urban riots of the 1960s shook the political system and quickened the pace of policy making.

also make you more appreciative of the obstacles that have stood in the way of some who shaped the nation's agenda and of their success in overcoming those obstacles. For example:

- The federal government accepted responsibility for ensuring the civil rights of blacks only after the Reverend Martin Luther King, Jr., and other black civil rights leaders marched, suffered, and persisted.
- The federal government moved more forcefully and generously to respond to the needs of the poor only after the poor organized themselves to bring about peaceful political pressure and only after elected policy makers better appreciated the depths of the social discontent that spilled over in urban riots during the late 1960s.
- The drive to deregulate American business picked up steam and began to win policy victories only after a broad segment of the public came to believe that excessive governmental regulations stifled the economy, increased unemployment, and made it harder for Americans to compete in the global economy.

This case, and others going on around you, show that policy making often is only the quick, dramatic cap that is placed on a much slower and less glamorous political process of changing people's perceptions, if not their values.

The policy process continues through the application of certain decision-making techniques. These, too, are less dramatic than you might have thought.

552   *SOCIAL WELFARE: ARE MOST AMERICANS BETTER OFF?*

Wise policy makers, we argued in chapter 9, know that they are struggling with an uncertain world, often full of forces that are beyond their control. To cope with uncertainty, while working to advance their goals, the wise policy maker acts incrementally, by being reactive, not proactive; by prefering marginal to radical changes in policy; by searching for policies that will remedy the problem, even if they do not eradicate it; and by tending to believe that good policies are those that can win popular approval.

Throughout American history, these tactics of incrementalism have characterized the making of domestic policy, as in these examples:

- Most new domestic policy proposals introduced in Congress, at least those that go somewhere, seek only a new program and a relatively small authorization and appropriation, in a manner reminiscent of the beginnings of the WIC program.
- After the passage of landmark or breakthrough legislation, such as the Civil Rights Act of 1964, there usually is a long period in which policy changes in other areas are simply brought into line with the breakthrough. This was the case with policy changes in education, employment, and credit, for example, following the 1964 breakthrough in civil rights for blacks.
- Under President Reagan, the popular reaction to radical proposals to sell off public lands caused many of those plans to be shelved.

In addition, nonincremental approaches to policy making often fail, either because their promise is too grandiose (President Johnson's War on Poverty), because their performance is too disappointing (President Johnson's Model Cities program, for example), or because they fail to take into account negative feedback (President Ford's swine flu immunization program, for example).

Goals and Policies. In the discussion in chapter 10 of economic policy, we distinguished between broad policy goals and the more narrow and specific policy means that can be used in the attempt to realize them.

In the case of the making of economic policy, there are many different goals, some of which often conflict, as, for example, the goal of economic growth appears to conflict with the goal of economic equality. In addition, the task of goal realization is complicated by (1) the state of knowledge about existing policy means; (2) the possibility that a policy that contributes to the realization of one goal may detract for the realization of another goal; and (3) political constraints on the use of a particular policy approach.

Much of domestic policy making seems to be a jumble of competing goals and conflicting means. For example:

- We remain deeply concerned over the growing trade deficit and deeply committed to governmental subsidies that keep the price of our agricultural products, way above their world market price.
- We are resentful of welfare benefits that are provided to unwed teenage mothers and reluctant to subsidize the dissemination of birth control information and devices in public schools.

In addition, the task of devising and implementing effective domestic policy is further complicated by many of the characteristics of the major national governmental institutions.

Governmental Institutions

The chapters of Part IV examined the four major institutions of American national government: (1) the presidency, (2) Congress, (3) the federal bureaucracy, and (4) the federal courts, especially the Supreme Court.

These four chapters described some of the characteristics of each institution and began the discussion of the ways in which these characteristics affect the making of public policy. This chapter extends that discussion, with a special focus on the making of domestic policy. (The next chapter does the same, but with a focus on foreign policy.)

Each of the major institutions of American national government has certain dominant organizational characteristics that affect the performance of the institution in the making of domestic policy. What are these dominant characteristics and what effects do they have?

The Presidency. As chapter 11 pointed out, the modern American presidency is becoming a more personalized, plebiscitary institution.

It is more of a personalized institution in that the President's popular appeal seems to matter more than it used to. Both President Carter and President Reagan ran successfully against Washington, both successfully convinced the public of their personal virtue, and both aspired to be more than caretaker Presidents. Once in office, however, they behaved totally differently. President Carter, we know from the subsequent reports of his key aides, acted as though he believed that sincerity was sufficient: if he believed in the substantive merits of a proposed policy, then interest groups should acquiesce, Congress should nod, the public should applaud, and the media should report the good news. President Reagan, however, acted as though he understood that good policies are those that can elicit the support of those most affected by them; if he carefully limited his agenda, carefully rationed his energies and influence, carefully packaged his proposals in appealing symbols, and claimed resounding success for both modest victories and real defeats, then he could enter future battles, empowered by the glow of public approval. Thus, the Reagan presidency made the point: personal appeal begets both modest policy success and, if carefully orchestrated, more personal appeal. Given the importance of personal appeal, it is not surprising that Presidents work so hard to cultivate it.

The modern presidency is a plebiscitary institution because of the skill with which the President's advisors employ the techniques of the permanent campaign. Through these techniques (described in the **Vantage Point** on page 248 of chapter 7), modern Presidents conduct what amounts to an ongoing referendum on their presidency. Under President Reagan, for example, (1) public opinion polls identified concerns about social problems (about the continuing degradation of the environment, for example) and doubts about the President's policies (about the strength of his commitment to preserving Social Security benefits, for example); (2) the President and his advisors designed and carried out events (appearances, speeches, personnel changes, for example) to demonstrate the President's personal commitment to the policy goal; (3) evaluated the impact of these activities with more public opinion polling; and, when necessary, (4) designed and carried out additional activities to heighten the belief that relief was on the way. In this manner, the techniques of the permanent campaign can make the President look more successful and actually be more successful, especially if he is as skilled as President Reagan was in translating the appearance of power into the fact of power.

Even though the plebiscitary President may look as though he is proactive and capable of exercising bold leadership, recall that he is reacting to public sentiments that he helped orchestrate and he is leading people where he has helped convince them they want to go. Keeping this in mind might cause you to adjust downward your future estimates of a President's influence over the policy-making process. In addition, you might wonder what would happen to the plebiscitary President's policy influence should the public ever figure out what was going on.

Congress.   As described in chapter 12, today's Congress is a very representative and highly fragmented institution. The organization of Congress makes it very representative, especially of constituent concerns. The organization of Congress, however, also makes it a highly fragmented institution in which congressional decision-making power is widely scattered.

These two organizational characteristics have mutually reinforcing effects on roles of individual members of Congress in the policy-making process. The representativeness of Congress encourages its members to respond to local constituent demands, as, for example, Representative Claude Pepper (D., Fla.) did for retirees in his district and as Senator Bob Packwood (R., Ore.) did for the timber industry in his home state. The fragmentation of congressional decision-making power makes it possible for members to respond successfully to constituent demands, by creating many different points at which members have great leverage over the policy-making process. Representative Pepper, for example, had a greater ability to protect the interests of the elderly by virtue of his position as chair of the House Rules Committee, the body through which most bills had to go on their way to the floor for a vote. Similarly, Senator Packwood's ability to protect his state's timber industry increased considerably after he became the chair of the Senate Finance Committee, given its influence over the drafting of tax legislation.

The pattern generally holds; there are many different fragments of congressional power and many members of Congress who wish to hold and use them to service the needs of those who determine their electoral future. Both organizational characteristics also affect the institution's role in the policy-making process, making it less able to initiate new broad policy initiatives and more likely to react to presidential ones, as it did in 1986, for example, in responding to President Reagan's call for tax reform.

According to David Stockman, President Reagan's first Director of the Office of Management and Budget, the tobacco subsidy "was the worst symbol of the old order we intended to overthrow." This photograph shows Stockman, left, at a breakfast meeting with Senator Helmes, at the time the chair of the Senate's Committee on Agriculture, Nutrition, and Forestry, and Jack Kemp, the Republican representative and presidential aspirant from New York.

The Bureaucracy. As chapter 13 showed, the federal bureaucracy is a very factious and inefficient place. It is factious because it is full of competing values and their advocates and it is inefficient because often vague laws have to be implemented over a large and diverse country and because usually no one trusts the bureaucracy enough to give it enough authority or staff to carry out its mission. These two characteristics of the federal bureaucracy mean that it is (1) highly susceptible to special alliances with key congressional committees and selected interest groups and (2) relatively immune to presidential leadership.

Lacking authority and endowed with at best dubious legitimacy, the federal bureaucracy relies on others for expertise, support, and clout. Often, these alliances are struck with those parts of Congress that are most concerned with the agency's mission and with those special interest groups most likely to be affected by the agency's actions. The Department of Agriculture, for example, maintains close working relationships with (1) the Senate's Agriculture, Nutrition, and Forestry Committee and especially the chair of its Subcommittee on Agricultural Production, Marketing, and Stabilization, (2) the House's Agriculture Committee and especially the chair of its Subcommittee on Tobacco and Peanuts, and representatives of the tobacco industry. These three-way alliances, referred to as iron triangles in chapter 13, help make many parts of the federal bureaucracy relatively immune to presidential influence.

The federal bureaucracy is relatively immune to presidential leadership. The President has limited capacity to make the bureaucracy and therefore, public policy responsive to popular preferences. Every in-coming new President in the last twenty years has promised to reorganize the federal bureaucracy. Every new President also soon abandoned the attempt as one that (1) was too difficult, (2) took too much of the President's time, energy, and political influence; and (3) was too politically unrewarding. The federal bureaucracy's relative invulnerability to presidential pressure is a mixed blessing. In the short run, invulnerability enhances the policy making discretion of federal bureaucrats. In the long run, however, the isolation that goes with invulnerability weakens the federal bureaucracy's claim to legitimacy and therefore its potential influence over the policy-making process.

The Courts. As chapter 14 showed, the federal courts and the Supreme Court in particular perform in a reactive and highly tentative manner.

Of all the major institutions of American national government, the Supreme Court is the most reactive, since, for the most part, it has to wait on others to press their claims up through the appeal process. Thus, the Supreme Court never moves if it does not have to, and even when it does, the Court usually moves in an especially tentative manner.

The Supreme Court has good reason to act tentatively, since its influence over the policy-making process rests on so fragile a basis, namely, its ability to convince others that it is acting in a manner consistent with the language and intent of the Constitution. The Court, moreover, works hard to maintain its hard-won and precious legitimacy, both by a tendency to rely on narrow

SOCIAL WELFARE: ARE MOST AMERICANS BETTER OFF?

interpretations of the issues before it and by trying to avoid the need to speak clearly on issues that deeply divide society. The Court, however, can avoid neither controversy nor action.

The Supreme Court is the last and, some argue, the best place in the political system where individual rights can be protected. This means that the Court, invariably, will be called on to defend unpopular minorities and causes against intolerant majorities. They have done this, for example, in cases involving those who argue in favor of the violent overthrow of the American political system, those who demand a free public education for the children of illegal immigrants, and those who insist that those improperly convicted should be released from prison. In all these and many other instances, the Supreme Court faced a dilemma: act in a manner that invited widespread popular disapproval or in a manner that was obviously inconsistent with the Constitution. Both are unattractive courses that threaten to erode the Court's fragile foundation of legitimacy.

Since the Supreme Court often finds itself in such awkward situations, you should expect to find that the Court (1) will try to avoid rushing into controversies where the society is deeply divided, such as the issue of abortion; (2) when it can no longer avoid action, will try to define the issue in narrow and, if possible, procedural terms, and (3) when it must act, will render a decision that makes only a marginal policy change.

Each of the major institutions of American national government, in other words, attempts to reach commendable policy goals, while seriously constrained by historical, cultural, political, and organizational forces.

■ Domestic policies in America are the product of a complex process, one shaped by our historical foundations, cultural expectations, political dynamics, and institutional arrangements. These various influences simultaneously push the political system toward difficult, if not impossible goals, while limiting its capacity to realize them. It is, therefore, perhaps inevitable that evaluations of the performance of American system of government are so critical. (For a discussion of the impact of discontent on the unending search for government's proper role, see the Epilogue.)

SUMMARY

Most Americans are better off today than they were thirty years ago, although there are some serious and troubling exceptions.

It is also relatively clear that Americans are better off because of the more expansive roles which all levels of government have played in the making of domestic policy. Nevertheless, it is also relatively clear that most Americans are better off because of three decades of extraordinary economic progress. The economic growth, however, did not come about without governmental assistance. To stimulate and sustain economic progress, all levels of government and the federal government in particular have intervened in many ways, indirectly, by providing, for example, universal public education and civil peace, and more directly, for example, by providing tax breaks and essential public services. The government's investment in the nation's economy benefited both: the economy grew as did government's role in providing for the welfare of society.

By the early 1980s, something changed. There emerged a sense that the private and public sectors were adversaries, not allies. Government came to be seen as the foe, not the friend, of economic progress. More and more people began to believe that it was time to stop passing out golden eggs and to start worrying about the health of the goose. By the mid-and late-1980s, they were still worrying.

Key Terms

feminization of poverty   entitlements
structural poverty   infrastructure
social safety net

Review and Reflection

1. Do you agree that most Americans are better off today than they seem to have been thirty years ago?

2. What exceptions, if any, do you think there are to this general improvement in the welfare of society?

3. President John F. Kennedy, in defense of an expanded social welfare role for the federal government, said: "A rising tide lifts all boats." By that he presumably meant that when society is better off, as it is after a period of vigorous economic growth, then everyone is better off. Do you agree?

4. What should be government's role if economic growth and social progress fail to improve the conditions of some? (What if some people have a hole in their boat?)

5. Do you think most Americans are better off because of what the major institutions of national government have done—or in spite of what they have done?

Supplemental Readings

When contemplating government's role in making domestic policy, it is natural to wonder about what works.

What works? You are at the tail end of an interesting phase in American public life. Between 1960 and 1980, America fell in and out of love with social engineering. When it was in love, America believed that government could alter the allocation of society's resources in ways that made everyone better off. As it fell out of love, America began to believe that the free market could do a better job. Since love is blind, however, both extremes are overstated. There have been many attempts to find the middle ground, by sorting out the successes and failures of this twenty year period. Here are some of the more interesting arguments about what works—and what does not.

Auletta, Ken. *The Underclass*. New York: Vintage, 1983.

Banfield, Edward C. *The Unheavenly City: The Nature and Future of Our Urban Crisis*. Boston: Little, Brown, 1970.

Bawden, D. Lee. *The Social Contract Revisited: Aims and Outcomes of President Reagan's Social Welfare Policy*. Washington, D.C.: The Urban Institute Press, 1984.

Ginzberg, Eli, and Robert M. Solow. *The Great Society*. New York: Basic Books, 1974.

Harrington, Michael. *The Other America: Poverty in the United States*. Baltimore, Penguin Books, 1972. (originally published in 1962).

Harrington, Michael. *The New American Poverty*. New York: Holt, Rinehart, 1984.

Himmelfarb, Gertrude. *The Idea of Poverty*. New York: Knopf, 1983.

Lucas, J. Anthony. *Common Ground: A Turbulent Decade in the Lives of Three American Families*. New York: Knopf, 1985.

Mead, Lawrence M. *Beyond Entitlement: The Social Obligations of Citizenship*. New York: The Free Press, 1986.

Morris, Charles R. *The Cost of Good Intentions: New York City and the Liberal Experiment, 1960–1975*. New York: McGraw-Hill, 1980.

Murray, Charles. *Losing Ground: American Social Policy, 1950–1980*. New York: Basic Books, 1984.

Patterson, James T. *America's Struggle against Poverty, 1900–1980*. Cambridge, Mass.: Harvard University Press, 1981.

Piven, Francis Fox, and Richard A. Cloward. *Regulating the Poor: The Functions of Public Welfare*. New York: Vintage, 1971, 1972.

Ryan, William. *Blaming the Victim*. New York: Vintage, 1976.

Schwarz, John E. *America's Hidden Success: A Reassessment of Twenty Years of Public Policy*. New York: W. W. Norton, 1983.

Stockman, David A. *The Triumph of Politics: Why the Reagan Revolution Failed*. New York: Harper & Row, 1986.

CHAPTER SIXTEEN

NATIONAL DEFENSE
IS AMERICA LESS SECURE?

*A*t the end of the Second World War, it was hard to imagine that America could be more secure.

America's military might stretched from Crete in the Mediterranean to Norway in the North Sea, from France to Berlin. In the Pacific theater, the American presence replaced Japan's, from Sumatra in the Indian Ocean to Tarawa in the South Pacific, from New Guinea to Tokyo.

America's economic strength at home mirrored the nation's military might abroad. The nation's industrial capacity had expanded to supply the war effort, and unlike those of every other industrial nation, America's factories stood untouched by the war.

America's diplomatic strength around the world was a logical extension of the nation's military, economic, and nuclear superiority. Except for the Communist controlled nations of Europe and Asia, and the generally ignored continent of Africa, America's allies encircled the globe.

Since then, the United States has become less dominant, the nation's adversaries less intimidated, the nation's allies less compliant. In many, but not all ways, America seems less secure today than at the end of the Second World War—and perhaps, less secure than in any time in the nation's history.

Some of these changes are revealed in the following Case, an examination of a current controversy between the United States and one of its allies. The Case suggests three insights. First, America's allies are much more independent than they used to be. Second, in spite of its loss of dominance, the nation has enjoyed some notable foreign policy accomplishments. Third, foreign policy calculations are intrinsically political.

NATIONAL DEFENSE

The days when a few big powers could
dominate the world are gone forever.
—*Zhao Ziyang, Prime Minister of
the People's Republic of
China, speaking to the General Assembly of the United
Nations, 1985*

The Case The Diplomatic War Between New Zealand and the United
States

Wellington, New Zealand, 1984. It seemed an unlikely place for an international
confrontation—especially between countries that were supposed to be allies.
Nevertheless, the confrontation came and threatened the United States' worldwide naval strategy.

On the surface, it did not appear as though anything New Zealand did, or did
not do, could affect the strategic interests of the United States. No closer to its
nearest neighbor, Australia, than France is to the Soviet Union, New Zealand
seemed to most Americans little more than a pleasant stopover—if one was on
an expedition seeking the South Pole or on an American warship making a port
call.

New Zealanders, however, like the citizens of most nations, resented actions
that wounded their pride and endangered their national security. For example,
they resented France's use of the South Pacific for tests of nuclear weapons and
the presence of American nuclear weapons inside their borders. Moreover, New
Zealand was committed to maintaining its status as a nuclear-free country—free
of nuclear weapons, nuclear energy, and hopefully, nuclear fallout. Beneath the
surface, therefore, it probably was inevitable that New Zealand would ban from
its harbors nuclear-armed or nuclear-powered American warships.

In July 1984, the Labor Party, led by David Lange, ran on a nuclear-free
platform and won a majority of seats in New Zealand's Parliament. Delivering on
one of his campaign promises, Prime Minister Lange promptly issued an executive order that banned all nuclear-armed or nuclear-powered ships from New
Zealand's waters. The ban started what was about to become a quick little
diplomatic war between New Zealand and the United States.

Immediately after Prime Minister Lange issued the ban, the United States
announced its intention to have one of its destroyers, the USS Buchanan, stop
over in New Zealand. Prime Minister Lange countered that the Buchanan would
be permitted entry only if the United States assured him that the ship was not
carrying nuclear weapons. The United States, responding that it was not its policy
to inform other countries of the armaments its ships carried, refused. Prime
Minister Lange, in turn, refused entry to the Buchanan. Then, in an apparently
well-orchestrated campaign, the United States canceled all planned military
maneuvers with New Zealand, discontinued the long-standing practice of shar-

The opposition of many New Zealanders to the presence of nuclear-armed and powered warships was made clear as early as March, 1984, as in this attempt to block the USS Queenfish from entering Auckland Harbor.

ing military intelligence with New Zealand, and publicly chastised New Zealand for its failure to carry out its obligations under the Anzus Treaty. (The treaty, in which the United States, Australia, and New Zealand pledged to consult one another about joint military action in the event any one country was attacked, had served as the basis for military cooperation for the previous thirty-four years.)

Informed of the decision to end bilateral military exercises and end the flow of military data between the two countries, Prime Minister Lange, obviously unimpressed, responded: "New Zealand's answer: That's heavy, we can cut it."[1] Undaunted by Prime Minister Lange's flippancy, the United States stepped up the pressure, by announcing the cancellation of the annual meeting of the Anzus alliance, scheduled to be held in Canberra, Australia, in July of 1985 and by expressing its intention to review its commitments to the defense of New Zealand. In the words of Paul D. Wolfowitz, the Assistant Secretary of State for East Asian and Pacific Affairs: "The American public will not long support commitments and alliances that protect others, if those others will not uphold their own responsibilities."[2]

To many, the United States' response seemed an overreaction to a trivial affront from a minor ally. American naval strategists saw the challenge differently, however (as did most American political cartoonists). From the American military's point of view, the Soviet threat meant that the United States had to maintain unrestricted passage through international waters and unimpaired access to the ports of its allies. From the American view, the need was dictated by the Soviet Navy's "blue water strategy," through which Soviet warships, based in ice-free ports, such as those at Cienfuegoes in Cuba and Cam Ranh Bay in Vietnam, freely operated throughout the world. To counter the Soviet deploy-

---

[1] Quoted in William Safire, "Friends, Allies No More," *New York Times*, 28 February 1985.

[2] Quoted in *The New York Times*, 27 February 1985.

New Zealand, by not automatically complying with U.S. wishes, refuted popular expectations of its traditional role in the Anzus Alliance.

ment, American naval strategists argued, the United States could not tolerate restrictions that hindered its mobility, especially ones imposed by its formal allies.

American naval strategists, therefore, were primarily concerned with the global implications of New Zealand's ban. If New Zealand got away with it, they feared, then other allies with more essential ports might follow suit. The danger seemed real in Japan, where the government had been able to finesse intense public opposition to nuclear weapons (and its own Constitution against their presence) by simply not asking whether or not incoming American ships carried them. Fully aware of the Japanese government's "see no evil approach" to U.S. warships, American naval strategists thought that New Zealand's policy had to be beaten down. In the words of William Safire, a political commentator with close ties to the Reagan administration, had we given an inch in New Zealand, "Japan's government would have been forced to demand a yard."[3]

In addition, the Reagan administration appeared to believe that if Japan succumbed to the pressure of its anti-nuclear activists, then our NATO allies would find it harder to resist the pressure of theirs. America's global security interests therefore required that it make an example of New Zealand. Events, however, soon conspired to discredit this approach and to force the United States to soften its stance toward New Zealand.

On July 10, 1985, the Rainbow Warrior, the flagship of Greenpeace, an international environmental action group, was bombed and severely damaged while harbored in New Zealand. The Rainbow Warrior had been preparing to sail in an attempt to prevent a French nuclear test on the atoll of Mururoa. Suspicion about those responsible for the bombing soon focused on France, and it gradually appeared as though French secret agents had bombed the ship to prevent it from either interfering with the test or from generating publicity adverse to France. The public outcry, in New Zealand and elsewhere, turned world opinion increasingly against France and made the American tough-guy stance more and more untenable.

Almost simultaneously, other events in New Zealand pushed Prime Minister David Lange into a more moderate position. His popularity reduced by soaring

---

[3] William Safire, "Friends, Allies No More," *New York Times*, 28 February 1985.

inflation and interest rates, Prime Minister Lange edged away from the extreme left wing of his Labor Party and toward most New Zealanders, who, according to a New Zealand newspaper poll, favored improved relations with the United States and retention of the Anzus pact.[4]

As the issue moved out of the headlines, most New Zealand observers expected that Prime Minister Lange would try to repair relations with Washington before the upcoming general elections in 1987. Simultaneously, American sources suggested that they were expecting Prime Minister Lange to agree to a policy, similar to that adopted by two of America's NATO allies, Norway and Denmark, which would bar ships with nuclear weapons only during wartime, not peacetime. As the uproar died down, both nations refocused their energies on more pressing foreign and domestic problems. In his observations on New Zealand's return to more mundane concerns, Tom Scott, a satirist with the *Auckland Star*, said: "It is a shame, really, because dealing with them is nowhere near as much fun as taking on the world."[5] Nevertheless, perhaps both New Zealand and the United States learned something from their little war, as we can.

Insights

Insight 1. *America's allies are much more independent than they used to be.* As this Case suggests, America's allies are not always quick to comply with American foreign policy wishes. Increasingly, America's allies, especially its strong and traditional ones in Europe, independently pursue their national interests, which they do not necessarily see as identical to the foreign policy goals of the United States.

Insight 2. *In spite of its loss of dominance, the United States has enjoyed some notable foreign policy accomplishments.* Since the end of the Second World War, the United States has lost influence over both allies and world events. Nevertheless, some foreign policy successes stand out. If, for example, one assumes that a major goal of America's foreign policy has been to avoid another world war or any nuclear war, then the nation has to be credited with a major accomplishment. Even though in spite of America's inability to dictate to its allies, the United States has conducted at least a moderately successful foreign policy since the end of the Second World War. Although that policy has had many specific goals, it most generally has been concerned with avoiding any worldwide war, especially one that might involve any of the major powers and thereby run the risk of a nuclear confrontation.

Insight 3. *Foreign policy calculations are intrinsically political.* In all cases, foreign policies are a part of a state's overall political processes. In this case, domestic political factors helped explain New Zealand's actions and the American response to them. Within New Zealand, domestic political pressures and

---

[4] Cited in *The New York Times*, 15 September 1985.

[5] Quoted in *The New York Times*, 22 September 1985.

partisan calculations of electoral advantage both pushed Prime Minister Lange into confrontation with the United States and pulled him back. In addition, American sensitivity to the domestic political pressures inside Japan and the countries of Western Europe helped shape the American policy response. Moreover, American sensitivity to international political pressures helped pull it back from its adversarial stance toward New Zealand. In general, both strategic doctrines and domestic political demands shape American foreign policy.

■ To elaborate these insights, the rest of this chapter focuses on changes in America's national security since the end of World War II and considers some of the ways in which various aspects of the American political system shape its foreign policy.

NATIONAL SECURITY

> A nation has neither permanent friends nor permanent enemies, only permanent interests.
> —Lord Palmerston, British Prime Minister (1784–1865)

Is America Less Secure Than in the Past?

Since the end of the Second World War, there have been three main historical periods that have provided different levels of national security. These are (1) a short period of **hegemony** in which the United States acted unilaterally and was able to dominate international events; (2) a longer period of **bipolarity** in which the United States and the Soviet Union, in concert with their allies, competed for dominance; and (3) a continuing period of **multipolarity** in which other states, such as France and China, and clusters of states, such as those in Western or Eastern Europe, have acted independently, thereby making it harder for either the United States or the Soviet Union to exercise control.

Hegemony. The United States emerged from World War II with unchallenged military might. In 1945, the United States had "the best equipped ground army, the greatest air force, the secret of the atomic bomb . . . (and) its navy was more powerful than any two other existing fleets."[6] In addition, the task of gearing up for the war effort had accelerated industrial development in the United States. Moreover, the nation's remoteness from the battle had protected its potent productive facilities from damage during the war. Thus, in

---

[6] Robert Dallek, "The Postwar World: Made in the USA," in Sanford J. Ungar, ed., *Estrangement: America and the World* (New York: Oxford University Press, 1985), p. 30.

In 1945, there was no better, or worse, symbol of America's unchallenged military might than the atomic bomb.

1946, the United States had, for a short time, the capacity to exercise unparalleled influence over world affairs. This it did, politically, economically, and militarily.

First, the United States exercised political influence over world affairs through a series of international agreements. These included:

- The Yalta Conference of 1945. Meeting in Yalta in the Crimea, President Franklin Roosevelt, Prime Minister Winston Churchill, and Marshall Joseph Stalin agreed on the occupation of Germany and approved preliminary plans for what became the United Nations.
- The Bretton Woods Agreement of 1944. Meeting in Bretton Woods, New Hampshire, the United States, along with Britain, China, France, the Soviet Union, and thirty-nine other nations attempted to create international economic order out of chaos. The International Bank for Reconstruction and Development (usually referred to as the World Bank) was formed to reconstruct the economies of Western Europe and in due course, to promote economic development in poorer, Third World, nations.
- The United Nations Treaty of 1945. By ratifying the Charter of the United Nations, the United States Senate signalled America's willingness to cooperate with other nations in maintaining world peace.

Second, the United States exercised economic influence over world affairs in a number of ways. Initially, the United States exercised economic influence through its role as the main financial backer of the United Nations. Subsequently, the United States became the main source of financial support for the

ΕΛΛΗΝΟΠΟΥΛΑ ΠΙΝΕΤΕ ΓΑΛΑ
ΕΙΝΑΙ ΔΥΝΑΜΩΤΙΚΟ ΚΑΙ ΩΦΕΛΙΜΟ

ΣΑΣ ΤΟ ΠΡΟΣΦΕΡΕΙ Η ΑΜΕΡΙΚΑΝΙΚΗ
ΑΠΟΣΤΟΛΗ ΒΟΗΘΕΙΑΣ ΔΙΑ ΤΗΝ ΕΛΛΑΔΑ
ΜΕ ΤΗΝ
ΣΥΝΕΡΓΑΣΙΑ ΤΗΣ ΕΛΛΗΝ. ΚΥΒΕΡΝΗΣΕΩΣ

In 1947, U.S. aid to Greece included milk for Greek children and guns for Greek soldiers.

reconstruction of the economies of Western European nations. Finally, the influence of the United States over international affairs was extended by the growth of large scale corporations that spanned national boundaries.

Third, the United States exercised military influence by maintaining an impressive defense capability and through a series of multilateral defense agreements with its former allies.

As the short period of hegemony ended, the United States relied more heavily on both economic and military forms of influence.

Bipolarity. The expansionist tendencies of the Soviet Union and the American determination to contain the spread of Communism quickly split the world into two hostile spheres. The Soviet challenge appeared soon after the war, as it dominated politically those portions of Eastern Europe it had just conquered militarily. Subsequently, the Soviet threat appeared on the shores of the Mediterranean, then in a perceived threat to the political independence of the states of Western Europe. In addition, the Soviet Union's development of nuclear weapons further eroded the West's sense of security.

The American response to the Soviet threat included a number of economic and military aid policies. These included:

- The Truman Doctrine of 1947. To assist the government of Greece against a communist-led rebellion and to help Turkey defend its border with the Soviet Union, President Harry Truman won congressional approval for a package of military and economic aid to contain the spread of Communism.
- The Marshall Plan of 1948. To assist in rebuilding the war-torn economies of the nations of western Europe and to make them politically more stable and militarily more able to defend themselves, the United States Congress accepted a plan proposed by Secretary of State George C. Marshall. Between 1948 and 1952, the Marshall Plan, formally known as European Recovery Program, funneled over 15 billion dollars in grants and loans into the sixteen nations of western Europe and later, into West Germany.
- To contain the spread of Communism, the United States entered into a series of multilateral defense agreements: the Rio Treaty of 1947 which established a mutual defense agreement among twenty-one American republics (under which an attack on one would be considered an attack on all); the North Atlantic Treaty of 1949 which established a mutual defense pact of fifteen (mostly European) nations under the North Atlantic Treaty Organization (NATO);[7] the Anzus Treaty with Australia and New Zealand (1952); and the Southeast Asian Collective Defense Treaty of 1954, the Southeast Asian equivalent of NATO.

Through these international agreements, the United States wove together a string of alliances that were meant to contain (the Russians would have said

[7] The original twelve NATO countries were Belgium, Britain, Canada, Denmark, France, Iceland, Italy, Luxembourg, the Netherlands, Norway, Portugal, and the United States. Three additional countries were added in the 1950s: Greece, Turkey, and West Germany.

"encircle") the Soviet Union. In the process, the United States helped create a bipolar world, with it and its allies on one side and, on the other, the Soviet Union and its East European allies and, after 1949, China.

The bipolar alliances gave the appearance of stability and therefore of relative security. Beneath the surface, however, both the United States and the Soviet Union had committed themselves to a nuclear arms race that would soon bring about only a balance of terror. With increasingly high levels of nuclear armaments on both sides, international security rested on what many viewed as a calculation too subject to human error: the **Mutual Assured Destruction** (MAD) doctrine which held that one side's security lay in its ability to assure the other that a nuclear attack would bring about its own destruction.

"Don't mind me—just go right on talking."
—from *The Herblock Book Beacon Press, 1952*)

"Don't mind me— just go right on talking."

While negotiators talk, the earth is having its measurements taken—for its own coffin.

Multipolarity. The bipolar world ended through a series of developments in both its spheres. In the Western camp, American dominance was eroded by the re-emergence of strong European nations, each with their own economic and military capabilities and by the re-emergence of Japan as a major world power. In the Eastern camp, Soviet dominance was eroded by the growing economic independence of Eastern European nations, by developing economic ties between Eastern and Western European states, and by the ideological split between the Soviet Union and China. Elsewhere, the bipolar world was fragmented further by the emergence of middle range powers, such as Brazil, Mexico, and India, and by the growing assertiveness of Third World states, such as Egypt and Indonesia.

The end of the bipolar and the arrival of the multipolar world was graphically illustrated by a number of developments:

- Beginning in the mid-1960s, NATO became a less secure shield, as the Soviet threat seemed to retreat, as member nations reduced their financial commitments, after France withdrew in 1966 to chart an independent foreign policy course, and after Greece cut back its participation in 1974 because of Turkey's use of NATO weapons to invade Cyprus.
- In the early- and mid-1960s, cracks appeared in the facade of the Organization of American States, after Cuba was expelled in 1962 for promoting Communist subversion in Latin America and after the United States acted unilaterally to intervene militarily to prevent what it referred to as a Communist takeover in the Dominican Republic in 1965.
- In 1977, SEATO dissolved after Pakistan withdrew in 1972 over the loss of Bangladesh and after South Vietnam fell to Communist aggression in 1975 in spite of the treaty.
- By the early- and mid-1980s, America's traditional allies seemed more and more unappreciative of past help and increasingly unresponsive to requests for support, as France was, for example, in refusing to let American airplanes fly over French territory on their way to bomb Libya in 1986.

As symbolized by such developments, the postwar alliance structures in the West began to unravel and even the alliances in the East began to look a bit

America's ailing alliances are a frequent source of material for editorial cartoonists, as in this example.

frayed, as China split off from the Soviet Union, as occasional border strife erupted between China and North Vietnam, and as waves of restlessness repeatedly swept across the captive nations of Eastern Europe. The dissolution of the bipolar alliances made some think that it signalled growing international instability and therefore the loss of security for all nations, and especially for the United States and the Soviet Union.

On the other hand, the disorderliness of the multipolar world, some believe, enhances the stability of the international system and therefore the security of the United States. In such a world, nations are free to act as Madisonian factions, each checking the fallible judgments of the other and restraining its possible excesses. Our European allies may have acted in this way by limiting the severity of the American response to Libya in 1986 after it was linked to acts of terrorism against Americans abroad. In this view, the United States is more, not less, secure, since its lack of compliant allies makes the United States act more prudently than it might otherwise.

Although it is difficult to date its beginning, the multipolar period continues on today and, if we are lucky, will continue tomorrow.

How Did America Become Less Secure?

Since the end of the Second World War, changes in America's level of national security have been the result of (1) its own foreign policy successes; (2) a resurgence of nationalism elsewhere; and (3) technological advances.

Foreign Policy Successes. To some extent, the United States today is less dominant but perhaps more secure because of its own foreign policy successes. In the West, at least, the alliance structures were supposed to shield nations which had been weakened by the war and which needed a chance to revive their economies and restructure their political systems. For those purposes, the Western alliances worked and they produced the intended result: free nations that often acted independently of one another. The results, therefore, were intended and indeed, may contribute to the stability of the international system and thereby to America's security.

Thus, apparent failures that distress Americans may turn out to be deeper, more significant successes. For example, on the surface, the United States, for the most part, failed in its attempt to rally European support for economic sanctions against Libya in 1986. The lukewarm European response distressed many Americans and provoked a popular outcry. For example, Ben Wattenberg, a political commentator, wrote: "Europeans have demonstrated again and again that they put money above principle."[8] Others, however, argued that the American response to Libya, American expectations about attainable levels of security, and American claims on its allies were excessive. For example, Christopher Makins, a former British diplomat who is now a U.S. citizen and commentator on American politics, said: "Never until the last 25 years has the United States faced a real, direct threat to its security. The level of security that the U.S. used to enjoy is no longer attainable, but that is not widely acknowledged."[9] To the extent this is true, allies who are free to force unpleasant realities upon American policy makers can only enhance American security.

Nationalism.   **Nationalism** is the desire of a people who share some common identity to have their own territory and their own state through which they exercise self-governance.[10] (Nationalism, in addition, often is associated with particular and typically unflattering views of the people of other nations, as shown in the **Vantage Point**: How Americans View Russians.) Since the end of the Second World War, this yearning and the willingness of people to die for it have had mixed effects on the stability of the international system and the security of the United States.[11]

Nationalism empowers a people who shared some common heritage and encourages them to form their own independent state. Since the end of the Second World War, for example, political independence movements and the breakup of colonial empires accelerated the formation of independent states. (Since its founding in 1945, membership in the United Nations has tripled.) Thus, after the war, nationalism encouraged peoples to form states that acted independently of other nation-states.

Nationalism became a potent force in the post war world because of economic and technological developments. In some cases, growing economic strength made it possible for states to assert themselves more forcefully, as, for

[8] Quoted in *The New York Times*, 19 January 1986.

[9] Quoted in *The New York Times*, 19 January 1986.

[10] For a similar definition of nationalism, see Theodore A. Couloumbis and James H. Wolfe, *Introduction to International Relations: Power and Justice* (Englewood Cliffs, NJ: Prentice-Hall, 1986), p. 65.

[11] On the resurgence of nationalism, see Barbara Ward. *Five Ideas that Change the World* (New York: Norton, 1959).

HOW AMERICANS VIEW RUSSIANS

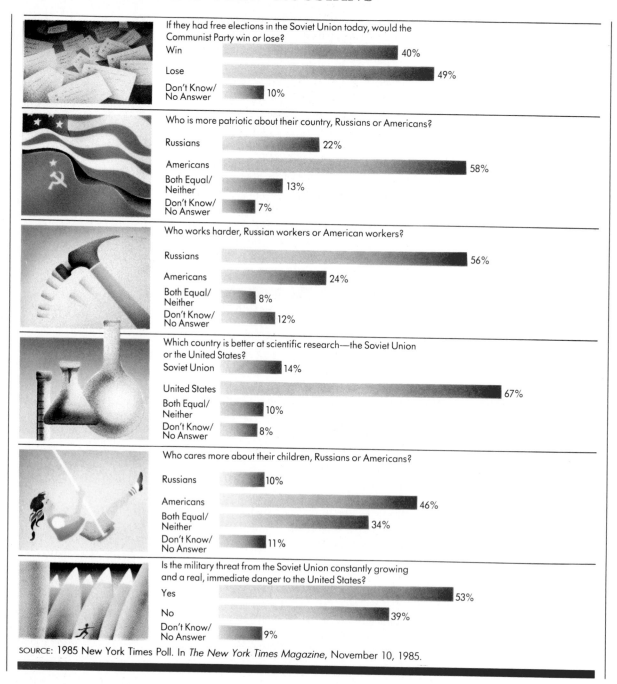

If they had free elections in the Soviet Union today, would the Communist Party win or lose?

Win 40%

Lose 49%

Don't Know/ No Answer 10%

Who is more patriotic about their country, Russians or Americans?

Russians 22%

Americans 58%

Both Equal/ Neither 13%

Don't Know/ No Answer 7%

Who works harder, Russian workers or American workers?

Russians 56%

Americans 24%

Both Equal/ Neither 8%

Don't Know/ No Answer 12%

Which country is better at scientific research—the Soviet Union or the United States?

Soviet Union 14%

United States 67%

Both Equal/ Neither 10%

Don't Know/ No Answer 8%

Who cares more about their children, Russians or Americans?

Russians 10%

Americans 46%

Both Equal/ Neither 34%

Don't Know/ No Answer 11%

Is the military threat from the Soviet Union constantly growing and a real, immediate danger to the United States?

Yes 53%

No 39%

Don't Know/ No Answer 9%

SOURCE: 1985 New York Times Poll. In *The New York Times Magazine*, November 10, 1985.

example, the Arab states of OPEC have in recent years. In other cases, new weapons technologies added significance to the claims of peoples who felt frustrated either in (1) their search for a national homeland, as, for example, was true of the Palestinians, or (2) their attempt to break away from some existing state and form their own state, as, for example, was true of the separatist campaigns of the Kurds in Iran, the Tamil insurgency in Sri Lanka, the Hmong tribe in Laos, and so on. (These and other conflicts are listed in **Table 16.1**: Factiousness Is Endemic Throughout the World.)

Overall, nationalism has had mixed effects on the stability of the international political system. In some cases, the sense of nationalism has contributed to the stability of the international system and, thereby, to the security of all nations, as, for example, when the United States must pause before it counts on the support of its NATO allies and when the Soviet Union must do the same before it takes for granted the support of its allies' governments.

In other cases, however, nationalism has tended to destabilize the international system, thereby endangering the security of many nations. This destabilizing effect has come about in two major ways. First, nationalism has fueled expansionist drives in which some nations have sought to extend their rule, as Germany did over Western Europe on the eve of the Second World War, or have sought to spread their ideology beyond existing borders, as the Soviet Union has done since the war. Second, nationalism has precipitated conflicts between the superpowers and their traditional allies. In the Soviet camp, for example, Czech nationalism was suppressed only through the Soviet Union's use of force in 1968. In the Western alliance, for example, France, ever since it pulled out of NATO, has asserted its independence with greater impunity.

Technological Advances.   Throughout history and especially since the end of the Second World War, technological advances have destabilized the international system and detracted from America's security, although some hope to reverse this trend. Technological progress is destabilizing because it permits the development of new and therefore unregulated weapons. For example, in the Strategic Arms Limitation Talks of 1972 (SALT I), the United States and the Soviet Union agreed to limits on numbers of intercontinental missiles and on protections that could be built into antiballistic-missile systems. But technological advances enabling missiles to carry additional warheads circumvented the first limitation and the prospect of a laser-based antiballistic missile system (popularly known as the **Star Wars technology**) threatened to render moot the second limitation.

Some technological advances are said to promise greater national security, although many doubt it. On the positive side, some technological advances facilitate international agreements, by making it easier to determine whether or not nations are living up to their treaty obligations. For example, sophisticated spy satellites permit more accurate monitoring of compliance with arms control and nuclear testing agreements. Also, some, especially some in President Reagan's Administration, argued that the technological advances embed-

TABLE 16.1 Factiousness is Endemic Throughout the World

In the 1980s, there were over forty small-scale wars going on throughout the world. Many of these were fueled by the desire of peoples to break away from some existing state to form their own. Others were the result of long-simmering disputes between neighboring states.

Here is a list of the wars that is circulating at the Defense Department, where no one person or office claims authorship. It was compiled from public sources and not from secret intelligence data, according to department officials, who said the descriptions are only shorthand and not intended as official pictures. Condensed, the list goes:

Sub-Saharan Africa	**Angola.** Insurgency; high-intensity conflict.
	Botswana. Low-intensity conflict; cross-border operations involving South Africa.
	Burkina Faso. Intense conflict with Mali over border; cease-fire in early January 1986.
	Central African Republic. Low-intensity conflict with dissidents in north and Chadian commandos.
	Chad. Insurgency; low-intensity conflict with southern commandos and Libyans.
	Ethiopia. Insurgency; high-intensity conflict with insurgents in Eritrea and Tigre plus border confrontations with Somalia.
	Lesotho. Cross-border operations with South Africa.
	Namibia. Low-intensity conflict with South Africa.
	Somalia. Low-intensity conflict with dissidents and border confrontations with Ethiopia.
	South Africa. Pre civil war.
	Sudan. Low-intensity conflict with dissidents in south.
	Uganda. Low-intensity conflict with dissidents.
	Zaire. Low-intensity conflict with dissidents in the east.
	Zimbabwe. Low-intensity conflict with dissidents in south.
Asia and the Pacific	**India.** Border skirmishes with Pakistan.
	Pakistan. Small-unit actions on Indian border; problems with Afridis tribe; heavily armed bandits, and air-space violations by Afghan aircraft.
	Sri Lanka. Tamil insurgent activity.
	China. Conflict on border with the Soviet Union, and Vietnam.
	North and South Korea. Cross-border operations; intense psychological warfare.
	Burma. Insurgent activity and problems with narcotics traffickers.
	Cambodia. Insurgents against Vietnamese and Republic of Kampuchea forces.
	Indonesia. Insurgent activity; occasional border incidents with Papua New Guinea.
	Laos. Problems with Hmong tribe, former Nationalist government troops, narcotics smugglers and bandits.
	Malaysia. Low-level Islamic dissidence.
	Papua New Guinea. Low-level border conflict with Indonesia.
	Philippines. Continued insurgent conflict.
	Vietnam. Forces occupying Cambodia and Laos are engaged in counterinsurgency.
Western Europe	**Ireland.** Sectarian conflict.
Warsaw Pact-Eastern Europe-Mongolia-Afghanistan	**Afghanistan.** Protracted conflict between Afghan resistance and the Soviets-Karmal regime.
Latin America	**Columbia.** Insurgency and acts of terrorism.
	Ecuador. Nascent terrorism; insurgency.
	El Salvador. Active insurgency.
	Guatemala. Active insurgency.
	Nicaragua. Active insurgency.
	Peru. Acts of terrorism; insurgency.
Middle East-North Africa-Persian Gulf	**Lebanon.** Civil war; Syrian presence; conflicts with Israel.
	Morocco. Conflict with Polisario over control of Western Sahara.
	Iran. War with Iraq; skirmishes with Kurds.
	Iraq. War with Iran; skirmishes with Kurds.
	South Yemen. Coup attempt.

SOURCE: Joanne Omang, "The Fabled 42 Wars Don't Equal WW III," *The Plain Dealer*, May 1, 1986.

NATIONAL DEFENSE: IS AMERICA LESS SECURE?

Do advances in weapons technology and production increase, or decrease, national security?

ded in their Star Wars proposals promised to enhance security by making intercontinental ballistic missiles obsolete. Others, however, argued that the Star Wars proposals detracted from world security, because they deluded the American people. By convincing them that a technological umbrella could protect them from incoming missiles, the Star Wars critics feared that the American people would become more willing to support a military buildup that could re-ignite the arms race and thereby endanger world peace.[12] Still others, such as some editorial cartoonists, took a more irreverent view of the Star Wars proposals.

Will America Be Even Less Secure in the Future?

Whether or not America will be less or more secure in the future will depend on the way in which we and others respond to threats to international peace. Although some of them have yet to be discovered (or invented), it is possible to identify four major contemporary threats: (1) nationalism; (2) the arms race; (3) economic distress; and (4) an impaired capacity to learn from the past.

The possibly destabilizing effects of nationalism and the arms race have already been discussed. In addition to these factors, economic distress, especially among the peoples of less developed countries and the failure to learn from the past can pose future threats to national security.

Economic Distress.   Many policy makers believe that economic distress is a perpetual source of international instability. In many parts of the less economically developed Third World, they believe, the appallingly poor quality of life can easily provoke desperate political acts. In addition, they assume, the startling contrast in the conditions of developed and developing countries

---

12 The point was made, for example, by Flora Lewis, an international affairs commentator for the *New York Times*, in her commencement address at Oberlin College on May 26, 1986.

TABLE 16.2 Resource Imbalances between Developed and Developing Countries

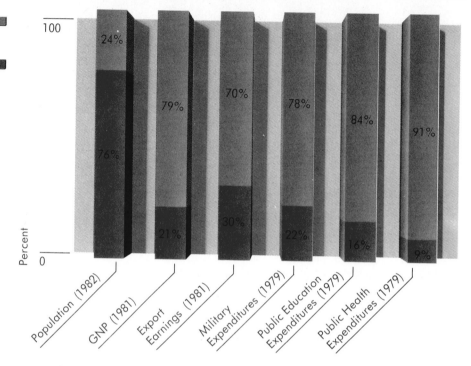

Notes: World population, 4.6 billion; world GNP, $12.2 trillion; total world export earnings, $1,965.1 billion; total world military expenditures, $478.0 billion; total world public education expenditures, $545.9 billion; and total world health expenditures, $313.5 billion.

SOURCE: *U.S. Foreign Policy and the Third World: Agenda 1983* edited by John P. Lewis and Valeriana Kallab. Copyright © 1983 Overseas Development Council. Reprinted by permission of Praeger Publishers. In Theodore A. Couloumbis and James H. Wolfe, *Introduction to International Relations: Power and Justice*, 3rd ed. (Englewood Cliffs, NJ: Prentice-Hall, 1986), p. 362.

(revealed in **Table 16.2**) can easily lead to envy, resentment, and hostility. Therefore, they argue, it is in the self-interest of richer nations to help poorer ones improve the living conditions of their people.[13]

These arguments ring true. In the last twenty years, most major strains in the Western alliance and most conflicts between the United States and the Soviet Union have been precipitated by Third World conflicts, in for example, Cuba, Vietnam, Central America, Iran, Lebanon, Libya, Afghanistan, and Angola.

The Capacity to Learn. As Lloyd Etheredge shows in his review of American policies toward Central America, many American foreign policy makers have

---

[13] For examples of such arguments, see Willy Brandt, et. al. *North-South: A Program for Survival* (Cambridge, Mass.: M.I.T. Press, 1980) and Robert S. McNamara, "Time Bomb or Myth: The Population Problem," *Foreign Affairs* 62 (1984): 1113–31.

failed to learn from the past and therefore continue to make mistakes that detract from America's security.[14]

Most of the failures to learn are rooted in some form of delusional thinking that over-estimates America's capacity to influence international events and underestimates obstacles that effectively constrain America's influence. Thus, for example, the administration of President Kennedy mistakenly assumed that an American-backed invasion of Cuba would ignite a mass uprising against Fidel Castro in the early 1960s; the administration of President Lyndon Johnson mistakenly assumed that American military force could shore up a South Vietnam that lacked leadership and the will to resist Communist aggression in the mid-1960s;[15] and the administration of President Reagan may be mistakenly assuming that American-backed guerrillas can topple the Communist government of Nicaragua in the mid-1980s.

The American tendency to over-estimate the efficacy of unilateral action also may detract from our willingness and ability to learn to rely on international organizations such as the United Nations to promote national security.

Anti-Sandinista guerrillas being trained in Honduras. Based in Honduras, this group makes strikes inside the border of northern Nicaragua.

■ To some extent, America's current level of national security is a product of good fortune: the fact that, because of ill health or internal economic distractions, no strong Soviet leader has emerged in recent years.[16] In the long run, however, the nation's security will depend more on our ability to cope with destabilizing influences, without over-reacting in ways that are themselves destabilizing. Nevertheless, the days of hegemony probably are gone forever, and therefore our security, to some extent, is dependent upon the actions of others—as theirs is on ours. The recognition of that interdependency may be the key to our joint survival.

FOREIGN POLICIES

> We are citizens of the world; and the tragedy of our times is that we do not know this.
> —Woodrow Wilson

As in the case of New Zealand's anti-nuclear stance and the American response to it, foreign policy is the product of many determinants. These include (1) factors that are a part of our historical foundations, (2) various parts of the

---

[14] Lloyd S. Etheredge, *Can Governments Learn?: American Foreign Policy and Central American Revolutions* (New York: Pergamon Press, 1985).

[15] For the counter-argument, that the Vietnam War may have been winable, see Fox Butterfield, "The New Vietnam Scholarship," *New York Times Magazine*, 13 February 1983.

[16] For an excellent discussion of the internal economic problems of the Soviet Union, see, for example, Seweryn Bialer, *The Soviet Paradox: External Expansion, Internal Decline* (New York: Knopf, 1986).

domestic political environment, (3) various characteristics of the process of assessing foreign threats and devising policy responses, and (4) characteristics of the major institutions of the national government. In general, however, and in contrast to the making of domestic policy, the making of foreign policy is a much more chaotic, unstructured affair.

Historical Foundations

Our historical foundations offer little unambiguous guidance for the making of foreign policy, primarily because, in the international arena, there is no commonly accepted form of legitimate authority. Lacking one, the task of making resource allocation decisions with effects that cross national borders often falls to multinational corporations, not international organizations.

Throughout our history, Americans have been able to reach little agreement about the proper role of the United States in the world community. In practice, its actual role, however, has been a reflection of its capacity to play one: when Americans have had the economic and military capacity, they have played a strongly interventionist role and when they felt unable to dominate international affairs, they have tended to assume a much more isolationist posture.[17]

In the absence of more precise directives, perhaps it would be useful for Americans to recall the words spoken by President George Washington in his farewell address on September 17, 1796, when he urged future leaders to avoid "permanent, inveterate antipathies against particular nations" and strive to cultivate "peace, harmony, and liberal intercourse" with all nations.

The task of foreign policy making is further complicated by some of those provisions of the American Constitution which we discussed in chapter 2. In general, as Edward S. Corwin, one of America's most eminent constitutional authorities, has written: "The Constitution . . . is an invitation to struggle for the privilege of directing American foreign policy."[18] Over time, many have responded to the invitation, especially the President and Congress. For example, the Constitution gives the President most of the authority for making foreign policy but also provides special grants of authority to the Senate to participate in treaty making and in approving ambassadors and, of course, general grants of authority to both houses, by virtue of their roles in the approval of expenditures and in the formal declaration of war.

As we discussed in chapter 3, the principle of federalism is another enduring, if ambiguous, foundation of American government. In this context, the principle has both direct and significant consequences for the making of defense policies and indirect, somewhat humorous consequences for the conduct of international diplomacy.

---

[17] See, for example, the discussion in Dallek, "The Postwar World," pp. 30–31.

[18] Edward S. Corwin, *The President: Office and Powers*, 5th rev. ed., Randall W. Bland et. al., eds. (New York: New York University Press, 1984).

"At last! A weapons system absolutely impervious to attack: It has components manufactured in all 435 Congressional districts!"

Federalism, you will recall, distributes formal governmental authority in various ways, including into the hands of members of Congress who must vote on military and economic aid to foreign governments and on the construction of military bases and weapons systems. Since the electoral fates of these members is tied, in part, to their ability to reward their supporters, it should not be surprising that the Defense Department tries to spread around defense contracts, as it appears to have done in the case of the MX missile. (See **Figure 16.1**.)

In other cases, federalism allows even local governments to attempt to intrude, complicating the conduct of diplomatic relations. For example, in May 1982, the Glen Cove City Council charged that the Russians were using a house in Glen Cove (New York) to spy on nearby defense industries. Besides, the Russians who lived in the house were using the city's public beaches and tennis courts even though the house they owned had diplomatic tax immunity. In reaction to both, the City Council banned the Russians from its beaches and tennis courts; to counter, the Justice Department filed suit in district court, seeking an injunction to force Glen Cove to open its beaches and tennis courts to the Russians. The injunction proved unnecessary, however. After the Russians agreed to make a voluntary contribution to the city, in lieu of taxes, the bans were lifted and a diplomatic crisis was avoided.

The American concern with civil liberties and civil rights, described more fully in chapter 4, sometimes spills over into the making of foreign policy. These determinants often infuse American foreign policy with a strong moralistic tone. This can be seen, for example, in public demands that the Soviet Union loosen restrictions on Russian Jews who wish to emigrate and in public opposition to the South African government's reliance on a policy of apartheid to segregate and control the indigenous population.

His immigration blocked for nine years, Anatoly Shcharansky finally left Soviet domination behind.

FIGURE 16.1
Guns and Butter

Since building guns and missiles means jobs for their constituents, members of Congress may be more likely to vote for weapons, as some members were to vote for construction of the MX missile system in the 1980s. Here is where the jobs and contracts are.

Who Is Building the MX Missile

Where the Jobs and Contracts Are

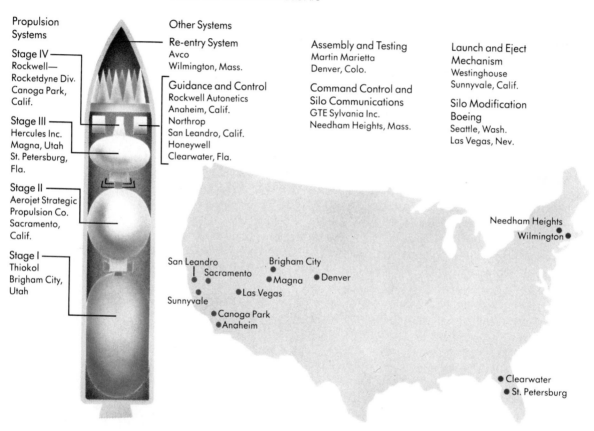

Propulsion Systems

Stage IV — Rockwell— Rocketdyne Div. Canoga Park, Calif.

Stage III — Hercules Inc. Magna, Utah St. Petersburg, Fla.

Stage II — Aerojet Strategic Propulsion Co. Sacramento, Calif.

Stage I — Thiokol Brigham City, Utah

Other Systems

Re-entry System Avco Wilmington, Mass.

Guidance and Control Rockwell Autonetics Anaheim, Calif. Northrop San Leandro, Calif. Honeywell Clearwater, Fla.

Assembly and Testing Martin Marietta Denver, Colo.

Command Control and Silo Communications GTE Sylvania Inc. Needham Heights, Mass.

Launch and Eject Mechanism Westinghouse Sunnyvale, Calif.

Silo Modification Boeing Seattle, Wash. Las Vegas, Nev.

SOURCE: United States Air Force. In *The New York Times*, March 19, 1985.

The Political Environment

The political environment includes three sources of possible influences over the making of foreign policy: (1) the political culture (described in chapter 5); (2) political interest groups and political parties (considered in chapter 6); and (3) the mass media and various forms of political participation (the subjects of chapter 7).

NATIONAL DEFENSE: IS AMERICA LESS SECURE?

The Political Culture.   As chapter 5 revealed, most Americans are not very well-informed about domestic, let alone international, political events. This limits the overall impact of public opinion on the making of foreign policy. Because Americans are ill informed, they are also easily swayed by symbolic appeals, especially ones that rely on strong, historical images of Soviet expansionism and Western appeasement. In addition, it is hard for most Americans to improve the level of their international awareness, since so relatively few Americans can read or speak a foreign language. (According to one informal estimate, there are more Japanese citizens doing business in New York City than there are Americans who can speak Japanese.)

In spite of their low level of knowledge of international affairs, Americans appear much more internationalist than isolationist. For example, a plurality of Americans believe it is worthwhile for the United States to work within the United Nations and prefer to see the United States use its UN membership to work for agreements on global issues, rather than simply respond to attacks. (See the **Vantage Point**: American Public Opinions about the United Nations.) Nevertheless, a persistent pattern of attacks against U.S. policy in the General Assembly, especially from nations that seem to contribute little, while receiving much, has begun to wear thin the patience of many Americans and has reduced their willingness to support the UN. Under the Reagan Administration, for example, the United States withheld some financial contributions to the UN and withdrew from UN-related international organizations.

Political Interest Groups and Political Parties.   The highly ambiguous nature of many foreign policy questions and the relative low interest in these matters by most members of the public create a void that many different kinds of political interest groups are quick to fill. All of the following, for example, exercise considerable influence over the making of foreign policy:

- Foreign governments themselves, through their legally retained and registered "foreign agents." Michael Deaver is an example of this; he was President Reagan's friend and advisor before he left to lobby on behalf of various clients, including the government of South Korea.
- Narrowly-based economic interest groups, especially defense contractors who lobby on behalf of programs and weapons systems. Sometimes, some defense contractors lobby against other defense contractors, with the public benefiting from the competition. For example, after losing out on a contract to build a piece of a mobile rocket launcher for the U.S. Army, the Morton Thiokol Corporation, a defense contractor with a plant in Louisiana, enlisted the aid of Senator J. Bennett Johnston (D., La.), who tried to pass legislation that would give them a piece of the action. In reaction, Vought, the Texas-based prime contractor of the rocket launcher, and the Army went public with their case. Vought purchased advertisements in Washington newspapers and an Army spokesperson referred to Senator Johnston's efforts as "another attempt by the losing contractor in a previous

AMERICAN PUBLIC OPINIONS ABOUT THE UNITED NATIONS

The American public is generally quite positive in their views of the United Nations, although there are some signs of waning support.

This impression is based on the results of a public opinion poll, conducted by the Roper Poll in 1983.

Here is a sampling of some of the questions and the responses:

1. Which one of these three statements comes closest to your feelings about the UN today?

The basic beliefs and decisions taken by UN members are largely compatible with our own interests.	11%
Although the US is frequently outvoted, enough common ground exists on most issues to make it worthwhile for the US to work within the UN.	49
The UN has become an anti-American organization where a hostile majority consistently comes to decisions against US interests	23
Don't know	18

2. Should the US increase or should it decrease its participation in the UN?

	1983	1980
Increase	32%	40%
Decrease	25	21
No change (volunteered)	25	26
Don't know	18	14

3. Some people say we should exercise more control over how our money is used at the UN by withholding part of our financial support when we do not agree with what the UN is doing. Of course, similar steps might be taken by other major contributors to cut programs we support. Do you think we should or should not withhold our financial support when the UN does things we disagree with?

Should withhold	51%
Should not	32
Don't know	17

head-to-head competition to politically reverse a well-conceived and workable acquisition strategy. . . ."[19]

• Other groups, with broader, noneconomic concerns also get involved in the making of defense and foreign policies. Although generally weaker than those that have immediate financial interests at stake, these noneconomic groups often are able to attract favorable publicity and thereby magnify their influence. For example, one poorly financed group, the Project on Military Procurement, has become a formidable source of public information about fraud and waste in the defense budget. Since this makes such excellent copy for reporters who often lack the time and the expertise for their own digging, the Project has successfully focused public and congressional attention on these problems. Moreover, its past successes encourage those in the know to leak damaging information, thereby augmenting the Project's future influence.

_____

[19] Quoted in *The New York Times*, 6 December 1982.

The foreign policy-making arena also attracts political parties, of course, and especially those rising political stars who wish to seek higher office. This arena is not without its dangers, however, since no politician can appear to be playing politics with the nation's security. Nevertheless, there are those who argue that the nation's security is a proper subject of partisan debate. If a policy really is in the nation's interest, then those who believe in it should be able to convince others of its merits. Besides, when policy makers fail to do so, it is too easy for them to fall prey to the kind of isolated, delusional thinking that can endanger world peace, as it may have when President Lyndon Johnson persisted in a Vietnam War policy long after he had lost popular support for it.[20]

The ambition that drives those who seek elective office also serves to introduce and to advance concerns that can only enrich, and perhaps improve, the making of foreign policy. In recent times, for example, partisan politics have helped focus public attention on the viability and cost of President Reagan's Star Wars proposals and on other, normally less visible concerns, such as the impact of drug and alcohol abuse on the state of military readiness.

Mass Media and Political Participation. As chapter 7 described it, the relationship between the mass media and governmental policy makers is frequently an adversarial one. This is especially true in the field of foreign relations, where hostility ranges between outright press accusations of lying and deception to administration allegations that the press is undercutting national security and should be prosecuted for publishing classified documents (to which the press responds that governmental officials overclassify materials to avoid embarrassment). Given the hostility of the press and their capacity to block effective policy making, those with major responsibility for making foreign policy today are working harder to influence the press' and the public's reactions. This practice was especially pronounced during the Reagan presidency, when, for example, carefully orchestrated ways of releasing information helped produce a favorable public reaction to the invasion of Grenada in 1983 and to the bombing of Libya in 1986.

In addition to the mass media, ordinary citizens are becoming more inclined and better able to participate in various indirect ways in the making of foreign policy. There is some evidence, for example, that voters are beginning to pay more attention to foreign policy matters. As Patrick Caddell, the pollster for President Carter and for Walter Mondale during his presidential campaign of 1984, reports: "Foreign affairs used to be near the bottom of voters' concerns. Now it ranks right behind inflation as the major thing on their minds."[21]

American citizens also find and invent various nonelectoral ways to participate in foreign policy making. Indeed, since there are so few good linkage mechanisms, public demands for participation often have to be exercised in an extraordinary manner, through, for example, various forms of protest.

---

20 David Halberstam. *The Best and the Brightest* (New York: Penguin, 1983).

21 Quoted in the *Wall Street Journal*, 26 February 1980.

In apparent recognition of the increasing prominence of international concerns, foreign policy makers have begun acting as though they alter their agendas to keep in, or, really *out*, of synch with the electoral cycle. For example, in the last year of its first term, the Reagan Administration cut back on overseas maneuvers and postponed proposed arms sales to Persian Gulf nations until after the 1984 elections. According to one unidentified Defense Department official: "We're not going to initiate anything on our own that would call attention to anything the military forces are doing."[22]

The Policy Process

The policy process, as it was described in chapters 8, 9, and 10, typically includes one or more policy organizations, some stages of agenda building, the reliance on certain decision-making techniques, and an often imprecise method for matching up policy goals and the means of reaching them.

Policy Organizations. There are two major kinds of policy organizations active in the making of foreign policy: informal ones that cluster around the consideration of particular policies and more formal ones that exercise some authority over a set of related policy matters. Examples of informal policy organizations are those that work to maintain the American commitment to Israel's national security, those whose information campaigns seek to buttress American public support for the United Nations, policy think tanks that provide detailed and well-reasoned critiques of defense strategy, and peace groups that work to end the arms race. Examples of formal policy organizations include a host of worldwide international organizations, such as the World Health Organization and the International Red Cross, and many regional organizations, such as the Organization of African Unity and the Organization of American States. All of these and many others, including some private international relief organizations, such as Oxfam, are active in a variety of concerns, touching on hunger, refugees, economic development, and so on.[23]

Policy Processes. The process of foreign policy making differs in many ways from the process of domestic policy making that was described in chapter 15. In general, foreign policy making, as compared to domestic policy making, is much more closed, involves fewer actors, greater pressures to respond quickly, fewer options with more irrevocable consequences, and therefore greater levels of uncertainty. As a result, foreign policy makers, compared to their domestic counterparts, are under even greater pressure to act incrementally, are more risk adverse, and are less likely to respond favorably to new or radically different policy ends or means. This generalization, however, must be quickly qualified, since the reverse is sometimes true. Sometimes, Presidents

---

[22] Quoted in *The New York Times*, 29 June 1984.

[23] On international organizations, see Robert O. Keohane and Joseph S. Nye, eds., *Transnational Relations and World Politics* (Cambridge, Mass.: Harvard University Press, 1972).

NATIONAL DEFENSE: IS AMERICA LESS SECURE?

are able to use bold foreign policy initiatives to deflect public attention from domestic problems, as President Nixon successfully did when he established diplomatic relations between the United States and Communist China.

Governmental Institutions

As is true of their role in the making of domestic policy, each of the major institutions of American national government has certain dominant tendencies that affect their participation in the making of foreign policy.

The Presidency. Modern American Presidents find it hard to achieve significant foreign policy successes and to avoid blame for troubling foreign policy failures. As a result, foreign policy waters can easily become a presidential graveyard, as Presidents Johnson and Carter discovered.

Modern American Presidents seem well-aware of the electoral pitfalls of foreign policy making and especially sensitive to popular expressions of disapproval—perhaps too aware, some feel. For example, their awareness and sensitivity may incline them to postpone tough foreign policy decisions until after their first term, unless foreign policy crises intrude, as Iran did during President Carter's term. In addition, their awareness and sensitivity may lock Presidents into foreign policies that win popular support, even if they do not significantly advance the nation's security. For example, President Carter's foreign policies were too driven by electoral imperatives: help the Israelis, pressure the Soviet Union, and increase the defense budget, according to the memoirs written by his Secretary of State, Cyrus Vance.[24] In a more generalized critique of the practice, Roger Fisher, a Harvard law school professor and expert on international negotiation, has written: "Good statesmanship requires concentrating on the road ahead. Good politics requires paying attention to the passengers. But a dangerous road becomes lethal if a driver keeps his eyes on the rear-view mirror, worrying about the passengers' wishes at every turn."[25]

Congress. Congress' role in the making of foreign policy is shaped both by its fragmented and representative character.

The fragmentation of legislative authority into the hands of the chairs of many different committees and subcommittees creates the possibility that members of Congress will acquire the kind of expertise and stature that allow them to play a meaningful role in the making of foreign policy. This, for example, seems true in a number of cases, including that of John Tower (R., Texas), when he chaired the Senate Armed Services Committee. Moreover, such committees can become an effective forum for challenging the President's conduct of national security policy. For example, under Senator Tower,

---

[24] Cyrus Vance, *Hard Choices: Four Critical Years in America's Foreign Policy* (New York: Simon & Schuster, 1983).

[25] Roger Fisher, "Watching the Road," *New York Times*, 2 May 1980.

THE WILDAVSKY—POLSBY DIALOGUE CONTINUED . . .

AUTHOR: How would you evaluate the federal government's performance in providing for national security, say, since the end of the Second World War?

WILDAVSKY: In the history of international affairs, this is one of the largest periods of relative peace among great powers, although of course, not in other parts of the world. You can say there have been no great confrontations similar to World War I. But how much of this is luck? How much is due to defense? How much is due to two scorpions in a bottle? The most moderate judgment I can think of is that we have navigated through these events with many blunders, but in relatively one piece. Democratic nations remain in the world, as we do. Not all epochs of history can claim the same.

POLSBY: Look, from 1918, the end of World War I, to 1940, the beginning of World War II, is 22 years. From 1945 to today is 42 years. So, after World War I, whether anyone realized it or not, we were really in the middle of a period of upheaval and war. At the end of World War II, we had no way of knowing but what we might be similarly situated. What we did, starting at the end of World War II, seems to me kind of interesting. The most significant thing we did was make a very substantial bet that the long term welfare of the United States would be greatly enhanced by, in effect, resuscitating Western Europe. And, today, Western Europe is an independent force in the world, not controlled by us, but, in most fundamentals, allied with us in support of the kind of values that we favor. It's also true we did the same thing in Japan.

WILDAVSKY: That must be counted as a very great success. Not everybody loves General Douglas MacArthur or his methods. But it's hard to think of how that could have conceivably turned out better.

POLSBY: Now, our overarching strategy was, I think, in historical terms, absolutely stunning: take former enemies and prostrate allies and turn them into independent actors in the world who are fundamentally in favor of the values that we favor. That is a gigantic achievement. Moreover, I think it has to be said directly that those were their intentions.

AUTHOR: That we would take the risk that they would not act like clients in the future but like independent nation-states?

POLSBY: That's right. We took that risk. We said, we share these common values so much that we'll let these states float free, even though, for example, they will become our commercial competitors.

AUTHOR: But to some extent, hasn't that allowed them to become less dependable allies?

POLSBY: Of course; that's right.

AUTHOR: Does that make us less secure?

POLSBY: No, that's the point I'm getting to. On the whole, my judgment is that we are better off in a world of independent actors sharing our values than in a world of subservient client states.

AUTHOR: Why?

WILDAVSKY: If you have satellites, then, in times of trouble, you can't rely on them at all, as is shown by the immense numbers of Soviet troops now occupying Eastern Europe. I see having other free and democratic nations in the world as about the most important thing we could do. But, if you want practical motives, consider such a matter as nuclear weapons. The fact that the English and the French have them complicates Soviet designs. Even if they were to be successful in catching us napping or whatever, there would still be independent forces in Europe. If we did not favor the existence of independent democratic states elsewhere, how could we favor it at home?

> *If we did not favor the existence of independent democratic states elsewhere, how could we favor it at home?* —**Wildavsky**

> *On the whole, my judgment is that we are better off in a world of independent actors sharing our values than in a world of subservient client states.* —**Polsby**

POLSBY: I suppose it's simply a view about human nature and human creativity. It's simply that the possibilities of human life are just greatly enhanced when that occurs. It's more interesting. It's more creative. I think it means that people will be economically stronger, will be better customers, better producers. We will have greater technological innovation, a greater possibility of controlling disease— all kinds of things that rely on human creativity.

1983 hearings of the Senate Armed Services Committee successfully surfaced a number of controversies surrounding rising military costs, bureaucratic infighting, and the vulnerability of command decision making mechanisms in the event of war. In general, as this example suggests and as chapter 12 showed in detail, contemporary Congresses have tended to become more insistent about their role in the foreign policy process—especially when there are a few presidential aspirants scattered through the Capitol.[26]

The representative nature of Congress increases opportunities for many different constituencies to advance their definitions of foreign problems and their preferred policies for dealing with them. For example, in dealing with the problems of international terrorism, Congress was encouraged to examine various aspects of the problem by American businesspersons with overseas operations, by representatives of airline pilots, by representatives of the tourism industry, and so on. In addition to those interest groups that press their claims upon Congress, the mass media can help focus Congress' attention. In the mid-1980s, for example, the press helped push the famine in Ethiopia onto Congress' policy agenda.

Bureaucracy.   As chapter 13 would lead you to expect, the federal bureaucracy further confounds presidential foreign policy making.[27] The confounding effects originate both within the White House and from the Cabinet Departments. Within the Reagan White House, for example, personality and policy conflicts between hard- and soft-liners often frustrated attempts to devise and pursue a consistent foreign policy for dealing with the Soviet Union.

The relationships between foreign policy advisors in the White House and those in the State Department add another, especially opaque layer of bureaucratic confusion. According to Alexander M. Haig, Jr., President Reagan's first Secretary of State, the Administration was "as mysterious as a ghost ship" in its charting of the nation's foreign policy course. Although the rigging creaked, the timbers groaned, and, occasionally, the crew appeared on deck, " . . . which of the crew had the helm? Was it Meese, was it Baker, was it someone else? It was impossible to know for sure?"[28]

The Cabinet Departments of the federal bureaucracy further complicate the making of foreign policy. By pursuing their own policy goals, Cabinet Departments invariably intrude on foreign policy considerations, as, for example, the Defense Department does when it encourages our allies to modernize their weapons systems, and as the Treasury Department does when it tries to encourage other nations to increase their imports of American products, and as the Agriculture Department does when it seeks to block the importation of

---

[26] On the perpetual strife over the conduct of foreign policy, see Cecil V. Crabb, Jr., and Pat M. Holt, *Invitation to Struggle: Congress, the President and Foreign Policy* 2nd ed. (Washington, D.C.: CQ Press, 1984).

[27] See, for example, Morton H. Halperin, *Bureaucratic Politics and Foreign Policy* (Washington, D.C.: The Brookings Institution, 1974).

[28] Alexander M. Haig, Jr., *Caveat: Realism, Reagan, and Foreign Policy* (New York: Macmillan, 1982).

foreign food stuffs. Moreover, as these examples suggest, departments can work at cross purposes and there is a need for some degree of overall coordination. Some had hoped that the National Security Council, established in 1947, would be able to integrate various recommendations and thereby help the President carry out a coherent foreign policy. Over time, however, and especially under Henry Kissinger, the National Security Council has tended to become another foreign policy actor, often at odds with other parts of the executive branch.

The Courts. As chapter 14 would lead you to predict, the federal courts only react to controversies that are pressed upon them. In the field of foreign policy, these usually are brought either by the President or members of Congress, arguing that one or the other has somehow infringed on their rightful role in the making of foreign policy, or by those who believe they have been adversely affected by some foreign policy action. In one relatively recent case, for example, the Supreme Court ruled that President Carter acted within his constitutional powers when, in exchange for the return of the American hostages, he returned some of Iran's assets and transfered others to a new international tribunal, even though that prevented Americans from filing claims against Iran in U.S. courts.

As this brief overview suggests, all the major institutions of American national government participate in the making of the nation's foreign policy, although the patterns by which they do so are quite varied and sometimes unpredictable.

■ When the United States was only a minor actor in the international political arena, foreign policy was more of a sidelight in the study of American government. Today, however, the United States is a major actor with many far-flung international involvements and obligations. It is perhaps inevitable, therefore, that those involvements and obligations will affect many domestic matters and that domestic and foreign policy making will become increasingly intertwined.

SUMMARY

America is less secure today than at the end of the Second World War.

The war began a short period of hegemony. During this period, the United States had unparalleled influence over international affairs. Its influence effectively challenged by the Soviet Union, the United States sought to maintain its security through a string of alliances. The alliances were meant to contain Communism, by reconstructing the economies and armies of our wartime enemies and allies.

The bipolar world of alliance politics was soon fractured, however, by the end of colonial empires and the emergence of new, nationalistic states, bent on asserting their independence. America's allies, too, increasingly acted like the strong, free nation-states we had helped them become once again. The result of these developments was a multipolar world in which many states of all sizes acted in their national self-interest, as they defined it.

From the perspective of the United States, the multipolar world is clearly a more complicated and confusing one. It is also clear that we find it harder to deal with economically strong and politically independent allies than with weak and dependent ones. Nevertheless, it may also be true that the multipolar world enhances American security. By constraining their freedom of action, for example, independent allies can force American foreign policies makers to proceed more cautiously than they might otherwise.

Key Terms

hegemony   Mutual Assured Destruction (MAD)
bipolarity   nationalism
multipolarity   Star Wars technology

Review and Reflection

1. Do you agree that the United States is less secure today than at the end of the Second World War?

2. Do you think the United States would be more or less secure if its allies were more compliant? Why?

3. Is the American failure to act more forcefully in the world due to the presence of constraints or the absence of courage? (Are you sure?)

4. What do you believe to be the proper role of the United States in the world community?

5. Do you think the United States will be more or less secure tomorrow?

6. What, if anything, are you going to do about it?

Supplemental Readings

In some ways, the study of international relations is the study of never-ending threats to world peace and of the ways different nations cope with those threats.

Threats exist at every turn, through escalation in the nuclear arms race, as *Schell* warns, and through attempts to appease the Soviet Union, as *Revel* argues.

Strategies for coping with threats to peace are dissected dispassionately by *Schelling* and *Halperin* and debated more heatedly in *Oye* et al. and in *Talbott*. Meanwhile, *Shevchenko* provides some useful insights on what the West has to cope with.

As *Etheredge* implies, America's and the world's security may depend mostly on the ability to learn from the past and to adapt those lessons to the future. Some of the best places to start looking are *Carr, Pearson* and *Rochester,* and *Spero.*

Carr, Edward Hallett. *The Twenty Years' Crisis, 1919–1939: An Introduction to the Study of International Relations.* New York: Harper Torchbooks, 1964.

Etheredge, Lloyd S. *Can Governments Learn?: American Foreign Policy and Central American Revolutions.* New York: Pergamon Press, 1985.

Oye, Kenneth A., Robert J. Lieber, and Donald Rothchild, eds. *Eagle Defiant: United States Foreign Policy in the 1980s.* Boston: Little, Brown and Company, 1983.

Pearson, Frederic S., and J. Martin Rochester. *International Relations: The Global Condition in the Late 20th Century.* Reading, Mass.: Addison-Wesley, 1984.

Revel, Jean-Francois. *How Democracies Perish.* New York: Harper & Row, 1984.

Schell, Jonathan. *The Fate of the Earth.* New York: Avon Books, 1982.

Schelling, Thomas C., and Morton H. Halperin. *Strategy and Arms Control.* Washington, D.C.: Pergamon-Brassey, 1985.

Shevchenko, Arkady N. *Breaking with Moscow.* New York: Knopf, 1985.

Spero, Joan E. *The Politics of International Economic Relations.* New York: St. Martins, 1985.

Talbott, Strobe. *Deadly Gambits: The Reagan Administration and the Stalemate in Nuclear Arms Control.* New York: Vintage, 1985.

THE UNENDING SEARCH FOR GOVERNMENT'S PROPER ROLE

*T*hus far, you have been a spectator in a story: the attempt of Americans to figure out what their governmental institutions should and should not do.

By now, you know the plot. In an attempt to maintain their legitimate right to make authoritative decisions about the uses of society's resources, democratic institutions try to improve the fit between their policies and the preferences of the people. The attempt, however, invariably falls short, because the institutions are constrained by law and traditions, because public policies produce public dissatisfaction, and because expectations about government's proper role constantly change.

Before the curtain falls, this chapter catches a glimpse of some contemporary dramas: retrenchment in the role of the federal government, renewal of faith in free enterprise, resurgence in the roles of state and local governments, and experimentation with new forms of private and public cooperation.

Only one thing remains: you have to figure out the part you will play in the story. Good luck.

PERPETUAL DISCONTENT

> The tide comes in; the tide goes out.
> —*Political maxim*

The Case   Leaving the Island of Despair

Robinson Crusoe, as you will recall from the Prologue to this textbook, knew perfect contentment on the Island of Despair.

After four years on the island, Robinson wrote:

> I had nothing to covet; for I had all that I was now capable of enjoying. I was lord of the whole manor; or if I pleased, I might call myself king, or emperor over the whole country which I had possession of. There were no rivals. I had no competitor, none to dispute sovereignty or command with me.[1]

Nevertheless, and quite in spite of his perfect contentment, Crusoe, after saving a captain of a ship and some of his men from an attempted mutiny, left the island.

Arriving in his native England over twenty-eight years after he had left it, Crusoe, at first, found little reason for returning:

> . . . I was as perfect a stranger to all the world as if I had never been known there.
>
> I went down afterward into Yorkshire; but my father was dead, and my mother and all the family extinct, except I found two sisters, and two of the children of one of my brothers; and as I had been long ago given over for dead, there had been no provision made for me; so that, in a word, I found nothing to relieve or assist me; and that little money I had would not do much for me as to settling in the world.[2]

Immediately, however, Crusoe's lot improved, with the receipt of a reward of two hundred pounds sterling from the owners of the ship he had saved from mutiny. Then Crusoe casually reported that he thought it would be a good idea to find out what had become of his business partner and their plantation in Brazil.

In his absence, fortune had smiled on Crusoe. His partner was alive and well, Crusoe's share of the plantation, and the income from it, had been put into a trust account, and those who controlled the account happily turned over its contents to him—along with 1200 chests of sugar and 800 rolls of tobacco!

Even the normally taciturn Crusoe could not help but reflect on the letters from his partner and trustees and on what they had sent him:

> It is impossible to express here the flutterings of my very heart when I looked over these letters, and especially when I found all my wealth about me; . . .

---

[1] Daniel Defoe, *Robinson Crusoe* (New York: New American Library, Signet Classic, 1961), p. 128–29.

[2] *Ibid.*, p. 272.

I was now master, all of a sudden, of about £5000 sterling in money, and had an estate, as I might well call it, in Brazil, of above a thousand pounds a year, . . .

But, in almost the same breath, Crusoe gave a hint of impending discontent:

. . . in a word, I was in a condition which I scarce knew how to understand, or how to compose myself for the enjoyment of it.[3]

And so, now a bit lost in his good fortune, Crusoe sold his estate, prepared to return to the Island of Despair, and tried to explain:

Anyone would think that in this state of complicated good fortune, I was past running any more hazards; and so indeed I had been, if other circumstances had concurred, but I was inured to a wandering life, had no family, not many relations, nor, however rich, had I contracted much acquaintance; and though I had sold my estate in Brazil, yet I could not keep the country out of my head, and had a great mind to be upon the wing again; especially I could not resist the strong inclination I had to see my island, and to know if the poor Spaniards were in being there, and how the rogues I left there had used them.[4]

Insights

Robinson Crusoe's account entertains and instructs, because it teaches us something about the ways we search for happiness, and never entirely satisfied with what we find, look elsewhere, often retracing our steps.

Insight 1. *Both the public and the private market can work.* Recall that (1) the public market is the one where government makes authoritative decisions about the use of society's resources; (2) the private market is the one where large numbers of buyers and sellers make voluntary resource allocation decisions; and (3) markets "work" when people approve of the results of these decisions. In Crusoe's case, both markets worked. The public market (his authoritative control of the island's resources) produced satisfying results, as did the private market (the competitive transactions of his trustees). Thus, for Crusoe, it was not the case that he found happiness only on the island or only in the world of commerce; he found happiness in both. Similarly, for us, it is not the case that we find happiness only through governmental action or private economic activity; both produce results that we value.

Insight 2. *Nevertheless, people will be dissatisfied with the workings of both government and the free enterprise system.* Crusoe found happiness both on and off the island. But he did not find total happiness in either place. Similarly, Americans have acted as though they too have been, from time to time, dissatisfied with the performance of one or another level of government, just as they have been, from time to time, dissatisfied with the workings of the private economic market.

---

[3] *Ibid.*, p. 278.
[4] *Ibid.*, p. 297.

Insight 3. *People, perpetually discontent, move back and forth, both toward and away from public and private solutions to their, and society's problems.* Crusoe, although once totally happy on the Island of Despair, was discontented enough to leave, and later, although awash in comforts, was sufficiently discontented to leave them as well. In a similar fashion, Americans, from time to time, dissatisfied with some aspects of government's role, have sought to deregulate the operations of the private market. Inevitably, dissatisfied with some of the casualties of capitalism have sought to increase government's regulation of the private market.

Taken together, these insights suggest that the search for the proper balance between a reliance on government and a reliance on the private economic market will be never ending.

THE UNENDING SEARCH FOR GOVERNMENT'S PROPER ROLE

> 'Tis not too late to seek a newer world.
> —*Alfred, Lord Tennyson,* Ulysses

Throughout their history, Americans have searched for government's proper role, for what it should and should not do. Especially since the early 1930s, that search led to a tremendous expansion in the operations of all levels of government and to an explosion of governmental programs and regulations. That search also helped bring about significant improvements in the social welfare of most Americans and a relatively long period of freedom from world war. Nevertheless, that search failed to meet expectations that rose faster than government's capacity to meet them. Ironically, while working harder and accomplishing more, government, and especially the federal government, was perceived as having failed most badly. Thus, by the early 1980s, many Americans acted as though they had lost confidence in national governmental institutions.[5] As a result, we entered a new period, one characterized by (1) federal retrenchment; (2) renewed economic faith; (3) state and local resurgence; and (4) private-public experiments.

Federal Retrenchment

The 1980s began a period of retrenchment in the role of the federal government. The retrenchment was justified by a widespread belief that the federal government, by stifling individual initiative, had become the cause of many of our social and economic problems, not the source of possible cures for them.

---

[5] See, for example, James L. Sundquist, "The Crisis of Competence in Our National Government," *Political Science Quarterly* 95 (1980): 183–208.

Throughout the administrations of President Reagan, the federal government drew back from a number of previous commitments.[6] For example:

- The Civil Aeronautics Board, established to encourage and develop civil aviation, was abolished.
- The United States Civil Rights Commission drifted so far from its original mandate that civil rights organizations called for an end to its funding.
- The Department of Justice intensified its opposition to affirmative action programs.
- The Supreme Court began to circumscribe the due process rights of criminal defendants.
- The Department of Agriculture tightened up regulations in ways that made it harder for the poor to qualify for food stamps.
- The Department of Education changed regulations in ways that made it harder for college students to qualify for an educational loan.
- General revenue sharing, through which the national government returned federal tax dollars to the states, gradually wound down.

As the federal government pulled back from these and other responsibilities for the nation's socioeconomic welfare, the immediate human costs mounted. But, many argued, the costs were (1) unavoidable, because of the need to rebuild the nation's defense arsenal, and (2) only temporary, because of the anticipated upturn of the nation's economy.

Renewed Economic Faith

The 1980s also saw a revival of faith in the principles of laissez-faire economics (see chapter 10). The principles held that the free-market, unregulated by government, would accelerate economic progress and thereby enhance social welfare. The principles, especially when articulated by a popular President, Ronald Reagan, and by a Nobel-laureate economist, Milton Friedman, made it seem as though less government meant more economic progress.[7]

The principles of laissez-faire economics had strong appeal at home and modest appeal abroad. At home, the principles were used to justify attacks on the welfare state. Abroad, the principles were used to explain the successes of the economies of Taiwan, South Korea, Hong Kong, and Singapore. In addition, the principles of laissez-faire economics were held up as an alternative to more tangible forms of foreign aid. For example, while addressing the 1981 annual meeting of the World Bank and International Monetary Fund, President Reagan encouraged the representatives of 141 nations to "believe in the magic of the marketplace."[8] The message was repeated five years later, after a United Nations report called on donor nations to contribute an additional $80

---

6 Some of the evidence is found in Lester M. Salamon and Michael S. Lund, eds., *The Reagan Presidency and the Governing of America* (Washington, D.C.: The Urban Institute Press, 1985); and D. Lee Bawden, ed., *The Social Contract Revisited: Aims and Outcomes of President Reagan's Social Welfare Policy* (Washington, D.C.: The Urban Institute Press, 1984).

7 Milton Friedman, *Free to Choose: A Personal Statement* (New York: Harcourt, 1980).

8 Quoted in *The New York Times*, 4 October 1981.

to \$100 billion to famine- and debt-stricken African nations. In subsequent remarks released by the White House, President Reagan suggested that free-market economic strategies could bring about "broad-based equitable development based on social justice, self-reliance and the proven skills of the African people"[9]

The renewed American commitment to laissez-faire capitalism carried with it the seeds of new discontents, however. The free-market world, it quickly appeared, was a harsh place, where people had to be free to choose *and* to fail. Failure, in pure capitalistic theory, was functional; it flushed out of the economic system those products that were unwanted and those producers who were inefficient. Laissez-faire capitalism, in other words, produced casualties, such as an estimated "one-quarter of all savings-and-loan institutions (that) went under during the shakeout stimulated by deregulation."[10] Adherence to the true principles of capitalism, therefore, tended to produce both winners and losers. Losers, being discontented, could be counted on to demand of government that it cushion their fall, or sustain them in their time of need, or, perhaps, even retreat from those principles that had caused their suffering.

As the nation moved through the 1980s, the casualties of capitalism grew more numerous, their expressions of discontent more strong. It was inevitable, therefore, that a democratic government could not long remain unresponsive to small farmers, steel workers, autoworkers, coal miners, and all the others who were unable to compete effectively in an international economy. Increasingly, the nation's political debate became focused: To what extent should government protect those who can not succeed in a competitive world? To a large extent, it was a question often answered through trial and error, often as state and local governments experimented with new public policies.

State and Local Resurgence

In the 1980s, many states and local governments re-asserted themselves as important actors in the policy-making process. Their capacity to do so had been enhanced over the last twenty years, partly in response to the administrative demands of federal programs and partly as a result of the infusion of policy professionals who found fewer attractive opportunities at the federal level. In addition, the will of state and local governments to play a more significant policy-making role had been strengthened by an infusion of new, enthusiastic talent; for example, the women, blacks, and ordinary citizens who found the barriers to service lower and the rewards greater than they had been in the past.

The 1980s, therefore, began what promised to be an era of state and local experimentation with innovative approaches to problem solving. In some cases, state and local efforts focused on different ways of protecting the environment. The California state legislature, for example, adopted new policies to protect

---

[9] Quoted in *The New York Times*, 28 May 1986.

[10] George F. Will, "The Casualties of Our Dynamism," *Newsweek*, 4 March 1985.

THE UNENDING SEARCH FOR GOVERNMENT'S PROPER ROLE

the quality of the air, by requiring special pollution-control equipment on automobiles and on gasoline pumps. In other cases, state governments experimented with training programs to move people off welfare programs and into productive jobs. In Massachusetts, for example, a vocational training program, fortunately coupled with a booming economy, compiled huge welfare savings, while generating both human pride and state revenues. Elsewhere, state governments experimented with contractual arrangements that allowed private firms to run state prisons at a profit and local governments contracted out the collection of fines on traffic tickets.

By the mid-1980s, policy experimentation at the state and local level was increasingly widespread. Eventually, the record of successes and failures will become clearer and more widely known. As it does, successful policy innovations should spill over state borders and perhaps, even trickle up for adoption at the federal level.

These experiments only scratch the surface, however. In addition to these predominantly governmental approaches to problem solving, there also were a large number of experiments with ways of involving non-governmental actors in social problem solving.

Private-Public Experimentation

During the 1980s, there was an upsurge of **volunteerism**, the practice in which private actors contribute money, expertise, and time to public causes. Throughout the 1980s, the spirit of volunteerism took many forms:

The volunteer fire fighters of the early 1900s epitomized the 1980s ideal of volunteerism.

The Statue of Liberty, as seen during restoration in time for the 100th birthday celebration and re-dedication ceremony on July 4, 1986.

- In time for the 100th birthday celebration, the Statue of Liberty and the surrounding grounds were completely restored, largely with funds raised through corporate contributions (made partly through altruism and partly in exchange for the right to use the Liberty logo in advertising campaigns).
- Along Louisiana's Gulf coast, the National Audubon Society acquired approximately 26,000 acres to establish the Paul J. Rainey Sanctuary for wildlife.
- In northern Nebraska, Nature Conservancy, a private conservation group, used an $11 million bequest to purchase 54,000 acres of unplowed prairie to create the Niobrara Valley Preserve.
- In Middletown, Ohio, the town's largest employer, Armco, a multi-national corporation involved in the production of specialty steels, used a share of its profits locally, to help expand a Y.M.C.A. and to purchase land for a branch of Miami University, and nationally, to subsidize Hispanic chambers of commerce and to help minorities and Native Americans attend professional schools in engineering, earth sciences, and business.
- In Lincoln, Nebraska, the Kawasaki Motor Corporation, rather than lay off workers when sales slowed, kept them on the payroll and loaned them to the municipal government.

However commendable, volunteerism, especially when practiced by corporations, was not without its critics. Some, for example, asked whether or not it was proper for private businesses to be so heavily involved in public endeavors.

THE UNENDING SEARCH FOR GOVERNMENT'S PROPER ROLE

Some thought the spirit of volunteerism was misplaced, after an anonymous donor contributed $209, 508 to purchase a 220 place setting of new china for the White House. This is a photograph of the place setting.

■During the 1980s, caught up in the shifting tides of a retrenchment in the role of the federal government, a bouyant, renewed faith in free enterprise, a resurgence in the roles of state and local governments, and a tangled mass of experimental relationships between government and the private sector, Americans seemed to be having an especially difficult time sorting out what their governments should and should not do.

SUMMARY

By now, you know that Americans have been preoccupied with a search for what they believe to be government's proper role in the making of resource allocation decisions.

But you also know that all answers are incomplete and tentative. Struggling to maintain their legitimacy and enhance their power, coping with value conflicts which they suspect are big enough to overwhelm them, poorly armed with limited and fragmented public power, and constantly buffeted by competing values and the resulting political pressures, democratic governmental institutions constantly make and remake public policy.

Therefore, there are no final answers. But there is an imperative that is directed to all citizens: search for ways that improve the fit between the actions of government and the preferences of its people.

There have been many who have responded; hopefully, so will you.

Key Term

volunteerism

Review and Reflection

1. What do you believe to be the proper role of government?

2. Justify your answer by drawing on information in this textbook.

Supplemental Readings

We should not let you go on the search for government's proper role without something for the road: some summer reading suggestions.

First, ask your instructor for some suggestions. (Have confidence that your inquiry will be welcomed.)

Second, you should start reading a good newspaper, something like *The New York Times*, the *Washington Post*, or the *Los Angeles Times*. (Subscribe or read the one in your library, where you will meet some interesting people.)

At first, reading the newspaper will be slow going—a little like trying to memorize the names of the dancers the first time you attend a performance of the Moscow Ballet. But after awhile, some interesting things will happen. Gradually, you will find that some stories are more interesting than others and you will begin to focus on them: federal aid to farmers, weapons development, the politics of your city, foreign aid, potholes, civil rights, or whatever. Then, the reading will go faster as you become more knowledgeable; knowing more, you will skim over repetitious parts of stories, looking for the new information. Next, you will start retaining more of what you read, as you begin building your own set of mental pigeon holes for information. Marvelously, you will begin to understand why the story is unfolding as it is. Finally, you will see in the stories you read interesting people doing interesting things, causing you to say: "People get paid for doing *that*?" Once you recover, you might even start thinking of some of these people as role models, inspiring you to become one of those that *we* read about.

Well, you are on your own now.

We hope this course and this textbook have given you the roots and wings you need to help you realize your potential and to help you help America realize hers.

DECLARATION OF INDEPENDENCE

In Congress, July 4, 1776

The unanimous Declaration of the thirteen united States of America,

When in the Course of human events, it becomes necessary for one people to dissolve the political bands which have connected them with another, and to assume among the Powers of the earth, the separate and equal station to which the Laws of Nature and of Nature's God entitle them, a decent respect to the opinions of mankind requires that they should declare the causes which impel them to the separation.

We hold these truths to be self-evident, that all men are created equal, that they are endowed by their Creator with certain unalienable Rights, that among these are Life, Liberty and the pursuit of Happiness. That to secure these rights, Governments are instituted among Men, deriving their just powers from the consent of the governed. That whenever any Form of Government becomes destructive of these ends, it is the Right of the People to alter or to abolish it, and to institute new Government, laying its foundation on such principles and organizing its powers in such form, as to them shall seem most likely to effect their Safety and Happiness. Prudence, indeed, will dictate that Governments long established should not be changed for light and transient causes; and accordingly all experience hath shown, that mankind are more disposed to suffer, while evils are sufferable, than to right themselves by abolishing the forms to which they are accustomed. But when a long train of abuses and usurpations, pursuing invariably the same Object evinces a design to reduce them under absolute Despotism, it is their right, it is their duty, to throw off such Government, and to provide new Guards for their future security.—Such has been the patient sufferance of these Colonies; and such is now the necessity which constrains them to alter their former Systems of Government. The history of the present King of Great Britain is a history of repeated injuries and usurpations, all having in direct object the establishment of an absolute Tyranny over these States. To prove this, let Facts be submitted to a candid world.

He has refused his Assent to Laws, the most wholesome and necessary for the public good.

He has forbidden his Governors to pass Laws of immediate and pressing importance, unless suspended in their operation till his Assent should be obtained; and when so suspended, he has utterly neglected to attend to them.

He has refused to pass other Laws for the accommodation of large districts of people, unless those people would relinquish the right of Representation in the Legislature, a right inestimable to them and formidable to tyrants only.

He has called together legislative bodies at places unusual, uncomfortable, and distant from the depository of their Public Records, for the sole purpose of fatiguing them into compliance with his measures.

He has dissolved Representative Houses repeatedly, for opposing with manly firmness his invasions on the rights of the people.

He has refused for a long time, after such dissolutions, to cause others to be elected; whereby the Legislative Powers, incapable of Annihilation, have returned to the People at large for their exercise; the State remaining in the mean time exposed to all the dangers of invasion from without, and convulsions within.

He has endeavoured to prevent the population of these States; for that purpose obstructing the Laws for Naturalization of Foreigners; refusing to pass others to encourage their migrations hither, and raising the conditions of new Appropriations of Lands.

He has obstructed the Administration of Justice, by refusing his Assent to Laws for establishing Judiciary Powers.

He has made Judges dependent on his Will alone, for the tenure of their offices, and the amount and payment of their salaries.

He has erected a multitude of New Offices, and sent hither swarms of Officers to harass our people, and eat out their substance.

He has kept among us, in times of peace, Standing Armies without the Consent of our legislatures.

He has affected to render the Military independent of and superior to the Civil Power.

He has combined with others to subject us to a jurisdiction foreign to our constitution, and unacknowledged by our laws; giving his Assent to their acts of pretended Legislation:

For quartering large bodies of armed troops among us:

For protecting them, by a mock Trial, from Punishment for any Murders which they should commit on the inhabitants of these States:

For cutting off our Trade with all parts of the world:

For imposing taxes on us without our Consent:

For depriving us in many cases, of the benefits of Trial by Jury:

For transporting us beyond Seas to be tried for pretended offences:

For abolishing the free System of English Laws in a neighbouring Province, establishing therein an Arbitrary government, and enlarging its Boundaries so as to render it at once an example and fit instrument for introducing the same absolute rule into these Colonies:

For taking away our Charters, abolishing our most valuable Laws, and altering fundamentally the Forms of our Governments:

For suspending our own Legislatures, and declaring themselves invested with Power to legislate for us in all cases whatsoever.

He has abdicated Government here, by declaring us out of his Protection and waging War against us.

He has plundered our seas, ravaged our Coasts, burnt our towns, and destroyed the lives of our people.

He is at this time transporting large armies of foreign mercenaries to compleat the works of death, desolation and tyranny, already begun with circumstances of Cruelty & perfidy scarcely paralleled in the most barbarous ages, and totally unworthy the Head of a civilized nation.

He has constrained our fellow Citizens taken Captive on the high Seas to bear Arms against their Country, to become the executioners of their friends and Brethren, or to fall themselves by their Hands.

He has excited domestic insurrections amongst us, and has endeavoured to bring on the inhabitants of our frontiers, the merciless Indian Savages, whose known rule of warfare, is an undistinguished destruction of all ages, sexes and conditions.

In every stage of these Oppressions We have Petitioned for Redress in the most humble terms: Our repeated Petitions have been answered only by repeated injury. A Prince, whose character is thus marked by every act which may define a Tyrant, is unfit to be the ruler of a free people.

Nor have We been wanting in attentions to our British brethren. We have warned them from time to time of attempts by their legislature to extend an unwarrantable jurisdiction over us. We have reminded them of the circumstances of our emigration and settlement here. We have appealed to their native justice and magnanimity, and we have conjured them by the ties of our common kindred to disavow these usurpations which, would inevitably interrupt our connections and correspondence. They too have been deaf to the voice of justice and of consanguinity. We must, therefore, acquiesce in the necessity, which denounces our Separation, and hold them, as we hold the rest of mankind, Enemies in War, in Peace Friends.

We, therefore, the Representatives of the united States of America, in General Congress, Assembled, appealing to the Supreme Judge of the world for the rectitude of our intentions, do, in the Name, and by authority of the good People of these Colonies, solemnly publish and declare, That these United Colonies are, and of Right ought to be Free and Independent States; that they are Absolved from all Allegiance to the British Crown, and that all political connection between them and the State of Great Britain, is and ought to be totally dissolved; and that as Free and Independent States, they have full power to levy War, conclude Peace, contract Alliances, establish Commerce, and to do all other Acts and Things which Independent States may of right do. And for the support of this Declaration, with a firm reliance on the Protection of Divine Providence, we mutually pledge to each other our Lives, our Fortunes and our sacred Honor.

THE CONSTITUTION

We the People of the United States, in Order to form a more perfect Union, establish justice, insure domestic Tranquility, provide for the common defence, promote the general Welfare, and secure the Blessings of Liberty to ourselves and our Posterity, do ordain and establish this Constitution for the United States of America.

ARTICLE 1

Section 1.

All legislative Powers herein granted shall be vested in a Congress of the United States, which shall consist of a Senate and House of Representatives.

Section 2.

The House of Representatives shall be composed of Members chosen every second Year by the People of the several States, and the Electors in each State shall have the Qualifications requisite for Electors of the most numerous Branch of the State Legislature.

No Person shall be a Representative who shall not have attained to the Age of twenty five Years, and been seven Years a Citizen of the United States, and who shall not, when elected, be an Inhabitant of that State in which he shall be chosen.

Representatives and direct Taxes shall be apportioned among the several States which may be included within this Union, according to their respective Numbers, which shall be determined by adding to the whole Number of free Persons, including those bound to Service for a Term of Years, and excluding Indians not taxed, three fifths of all other Persons.[1] The actual Enumeration shall be made within three years after the first Meeting of the Congress of the United States, and within every subsequent Term of ten Years, in such Manner as they shall by Law direct. The Number of Representatives shall not exceed one for every thirty Thousand, but each State shall have at Least one Representative; and until such enumeration shall be made, the State of New Hampshire shall be entitled to chuse three, Massachusetts eight, Rhode-Island and Providence Plantations one, Connecticut five, New-York six, New Jersey four, Pennsylvania eight, Delaware one, Maryland six, Virginia ten, North Carolina five, South Carolina five, and Georgia three.

When vacancies happen in the Representation from any State, the Executive Authority thereof shall issue Writs of Election to fill such Vacancies.

The House of Representatives shall chuse their Speaker and other Officers; and shall have the sole Power of Impeachment.

Section 3.

The Senate of the United States shall be composed of two Senators from each State, chosen by the Legislature thereof, for six Years; and each Senator shall have one Vote.

Immediately after they shall be assembled in Consequence of the first Election, they shall be divided as equally as may be into three Classes. The Seats of the Senators of the first Class shall be vacated at the Expiration of the second Year, of the second Class at the Expiration of the fourth Year, and of the third Class at the Expiration of the Sixth Year, so that one third may be chosen every second Year; and if Vacancies happen by Resignation, or otherwise, during the Recess of the Legislature of any State, the Executive thereof may make temporary Appointments until the next Meeting of the Legislature, which shall then fill such Vacancies.[2]

No Person shall be a Senator who shall not have attained to the Age of thirty Years, and been nine Years a Citizen of the United States, and who shall not, when elected, be an Inhabitant of that State for which he shall be chosen.

The Vice President of the United States shall be President of the Senate, but shall have no Vote, unless they be equally divided.

The Senate shall chuse their other Officers, and also a President pro tempore, in the Absence of the Vice President, or when he shall exercise the Office of President of the United States.

The Senate shall have the sole Power to try all impeachments. When sitting for that Purpose, they shall be on Oath or Affirmation. When the President of the United States is tried the Chief Justice shall preside: And no Person shall be convicted without the Concurrence of two thirds of the Members present.

Judgment in Cases of Impeachment shall not extend further than to removal from Office, and disqualification to hold and enjoy any Office of honor, Trust or Profit under the United States: but the Party convicted shall nevertheless be liable and subject to Indictment, Trial, Judgment and Punishment, according to Law.

Section 4.

The Times, Places and Manner of holding Elections for Senators and Representatives, shall be prescribed in each State by the Legislature thereof; but the Congress may at any time by Law make or alter such Regulations, except as to the Places of chusing Senators.

The Congress shall assemble at least once in every Year, and such Meeting shall be on the first Monday in December, unless they shall by Law appoint a different Day.[3]

Section 5

Each House shall be the Judge of the Elections, Returns and Qualifications of its own Members, and a Majority of each shall constitute a Quorum to do Business; but a smaller Number may adjourn from day to day, and may be authorized to compel the Attendance of absent Members, in such Manner, and under such Penalties as each House may provide.

Each House may determine the Rules of its Proceedings, punish its Members for disorderly Behaviour, and, with the Concurrence of two thirds, expel a Member.

Each House shall keep a Journal of its Proceedings, and from time to time publish the same, excepting such Parts as may in their Judgment require Secrecy; and the Yeas and Nays of the Members of either House on any question shall, at the Desire of one fifth of those Present, be entered on the Journal.

Neither House, during the Session of Congress, shall, without the Consent of the other, adjourn for more than three days, nor to any other Place than that in which the two Houses shall be sitting.

Section 6.

The Senators and Representatives shall receive a Compensation for their Services, to be ascertained by Law, and paid out of the Treasury of the United States. They shall in all Cases, except Treason, Felony and Breach of the Peace, be privileged from Arrest during their Attendance at the Session of their respective Houses, and in going to and returning from the same; and for any Speech or Debate in either House, they shall not be questioned in any other Place.

No Senator or Representative shall, during the Time for which he was elected, be appointed to any civil Office under the Authority of the United States, which shall have been created, or the Emoluments whereof shall have been encreased during such time; and no Person holding any Office under the United States, shall be a Member of either House during his Continuance in Office.

Section 7.

All Bills for raising Revenue shall originate in the House of Representatives; but the Senate may propose or concur with Amendments as on other Bills.

Every Bill which shall have passed the House of Representatives and

---

[1]"Other Persons" being black slaves. Modified by Amendment XIV, Section 2.
[2]Provisions changed by Amendment XVII.

[3]Provision changed by Amendment XX, Section 2.

the Senate, shall, before it become a Law, be presented to the President of the United States; If he approve he shall sign it, but if not he shall return it, with his Objections to that House in which it shall have originated, who shall enter the Objections at large on their Journal, and proceed to reconsider it. If after such Reconsideration two thirds of that House shall agree to pass the Bill, it shall be sent, together with the Objections, to the other House, by which it shall likewise to be reconsidered, and if approved by two thirds of that House, it shall become a Law. But in all such Cases the Votes of both Houses shall be determined by yeas and Nays, and the Names of the Persons voting for and against the Bill shall be entered on the Journal of each House respectively. If any Bill shall not be returned by the President within ten Days (Sundays excepted) after it shall have been presented to him, the Same shall be a Law, in like Manner as if he had signed it, unless the Congress by their Adjournment prevent its Return, in which Case it shall not be a Law.

Every Order, Resolution, or Vote to which the Concurrence of the Senate and House of Representatives may be necessary (except on a question of Adjournment) shall be presented to the President of the United States; and before the Same shall take Effect, shall be approved by him, or being disapproved by him, shall be repassed by two thirds of the Senate and House of Representatives, according to the Rules and Limitations prescribed in the Case of a Bill.

Section 8.

The Congress shall have Power To lay and collect Taxes, Duties, Imposts and Excises, to pay the Debts and provide for the common Defence and general Welfare of the United States; but all Duties, Imposts and Excises shall be uniform throughout the United States;

To borrow Money on the credit of the United States;

To regulate Commerce with foreign Nations, and among the several States, and with the Indian Tribes;

To establish an uniform Rule of Naturalization, and uniform Laws on the subject of Bankruptcies throughout the United States;

To coin Money, regulate the Value thereof, and of foreign Coin, and fix the Standard of Weights and Measures;

To provide for the Punishment of counterfeiting the Securities and current Coin of the United States;

To establish Post Offices and post Roads;

To promote the Progress of Science and useful Arts, by securing for limited Times to Authors and Inventors the exclusive Right to their respective Writings and Discoveries;

To constitute Tribunals inferior to the supreme Court;

To define and punish Piracies and Felonies committed on the high Seas, and Offences against the Law of Nations;

To declare War, grant Letters of Marque and Reprisal, and make Rules concerning Captures on Land and Water;

To raise and support Armies, but no Appropriation of Money to that Use shall be for a longer Term than two Years;

To provide and maintain a Navy;

To make Rules for the Government and Regulation of the land and naval Forces;

To provide for calling forth the Militia to execute the Laws of the Union, suppress Insurrections and repel Invasions;

To provide for organizing, arming, and disciplining, the Militia, and for governing such Part of them as may be employed in the Service of the United States, reserving to the States respectively, the Appointment of the Officers, and the Authority of training the Militia according to the discipline prescribed by Congress;

To exercise exclusive Legislation in all Cases whatsoever, over such District (not exceeding ten Miles square) as may, by Cession of particular States, and the Acceptance of Congress, become the Seat of the Government of the United States, and to exercise like Authority over all Places purchased by the Consent of the Legislature of the State in which the Same shall be, for the Erection of Forts, Magazines, Arsenals, dock-Yards, and other needful Buildings;—And

To make all Laws which shall be necessary and proper for carrying into Execution the foregoing Powers, and all other Powers vested by this Constitution in the Government of the United States, or in any Department or Officer thereof.

Section 9.

The Migration or Importation of such Persons as any of the States now existing shall think proper to admit, shall not be prohibited by the Congress prior to the Year one thousand eight hundred and eight, but a Tax, or duty may be imposed on such Importation, not exceeding ten dollars for each Person.

The Privilege of the Writ of Habeas Corpus shall not be suspended, unless when in Cases of Rebellion or Invasion the public Safety may require it.

No Bill of Attainder or ex post facto Law shall be passed.

No Capitation, or other direct, Tax shall be laid, unless in Proportion to the Census or Enumeration herein before directed to be taken.

No Tax or Duty shall be laid on Articles exported from any State.

No Preference shall be given by any Regulation of Commerce or Revenue to the Ports of one State over those of another; nor shall Vessels bound to, or from, one State, be obliged to enter, clear, or pay Duties in another.

No Money shall be drawn from the Treasury, but in Consequence of Appropriations made by Law; and a regular Statement and Account of the Receipts and Expenditures of all public Money shall be published from time to time.

No Title of Nobility shall be granted by the United States: And no Person holding any Office of Profit or Trust under them, shall, without the Consent of the Congress, accept of any present, Emolument, Office, or Title, of any kind whatever, from any King, Prince, or foreign State.

Section 10.

No State shall enter into any Treaty, Alliance, or Confederation; grant Letters of Marque and Reprisal; coin Money; emit Bills of Credit; make any Thing but gold and silver Coin a Tender in Payment of Debts; pass any Bill of Attainder, ex post facto Law, or Law impairing the Obligation of Contracts, or grant any Title of Nobility.

No State shall, without the Consent of the Congress, lay any Imposts or Duties on Imports or Exports, except what may be absolutely necessary for executing its inspection Laws: and the net Produce of all Duties and Imposts, laid by any State on Imports or Exports, shall be for the Use of the Treasury of the United States; and all such Laws shall be subject to the Revision and Controul of the Congress.

No State shall, without the Consent of Congress, lay any Duty of Tonnage, keep Troops, or Ships of War in time of Peace, enter into any Agreement or Compact with another State, or with a foreign Power, or engage in War, unless actually invaded, or in such imminent Danger as will not admit of delay.

ARTICLE II

Section 1.

The executive Power shall be vested in a President of the United States of America. He shall hold his Office during the Term of four Years, and, together with the Vice President, chosen for the same Term, be elected, as follows:

Each State shall appoint, in such Manner as the Legislature thereof may direct, a Number of Electors, equal to the whole Number of Senators and Representatives to which the State may be entitled in Congress: but no Senator or Representative, or Person holding an Office of Trust or Profit under the United States, shall be appointed an Elector.

The Electors shall meet in their respective States, and vote by Ballot for two Persons, of whom one at least shall not be an Inhabitant of the same State with themselves. And they shall make a List of all the Persons voted for, and of the Number of Votes for each; which List they shall sign and certify, and transmit sealed to the Seat of the

Government of the United States, directed to the President of the Senate. The President of the Senate shall, in the Presence of the Senate and House of Representatives, open all the Certificates, and the Votes shall then be counted. The Person having the greatest Number of Votes shall be the President, if such Number be a Majority of the whole Number of Electors appointed; and if there be more than one who have such Majority, and have an equal Number of Votes, then the House of Representatives shall immediately chuse by Ballot one of them for President; and if no Person have a Majority, then from the five highest on the List the said House shall in like Manner chuse the President. But in chusing the President, the Votes shall be taken by States, the Representation from each State having one Vote; A quorum for this Purpose shall consist of a Member or Members from two thirds of the States, and a Majority of all the States shall be necessary to a Choice. In every Case, after the Choice of the President, the Person having the greatest Number of Votes of the Electors shall be the Vice President. But if there should remain two or more who have equal Votes, the Senate shall chuse from them by Ballot the Vice President.[4]

The Congress may determine the Time of chusing the Electors, and the Day on which they shall give their Votes; which Day shall be the same throughout the United States.

No Person except a natural born Citizen, or a Citizen of the United States, at the time of the Adoption of this Constitution, shall be eligible to the Office of President; neither shall any Person be eligible to that Office who shall not have attained to the Age of thirty five Years, and been fourteen Years a Resident within the United States.

In Case of the Removal of the President from Office, or of his Death, Resignation, or Inability to discharge the Powers and Duties of the said Office, the Same shall devolve on the Vice President, and the Congress may by Law provide for the Case of Removal, Death, Resignation or Inability, both of the President and Vice President, declaring what Officer shall then act as President, and such Officer shall act accordingly, until the Disability be removed, or a President shall be elected.

The President shall, at stated Times, receive for his Services, a Compensation, which shall neither be encreased nor diminished during the Period for which he shall have been elected, and he shall not receive within that Period any other Emolument from the United States, or any of them.

Before he enter on the Execution of his Office, he shall take the following Oath or Affirmation:—"I do solemnly swear (or affirm) that I will faithfully execute the Office of President of the United States, and will to the best of my Ability, preserve, protect and defend the Constitution of the United States."

Section 2.

The President shall be Commander in Chief of the Army and Navy of the United States, and of the Militia of the several States, when called into the actual Service of the United States; he may require the Opinion, in writing, of the principal Officer in each of the executive Departments, upon any Subject relating to the Duties of their respective Offices, and he shall have Power to grant Reprieves and Pardons for Offences against the United States, except in Cases of Impeachment.

He shall have Power, by and with the Advice and Consent of the Senate, to make Treaties, provided two thirds of the Senators present concur; and he shall nominate, and by and with the Advice and Consent of the Senate, shall appoint Ambassadors, other public Ministers and Consuls, Judges of the supreme Court, and all other Officers of the United States, whose Appointments are not herein otherwise provided for, and which shall be established by Law: but the Congress may by Law vest the Appointment of such inferior Officers, as they think proper, in the President alone, in the Courts of Law, or in the Heads of Departments.

The President shall have Power to fill up all Vacancies that may happen during the Recess of the Senate, by granting Commissions which shall expire at the end of their next Session.

Section 3.

He shall from time to time give to the Congress Information of the State of the Union, and recommend to their Consideration such Measures as he shall judge necessary and expedient; he may, on extraordinary Occasions, convene both Houses, or either of them, and in Case of Disagreement between them, with Respect to the Time of Adjournment, he may adjourn them to such Time as he shall think proper; he shall receive Ambassadors and other public Ministers; he shall take Care that Laws be faithfully executed, and shall Commission all the Officers of the United States.

Section 4.

The President, Vice President and all civil Officers of the United States, shall be removed from Office on Impeachment for, and Conviction of, Treason, Bribery, or other high Crimes and Misdemeanors.

ARTICLE III

Section 1.

The judicial Power of the United States, shall be vested in one supreme Court, and in such inferior Courts as the Congress may from time to time ordain and establish. The Judges, both of the supreme and inferior Courts, shall hold their Offices during good Behaviour, and shall, at stated Times, receive for their Services, a Compensation, which shall not be diminished during their Continuance in Office.

Section 2.

The judicial Power shall extend to all Cases in Law and Equity, arising under this Constitution, the Laws of the United States, and Treaties made, or which shall be made, under their Authority;—to all Cases affecting Ambassadors, other public Ministers and Consuls;—to all Cases of admiralty and maritime Jurisdiction;—to Controversies to which the United States shall be a Party;—to Controversies between two or more states;—between a State and Citizens of another State;—between Citizens of different States;—between Citizens of the same State claiming Lands under Grants of different States, and between a State, or the Citizens thereof, and foreign States, Citizens or Subjects.[5]

In all Cases affecting Ambassadors, other public Ministers and Consuls, and those in which a State shall be Party, the supreme Court shall have original Jurisdiction. In all the other Cases before mentioned, the supreme Court shall have appellate Jurisdiction, both as to Law and Fact, with such Exceptions, and under such Regulations as the Congress shall make.

The Trial of all Crimes, except in Cases of Impeachment, shall be by Jury; and such Trial shall be held in the State where the said Crimes shall have been committed, but when not committed within any State, the Trial shall be at such Place or Places as the Congress may by Law have directed.

Section 3.

Treason against the United States, shall consist only in levying War against them, or in adhering to their Enemies, giving them Aid and Comfort. No person shall be convicted of Treason unless on the Testimony of two Witnesses to the same overt Act, or on Confession in open Court.

The Congress shall have Power to declare the Punishment of Treason, but no Attainder of Treason shall work Corruption of Blood, or Forfeiture except during the Life of the Person attainted.

ARTICLE IV

Section 1.

Full Faith and Credit shall be given in each State to the public Acts, Records, and judicial Proceedings of every other State. And the Congress may by general Laws prescribe the Manner in which such Acts, Records and Proceedings shall be proved, and the Effect thereof.

---

[4]Provisions superseded by Amendment XII.

[5]Clause changed by Amendment XI.

Section 2.

The Citizens of each State shall be entitled to all Privileges and Immunities of Citizens in the several States.

A Person charged in any State with Treason, Felony, or other Crime, who shall flee from Justice, and be found in another State, shall on Demand of the executive Authority of the State from which he fled, be delivered up, to be removed to the State having Jurisdiction of the Crime.

No Person held to Service or Labour in one State, under the Laws thereof, escaping into another, shall, in Consequence of any Law or Regulation therein, be discharged from such Service or Labour, but shall be delivered up on Claim of the Party to whom such Service or Labour may be due.

Section 3.

New States may be admitted by the Congress into this Union; but no new State shall be formed or erected within the jurisdiction of any other State; nor any State be formed by the Junction of two or more States, or Parts of States, without the Consent of the Legislatures of the States concerned as well as of the Congress.

The Congress shall have Power to dispose of and make all needful Rules and Regulations respecting the Territory or other Property belonging to the United States; and nothing in this Constitution shall be so construed as to Prejudice any Claims of the United States, or of any particular State.

Section 4.

The United States shall guarantee to every State in this Union a Republican Form of Government, and shall protect each of them against Invasion; and on Application of the Legislature, or of the Executive (when the Legislature cannot be convened) against domestic Violence.

ARTICLE V

The Congress, whenever two thirds of both Houses shall deem it necessary, shall propose Amendments to this Constitution, or, on the Application of the Legislatures of two thirds of the several States, shall call a Convention for proposing Amendments, which, in either Case, shall be valid to all Intents and Purposes, as Part of this Constitution, when ratified by the Legislatures of three fourths of the several States,

or by Conventions in three fourths thereof, as the one or the other Mode of Ratification may be proposed by the Congress; Provided that no Amendment which may be made prior to the Year One thousand eight hundred and eight shall in any Manner affect the first and fourth Clauses in the Ninth Section of the first Article; and that no State, without its Consent, shall be deprived of its equal Suffrage in the Senate.

ARTICLE VI

All Debts contracted and Engagements entered into, before the Adoption of this Constitution, shall be as valid against the United States under this Constitution, as under the Confederation.

This Constitution, and the Laws of the United States which shall be made in Pursuance thereof; and all Treaties made, or which shall be made, under the Authority of the United States, shall be the supreme Law of the Land; and the Judges in every State shall be bound thereby, any Thing in the Constitution or Laws of any State to the Contrary notwithstanding.

The Senators and Representatives before mentioned, and the Members of the several State Legislatures, and all executive and judicial Officers, both of the United States and of the several States, shall be bound by Oath or Affirmation, to support this Constitution; but no religious Test shall ever be required as a Qualification to any Office or public Trust under the United States.

ARTICLE VII

The Ratification of the Conventions of nine States shall be sufficient for the Establishment of this Constitution between the States so ratifying the Same.

done in Convention by the Unanimous Consent of the States present the Seventeenth Day of September in the Year of our Lord one thousand seven hundred and Eighty seven and of the Independence of the United States of America and the Twelfth[6] IN WITNESS whereof We have here unto subscribed our Names.

---

[6]The Constitution was submitted on September 17, 1787, by the Constitutional Convention, was ratified by the conventions of several states at various dates up to May 29, 1790, and became effective on March 4, 1789.

[AMENDMENT I]

Congress shall make no law respecting an establishment of religion, or prohibiting the free exercise thereof; or abridging the freedom of speech, or of the press, or the right of the people peaceably to assemble, and to petition the Government for a redress of grievances.

[AMENDMENT II]

A well regulated Militia being necessary to the security of a free State, the right of the people to keep and bear Arms, shall not be infringed.

[AMENDMENT III]

No Soldier shall, in time of peace be quartered in any house, without the consent of the Owner, nor in time of war, but in a manner to be prescribed by law.

[AMENDMENT IV]

The right of the people to be secure in their persons, houses, papers, and effects, against unreasonable searches and seizures, shall not be violated, and no Warrants shall issue, but upon probable cause, supported by Oath or affirmation, and particularly describing the place to be searched, and the persons or things to be seized.

[AMENDMENT V]

No person shall be held to answer for a capital, or otherwise infamous crime, unless on a presentment or indictment of a Grand Jury, except in cases arising in the land or naval forces, or in the Militia, when in actual service in time of War or public danger; nor shall any person be subject for the same offense to be twice put in jeopardy of life or limb; nor shall be compelled in any criminal case to be a witness against himself, nor be deprived of life, liberty, or property, without due process of law; nor shall private property be taken for public use, without just compensation.

[AMENDMENT VI]

In all criminal prosecutions, the accused shall enjoy the right to a speedy and public trial, by an impartial jury of the State and district wherein the crime shall have been committed, which district shall have been previously ascertained by law, and to be informed of the nature and cause of the accusation; to be confronted with the witnesses against him; to have compulsory process for obtaining witnesses in his favor, and to have the Assistance of Counsel for his defence.

[AMENDMENT VII]

In Suits at common law, where the value in controversy shall exceed twenty dollars, the right of trial by jury shall be preserved, and no fact tried by a jury, shall be otherwise re-examined in any court of the United States, than according to the rules of the common law.

[AMENDMENT VIII]

Excessive bail shall not be required, nor excessive fines imposed, nor cruel and unusual punishments inflicted.

[AMENDMENT IX]

The enumeration in the Constitution, of certain rights, shall not be construed to deny or disparage others retained by the people.

[AMENDMENT X]

The powers not delegated to the United States by the Constitution, nor prohibited by it to the States, are reserved to the States respectively, or to the people.[7]

[AMENDMENT XI]

The Judicial power of the United States shall not be construed to extend to any suit in law or equity, commenced or prosecuted against one of the United States by Citizens of another State, or by Citizens or Subjects of any Foreign State.[8]

[AMENDMENT XII]

The Electors shall meet in their respective states, and vote by ballot for President and Vice-President, one of whom, at least, shall not be an inhabitant of the same state with themselves; they shall name in their ballots the person voted for as President, and in distinct ballots the person voted for as Vice-President, and they shall make distinct lists of all persons voted for as President, and of all persons voted for as Vice-President, and of the number of votes for each, which lists they shall sign and certify, and transmit sealed to the seat of the government of the United States, directed to the President of the Senate;—The President of the Senate shall, in the presence of the Senate and House of Representatives, open all the certificates and the votes shall then be counted;—The person having the greatest number of votes for President, shall be the President, if such number be a majority of the whole number of Electors appointed; and if no person have such majority, then from the persons having the highest numbers not exceeding three on the list of those voted for as President, the House of Representatives shall choose immediately, by ballot, the President. But in choosing the President, the votes shall be taken by states, the representation from each state having one vote; a quorum for this purpose shall consist of a member or members from two-thirds of the states, and a majority of all the states shall be necessary to a choice. And if the House of Representatives shall not choose a President whenever the right of choice shall devolve upon them, before the fourth day of March next following, then the Vice-President shall act as President, as in the case of the death or other constitutional disability of the President.—The person having the greatest number of votes as Vice-President, shall be the Vice-President, if such number be a majority of the whole number of Electors appointed, and if no person have a majority, then from the two highest numbers on the list, the Senate shall choose the Vice-President; a quorum for the purpose shall consist of two-thirds of the whole number of Senators, and a majority of the whole number shall be necessary to a choice. But no person constitutionally ineligible to the office of President shall be eligible to that of Vice-President of the United States.[9]

[AMENDMENT XIII]

Section 1.

Neither slavery nor involuntary servitude, except as a punishment for crime whereof the party shall have been duly convicted, shall exist within the United States, or any place subject to their jurisdiction.

Section 2.

Congress shall have power to enforce this article by appropriate legislation.[10]

[AMENDMENT XIV]

Section 1.

All persons born or naturalized in the United States and subject to the jurisdiction thereof, are citizens of the United States and the State wherein they reside. No State shall make or enforce any law which shall abridge the privileges or immunities of citizens of the United States; nor shall any State deprive any person of life, liberty, or property, without due process of law; nor deny to any person within its jurisdiction the equal protection of the laws.

Section 2.

Representatives shall be apportioned among the several States according to their respective numbers counting the whole number of

---

[7]The first ten amendments were all proposed by Congress on September 25, 1789, and were ratified and adoption certified on December 15, 1791.

[8]Proposed by Congress on March 4, 1794, and declared ratified on January 8, 1798.
[9]Proposed by Congress on December 9, 1803; declared ratified on September 25, 1804; supplemented by Amendments XX and XXIII.
[10]Proposed by Congress on January 31, 1865; declared ratified on December 18, 1865.

persons in each State, excluding Indians not taxed. But when the right to vote at any election for the choice of electors for President and Vice-President of the United States, Representatives in Congress, the Executive and Judicial officers of a State, or the members of the Legislature thereof, is denied to any of the male inhabitants of such State being twenty-one years of age and citizens of the United States, or in any way abridged, except for participation in rebellion or other crime, the basis of representation therein shall be reduced in the proportion which the number of such male citizens shall bear to the whole number of male citizens twenty-one years of age in such State.

Section 3.

No person shall be a Senator or Representative in Congress, or elector of President and Vice President or hold any office, civil or military, under the United States or under any State, who, having previously taken an oath, as a member of Congress, or as an officer of the United States, or as a member of any State legislature or as an executive or judicial officer of any State to support the Constitution of the United States, shall have engaged in insurrection or rebellion against the same, or given aid or comfort to the enemies thereof. But Congress may by a vote of two-thirds of each House, remove such disability.

Section 4.

The validity of the public debt of the United States authorized by law, including debts incurred for payment of pensions and bounties for services in suppressing insurrection or rebellion, shall not be questioned. But neither the United States nor any State shall assume or pay any debt or obligation incurred in aid of insurrection or rebellion against the United States, or any claim for the loss or emancipation of any slave; but all such debts, obligations and claims shall be held illegal and void.

Section 5.

The Congress shall have power to enforce, by appropriate legislation, the provisions of this article.[11]

[AMENDMENT XV]
Section 1.

The right of citizens of the United States to vote shall not be denied or abridged by the United States or by any State on account of race, color, or previous condition of servitude.

Section.

The Congress shall have power to enforce this article by appropriate legislation.[12]

[AMENDMENT XVI]

The Congress shall have power to lay and collect taxes on incomes, from whatever source derived, without apportionment among the several States, and without regard to any census or enumeration.[13]

[AMENDMENT XVII]

The Senate of the United States shall be composed of two Senators from each State, elected by the people thereof, for six years; and each Senator shall have one vote. The electors in each State shall have the qualifications requisite for electors of the most numerous branch of the State legislatures.

When vacancies happen in the representation of any State in the Senate, the executive authority of such State shall issue writs of election to fill such vacancies: *Provided*, That the legislature of any State may empower the executive thereof to make temporary appointments until the people fill the vacancies by election as the legislature may direct.

This amendment shall not be so construed as to affect the election or

term of any Senator chosen before it becomes valid as part of the Constitution.[14]

[AMENDMENT XVIII]
Section 1.

After one year from the ratification of this article the manufacture, sale, or transportation of intoxicating liquors within, the importation thereof into, or the exportation thereof from the United States and all territory subject to the jurisdiction thereof for beverage purposes is hereby prohibited.

Section 2.

The Congress and the several States shall have concurrent power to enforce this article by appropriate legislation.

Section 3.

This article shall be inoperative unless it shall have been ratified as an amendment to the Constitution by the legislatures of the several States, as provided in the Constitution, within seven years from the date of the submission hereof to the States by the Congress.[15]

[AMENDMENT XIX]

The right of citizens of the United States to vote shall not be denied or abridged by the United States or by any State on account of sex.

Congress shall have power to enforce this article by appropriate legislation.[16]

[AMENDMENT XX]
Section 1.

The terms of the President and Vice President shall end at noon on the 20th day of January, and the terms of Senators and Representatives at noon on the 3d day of January, of the years in which such terms would have ended if this article had not been ratified; and the terms of their successors shall then begin.

Section 2.

The Congress shall assemble at least once in every year, and such meeting shall begin at noon on the 3d day of January, unless they shall by law appoint a different day.

Section 3.

If, at the time fixed for the beginning of the term of the President, the President elect shall have died, the Vice President elect shall become President. If a President shall not have been chosen before the time fixed for the beginning of his term, or if the President elect shall have failed to qualify, then the Vice President elect shall act as President until a President shall have qualified; and the Congress may by law provide for the case wherein neither a President elect nor a Vice President elect shall have qualified, declaring who shall then act as President, or the manner in which one who is to act shall be selected, and such person shall act accordingly until a President or Vice President shall have qualified.

Section 4.

The Congress may by law provide for the case of the death of any of the persons from whom the House of Representatives may choose a President whenever the right of choice shall have devolved upon them, and for the case of the death of any of the persons from whom the Senate may choose a Vice President whenever the right of choice shall have devolved upon them.

Section 5.

Sections 1 and 2 shall take effect on the 15th day of October following the ratification of this article.

---

[11]Proposed by Congress on June 13, 1866; declared ratified on July 28, 1868.
[12]Proposed by Congress on February 26, 1869; declared ratified on March 30, 1870.
[13]Proposed by Congress on July 12, 1909; declared ratified on February 25, 1913.

[14]Proposed by Congress on May 13, 1912; declared ratified on May 31, 1913.
[15]Proposed by Congress on December 18, 1917; declared ratified on January 29, 1919; repealed by Amendment XXI.
[16]Proposed by Congress on June 4, 1919; declared ratified on August 26, 1920.

Section 6.

This article shall be inoperative unless it shall have been ratified as an amendment to the Constitution by the legislatures of three-fourths of the several States within seven years from the date of its submission.[17]

[AMENDMENT XXI]

Section 1.

The eighteenth article of amendment to the Constitution of the United States is hereby repealed.

Section 2.

The transportation or importation into any States, Territory, or possession of the United States for delivery or use therein of intoxicating liquors, in violation of the laws thereof, is hereby prohibited.

Section 3.

This article shall be inoperative unless it shall have been ratified as an amendment to the Constitution by conventions in the several States, as provided in the Constitution, within seven years from the date of the submission hereof to the States by the Congress.[18]

[AMENDMENT XXII]

Section 1.

No person shall be elected to the office of the President more than twice, and no person who has held the office of President, or acted as President, for more than two years of a term to which some other person was elected President shall be elected to the office of the President more than once. But this Article shall not apply to any person holding the office of President when the Article was proposed by the Congress, and shall not prevent any person who may be holding the office of President, or acting as President, during the term within which this Article becomes operative from holding the office of President or acting as President during the remainder of such term.

Section 2.

This article shall be inoperative unless it shall have been ratified as an amendment to the Constitution by the legislatures of three-fourths of the several States within seven years from the date of its submission to the States by the Congress.[19]

[AMENDMENT XXIII]

Section 1.

The District constituting the seat of Government of the United States shall appoint in such manner as the Congress shall direct:

A number of electors of President and Vice President equal to the whole number of Senators and Representatives in Congress to which the District would be entitled if it were a State, but in no event more than the least populous State; they shall be in addition to those appointed by the States, but they shall be considered, for the purposes of the election of President and Vice President, to be electors appointed by a State; and they shall meet in the District and perform such duties as provided by the twelfth article of amendment.

Section 2.

The Congress shall have power to enforce this article by appropriate legislation.[20]

[AMENDMENT XXIV]

Section 1.

The right of citizens of the United States to vote in any primary or other election for President or Vice President, for electors for President or Vice President, or for Senator or Representative in Congress, shall not be denied or abridged by the United States or any state by reason of failure to pay any poll tax or other tax.

Section 2.

The Congress shall have the power to enforce this article by appropriate legislation.[21]

[AMENDMENT XXV]

Section 1.

In case of the removal of the President from office or his death or resignation, the Vice President shall become President.

Section 2.

Whenever there is a vacancy in the office of the Vice President, the President shall nominate a Vice President who shall take the office upon confirmation by a majority vote of both houses of Congress.

Section 3.

Whenever the President transmits to the President pro tempore of the Senate and the Speaker of the House of Representatives his written declaration that he is unable to discharge the powers and duties of his office, and until he transmits to them a written declaration to the contrary, such powers and duties shall be discharged by the Vice President as Acting President.

Section 4.

Whenever the Vice President and a majority of either the principal officers of the executive departments or of such other body as Congress may by law provide, transmit to the President pro tempore of the Senate and the Speaker of the House of Representatives their written declaration that the President is unable to discharge the powers and duties of his office, the Vice President shall immediately assume the powers and duties of the office as Acting President.

Thereafter, when the President transmits to the President pro tempore of the Senate and the Speaker of the House of Representatives his written declaration that no inability exists, he shall resume the powers and duties of his office unless the Vice President and a majority of either the principal officers of the executive department or of such other body as Congress may by law provide, transmit within four days to the President pro tempore of the Senate and the Speaker of the House of Representatives their written delcaration that the President is unable to discharge the powers and duties of his office. Thereupon Congress shall decide the issue, assembling within 48 hours for that purpose if not in session. If the Congress, within 21 days after receipt of the latter written declaration, or, if Congress is not in session, within 21 days after Congress is required to assemble, determines by two-thirds vote of both houses that the President is unable to discharge the powers and duties of his office, the Vice President shall continue to discharge the same as Acting President; otherwise, the President shall resume the powers and duties of his office.[22]

[AMENDMENT XXVI]

Section 1.

The right of citizens of the United States, who are 18 years of age or older, to vote shall not be denied or abridged by the United States or any state on account of age.

Section 2.

The Congress shall have the power to enforce this article by appropriate legislation.[23]

[17]Proposed by Congress on March 2, 1932; declared ratified on February 6, 1933.
[18]Proposed by Congress on February 20, 1933; declared ratified on December 5, 1933.
[19]Proposed by Congress on March 24, 1947; declared ratified on March 1, 1951.
[20]Proposed by Congress on June 16, 1960; declared ratified on April 3, 1961.

[21]Proposed by Congress on August 27, 1962; declared ratified on January 23, 1963.
[22]Proposed by Congress on July 6, 1965; declared ratified on February 10, 1967.
[23]Proposed by Congress on March 23, 1971; declared ratified on June 30, 1971.

GLOSSARY

Administrative routines—Regularized and repetitive tasks that can be handled impersonally, according to objective criteria. (p. 472)

Affirmative action—Employers' agreements to compensate people for past wrongs against all members of their race or sex by giving them preferential treatment in hiring and promotions. (p. 136)

Agenda building—A political process that defines the problem, legitimizes it as a proper matter of public concern, specifies alternative policies, and prods government into accepting responsibility for seeking a solution. (p. 305)

Agenda change—When policy makers focus their attention on some new problem or policy. (p. 438)

Antifederalists—Those who, during the founding, favored modest reform in the Articles of Confederation and who feared that a strong central government would suppress personal liberty. (Contrast with **Federalists**. (p. 52)

Appellants—**Litigants** involved in the appeal of some court decision. *See* **litigants.** (p. 500)

Appellate jurisdiction—A court's right to hear cases on appeal. (Contrast with **original jurisdiction.**) (p. 500)

Appropriations process—The process for authorizing expenditures. (p. 440)

Bicameralism—The division of legislative authority between two houses. (pp. 61, 427)

Bill—A draft of a proposed law. (p. 439)

Bipolarity—An international political system in which two superpowers and their allies compete for dominance. (Contrast with **multipolarity.**) (p. 566)

Block grants—A federal grant, awarded on the basis of some objective formula, for some broadly defined public purpose, such as health training. (Contrast with **categorical** and **project grants.**) (p. 108)

Budget-making process—A sequence of events through which the President develops a comprehensive budget, the budget is broken down into specific legislative proposals, Congress considers and may approve specific proposals, and the President approves Congress' actions. (p. 369)

Bureaucracy—Any organization with people in positions of authority, experts, procedures, and formal criteria for making decisions. (p. 453)

Cabinet departments—The major administrative units of the federal government, each with responsibility over a broad area of public policy (Agriculture, Commerce, Defense, Education, Energy, Health and Human Services, Housing and Urban Development, Interior, Justice, Labor, State, Transportation, Treasury). (p. 467)

Capitalism—The view that private persons should own society's resources and that economic competition should be the force which determines how they are used. (Contrast with **socialism.**) (p. 337)

Case law—Legal precedents that are derived from judges' decisions. (Contrast with **statutory law.**) (p. 501)

Casework—Favors that legislators do for their constituents. (p. 436)

Categorical grants—A federal grant, awarded on the basis of some objective formula, for a narrowly defined purpose, such as educating the children of federal employees. (Contrast with **block** and **project grants.**) (p. 108)

Caucus—An informal gathering of the party faithful, called to select delegates to a party's nominating convention. (Contrast with **primary elections.**) (p. 255)

Checks and balances—An arrangement in which authority is shared so that the actions of any one governmental official are constrained by other officials. (p. 71)

Civil laws—Laws that define the rights and obligations between private persons, such as those embodied in contracts. (Contrast with **criminal laws.**) (p. 499)

Civil liberties—Guarantees that government will not interfere arbitrarily with people, their opinions, and their property. (Contrast with **civil rights.**) (p. 117)

Civil rights—Guarantees that government will protect people against discrimination, either by other persons or by some other part of the government. (Contrast with **civil liberties.**) (p. 117)

Civil Service Reform Act of 1883—A federal law (also called the Pendleton Act) mandating that appointed positions be filled on the basis of merit, as measured by competitive examinations. *See* **merit principle.** (p. 462)

Classical liberalism—The doctrine justifying personal freedom which holds that the well-being of individual persons is more important than anything else, it is necessary to rely on individuals to know what is good for them, and individuals, if left free to decide upon and pursue their own interests, will do that which is good for them and thereby, for society. (p. 121)

Closed primaries—A party's **primary election** in which the only people who can vote are those who declare that they are a member of that party. (Contrast with **open primaries.**) (p. 255)

Cognitive dissonance—A psychological state of tension produced by the discrepancy between perceptions of the way things are and beliefs about the way they should be. (p. 313)

Comity—The informal norm of mutual courtesy and deference, especially strong in the U.S. Senate. (p. 428)

Commerce clause—The portion of Article I, Section 8 that provides the constitutional basis of the national government's **commerce powers.** (p. 92)

Commerce powers—The national government's right to regulate various forms of economic activity. (p. 92)

Conference committees—Temporary committees, consisting of members of both the House and the Senate, used to iron out differences between House- and Senate-passed bills. (p. 432)

Congressional agencies—A federal agency whose actions have significant effects on the constituents of members of Congress and, therefore, on the members' chances of being reelected; for example, the Army Corps of Engineers, the Small Business Administration, the Veterans' Administration. (p. 481)

Constitution—Law that describes the structure of government, its authority to maintain order, and its proper relationship to a people. (p. 47)

Constitutionalism—The principle that holds that the proper role of government is circumscribed by a written constitution. (p. 67)

Contempt—A judge's ruling that someone filed to abide by the court's decision in a civil proceeding or that they interfered in some way in a criminal proceeding. (p. 519)

Contract clause—The section of Article I, Section 10 of the U.S. Constitution which prevents states from passing laws that relieve private persons (such as debtors) of their contractual obligations. (p. 93)

Cooptation—The practice of including those likely to be affected in the making of decisions, so as to win their support or, at least, neutralize their opposition. (p. 485)

Corporatism—A doctrine which holds that the state should assume substantial responsibility, along with private business and organized labor, for the development of a strong economy. *See* **industrial policy.** (p. 341)

Cost-benefit analysis—A way of determining whether the costs of a policy are less than the benefits it provides to consumers or to society as a whole. (p. 360)

Criminal laws—Laws that prohibit certain private actions against society, such as theft or murder. (Contrast with **civil laws.**) (p. 500)

Crosscutting cleavages—Cultural divisions that intersect, rather than overlap; for example, not all who are white are also rich. (p. 173)

Cultural environment—Broad public expectations about what government should and should not do. *See also* **institutional, policy,** and **political environments.**) (p. 297)

Demand—The amount of goods and services people are willing and able to buy (and sell) at a particular price. (p. 356)

Demand-side fiscal techniques—Governmental actions that try to increase consumption. (p. 356)

Democracy—A political system in which government's right to rule depends on maintaining the consent of the governed. (p. 29)

Depression—A sustained period of falling economic growth. (p. 342)

Deregulation—The practice of deemphasizing government's role by returning to the principles of **laissez-faire** economics. *See* **privatization.** (p. 477)

Distributive policies—Governmental programs that reward certain persons and activities, without obviously disadvantaging others: for example, federal guarantees on student loans. (Contrast with **redistributive policies.**) (pp. 75, 435)

Doctrine of implied powers—The view that the national government can do whatever is necessary and proper (or even just convenient) to carry out its constitutionally explicit powers. *See McCulloch v. Maryland.* (p. 90)

Due process of law—Procedural protections against arbitrary governmental actions. (pp. 126, 511)

Economic efficiency—The allocation of resources in such a way so as to reduce waste and increase human welfare. (pp. 9, 349)

Economic equality—The condition that exists when the wealth of a society is uniformly distributed over the entire population. (p. 350)

Electoral participation—A composite set of political behaviors which are associated with the act of voting, including registering to vote, arranging for time to register and vote, donating time and money to election campaigns, voting, and so on. (Contrast with **nonelectoral forms of political activity.**) (p. 248)

Elitist democracy—A democratic system of government in which the few are expected to act in the interests of the many. (Contrast **participatory** and **representative democracy.**) (p. 29)

Entitlements—Federal social welfare policies that provide benefits to all who meet legal eligibility requirements: for example, Social Security payments and federally guaranteed student loans. (p. 539)

Entrepreneurial members—The members of a **policy organization** who bring energy, assertiveness, and "people" skills of organizing and management (for a federal tax reform policy organization, examples might include the leadership of the Senate and the House of Representatives, as well as those members of Congress who popularize the cause, sometimes because of their presidential ambitions). *See also* **political** and **technical members.** (p. 291)

Equality—In America, usually refers to equality of opportunity, not necessarily equality of result; the chance to succeed, not a guarantee of success. (p. 162)

Executive agreements—International understandings between the President and the head of a foreign nation which do not require senatorial approval but which can be nullified by congressional action and ignored by future Presidents. (p. 399)

Executive orders—Administrative regulations that serve as guidelines for the implementation of policy and that have the force of law. (p. 400)

Executive privilege—The right of a President (and those he gives it to) to refuse to appear before congressional committees or provide them with requested information. (p. 400)

Faction—A group of people who share some common interest, actually try to realize it, and in the process, disadvantage others. (p. 193)

Factional party—A political party that has split off from a major political party over some policy dispute, such as the American Independent Party which split off from the Democrats in 1968, largely over civil rights issues. (p. 202)

Fairness—The distribution of goods and services in a manner that society approves of. (p. 12)

Federal bureaucracy—Normally, refers to all parts of the federal government other than the President, Congress, and the Supreme Court; that is, **cabinet departments, independent executive agencies, government corporations,** and **independent regulatory commissions.** (p. 455)

Federal circuit courts—Federal courts that hear cases on appeal. (p. 505)

Federal district courts—Federal courts that act as trial courts. (p. 505)

Federal governments—Those that distribute governmental responsibilities among various levels: for example, those in the

United States, Canada, West Germany, and Australia. (Contrast with **unitary governments.**) (p. 85)

Federalism—A way of distributing authority among national, state, and local governments so that all have some degree of independence from one another. (p. 81)

Federalists—Those who, during the founding, wished to create a new constitution and a strong central government. (Contrast with **Antifederalists.**) (p. 52)

Feedback—Information about consequences that can be used to adjust policy. (p. 323)

Feminization of poverty—The tendency of the ranks of the poor to be filled with female-headed families. (p. 530)

Fiscal federalism—The network of interdependent relationships among different levels of government that has been stitched together through different ways of using public revenues. (p. 106)

Fiscal policies—Attempts to realize economic goals through governmental spending, taxing, and borrowing. (p. 356)

Fiscal subsidy—A governmental action that encourages production by compensating producers for their efforts. (p. 356)

Goal displacement—The re-direction of energy and concern away from long and even short-term institutional goals toward the more immediate and political goals of the members of the institution: for example, when members of Congress act as though they are more concerned with re-election than with solving public problems. (p. 294)

Government corporations—Federal agencies that perform business-like activities, such as delivering the mail, generating and distributing electricity in the Tennessee Valley, and insuring savings deposits: for example, the Pension Benefit Guaranty Corporation. (p. 470)

Governmental institutions—Places where binding decisions are made about the use of society's resources. (p. 19)

Gramm-Rudman Act—A law (also the Gramm-Rudman-Hollings Act) that attempted to reduce the federal deficit by automatic across-the-board budget cuts. (p. 416)

Grants-in-aid—Financial grants made by the national government to aid state and local governments in carrying out certain responsibilities. (p. 106)

Great Compromise—The proposal advanced to break the deadlock over the **New Jersey** and **Virginia Plans;** the Great Compromise guaranteed states equal representation in the U.S. Senate and the people proportional representation in the U.S. House of Representatives (also called the Connecticut Compromise). (p. 49)

Hegemony—The ability of a nation-state to dominate international events through unilateral action. (p. 566)

Ideological party—A political party that is organized around some coherent view of the proper relationship of government and society, such as the Marxist view taken by the Socialist Workers Party. (p. 202)

Impoundment—The refusal of a President to spend money that has been appropriated by Congress. (p. 401)

Incrementalism—A reactive strategy of decision making which leads government officials to prefer **marginal changes,** to search for remedies, not cures, and to define good public policy as that which wins popular approval. *See* **marginal changes.** (p. 305)

Independent executive agencies—A part of the federal government with narrowly defined functions, such as environmental protection, caring for veterans, and so on. Like **Cabinet departments,** independent executive agencies are headed by people who report directly to the President. Unlike Cabinet departments, independent executive agencies have less broad responsibilities. Examples of independent executive agencies include the Central Intelligence Agency, the National Science Foundation, and the U.S. Arms Control and Disarmament Agency. (p. 469)

Independent regulatory commissions—Federal organizations that are separate from all the departments and agencies of the executive branch. Unlike **independent executive agencies** that provide services, independent regulatory commissions produce rules and regulations to protect the public from various economic activities. Examples include the Federal Trade Commission, the Securities and Exchange Commission, and the Federal Reserve Board. (p. 470)

Individualism—A value that glorifies the process by which unfettered individuals pursue what they judge to be their self-interest. (p. 161)

Industrial policy—Governmental actions to revitalize companies that manufacture goods, rather than those that provide services. *See* **corporatism.** (p. 343)

Infrastructure—Capital projects that provide the basis for economic development: for example, roads, water and sewage systems. (p. 541)

Institutional environment—The set of public and private organizations that must agree before a particular policy change can take effect. *See also* **cultural, policy,** and **political environment.** (p. 298)

Institutionalized presidency—The set of relatively permanent expectations that are imposed on any President. (p. 376)

Interest aggregation—The process of integrating political demands into a broader set of policy proposals. *See* **interest articulation.** (p. 194)

Interest articulation—The act of expressing expectations about what government should do. *See* **interest aggregation.** (p. 194)

Iron triangle—An informal alliance (of a special interest group, a bureaucratic agency, and a congressional committee or subcommittee) which works to advance a particular policy. (pp. 381, 475)

Item veto—The ability of an executive officer to veto a portion of an appropriation, without vetoing the whole thing (sought after, but not currently enjoyed, by modern Presidents). Also called line-item veto. (p. 402)

Joint committees—Congressional committees consisting of members of both the House and the Senate, used to coordinate policy making on broad national concerns. (p. 432)

Judicial activism—The principle that a court, and especially the Supreme Court, should try to decide cases by interpreting the Constitution broadly, even though that may entail departures from current policies. (Contrast with **judicial restraint.**) (p. 501)

Judicial restraint—The principle that a court, and especially the Supreme Court, should try to decide cases on narrow, technical grounds, without itself making new public policies. *See* **stare decisis** and contrast with **judicial activism.** (p. 501)

Judicial review—The principle that federal courts, and especially the Supreme Court, has the right and the duty to invalidate executive and legislative actions that violate the Constitution. (pp. 68, 503)

Jurisdiction—A court's formal authority to hear and decide a case. (p. 500)

Keynesian economics—The economic theory that justifies governmental intervention into the economy, especially to reverse an economic slowdown. (p. 333)

Laissez-faire—The view that government should leave alone the operation of the free economic market. (p. 337)

Legislative veto—A requirement, written into a law, that some of the bureaucratic decisions that are required by the law can not go into effect until after Congress has had a chance to cancel them. (p. 481)

Legitimacy—A collective sense that governmental actions are consistent with popular preferences. (p. 25)

Liberty—A valued means and end; a way of striving and, once attained, something to be enjoyed for its own sake. (p. 161)

Line-item veto—*See* **item veto.**

Litigants—The plaintiff who brings a legal suit and the defendant against whom it is brought. (p. 500)

McCarthyism—A style of political discourse which impugns the loyalty of one's opponents. (p. 143)

McCulloch v. Maryland—An early decision of the Supreme Court which established the **doctrine of implied powers** and the **principle of national supremacy**. *See also* **Marbury v. Madison.** (p. 90)

Macroeconomic policies—**Fiscal** and **monetary policies** that attempt to alter the performance of the economy as a whole. (Contrast with **microeconomic policies.**) (p. 360)

Majority leader—The leader of the majority party and the most important official in the U.S. Senate. (p. 426)

Majority whip—The **majority leader's** second in command. (p. 426)

Management tasks—Those things a **policy organization** must do to maintain the organization, for example, facilitate communications among members. *See also* **policy** and **research tasks.** (p. 294)

Mandatory social decision—One of the decisions that every society must make about the allocation of its resources. (p. 5)

Marbury v. Madison—An early decision of the Supreme Court which established its power of **judicial review.** *See also* **McCulloch v. Maryland.** (p. 88)

Marginal changes—Customary and small, rather than radical and large, modifications in public policy. *See* **incrementalism.** (p. 323)

Market failure—Whenever the private market does not allocate resources efficiently, or when the market does not distribute goods and services fairly, or when the market does not promote other things of value to society. (p. 11)

Market imperfections—Defects that keep the private market from operating efficiently: for example, consumer ignorance. (p. 102)

Media—Forms of communication between political masses and political elites. (p. 237)

Media party—A minor political party which probably exists only because television is such an important part of the political process, as probably was true of the National Unity Ticket, under which John B. Anderson ran for the presidency in 1980. (p. 202)

Mercantilism—A doctrine that justified governmental regulation of all aspects of the economy. (p. 337)

Merit principle—The idea that appointed positions should be staffed by those who are most qualified for them. (Contrast with **nepotism, patronage, spoils system.**) (p. 462)

Merit System Protection Board—The federal agency which is supposed to protect civil service employees from political pressure. (p. 460)

Microeconomic policies—Governmental attempts to alter the behavior of individual economic actors. (Contrast with **macroeconomic policies.**) (p. 360)

Minority leader—The leader of the minority party in the U.S. House or in the U.S. Senate. (p. 426)

Minority whip—The **minority leader's** second in command. (p. 426)

Mixed economy—An economic system, like the United States, which relies primarily on capitalistic forces, while allowing for a substantial governmental role in the regulation of most economic activities and in the production and distribution of some goods and services. (p. 339)

Monetarists—Those economists who argue that the rate of growth of the money supply is the main, if not the sole, determinant of economic growth. (p. 359)

Multipolarity—An international political system in which many nation-states independently pursue their own (often different) national self-interests. (Contrast with **bipolarity.**) (p. 566)

Mutual Assured Destruction (MAD)—The military doctrine which holds that nation-states are secure from nuclear attack as long as they retain the ability to launch an equally, if not more, devastating counter-attack. (p. 569)

National supremacy—The principle that federal laws are supreme over state laws. (p. 503)

Nationalism—The desire of a people who share some common identity to have their own territory and their own government. (p. 571)

Natural law—The set of immutable principles that should govern human relations. (p. 65)

Natural rights—Those guaranteed by **natural law,** including life, liberty, and the right to hold property. (p. 65)

Necessary and proper clause—Article I, Section 8 of the U.S. Constitution, giving the national government the right to make whatever laws are "necessary and proper" to carry out its responsibilities. (p. 91)

Negative rights—Personal rights that emphasize the absence of interference. (Contrast with **positive rights.**) (p. 129)

Nepotism—The practice of appointing relatives to public office. *See also* **patronage** and contrast with **merit principle.** (p. 381)

New Jersey Plan—As an alternative to the **Virginia Plan,** the New Jersey Plan would have only reformed the Articles of Confederation, while preserving the independence of the states. *See* **Great Compromise.** (p. 49)

Nonelectoral forms of political participation—All forms of political activity other than those associated with voting: for example, observing, discussing, and writing about politics and policymaking. (Contrast with **electoral forms of participation.**) (p. 249)

Office of Management and Budget—The federal agency in charge of preparing the President's budget and, in recent years, of deciding whether proposed administrative regulations should be adopted. (p. 467)

Office of Personnel Management—The federal agency in charge of hiring persons for civil service positions. (p. 460)

Open primaries—A party's **primary election** in which anyone can vote, whether or not they consider themselves to be a member of that party. (Contrast with **closed primaries**.) (p. 255)

Organizational set—Those parts of a **policy organization's** environment that can do the most to aid, or block, the realization of its goals. (p. 300)

Original jurisdiction—The right to act as a trial court on a case that no other court has heard. (Contrast with **appellate jurisdiction**.) (pp. 89, 500)

Oversight—Congressional efforts to gather and evaluate information on the implementation of public policy. (p. 436)

Participation rights—Prohibitions against artificial restrictions on one's right to participate in government and in the making of public policy. *See also* **privacy** and **punishment rights**. (p. 125)

Participatory democracy—A form of democracy in which the people are expected to represent their own interests. (Contrast **elitist** and **representative democracy**.) (p. 30)

Party delegates—Those who attend their political party's nominating convention. (p. 204)

Party identification—A person's psychological attachment to a **political party**. (pp. 204, 259)

Party identifiers—People who consider themselves to be members of a **political party**. (p. 204)

Party-line voting—A legislative vote in which a majority of one party votes one way and a majority of the other party votes the other way. (p. 442)

Passive representation—The practice of making a **bureaucracy** more representative by staffing it with people who mirror the characteristics of the citizenry. (p. 478)

Patronage—The practice of appointing political supporters to public office. *See also* **nepotism** and contrast with **merit principle**. (pp. 381, 462)

Permanent campaign—A process by which political actors win popular support by continuously monitoring public opinion and adjusting their media appeal. (p. 231)

Personal values—Intense personal beliefs about goals worth realizing and preferred ways of trying to reach them. (p. 160)

Plebiscitary presidency—The popular view that the President is the source of all solutions to society's problems. (p. 404)

Policy environment—The set of all **policy organizations** that compete with one another. *See also* **cultural, institutional,** and **policy environment**. (p. 298)

Policy inducements—Governmental actions that encourage certain economic behaviors by rewarding them: for example, providing financial rewards to those who turn in tax cheats. (Contrast with **policy sanctions**.) (p. 349)

Policy organization—A set of public and private actors who work together to shape some aspect of government's role: for example, all government officials, interest groups, Washington lawyers, and representatives of the press. (p. 279)

Policy sanctions—Governmental actions that discourage certain economic behaviors by punishing them: for example, imposing tax penalties on those who fail to pay their taxes on time. (Contrast with **policy inducements**.) (p. 349)

Policy tasks—Those things a **policy organization** must do to link its goals to those of official policy makers: for example, giving testimony at legislative hearings. *See also* **management** and **research tasks**. (p. 294)

Political Action Committee (PAC)—A political interest group which tries to achieve its policy objective by influencing the electoral process, either directly, through their own campaigns for or against particular candidates or indirectly, through cash contributions to particular candidates. (p. 210)

Political Activities Act of 1939—A law prohibiting federal employees from engaging in certain political activities. Also called the Hatch Act. (p. 463)

Political attitudes—Emotionally charged personal reactions toward objects in one's political environment. (p. 160)

Political culture—People's collective sense of what government should do and how it should do it. (p. 153)

Political environment—All those who stand to win or lose something from a particular policy change. *See also* **cultural, institutional,** and **policy environment**. (p. 298)

Political ideology—A well-organized and coherent set of **political attitudes** and **public opinions** about government's proper role. (p. 175)

Political interest group—A relatively tight coalition of people who are organized primarily for the purpose of influencing public policy. (Contrast with **political party**.) (p. 187)

Political members—The members of a **policy organization** who know how to exercise power, to persuade, to craft legislation, and to line up votes. For a federal tax reform policy organization, examples might include the members of the Senate Finance and House Ways and Means Committees, some of their staff persons, and the President and some of his advisers. *See also* **entrepreneurial** and **technical members**. (p. 291)

Political party—A loose coalition of both principled and ambitious people who are organized for the purpose of winning elective office. (Contrast with **interest group**.) (p. 187)

Political socialization—The way people learn about, and develop psychological reactions to, their political surroundings. (p. 153)

Political values—Beliefs about the proper role of government. (p. 153)

Politics—The way people fight over what government should, and should not, do. (p. 19)

Popular sovereignty—The right of a people to create, alter, or abolish government or any of its policies. (pp. 29, 66)

Positive rights—Personal rights that emphasize the provision of tangible benefits. (Contrast with **negative rights**.) (p. 129)

Power brokering—The practice by which governmental agencies provide benefits to their clients who, in exchange, provide political support for the agency and its policies. (p. 488)

President pro tempore—In the absence of the Vice-President of the United States, the presiding officer of the U.S. Senate. (p. 426)

Presidential power—Mostly, the ability to persuade. (p. 383)

Primary election—An election that selects either the candidates who will appear on the general election ballot or the delegates who, at a political party's nominating convention, will select the candidates. *See* **closed** and **open primaries**. (Contrast with **caucus**.) (p. 255)

Principle of national supremacy—The view that the laws that result from the national government's exercise of its powers are supreme over the laws of the states. *See **McCulloch v. Maryland**.* (p. 91)

Prior restraint—Court orders that prevent publication of news stories deemed damaging to the public interest. (p. 267)

Privacy rights—Protections against arbitrary governmental interference in one's personal affairs. *See also* **participation** and **punishment rights.** (p. 124)

Private economic market—The voluntary transactions of buyers and sellers which result in decisions about the allocation of societal resources. (Contrast with **governmental institutions.**) (p. 9)

Private goods—Goods which, once consumed by someone, can not be consumed by anyone else: for example, a pencil or a hot dog. (Contrast with **public goods.**) (p. 6)

Privatization—The practice of letting private economic actors perform what used to be governmental responsibilities: for example, letting airlines decide their own routes and fares, rather than have that done by the (now defunct) Civil Aeronautics Board. (pp. 320, 478)

Progressive tax—One that taxes people on the basis of their ability to pay: for example, the federal income tax which has higher rates for those with higher personal incomes. (Contrast with **regressive tax.**) (p. 351)

Project grants—Federal grants, given on application, for some specific purpose, such as highway construction. (Contrast with **block** and **categorical grants.**) (p. 108)

Protest party—A minor political party that typically reflects regionally based dissatisfaction with economic conditions, such as the Populist Party of 1892–1908. (p. 202)

Public goods—Goods which, even though consumed by some, are still available to be consumed by others: for example, freedom from fear of crime. (Contrast with **private goods.**) (p. 6)

Public opinions—Verbal expressions of underlying attitudes and values. (p. 153)

Public policies—Governmental attempts to remedy societal problems. (p. 19)

Punishment rights—Protections against the arbitrary lose of life, liberty, or property. *See also* **participation** and **privacy rights.** (p. 126)

Reactive campaigning—Quick adjustments in campaign strategy that are made in response to an opponent's election campaign. (p. 262)

Reconciliation process—The congressional budget-making procedure through which the initial budget requests of committees are reduced. *See* **budget-making process.** (p. 369)

Redistributive policies—Governmental programs that reward certain persons and activities, while obviously taking away from some others: for example, Social Security payments to the elderly that are financed out of the wages of younger workers. (Contrast with **distributive policies.**) (pp. 75, 435)

Regressive tax—One that taxes all persons the same, without regard to their ability to pay: for example, a sales tax. (Contrast with **progressive tax.**) (p. 351)

Representative democracy—A form of democracy in which the people participate indirectly, through elected representatives. (Contrast with **elitist** and **participatory democracy.**) (p. 31)

Republic—A form of government in which sovereign power belongs to the people, although it is exercised by governmental officials. (p. 29)

Republicanism—The doctrine which holds that the power to rule resides in the people and is only exercised by elected representatives who are responsible to the people. (p. 66)

Research tasks—Those things a **policy organization** must do to justify the organization's policy recommendations: for example, gathering and analyzing information on the extent of a problem or the likely impact of some policy change. *See also* **management** and **policy tasks.** (p. 294)

Revenue sharing—Federal funds that are awarded, with few strings attached, to state governments and local governmental jurisdictions. (p. 108)

Roll-call votes—The recorded floor votes of the House and Senate. (p. 440)

Routine issues—Matters that come before policy makers on a regular basis, such as governmental budgets. (p. 317)

Rules Committee—The committee in the U.S. House of Representatives which regulates the flow of committee bills onto the floor for debate and a vote. (p. 431)

Scarcity—Not enough of what people desire. (p. 5)

Select committee—A congressional committee that is established for a limited period to examine a particular problem. Also called a Special committee. (p. 431)

Seniority rule—The practice of assigning the chairmanship of a committee to the person who has been on it the longest, assuming they are a member of the majority party. (p. 432)

Separation of powers—The division of governmental authority among the executive, legislative, and judicial branches of government. (p. 61)

Single-issue party—A minor political party that typically opposes a specific policy, such as the Prohibition Party which opposes the sale of liquor. (p. 202)

Social contract—An agreement to form a civil society that will guarantee **natural rights.** (p. 65)

Social safety net—A set of federal social welfare policies that are intended to protect people against a sudden and catastrophic loss of income. (p. 539)

Socialism—An economic doctrine which holds that the state should own all of society's resources, in the name of the people, and should decide how they will be used, presumably in the service of the people. (Contrast with **capitalism.**) (p. 337)

Speaker—The leader of the majority party and the most important official of the U.S. House of Representatives. (p. 426)

Spoils system—The practice of rewarding political supporters, typically with employment. *See* **patronage** and contrast with **merit principle.** (p. 462)

Standing committees—The main substantive committees of Congress. (p. 431)

Star Wars technology—The possibility that lasers can be used to destroy incoming ballistic missiles. (p. 573)

Stare decisis—The judicial principle that precedents from prior cases should be applied to subsequent ones. *See* **judicial restraint.** (p. 501)

Statism—A doctrine which holds that government should have primary responsibility for the allocation of resources and the reallocation of personal wealth. (p. 340)

Statutory laws—Laws passed by a legislature. (Contrast with **case law.**) (p. 501)

Structural poverty—A permanent condition of poverty, not lessened by economic growth or by job training programs.

Subgovernments—Alliances between special interests and bureaucratic agencies. (p. 443)

Supply-side economics—The theory that, by reducing taxes, the federal government can encourage investment in productive enterprises, thereby stimulating economic growth. (p. 369)

Tax preferences—Provisions of the tax code that encourage certain behaviors by reducing the tax liability that is associated with them: for example, encouraging charitable contributions by making them tax deductible. (p. 357)

Technical members—The members of a **policy organization** who have the knowledge of what must be done and the sort of "nuts-and-bolts" grip on procedures so that they know how to do it. For a federal tax reform policy organization, technical members might include the staff of the Senate Finance and House Ways and Means Committees, at least some of the members of those committees, some of their personal staff, members of the Executive Branch, especially those who work in the White House and at the Treasury Department, and the lawyers and accountants who work for those interests likely to be affected by a policy change. *See also* **entrepreneurial** and **political members.** (p. 291)

Transfer payment—A direct payment from the government to a private person, provided as a matter of law. (p. 351)

Unitary governments—Those that concentrate governmental responsibilities at one level: for example, Great Britain and Japan. (Contrast with federal governments.) (p. 85)

Virginia Plan—A plan proposed during the Constitutional Convention which would have established a very strong national government, one armed with the power to overturn state laws. (Contrast with **New Jersey Plan** and *see* **Great Compromise.**) (p. 49)

Volunteerism—The practice of private actors contributing money, expertise, and time to public causes. (p. 597)

War powers—The President's claimed prerogative to do what is necessary to protect national security. (pp. 401–402)

Writ—A formal, written court order. (p. 518)

Writ of certiorari—A court's written order to a lower court to deliver up material on a case for higher court review. (p. 500)

Writ of habeas corpus—A court order that requires that a governmental official who is holding someone in custody justify the continued detention of that person. (p. 518)

Writ of mandamus—A court order that compels the performance of an official duty. (p. 89)

ACKNOWLEDGMENTS

Photographs and Cartoons

Positions of the photographs are indicated in abbreviated form as follows: top (t), bottom (b), center (c), left (l), right (r).
Cover: Don Hamerman.
All Dialogue photographs are by Linda B. Dawson.
P 1: 17, Paul Conklin; **Prologue:** 3, The Museum of Modern Art/Film Stills Archive; 4, Bettmann Archive; 5, Roger Sandler/NYT Pictures; 6, Betty Barry/The Picture Cube; **7(t),** UPI/Bettmann Newsphotos; **7(b),** Linda B. Dawson; 12, Prints Division, New York Public Library, Astor, Lenox and Tilden Foundations; **Chapter 1:** 18, Fredrik D. Bodin/Stock, Boston; 21, 24, Library of Congress; 25, 31, Paul Conklin; **28(t),** From R.M. Devens *Our First Century;* **28(b),** Courtesy, Henry Francis du Pont Winterthur Museum; 33, OLIPHANT COPYRIGHT UNIVERSAL PRESS SYNDICATE. Reprinted with permission. All rights reserved; 34, Margaret Bourke-White, Life Magazine © 1937 Time Inc.; 37, UPI/Bettmann Newsphotos; 41, © 1980 News America Syndicate; 42, Salk in *Minneapolis Tribune;* **Chapter 2:** 46, Scott, Foresman and Company; 48, U.S. Bureau of Printing and Engraving; 49, Bowdoin Museum of Fine Arts, Bowdoin College, Brunswick, ME; 50, 51, 69, Independence National Historical Park Collection, Eastern National Park and Monument Association; 61, Library of Congress; 62, Historical Society of Pennsylvania; 67, St. Louis Art Museum; 73, Sygma; **Chapter 3:** 80, © Andrew Popper 1980/Picture Group; 82, 89, Supreme Court Historical Society; 83, 95, Library of Congress; 91, Smithsonian Institution; 94, U.S. Bureau of Printing and Engraving; **99(t),** *Harper's Weekly,* November 16, 1867; **99(b),** Wide World; 105, DOONESBURY COPYRIGHT 1981 G.B. Trudeau. Reprinted with permission of Universal Press Syndicate. All rights reserved; **106(l),** Keefe, *The Denver Post* © 1982; **Chapter 4:** 116, Bruce Davidson/Magnum; 119, Ted Cowell/Black Star; 122, Shelburne Museum, Inc., Shelburne, Vermont; 125, **136(l),** UPI/Bettmann Newsphotos; 126, Courtesy of H.R. Rodgers; 127, David S. Strickler/The Picture Cube; 128, Flip Schulke, Life Magazine © 1964 Time Inc.; 131, Reprinted by permission of United Feature Syndicate, Inc.; 135, Carl Iwasaki, Life Magazine © Time Inc.; **136(r),** Linda L. Richardson; 143, National Archives; 145, Copyright Herblock in the Washington Post; **P 2:** 151, Robert Llewellyn; **Chapter 5:** 152, David Powers/Stock, Boston; 154, Beinecke Rare Books and Manuscripts Library, Yale University; 157, Library of Congress; 160, © 1981, Washington Post Writers Group, reprinted with permission; **163(l),** Wide World; **163(r),** Photo by Richard Blomgren, Courtesy of Helen Boosalis for Governor; 165, Reprinted by permission of Newspaper Enterprise Association, Inc.; 168, © 1981 James Mason/Black Star; 170, HERMAN COPYRIGHT 1984 UNIVERSAL PRESS SYNDICATE. Reprinted with permission. All rights reserved; 175, DOONESBURY COPYRIGHT 1971 G.B. Trudeau. Reprinted with permission of Universal Press Syndicate. All rights reserved; **Chapter 6:** 186, Mike Mazzaschi/Stock, Boston; 189, 217, Wide World; 196 (both), Courtesy of The New-York Historical Society, New York City; 197, Library of Congress; 200, *Colliers Weekly,* November 10, 1906; 207, Reprinted with permission: Tribune Media Services; **210(b),** Timothy A. Murphy/U.S. News & World Report; 213, Drawing by Bassett. Reprinted with permission; 215, The Picture Cube; 220, Brad Markel/Gamma-Liaison **Chapter 7:** 230, Robert Kalfus/Gamma-Liaison 232, Ledru/Sygma; 234, Reprinted by permission of United Feature Syndicate, Inc.; 235, Chuck Ayers/Courtesy Akron Beacon Journal; 236, Wide World; 239, DOONESBURY COPYRIGHT 1980 G.B. Trudeau. Reprinted with permission of Universal Press Syndicate. All rights reserved; 240, 250, Paul Conklin; 241, George Bellerose/Stock, Boston; 242, David Burnett/Contact Press; **249(l),** Rich-

ard A. Bloom; **249(r),** Ken Heinen; 259, Eli Reed/Magnum; 258, Picture Collection, New York Public Library, Astor, Lenox and Tilden Foundations; 263, Lyndon Baines Johnson Library; 264, Krokodil/Sovfoto; 268, Dennis Brack/Black Star; **P 3:** 277, Mark Antman/The Image Works; **Chapter 8:** 278, The Jacob A. Riis Collection, Museum of the City of New York; 281, Thomas England/PEOPLE Weekly © 1983 Time Inc.; 283, Enright/New York American; 284, Courtesy of the Office of Economic Opportunity; 285, Des Moines Register and Tribune; 289, Marilyn K. Yee/NYT Pictures; 293, Paul Conklin; **Chapter 9:** 304, Frank Siteman/Stock, Boston; 307, Wide World; 308, UPI/Bettmann Newsphotos; 311, 317, OLIPHANT COPYRIGHT UNIVERSAL PRESS SYNDICATE. Reprinted with permission; 313, "After all, we've only been here a little over four years"...copyright 1985 by Herblock in the Washington Post; 314, Bruce Roberts/Photo Researchers; 315, A.F.P. from Pictorial Parade; 320, © 1984, Washington Post Writers Group, reprinted with permission; 326, © 1984 Stephen Shames/Visions; **Chapter 10:** 330, Bill Fitz-Patrick/The White House; 335, 361, King Features Syndicate; 340, Prints Division, New York Public Library, Astor, Lenox and Tilden Foundations; **341(l),** Mickey Osterreicher; **341(r),** 343, UPI/Bettmann Newsphotos; 342, Hoda Bakhshandagi; 344, Reprinted with permission: Tribune Media Services; 347, Union Pacific Museum Collection; **350(t),** J.P. Laffont/Sygma; **350(b),** Gorrell 1981 The Charlotte News; **P 4:** 365, Paul Conklin; **Chapter 11:** 366, Enrico Ferorelli/Dot; 370, Jim Mazzotta/Ft. Meyers News-Press; 374, Reprinted by permission of United Feature Syndicate, Inc.; 375, UPI/Bettmann Newsphotos; 379, COPYRIGHT 1968 FEIFER COPYRIGHT UNIVERSAL PRESS SYNDICATE. Reprinted with permission. All rights reserved; 382, © 1981 Washington Post Writers Group, reprinted with permission; 385, Brown Brothers; 387, Teresa Zabala/NYT Pictures; 389, © 1975 The Washington Post Writers Group, reprinted with permission; **391(all),** National Archives; 392, © Engelhardt in the St. Louis Post-Dispatch/Reprinted with permission; **397(l),** Illingworth/News of the World; **397(r),** Bensfield; 398, Sygma; 401, J.L. Atlan/Sygma; **405(tl, tr),** Wide World; **405(b),** David Levine/Reprinted with permission from The New York Review of Books © 1966 NYREV Inc.; 407, Bill Fitz-Patrick/The White House; **Chapter 12:** 412, J.L. Atlan/Sygma; 414, UPI/Bettmann Newsphotos; 418, OLIPHANT COPYRIGHT UNIVERSAL PRESS SYNDICATE. Reprinted with permission. All rights reserved; 423, Courtesy of The New-York Historical Society, New York City; 425, *Harper's Weekly;* **429(top left to right),** Courtesy of the office of Tip O'Neill, UPI/Bettmann Newsphotos, UPI/Bettmann Newsphotos, Wide World; **429(bottom left to right),** Courtesy of the office of Robert Dole, Wide World, UPI/Bettmann Newsphotos, UPI/Bettmann Newsphotos; 431, Agence France-Presse; 432, Tom Darcy/Newsday, Inc.; 433, Reprinted by permission of Newspaper Enterprise Association, Inc.; 448, Paul Conklin; **Chapter 13:** 452, Ted Wathen/Marketing and Design Services; 455, Frank Siteman/The Picture Cube; 462, Darryl Heikes/U.S. News & World Report; 463, *Harper's Weekly,* October 20, 1877; 464, 475, Reprinted by permission: Tribune Media Services; 465, Krokodil/Sovfoto; 477, Wide World; 482, Robert Graysmith/San Francisco Chronicle; 484, Eddie Adams/Gamma-Liaison; **Chapter 14:** 492, Fred Ward/Black Star; 495, Vint Lawrence/The Washington Monthly; 499, 501, **504(b),** 505, Supreme Court Historical Society; 503, **511(l),** Library of Congress; **504(t),** Franklin D. Roosevelt Library; **511(r),** Reprinted with permission: Tribune Media Services; 517, OLIPHANT COPYRIGHT UNIVERSAL PRESS SYNDICATE. Reprinted with permission. All rights reserved;

520, News America Syndicate; **P 5: 525,** Paul Conklin; **Chapter 15: 526,** Cary Wolinsky/Stock, Boston; **528,** Mary Ellen Mark/Archive; **532,** Michael Weisbrot/Stock, Boston; **533,** Bryce Flynn/Stock, Boston; **536(l), 545, 554,** UPI/Bettmann Newsphotos; **536(r),** Brown Brothers; **541,** Ellis Herwig/Stock, Boston; **550,** Burt Glinn/Magnum; **Chapter 16: 560,** Harald Sund; **563, 568,** Wide World; **564,** King Features Syndicate, Inc.; **567,** Joint Task Force One photo; **569,** "Don't mind me...just go right on talking....from *The Herblock Book* (Beacon Press, 1952); **570, 579(t),** News America Syndicate; **575,** Cornell Capa/Magnum; **577;** Claudio Urraca/Sygma; **579(b),** Reuters/Bettmann Newsphotos; **Epilogue: 599,** Bettmann Archive; **600,** Ulrike Welsch/Stock, Boston; **601,** UPI/Bettmann Newsphotos. All stamps are from the collection of Ronald C. Kahn.

Color Essay I: Participation; **Plate 1** Kennedy Galleries, Inc.; **Plate 2(t),** © 1984 Christopher Morris/Black Star; **(b),** Tom Bytes/Sygma; **Plate 3(t),** Owen Franken/Stock, Boston; **(b),** Max Winter/Picture Group; **Plate 4(t),** Wally McNamee/Woodfin Camp; **(b),** David R. Frazier.

Color Essay II: Policy Symbols; **Plate 1(t),** Robin E. Bowman; **(b),** American Antiquarian Society; **Plate 2(t),** Cary Wolinsky/Stock, Boston; **(b),** National Park Service History Collection, Harpers Ferry Center, Harpers Ferry, West Virginia; **Plate 3(t),** Library of Congress; **(b1),** © 1983 James Nachtwey/Black Star; **(br),** Robert W. Kelley, Life Magazine © 1970, Time Inc.; **Plate 4(t),** Trustees of the Imperial War Museum; **(c),** Official U.S. Army photo; **(b),** Lyndon Baines Johnson Library.

Literary, Figures, and Tables

Chapter 5: 159(t) From "Opinion Roundup" in *Public Opinion*, June/July 1981, p. 25. Copyright © 1981 by the American Enterprise Institute. Reprinted by permission. **159(b)** From "Patriotism's Pulse" in *The New York Times Magazine*, December 11, 1983. Copyright © 1983 by The New York Times Company. Reprinted by permission. **162** "Public Opinions Toward Affirmative Action" from The Gallup Report, No. 224, May 1984. Copyright © 1984 by The Gallup Poll. Reprinted by permission. **167** From "Opinion Roundup" in *Public Opinion*, August/September, 1980, p. 40. Copyright © 1980 by the American Enterprise Institute. Reprinted by permission. **171** From "Opinion Roundup" in *Public Opinion*, June/July, 1979, p. 40. Copyright © 1979 by the American Enterprise Institute. Reprinted by permission. **172** American Institute of Public Opinion (Gallup); Center for Political Studies; Lou Harris and Associates; National Opinion Research Center, CBS/NYT. **173** From "Opinion Roundup" in *Public Opinion*, December/January, 1982, p. 36. Copyright © 1982 by the American Enterprise Institute. Reprinted by permission. **183** From "Differences of Opinion on Major Issues Between Blacks and Whites" in *The New York Times*, August 28, 1981. Copyright © 1981 by The New York Times Company. Reprinted by permission. **Chapter 6: 211** From *The Interest Group Society* by Jeffrey M. Berry, p. 161. Copyright © 1984 by Jeffrey M. Berry. Reprinted by permission of Little, Brown and Company. **212** From *The Washington Lobby*, fourth edition. Copyright © 1982 by Congressional Quarterly Inc. Reprinted by permission. **Chapter 7: 251** From *Political Participation*, second edition, by Lester W. Milbrath and M. L. Goel. Copyright © 1977 by Houghton Mifflin Company.

Reprinted by permission. **Chapter 9: 306–7** Excerpt from pp. 82–84 of Letter From Birmingham Jail, April 16, 1963 in *Why We Can't Wait* by Martin Luther King, Jr. © 1963 by Martin Luther King, Jr. Reprinted by Harper & Row, Publishers, Inc. **Chapter 10: 338, 339** Reprinted by permission of the publisher, from *The U.S. Economy Demystified* by Albert T. Sommers (Lexington, Mass.: Lexington Books, D.C. Heath and Company). Copyright © 1985 by D.C. Heath and Company. **348** "The Relation Between Savings and Growth" from *The New York Times*, November 3, 1985. Copyright © 1985 by The New York Times Company. Reprinted by permission. **351** From *The Personal Distribution of Income and Wealth*, edited by James D. Smith. Copyright © 1975 by the National Bureau of Economic Research, Inc. Reprinted by permission. **352** From *The New Politics of Inequality* by Thomas Byrne Edsall. Copyright © 1984 by Thomas Byrne Edsall. Reprinted by permission of W. W. Norton & Company. **Chapter 12: 419** "The Federal Budget Process" from *The New York Times*, February 2, 1984. Copyright © 1984 by The New York Times Company. Reprinted by permission. **422** "Confidence in Institutions" from The Gallup Report, July 14, 1985. Copyright © 1985 by The Gallup Poll. Reprinted by permission. **441** Figure 12.1 illustration by Hans Zander. **442** From *Congressional Quarterly Weekly Report*, January 11, 1986. Copyright © 1986 by Congressional Quarterly Inc. Reprinted by permission. **Chapter 13: 459** From "Issue Networks and the Executive Establishment" by Hugh Heclo in *The New American Political System*, edited by Anthony King. Copyright © 1978 by American Enterprise Institute for Public Policy Research, Washington, D.C. Reprinted by permission. **466** "NASA Wasted Billions in Space Projects, U.S. Audits Show" from *The New York Times*, April 23, 1986. Copyright © 1986 by The New York Times Company. Reprinted by permission. **Chapter 14: 506** "The Thirteen Federal Judicial Circuits" from *The Federal Reporter*, second series, Vol. 779 F.2d, 1986. Copyright © 1986 by West Publishing Company. Reprinted by permission. **509** From *The Supreme Court*, second edition, by Lawrence Baum. Copyright © 1985 by Congressional Quarterly Inc. Reprinted by permission. **Chapter 15: 529** From *Los Angeles Times* survey reported in "Hard Times: The Public on Poverty" by I. A. Lewis and William Schneider in *Public Opinion*, June/July 1985. Copyright © 1985 by American Enterprise Institute for Public Policy Research, Washington, D.C. Reprinted by permission. **540** "Key Antipoverty Programs, 1980" from "The War on Poverty: 1965–1980" by Charles Murray in *The Wilson Quarterly*, Autumn, 1984. Copyright © 1984 by the Woodrow Wilson International Center for Scholars. Reprinted by permission. **543** From "When Government Was a Friend in Need" by Thomas P. O'Neill, Jr. in *The New York Times*, May 16, 1986. Copyright © 1986 by The New York Times Company. Reprinted by permission. **Chapter 16: 572** From *The New York Times Magazine*, November 10, 1985. Copyright © 1985 by the New York Times Company. Reprinted by permission. **574** From "The Fabled 42 Wars Don't Equal WWIII" by Joanne Omang in *The Plain Dealer*, May 1, 1986. Reprinted by permission of The Washington Post Writer's Group. **576** From *U.S. Foreign Policy and the Third World: Agenda 1983*, edited by John P. Lewis and Valeriena Kallab. Copyright © 1983 by Overseas Development Council. Reprinted by permission of Praeger Publishers. **580** "Who Is Building the MX Missile" from *The New York Times*, March 19, 1985. Copyright © 1985 by The New York Times Company. Reprinted by permission.

state, 63
supremacy of, 67–68, 543
Constitutional Convention, 47–50, 192, 269
Constitutionalism, 67–68, 69, 545–46
Contempt, 519
Continental Congress, 62, 283
Contract clause, 93
Convention, 256–57, 264
Convention delegate, 264
Coolidge, Calvin, 376
Cooptation, 485
Corporatism, 341–43
Corwin, Edwin S., 578
Cost-benefit analysis, 360
Council of Economic Advisors (CEA), 345
Counter-cyclical spending, 332
Court martial, 498
Court of Appeals, 505
Courts, 68, 498
as constraint on presidency, 397
and foreign policy, 589
role of federal, 146–47
See also Federal circuit courts; Federal district courts; Judicial system; Supreme Court
Cranston, Alan, 264
Crime and criminals, 126–27, 142, 144–45, 326, 513, 597
Criminal laws, 500
Cronin, Thomas, 400
Cronkite, Walter, 244
Crosscutting cleavages, 173–75, 179–83
Cruel and unusual punishment, 124, 127
Crusoe, Robinson, 1, 2–3, 4, 7, 8, 9, 10, 594–96
Cultural environment, 297–98
Cultural values, 385
Culver, John, 219
Cutler, Lloyd N., 396

D
Daley, Richard J., 200, 319
Dallek, Robert, 385
Darmen, Richard G., 344
Davidson, Roger, 434
Dawson, Paul, 262–63
Death penalty. *See* Capital punishment
Deaver, Michael, 581
Decision making, government's role in, 4–5, 6–8
Declaration of Independence, 33, 62–63
Defense spending
in developed versus developing countries, 576
in United States, 39, 284, 538, 580, 582, 597
Defoe, Daniel, 3, 4
Demand, 356
Demand-side fiscal techniques, 356
Democracy, 29
characteristics of, 25–35
excesses of, 70–72
and political culture, 157–58, 164
Democracy in America, 154, 157, 423
Democratic party
Andrew Jackson and, 195, 196
composition of, 198
and domestic policy, 550

goals of, 202
members of, 205, 206, 251
and New Deal, 195, 290
nominating process in, 207, 256
1984 platform of, 204, 255
and Reconstruction, 196, 197
and Robert F. Kennedy, 187, 188, 189, 190, 191
since 1952, 197
Democratic-Republican party, 195
Denton, Jeremiah, 533
Department of Agriculture, 468, 481, 556, 597
Department of Commerce, 468
Department of Defense, 460, 485
Department of Education, 597
Department of Housing and Urban Development (HUD), 108–9
Department of the Interior, 24, 481, 485
Department of Justice, 464, 467, 472, 597
Department of State, 467
Department of Transportation, 463–64
Department of the Treasury, 467
Department of War, 467
Depression, 342. *See also* Great Depression
Deregulation, 102, 477–78, 598
Dewey, Thomas, 265
Dialogue, 26–27, 140–41, 180–81, 222–23, 270–71, 354–55, 394–95, 486–87, 548–49, 586–87
Diamond, Edwin, 246
Discrimination, 130–31, 138–39, 307
against blacks and women, 542
in education, 285
job, 136–37
See also Civil rights
Distributive public policy, 75, 435
District of Columbia, 142
Doctrine of implied powers, 90–92
Dole, Robert, 393, 416, 433
Domestic policy, 543–57
Congress and, 555
courts and, 556–57
federal bureaucracy and, 556
history of, 543–47
political environment of, 547–50
President and, 554–55
process, 551–54
Douglas, Paul, 215
Douglas, William O., 496
Douglass, Frederick, 312
Downs, Anthony, 198
Dred Scot decision, 95, 497, 503, 516
Due process of law, 126–27, 128–29, **511**–12, 597
Duverger, Maurice, 199

E
Economic efficiency, 9–10, 348–**49**
as American value, 100, 101–2, 103–4
Economic equality, 350–53
Economic policy
fiscal, 356–59
monetary, 359–60
regulatory, 360
trade, 360–62
Economic Policy Council, 345
Economic powers, 337

Economic productivity, 283
Economy (U.S.)
capitalism and, 336–39
corporatism and, 341–43
and electoral success, 257, 259
federal policy makers in, 343–46
fiscal policy, 356–59
goals, 346–53
growth, 347–53
growth since World War II, 538
monetary policy, 359–60
policy and, 340–41
regulation of, 39, 360, 476–78, 512
statism and, 340–41, 342–43
trade policy, 360–62
Edsall, Thomas, 353
Education
civil liberties in, 285–86
and future of America, 536–37, 541
at home, 285
social goals of, 282–86
Education Amendments (1972), 133
Ehrlichman, John, 380
Eisenhower, Dwight D.
as advisor, 374
as bureaucrat, 376, 383
election of, 197
and media, 243
and political interest groups, 208, 225
as President, 34, 368, 379, 387, 407, 515
Elastic clause, 447
Elastic powers, 75
Elazar, Daniel, 87
Elderly, 131
Election laws, 257, 258–59
Elections, 254–55
financing, 214, 258
local preferences in, 265
presidential, 255–57
purpose of, 273–74
Supreme Court on, 513
Electoral college, 260–61
Electoral participation, 248–49. *See also* Voting
Electoral system, as constraint on presidency, 393–96
Electorate, 257, 259, 517
apathy in, 269–72
Elitist democracy, 29–30
Emancipation Proclamation, 22, 35, 39
Employment Act (1946), 345
Entitlements, 539
Entrepreneurial members, 291
Enumerated powers, 446–47
Environment, 598–99
Environmental Protection Agency, 400, 464
Epstein, Leon, 198
Equal Credit Opportunity Act (1974), 133
Equal Educational Opportunities Act (1974), 133
Equal Employment Opportunity Commission, 132
Equality, 162–64
as American value, 100, 102–3, 104, 158
education and, 284–85
and liberty, 156, 178

and political parties, 194
and political socialization, 168–69
popular dissatisfaction with, 32–35, 593,
    595–96
and protection of freedom, 147–48
role of, 2, 4–5, 22, 23–25, 40–43, 59,
    72, 158, 593–601
role of individuals in, 85–88
Government corporations, 470
Government in the Sunshine Act (1976),
    483
Governmental institutions, 19, 30
Gramm-Rudman Act, 416, 510
Grant, Ulysses S., 20
Grants, 106, 108–9
Grants-in-aid, 106–8
Grassley, Charles, 416
Gray, William H., III, 384–85, 414–15
Gray v. *Sanders,* 513
Great Compromise, 49–50, 427
Great Depression, 9, 197, 348
  government's role in, 22, 29, 438
Great Society, 96, 320, 340–41, 396,
    538–39
Greeley, Horace, 21, 23
Greenfield, Jeff, 241
Greenfield, Meg, 239
Greenstein, Fred, 387
Grenada, 241, 583
Grodzins, Morton, 86
Grossman, Michael B., 238
Gross National Product, 87, 324, 325, 458,
    538, 539
Grove City College v. *Bell,* 516
Gun control, 217

H
Habeas corpus. See Writ of *habeas corpus*
Habeas Corpus Act, 61
Hacker, Andrew, 170
Haig, Alexander M., Jr., 588
Halberstam, David, 321
Hamilton, Alexander
  on federalism, 94, 101, 195, 337
  as Founder, 51
  as policy maker, 421
  on presidency, 371, 383–84
  use of mass media, 269
Hand, Learned, 543
Handicapped
  civil liberties of, 127
  and civil rights, 131
Harlan, John Marshall, 514
Harris, Louis, 172, 176, 240
Hart, Gary S., 241, 242, 243, 264
Hartz, Louis, 100
Hatch Act (1939), 463
Hawkins, Paula, 438
Haynsworth, Clement, Jr., 515
Heclo, Hugh, 386
Hegemony, 566–68, 577
Helms, Jesse, 263
Henderson, Margaret, 118
Henry, Patrick, 122
Henson, Charles, 135
Heritage Foundation, 551
Hess, Stephen, 245
Higher education, 284–85
Hirschman, Albert, 320

Hispanics, 131, 600
Hobbes, Thomas, 403
Homosexuals, 144, 146
Hoover, Herbert, 232, 332, 405–6
Hoover, J. Edgar, 483–84
House of Representatives
  committee system in, 431–32
  leadership in, 426, 428–30
  organization of, 421, 426
  as "people's branch" of government,
    420
  size, 427, 428
Huddleston, Walter D. "Dee," 231,
    245–46, 248
Humphrey, Hubert H., 188, 189, 190,
    191, 197, 200, 202, 215
Humphrey's Executor v. *United States,*
    483
Hunt, James, 263
Huntington, Samuel P., 164, 476

I
Ideological parties, 202
Illegal aliens, 127, 145, 285, 392
Illegitimate children, 512, 528, 530–32,
    533
Illiteracy, 280
Immigration, 158, 172
  and education, 283–84
Immigration and Naturalization Service v.
    Chadha, 510
Impeachment, 375, 516
Implied powers. *See* Doctrine of implied
    powers
Implied right, 74
Imports, 54–55. *See also* Tariffs
Impoundment, 400–401
Income tax, 75, 102, 350–51, 352–53, 445
Incrementalism, 305, 308, 321–27
Incumbency, and electoral success,
    259–60
Independent executive agencies, 469
Independent regulatory commissions,
    470
Independents, 166, 204–5
Indians. *See* American Indians
Individualism, 161, 164
  as political value, 158
Industrialization, 196–97
Industrial policy, 343
Infant mortality, 536, 537
Inflation, 37
Infrastructure, 541
Institute for Policy Studies, 218
Institutional environment, 298
Institutionalized presidency, 376–77
Integration
  government's role in, 22, 24, 34
  school, 134, 135
Interest aggregation, 194, 198
Interest articulation, 194, 198
Interest groups, 38, 209
  and bureaucracy, 474–76
  as constraint on Congress, 443–44
  as constraint on presidency, 392–93
  and foreign policy, 581–83
  formation of, 210
  and policy making, 178, 300, 550
  and political socialization, 168–69

See also Political interest groups
Intergovernmental relations, 105–6
Internal Security Act (1950), 143
International Bank for Reconstruction and
    Development (World Bank), 567, 597
International Monetary Fund, 597
International Red Cross, 584
International trade. *See* Foreign policy
Interstate commerce, 92, 98
Interstate Commerce Act (1887), 425
Interstate Commerce Commission, 214,
    425
Iran hostage crisis, 24, 40, 232–33, 260,
    396, 585, 589
Iron triangles, 381, 475
Item veto, 402
Iyengar, Shanto, 268

J
Jackson, Andrew, 156, 195, 196, 284, 290,
    462
Jackson, Henry "Scoop," 265, 393
Jackson, Jesse, 167, 265, 397
Jacob, Herbert, 498
Jacobson, Gary, 257, 259, 447
Japanese-Americans, 143, 145
Jascalevich, Mario, 118, 119, 120, 121,
    122, 123, 127, 144, 146, 147
Jay, John, 82, 83, 269
Jefferson, Thomas
  on Constitution, 51, 66
  and federalism, 94, 337
  as Founder, 52, 58
  on government, 8, 10, 74, 321
  and John Marshall, 83, 84, 89, 90
  as opponent of Alexander Hamilton,
    195, 421–22
Jennings, M. Kent, 168
Jepsen, Roger, 262
Job discrimination, 136–37
Johnston, Andrew, 375
Johnson, Lyndon B.
  campaign of, 188, 189, 262, 393
  and civil rights, 132
  election of, 142
  and Great Society, 96, 320, 538
  as policy maker, 553
  as President, 272, 379, 396, 405, 424,
    516
  and Vietnam War, 29, 146, 368, 396,
    401–2, 407, 577, 583, 585
  and War on Poverty, 108, 285, 379,
    392, 396, 544
Johnston, J. Bennett, 581
Joint committees, 432
Jordan, Hamilton, 232, 233, 384
Judges
  appointment of, 498
  Supreme Court (justices), 390, 498–99,
    515
Judicial activism, 501–2, 505
Judicial Conference of the United States,
    510
Judicial restraint, 501, 505
Judicial review, 68–69, 73, 88–90, **503**
  in *Dred Scot* decision, 95
  and policy changes, 326
  and Supreme Court, 518
Judicial system, 68, 88, 508

Medicaid, 541
Medicare, 319
Meese, Edwin III, 138, 515, 588
Mencken, H. L., 243, 256–57, 267
Mercantilism, 337
Merit principle, 462
Merit System Protection Board (MSPB), 460
Merriam, Charles, 198–99
Merriam, Robert E., 104
Miami University, 600
Microeconomic policies, 360–62
Milbrath, Lester, 218–19
Militants, 125
Military spending. *See* Defense spending
Mill, John Stuart, 315
Miller, "Fishbait," 420, 426
Minimum wage, 96
Minorities, 110–11, 131
  and civil liberties, 144, 145–46
  education of, 600
  hiring of, 138
  interest groups and, 215
  proficiency testing of, 282
Minority leader, 426
Minority whip, 426
Miranda, Ernesto, 128–29
Miranda v. *Arizona*, 128–29, 504
Missouri Compromise (1820), 95, 422
Mixed economy, 339
Model Cities program, 109, 539, 553
Modigliani, Franco, 348
Mondale, Walter F.
  campaign of, 36, 42, 197, 233–34, 243, 264, 370
  nomination of, 256
  as Vice-President, 233–34, 393
Monetarists, 359–60
Money, 68
Monroe, James, 422
Moral Majority, 167–68
Morison, Samuel Eliot, 33
Morrill Act (1862), 284
Morris, Robert, 51
Morton Thiokol Corporation, 581
Moses, Robert, 488
Mosher, Charles, 446
Mosher, Frederick, 479
Mothers Against Drunk Driving (MADD), 296
Moynihan, Daniel Patrick, 165, 403, 538
Mudd, Roger, 243
Multipolarity, 566, 569–70
Murphy, Bruce Allen, 497, 513
Murray, Charles, 534
Muskie, Edmund, 265
Mussolini, Benito, 310
Mutual Assured Destruction (MAD), 569
MX missile, 579, 580
Myrdal, Gunnar, 158, 164

N

Nader, Ralph, 215, 240, 268, 300, 551
National Advisory Council on Economic Opportunity, 531
National Aeronautics and Space Administration (NASA), 465, 466
National Association for the Advancement of Colored People (NAACP), 215, 296
National Audubon Society, 600
National bank, 74, 91
National Committee for an Effective Congress (NCEC), 215
National Conservative Political Action Committee (NCPAC), 215, 216
National Council of Counties, 215
National debt, 331–36, 385, 541
National government, 102–3. *See also* Federalism; Virginia Plan
National Governors' Association, 215
National Gray Panthers, 215
National League of Cities, 215
National Park Service, 99
National Rifle Association, 217
National Science Foundation, 469
National security
  changes in, 570–75
  future of, 575–77
  throughout history, 566–70
  technology and, 573–75
  and world economy, 575–76
  See also Foreign policy
National Security Agency, 145
National Security Council, 589
National strength, as American value, 100, 101, 103–4
National supremacy, 95, 96, **503**
National unity, and public opinion, 178–79
National Unity Ticket, 202
National Welfare Rights Organization, 215
National Women's Political Caucus, 182
Nationalism, 571–73
Native Americans. *See* American Indians
NATO. *See* North Atlantic Treaty Organization
Natural law, 65
  in Constitution, 74
Natural rights, 65
Nature conservancy, 600
Necessary and proper clause, 74, **91,** 447
Negative rights, 129
Nepotism, 381
Neustadt, Richard E., 382, 383, 454, 455, 464
New Deal, 33, 40, 96, 195, 197, 290, 323, 342–43, 462–63, 503
New Federalism, 97
New Jersey Plan, 49
Newspapers, 237, 238, 241, 243, 244, 269
News services, 237, 238
New York Times, 117, 119, 120
New York Tribune, 21, 22
New Zealand, 562–66, 568, 577
Nicaragua, 577
Nienaber, Jeanne, 485
Nix v. *Williams,* 129
Nixon, Richard M.
  as advisor, 374
  as bureaucrat, 380, 463, 481, 488
  on Congress, 414
  election of, 41, 96, 191, 240, 495
  as foreign policy maker, 407, 585
  and media, 241, 244
  as President, 109, 424, 538
  and Supreme Court, 505, 515
  and Vietnam War, 401–2
  and Watergate scandal, 29, 40, 368, 375, 400, 407, 496, 508–10
Nofziger, Lyn, 388
Nomination process, 200
  presidential, 255–56
Nonelectoral forms of political activity, 249–50
North Atlantic Treaty Organization (NATO), 568, 569

O

Obscenity, 125
Occupational Safety and Health Act (1970), 342
Occupational Safety and Health Administration (OSHA), 474, 488
O'Connor, Sandra Day, 96, 385, 494, 514
Office of Economic Opportunity, 538–39
Office of Management and Budget (OMB), 345, 376, **467,** 477, 484
Office of Personnel Management (OPM), 460
Okun, Arthur, 104
Oleszek, Walter, 434
Olson, Mancur, 212
O'Neill, Thomas P. "Tip," 415, 416, 429–30, 542, 543
Open market operations, 359
Open primaries, 255
Opinion (Supreme Court), 495, 500–501, 518, 519, 520. *See also* Public opinion
Organizational set, 300–301
Organization of African Unity, 584
Organization of American States, 569, 584
Original jurisdiction, 89, 500
Ortega y Gasset, José, 310
Oversight, 436–37, 481

P

Packwood, Robert, 555
Paine, Thomas, 121
Palmerston, Lord, 566
Parks, Rosa, 122, 309
Participation rights, 125–26, 142, 512–13
Participatory democracy, 30–31
Party delegates, 205–6
Party identification, 204–6, 255, **259**
  and families, 166
Party identifiers, 205–6
Party-line voting, 442
Passive representation, 478–79
Patriotism, 159
Patronage, 381, 459–**62**
Pearl Harbor, 36, 143
Pendleton Act (1883), 462
Pennsylvania Avenue Development Corporation, 470
Pension Reform Act (1974), 342
Pepper, Claude, 555
Percy, Charles, 249
Pericles, 247
Permanent campaign, 231, 235–36, 248–49, 408–9
Personal freedoms, 121–23, 130. *See also* Civil liberties

and timing, 406–7
of United States (table), 372–73
use of public opinion, 384–86, 408–9
veto, 399, 402
war powers of, 399, 400, 401–2
See also Presidency
President pro tempore, 374, 426
Presidential power, 383
Press, and public opinion, 177. *See also*
    Mass media
"Pre-Warren Court," 503
Price fixing, 338–39
Primary elections, 255
Principle of national supremacy, 90,
    91, 92
Print journalism, 237, 238–40
Prior restraint, 267
Privacy rights, 124–25, 129–30
Private economic market, 9, 10–13
Private goods, 6, 7
Private morality, 156, 158
Private sector,87
Privatization, 320, 478
Problem definition, 312–15
Production of, 6–7, 8
Proficiency testing, 280–82, 290, 293,
    297–98
Progressive party, 380–81
Progressive tax, 351
Prohibition, 74
Prohibition party, 202
Project grants, 108
Project on Military Procurement, 582
Pro-Life Action Council, 219, 272
Property rights, 92–93, 125, 126
Protest parties, 202
Proxmire, William, 242, 272, 436
Public assistance. *See* Welfare
Public goods, 6–7
Public Health Service Act (1981), 532–33
Public opinion(s), 153, 169–83
    on affirmative action, 162
    and apolitical attitudes in America,
        170–72
    and civil liberties, 146–47
    as constraint on presidency, 392
    as constraint on Supreme Court, 517
    differences in, along racial lines, 183
    and distrust of government, 300, 301
    effect of, on political system, 177–83
    and federal bureaucracy 485–89,
        595–97
    and media, 177
    and permanent campaign, 231
    pluralism in, 172–77
    and policy making, 321–22, 438–39, 550
    polls, 237, 238, 240
    presidential use of, 385–86
    private nature of, 169–72
Public policies, 19, 22–23, **30,** 40–43
    Constitution and, 75–76
    dissatisfaction with, 593, 595–96
    and federalism, 110–12
    and legitimacy, 545
    makers of, 286–87
    people's preferences in, 25, 28–29
    and policy organizations, 282
    and special interest groups, 178
    values and, 178

See also Policy organization
Public Works Employment Act (1977),
    133
Punishment rights, 126–27
Pye, Lucian, 159

Q

Quality of life, in United States, 535–38

R

Race, as crosscutting cleavage, 182–83
Radio, 237, 240
Railroads, 498
Rainbow Warrior, 564
Rainey, Paul J., Sanctuary, 600
Rakove, Jack, 57
Reactive campaigning, 262–63
Reagan, Maureen, 265
Reagan, Michael, 108
Reagan, Nancy, 374
Reagan, Ronald
    and affirmative action, 138
    as agenda builder, 314, 315
    assassination attempt on, 144
    and budget, 368–71, 401, 407, 416, 439
    as bureaucrat, 206, 368–71, 376, 379,
        380, 381, 458, 460, 464, 467, 481,
        531, 597
    campaign of, 36–37, 40, 41, 42, 387
    and Congress, 445, 482
    and courts, 147
    and deregulation, 477
    as economic policy maker, 344–45, 346,
        349–50, 352–53, 597–98
    election of, 34, 96, 202, 231, 232, 233,
        234, 235, 237, 240, 244, 259–60,
        262, 264
    and federalism, 102, 103, 106, 107, 110
    and foreign policy, 581, 583, 584, 588
    and gender gap, 179–82, 248
    and interest groups, 218, 220, 221
    and liberty, 162
    and media, 241, 242, 244, 246, 267,
        268, 269, 396, 406–7, 583
    and New Federalism, 97
    and New Zealand, 564
    and Nicaragua, 577
    as policy maker, 321, 386–87, 393,
        402–3, 407, 408, 551, 553, 554
    as President, 261–62, 273, 311, 384,
        385, 400, 402
    and presidential power, 402–4, 408–9
    and public opinion, 99
    and Star Wars technology, 583
    and Supreme Court, 515
    and taxation, 334, 335
    and veto, 402
    and welfare expenditures, 109, 175,
        351, 353, 368–69, 532, 541,
        597
    White House staff of, 374
Reapportionment, 126, 142, 513
Reconciliation process, 369–70
Reconstruction, 196, 197, 424
Redistributive policy, 75, 103, 435
Regan, Donald T., 344
Regents of the University of California v.
    Bakke, 138
Regressive tax, 351

Regulation, of economic activity, 476–78
Regulatory policies, 360
Rehabilitation Act (1973), 133
Rehnquist, William, 96
Religion
    as crosscutting cleavage, 182
    freedom of, 124, 125
    organized, 122
    and political socialization, 167–68
    See also Prayer
Representative democracy, 31–32
Republic, 29
Republicanism, 66–67, 69
Republican party
    cleavages in, 179–82
    conservatism in, 202. *See also*
        Conservatives
    historical perspective on, 195, 196–97,
        198, 462
    in 1984, 204, 205–6, 255
    nominating process in, 207
    nonvoters in, 251
    and Watergate scandal, 496
Research tasks, 294
Reserve requirement, 359
Resources
    allocation of, 7–8, 9–13, 39, 100, 102–3
    decisions about, 4–5
    and federalism, 105–6
Reston, James, 188, 239
Revenue sharing, 108, 109, 597
Reverse discrimination, 138
Revolutionary period, 62–63
Revolutionary War, 33, 41, 51, 54
Richardson, Joy, 281
Rights
    individual, 72
    natural, 65
Riker, William H., 88, 290
Rio Treaty (1947), 568
Ripley, Randall, 436
Roche, John, 51, 97
Rogers, Will, 198
Roll-call votes, 440
Roosevelt, Eleanor, 215, 374
Roosevelt, Franklin D.
    and balanced budget, 332
    as bureaucrat, 376, 462–63
    election of, 96
    and internment of Japanese-Americans,
        143
    and media, 405–6
    and New Deal, 33, 174, 195, 197, 323
    on policy making, 36
    on poverty, 10 535–36, 543
    on presidency, 378, 388
    as President, 42, 375, 379, 384, 385,
        386, 399–400, 404, 424
    and Social Security, 547
    and Supreme Court, 503
    at Yalta Conference, 567
Roosevelt, Theodore, 42, 48, 388, 424
Roper Center for Public Opinion
    Research, 240
Ross, Kevin, 280, 282
Rossiter, Clinton, 196
Rostenkowski, Daniel, 218
Routine issues, 317
Rudman, Warren B., 416

Rules Committee, 431
Russell, Mark, 239

S

Safire, William, 564
SALT I. *See* Strategic Arms Limitation
    Talks (1972)
Savino, Nancy, 118
Scarcity, 5–6
Schattschneider, E. E., 192, 221, 314, 316
Schlafly, Phyllis, 147
Schlesinger, Arthur, Jr., 42
Schlesinger, Joseph, 199–200
Schools, 282–86. *See also* Education
Schroeder, Patricia, 404
Schumpeter, Joseph, 32
Schwartz, Bernard, 514
Schwartz, Thomas, 436–37
Schwartz, Tony, 262
Schweiker, Richard S., 456
Scott, Tom, 565
SEATO. *See* Southeast Asian Treaty
    Organization
Secretary of State, 374
Segregation, 134, 142, 511
Select (special) committees, 431–32
Selznick, Philip, 299, 485
Senate
    committee structure of, 431
    confirmation of appointments, 469, 470
    and election of senators, 424
    evolution of, 421–23
    organization of, 421, 426
    size of, 427–28
Sencer, David J., 454–56
Seniority rule, 432
Separation of powers, 61
Sex, as crosscutting cleavage, 179–82
Shah of Iran, 396
Shaw, Eileen, 118
Shaw, George Bernard, 169
Sherman Act (1890), 338, 472
Shultz, George P., 344
Sidey, Hugh, 392
Simon, Herbert, 322
Simon, Paul, 249
Sinclair, Barbara, 438, 439
Sinclair, Upton, 240
Single-issue parties, 202
Sirhan, Sirhan B., 188, 190
Slavery
    and *Dred Scot* decision, 94–95, 497,
        503, 516
    and Emancipation Proclamation, 21–23
    and Free Soil party, 202
    and Kansas-Nebraska Act, 196
    and Missouri Compromise, 422
    as policy issue, 36
    and Republican party, 195
    and slave trade, 68
    and Thirteenth Amendment, 98, 142
    as threat to democracy, 182
Small Business Administration, 481
Smith, Adam, 56, 337
Smith, Hedrick, 407
Smith, Linda Brown, 135
Smith Act, 143
Smoking, 99
Social conscience. *See* Public opinion

Social contract, 65
Socialism, 337
Socialist Workers party, 202
Socialization. *See* Political socialization
Social safety net, 539, 541
Social Security, 319, 351, 352, 386, 393,
    541, 547
Social Security Act (1935), 533
Social welfare policies. *See* Welfare
Society, as decision maker, 4–8
Solow, Robert M., 332
Southeast Asian Collective Defense Treaty
    (1854), 568
Southeast Asian Treaty Organization
    (SEATO), 569
Sovereignty. *See* Popular sovereignty
Soviet Union, 568, 569, 570, 572, 573–75,
    576–77, 585, 588
Sowell, Thomas, 138
Speaker (of the House), 394, **426**
Special Supplemental Food Program for
    Women, Infants, and Children,
    533–34
Spitzer, Robert J., 397
"Split-ticket" voting, 393–96
Spoils system, 462
Stalin, Joseph, 567
Standing committees, 424, 431, 434
Star Wars technology, 573–75, 583
Stare decisis, 501, 519
State legislatures, 48, 55, 56–57
State of the Union message, 317
States
    autonomy of, 62–63
    and federal aid, 106–9, 598–99
    and national economy, 97–100, 598–99
States' rights, 91–92, 95–96, 510, 546
Statism, 340–41
Statue of Liberty, 24, 600
Statutory law, 501
Stevenson, Adlai, 23
Stewart, Potter, 513
Stockman, David, 162, 369, 376, 403, 416,
    435, 460
Stowe, Harriet Beecher, 240
Strategic Arms Limitation Talks (1972),
    573
Structural poverty, 534
Students Against Drunk Driving (SADD),
    296
Subgovernments, 443
Succession Act (1947), 374
Supplemental Security Income, 541
Supply-side economics, 332, 335, 356,
    369
Supreme Court
    on abortion, 495, 511
    and *The Brethren,* 493–98
    and capital punishment, 511
    cases heard by, 499–501
    characteristics of justices, 497–98, 505
    and civil rights, 139
    and Communist Party, 143
    Congress and, 445, 515–16
    constraints on, 497–98, 514–18
    and contempt of court, 519
    and *Dred Scot* decision, 95, 497, 503,
        516
    and due process, 128–29, 511–12, 597

and economy, 512
on election campaigns, 513
and fear of crime, 145
and federalism, 88–93, 95–96, 508–10
governance goals of, 497, 507, 508–10
history of, 502–5
on Iran hostage crisis, 589
and Judicial Conference, 510
judicial constraints on, 516–17
judicial powers of, 508
and judicial review, 68–69, 73, 88–90,
    95, 326, 518
justices, 498–99, 502, 505, 513–14,
    515–16
and legislative veto, 482
legitimacy of, 501–2, 505, 517–18,
    556–57
Marshall Court, 82, 83–84, 88, 89–90
and media, 518
and New Deal, 503
nomination of justices, 390, 515
and participation rights, 138, 512–13
policy goals of, 497, 507, 508–10
as policy maker, 445, 510–12, 556–57
and Political Action Committees, 214
political goals of, 497, 507, 512–14
political power of, 519–21
powers of, 75, 497–98, 513, 518–19
President and, 515, 516
and presidential appointments, 483
and presidential (executive) privilege,
    508–10
and public opinion, 517–18
and reapportionment, 513
and right to vote, 512–13
rulings of unconstitutionality by, 509,
    518
and segregation, 511
and slavery, 503
writs issued by, 518–19
Swann v. *Charlotte-Mecklenburg Board of
    Education,* 133
Swine flu, 316, 454–56, 465, 553
Symington, Stuart, 393

T

Taft, Robert, 387
Taney, Roger, 94–95, 503, 514
Tariffs, 40, 68, 542
Taxation
    disputes, 498
    and policy goals, 350–53, 356
    Reagan and, 369–70
    See also Income tax; Poll tax
Tax credits, 110, 111
Tax preferences, 357–59
Technical members, 291
Technology
    and civil liberties, 145
    education and, 283
    and foreign policy, 573–75
    and media, 237, 247
    and political interest groups, 214
Teenage pregnancy, 528–30, 532, 533,
    553
Television, 237, 238, 241, 243, 244, 245,
    256, 262
Tennessee Valley Authority, 299, 485
Tennyson, Alfred Lord, 596

Territories (U.S.), 498
Third party, 196. *See also* Political parties
Third World countries, 567, 569, 570, 571, 574, 575, 576, 597–98
Tocqueville, Alexis de, 30–31, 153, 154, 155, 156, 163, 164, 169, 176, 178, 179, 182, 183, 423
Tolchin, Martin, 242
Tory, 192
Totenberg, Nina, 494
Tower, John, 585–88
Tozzi, Jim T., 479
Trade policies. *See* Foreign policy
Trade deficit, 553
Transfer payment, 350, **351**
Traugott, Michael, 257
Treason, during Civil War, 95
Treaties, 68, 390, 508
Treatise of Civil Government, 65
Truman, David B., 110, 209, 210, 212, 216
Truman, Harry S., 25, 238
  on politics, 387
  on presidency, 383
  as President, 376, 381, 400
  and Truman Doctrine, 568
Truman Doctrine (1947), 568
Twain, Mark, 426
Two-party system, 196, 197–98

U

Unemployment (workmen's) compensation, 351, 353, 541
Unemployment, 37, 137
Union. *See* Labor union
Union Army, 20
Unitary government, 85
United Nations, 567–68, 571, 581, 582, 584, 597–98
United Nations Treaty (1945), 567
United States v. *Nixon,* 73, 509–10
U.S. Arms Control and Disarmament Agency, 469
U.S. Conference of Mayors, 215
Unwed mothers, 553. *See also* Teenage pregnancy

V

Values
  changing, 94–96
  conflicts in, 39–43, 209–10, 267
  cultural, 385
  and federalism, 84, 94–96, 100–104
  and policy making, 178
  political, 153, 158, 164
  societal, 10, 11, 38, 39
  triumvirate of, 161–64
  See also Personal values
Vance, Cyrus, 232, 585
Verba, Sidney, 159, 168
Veterans' Administration, 481, 488
Veterans' disability, 351, 541
Veto, 68, 440
  legislative, 481–82, 510
  line-item, 402
  presidential, 399, 402

Vice-President, 374
Vietnam Veterans Readjustment Act (1974), 133
Vietnam War
  American opposition to, 145–46, 188, 244
  Lyndon Johnson and, 29, 145–46, 188, 190, 577, 583
  role of public opinion in, 178, 401–2
  veterans, 131
  withdrawal from, 40
Viguerie, Richard A., 214
Virginia Plan, 49, 58
Volcker, Paul A., 344
Volunteerism, 458, **599**–601
Voter registration laws, 257, 258–59
Voting
  age, 126, 142, 445
  behavior, 251–54
  of blacks, 134–36, 142
  in Congress, 440–43
  participation rates, 252–54, 256
  rights, 142, 512–13
  and work of political parties, 207
Voting Rights Act (1965), 132, 134–36, 142, 456, 457, 512–13

W

Wages, 92
Walker, Charles E., 221
Walker, Jack, 213, 319
Wallace, George, 255, 272
Walters, Barbara, 234–35
Walzer, Michael, 138
War, 68
  and role of government, 178, 438–39
  See also specific war, such as Korean War; Vietnam War; *and so forth*
War on Poverty, 108–9, 379, 392, 396, 473, 544, 553
War powers, 401–2
War Powers Resolution (1973), 402, 424
Warren, Earl, 142, 499, 504, 514, 517
Washington, George
  Cabinet of, 467
  on foreign policy, 578
  as Founder, 48, 51, 64
  on political parties, 195, 225
  as President, 159, 231, 375, 387, 421
Washington, Harold, 136
Watergate scandal, 29, 40, 168, 496
Watt, James B., 220, 485
Wattenberg, Ben, 571
Waxman, Henry, 544
Wealth, redistribution of, 39, 103
Weaver, Suzanne, 472
Weber, Max, 100, 453, 484
Webster, Daniel, 196, 422
Weicker, Lowell, 272
Weidenbaum, Murray L., 218, 353
Weinberger, Caspar, 460
Welfare
  Aid to Families with Dependent Children (AFDC), 533, 541, 553
  food programs, 533–34, 541, 597
  government's role in, 178, 597

housing programs, 540, 541
  as national policy, 103, 351, 353, 528–32, 535
  Reagan Administration and, 109, 175, 351, 353, 368–69, 532, 541, 597
  spending, 534–35, 538–41
  Supreme Court on, 505
Whig party, 195, 196
Whiskey Rebellion, 28
Wicker, Tom, 239
Wildavsky, Aaron B., 25, 26–27, 101, 110, 140–41, 180–81, 222–23, 257, 270–71, 350, 354–55, 418–19, 446, 586–87
Wilder, L. Douglas, 136
Will, George, 239, 244
Williams, Robert, 129
Wilson, John, 266
Wilson, Kathy, 182
Wilson, Woodrow, 197, 424, 430–31, 467, 472, 577
Wirt, Frederick M., 104
Wirthlin, Richard, 240
Witcover, Jules, 246–47
Wolfe, Alan, 384
Wolfowitz, Paul D., 563
Woll, Peter, 478
Women
  abortion rights of, 505, 511, 516, 528
  and affirmative action, 138, 145
  civil liberties of, 127
  and civil rights, 131, 142, 285, 510
  discrimination against, 516, 542
  in government, 598
  as head of household, 528, 530–32
  as political candidates, 265
  as political constituency, 179–82
  poverty among, 530–32, 538
  in Supreme Court, 499
Woodruff, Judy, 403
Woodward, Bob, 493, 494, 496, 498, 506
Working conditions, 95–96
World Bank, 567, 597
World Health Organization, 584
World War I, 143
World War II, 36, 145
  U.S. foreign policy since, 565, 566–67, 570, 571
Wright, Jim, 444
Writ, 518–19
Writ of *certiorari,* **500**
Writ of *habeas corpus,* **518**–19
Writ of *mandamus,* **89,** 90

Y

Yalta Conference, 567
Yorktown, Battle of, 63
Young, Coleman, 136
Young Men's Christian Association (YMCA), 600

Z

Zeckhauser, Richard, 2
Zinser, James, 262–63
Ziyang, Zhao, 562

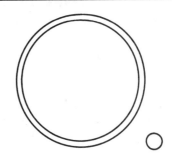

James C. Foster
to accompany

AMERICAN GOVERNMENT

Paul A. Dawson

STUDY-WARE

School is tough enough. Get an edge on studying this semester with Study-Ware.

Study-Ware is an electronic learning system that not only evaluates your knowledge of text content but also helps diagnose your specific learning skills. Designed for the Apple 11+, 11e, and 11c, Macintosh, and the IBM PC computers, Study-Ware is keyed directly to AMERICAN GOVERNMENT for easy reference and learning.

After reading each chapter in the text, Study-Ware allows you to check how much you have learned with true-false, fill-in-the-blank, and multiple-choice self-tests.

Automatic scoring allows you to check yourself as you learn.

And Study-Ware is easy to use. Three simple keystrokes are all you need to get started.

The system was designed for use on your own computer or any computer available to you on campus.

To order, complete and mail the card below. Be sure to indicate the type of computer disk you want and your method of payment.

Name _____ School _____

Address _____

City _____ State _____ Zip _____

Please send me Study-Ware for **AMERICAN GOVERNMENT** by Paul A. Dawson

_____ Apple $14.95   _____ IBM $14.95

Year in College _____
　　　　　　SR　　JR　　SO　　FR
　　　　　　　　(circle one)

My Major _____

Other courses I'd like to have Study-Ware for _____

_____

_____

Please indicate method of payment

_____ Personal Check

_____ VISA   _____ MasterCard

Acct. # _____

Expiration Date _____

Signature _____
　　　　　　(required on all charges)

Make checks payable to
Soft Productions, Inc.
Indiana residents add sales tax.

POWER . . . .

JACK FRENCH KEMP
United States Representative
(R—New York)

The identities and titles, at the time these photographs were taken, of the people in power pictured on the inside of the front cover.

KATHARINE GRAHAM
Chairman of the Board,
The Washington Post Company

PAUL ADOLPH VOLCKER
Chairman, Federal Reserve Board

CLAUDE DENSON PEPPER
United States Representative
(D—Florida)

SANDRA DAY O'CONNOR
United States Supreme Court
Associate Justice

RONALD WILSON REAGAN
President of the United States